*Dictionary of
British Naval Battles*

Dictionary of British Naval Battles

John D. Grainger

THE BOYDELL PRESS

© John D. Grainger 2012

All Rights Reserved. Except as permitted under current legislation no part of this work may be photocopied, stored in a retrieval system, published, performed in public, adapted, broadcast, transmitted, recorded or reproduced in any form or by any means, without the prior permission of the copyright owner

The right of John D. Grainger to be identified as the author of this work has been asserted in accordance with sections 77 and 78 of the Copyright, Designs and Patents Act 1988

First published 2012
The Boydell Press, Woodbridge

ISBN 978 1 84383 704 6

The Boydell Press is an imprint of Boydell & Brewer Ltd
PO Box 9, Woodbridge, Suffolk IP12 3DF, UK
and of Boydell & Brewer Inc.
668 Mount Hope Ave, Rochester, NY 14620, USA
website: www.boydellandbrewer.com

A catalogue record for this book is available
from the British Library

The publisher has no responsibility for the continued existence or accuracy of URLs for external or third-party internet websites referred to in this book, and does not guarantee that any content on such websites is, or will remain, accurate or appropriate.

Papers used by Boydell & Brewer Ltd are natural, recyclable products made from wood grown in sustainable forests

Printed and bound in the United States of America
by Edwards Brothers Malloy

Contents

Introduction	vii
References	x
Abbreviations and Glossary	xiii
DICTIONARY	1
Maps	505
Index	511

Introduction

In producing a *Dictionary of British Naval Battles* a whole series of preliminary definitions is needed. 'Dictionary' is straightforward: an alphabetical list. 'British' is more difficult, since British naval activity has been worldwide, and the navy did not exist as a unit until 1707. The word 'naval' is to be seen as referring to governmental sea power, rather than private, and so 'British' must include such countries as Canada, India, Australia, New Zealand, and South Africa, all of whose navies were more or less under British command. But those countries became fully independent in or soon after the Second World War, so a cut-off date of 1945 has been imposed, after which the navies of the dominions are regarded as separate. 'British' must also apply to all parts of the British Isles, so Scotland before 1707, Ireland before 1801, Wales before 1542, must be included – and that means such states as the Irish kingdoms, the Earldom of Orkney, the Lords of the Isles, the Welsh kings, and the Anglo-Saxon kingdoms. All of these disposed of, or were subject to, naval power at times, and must be included, even though they are not well recorded. (Roman naval activity in and about the British Isles has been excluded.) The East India Company, the Levant Company, and others have been included – they were essentially extensions of the British state.

However, it is the deceptively simple word 'battles' which causes most difficulty. One thinks, of course, of Trafalgar and Jutland, the Spanish Armada and so on, great thunderous clashes between immense fleets. But how 'big' must a 'battle' be to be included? What size of force is the minimum to count as a battle? The basic concept must be of naval vessels fighting each other. It is obvious that a fight such as that of Capt. Pellew's *Indefatigable* against the *Droits de l'Homme*, lasting over a day, must be counted as a battle. So the minimum size of a battle is one ship fighting another. The number of such encounters is very large, though finite.

Yet there are other naval conflicts which were not necessarily ship-to-ship encounters. D-Day in 1944 clearly was a naval event, though hardly any fighting at sea took place. So landings on hostile shores must be included, and therefore so must seaborne raids – think of Zeebrugge or St Nazaire – and bombardments of the land from the sea. There are even naval events which need to be included which did not involve an exchange of fire – the sinking of a ship by a submarine's torpedo, for example – and some which are famous, or notorious, which would fall outside all these categories if strict boundaries were drawn – Francis Drake in several of his exploits in the Caribbean was operating as a private individual, and *Lusitania* was not a warship.

So, given the broad categories of 'British', 'naval', and 'battle', it has been necessary to be flexible, and to leave the precise boundaries of all of these categories fuzzy. I have drawn the line at ships sunk by aircraft – unless in the context of a greater battle – and at including privateering, though when a Royal Navy ship fought a privateer it has been included. The records of individual privateers are poor, to say the least, so in general they have to be omitted. The sinking of merchant ships by submarines and aircraft has also been generally excluded – a twentieth-century version of privateering – except in the case of defended convoys, which were in fact some of the larger battles of the Second World War.

No doubt, also, this catalogue is incomplete. For certain periods – the French Revolutionary and Napoleonic Wars, the Second World War – records are good, but even here sources are contradictory at times. I have endeavoured to be as complete as possible, but too many battles are recorded as little more than 'ship x sank ship y', or 'ship A fought ship B'.

The layout of the entries is as follows: ships' names are italicised; in single ship or squadron actions the British ship or unit is always named first in the heading, even when it loses; major battles are given capital letters (there is room for disagreement here also – I have used long-term importance as one means of categorising an event as a major battle, so that the near non-battle of Largs is included, largely due to its reputation and political results). I have gathered together certain sets of actions – Second World War convoys in the Atlantic, to Russia, to Malta – and certain geographical regions which saw repeated minor fighting. The most notable of these are the English Channel and the North Sea, of course, but also the Adriatic, the Persian Gulf and West Indian islands, for instance. In these instances the listing is chronological. On the other hand, the recurrence of ships' names I have left separate; so there is a single joint entry for Acre, for example, but several for *Active*. Partly this is because the entries of the same ship's name often refer to different ships (noted in the index), and because the actions usually occurred in different places.

I have tried to name the ships' captains where possible. This is the standard practice with the sailing navy, but much less so in the mechanical, and in early periods it is not always possible to find out captains' names. Practice has therefore to be inconsistent (as in so many marginal areas). Ships are also identified as to their power. In the sailing navy the practice was to state the number of guns a ship was rated to carry – so '*Indefatigable* (38)', for example. (This is not necessarily an accurate statement of the guns a ship actually carried, for captains tended to acquire extra guns as they went along.) In the mechanical navy the classification at first was the means of propulsion, so ships were defined as 'screw' or 'paddle' craft. So in the entries, if guns are quoted, the ship was a sailing ship. (For much of the nineteenth century, the only ships which saw action tended to be the smaller vessels, 'gunboats' in popular parlance.) By the end of the nineteenth century, the classification by type and size – battleships, cruisers, and so on – had stabilised.

The sources for this information are very largely secondary, in the accounts of wars and naval operations which have been published. It would be beyond the capacity of one man to consult all the relevant original materials, from the Anglo-Saxon Chronicle to detailed Admiralty records. As a result there will be mistakes and gaps, but the former have been corrected where possible, while the latter are only minor. The sources I have consulted for each incident are noted in the entries, in parentheses at the end.

References

The following abbreviations are used for the authorities in the entries:

Anderson – R.C. Anderson, *Naval Wars in the Baltic*, London 1969.
Andrews – K.R. Andrews, *Drake's Voyages*, London 1967.
Aubrey – P. Aubrey, *The Defeat of James II's Armada, 1692*, Leicester 1979.
Barker – Juliet Barker, *Conquest: The English Kingdom in France*, London 2009.
Barrow – G.W.S. Barrow, *Robert Bruce*, Edinburgh 1976.
Belich – J. Belich, *The New Zealand Wars*, Auckland 1986.
Bennett – G. Bennett, *Freeing the Baltic*, Edinburgh 2002.
Bethell – L. Bethell, *The Abolition of the Brazilian Slave Trade*, Cambridge 1970.
Cable – James Cable, *Gunboat Diplomacy 1919–1979: Political Applications of Limited Naval Force*, 2nd edn, London 1981.
Capp – B. Capp, *Cromwell's Navy*, Oxford 1989.
Childs – J. Childs, *The Williamite Wars in Ireland*, London 2003.
Clowes – William Laird Clowes, *The Royal Navy: A History from the Earliest Times to 1900*, 7 vols, London 1897–1903.
Colledge – J.J. Colledge and B. Warlow, *Ships of the Royal Navy*, 3rd edn, Philadelphia and Newbury 2003.
Corbett – Julian S. Corbett, *History of the Great War: Naval Operations*, vols 1–3, London 1920–1931.
Corbett, *Mediterranean* – J.S. Corbett, *England in the Mediterranean, 1603–1714*, 2 vols, London 1917.
Dike – K.O. Dike, *Trade and Politics in the Niger Delta, 1830–1885*, Oxford 1956.
Duffy – M. Duffy, *Soldiers, Sugar and Seapower*, Oxford 1987.
Duncan – A.A.M. Duncan, *Scotland: The Making of the Kingdom*, Edinburgh 1975.
Earle – Peter Earle, *The Pirate Wars*, London 2003.
Foster – Sir W. Foster, *England's Quest of Eastern Trade*, London 1933.
Francis – D. Francis, *The First Peninsular War 1702–1713*, London 1975.
Gillingham – John Gillingham, *The Wars of the Roses*, London 1981.
Gordon – Iain Gordon, *Admiral of the Blue: The Life and Times of Admiral John Child Purvis, 1747–1825*, Barnsley 2005.
Graham – G.S. Graham, *The China Station*, Oxford 1978.
Grant – Robert M. Grant, *U-boats Destroyed*, Penzance 2002.
Greene and Massignani – J. Greene and A. Massignani, *The Naval War in the Mediterranean, 1940–1943*, London 1998.
Hall – Christopher Hall, *Wellington's Navy*, London 2004.

Halpern, *Mediterranean* – Paul G. Halpern, *The Royal Navy in the Mediterranean, 1915–1918*, NRS 1987.
Halpern, *Naval History* – Paul G. Halpern, *A Naval History of World War I*, London 1994.
Hore – P. Hore, *Sydney, Cipher and Search*, Rendlesham 2009.
Hore, *Seapower* – P. Hore (ed.), *Seapower Ashore*, London 2001.
Howell – Raymond C. Howell, *The Royal Navy and the Slave Trade*, London 1987.
Hudson – Benjamin Hudson, *Viking Pirates and Christian Princes: Dynasty, Religion and Empire in the North Atlantic*, Oxford 2005.
James – William James, *Naval History of Great Britain*, 6 vols, plus index, London 1902.
Keay – John Keay, *The Honourable Company*, London 1991.
Lambert – Andrew Lambert, *The Crimean War*, Manchester 1990.
Loades – D.M. Loades, *The Tudor Navy: An Administrative, Political and Military History*, Aldershot 1992.
Lloyd – C. Lloyd, *The Navy and the Slave Trade*, London 1949.
Low – Charles Rathbone Low, *The History of the Indian Navy 1613–1863*, 1877, repr. London 1990.
MacDonald – R. Andrew MacDonald, *The Kingdom of the Isles: Scotland's Western Seaboard, c.1100 – c.1336*, East Linton, East Lothian 1997.
MacDougall – N. MacDougall, *James IV*, Edinburgh 1989.
Macintyre – Donald Macintyre, *The Battle of the Atlantic*, London 1961.
Mackesy, *America* – Piers Mackesy, *The War for America 1775–1783*, London 1964.
Mackesy, *Mediterranean* – Piers Mackesy, *The War in the Mediterranean, 1803–1810*, Cambridge, MA 1957.
Mahan – Alfred T. Mahan, *The Influence of Seapower on History, 1660–1783*, Boston, MA 1890.
Massie – Robert K. Massie, *Castles of Steel*, London 2003.
Maund – K.L. Maund, *Ireland, Wales and England in the Eleventh Century*, London 1991.
Milner – Marc Milner, *Battle of the Atlantic*, Stroud 2005.
Morriss – Roger Morriss, *Cockburn and the British Navy in Transition*, Exeter 1997.
Newbolt – Henry Newbolt, *History of the Great War: Naval Operations*, vols 4–5, London 1920–1931.
Nicholson – R. Nicholson, *Scotland: The Later Middle Ages*, Edinburgh 1974.
NRS, *Blockade of Brest* – R.A. Morriss (ed.), *The Channel Fleet and the Blockade of Brest, 1793–1801*, NRS 2001.
NRS, *Hawke* – R.F. Mackay (ed.), *The Hawke Papers*, NRS 1990.
NRS, *Maritime Blockade* – J.D. Grainger (ed.), *The Maritime Blockade of Germany in the Great War*, NRS 1996.
NRS, *Misc* – *Miscellany* I–VII.
NRS, *Piracy* – Lt-Cmdr C.G. Pitcairn Jones, *Piracy in the Levant 1827–8*, NRS 1934.
NRS, *Rodney* – D. Syrett (ed.), *The Rodney Papers*, 2 vols, NRS 2005–2007.
Oram – Richard Oram, *The Lordship of Galloway*, Edinburgh 2000.

Owen – J.H. Owen, *War at Sea under Queen Anne*, Cambridge 1938.
Parkinson – C.N. Parkinson, *War in the Eastern Seas, 1793–1815*, London 1954.
Phillips – Gervase Phillips, *The Anglo-Scots Wars, 1513–1550*, Woodbridge 1999.
Powell – J.R. Powell, *Robert Blake, General-at-Sea*, New York 1972.
Powley – E.B. Powley, *The Naval Side of King William's War*, London 1972.
Prestwich – M. Prestwich, *Edward I*, London 1988.
Rodger – A.B. Rodger, *The War of the Second Coalition 1708–1801*, Oxford 1964.
Rodger 1, Rodger 2 – N.A.M. Rodger, *The Sovereign of the Seas*, London 1999; *The Command of the Ocean*, London 2004.
Rohwer – J. Rohwer, *Chronology of the War at Sea, 1939–1945*, London 2005.
Rose – Susan Rose, *Medieval Naval Warfare, 1000–1500*, London 2002.
Roskill – S.W. Roskill, *The War at Sea 1939–1945*, 3 vols, London 1954–1961.
Schofield – B.B. Schofield, *The Russian Convoys*, London 1964.
Sebag-Montefiore – H. Sebag-Montefiore, *Enigma: The Battle for the Code*, London 2000.
Silke – J. J. Silke, *Kinsale*, Liverpool 1970.
Smyth, *Dublin* – A.P. Smyth, *Scandinavian York and Dublin*, 2 vols, Dublin 1979.
Smyth, *Kings* – A.P. Smyth, *Scandinavian Kings in the British Isles*, Oxford 1977.
Smyth, *Warlords* – A.P. Smyth, *Warlords and Holy Men*, Edinburgh 1984.
Spence – Richard T. Spence, *The Privateering Earl: George Clifford, 3rd Earl of Cumberland, 1558–1605*, Stroud 1995.
Sumption – Jonathan Sumption, *The Hundred Years War*, vol. 1, *Trial by Battle*, vol. 2, *Trial by Fire*; vol. 3, *Divided Families*, London 1990, 1999, 2009 (cited as '1', '2' and '3').
Syrett, *American* – D. Syrett, *The Royal Navy in American Waters in the American Revolutionary War*, Aldershot 1989.
Syrett, *European* – D. Syrett, *The Royal Navy in European Waters during the American Revolutionary War*, Columbia, SC 1998.
Syrett, *Howe* – D. Syrett, *Admiral Lord Howe*, Stroud 2006.
Terraine – John Terraine, *Business in Great Waters: The U-boat Wars 1916–1945*, London 1989.
Thomas – D. Thomas, *Cochrane: Britannia's Sea Wolf*, London 1978.
Thompson – William P.L. Thompson, *History of Orkney*, Edinburgh 1987.
Tunstall – Brian Tunstall, *Naval Warfare in the Age of Sail*, ed. N. Tracy, London 1990.
Ward – W.E.F. Ward. *The Royal Navy and the Slavers*, London 1969.
Warner – O. Warner, *Nelson's Battles*, London 1965.
Wettern – D. Wettern, *The Decline of British Sea Power*, London 1982.
Williamson – J.A. Williamson, *The Age of Drake*, Cleveland, OH 1965.

Abbreviations and Glossary

AA – Anti-aircraft
AMC – armed merchant cruiser
ASC – Anglo-Saxon Chronicle
ASW – anti-submarine warfare
balinger – a small coasting vessel
battle-cruiser – a fast battleship, the greater speed acquired at the cost of armour
battleship – a heavily armed and armoured vessel, queen of the battlefield until proved to be all too vulnerable to air and submarine attack
BM – Bombay Marine
bomb – a vessel armed, usually, with a mortar for
brig – a two-masted coasting ship
Capt. – Captain
carrack – a large three-masted trading ship, particularly used by Spain and Portugal in trading with eastern lands
carrier – a ship designed to carry and launch aircraft
chasse-marée – a French government coastguard vessel
Cmdr – Commander
corvette – a small warship, smaller than a frigate, but fast and weatherly; the term was re-used from 1939 for small fast anti-submarine warships
cutter – a small, single-masted ship, often used as a coastguard vessel
destroyer – a fast armed ship originally designed to counter torpedo boats, later used in anti-submarine warfare
D/F – direction finding by radio interception
dhow – a lateen-rigged trading ship of the Indian Ocean
dogger – a Dutch fishing vessel
EIC – East India Company
en flute – a warship whose armament has been much reduced to enable it to carry goods or a large numbers of soldiers
felucca – a small Mediterranean coastal trading ship, sailed or rowed
frigate – a medium-sized warship developed in the eighteenth century, carrying 38 to 44 guns, usually used as lookouts and independent cruisers
galivat – an Indian Ocean warship of medium size
grab – a small Indian trading ship, convertible to a warship
guarda costa – a Spanish coastguard vessel in the Caribbean
gunboat – a lightly-armed small vessel, often with only one gun, useful especially in narrow and shallow waters; the term became used for a class of British steamships capable of dominating poorly armed 'native' powers in eastern seas
LCT – Landing craft, tank

line-of-battle ship – the main warship of European navies from the seventeenth century onwards, well armed, with from 60 to 130 guns
LST – Landing Ship, tank
Lt – Lieutenant
lugger – a small sailing vessel specially favoured by privateers
MGB – motor gunboat
mistico – a small coastal trading ship in the Mediterranean
ML – motor launch
MM – The Mariner's Mirror
MTB – motor torpedo boat
NC – Naval Chronicle
NHI – National History of Ireland
NRS – Navy Records Society
pink – a small warship
prame – a lighter used to ferry goods from ship to shore mainly in Dutch and Baltic waters; later, when armed, used in the French navy as a coastal defence gunboat
prau – a small trading vessel in Malayan and Indonesian waters
privateer – a privately owned armed vessel licensed by a government at war to attack enemy vessels and keep the profits
Q-ship – an armed ship disguised as an unarmed vessel
RAN – Royal Australian Navy
RCN – Royal Canadian Navy
RIN – Royal Indian Navy
RNZN – Royal New Zealand Navy
S-boat – '*schnellboot*', the German MTB, called by the British an 'E-boat'
schooner – a fast, lightly crewed ship, mainly commercial, though it could be armed
schuyt – a Dutch coasting vessel
settee – a two-masted sailing ship of the eastern Mediterranean
sloop – a loose term for a variety of small naval craft, generally with one mast and about ten guns
tartan – a small single-masted Mediterranean trading ship
TB – torpedo boat
trabacolo – a small trading vessel, mainly used in the Adriatic
xebec – a small three-masted trading vessel in the Mediterranean

A

***Aboukir*, *Cressy* and *Hogue* v. *U-9*, 22 September 1914**
Three old cruisers patrolled the Dogger Bank area of the North Sea. *U-9* torpedoed *Aboukir*, and then *Hogue* when it stopped to lower boats for the rescue; *Cressy* lay stationary nearby and was also torpedoed. All three ships sank. Many of the men were rescued by Dutch steamers, but nearly 1400 died. (Corbett 1.174–177)

ABOUKIR BAY, Egypt, 8 March 1801
An expeditionary force of 16,000 British soldiers landed from transports shepherded by the Mediterranean fleet commanded by Admiral Lord Keith, seven line-of-battle ships and sixty or so lesser vessels. The landing, in the face of considerable French resistance, was accomplished in a highly professional manner, thanks to good planning by General Sir Ralph Abercromby, and the care of the sailors. In the campaign which followed, sailors manned guns and gunboats on Aboukir Lake, and a division of seamen and marines under Capt. Sir Sidney Smith's command fought alongside the soldiers. (James 3.81–90; P. Mackesy, *British Victory in Egypt*, London 1995; *NC* 2.198–217)

Aboukir Bay, Egypt, 7–10 March 1807
In order to attack Alexandria, a landing was made from a fleet commanded by Rear-Admiral Sir John Duckworth at Aboukir Bay; 5000 soldiers commanded by Major-General Frazer were landed three days later, at which point Alexandria surrendered. The troops were evacuated in September. (James 4.232–233; *NC* 4.35–36)

Abyssinia (Ethiopia), 1868
The detention of a British consul by the Ethiopian Emperor Tewodros produced a full-scale imperial rescue expedition by the Indian army, commanded by General Sir Robert Napier. Three hundred ships conveyed 13,000 troops and 15,000 animals from Bombay to the Red Sea, escorted by the screw frigate *Octavia*, the screw corvette *Satellite* and seven smaller steamships under Capt. Leopold Heath. The Ethiopians had no ships so the naval expedition was essentially a logistical exercise. The expedition landed at Zula, south of Massawa. A hundred officers and seamen from the warships formed a Naval Brigade, whose duty was principally to fire rockets. No naval casualties were incurred. (Clowes 7.218–220; A. Moorehead, *The Blue Nile*, London 1962, part 4)

Acadia (Nova Scotia), Canada, May 1690
A force of soldiers recruited in New England sailed under the command of Sir William Phipps, governor of Massachusetts, to seize control of the French bases at Port Royal and elsewhere in Acadia. The flotilla sailed on 28 April and returned home, successful, on 30 May. (Clowes 2.464)

Acasta v. *Serpent*, 17 July 1808

The frigate *Acasta* (40; Capt. Philip Beaver) captured the French brig *Serpent* (18) at La Guaira, Spanish Main. (Clowes 5.424)

Acheron v. French ship(s), 3 February 1805

The bomb *Acheron* (8) was captured and burnt by the French in the Mediterranean. (Colledge 2)

Achilles v. Spanish ship, 14 November 1745

The sloop *Achilles* was captured by a Spanish ship near Jamaica. (Clowes 3.311; College 2)

Achilles v. *Comte de St Florentine*, 4 April 1759

The French privateer *Comte de St Florentine* (60) was captured near Finisterre by *Achilles* (60; Capt. Hon. Samuel Barrington). (Clowes 3.301–302)

Achilles and *Dundee* v. *Leopard*, 16 March 1917

The German raider *Leopard*, disguised as the Norwegian ship *Rena*, was intercepted by the cruiser *Achilles* (Capt. Leake) and the armed boarding steamer *Dundee* (Capt. S.M. Day). A boarding party was sent but after an hour the raider opened fire on *Dundee*, which was both suspicious and ready. *Dundee* inflicted some damage, then *Achilles* sank the ship. None on *Leopard*, including the boarding party, survived. (Newbolt 4.193–195)

Acorn v. *Gabriel*, 6 July 1841

The brig *Acorn* (16; Cmdr John Adams) captured the slaver *Gabriel* off West Africa. (Clowes 6.306)

Acorn in Sierra Leone, November 1887

A party of men from the screw sloop *Acorn* (Cmdr William Atkinson) formed part of the force which struggled through forest to attack Robari, the main town of the Yoni, who were deemed to be in rebellion. The town was shelled and burnt, as were some villages nearby. (Clowes 7.388–389)

ACRE, Palestine

1798 (Siege of ACRE) General Bonaparte and a French army marched from Egypt into Syria in 1798. Jezzar Pasha, the Ottoman governor in Palestine, received assistance from Capt. Sir Sidney Smith, who had contacts in Constantinople (his brother was the British envoy there). Acre, Jezzar's capital and the only strongly fortified place in the region, was besieged by the French.

Smith captured a French flotilla and landed the guns it carried at Acre. The French army at Acre was thus short of artillery, and was faced by the fire of its own guns. Sailors and marines from Smith's squadron (*Tigre* (74), *Theseus* (74), the storeship *Alliance*, and two gun vessels) assisted in the repulse of the besiegers, who were also harassed by fire from the British ships. A French squadron of frigates managed to land guns and ammunition at Jaffa, but repeated French assaults on the small breaches in Acre's walls were beaten off. *Theseus* chased the French frigates, but suffered an explosion of shells which had been brought on deck, with many casualties. Casualties in the city were heavy, but Turkish reinforcements arrived. Finally, after several assaults, and faced with plague among his troops, Bonaparte withdrew to Egypt. British naval casualties were substantial: almost 100 killed and 180 wounded; 100 more were taken prisoner. (*NC* 2.15–29; Clowes 4.400–404; James 2.321–332; T. Pocock, *A Thirst for Glory*, London 1996, 90–114; D. Chandler, *The Campaigns of Napoleon*, London 1966, 237–241; Hore, *Seapower* 26–38)

1840 A fleet of British, Austrian, and Turkish ships, including eight line-of-battle ships, commanded by Admiral Hon. Sir Robert Stopford, attacked the fortified city of Acre in order to drive out the Egyptian garrison. The bombardment lasted several hours. The Egyptian magazine was hit, depriving the defenders of much of their powder and killing perhaps 1200 soldiers. That night the city was evacuated. (Clowes 6.318–323; Hore, *Seapower* 85–93)

Active and *Favourite* v. *Hermione*, 17 March 1762
Hermione, a Spanish ship, carried part of the annual treasure from Peru to Cadiz, not knowing that Spain was at war with Britain. The frigate *Active* (28; Capt. Herbert Sawyer) and the sloop *Favourite* (14; Cmdr Philemon Pownoll), part of the Cadiz blockading squadron, demanded *Hermione*'s surrender. *Hermione* did not fight, and treasure worth £500,000 was captured. (Clowes 3.308)

Active v. *Charmante* and *Dedaigneuse*, 1 September 1778
Active (26; Capt. William Williams), damaged and partly disarmed by a storm, was attacked by the French ships *Charmante* (58) and *Dedaigneuse* (26) near St Domingue; unable to defend herself, *Active* quickly surrendered. (Clowes 4.19)

Active v. French fleet, 16 August 1781
The brig *Active* (14), carrying dispatches from Admiral Rodney to New York, was captured by the French fleet of Admiral de Grasse. This loss helped delay Admiral Graves's sailing for the Chesapeake. (Clowes 3.495)

Active in the Ems River, Germany, 23 November 1800
The cutter *Active* (Lt J. Hamilton) was captured by French and Dutch ships in the Ems estuary. (Clowes 4.551)

Active v. *U-179*, 8 October 1942
U-179 was sunk by the destroyer *Active* in a combined depth-charge and ramming attack. (Rohwer 200)

Active and others v. *U-340*, 1 November 1943
U-340 was damaged by air attack and by attacks from the destroyers *Active* (Lt-Cmdr Merriman) and *Witherington* (Lt-Cmdr Tarrant) and the sloop

Fleetwood (Cmdr Piggott), and was then scuttled. The crew, rescued by a Spanish fishing boat, were taken prisoner by *Fleetwood*. (Rohwer 284)

Acton v. *UC-72*, 20 August 1917
Acton, a Q-ship, encountered *UC-72* in the Bay of Biscay. The crew acted out a panicky abandonment; when *UC-72* surfaced she was sunk by gunfire. (Grant 66)

Aden, Yemen, January 1839
The Emir of Lahej reneged on an agreement to rent out Aden to the EIC for a coaling station; when the Indian Navy corvette *Coote* (18) arrived to implement the agreement she was resisted. She was joined by an expeditionary force of 2000 soldiers, the RN ships *Cruizer* (16) and *Volage* (28) and the EIC schooner *Mahé*. Negotiations failed. The ships bombarded a battery and a tower which prevented landing, but the ruins of these buildings then provided cover for local marksmen. These were driven out by a landing by some of the troops, and the rest then landed. The town and harbour were secured, but resistance by local Arabs to British rule continued for many years. (Low 1.112–113; Clowes 6.277–279)

***Admiral Pasley* v. Spanish gunboats, 10 December 1800**
The brig *Admiral Pasley* (Lt Charles Nevin) was attacked by two Spanish gunboats off Ceuta, Morocco. They bombarded the brig from a distance until it surrendered. (James 3.37–38)

***Admiral Rainier* v. gunboats, 28 and 30 October 1800**
The brig *Admiral Rainier* (Lt Hugh Dobbie) destroyed several gunboats in two attacks. (Clowes 5.560)

Admiralty Islands, Melanesia, 29 February–9 March 1944
The RAN destroyers *Warramunga* and *Arunta* took part in landings at Los Negros on Manus Island. (Rohwer 309)

Adour River Crossing, 23–24 February 1814
The advance of Wellington's army from Spain into southern France was hindered by the many rivers crossing its front. A small squadron hovered off the mouth of the River Adour to assist, but heavy surf made access to the river difficult. Repeated attempts to land failed until one commanded by Lt George Cheyne in the gun brig *Woodlark* found a safe channel; the others thereupon followed. The army's crossing of the river was facilitated, but the cost to the navy was four boats sunk and thirteen sailors drowned; an unknown number of civilians in the transports also drowned. (James 6.120; Hall 225–228)

ADRIATIC SEA
The Adriatic Sea was of interest to the Royal Navy only in the Napoleonic and the two World Wars.

Napoleonic War

1807 *Porcupine* (22; Capt. Hon. Henry Duncan) raided places along the Dalmatian seacoast between Ragusa and Curzola Island, capturing local vessels including, on 7 October, *Safo*, a Venetian gunboat, and a vessel which had run into Zupiano harbour carrying guns and ammunition to a battery. The sloop *Herald* (Cmdr George Hony) sent boats to take out the privateer *César* from beneath the fortress at Otranto on 25 October. The crew fought until the British boats were alongside, then fled. (James 4.268–269; Clowes 5.403)

1808 Capt. William Hoste commanded British forces in the Adriatic between 1808 and 1813. *Unite* (40; Capt. Patrick Campbell) enforced the blockade of the northern Adriatic, from Ragusa to Ancona, from July 1806. On 2 May 1808 he met and captured the corvette *Ronco* (16), and on 31 May, off Zara, chased and defeated three gun brigs, two of which, *Nettuno* and *Teulie*, were captured. (James 4.342–343; Clowes 5.418)

On 26 June boats from *Standard* (64; Capt. Thomas Harvey) chased the Neapolitan gun vessel V*olpe* and the dispatch boat *Léger* near Corfu. *Volpe* was captured and *Léger* driven ashore. Despite both sides firing vigorously at each other, no one was even wounded. (James 4.347; Clowes 5.421)

1809 On 8 February *Amphion* (32; Capt. Hoste) and *Redwing* (18; Cmdr Edward Down) intercepted a French attempt to move troops and supplies onto the island of Melada; a broadside dispersed troops on shore and a landing party raided the stores. The frigate *Topaze* (38; Capt. Anselm Griffiths) came up with and fought the French frigates *Danae* (40) and *Flore* (40) near Paxo in the Adriatic on 17 March; the French ships failed to co-ordinate their attacks, but soon escaped. On 1 April boats from the frigate *Mercury* (Capt. Hon. Henry Duncan) went into the port of Rovigno, Istria, to cut out two gunboats. A fog prevented the full attack being accomplished, but one boat, *Leda*, was captured and brought out.

The frigates *Spartan* (38; Capt. Jahleel Brenton) and *Mercury* bombarded batteries at Cesenatico into silence on 2 May, then sent boats into the harbour, blew up the castle and a battery, and captured twelve laden merchant vessels. On 15 May *Mercury* bombarded the town of Rodi, and sent boat parties into the harbour, where seven coasters were destroyed. On 31 May *Topaze* discovered a convoy sheltering under a fortress at Santa Maura. Boats went in, and the whole convoy, nine ships, was captured.

On 28 July boats from *Excellent* (74; Capt. John West) with the sloops *Acorn* (Cmdr Robert Clephane) and *Bustard* (Cmdr John Markland) went in to seize a convoy at Duin, near Trieste. Marines were landed to prevent interference; six gunboats and ten coasters were brought out. On 27 August *Amphion* raided the Piave River estuary at Cortellazzo; six gunboats and seven coasters were destroyed or taken. *Mercury* sent boats into Bartella harbour on 7 September, where the schooner *Pugliese* (7) was boarded and captured. (James 5.29–32, 35–38; Clowes 5.433, 435, 437–438, 442–443)

1810 On 28 June *Amphion* and *Active* (38; Capt James Gordon) chased a convoy into the Venetian harbour of Grado; next day *Amphion* and *Cerberus*

(32; Capt. Henry Whitby) sent in boats, which menaced the town and defeated a small force of French troops who tried to stop them; the ships were brought out after some of the cargoes were transferred. (*NC* 4.348–349; James 5.120–121; Clowes 5.456)

1811 On 4 February *Cerberus* and *Active* sent a raiding party into Pescara in Istria, which brought out three merchant ships; eight days later they raided Ortona, capturing a defensive post and ten ships from the harbour, including a Venetian trabacolo; a large quantity of military stores was burned. On 4–5 May the frigates *Belle Poule* (38; Capt. James Brisbane) and *Alceste* (38; Capt. Murray Maxwell) went into the port of Parenza to attack a French gun brig (18) laden with supplies for Ragusa; the brig was driven on shore, and next day destroyed by gunfire. On 27 July *Active* raided Ragosniza, also in Istria, and having captured a high point, took three gunboats and a convoy of ten grain ships. The line-of-battle ship *Eagle* (74; Capt. Charles Rowley) chased three French ships heading for Corfu on 27 November; *Corceyre*, a frigate *en flute*, carrying wheat and military stores, was captured. (James 5.232–233, 247–248, 260–261; Clowes 5.484–488, 560)
See also: **Lissa**.

1812 The French ship *Rivoli* (74), three brigs and two gunboats sailed from Venice for Pola; on 21 February *Victorious* (74; Capt. John Talbot) sent the sloop *Weazel* (18; Lt. John Andrew) to attack two of the brigs, and attacked *Rivoli* itself. *Weazel* sank one brig; the other sailed away. *Rivoli* was battered by *Victorious*, and when *Weazel* came up and added its broadsides, *Rivoli* surrendered.

The frigate *Bacchante* (38; Capt. Hoste) sent boats into Port Lemo on 31 August to capture ships laden with ship timber. Seven of these were taken, along with the xebec *Tisiphone* (3) and two gunboats. Boats from *Eagle* (74; Capt. Charles Rowley) went to attack a convoy in Goro, near Ancona, on 16 September; two gunboats were captured, then the convoy, of which six were burnt and sixteen brought out. On 18 September *Bacchante* sent six boats against a convoy of eighteen merchant ships and six gunboats off Apulia. Despite a strong defence the sailors captured all the ships. On 20 September the frigate *Apollo* (Capt. Bridges Taylor) captured *Ulysse*, a xebec, near Corfu. On 21 December San Cataldo in Apulia was raided by *Apollo* and *Weazel* in pursuit of a trabacolo; the fortified tower under which it sheltered was blown up. On 6 January 1813 *Bacchante* with *Weazel* attacked a group of gunboats near Cape Otranto; all five were taken. On the same day, further north, *Havannah* (36; Capt. Hon. George Cadogan) captured *Gun Vessel no. 8* along with three merchant ships. (James 5. 336–341, 348–361, 6.26–27, 268; Clowes 5.501–502, 514–516)

1813–1814 Rear-Admiral Thomas Fremantle commanded in the Adriatic in 1813–1814. On 18 January 1813 he, with *Apollo*, the privateer *Esperanza*, and four gunboats, attacked Lagosta Island and on 1 February Curzola Island. A series of landings ensured that both islands were conquered and then garrisoned. Along with the garrison in Lissa Island, this ensured that the middle passage from Ancona to Cattaro and Ragusa was under British control.

Cerberus (32; Capt. Thomas Garth) captured the gunboat *Veloce* on 29 January 1813. The Brindisi–Corfu route was one the British were concerned to interrupt. On 14 February *Bacchante* captured the French gunboats *Alcinous* and *Vigilante* and part of a convoy heading for Corfu from Italy. On 17 February *Cerberus* captured a ship near Brindisi. The sloop *Kingfisher* (18; Cmdr Ewell Tritton) sent boats to intercept ships heading for Corfu; one was captured, nine driven on shore. Boats from *Apollo* and *Cerberus* took control of Devil's Island, north of Corfu, on 11 April, and from there captured ships heading for Corfu; three days later they raided Malero, but the eight vessels there had been scuttled.

Cerberus's boats raided the Apulian coast on 17 May after a ship was run ashore while attempting to escape. After driving off a party of soldiers and braving the fire of a Martello tower, the ship was brought out. At San Cataldo on 24 April, *Apollo* landed troops while her sailors seized a felucca. Two days earlier *Weazel* had scattered a convoy near Zibara Island, taking or destroying most of it, but a day-long battle with shore guns and gunboats left *Weazel* heavily damaged. The xebec *Aigle* was captured by a boat party from *Elizabeth* (74; Capt. Edward Leveson Gower) off Corfu on 25 May, and on the 27th, *Cerberus* sent boats to attack a convoy protected by eleven gunboats at Otranto; three gunboats and four of the convoy were captured. Also off Otranto on 23 August *Weazel* captured the gunboats *Tonnante* and *Auguste*.

Admiral Fremantle's squadron raided the Istrian coast – Porto-Re on 5 July, Farasina fortress (by *Eagle* (74)) on 7 July, Rovigno on 2 August, where the town was captured, a battery disabled and a convoy of 21 ships destroyed or removed, and Ragosniza on 4 August (by *Milford* (74; Capt. John Markland) and *Weazel*), where a battery and a signal tower were destroyed. Further north, *Havannah* took two ships near Vasto and ten more at the mouth of the Fortone River: the cargoes were oil and salt.

Venice was a major shipbuilding centre for Napoleon's effort to revive the imperial navy, and the patrol in the north of the Adriatic was given to two 74s, *Elizabeth* and *Eagle*. They raided convoys at Goro and Omago in Istria on 29 April and 8 June, the latter requiring a landing and the destruction of a battery. *Bacchante* destroyed a battery in a raid on Karlebago on 15 May. A month later, on the Italian coast, Hoste sent in boats to attack a convoy at Giulia Nova, where there were fourteen merchant vessels protected by ten gunboats and troops on shore; the ships were successfully taken. Five days later, on 17 June, *Havannah* took ten merchant ships at Vasto. On the same day *Saracen* (18; Cmdr John Harper) raided the island of Giuppana, while *Weazel* (Cmdr James Black) did the same at Mezzo, both in Dalmatia.

Fremantle, with *Milford*, *Elizabeth*, *Eagle*, *Bacchante*, and the gun brig *Haughty* (12; Lt James Hanway), sailed into the approaches of Fiume. A battery on the mole and a line of other batteries protecting the harbour were bombarded and taken. A party of seamen and marines stormed the town, capturing artillery and turning these guns on the last enemy holdouts. The French garrison left; ninety ships were captured in the harbour.

In October Fremantle with *Milford* and *Eagle* blockaded Trieste, which was also under siege on land by Austrian troops. Sailors and marines were landed on 5 October with cannon from the ships to assist in the siege of the castle after the town was taken. Bombardment continued for a full fortnight until the French finally surrendered. (James 6.22–33; Clowes 5.525–526, 531–534, 561–562; *NC* 5.191–192)
See also: **Cattaro, Ragusa, Ionian Islands**.

The Great War, 1914–1918 – see: *Dartmouth*, Durazzo, Otranto Barrage, *Weymouth*.

Hitler's War, 1940–1945
1940–1941 During the Greek and Yugoslav campaigns in 1940–1941 the British submarine *Osiris* (Lt-Cmdr Harvey) attacked an Italian convoy off Durazzo on 22 September 1940, and sank the escorting TB *Palestro*. Valona was shelled by the battleships *Warspite* and *Valiant* on 18–19 December. The submarine *Triumph* (Lt-Cmdr Woods) landed a raiding party in Apulia on 19 February 1941 to cut an important water main near the Italian air base at Foggia. (Rohwer 41, 52, 58)

1943–1945 British ships could operate into the Adriatic once Brindisi and Taranto had been captured. The German cruiser *Niobe* grounded on Silba Island on 19 December 1943, and was destroyed by two British MTBs on the 22nd. Durazzo was shelled by the destroyers *Blackmore* and *Ledbury* on 15–16 January 1944 and Curzola by the destroyers *Troubridge* and *Tumult* next night, on 18–19 January and on 12 February. Recanati and Pedaso were shelled by the destroyers *Tenacious* and *Tumult* on 1–2 February 1944. (Rohwer 294, 301)

***Adventure* v. French ships, July 1650**
Three French ships were found by an English detachment in Lagos Bay, Portugal; *Adventure* (Capt. Ball) fought one of them and captured her, though the French ship was badly damaged in the encounter. (Powell 97)

***Adventure* v. enemy squadrons, 28–31 December 1666**
Adventure (38; Capt. John Torpley) encountered four French warships in the English Channel. Unable to escape, she turned to fight, disabled three of them, and finally got away. Three days later *Adventure* met three Dutch warships from Flushing, who attacked. One of the ships was so badly damaged it probably sank; the other two were driven off. (Clowes 2.430–431)

***Adventure* and others v. Algerine ships, 1680–1681**
Adventure (40; Capt. William Booth) and *Hampshire* (46; Capt. Edward Pinn) fought four Algerine warships in a fight lasting ten hours. One Algerine escaped, but *Orange Tree* (28) was run ashore at Tangier, *Calabash* (28) was captured, and the third ran onto the bar at Sallee. On 8 April 1681 *Adventure* met and fought the Algerine ship *Golden Horse* (46) near Cape de Gata. The fighting continued through the night until another English ship, *Nonsuch* (40; Capt. Francis Wheler), arrived, at which point *Golden Horse*

surrendered. In December *Adventure* and the *James* galley (30; Capt. Cloudisley Shovell) fought the Algerine ship *Flower-pot* (30) and drove her ashore near Mazagran. (Clowes 2.454–457)

Adventure and *Tartar* v. French warship, July 1706
Adventure (40; Capt. Edmund Hicks) and *Tartar* (32; Capt. Richard Leake) captured a French ship of 24 guns in the North Sea; it was taken into the navy. (Clowes 2.510)

Adventure v. French ships, 1 March 1709
Adventure (40; Capt. Robert Clarke), cruising in the West Indies, was captured by the French. Clarke was killed. (Clowes 2.518)

Adventure v. *Infernal*, 1756
The brig *Adventure* (6; Lt James Orrok) was captured by the French privateer *Infernal* out of Le Havre after a fight. (Clowes 2.293, 311)

Advice v. French warship, 19 June 1704
Advice (50; Capt. Salmon Morrice) captured a French 18-gun warship, which was taken into the navy as *Advice Prize*. (Clowes 2.506)

Advice v. French privateer, 27 June 1711
A privateer out of Dunkirk raided a convoy from Virginia in the English Channel, and on her return met and captured *Advice* (46; Capt. Lord Duffus) off Yarmouth. (Clowes 2.532)

AE-2 v. *Sultan Hissar*, 30 April 1915
The Australian submarine *AE-2* was damaged by gunfire from the Turkish TB *Sultan Hissar* in the Sea of Marmara, and was later scuttled. (Colledge 122)

Aetna v. French ship, 18 April 1697
The fireship *Aetna* (8; Capt. Kenneth Anderson) was captured by the French. Anderson was killed. (Clowes 2.495)

Affleck and others v. *U-91* and *U-358*, 25–26 February 1944
The 1st Support Group (six ships) attacked U-boats of the *Preussen* pack west of Ireland. *U-91* was sunk by the destroyers *Affleck*, *Gore* and *Gould*, *U-358* sank *Gould*, but then was sunk by *Affleck*. (Rohwer 308)

Africa v. French privateers, October 1694
Africa (46; Capt. John Knapp), escorting a convoy towards New England, successfully fought off attacks by three French privateers (of 50, 30 and 24 guns). (Clowes 2.480–481)

Africa v. Danish gunboats, August–October 1808
Twelve Danish gunboats attacked *Africa* (64; Capt. John Barrett) off Copenhagen, and forced her to take refuge in Malmo. On her return voyage with

the *Thunder* bomb vessel and a gunboat, escorting a large convoy from the Baltic, she was attacked again in the Sound by a squadron of Danish gunboats and armed launches. Their bombardment of *Africa* lasted several hours, and the ship was so badly damaged that she had to return to Karlskrona for repair. The convoy largely survived. (James 4.369–370; Clowes 5.420; Anderson 326–327)

Agamemnon v. French frigates, 22 October 1793
Off the coast of Sardinia, *Agamemnon* (64; Capt. Horatio Nelson) came upon a squadron of French frigates. One of these was attacked, but replied by hitting *Agamemnon*'s masts and yards so successfully that she had to back off to make repairs. (James 1.117–118; Clowes 4.480)

Agamemnon and *Carysfort* v. *Lutine*, 24 March 1806
Agamemnon (64) and *Carysfort* (28) captured the French *Lutine* (18) in the Leeward Islands. (Clowes 5.557)

Aigle v. *Harriette*, 12 June 1797
The frigate *Aigle* (38; Capt. Charles Tyler) captured *Harriette* off Lisbon. (Clowes 4.555)

Aigle v. *Charente* and *Joie*, 12 July 1804
The frigate *Aigle* (36; Capt. George Wolfe) chased the *Charente* (20) and *Joie* (8) southwards from the Gironde estuary. Both French vessels ran themselves aground to avoid capture, and were destroyed by *Aigle*'s men. (James 3.342; Clowes 5.346)

Aigle at Lorient, 22 March 1808
Aigle (36; Capt. George Wolfe) ran into the approaches to Lorient attempting to cut off a French frigate squadron. One frigate took shelter under a battery on Ile Groix, the other fought and got away. (Clowes 5.413; James 4.313–314)

Aimable v. *Moselle*, 23 May 1794
The frigate *Aimable* (32; Capt. Sir Harry Burrard) captured the French sloop *Moselle* (24) off Hyères. (Clowes 4.553)

Aimable v. *Sans Culotte*, 22 September 1795
The frigate *Aimable* (32; Capt Charles Davers) captured and burnt the French sloop *Sans Culotte* in the West Indies. (Clowes 4.554)

Aimable v. *Pensee*, 22–23 July 1796
The frigate *Aimable* (32; Capt. Jemmett Mainwaring) encountered the French frigate *Pensee* (36) off Guadeloupe, and chased her for two days; *Pensee* was the faster ship and got away. *Aimable* suffered only two men wounded; *Pensee* is said to have had ninety casualties. (James 1.377–378; Clowes 4.501)

Aimable v. *Iris*, 2–3 January 1809
The frigate *Aimable* (32; Capt. Lord George Stuart) chased and captured

the French *Iris* (24) off the Dutch coast; *Iris* was carrying a cargo of flour to Martinique. (Clowes 5.430; James 5.2)

Aix Roads, Bay of Biscay, June–July 1799
A squadron of five Spanish line-of-battle ships entered Aix Roads near Rochefort. There they were blockaded by a British squadron commanded by Admiral Sir Alan Gardner and later by Rear-Admiral Hon. George Berkeley. Tentative attacks were made by both sides without result. The Spanish ships eventually got away to Ferrol. (Clowes 4.388–389; James 301–303)

Ajax and *Unite* v. *Dromedaire*, 31 March 1811
The French frigates *Amelie* (40) and *Adrienne* (40) came out of Toulon to carry stores to Corfu. They were intercepted by *Ajax* (74; Capt. Robert Otway) and *Unite* (38; Capt. Edwin Chamberlayne). The large storeship *Dromédaire* (20) was captured but the two frigates got into Porto Ferraio. (Clowes 5.483; James 5.245–246)

Ajax v. *Alcion*, 17 March 1814
Ajax (74; Capt. Robert Otway) captured the French sloop *Alcion* (18). (Clowes 5.562)

Alaart v. Danish flotilla, 18 August 1809
The sloop *Alaart* (16; Cmdr James Tillard), formerly Danish, was recaptured by a flotilla of Danish gunboats. (Clowes 5.553; Anderson 339)

Alacrity v. *Abeille*, 26 May 1811
Alacrity (18; Cmdr Nisbet Palmer) chased *Abeille* (20) near Corsica. The two ships fought for an hour, then *Alacrity* surrendered, largely because of Palmer's fears. The captain later died. (Clowes 5.485–486; James 5.248–249)

Alacrity v. Greek pirates, 9–10 April 1826
Alacrity (10; Cmdr George Johnstone) sent in boats to attack three Greek pirate ships at Psara, Greece. Forty pirates were killed and seventy captured; their ships were burnt. (Clowes 6.251)

Alarm v. *Liberte*, 30 May 1795
The frigate *Alarm* (32; Cmdr David Milne) fought and sank the sloop *Liberté* off Puerto Rico. (Clowes 4.553)

Alarm v. *Galgo*, 23 November 1796
The frigate *Alarm* (32; Capt. Edward Fellowes) captured the Spanish sloop *Galgo* off the Gironde estuary. (Clowes 4.560)

Alarm in the West Indies, 1799–1800
The Spanish packet *Pajaro* was captured by *Alarm* (32; Capt. Robert Rolles) in the Gulf of Florida in May 1799, the brig *Feliz* in July, and *Cuervo* (4) in February 1800. (Clowes 4.560–561)

Albacore v. *Athénienne*, 8 May 1796
The sloop *Albacore* (16; Cmdr Robert Winthrop) captured the French brig *Athénienne* off Barbados. (Clowes 4.554)

Albacore v. *Gloire*, 18 December 1812
The sloop *Albacore* (18; Cmdr Henry Davies) along with *Pickle* (14; Lt William Figg) chased the frigate *Gloire* (40) which was bound for the West Indies. The chase took place west of the Lizard, but ceased when *Albacore* was disabled. (Clowes 5.517; James 6.7)

Alban v. Danish gunboats, 24 May 1810
The schooner *Alban* (12; Lt Samuel Thomas) was attacked by a flotilla of seven Danish gunboats near Skagen; *Alban* was captured after a fight of three hours. Thomas was killed. (Clowes 5.553; James 5.445)

Albany v. French ships, 1746
The brig *Albany* (14; Cmdr Stephen Colby) was captured by French ships in North American waters. (Clowes 3.311)

Albion at Sarawak, December 1963
A strong incursion of Indonesians into Sarawak was defeated by RAF air attacks and by troops landed from the Commando ship *Albion*. (Wettern 227)

Alcantara v. *Greif*, 29 February 1916
The AMC *Alcantara* (Capt. Wardle), of the Northern Patrol, intercepted and fought the German raider *Greif*. The arrival of the AMC *Andes* (Capt. Young) ended the fight just as *Greif* sank. (NRS, *Maritime Blockade*, 383–389; Hore 254; Corbett 3.270–271)

Alcantara v. *Thor*, 28 July 1940
The AMC *Alcantara* (Capt. Ingham) was badly damaged in an engagement off the coast of Brazil with the German auxiliary cruiser *Thor*, and had to put into Rio de Janeiro for repairs. (Rohwer 54; Hore 254)

Alceste at Agay, Provence, 22 May 1810
The frigate *Alceste* (38; Capt. Murray Maxwell) raided the batteries at Agay, near Frejus, capturing one. Leaving a boat party hidden nearby, Maxwell took *Alceste* out to sea. The boat party captured four feluccas when they came out. (James 5.119–120)

Alceste and *Active* v. *Pomone* and *Pauline*, 29 November 1811
The frigates *Alceste* (38; Capt. Murray Maxwell) and *Active* (38; Capt. James Gordon) pursued a small French squadron. One ship turned away and escaped, but the British vessels fought *Pomone* (40) and *Pauline* (40). The British ships were seriously damaged but *Pomone* was captured; *Pauline* escaped. (Clowes 5.496–497; James 5.247–248)

Alceste at Pulo Leat, 18 February–3 March 1817
The frigate *Alceste* (46; Capt. Murray Maxwell) carrying Lord Amherst, appointed as ambassador to China, was wrecked on a reef off Pulo Leat, Strait of Gaspar, Indonesia. The crew landed and fortified the island. Malays unsuccessfully attacked the sailors, but burnt the wreck. The crew were rescued by the EIC cruiser *Ternate*. (Low 1.271–271; Clowes 6.232–233)

Alcide and *Actaeon* v. *Robuste*, 1758
Robuste (74; *en flute*) was captured by *Alcide* (64) and *Actaeon* (28). (Clowes 3.313)

Alcmene v. *Légère*, 22 August 1798
Alcmene (32; Capt. Henry Digby) captured the French gunboat *Légère* (6) near Egypt; two seamen dived into the water to recover dispatches thrown overboard by a French officer as her capture became inevitable. (Clowes 4.376; James 2.215)

Alcmene v. *Courageux*, 22–26 June 1799
Near the Azores *Alcmene* (32; Capt. Henry Digby) chased the Bordeaux privateer *Courageux* (28). The chase was slow because of calm weather. Little damage was done to either ship, but *Courageux* eventually surrendered; there were no casualties. (James 2.380–381)

Alcmene v. *Agile*, 8 June 1813
The frigate *Alcmene* (38; Capt. Edwards Graham) captured the French *Agile* (8). (Clowes 5.561)

Alert v. *Lexington*, 19 September 1777
Alert (10; Lt John Bazeley) encountered the rebel American brig *Lexington* (16) in the English Channel. The two fought from daybreak until mid-afternoon until *Lexington*, out of ammunition, surrendered. (Clowes 4.8–10)

Alert v. *Junon*, July 1778
Alert (10; Lt William Fairfax) was intercepted by the frigate *Junon* (32) and captured. (Clowes 4.15–16)

Alert v. *Unité*, 10 May 1794
The sloop *Alert* (16; Cmdr Charles Smith) was captured by the French frigate *Unité* (40) off the Irish coast. (Clowes 4.548; James 1.439)

Alert at Khanderi, 1799
The BM schooner *Alert* (14; Lt John Hayes) raided the island of Khanderi near Bombay, seizing ships and loot. (Low 1.203)

Alert v. *Essex*, 13 August 1812
The sloop *Alert* (16; Capt. Thomas Laugharne) attacked the US frigate *Essex* (32), which captured her. (James 5.365–366)

Alerte at Toulon, 14 December 1793
The sloop *Alerte* (14), seized from the French at the capture of Toulon, was retaken when the base was evacuated. (Clowes 4.548)

Alexander v. *Solebay*, 10 April 1746
The privateer *Alexander* (Phillips, master) attacked and captured the French *Solebay* (20) off the Ile de Ré. (Clowes 3.282)

Alexander v. French squadron, 6 November 1794
Alexander (74; Capt. Richard Bligh) was attacked in succession by five French line-of-battle ships. *Canada* (74; Capt. Charles Hamilton), which had been in company with *Alexander*, was kept away by one of the French ships, and *Alexander* surrendered after fighting for several hours. She was taken into Brest in a near-sinking condition. (*NC* 1.112–114; James 1.203–205; Clowes 4.241–242)

Alexander and *Success* v. *Genereux*, 18 February 1800
A French squadron attempted to run supplies into besieged Valetta, Malta, but was intercepted by ships of the British blockading squadron. *Alexander* (74; Lt William Harrington) and *Success* (32; Capt. Shuldham Peard) joined in attacking *Genereux* (74), which resisted strongly until *Foudroyant* (74; Admiral Lord Nelson) arrived. *Genereux* then surrendered. (*NC* 2.70–72; Clowes 2.438–439; James 2.438–439)

ALEXANDRIA, Egypt

1882 The Mediterranean fleet, commanded by Admiral Sir Beauchamp Seymour, bombarded batteries and forts in Alexandria harbour from 11 to 13 June. The Khedival government had given way to a nationalist government under Arabi Pasha, and this was the beginning of the British attempt to return to dominate Egypt. The bombardment was laborious, and showed up serious inadequacies in British armament, shells, guns, and training. Nor did it seriously inconvenience the Egyptian government. It was necessary to land forces in Alexandria to keep order after the bombardment. (Clowes 7.323–337)

1941 The Italian submarine *Scire* launched three human torpedoes (six men) through the boom in Alexandria harbour on the night of 18 December; the battleships *Queen Elizabeth* and *Valiant*, a tanker and the destroyer *Jervis* were badly damaged, though they could be repaired. (Rohwer 125; Greene and Massignani 202–204)

Alexandria v. *President*, 19–23 July 1813
The US frigate *President* (44) was chased by the frigate *Alexandria* (32; Capt. Robert Cathcart) and *Spitfire* (16; Capt. John Ellis). The US Commodore Rodgers evidently mistook these for a line-of-battle ship and a frigate. *President* eventually escaped after a five-day chase. (James 6.70–72)

Alexandrian v. *Coq*, **15 August 1797**
The schooner *Alexandrian* (6; Lt William Senhouse) fought and captured the French privateer *Coq* (6) off Martinique. (James 2.99)

Alexandrian v. *Epicharis*, **4 October 1799**
Near Barbados the schooner *Alexandrian* (6; Lt William Senhouse) found the French privateer schooner *Epicharis* and chased and captured her. (James 2.101)

Alfred v. *Favorite*, **March 1796**
Alfred (74; Capt. Thomas Drury) captured the French *Favorite* (22) off Cape Finisterre. (Clowes 4.554)

Alfred v. *Renommée*, **12 July 1796**
Alfred (74; Capt. Thomas Drury) encountered *Renommée* (36) off St Domingue and compelled her to surrender in a brief fight. (Clowes 4.500–501; James 2.453)

Alfred v. *Scipion*, **16 February 1798**
The French sloop *Scipion* (20) was captured by *Alfred* (74; Capt. Thomas Totty) near Guadeloupe. (Clowes 4.555)

Algeciras, Spain

1756 A British merchantman, captured by a French privateer, was held at neutral Algeciras. Admiral Sir Edward Hawke sent in boats to cut her out. The privateer was supported by Spanish gunfire and, although the ship was brought out, the fleet suffered 150 casualties. (Clowes 3.292)

1801 (Battle of ALGECIRAS) A French squadron of three line-of-battle ships and a frigate under Rear-Admiral Linois sailed from Toulon to Algeciras. The British squadron blockading Cadiz, six line-of-battle ships under Rear-Admiral Sir James Saumarez, attacked them in Gibraltar Bay on 4 July. The French ships were protected by shore batteries and forts and the British attack was unsuccessful; *Hannibal* (74; Capt. Solomon Ferris) went aground and was surrendered. Both sides suffered much damage and had serious casualties.

The British worked to repair their ships. Spanish ships came to reinforce the French, and more 74s came from the blockade of Cadiz to reinforce Saumarez's fleet. The British had five line-of-battle ships, the allies nine. The second phase of the battle began on 12 July. The Franco-Spanish fleet came out of the bay late in the day, and the fight, in darkness, was a chase. *Superb* (74; Capt. Richard Keats) went on ahead to head off and delay the allies, and the rest came up in succession. Two Spanish three-deckers, *Real Carlos* and *San Hermenegildo* (both 112 guns), caught fire and blew up, while the British *Venerable* (74; Capt. Samuel Hood) was dismasted and almost captured. Both sides claimed victory, the British with marginally more justification. (*NC* 2.218–233; Clowes 4.459–470; James 3.97–107; Tunstall 245)

Algerine v. pirates, Mirs Bay, China, May–July 1868
The screw gunship *Algerine* (Lt Compton Domville) attacked and burned two pirate vessels on 26 May. On 31 May she met and fought a squadron of thirteen ships; one was captured, but they were later deemed to be traders. *Algerine* captured three real pirates in July. (Clowes 7.220)

Algier v. Dutch privateer, September 1672
Algier (Capt. Thomas Knyvett), cruising alone in the North Sea, enticed a Dutch privateer close, and a sudden broadside brought a quick surrender. (Clowes 2.445)

Algiers
As the base for the Barbary pirates, supported and sponsored by the Dey, Algiers was the object of repeated attacks. The usual aim was to obtain exemption from attack for British ships, but achieving this invariably required force.

1621 An English fleet commanded by Admiral Robert Mansell tried to negotiate a treaty with the Dey but failed. In June two fireship attacks were made on ships in the harbour with little success. (Clowes 2.51–54)

1661 The Earl of Sandwich with eighteen warships attempted negotiations, but on 29 June fighting began and he withdrew having suffered some damage. Sir John Lawson with some ships remained for a time, but was then recalled. (Clowes 2.422)

1669–1670 The Dey of Algiers broke a treaty he had made in 1668 with Admiral Sir Thomas Allin. Allin returned in 1669 to take action in reprisal. *Pearl* (22; Capt. John Berry) fought *Gilt Lime Tree* (36), driving her ashore and burning her; *Mary Rose* (40; Rear-Admiral John Kempthorne) drove off an attack on the convoy she was escorting; and *Active* (Capt. Benjamin Young) and *Guernsey* (22; Capt. Argenton Allington) also defeated an attack by seven Algerine ships on their convoy. (Clowes 2.437–438)

1677–1679 Admiral Sir John Narbrough's campaign steadily reduced the Algerine fleet. Three ships were taken by his own ship in March 1678, and in November the Dey sent out his whole fleet, which was captured in its entirety. Narbrough returned to England next year. (Clowes 2.453–454; Rodger 2.89–91)

1816 (Battle of ALGIERS) Admiral Lord Exmouth commanded a joint British and Dutch bombardment of the city, lasting several days: ships in the harbour were largely destroyed. Fire was returned from the shore, and the allies suffered over 800 casualties. An agreement to release Christian slaves followed, but it was not possible to persuade the Dey to stop his corsairs working. Only the French conquest in 1830 did that. (Clowes 6.226–231; James 6.278–291; R. Perkins and K.J. Douglas-Morris, *Gunfire in Barbary*, London 1982)

Alicante, Spain

1704–1709 A force of 400 marines landed at Alicante from the Mediterranean fleet in 1704. Two small forts were captured, and the city's governor, of whose oppression the citizens had complained, was removed and put on shore some distance away with a warning not to repeat his transgressions. On 26–28 June 1706 the Mediterranean fleet under Vice-Admiral Sir John Leake bombarded the city to assist the siege; when the city was stormed on the 28th, seamen from the fleet took part. It proved impossible, however, to hold the city, and when it was about to fall, in March 1709, the garrison was evacuated by the Mediterranean fleet under Vice-Admiral Sir George Byng. (Clowes 2.409, 414; Francis 108, 272–273)

1812 A British army was transported from Sicily to land at Alicante to pursue the war against the French in the Peninsula. The aim had been to land further north, but Alicante provided a good harbour and a safe base for the army. (Hall 184)

Alligator v. *Fée*, 26 June 1782

The sloop *Alligator* (14; Cmdr John Frodsham), returning to Britain from West Africa with dispatches, was attacked and captured by *Fée* (32) off the Lizard after a sharp fight. (Clowes 4.83)

Alligator v. *Liberté*, 28 March 1794

The frigate *Alligator* (28; Capt. Thomas Surridge) captured *Liberté* (14) near Jamaica. (Clowes 4.592)

Allin's squadron v. *Rubis*, 18 September 1666

The French ship *Rubis* (50) was captured by the English squadron of Admiral Sir Thomas Allin off Dungeness; she was retained, renamed *French Ruby*, and taken into the navy. (Clowes 2.286)

Alphaea v. *Renard*, 9–10 September 1813

The schooner *Alphaea* (8; Lt Thomas Jones) chased the French Cherbourg privateer *Renard* (14). The ships fought through the night until *Alphaea*, attacked several times with hand grenades, blew up. All the men in *Alphaea* died; *Renard* also suffered badly. (James 6.9–10)

Amaranthe v. *Vengeur*, 13 April 1799

The sloop *Amaranthe* (14; Cmdr Francis Vesey) met and fought the French schooner privateer *Vengeur* (6) off Jamaica; *Vengeur* fought for an hour before surrendering. (James 2.378)

Amaranthe v. *Cygne*, 1 December 1808

The French ship *Cygne* (16), already battered by a fight with *Loire* (32) and other ships, was finally destroyed by a boat party from *Amaranthe* (18; Cmdr Edward Brenton). (Clowes 5.429–430)

Amazon v. Loup, 1747
Amazon (26; Capt. Samuel Faulkner), formerly the French *Subtile*, captured *Loup*, a privateer formerly the British *Wolf* (14). *Loup*, re-renamed, returned to British service. (Clowes 3.284)

Amazon and Dover v. Renommée, 12–13 September 1747
Amazon (26; Capt. Samuel Faulkner) fell in with and fought *Renommée*; both ships were badly damaged. Next day *Renommée* met *Dover* (50; Capt. Hon. Washington Shirley), which captured her. (Clowes 3.284)

Amazon v. Trois Couleurs and Betsy, 11 June 1796
The French corvettes *Trois Couleurs* and *Betsy* were captured by the frigate *Amazon* (36; Capt. Robert Reynolds) off Brest. (Clowes 4.499)

Amazon v. Félix, 26 July 1803
Amazon (38; Capt. William Parker) captured the French privateer schooner *Félix*, which was taken into the navy. (Colledge 141)

Amazon at Ferrol, 26 June 1809
Amazon (38) landed a party at Ferrol primarily to secure British armaments there, which might be used by French forces. (Hall 88–89)

Ambuscade v. Vainqueur, 1757
Ambuscade (32; Capt. Richard Gwynn) captured the French privateer *Vainqueur* (24). (Clowes 3.296)

Ambuscade v. Hélène, 22 June 1779
The frigate *Ambuscade* (32; Capt. Hon. Charles Phipps) captured the French brig *Hélène* (16) in the English Channel. (Clowes 4.27)

Ambuscade v. Bayonnaise, 14 December 1798
Ambuscade (32; Capt. Henry Jenkins) fought the French frigate *Bayonnaise* (32) off Bordeaux. *Ambuscade*, undermanned, was damaged when a gun burst. *Bayonnaise* deliberately ran afoul and boarded her, and in the fight which followed most of *Ambuscade*'s officers were killed or wounded. A fire and another inadvertent explosion allowed the French to rush the ship and capture it. (James 2.273–276)

Amelia and San Fiorenzo v. French frigates, 9 April 1799
Near Belle Isle the frigate *Amelia* (38; Capt. Hon. Charles Herbert) was damaged in a squall, and was then attacked by three French frigates, *Cornélie* (40), *Semillante* (36), and *Vengeance* (40). The frigate *San Fiorenzo* (36; Capt. Sir Harry Neale) assisted *Amelia* and the French ships eventually withdrew. (Clowes 4.522; James 2.376–377)

Amelia and Statira v. Mouche and Rejouie, 10–17 June 1809
The French corvette *Mouche* (16) was driven into Santander, Spain, and captured by *Amelia* (38; Capt. Hon. Frederick Irby) and *Statira* (38; Capt.

Charles Boys). A week later they captured *Rejouie* (14) and three smaller vessels off the same port. (Hall 76; James 5.27; Clowes 5.559)

Amelia v. *Aréthuse*, 7 February 1813

Amelia (38; Capt. Hon. Frederick Irby) at Freetown, Sierra Leone, learned of the near presence of the French frigates *Aréthuse* (40) and *Rubis* (40). They were found, *Rubis* having run aground. *Amelia* fought *Aréthuse* until both were so damaged as to be virtually unmanageable. *Amelia* had fifty-one men killed and *Aréthuse* thirty-one. (*NC* 5.150–154; Clowes 6.519–521; James 6.37–41)

America v. *Hussard*, October 1798

America (64) captured the French privateer *Hussard*, which was taken into the navy as the sloop *Hussar* (14). (Colledge 190)

Amethyst v. *Mars*, 1 April 1800

The frigate *Amethyst* (36; Capt. John Cooke) captured the French privateer *Mars*, which was taken into the navy as *Garland* (22). (Colledge 156)

Amethyst v. *Général Brune*, 9 April 1801

The frigate *Amethyst* (36; Capt. John Cooke) captured the French brig *Général Brune* in the English Channel. (Clowes 4.558)

Amethyst v. *Thétis*, 10–11 November 1808

The French frigate *Thétis* (40) came out of Lorient and was chased by the frigate *Amethyst* (36; Capt. Michael Seymour). The two ships manoeuvred and fought each other for several hours. *Thétis* at last aimed to board, but *Amethyst* frustrated that move by rapid and destructive gunnery, then boarded and captured *Thétis*, which had suffered almost 240 casualties. (Clowes 5.427–428; James 4.376–380)

Amethyst v. *Niemen*, 6 April 1809

The frigate *Amethyst* (36; Capt. Michael Seymour) chased the French frigate *Niemen* (40) in the Bay of Biscay. The two ships fought for two hours. *Niemen* caught fire, but by then both ships had lost their mainmasts. *Arethusa* (38; Capt. Robert Mends) arrived and took *Niemen*'s surrender. (Clowes 5.433–435; James 5.13–15)

Amethyst in the Yangzi River, April–July 1949

The frigate *Amethyst*, heading for Nanking to relieve the destroyer *Consort*, was shelled and driven aground by Communist artillery on 20 April. She remained stranded until July, when she was brought out by surprise at night. (Wettern 14–16)

Amoy, China

1840 Capt. Thomas Bourchier in *Blonde* (46) on 6 July attempted to deliver a letter to the Chinese government through the authorities at Amoy on 6 July, who refused to accept it. When the ship's boat was fired on, Bourchier bombarded the fortifications. (Clowes 6.283; Graham 24)

1841 An attack was made on Amoy on 24 August by a joint naval and army force. *Wellesley* (74) and *Blenheim* (74) bombarded batteries on Kolangsu Island, and landing parties were put ashore, who easily captured the batteries. Amoy, abandoned, was then occupied. A garrison was left on Kolangsu Island. (Clowes 6.293–294; Low 2.144–145; Graham 181–183)

Amphion v. *Bonetta*, 2 January 1782
Amphion (32; Capt. John Bazely) recaptured *Bonetta* (14), recently taken at Yorktown. (Clowes 4.76)

Amphion v. *Baleine*, 12 May 1808
The frigate *Amphion* (32; Capt. William Hoste) found the French storeship *Baleine* (26) in the harbour at Rosas, Spain; Spanish batteries on shore foiled *Amphion*'s attack. (Clowes 5.419; James 4.344–345)

Anatolian coast, 30 April–1 May 1916
The minesweepers *Whitby Abbey* and *Aster* towed sixteen caiques manned by armed Turkish refugees to raid the coast of Anatolia south of Samos. The raiders rustled 1870 animals. (Halpern, *Mediterranean* 291)

Anchusa v. *U-54*, 16 July 1918
The sloop *Anchusa* was sunk by *U-54* off the north coast of Ireland. (Colledge 6)

Andaman Islands, 1945
The destroyers *Rapid*, *Rodent*, *Roebuck*, and *Rotherham* shelled Japanese positions on 24–25 February and 3 March, and *Saumarez*, *Rapid*, and *Volage* bombarded Port Blair on 19 March; *Rapid* was damaged by a shore battery in shelling a Japanese position. A Japanese convoy was destroyed on 26 March – one ship was sunk by air attack, and three ships and the submarine chaser *Ch-34* by destroyers. Port Blair was shelled by Task Force 63 on 30 April and 1 May and a Japanese convoy of nine ships was destroyed in the process. The Indian sloop *Narbada* received the surrender of Japanese forces in the islands on 26 September 1945. (Rohwer 395, 401, 408, 412, 431)

Andania v. *U-A*, 16 June 1940
The AMC *Andania* was sunk by *U-A* in the North Atlantic, at the second attempt. (Rohwer 28)

Andromache v. Algerine ship, 31 January 1797
A mutual misunderstanding led to *Andromache* (32; Capt. Charles Mansfield) fighting an Algerine ship (24). The Algerine, having failed to board, surrendered, at which point the mistake was discovered. Three British sailors died and six were wounded, and the Algerine had sixty-six killed and fifty or more wounded. (James 2.90)

Andromache and Cleopatra at Cevita Bay, 22–23 March 1801
The frigates *Andromache* (Capt. Israel Pellew) and *Cleopatra* (Capt. Robert Lawrie) discovered a convoy in Cevita Bay, Cuba. Boats were sent in after dark, but only one ship, a galley of the escort, was taken. (James 3.129–130)

Andromache v. Trave, 23 October 1813
The Franco-Batavian frigate *Trave* (40), already dismasted by a storm, met the brig *Achates* (Cmdr Isaac Morrison) and the frigate *Andromache* (32; Capt. George Tobin) in the Bay of Biscay. *Andromache* closed before firing; *Trave* lost the rest of her masts and quickly surrendered. (*NC* 5.171; James 6.14)

Andromache v. Prospère, 20 December 1813
The French schooner *Prospère* (2) was captured by the frigate *Andromache* (38; Capt. George Tobin) off the French coast. (Clowes 5.561)

Anglesey v. St Louis, October 1694
Anglesey (46; Capt. William Prower) captured the privateer *St Louis* (38) after a fight lasting an hour. (Clowes 2.480)

Anglesey and Hope v. François and squadron, 16 April 1695
Anglesey (48; Capt. William Prower) and *Hope* (70; Capt. Henry Robinson) became separated from a convoy they were escorting, and were attacked by a French squadron commanded by Capt. Duguay-Trouin in *François*. *Hope* was forced to surrender after a long fight. *Anglesey* (and fireship *Roebuck*) escaped. (Clowes 2.484)

Anglesey and Fowey v. Scarborough, 1 November 1710
The French frigate *Scarborough* (34) was captured by *Anglesey* (50; Capt. Thomas Legge) and *Fowey* (40; Capt. Robert Chadwick) in the West Indies. (Clowes 2.531)

Anglesey v. Apollon, 28 March 1745
Anglesey (44; Capt. Jacob Elton) near Kinsale was surprised by the French privateer *Apollon* (50) which Elton had mistaken for a British ship; the captain, first lieutenant, and many men were casualties in the first minutes of the fight; the second lieutenant, in consultation, surrendered. (Clowes 3.278–279)

Anholt Island, Denmark, 1809–1811
Anholt had a lighthouse very useful for navigating the Kattegat. On 18 May 1809 the frigate *Owen Glendower* (36; Capt. William Selby) landed a party of marines and sailors and seized the island, with little resistance. On 27 March 1811 a Danish landing attempted to retake the island, but the ships *Tartar* (32; Capt. Joseph Baker) and *Sheldrake* (16; Cmdr James Stewart) arrived opportunely and assisted the defence. The Danish attackers either surrendered or were evacuated. *Tartar* captured two gunboats and *Sheldrake* sank one. (Clowes 5.290, 481–483; James 5.222–226; Anderson 338, 343–344)

Annan v. U-1006, 16 October 1944
U-1006 was sunk by the Canadian frigate *Annan*, near Iceland. (Rohwer 360)

Anne v. Spanish gunboats, 24 November 1807
The brig *Anne* (10; Lt James McKenzie) captured the lugger *Vencejo*, and was then attacked off Tarifa, Spain, by ten gunboats. The lugger was quickly retaken, but *Anne* escaped. (Clowes 5.403–404; James 4.269–270)

Anson's squadron and Spanish America, 1741–1742
Capt. George Anson, in command of a squadron, harassed Spanish territories in the Pacific. Of his eight ships only three made the rendezvous at Juan Fernandez Island, all with sickly crews. By capturing prizes Anson was able to continue the voyage; he raided and burned the town of Payta, securing there, and in the ships, considerable plunder. Anson went on to cross the Pacific to the Philippines. (Clowes 3.320–324; G. Williams, *The Prize of all the Oceans*, London 1999)

Anson and Sylph v. Calliope and Réolaise, July–August 1797
The French frigate *Calliope* (26), unable to escape *Anson* (44; Capt. Philip Durham) off Ushant, ran herself aground on the Penmarcks. *Anson* could not get close enough to cause serious damage; *Sylph* (18; Cmdr John White), with its shallower draft, sailed in closer and bombarded her. *Sylph* was recalled in the evening, but *Calliope* was so damaged that she fell to pieces next day. On 11 August *Sylph* attacked a French gunvessel and the corvette *Réolaise* at Sables d'Olonne, Bay of Biscay, though they were protected by a fort. The gunvessel sank; the corvette was damaged. (James 2.95–96; Clowes 4.507–508)

Anson v. Daphne, 29 December 1797
Anson (44; Capt. Philip Durham) met *Daphne* (20) off the coast of France, and forced her surrender after a brief exchange of fire. (James 2.106)

Anson and Kangaroo v. Loire, 18 October 1798
The French frigate *Loire* (40), already damaged, met *Anson* (44; Capt. Philip Durham), also damaged, and *Kangaroo* (18; Cmdr Edward Brace) off the Donegal coast. *Anson* and *Loire* fought each other for an hour until both were disabled; *Kangaroo* came up, fired a single broadside which brought down *Loire*'s mizen, and the French ship surrendered. (James 2.158–159; Clowes 4.350)

Anson v. Gibraltar and Salvador, 29 June 1800
The frigate *Anson* (44; Capt. Philip Durham) captured the Spanish gunboats *Gibraltar* (10) and *Salvador* (10) off Gibraltar. (Clowes 4.561)

Anson v. Foudroyant, 15 September 1806
The French ship *Foudroyant* (80), carrying Rear-Admiral Willaumez, separated from its squadron in a hurricane, made for Havana. *Anson* (44; Capt. Charles Lydiard) attacked her approaching the port, but, outmatched,

outgunned, and damaged, *Anson* retired after half an hour. *Foudroyant* went into Havana, scarcely hurt. (Clowes 4.195; James 4.114–115)

Antelope v. *Happy Entrance*, Helvoetsluis, June 1649
The *Antelope* galleon, the only Royalist ship left in the Netherlands after Prince Rupert's squadron sailed, was captured by a boat party commanded by Anthony Young of the Parliamentary ship *Happy Entrance* (30); *Antelope* was captured and blown up. (Capp 66; Clowes 2.120)

Antelope v. Dutch convoy, September 1672
Antelope (40; Capt. Richard White), escorting a convoy from Hamburg, met a Dutch convoy; she fought off two Dutch escorting ships, and captured one warship and two merchantmen. (Clowes 2.444–445)

Antelope v. French warship, November 1705
Antelope (50; Capt. Philip Cavendish) fought a 70-gun French warship; in the end she pulled away, leaving *Antelope* damaged but free. (Clowes 2.509)

Antelope v. Coolie pirates, 1734
Antelope, a BM galivat, escorting a convoy from Bombay to Cambay, was attacked and captured by a force of Coolie pirates from Sultanpur. (Low 1.116–117)

Antelope v. *Aquilon*, 14 May 1757
The frigate *Antelope* (50; Capt. Alexander Hood) met and fought *Aquilon* (50), which ran aground in Audierne Bay and was wrecked. (Clowes 3.293)

Antelope v. *Belliqueux*, October 1758
Antelope (50) captured *Belliqueux* (64) off Ilfracombe, Devon. Both ships were of squadrons returning from Québec, Canada. (Clowes 3.186)

Antelope v. *Atalante*, 1–2 December 1793
The packet *Antelope* (6; Capt. Curtis), off Cuba, was chased by two privateers, one of which, *Atalante* (8), caught up when the wind failed. The privateer attacked under the red flag, signifying no quarter. *Antelope*'s officers were wounded and the boatswain forced to surrender. *Antelope* had seven casualties, *Atalante* forty. (James 1.122–124; Clowes 4.482)

Antelope and others in the Scheldt, 1813
Antelope (50; Capt. Samuel Butcher), with the Russian frigate *Sweaborg* and the cutter *Resolution*, sailed into the Scheldt estuary. They came under bombardment from two powerful forts (Bonaparte and Imperial), and *Antelope* ran aground. It took two days to refloat her, under fire all the time. (*NC* 5.210–212)

Antelope and others v. pirates, 1818–1819
The EIC brig *Antelope* (Lt Tanner) headed a squadron of small vessels cruising the coast of Cutch and Sind to suppress piracy; several pirate ships were destroyed. (Low 1.280)

Anthony and ***Wishart*** v. ***U-761***, 24 February 1944
U-761 was located by air reconnaissance off Morocco; under attack from the air and from the destroyers *Anthony* and *Wishart*, she was forced to scuttle. (Rohwer 303)

Antibes, Provence, 1747
The Austrian army invaded Provence and besieged Antibes. A British squadron under Vice-Admiral Henry Medley assisted by blockade and bombardment. Then Genoa revolted against Austrian occupation, and the siege was abandoned. (M.S. Anderson, *The War of Austrian Succession, 1740–1748*, Harlow 1995, 168–169; Clowes 3.123)

Antigua v. privateers, February 1762
The sloop *Antigua* (14; Lt Samuel Marshall) while near Guadeloupe was boarded at night by men from two French privateers. The boarders were driven off, and one of the privateers' ships was captured. The boarders had thirty-four men killed, *Antigua* only seven. (NRS, *Rodney*, nos. 906, 914)

Antigua v. French ship, May 1781
The sloop *Antigua* (14; Cmdr John Hutt) was captured by the French in the West Indies. (Clowes 4.111)

Anzio, Italy

1813 A squadron headed by *Edinburgh* (74; Capt. George Dundas) mounted an assault on a convoy of twenty-nine ships in Anzio harbour on 15 October, using information from prisoners taken in a raid by Capt. Hon. Henry Duncan of *Impérieuse* (38) a few days before. Batteries and towers were bombarded by the squadron, and a landing was made. The convoy was captured, and the ships' defences blown up. (James 6.34–35; Clowes 5.535)

1944 ANZIO Landing. A landing by the British 1st and US 3rd Divisions, with elements of British Commandos and US Rangers, was made at Anzio, intended to cut the German communications between Rome and their defences to the south (Operation Shingle). The naval forces involved were mainly transport craft, since the enemy had no significant naval forces in the region; shore bombardment was carried out by British and US cruisers and destroyers.

The troops were put ashore without loss, the Germans being taken completely by surprise. Major-General John P. Lucas, US Army, attended first to his defences, a priority for which he was heavily criticised, not least by Churchill, who compared the force on shore to a 'stranded whale'. But these defences held against the German attack. By attracting considerable German forces the main German defence on the Garigliano was weakened.

Naval casualties in the initial phase included the minesweeper *Portent* and the AA ship *Palomares*, damaged by mines, and the destroyer *Janus*, sunk by air attack; the destroyers *Jervis* and *Mayo*, the minesweeper *Prevail*, and the cruiser *Spartan* were damaged. Air and U-boat attacks continued after the initial landing: the destroyer *Inglefield* and the cruiser *Penelope* were sunk, as were several LSTs and transports. (L. Truscott, *Command Missions*, London 1946; F. Majdalany, *Cassino, Portrait of a Battle*, London 1957, 71–80; Rohwer 301–302)

Apollo v. *Oiseau*, 31 January 1779
Apollo (32; Capt. Philemon Pownoll) attacked the French *Oiseau* (28), which was escorting a convoy off Brittany; the convoy scattered to safety, while *Oiseau* was pounded into defeat and captured in a battle lasting several hours. (Clowes 4.22–23)

Apollo v. *Stanislas*, 15 June 1780
Apollo (32; Capt. Philemon Pownoll) fought the French privateer *Stanislas*, which ran aground near Ostend but was later refloated. Pownoll was killed. (Clowes 4.52)

Apollo and *Doris* v. *Légère*, 22 June 1796
Légère (18) was captured by *Apollo* (38; Capt. John Manley) and *Doris* (36; Capt. Hon. Charles Jones) off Brest; a few shots only were fired. (*NC* 1.11; James 1.370)

Apollo in the West Indies, 1800
The frigate *Apollo* (36; Capt. Peter Halkett) captured the Spanish sloop *Cantabro* (18) near Havana, Cuba, on 27 July, and on 10 November destroyed the Spanish sloop *Resolucion* (18) in a fight in the Gulf of Mexico. (Clowes 4.561)

Apollo v. *Dart*, 29 June 1803
The French lugger *Dart* (8) was captured by the frigate *Apollo* (36) in the Bay of Biscay. (Clowes 5.555)

Apollo v. *Merinos*, 13 February 1812
Apollo (38; Capt. Bridges Taylor) chased the storeship *Merinos* (20) and a corvette near Cape Corso. The corvette got away, but the storeship surrendered after a short fight. (James 5.338; Clowes 5.501)

Arab v. *Cuba*, June 1857
The brig *Arab* (16) captured the slaver sloop *Cuba*. (Colledge 97)

Arabic v. *U-24*, 19 August 1915
The White Star liner *Arabic* was torpedoed by *U-24* south of Kinsale, Ireland. Most of the people on board were saved. This was the incident which finally brought the Germans to suspend their unrestricted submarine campaign. (Corbett 3.130–131; Halpern, *Naval History* 301–303)

Arabis v. German destroyers, 10–11 February 1916
The sloop *Arabis* (Lt-Cmdr Hallowell-Carew), one of four ships sweeping a lane clear of mines along the Yorkshire coast, was bombarded by three German destroyers (after a torpedo attack failed), and then by not less than

six more destroyers. In the end she was sunk by torpedo. (Corbett 3.274–276; Halpern, *Naval History* 311)

Arabis v. *U-22*, 23 June 1940
The corvette *Arabis* sank *U-22* in the North Channel. (Rohwer 28).

Aragon and *Attack* v. *UC-34*, 30 December 1917
The troopship *Aragon* was torpedoed and sunk by *UC-34* off Alexandria, Egypt. The destroyer *Attack* was rescuing survivors when it either hit a mine or was torpedoed. Over 600 men died. (Halpern, *Mediterranean* 399).

Arbutus v. *UB-65*, 16 December 1917
The sloop *Arbutus* was sunk by *UB-65* in the St George's Channel. (Colledge 20)

Arcachon, France

1807   Capt. Lord Cochrane of *Impérieuse* (38) sent in a boat party to raid Arcachon port on 7 January. The protecting fort was stormed and shipping destroyed; no British casualties were incurred. (James 4.239; Clowes 5.395)

1812   Capt. Hon. Pleydell Bouverie of *Medusa* (32) sent a boat party to cut out the French storeship *Dorade* (14) in Arcachon harbour on 4 June. The ship was captured after a fierce fight, but grounded as the tide ebbed and had to be destroyed. (James 5.331; Clowes 5.507)

Arcadian v. *UC-74*, 15 April 1917
The troopship *Arcadian* was sunk by *UC-74* near Melos in the Aegean; 279 men died. (Halpern, *Mediterranean* 338–339; Newbolt 4.285–286)

Archer v. *Lugger No. 432*, 3 January 1804
The brig *Archer* (14; Lt John Sherriff) captured the French *Lugger No. 432*. (Clowes 5.556)

Archer v. pirates, Congo River, 1865
Boats from the screw sloop *Archer* (Capt. Francis Marten) were sent into the Congo River estuary to suppress a group of river pirates. (Clowes 7.209)

Ardent v. *Bayonnaise*, 28 November 1803
Ardent (64; Capt. Robert Winthrop) pursued *Bayonnaise* (32; *en flute*) until she ran ashore near Cape Finisterre, and was burnt by the crew. (Clowes 5.332)

Arethusa and *Alert* v. *Belle Poule* and *Coureur*, 18 June 1778
The frigate *Arethusa* (32; Capt. Samuel Marshall) and the cutter *Alert* (12; Cmdr William Fairfax) pursued the French frigate *Belle Poule* (36) and the cutter *Coureur* (10). When *Arethusa* caught up with *Belle Poule*, the captain refused to go with him to the Channel Fleet – it was still technically a time of peace. The two frigates fought each other for two hours before *Belle Poule*

got away. *Alert* meanwhile fought *Coureur* and forced her surrender. (Syrett, *European* 38; Clowes 3.397, 4.14–15)

Arethusa v. *Aigrette*, 19 March 1779
Arethusa (32; Capt. Charles Everitt) attacked the French frigate *Aigrette* (32) near Ushant. The fighting was indecisive and ended when a second French ship approached to assist *Aigrette*. *Arethusa* then struck a rock and her crew were taken prisoner. (Clowes 4.24–25)

Arethusa v. *Gaieté*, 10 August 1797
Arethusa (44; Capt. Thomas Wolley) was attacked by *Gaieté* (20) while on passage near Bermuda. *Gaieté* was beaten and captured in half an hour, and taken into the navy. (James 2.98–99; Clowes 4.507–508)

Arethusa and *Anson* v. *Pomona* and gunboats, 23 August 1806
The frigates *Arethusa* (38; Capt. Charles Brisbane) and *Anson* (44; Capt. Charles Lydiard) attacked the Spanish frigate *Pomona* in Havana, which was defended by twelve gunboats and the guns of Moro castle. The two British ships came as close as possible and bombarded all these targets: the gunboats were all sunk or destroyed, and *Pomona* surrendered. She had been carrying specie from Mexico, but most of this had been landed before the action. (James 4.169–170)

Arethusa on the Basque coast, Spain, 15–20 March 1809
The frigate *Arethusa* (38; Capt. Robert Mends) sent parties ashore to destroy a 20-gun battery at Lequitio and signal posts near Passages. Ships laden with brandy and wood were captured. (James 5.12–13)

Argo v. *Dauphin*, 1782
Argo (44; Capt. John Butchart) captured *Dauphin* (64; *en flute*) in the West Indies. (Clowes 4.115)

Argo v. *Nymphe* and *Amphitrite*, 16 February 1783
Argo (44; Capt. John Butchart), partly disabled, was attacked by *Nymphe* (36) and *Amphitrite* (32), but resisted for several hours before surrendering; she was retaken by a British ship three days later. (Clowes 4.94)

Argo v. *Peterel*, 13 November 1798
The frigate *Argo* (44; Capt. James Bowen) recaptured the sloop *Peterel* (16) which had been earlier taken by the Spaniards. (Clowes 4.560)

Argo v. *Santa Teresa*, 6–7 February 1799
Argo (44; Capt. James Bowen) went in chase of the Spanish frigate *Santa Teresa* (34), off Majorca. *Argo* was followed by *Leviathan* (74; Capt. John Buchanan), and *Santa Teresa* was accompanied by *Proserpine* (34). The two Spanish ships separated. *Argo* caught up with *Santa Teresa* at midnight; the latter, seeing *Leviathan* approaching, surrendered after receiving a single broadside. (James 2.359; Clowes 4.519)

Argo v. Infanta Amalia, 6 August 1799
Argo (44; Capt. James Bowen) captured the Spanish brig *Infanta Amalia* off the Portuguese coast. (Clowes 4.560)

Argo v. Joseph, 10 March 1809
A boat party was sent in by *Argo* (44) to cut out the felucca *Joseph* at San Domingo. (Clowes 5.559)

Argonaut v. Esperance, 8 January 1795
Argonaut (64; Capt. Alexander Ball) captured the French sloop *Esperance* (22) off the Chesapeake. (Clowes 4.490)

Argonaut v. Mocenigo, 14 December 1942
The cruiser *Argonaut* was badly damaged by an attack by the Italian submarine *Mocenigo*. (Rohwer 216)

Ariadne and Ceres v. Alfred and Raleigh, 9 March 1778
Ariadne (20; Capt. Thomas Pringle) and *Ceres* (18; Cmdr James Dacres) chased the rebel American ships *Alfred* (20) and *Raleigh* (32) in the West Indies. *Alfred* surrendered after a short fight; *Raleigh* escaped. (Clowes 4.10)

Ariadne and Queen v. privateers, 30 April 1780
Ariadne (20; Capt. Matthew Squire) and *Queen* (28; Cmdr Richard Trotten), off Flamborough Head, chased and attacked three French privateers. These defended themselves well, damaged *Queen* badly, and got away. (Clowes 4.51)

Ariadne v. UC-65, 25 July 1917
The cruiser *Ariadne* was torpedoed and sunk by *UC-65* off Beachy Head. (Colledge 22)

Ariel v. Amazone, 10 September 1779
Ariel (28; Capt. Thomas Mackenzie) encountered the French fleet off the American coast and was chased and captured by *Amazone* (26) after a stubborn fight. (Clowes 4.31–32)

Ariel v. slavers, 1862–1864
The screw sloop *Ariel* on the west coast of Africa captured eighteen slavers in the years 1862 to 1864 under successive Cmdrs John Alexander and William Chapman. (Clowes 7.189)

Ariel v. U-12, 10 March 1915
U-12 was searched for along the east coast of Scotland for four days, and eventually found by a group of destroyers. *Ariel* (Lt-Cmdr Tippet) rammed her, and when she surfaced the others opened fire; the submarine quickly sank. (Corbett 2.279–280; Grant 22)

Ariel v. UC-19, 6 December 1916
The destroyer *Ariel* (Lt-Cmdr Tippet) sighted *UC-19*, which dived, but was sunk by *Ariel*'s high-speed sweep. (Grant 39)

Ark Royal **and others v.** *U-39,* **14 September 1939**
The aircraft carrier *Ark Royal,* with a destroyer escort, was attacked by *U-39* off the Hebrides. The U-boat's torpedo attack missed and the destroyers *Faulknor, Foxhound,* and *Firedrake* counter-attacked. The U-boat was sunk; the crew were captured. (Rohwer 3)

Arran Island, Scotland, 1477–1478
Men from the Western Isles, probably instigated by Angus Og MacDonald as part of his quarrel with his father, raided Arran more than once in these two years. (Nicholson 481)

Arrogant **and** *Victorious* **v. French squadron, 8–9 September 1796**
A squadron of French frigates under Rear-Admiral Sercey encountered *Arrogant* (74; Capt. Richard Lucas) and *Victorious* (74; Capt. William Clark) off the north coast of Sumatra. The British captains stalked the French squadron and next day decided to attack. They faced *Cybèle* (40), *Forte* (44), *Seine* (40; *en flute*), *Vertu* (40), *Prudente* (32), and *Regenerée* (38). In the fight *Victorious* was at first masked by *Arrogant,* which received the fire of all the French ships in succession, being thereby disabled. *Victorious* was then given the same treatment. Of the French, *Vertu* was damaged; they then sailed away. (James 1.389–395; Parkinson, 104–105; Clowes 4.502–503)

Arrogant **and** *Orpheus* **v. Dutch brig, 24 May 1799**
Arrogant (74; Capt. Edward Osborn) and *Orpheus* (32) captured a Dutch brig (6) in the East Indies. (Clowes 4.559)

Arrogant **v.** *Laurette,* **April 1801**
Arrogant (74; Capt. Edward Osborn) captured the French corvette *Laurette* (26) in the East Indies. (Clowes 4.558)

Arrogant **and** *Hecla* **at Eckness, Finland, 19 May 1854**
The screw frigate *Arrogant* (Capt. Hastings Yelverton) and the paddle sloop *Hecla* (Capt. William Hall) raided Eckness, where they destroyed four field guns on the approach and cut out a merchantman. (Clowes 6.417–418)

Arrow **and** *Acheron* **v.** *Hortense* **and** *Incorruptable,* **3 February 1805**
Arrow (28; Cmdr Richard Vincent) and *Acheron* (bomb; Cmdr Arthur Farquhar), escorting a convoy from Malta towards Gibraltar, met *Hortense* (40) and *Incorruptable* (38) near the Spanish coast. *Arrow* and *Acheron* turned to meet them, sending the convoy on. The French frigates fired at them briefly and passed on towards the convoy, but the British ships followed and insisted on fighting. Both were reduced to wrecks and surrendered; *Arrow* sank, and *Acheron* was so damaged that her captors burned her. Most of the convoy escaped. (James 4.13–17; Clowes 5.353–356)

Arrow **and** *Griffin* **v. German armed trawlers, 26 April 1940**
Off Romsdal, Norway, the German armed trawlers *Schiff 37* and *36* were

sunk by the destroyers *Arrow* and *Griffin*; valuable documents were found on the second trawler. (Rohwer 21)

Arthur v. French squadron, February 1805
The cutter *Arthur* (6; Lt R. Cooban) was captured by a French squadron in the Mediterranean. (Clowes 5.550)

Artois v. Revolutionnaire, 21 October 1794
Artois (38; Capt. Edmund Nagle) was part of a frigate squadron which met *Revolutionnaire* (44) off Ushant. *Artois* outsailed her companions to bring the French ship to action. *Diamond* came up, but left the fighting to *Artois*, which forced *Revolutionnaire* to surrender. (Clowes 4.487)

Asama v. U-boat, 16 July 1917
The trawler *Asama*, acting as a decoy ship, was sunk by a U-boat. (Colledge 25)

Ascension v. U-322, 24 November 1944
U-322, located and bombed from the air, was sunk by the frigate *Ascension* west of Shetland. (Rohwer 373).

Ascot v. UB-67, 10 November 1918
The paddle minesweeper *Ascot* was sunk by *UB-67* off the Earn Islands, Ireland. (Colledge 25)

Ashanti War, 1873–1874
In operations along the coast before the main expedition went inland to attack the Ashanti capital at Kumasi, a squadron of ships bombarded hostile villages and made landings to assist formed garrisons on shore. A Naval Brigade was formed and took part in the march to Kumasi and in the battles before its capture. (Clowes 7.256–262)

Assiniboine and others v. Speerbrecher 157 and others, 12 August 1944
In the Bay of Biscay the 12th Support Group, led by RCN *Assiniboine*, and including one British and three more Canadian destroyers, attacked *Speerbrecher 157* and two patrol boats. All three German ships survived, but damaged. (Rohwer 347)

Assistance v. French privateer, 1697
Assistance (42; Capt. James Davidson), protecting the fishing fleet off Iceland, captured a large French privateer which made an attack. (Clowes 2.495)

Assurance and others v. French squadron, 1709
A convoy from Cork to England, guarded by three warships, was attacked by a French squadron out of Brest commanded by Duguay-Trouin. The brunt of the attack fell on *Assurance* (70; Capt. Anthony Tollat), which suffered nearly eighty casualties; *Hampshire* (50) and *Assistance* (50) also suffered. All three survived, but five merchantmen were captured. (Clowes 2.520–521)

Assurance v. *Rattlesnake*, 1781
The frigate *Assurance* (44) captured the rebel American sloop *Rattlesnake* (12). (Colledge 90)

Asturias v. *Cagni*, 25 July 1943
The Italian submarine *Cagni* sank the AMC *Asturias* near South Africa; *Cagni* then surrendered at Durban on 20 September. (Rohwer 273)

Atalanta and *Trepassy* v. *Alliance*, 27 May 1781
The brigs *Atalanta* (16; Cmdr Sampson Edwards) and *Trepassy* (14; Cmdr James Smyth) were chased by the rebel American frigate *Alliance* (38). Unable to get away they turned to fight; the battle lasted several hours until both were captured, though *Atalanta* was soon retaken. (Clowes 4.65–66)

Atalante v. *Eveille*, 10 August 1801
The French lugger *Eveille* (6), sheltering in Quiberon Bay, was seized by a cutter sent in by *Atalante* (16; Cmdr Anselm Griffiths). (James 3.142)

Atalante v. French vessels, 9 October 1803
Two ketches and a brig took refuge from *Atalante* (16; Cmdr Joseph Masefield) at the mouth of the River Pennerf in Brittany. Two cutters went in after dark and captured one ketch and the brig, but they could not be refloated. (James 3.194–195)

Athenia v. *U-30*, 3 September 1939
On the first day of the Second World War, the liner *Athenia* was sunk without warning northwest of Ireland by *U-30*; 112 lives were lost. Lt Lemp, commander of *U-30*, said he thought the ship was an AMC. The Germans claimed it was a British plot, and altered *U-30*'s log. (Terraine 215–216; Rohwer 2)

ATLANTIC CONVOYS, 1939–1945 (Battle of the Atlantic)
The need for Britain to import supplies of all sorts, and later for the transportation to Europe of US troops, meant that the North Atlantic became a major battleground in Hitler's War. Both sides built on lessons learned in the Great War: the Germans relied on submarines, the British (and later the US) on protected convoys. Many convoys had to fight their way through and each of these encounters was a substantial battle. These encounters are here listed in chronological order. The dates are those in which the convoys were in action. Convoys not listed (the majority) passed without challenge.
See also: ***Bismarck*, Indian Ocean Convoys, Malta Convoys, North African Convoys, Russian Convoys.**
   Convoys were designated by letter and number, the most important of which were:
HG – Gibraltar to UK, HX – Halifax to UK
KM – UK to North Africa, MK – North Africa to UK
OG – UK to Gibraltar, 1939–1943, UG – US to Gibraltar (troops)

OB – Liverpool outward, 1939–1941, ON – UK to North America, from 1941, SC – Sydney, Nova Scotia to UK from 1940
OS – UK to West Africa, SL – Sierra Leone to UK
WS – 'Winston special' – UK to Middle East
F, M, S added to these – Fast, Medium, Slow

OB-4, 15–16 September 1939
This convoy was attacked by *U-31*, which sank one ship. (Rohwer 6)

OB-17, 13 October 1939
The escort destroyers *Ilex* and *Imogen* sank *U-42* when it attacked this convoy. (Rohwer 6)

KJF-3, 14 October 1939
This convoy was attacked by *U-45* south of Ireland, but she was sunk by the escort destroyers *Icarus, Inglefield, Intrepid,* and *Ivanhoe*. (Rohwer 6)

HG-3, 17 October 1939
This convoy was attacked by *U-37, U-47,* and *U-48* in an early attempt at pack tactics. It was without an escort, and three ships were sunk, one by each submarine. (Milner 28; Rohwer 6)

OG-16, 30 January 1940
This convoy was attacked by *U-55* west of the English Channel. Three ships were sunk, but *U-55* was then damaged by depth charges from the destroyer *Fowey*. She surfaced and was attacked by a Sunderland aircraft; a final attack by the destroyer *Whitshed* and the French destroyer *Valmy* led to her being scuttled. (Rohwer 14)

OA-84, 5 February 1940
U-41 attacked this convoy south of Ireland. One ship was sunk; then *U-41* was itself sunk by the destroyer *Antelope*. (Roskill 1.131; Rohwer 14)

OG-18, 17 February 1940
U-37 and *U-53* attacked this convoy off Cape Finisterre; four ships were sunk. (Roskill 1.132; Rohwer 15)

HN-14, 25 February 1940
This convoy was attacked by *U-63*, which was spotted and sunk by the destroyers *Escort, Imogen,* and *Inglefield*. (Rohwer 16)

ON-25, 7–9 April 1940
This convoy was ordered to return to Britain when news came of the German invasion of Norway, and its escort was taken away. Many of the ships went on, having lost touch with the rest; eleven were sunk or captured. (Roskill 1.148)

NP-1, 14–15 April 1940
This was a troop convoy heading for Harstad in Norway. It was attacked unsuccessfully by *U-58, U-65,* and *U-38*. The destroyers *Brazen* and *Fearless* located *U-49* on 15 April, and sank her, the credit going to *Fearless*. (Rohwer 20)

HX-48/HGF-34/HX-49, 12–15 June 1940
These convoys were attacked by the *Prien* pack (seven U-boats). They sank twenty-eight merchant ships between them, amounting to 150,000 tons of shipping; also sunk was the AMC *Scotstoun* (by *U-25*). The casualties included the ship *Arandora Star* which was carrying German and Italian civilian internees to Canada, sunk by *U-47*. (Rohwer 26)

SL-36, 1 July 1940
This convoy was attacked by *U-102*, which sank one ship, and was itself sunk by the destroyer *Vansittart*. (Rohwer 28)

OA-175, 1 July 1940
Southwest of Ireland, this convoy was attacked by *U-26*, which sank one ship; she was then sunk by the corvette *Gladiolus* and a Sunderland flying boat. (Rohwer 28)

OB-188, 26–27 July 1940
This convoy was attacked by *U-34*, which sank four of its ships. (Rohwer 34)

OB-191, 28 July 1940
Three tankers in this convoy were sunk by *U-99*. (Rohwer 34)

OB-193, 4 August 1940
U-56 sank one ship out of this convoy. (Rohwer 34)

SL-40, 4 August 1940
U-58 sank one ship from this convoy. (Rohwer 34)

HX-60, 4–7 August 1940
Three U-boats attacked this convoy in the Northwest Approaches; six ships were sunk. (Rohwer 34)

OB-197/OB-198/OA-198, mid-August 1940
These convoys were all attacked in the North Channel by U-boats. Several ships were sunk. (Rohwer 35)

OB-202, 24 August 1940
This convoy was attacked by *U-53*, which sank two ships and damaged another. (Rohwer 36)

SC-1, 24–27 August 1940
This convoy was attacked on 24–25 August by *U-37*; one ship and the destroyer *Penzance* were sunk; a second ship was sunk by *U-28* on 27 August. (Roskill 1.344; Rohwer 36)

HX-65, 25–26 August 1940
This convoy was attacked on 25 August by *U-48*, which sank two merchant ships, and later that day by *U-124*, which sank two more; another two were sunk by air attack on 26 August. (Rohwer 36)

OA-204, 29 August 1940
This convoy was attacked by *U-100*, which sank two ships, damaged one, and then sank two stragglers. (Rohwer 36)

HX-66A, 30 August 1940
This convoy was attacked by *U-32*, which sank three of the ships. (Rohwer 35)

OB-205, 30–31 August 1940
This convoy was attacked by four U-boats in succession; between them they sank one ship and damaged three more. (Rohwer 36)

SC-2, 6–10 September 1940
This convoy's position was detected by German radio decryption and four submarines were directed to attack. A first attack by *U-65* was foiled by the convoy escorts, but later *U-47* sank three ships. Later attempts were deterred by an escorting aircraft, but *U-47* sank a fourth ship on 8 September. (Terraine, 262–263; Rohwer 38)

OA-210, 11 September 1940
This convoy was attacked by *U-28*, which failed to make any kills. (Rohwer 40)

SC-3, 15 September 1940
This convoy was attacked by *U-48*, which sank the destroyer *Dundee*. (Roskill 1.344; Rohwer 40)

OB-216, 20–21 September 1940
U-136 attacked this convoy, but failed to sink any ships. (Rohwer 40)

HX-72, 21–22 September 1940
U-47 located this convoy west of Ireland and brought five other U-boats to the attack. The convoy lost twelve ships out of forty-one, with two more damaged. The escorts, first four ships, then six, failed to locate any of the submarines. (Terraine 263; Macintyre 41; Rohwer 40)

HX-76, 10 October 1940
U-58 sank one straggler from this convoy, which was otherwise unscathed. (Rohwer 43)

HX-77, 11–12 October 1940
This convoy was attacked by *U-48*, which sank three ships. (Rohwer 44)

OB-227, 15 October 1940
U-93 sank one ship from this convoy. (Rohwer 44)

OB-228, 15–17 October 1940
This convoy was attacked by *U-138* and *U-93*; they sank four ships between them. (Rohwer 44)

SC-7, 16–19 October 1940
This convoy was located by *U-48*, which torpedoed two ships, then was driven off by an aircraft. A pack of five more submarines arrived and on 18–19 October they sank fourteen merchant ships, and damaged four (thirty-five had set out). Four ships separated off early on in a storm, and three of these were sunk. The escorts, only four ships at any one time, failed to find

or deter any of the U-boats. (Terraine 265–268; Roskill 1.350; Macintyre 40–51; Milner 42–44; Rohwer 44)

HX-79, 19 October 1940
This convoy was located by five U-boats. A substantial escort force of ten ships failed to find any of them. Twelve merchant ships (out of forty-nine) were sunk, and one was damaged. (Terraine 268; Roskill 1.350; Macintyre 52–55; Milner 92–93; Rohwer 44)

OB-237, 2 November 1940
U-31 made an attack on this convoy, but it was sunk by the destroyer *Antelope*. (Rohwer 46)

HX-84, 5 November 1940
Sighted by an aircraft launched from the pocket battleship *Admiral Scheer*, this convoy was shelled by that ship. *Scheer* was attacked by the AMC escort ship *Jervis Bay*, which was quickly sunk, but meanwhile most of the convoy scattered, helped by a smokescreen, so *Scheer* sank only five ships. The whole convoy pattern was disrupted when the *Scheer*'s exploit was appreciated. One ship, the tanker *San Demetrio*, set on fire and abandoned, was later recovered by some of the crew and brought to port successfully; the exploit was later made into a notable film. (Terraine 295–296; Roskill 1.287–289; Macintyre 62; Milner 45; Rohwer 48)

OB-244, 20–22 November 1940
This convoy was attacked by *U-103*, which sank two ships on 20 November; two days later *U-123* sank five. During this convoy for the first time airborne radar was able to locate a submarine. (Rohwer 48)

SC-11, 22–23 November 1940
This convoy was attacked by *U-100* close to Ireland. Seven ships of the convoy were sunk in repeated attacks. (Milner 45–46; Rohwer 48)

HX-90, 1–2 December 1940
This convoy had only one escort ship when it came under attack by three U-boats. *U-101* sank two ships, *U-47* one, and *U-52* two; three ships were damaged that night. Despite four more escorts arriving, a second attack, by *U-94*, on the afternoon of 2 December sank two more ships. In total nine ships were sunk and three damaged. (Roskill 1.353; Macintyre 61; Milner 46; Rohwer 49)

HG-47, 1–2 December 1940
Near Rockall the Canadian escort ship *Saguenay* was hit by a torpedo from the Italian submarine *Argo*; *U-99* sank five merchant ships and the AMC *Forfar*. (Rohwer 49)

HX-92, 11–12 December 1940
U-96 attacked this convoy near Rockall, sinking four ships. (Rohwer 51)

OG-47, 21 December 1940
This convoy was attacked by the Italian submarine *Mocenigo* off the Azores; one ship was sunk. (Rohwer 50)

WS-5A, 25 December 1940
West of Cape Finisterre the German cruiser *Admiral Hipper* encountered this convoy. She had an exchange of fire with the cruiser *Berwick*, which was damaged, as were two of the troop transports in the convoy. (Terraine 297; Roskill 1.291, 369; Milner 47; Rohwer 53)

HX-99, 7 January 1941
This convoy was attacked by the Italian submarines *Nani* and *Glauco*; *Nani* was sunk by the corvette *Anemone*. (Rohwer 54)

OB-272, 15–16 January 1941
This convoy was located by *U-105* and later attacked by the Italian submarine *Torelli*, which sank three ships. (Rohwer 55)

SC-19, 28–29 January 1941
This convoy was located by air near the North Channel; two ships were sunk by aircraft and five by three U-boats. (Rohwer 55)

OB-279, 3 February 1941
This convoy was sighted and reported by *U-107*, which sank two ships; other U-boats failed to reach it. (Rohwer 57)

HX-106, 8 February 1941
This convoy was encountered east of Newfoundland by the German battle-cruisers *Gneisenau* and *Scharnhorst*, which were deterred from attacking by the presence of the British battleship *Ramillies*. (Terraine 297; Roskill 1.374; Macintyre 74; Rohwer 58)

HG-53, 9–11 February 1941
U-37 located this convoy on 9 February and sank two ships. Condor aircraft continued the attack, and these sank five ships; the cruiser *Admiral Hipper* sank a straggler. (Macintyre 72; Milner 47–48; Rohwer 58)

SLS-64, 10 February 1941
This convoy, without an escort, was found by the cruiser *Admiral Hipper* which sank seven and damaged two of the nineteen ships. (Roskill 1.372; Rohwer 59)

OB-287, 19–21 February 1941
This convoy was located by a Condor aircraft which sank two ships, and summoned U-boats, which failed to find the convoy; other planes damaged five ships and one was later finished off by *U-96*. The Italian submarine *Marcello* was sunk by the escorting destroyer *Montgomery*. (Rohwer 60)

OB-288, 22–24 February 1941
This convoy was located west of Ireland by a Condor aircraft, which sank two ships; *U-69* and *U-93* sank two more. The convoy scattered; four U-boats then sank one ship each and two sailing independently – ten ships were lost in all. (Macintyre 73; Milner 48; Rohwer 60)

OB-290, 26 February 1941
This convoy, near the north coast of Ireland, was located by *U-47*, which sank two ships at once; five more ships were sunk by aircraft and by the

Italian submarine *Bianchi*, and another by *U-47* later. (Macintyre 73; Milner 48–49; Rohwer 61)

OB-289, 28 February 1941
This convoy was located by *U-552* west of Ireland, but only *U-97* could find it; she sank three ships. (Terraine 313; Milner 48; Rohwer 60)

OB-292, 2–5 March 1941
Located by a Condor aircraft which sank one ship, this convoy avoided later attempted attacks by other submarines and aircraft. (Rohwer 61)

HX-109, 3–4 March 1941
This convoy was attacked by at least four U-boats, which sank three ships. (Rohwer 60)

OB-293, 6–9 March 1941
Located by *U-47*, which brought four more boats to the attack, this convoy lost five ships sunk. The convoy escort drove off the attackers and the corvettes *Arbutus* and *Camellia* sank *U-70*; *U-47* was sunk, possibly by the destroyer *Wolverine*, which certainly damaged *U-99* and *U-A*. (Terraine 313–314; Roskill 1.365; Macintyre 79; Milner 52; Rohwer 62)

SL-67, 7–8 March 1941
Located by the German battle-cruisers *Scharnhorst* and *Gneisenau* off West Africa, this convoy was attacked by *U-105* and *U-124*, which had refuelled at Las Palmas in the Canary Islands. The presence of the battleship *Malaya* deterred the battle-cruisers, but five vessels were sunk during the night; the U-boats were driven off in daylight. (Roskill 1.376; Rohwer 62)

HX-112, 7–8 March 1941
Attacked by several U-boats while south of Iceland, this convoy lost six ships. The destroyer *Vanoc* (using radar) found and sank *U-100*, and the destroyers *Walker* and *Vanoc* together sank *U-99*. (Terraine 314–316; Roskill 1.365; Rohwer 63)

HX-114, 16 March 1941
This convoy was escorted by the battleship *Rodney*, and encountered the battle-cruiser *Gneisenau*, which evaded. (Rohwer 63)

SL-68, 17–22 March 1941
Located off West Africa by *U-106*, this convoy was also attacked by *U-105*; between them they sank seven ships and damaged the battleship *Malaya*. (Terraine 121; Rohwer 63–64)

OG-56, 23–24 March 1941
U-97 and the Italian submarine *Verniero* sank three ships from this convoy. (Rohwer 64)

HX-115, 29 March 1941
This convoy was attacked by *U-48*, which sank four ships in a series of attacks. (Rohwer 65)

OB-302, 29–30 March 1941
Located by *U-69*, and also attacked by *U-46*, three ships were sunk from this convoy. (Rohwer 65)

SC-26, 2–3 April 1941
Attacked south of Greenland by a pack of seven U-boats, this convoy lost eleven ships; the AMC *Worcestershire* was damaged by *U-74*; the destroyers *Wolverine* and *Scarborough* sank *U-76*. The attacks ceased when the escort arrived, which encouraged the Admiralty to extend escorts further west. (Terraine 344; Roskill 1.463; Macintyre 85)

OG-57, 8–9 April 1941
This convoy was attacked by *U-105* and *U-107* off West Africa; three ships were sunk. (Rohwer 70)

HX-121, 28 April–2 May 1941
Three U-boats attacked this convoy. One was driven off, but five ships were sunk; *U-65* was in turn sunk by the destroyer *Douglas*. (Roskill 1.463; Rohwer 68)

OB-318, 7–10 May 1941
This convoy was sighted south of Iceland by *U-94*, which sank two ships, but was damaged in attacks by the escorts. *U-110* arrived and also sank two ships before it was forced to the surface by the corvette *Aubrietia* and captured by the destroyers *Bulldog* and *Broadway*. The current codes and an Enigma machine were recovered from this U-boat, opening the way to decrypting Enigma signal traffic. *U-201* sank one ship and damaged another, and was itself damaged by the escorts. *U-556* continued the attack on 10 May and sank two ships and damaged another. (Terraine 326; Rohwer 71; Sebag-Montefiore 150–161)

SC-30, 13 May 1941
U-98 sank the AMC *Salopian* when this convoy was south of Greenland. (Rohwer 73)

SL-73, 19 May 1941
This convoy was attacked by the Italian submarine *Octavia*, which sank one ship. (Rohwer 73)

HX-126, 19–22 May 1941
Successive attacks by ten U-boats on this convoy sank four ships and damaged one. The escort commander ordered the ships to scatter, but four more ships were sunk. *U-74* was damaged in a depth-charge attack. One result of this battle was that escorts were now to be provided right across the Atlantic. (Terraine 345; Roskill 1.459, 463; Macintyre 87; Milner 65–66; Rohwer 73)

OB-239, 2 June 1941
U-147 attacked this convoy north of Ireland, sank one ship and damaged another, and was then sunk by the destroyer *Wanderer* and the corvette *Periwinkle*. (Rohwer 77)

OG-63, 5–6 June 1941
Three Italian submarines attacked this convoy; they sank two ships. (Rohwer 76)

SL-76, 13 June 1941
Two ships from this convoy were sunk by the Italian submarine *Brin* east of the Azores. (Rohwer 76)

HX-133, 23–26 June 1941
This convoy was located by a pack of ten U-boats south of Greenland. The escort included Canadian Navy ships for the first time and this was the first convoy to have its attackers' reports intercepted and decrypted at Bletchley Park in time for effective reaction. Six ships of the convoy were sunk. *U-556* was sunk by the corvettes *Nasturtium*, *Celandine*, and *Gladiolus*, and *U-651* was sunk by *Malcolm*, *Violet*, *Scimitar*, *Arabis*, and *Speedwell*. (Terraine 348–350; Roskill 1.466–467; Macintyre 87; Rohwer 79–80)

OB-336, 24 June 1941
This convoy was attacked by several U-boats; three ships were sunk. (Rohwer 79)

OG-66, 29 June–3 July 1941
Several sightings were made of this convoy by German aircraft and several attacks were attempted, but they all failed. (Rohwer 84)

OG-69, 26–30 July 1941
Located by air reconnaissance, this convoy was attacked by several U-boats. Seven ships were sunk, though some attacks failed due to the vigilance of the escort ships. (Milner 66–67; Rohwer 87)

OS-1, 26–30 July 1941
U-141 sank one ship from this convoy, but was then hunted and depth-charged for twenty hours; *U-371* also found the convoy and sank two ships. (Rohwer 87)

SL-81, 3–5 August 1941
This convoy was the first of this series to be escorted all through its voyage and it was tenaciously defended by its escort; in addition a German reconnaissance plane was shot down by a catapulted Hurricane from the catapult ship *Maplin*. In the end several U-boats penetrated the screen and sank six ships, but *U-401* was sunk by *Wanderer*, *St Albans*, and *Hydrangea*. (Terraine 265–268; Roskill 1.453; Milner 67; Rohwer 89)

HG-69, 10–14 August 1941
One ship was sunk out of this convoy by a Condor aircraft, but all the U-boat attacks, in which eleven boats were involved, were foiled or driven off by the escort. (Rohwer 91)

ONS-4, 12 August 1941
Attacked west of the North Channel, this convoy lost four ships, and the corvette *Picotee* was sunk by *U-568*. (Macintyre 185; Rohwer 90)

OG-71, 18–23 August
A long series of attacks by air and by U-boats on this convoy resulted in nine merchant ships being sunk, and two escorts as well – *Bath* by *U-204*, and *Zinnia* by *U-564*. (Milner 67–68; Rohwer 91–92)

OS-3, 26–28 August 1941
This convoy was attacked by *U-557*, which sank four ships in its first attack; another was sunk by *U-558*. (Rohwer 94)

HX-145, 27 August 1941
A group of U-boats menaced this convoy, unsuccessfully. *U-570* was stranded, unable to dive, and was found by the trawler *Northern Chief*, then forced to surrender to the destroyer *Burwell* and aircraft of 269 squadron of Coastal Command; she was taken into the navy as HMS *Graph*. (Rohwer 90; Sebag-Montefiore 185–189)

SC-41, 9 September 1941
One ship from this convoy was sunk by *U-81*. (Rohwer 96)

SC-42, 9–12 September 1941
This convoy was located by a U-boat south of Greenland and attacked by several boats, despite repeated attempts to drive them away. Seventeen ships were sunk, and two damaged. *U-207* was sunk by *Leamington* and *Veteran*, and *U-501* by the Canadians *Chambly* and *Moose Jaw*. For a time three US destroyers joined the escort. (Terraine 373–382; Roskill 1.468–469; Macintyre 95–108; Milner 70–72; Rohwer 96; Sebag-Montefiore 192–196)

HG-72, 11–12 September 1941
This convoy was attacked by four Italian submarines, which were driven away by the escorts. (Rohwer 97)

ON-14, 15 September 1941
Three ships straggling from this convoy were sunk by *U-94*. (Rohwer 100)

SC-44, 18–19 September 1941
This convoy was subjected to repeated attacks by several U-boats, and four ships were sunk. HMCS *Levis* was sunk by *U-74*. (Terraine 382; Roskill 1.468; Macintyre 108; Rohwer 100)

OG-74, 20 September 1941
This convoy was accompanied by the first of the escort carriers, *Audacity*. Its planes forced several U-boats to submerge, and shot down a Condor aircraft, but six ships were sunk. (Terraine 386; Roskill 1.478; Macintyre 112–114; Milner 72; Rohwer 101)

SL-87, 22–24 September 1941
Located in the south central Atlantic by *U-107*, and attacked by four U-boats, this convoy lost seven out of twelve ships. (Terraine 383; Rohwer 103)

HG-73, 25–26 September 1941
Located by aircraft off Cape St Vincent, this convoy was attacked by three U-boats, which sank nine of its ships, a heavy loss partly attributable to the

breakdown of the radar in the escorts, but mainly to the lack of air cover. The Italian submarine *Malaspina* was sunk, possibly by a Sunderland aircraft, and *Torelli* was damaged by *Vimy*. The catapult ship *Springbank* was sunk by *U-201*. (Terraine 383–385; Roskill 1.468, 477; Macintyre 114; Rohwer 101)

SC-46, September 1941
This convoy was attacked by *U-562*, which sank one ship. (Rohwer 103)

OG-75, 5–12 October 1941
This convoy was located from the air. One ship was sunk by a German aircraft, and three others by submarines. The corvette *Fleur de Lys* was sunk near Gibraltar by *U-206*. (Rohwer 105)

HX-152, 9 October 1941
One ship straggling from this convoy was sunk by *U-562*. (Rohwer 104)

SC-48, 15–17 October 1941
Battered by storms and attacked by a U-boat pack, many ships of this convoy straggled. Nine merchant ships were sunk, as were the destroyer *Broadwater* and the corvette *Gladiolus*, by *U-103* and *U-553* respectively. USS *Kearny*, part of the substantial US section of the escort, was badly damaged by a torpedo. (Terraine 393; Milner 73; Rohwer 107)

ONS-19, 20 October 1941
This convoy was attacked by *U-562*, which sank a tanker and the catapult ship *Empire Wave*. (Rohwer 100)

SL-89, 21–23 October 1941
This convoy was located by *U-84*. Two merchant ships were sunk by *U-82*, and the AMC *Aurania* by *U-123*. The U-boats were driven off by the escort on 23 October. (Rohwer 109)

HG-75, 23–28 October 1941
This convoy was attacked by several German and Italian submarines. Four ships were sunk, as were the destroyer *Cossack* (by *U-563*) and the catapult ship *Ariguani* (by *U-83*). Two Italian submarines were sunk, *Ferraris* in a gun duel with the destroyer *Lamerton*, and *Marconi* by the destroyer *Duncan*. (Milner 73; Rohwer 109)

HX-156, 31 October 1941
This convoy was located by *U-552*, which torpedoed the US destroyer *Reuben James*, the first US ship to be sunk in this war. Other U-boat attacks on the convoy failed. (Roskill 1.472; Rohwer 111)

OS-10, 31 October 1941
This convoy met *U-96* which sank one ship; other U-boats failed to find the convoy. (Rohwer 111)

SC-52, 1–3 November 1941
This convoy was sighted by *U-374* and was intercepted by the *Raubritter* pack off Newfoundland. Four ships were sunk: the convoy was ordered to return to Canada. (Terraine 395; Rohwer 112)

SL-91, 8 November 1941

This convoy was searched for by Condor aircraft, and planes from the escort carrier *Audacity* successfully shot down two of these attackers; two others failed to find the convoy, which was unscathed on arrival in Gibraltar. (Terraine 395–396; Rohwer 112)

SC-53, 16 November 1941

This convoy was missed by the waiting U-boats, but *U-561* sank two stragglers. (Rohwer 113)

OS-12, 29 November 1941

One ship from this convoy was sunk by *U-43*. (Rohwer 115)

WS-13, 30 November 1941

One ship was sunk from this troop convoy by *U-43* west of Gibraltar. (Rohwer 115)

HG-76, 15–21 December 1941

This convoy was attacked by the *Seerauber* pack. The Australian destroyer *Nestor* sank *U-127* close to Gibraltar on the first day of the voyage, and a combination of aircraft from the escort carrier *Audacity* and the escort ships *Exmoor, Blankney, Stork, Stanley,* and *Pentstemon* sank *U-131* on the 17th. The destroyers *Stanley* and *Blankney* sank *U-434* next day. *Stork* sank *U-574* in a combined depth-charge, gun, and ramming fight, just after the boat had sunk *Stanley*. One Condor was shot down by *Audacity*'s aircraft, and two damaged. *Audacity* itself was sunk on the night of the 21st by *U-567*, which in turn was sunk by the sloops *Deptford* and *Samphire*. Two merchant ships were also sunk. This was one of the most eventful of convoys, in which an escort carrier's effectiveness was demonstrated by *Audacity*. (Terraine 396–399; Roskill 1.478; Macintyre 119; Milner 81–83; Rohwer 126)

SC-57, December 1941

U-130 met this convoy by chance, and sank three ships. (Rohwer 117)

HX-168, 12 January 1942

U-43 sank one straggler from this convoy. (Rohwer 124)

ON-55, 12–14 January 1942

U-333 sank one ship from this convoy, and two stragglers were sunk by *U-43* after it dispersed. (Rohwer 129, 132, 135)

HG-78, 15 January 1942

This convoy was attacked by three U-boats, which were driven off by the escort; the destroyer *Hesperus* sank *U-93*. (Roskill 2.94; Rohwer 135)

ONS-52, 17–19 January 1942

When this convoy dispersed, *U-553* and *U-87* sank a ship each, and *U-86* damaged another. (Rohwer 124)

ONS-54, 19–21 January 1942

U-135 sank one ship from this convoy after it had dispersed. (Rohwer 132)

ONS-56, 23–26 January 1942
Two ships from this convoy were sunk, by *U-82* and *U-582*. (Rohwer 129)

SC-63, 28 January 1942
U-84 and *U-588* each sank a straggler from this convoy and *U-333* sank a ship from the convoy itself. (Rohwer 132, 135)

SL-98, 31 January 1942
This convoy was attacked in the Bay of Biscay by *U-105*, which sank the US coastguard cutter *Culver*. (Rohwer 140)

NA-2, 31 January 1942
This convoy was sighted by *U-82*, which sank the destroyer *Belmont*. (Rohwer 140)

HX-173, 4–13 February 1942
One ship from this convoy was sunk by *U-751*. (Rohwer 132)

ON-63, 5 February 1942
This convoy was located near Rockall; the corvette *Arbutus* was sunk by *U-136*. (Roskill 2.101; Rohwer 132, 139)

OS-18, 6 February 1942
This convoy was located by a Condor aircraft, which was shot down by AA fire from the corvette *Genista*. *U-82* was sunk by the sloop *Rochester* and the corvette *Tamarisk* while attacking. (Roskill 2.102; Rohwer 141)

ONS-68, 8–10 February 1942
Attacked by *U-654*, this convoy largely escaped damage, but the Free French corvette *Alysse* was sunk. (Rohwer 141)

HX-174, 9–19 February 1942
One ship straggling from this convoy was sunk by *U-136*. (Rohwer 132)

ON-65, 10–24 February 1942
U-107 sank one ship from this convoy. (Rohwer 132)

SC-67, 11 February 1942
The RCN corvette *Spikenard* was sunk by *U-136*, and one ship from the convoy was sunk by *U-591*. (Roskill 2.10; Rohwer 139)

ON-67, 21–25 February 1942
Off Cape Race this convoy was located by *U-155*, which sank two ships; other U-boats arrived and sank seven more. Six of the victims were tankers. (Roskill 2.96; Rohwer 146)

HX-175, 22 February 1942
This convoy was reported by *U-154*; attacks by several U-boats sank three ships. Effective defensive manoeuvring by the convoy frustrated several other attacks. (Roskill 2.101; Rohwer 139)

ON-77, 24–25 March 1942
The convoy was sighted by *U-203*; *U-94* sank a tanker. (Rohwer 154)

WS-17, 27 March 1942
U-587 reported sighting this convoy, which carried the forces for the attack on Madagascar. The U-boat was then itself located by D/F and sunk by the destroyers *Aldenham, Grove, Leamington,* and *Volunteer*. (Roskill 2.102, 106–107; Rohwer 155)

OG-82, 14 April 1942
U-252 met this convoy, but was located by the corvette *Vetch* (using a new radar system) and was sunk by *Vetch* and the sloop *Stork*. (Roskill 2.102; Rohwer 155)

SL-109, 11–14 May 1942
This convoy was located by chance by three U-boats; *U-128* sank one ship. (Rohwer 165)

ONS-92, 11–13 May 1942
This convoy ran into the recently organised *Hecht* U-boat pack (six boats). Seven ships were sunk by two of the U-boats; the escorts were generally incompetently commanded. (Terraine 446–448; Roskill 2.106; Rohwer 165)

ONS-94, 20 May 1942
This convoy was located by *U-406*, which was driven off; other boats failed to find the convoy. (Rohwer 165)

OS-28, 21 May 1942
This convoy was attacked by *U-159*, which sank two ships. (Rohwer 167)

ONS-100, 8–12 June 1942
The *Hecht* pack attacked this convoy several times in difficult weather. The Free French corvette *Mimose* was sunk, as well as four ships from the convoy. (Terraine 450–451; Roskill 2.106; Rohwer 165)

HG-84, 11–16 June 1942
Located by aircraft, this convoy was attacked by three U-boats, which were driven off by the escorts. *U-552* later sank three ships, but other attacks were driven off. (Milner 90; Roskill 2.106; Rohwer 173)

ONS-102, 16–18 June 1942
The *Hecht* pack attacked this convoy but the U-boats were driven off, *U-94* and *U-590* damaged. *U-124* found the convoy again on 18 June and sank one ship. (Terraine 450–453; Milner 90; Rohwer 165)

BA-2, 3 July 1942
U-215 sank a ship from this convoy south of Nova Scotia; the submarine itself was then sunk by the trawler *Le Tiger*. (Rohwer 178)

QS-15, 6 July 1942
U-132 attacked this convoy in the Gulf of St Lawrence, and sank six of its ships. (Rohwer 178)

OS-33, 11–15 July 1942
This convoy was located by the U-tanker *U-116*, which with two other U-boats sank three of the ships. The frigate *Spey*, the sloop *Pelican*, and the

Free French destroyer *Leopard* sank *U-136*; four more ships from the convoy were also sunk. (Rohwer 179)

ON-111, 13 July 1942
This convoy was located by *U-71*, but most of the *Wolf* pack missed it; two U-boats were driven off by the escort. (Rohwer 180)

SL-115, 14 July 1942
This convoy was approached by the Italian submarine *Calvi* which fought the sloop *Lulworth* on the surface until she was sunk; *U-130* then attacked *Lulworth* without success. (Rohwer 180)

OS-34, 17–20 July 1942
Located by *U-202*, which was driven off quickly by the escort, this convoy was attacked later by other boats, which found attacking even at night very difficult; one ship was sunk. (Rohwer 181)

QS-19, 20 July 1942
U-132 sank one ship from this convoy in the Gulf of St Lawrence. (Rohwer 178)

ON-113, 24–29 July 1942
This convoy was located by signal decrypt and *U-552*. *U-90* was sunk by the RCN destroyer *St Croix*; three ships from the convoy were sunk. (Terraine 461–462; Roskill 2.108; Milner 112; Rohwer 180)

ON-115, 29 July–August 1942
This convoy was located by *U-210* and attacked by five boats; for several days the escort drove off every attack, and *U-588* was sunk by the RCN destroyer *Wetaskiwin*; later attacks sank three ships. (Milner 123–125; Rohwer 183)

SC-94, 6–8 August 1942
U-593 located this convoy and sank one ship but was then driven off; *U-595* and *U-454* were damaged by depth-charges and *U-210* was forced to the surface and rammed and sunk by the RCN destroyer *Assiniboine*. On 8 August other attacks sank five ships and three ships were abandoned in panic, one of which was later sunk. *U-379* was sunk by the corvette *Dianthus*. The escorts stayed behind to keep the U-boats away, but two boats sank four more ships in the absence of the escorts. (Terraine 476–478; Roskill 2.209–210; Macintyre 150–156; Milner 127–128; Rohwer 185)

TAW-12/WAT-13, 14 August 1942
These convoys, under escort of US and British ships in the Windward Passage, were seen and attacked by three U-boats which sank five of their ships. (Rohwer 188)

SC-95, 15–16 August 1942
Four U-boats attacked this convoy and sank two ships; contact was then lost. (Rohwer 188)

SL-118, 1–20 August 1942
This convoy was attacked by the *Blucher* pack (seven boats) off West Africa; four ships were sunk and the AMC *Cheshire* was damaged; three U-boats

were damaged by various attacks. (Roskill 2.200, 210; Milner 128; Rohwer 189)

ONS-122, 22–26 August 1942
This convoy was located by chance by *U-135*, which summoned several more boats of the *Lohs* pack. Early attacks were driven off but during the night of 24–25 August nine U-boats were in contact with the convoy. Two ships were sunk that night, and *U-605* and *U-256* were damaged. Two more ships were sunk before contact was lost. (Terraine 484–485; Milner 127–128; Rohwer 188–189)

SL-119, 25–29 August 1942
This convoy was located off West Africa by *U-214*, which summoned the U-boats of the *Iltis* and *Eisbar* packs (eight boats in all); three ships were sunk; *U-566* was damaged. (Rohwer 191)

TAW-15, 27 August 1942
This convoy was attacked in the Windward Passage. *U-94* was depth-charged to the surface by a Catalina aircraft and then rammed three times by the RCN corvette *Oakville*, and finally sunk. *U-511* sank two ships. (Rohwer 192)

SC-97, 31 August 1942
This convoy was attacked by the *Vorwarts* pack (ten boats). Two ships were sunk by *U-609*, which had first sighted the convoy; air patrols and the attentive escort successfully frustrated later attacks; *U-756* was sunk by the RCN corvette *Morden*. (Terraine 478; Rohwer 192)

NL-6/NL-7, 3–7 September 1942
In the St Lawrence River *U-517* sank one ship out of these convoys and the corvette *Charlottetown*. (Rohwer 190)

ON-127, 4–14 September 1942
This convoy was attacked by the *Vorwarts* pack (thirteen boats) approaching Newfoundland. Eight ships were sunk and four damaged. The RCN destroyer *Ottawa* was sunk by *U-91*. Air surveillance deterred daylight attacks, but the failure of the convoy's radar system allowed night-time attacks to succeed. (Terraine 485; Roskill 2.210; Milner 133; Rohwer 192–193)

QS-33, 6 September 1942
In the St Lawrence River *U-517* sank four ships from this convoy. (Rohwer 190)

NL-9, 9 September 1942
U-69 sank two ships from this convoy in the Gulf of St Lawrence. (Rohwer 193)

SC-99, 13–15 September 1942
This convoy was located by *U-216*, which summoned seven other boats, whose attacks were driven off; *U-440* was damaged by a depth-charge attack and *U-261* was sunk by air attack. (Rohwer 196)

SQ-36, 15–16 September 1942
This convoy, in the Gulf of St Lawrence, was attacked by *U-517* and *U-156*; they sank four ships and damaged another. (Rohwer 190)

ON-129, 16 September 1942
This convoy was briefly found by U-boats but they were driven off by the escort when attempting to attack. (Rohwer 196)

SC-100, 18–25 September 1942
This convoy was attacked by the *Pfiel* pack; four ships were sunk. (Rohwer 194)

SC-101, 23 September 1942
U-610 sank a straggler from this convoy. (Rohwer 199)

R-1, 24–26 September 1942
This convoy was located by the *Vorwarts* pack. Of the eight passenger steamers in the convoy three were sunk, as was the destroyer *Veteran*, by *U-404*. (Rohwer 197)

ON-131, 26–30 September 1942
U-617 sighted this convoy, and summoned the *Tiger* pack (fifteen boats). However, *U-617*'s attacks failed and the other U-boats could not find the convoy. (Rohwer 198)

HX-209, 2–4 October 1942
This convoy was sighted by *U-260*, and the *Luchs* pack (seventeen boats) pursued it, but with little success; an abandoned tanker was sunk, but the boats could not catch the convoy; two submarines were sunk and one was damaged by an air attack. (Roskill 2.210; Rohwer 199)

ONS-136, 11–14 October 1942
This convoy was attacked by the *Leopard* pack (nine boats) during a heavy storm; two ships were sunk; *U-597* was sunk by air attack. (Rohwer 200)

SC-104, 12–15 October 1942
U-221 attacked and sank three ships, and summoned the *Wotan* pack (eight boats), but the next attack was driven off by the escorts. Four more ships were then sunk, but other attacks failed, with two U-boats damaged. Several more U-boats were damaged on the 14th by air attack, by ramming – *U-619* was sunk by the destroyer *Viscount* in this way – and by depth-charges. *U-353* was sunk by the destroyer *Fame*, and yet another U-boat was damaged by gunfire. *U-661* was sunk by air attack nearby. (Terraine 489–490; Roskill 2.212–213; Macintyre 162; Milner 104–105; Rohwer 200)

ON-137, 16–18 October 1942
This convoy was attacked by the *Panther* and *Wotan* packs (twenty-two boats in all), but it escaped with the loss of only one straggler. (Rohwer 203)

ONS-139, 22 October 1942
U-443 attacked this convoy and sank two ships, but other boats could not reach it. (Rohwer 203)

HX-212, 26–29 October 1942

This convoy ran on to the *Puma* pack (seven boats), and three ships were sunk on the 26th. Later attacks were driven off or were frustrated by the escorts or aircraft, but another ship and one straggler were sunk. (Terraine 490; Roskill 2.213; Milner 136; Rohwer 203)

SL-125, 27–31 October 1942

This convoy was attacked near Madeira by four U-boats, which later were reinforced by seven more. Nine ships were sunk; eventually aircraft drove the attackers away. (Terraine 492–493; Roskill 2.213; Macintyre 161; Rohwer 206)

SC-107, 30 October–5 November 1942

This convoy was attacked by the *Vielchen* pack (thirteen boats), from which *U-520* and *U-658* were sunk by an attack on 31 October. A good half of the attacks were foiled by the escorts, but sixteen ships out of forty-two were sunk. *U-132* disappeared, probably sunk when a nearby ammunition ship exploded. (Terraine 490–492; Roskill 2.215–216; Macintyre 137–141; Rohwer 204)

ONS-143, 7 November 1942

This convoy was located by two U-boats of the *Natter* pack, which sank two stragglers. (Rohwer 208)

MFK-1, 14–16 November 1942

This convoy, returning from the North African Torch landings with a strong escort, was attacked in the Atlantic by U-boats of the *Westwall* pack. Two troop transports were sunk, and *U-155* sank the carrier *Avenger* and another transport. *U-92* sank another ship, but *U-218* was damaged in trying an attack. (Rohwer 212)

ONS-144, 15–19 November 1942

This convoy was attacked by the *Kreuzotter* pack (eight boats). Five ships were sunk, as was the Norwegian corvette *Montbretia* (by *U-262*). *U-184* was lost during the operation, probably by accident. (Terraine 505; Milner 137–138; Rohwer 212)

HX-217, 6–8 December 1942

After several fruitless attempts to attack this convoy, the *Panther* pack (seven boats) was joined by the *Draufganger* pack (nine boats) and they sank two ships; *U-611* and *U-254* were sunk and three other boats were damaged in the operation. (Terraine 505–506; Roskill 2.216; Milner 110–111; Rohwer 215)

HX-218, 13 December 1942

Attacked by the *Buffel* pack on 13 December this convoy's escorts drove the boats away; the *Ungestum* pack next attempted an attack but also failed. (Rohwer 218)

ONS-152, 15 December 1942

This convoy met *U-373* near Iceland, but only one ship was sunk; later, *U-626* was sunk by the US Coast Guard cutter *Ingham*. (Rohwer 218, 219)

ON-153, 16–18 December 1942
This convoy was located by *U-609*, which brought up the *Raufbold* pack (eleven boats). Six ships were sunk; the destroyer *Firedrake* was sunk by *U-211*. (Rohwer 219)

ONS-154, 26–30 December 1942
This convoy was attacked by the *Spitz* (ten boats) and *Ungestum* (nine boats) packs. The convoy had been routed southwards to avoid bad weather and encountered the packs as a result. The U-boats several times managed to get among the ships of the convoy, and shortage of fuel reduced the escort to only four ships at one point. Fourteen ships were sunk, as was the auxiliary warship *Fidelity* (by *U-435*); *U-356* was sunk by four of the convoy's escort ships. (Terraine 510–511, 537–538; Roskill 2.216; Milner 143–144; Rohwer 220)

HX-219, 26–27 December 1942
U-357 met this convoy, but was located by the escorts before she could attack, and was then sunk by the destroyers *Hesperus* and *Vanessa*. (Rohwer 220)

TN-1, 29 December 1942–10 January 1943
This convoy of tankers sailed from Trinidad in two parts; one section of two tankers and a corvette evaded an early attack; the full convoy was located in mid-Atlantic on 3 January by *U-514*, which sank one tanker at once. The convoy then ran on to the *Delphin* pack (ten boats) on 8 January. Of the eight tankers still in the convoy six were sunk by 10 January. (Rohwer 220–221)

UGS-3, 10 January 1943
This convoy lost one ship, a straggler which was sunk by *U-632*. (Rohwer 223)

HX-222, 17 January 1943
U-268 sank one ship from this convoy, a former whale factory ship which was carrying three LCTs. (Roskill 2.356; Rohwer 225)

SC-117, 22–25 January 1943
U-413, which sank two stragglers, was unable to communicate the convoy's position clearly to the other submarines in the *Jaguar* pack. (Rohwer 226)

UGS-4, 25 January 1943
This convoy was attacked by the *Delphin* pack (fifteen boats), losing three ships. (Rohwer 227)

HX-223, 26 January 1943
U-boats from the *Handegen* pack attacked this convoy. Already scattered by a storm, it lost two ships. (Rohwer 227)

HX-224, 1–3 February 1943
This convoy was located by *U-456*, which sank two ships; other boats arrived but could sink only one more ship. *U-265* was sunk by air attack. (Terraine 524; Roskill 2.356; Milner 148; Rohwer 227, 228)

SC-118, 2–9 February 1943

This convoy, sixty-one ships with eight escorts, was located by the German command from decrypted signals and information from a prisoner; it was found by the centre boat of the *Pfiel* pack (twenty boats), but first blood went to the escorts, when the destroyers *Vimy* and *Beverley* sank *U-187*. Two ships were sunk, though other attacks were driven off by the escorts and later by aircraft. On 7 February, *U-402* at last got past the escorts and sank six ships, and another was sunk by *U-614*. *U-679* was sunk by air attack, but *U-402* sank another ship from the convoy. Several of the U-boats were badly damaged in these attacks. (Terraine 529–531; Roskill 2.356; Milner 149–150; Rohwer 228–229)

Gibr-2, 7 February 1943

This convoy was attacked by *U-521*, which sank the ASW trawler *Bredon*; the arrival of more protection prevented further attacks. (Rohwer 227)

Krk-9, 12–14 February 1943

This convoy was attacked off Cape St Vincent. Aircraft assisted the defence and sank *U-442* and *U-620*. (Rohwer 227)

ONS-165, 17–20 February 1943

U-69 found this convoy but was herself located by D/F and sunk by the destroyer *Fame*; the next boat to arrive, *U-201*, was rammed and sunk by the destroyer *Viscount*. Other boats made occasional contact; two of the convoy's ships were sunk. (Terraine 531–532; Roskill 2.357; Rohwer 230–231)

ON-166, 20–25 February 1943

Located by *U-604*, this convoy was attacked by many U-boats. Early attacks were foiled by the escorts and by aircraft, and *U-623* was sunk by the latter. Three ships were sunk on 21 February, for the loss of *U-529*, sunk by the US Coast Guard cutter *Spencer*. *U-606* sank three ships on the 22nd, but then, under attack herself, collided with the cutter *Campbell* and sank. Five more ships were sunk on the 23rd, but a sudden change of course on the night of 23–24 February evaded most of the U-boats; two stragglers were sunk on the 24th, and one more from the convoy. It was located again, and another ship was sunk, but air cover and reinforcements deterred more U-boat attacks. Out of the forty ships in the original convoy fifteen were sunk; three U-boats were also sunk out of the twenty-one employed in the several attacks. (Terraine 532–534; Roskill 2.357; Rohwer 232)

ONS-167, 21–25 February 1943

Sighted by *U-664*, which sank two ships, this convoy was then attacked by other boats, though without loss. (Roskill 2.357; Rohwer 234)

UC-1, 23 February 1943

This tanker convoy was attacked by the *Rochen* pack and other U-boats. Five tankers were sunk; *U-522* was sunk by the sloop *Totland*. (Rohwer 233)

HX-227, 27–28 February 1943

This convoy was located by the northernmost boat of the *Neptun* pack, but it largely avoided other attacks, so that only one ship was sunk. (Rohwer 233)

DN-21, 3 March 1943
Off South Africa *U-160* sank four ships out of this convoy and damaged two more. (Rohwer 230)

KMS-10/XK-2, 4–5 March 1943
These convoys were located from the air and attacked by aircraft and by boats of the *Robbe* pack. *U-87* was sunk by the RCN destroyer *St Croix* and the corvette *Shediac* before the main contact. One ship was sunk by *U-410*, but others were either unable to find the convoys or were forced to submerge. (Rohwer 235)

SC-121, 6–11 March 1943
This convoy of fifty-nine ships became scattered by a storm, and was then attacked by *U-405* of the *Westmark* pack and twenty-six U-boats concentrated for the attack. The storm prevented many of the assaults, but a varying number of boats did succeed in sinking ships – twelve in all. The contact boat was driven off at last on 11 March, and the whole pack thereby lost contact also. (Terraine 546–550; Roskill 2.365; Macintyre 175; Milner 156; Rohwer 234–235)

ONS-168/169/170, 7–14 March 1943
The *Raubgraf* pack of fifteen U-boats attacked these three convoys over a brief period, during which German decrypts provided location information while Ultra signals could not be decrypted. There was also a heavy storm at the time and the escorts were generally short of fuel. Three ships from ONS-168 were sunk – two stragglers and one which broke up in the storm – but ONS-169 was completely missed by the submarines, and the highly skilled escorts of ONS-170 prevented any attacks from succeeding. (Rohwer 237)

HX-228, 10–11 March 1943
Located by *U-336*, this convoy was attacked by boats of the *Neuland* pack (sixteen boats plus five additions), but after two ships were sunk by *U-221*, other attacks were largely unsuccessful. The destroyer *Harvester* rammed *U-444*, a collision which grievously damaged both vessels: *U-444* was later sunk by the Free French corvette *Aconit*, and *Harvester* by *U-432*. Two more ships were meanwhile sunk, though several other attacks were blocked or driven off. The convoy was originally intercepted in part because the decryption of Ultra signals had temporarily failed. (Terraine 550–553; Roskill 2.365; Macintyre 176; Milner 156; Rohwer 238)

OS-44, 12–13 March 1943
This convoy was detected by signal decrypts, and was attacked by *U-107*, which sank four ships, but no other submarines reached it. (Rohwer 235)

MKS-9, 13 March 1943
Several U-boats hunted for this convoy, but the only one to find it, *U-163*, was sunk by the corvette *Prescott*. (Rohwer 225)

HX-229/SC-122, 16–20 March 1943
Hampered by the inability to decipher the German radio signals, these two

convoys, with a total of ninety ships between them, were faced by three U-boat packs, *Raubgraf, Sturmer,* and *Dranger,* a total of thirty-nine boats, though not all of these made contact. In addition escorts were in short supply, with only eleven ships to cover both convoys

The attack began with the *Raubgraf* pack (eight boats) and part of the *Sturmer* pack (eleven boats) targeting HX-229 (thirty-nine ships with four escorts) on the night of 16–17 March; eight ships were sunk. The rest of the *Sturmer* pack (seven boats) meanwhile located SC-122 (fifty-one ships) and *U-338* sank three ships. The *Dranger* pack (eleven boats) joined the attack. Aircraft from Aldergrove in Northern Ireland arrived to assist the defence, so that many of the boats were forced to submerge; nevertheless three ships from HX-229 and two more from SC-122 were sunk

On 18 March aircraft again protected the convoys, though two ships from HX-229 were sunk. Three more escorts also arrived, but there were thirty U-boats available to make attacks. Two more ships were sunk on the night of 18–19 March, and a straggler on the morning of the 19th. More escorts joined and air protection was increased, so that *U-384* was sunk, and two other U-boats damaged. On 20 March, the U-boat attack was called off, the result largely of the increased air presence and the general failure to secure any further hits. Twenty-one ships had been sunk from the two convoys. As a result of this battle Support Groups of destroyers from the Home Fleet were formed to provide escort support for particularly menaced convoys. And, on 19 March, the new German cypher, code-named *Triton,* was broken. (Terraine 553–556; Roskill 2.365–366, 401; Macintyre 178; Milner 156; Rohwer 238)

HX-230, 27–30 March 1943

This convoy was approached by U-boats from the *Seeteufel* and *Seewolf* packs, but its escort was reinforced by one of the new Support Groups. Only nine boats actually got near the convoy, and were faced by fourteen escort ships and air cover. D/F equipment enabled the escort to find the reporting U-boat and force it to submerge, so that contact was lost. One ship was sunk. (Terraine 589–591; Roskill 2.366; Milner 158; Sir P. Gretton, *Crisis Convoy,* London 1974; Rohwer 240)

RS-3, 28–29 March 1943

This coastal convoy was attacked by the seven boats of the *Seerauber* pack; three ships were sunk; air cover chased the U-boats away. (Rohwer 240)

SL-126, 29–30 March 1943

Located by air this convoy was attacked by five U-boats. Four ships were sunk out of thirty-seven. (Rohwer 241)

OS-45, 2 April 1943

U-124 attacked this convoy and sank two ships, but was then itself sunk by the corvette *Stonecrop* and the sloop *Black Swan.* (Rohwer 242)

HX-231, 3–7 April 1943

This convoy (sixty-one ships) was attacked by boats of the *Lowenherz* pack (thirteen boats). Three ships were sunk on 5 April and one U-boat was damaged. Then air cover arrived. Two more ships and two U-boats were sunk. (Milner 158; Rohwer 243)

ON-176/ONS-2, 10 April 1943

These convoys were both attacked by the *Adler* pack (ten boats). The destroyer *Beverley* was sunk by *U-188*; three ships from ONS-2 were sunk. Later attempts to approach the convoys were driven off by air cover and the active escorts; five U-boats were damaged. (Terraine 591; Rohwer 242)

HX-232, 11–13 April 1943

This convoy was located by *U-584*, which brought the boats of the *Lerche* pack to the attack; three ships were sunk, but later attacks were driven off. (Terraine 591; Rohwer 244)

HX-233, 15–18 April 1943

This convoy was located by *U-262*, which called up other boats but was driven off before they arrived. *U-175* located the convoy again later, and two more boats arrived, sinking one ship. *U-175* was then sunk by the US Coast Guard cutter *Spencer*, and the arrival of a Support Group drove off the other attackers. (Roskill 2.372; Rohwer 245–246)

HX-234/ONS-3/ON-178/ONS-4/ON-179, 21–25 April 1943

These convoys, close together, were attacked by U-boats from the *Meise* pack (twenty-one boats). Two ships were sunk from HX-234 and two from ON-178. A large set of escorts then drove off their attackers. *U-189* was sunk by an air attack, and *U-191* by the destroyer *Hesperus*. The submarines found it very difficult to maintain contact with the convoys, but the large number of convoys in the area tended to lead to new contacts almost haphazardly. *U-203*, located by aircraft from the carrier *Biter*, was sunk by the destroyer *Pathfinder*, and *U-710* by air attack. Only two ships were sunk, but five U-boats were destroyed. (Terraine 592; Rohwer 244–245)

RU-71, 24 April 1943

This convoy was attacked by *U-386*, which sank one ship. (Rohwer 246)

ONS-5, 28 April–6 May 1943

This convoy was reported by *U-386*, which was joined by two other U-boats, but all three were at first driven off; one ship was sunk, but most attacks failed. Contact was lost for a time, but regained on 4 May. The convoy had hove-to in a storm during which several ships had separated, so that seven ships were sunk that night. Five more were sunk on 5 May, but attempts at a night attack screened by mist led to the sinking of *U-192* by the corvette *Loosestrife*, *U-531* by the corvette *Snowflake* and the destroyer *Vidette*, *U-125* by the destroyer *Oribi* and *Snowflake*, *U-438* by the sloop *Pelican* and the frigate *Jed*, and *U-630* by *Vidette*. The secret of the success of the escorts was their possession of radar which penetrated the mist, while the U-boat commanders thought the mist hid them. For the loss of thirteen ships, six U-boats were sunk. (Terraine 594–600; Roskill 2.373–375; Macintyre 186, 193; Milner 159–160, 177; Rohwer 245)

TS-37, 30 April–1 May 1943
This convoy was located by *U-515* off West Africa. Three ships were sunk but the escorts, together with a support group, prevented further attacks. (Roskill 2.371, 372; Rohwer 242)

SL-128 and LST convoy, 3–7 May 1943
These two convoys were located by air reconnaissance west of Spain. The LST convoy was attacked in vain, and during this *U-659* and *U-439* collided and sank. The attack on SL-128 was also foiled partly by the escort and partly by air cover, during which *U-447* was sunk. *U-89* managed to sink one ship. (Rohwer 248)

HX-237, 10–13 May 1943
This convoy was detected by *U-403*, but air support from the US carrier *Biter* forced the U-boats in contact to dive, and the convoy avoided attack by the *Rhein* pack (twelve boats). The *Elbe-1* pack was then formed and the convoy was located again. *U-89* was sunk by the destroyer *Broadway* and the frigate *Lagan*; *U-456*, already damaged, sank when trying to avoid the new attack. Next day *U-753* was sunk by *Lagan* and the corvette *Drumheller*. Three of the convoy's ships were sunk. (Terraine 600–601; Roskill 2.375; Macintyre 193; Milner 178–179; Rohwer 250)

SC-129, 11–15 May 1943
This convoy was located by *U-504*, which was quickly driven away, but *U-402* then arrived and sank two ships. In the night the attacking U-boats were driven off, including *U-223*, which had a combined gun, depth-charge, and ramming duel with the destroyer *Hesperus*, which both survived. But *Hesperus* then sank *U-186*, and on 13 May air cover arrived. On 15 May *U-266* was sunk by air attack. (Rohwer 250)

ONS-7, 11–19 May 1943
Sighted by *U-640*, this convoy was repeatedly threatened with attack, until *U-640* was sunk by an aircraft. Located again on 16 May, the convoy was defended by air patrols, the escorts, and a Support Group. *U-657* sank one ship, but was then itself sunk by the frigate *Swale*, and *U-646* and *U-273* were sunk by aircraft. (Rohwer 250)

LMD-17, 17 May 1943
One ship was sunk from this convoy by *U-198*. (Rohwer 243)

SC-130, 18 May 1943
This convoy was attacked by the *Oder* pack (eight boats). *U-952* was damaged by the frigate *Tay*, and *U-381* was sunk; *U-954* was sunk by the sloop *Severn* and the frigate *Jed*. Aircraft and the escorts successfully forced all nearby U-boats to submerge and contact was eventually cut. *U-258* was sunk by aircraft. (Roskill 2.375–376; Macintyre 194; Milner 179; Rohwer 251)

ON-184, 21 May 1943
This convoy drove straight at the line of the *Mosel* pack (twenty-one boats) and by bombing and depth-charging forced the boats to submerge. Two

U-boats were damaged, and *U-569* was sunk by aircraft from the carrier US *Bogue*. (Milner 179; Rohwer 251)

HX-239, 22 May 1943
Boats from the *Mosel* and *Donau* packs threatened this joint convoy. Several U-boats were attacked by aircraft, and fought off the attacks with some success. *U-752* was damaged and then scuttled. None of the convoy was lost. (Terraine 607–608; Roskill 2.376; Macintyre 194; Rohwer 251)

WS-30/KMF-15, 24 May 1943
The Italian submarine *Leonardo da Vinci* encountered this convoy but was sunk by the frigate *Ness* and the destroyer *Active*. This submarine was probably the most successful Italian submarine of the war. (Rohwer 243)

KS-10, 26 May 1943
This convoy encountered *U-436* off Cape Finisterre but the boat was sunk by the frigate *Test* and the RIN corvette *Hyderabad*. (Rohwer 252)

CD-20, 28 May–1 June 1943
Two ships were sunk in separate attacks on this convoy by *U-177* and *U-178*. (Rohwer 243)

HX-240, 1 June 1943
This convoy found two U-boats near its route; *U-304* was sunk by air attack and *U-202* by the sloop *Starling*. (Rohwer 252)

SC-132, 8 June 1943
This convoy located *U-535*, which was then attacked from the air and damaged. (Rohwer 255)

ONS-10, 14 June 1943
U-334 was sunk by the frigate *Jed* and the sloop *Pelican*. (Rohwer 255)

ONS-11, 24 June 1943
This convoy encountered *U-194*, which was then sunk by air attack. (Rohwer 258)

OS-51, 15 July 1943
U-135 attacked this convoy and torpedoed one ship, but was then itself sunk by the sloop *Rochester* and the corvettes *Balsam* and *Mignonette*. (Rohwer 254)

BC-2, 1 August 1943
This convoy was attacked by *U-196*, which sank one ship. (Rohwer 243)

CB-21, 2 August 1943
This convoy was attacked by *U-196*, which sank one ship. (Rohwer 243)

OG-92/KMS-24, 25 August 1943
U-523 encountered this joint convoy west of Cape Finisterre, and was sunk by the corvette *Wallflower* and the destroyer *Wanderer*. (Rohwer 268)

MKS-22/SL-135, 30 August 1943
This joint convoy was encountered by *U-634* west of Spain; the submarine was sunk by the sloop *Stork* and the corvette *Stonecrop*. (Rohwer 268)

MKF-22, 4 September 1943
U-515 was attacked by the escort of this convoy and damaged; it returned to France. (Rohwer 269)

ONS-18/ON-202, 19–23 September 1943
ONS-18 was located by several U-boats on 19 September and next day ON-202 was also encountered. *U-270* damaged the frigate *Lagan*, and the destroyer *Escapade* was also damaged. *U-238*, at first driven off by the corvette *Polyanthus*, returned to sink two ships. *U-338* was sunk by air attack. The convoys joined up at this point but were again located. The RCN destroyer *St Croix* was sunk by *U-305*, and *Polyanthus* was sunk by *U-952*. On 21 September a mass attack by seven U-boats failed, and *U-229* was sunk by the destroyer *Keppel*. On 22 September the U-boats managed to fight off an air attack which was launched in part from the merchant aircraft carrier *Empire MacAlpine*; *U-260* sank the RCN frigate *Itchen* and *U-238* penetrated the escorts' guard to sink three ships in the convoy. One more ship was sunk on 23 September. (Terraine 637–638; Milner 196–199; Rohwer 276)

SC-143, 6–9 October 1943
The 3rd Support Group covered this convoy, which was located by *U-448* on 7 October. The Polish destroyer *Orkan* was sunk by *U-378*; an air attack sank *U-419*, *U-643*, and *U-610*; one of the convoy was sunk in a chance encounter with *U-645*. (Rohwer 281)

ON-206, 15 October 1943
U-844 located this convoy, but was driven off almost at once by the destroyers *Vanquisher* and *Duncan*; four more attacks were blocked by the escort. (Rohwer 281)

ONS-20, 16–18 October 1943
This convoy was located by *U-964*. Nearby U-boats attempted to fight through the air and ship escort, but *U-964*, *U-844*, and *U-470* were sunk by air attack – and one plane was shot down. One ship was sunk in the convoy, and *U-631* by the corvette *Sunflower*. There were still twelve U-boats in the area, but none was able to reach the convoy; *U-540* was sunk in an air attack, and *U-841* by the destroyer *Bayard*. (Milner 200; Rohwer 281)

ON-207, 23 October 1943
U-274 was encountered by and sunk by the destroyers *Duncan* and *Vidette*. (Rohwer 283)

ON-208, 29 October 1943
The corvette *Sunflower* sank *U-282* near this convoy. (Rohwer 283)

MKS-28, 31 October 1943
Located by repeated air reconnaissance, this convoy was attacked by boats of the *Schill* pack (eight boats). One ship was sunk; *U-306* was sunk by the destroyer *Whitehall* and the corvette *Geranium*, and *U-441* was damaged. (Milner 202; Rohwer 283)

HX-264, 6 November 1943
The sloops *Woodcock* and *Starling* of the 2nd Escort Group detected and

sank *U-226*, and *Wild Goose* and *Starling* later sank *U-842*. The convoy was unharmed. (Rohwer 283)

MKS-29A, 8–9 November 1943
This convoy ran into the *Schill* pack; *U-707* was sunk by an air attack, and no ships in the convoy or the escort were hit. (Rohwer 284)

MKS-30/SL-139, 18–21 November 1943
Located by air reconnaissance this joint convoy was attacked by boats of the *Schill-1* pack (seven boats). The frigate *Exe* damaged *U-333* by ramming; *U-515* hit the sloop *Chanticleer*, which had to be towed to the Azores. *U-211* was sunk by an air attack. A new pack, *Schill-2* (nine boats), was formed in front of the convoy on 19 November. *U-238* was overrun by the convoy and attacked it without success; *U-536* was forced to the surface by attacks from the RCN corvettes *Calgary* and *Snowberry* and the British corvette *Nene*; it was sunk by gunfire. *U-538* was sunk by the frigate *Foley* and the sloop *Crane*. The *Schill-3* pack was evaded, partly thanks to air surveillance. A final German air attack sank one and damaged another ship from the convoy. (Milner 203)

KMS-30/OG-95, 22–25 November 1943
This joint convoy was attacked by boats of the *Weddigen* pack (fifteen boats). *U-648* was sunk by the frigates *Bazely*, *Blackwood*, and *Drury* on 22 November; on the 25th *Bazely* and *Blackwood* sank *U-600*. The convoy was not seriously menaced. (Rohwer 289)

MKS-31/SL-140, 26 November 1943
This joint convoy was attacked by boats of the *Weddigen* pack, but the attacks were either evaded or unsuccessful; *U-542* and *U-86* were sunk by air attacks. (Rohwer 289–290)

OS-62/KMS-36, 26 December 1943
These convoys encountered the *Borkum* pack; the destroyer *Hurricane* was sunk by *U-415*. (Rohwer 292)

ON-217, 30 December 1943
One straggler from this convoy was sunk by one of a group of U-boats. (Rohwer 294)

OS-64/KMS-38, 8 January 1944
The destroyer *Bayntun* and the Canadian corvette *Camrose* sank *U-757* defending these convoys. (Rohwer 294, 298)

MKS-35/SL-144, 11 January 1944
These convoys were attacked by boats of the *Borkum* pack (ten boats) without success. All the boats survived attacks by the escorts, but *U-231* was sunk by air attack. (Rohwer 298)

OS-65/KMS-39, 19 January 1944
These convoys was attacked by *U-641*, which was sunk by the corvette *Violet*. (Rohwer 298)

SL-147/MKS-30, 8–11 February 1944

The *Igel* pack (twenty-one boats) menaced this joint convoy, but was itself attacked by the 2nd Escort Group: the sloops *Wild Goose* and *Woodpecker* sank *U-762*, *U-734* was sunk by *Wild Goose* and *Starling*, and *U-238* by *Kite*, *Magpie*, and *Starling*; two days later *Wild Goose* and *Woodpecker* sank *U-424*. (Milner 210; Rohwer 304)

ONS-29, 18–19 February 1944

Located by air reconnaissance this convoy evaded the *Hai* pack (twenty-one boats) by passing it to the south, but the escorts found and sank several U-boats – *U-406* was sunk by the frigate *Spey*, which also sank *U-386*; *U-264* was sunk by the sloops *Woodpecker* and *Starling*; *U-256* torpedoed *Woodpecker*, which later sank. (Rohwer 304)

SC-153, 24 February 1944

U-257 encountered the convoy and was sunk by the frigates *Waskesiu* (RCN) and *Nene*. (Rohwer 308)

HX-280, 5–6 March 1944

The escorts from this convoy hunted *U-744* for thirty hours; the submarine was at last sunk by the RCN frigate *St Catherines*, the RCN destroyers *Gatineau* and *Chaudiere*, and *Icarus* (RN), the corvettes *Chilliwack* and *Fennel*, and the British corvette *Kenilworth Castle*. (Rohwer 308; Sebag-Montefiore 322–326)

SL-150/MKS-41, 9 March 1944

This joint convoy was attacked by *U-575*, which sank the corvette *Asphodel* from the escort, but none of the convoy's ships. (Rohwer 308)

CU-14, 9 March 1944

This convoy was attacked by *U-255*, which sank the destroyer *Leopold*. (Rohwer 308–309)

SC-154, 10–11 March 1944

U-845 was detected close to this convoy; after a long hunt, she was sunk by the destroyer *Forester*, the RCN destroyer *St Laurent*, the frigate *Swansea*, and the corvette *Owen Sound*. (Rohwer 309)

CU-17, 17 March 1944

This convoy was attacked by *U-311*, which sank one ship; *U-415* was damaged in the action. (Rohwer 309)

SC-156, 5–8 April 1944

U-302 sank two ships in this convoy, but was then itself sunk by the frigate *Swale*; the sloops *Crane* and *Cygnet* sank *U-962*. (Rohwer 313)

SC-157, April 1944

U-859 sank one ship which was straggling from this convoy. (Rohwer 316)

ONM-234, 7 May 1944

This convoy was attacked by *U-548*, which sank the Canadian frigate *Valleyfield*. (Rohwer 316)

CU-36/ONS-251/HX-305, 27 August–8 September 1944
U-482 sank a tanker, three other ships, and the corvette *Hurst Castle* from these convoys. (Rohwer 353)

ONF-252, 9–11 September 1944
This convoy was threatened by *U-484*, which was sunk by the corvette *Portchester Castle* and the frigate *Helmsdale*. (Rohwer 353)

ONS-33, 4 October 1944
U-1223 torpedoed the Canadian escort frigate *Magog* off Halifax; from the same convoy as it neared Britain the corvette *Cheboque* was torpedoed by *U-1227*. (Rohwer 360)

UR-143, 10 November 1944
U-300 sank two ships from this convoy, near Reykjavik. (Rohwer 360)

HX-327, 27 December 1944
This convoy was met by *U-877* but the Canadian corvettes *St Thomas* and *Edmondston* sank her. (Rohwer 373)

TBC-1, 29–30 December 1944
U-772 sank two ships from this convoy, and three from others, but was then sunk by air attack. (Rohwer 373)

UGS-72, 17 February 1945
U-300 sank two ships from this convoy off Gibraltar, but was then sunk on 22 February by three minesweepers, the US *Recruit* and *Invade*, and the British *Pincher*. (Rohwer 391)

HX-337, 20 February 1945
U-1276 sank the corvette *Vervain* from this convoy, but was then sunk by the sloop *Amethyst*. (Rohwer 391)

SC-117, 2–7 March 1945
U-1302 sank three ships from this convoy, but was then hunted for a long time and sunk by the Canadian frigates *La Hulloise*, *Strathadam*, and *Thetford Mines*. (Rohwer 391)

TBC-103, 29 March 1945
U-246 sank a ship from this convoy and damaged the frigate *Teme* beyond repair. (Rohwer 397)

TBC-126, 15 April 1945
U-1063 was sunk by the frigate *Loch Killin* from this convoy. (Rohwer 406)

***Attack* v. French ship, 4–5 July 1812**
The brig *Attack* (Lt Richard Simonds) sent her gig to attack a transport seen leaving Calais. The transport was under tow by a privateer when the gig arrived and boarded. The two parties fought it out on her deck until the '*Attacks*' won. (James 5.329–330)

***Attack* and *Wrangler* v. Danish gunboats, 19 August 1812**
In the Kattegat the brigs *Attack* (Lt Richard Simonds) and *Wrangler* were

attacked by flotillas of Danish gunboats. *Wrangler* got away in the dark, but *Attack* was bombarded into a sinking wreck and surrendered. (James 5.350–351; Anderson 346)

Attack and others v. *U-12*, 15 March 1915
U-12, seen several times off the coast of Fife, was hunted by the destroyers *Acheron* (Lt-Cmdr C. Lithgow), *Attack* (Cmdr B.M. Money), and *Ariel* (Lt-Cmdr J.V. Creagh). *Attack* found her and sank her by ramming. (Corbett 2.279–280)

Attack v. *UC-34*, 30 December 1917
The destroyer *Attack* was torpedoed and sunk off Alexandria by *UC-34*. (Colledge 28)

Attentive and others in the White Sea, 1918
The revolutionary Soviet in Archangel held stores deemed to be Allied property. On 1 May the light cruiser *Attentive* (Capt. E. Altham) and the seaplane carrier *Nairana* from Murmansk bombarded the fort on Mudyugski Island and occupied it. *Attentive* was damaged. Next Archangel itself was occupied. *Attentive* captured a Bolshevik yacht which was firing on the town, and on 3 May the cruiser fired at a Bolshevik force approaching by rail. *Attentive* now operated in the White Sea in support of the Allied intervention force, and drove Bolshevik forces from Soroka. River gunboats were acquired, armed, and manned by men from *Attentive* and other British ships, and from Russian volunteers at Archangel. The monitor *M-25* and these gunboats made an expedition up the Dvina River for almost 200 miles. The whole force was withdrawn in early October before the sea froze. (Newbolt 5.311–320, 327–333; Halpern, *Naval History* 137)

Auckland at Namsos, Norway, 20 April 1940
The sloop *Auckland* and the trawler *Rutlandshire* were damaged by bombs; *Rutlandshire* ran aground and was abandoned. (Rohwer 21)

Augusta, Sicily, 10–16 July 1940
On 10 July aircraft from the carrier *Eagle* sank the Italian destroyer *Pancaldo* off Augusta; on 16 July the British submarine *Phoenix* was sunk by the Italian TB *Albatros*. (Rohwer 32)

Aurora v. *Narcisse*, 18 June 1794
The frigate *Aurora* (28; Capt. William Essington) captured the French cutter *Narcisse* off Shetland. (Clowes 4.553)

Aurora on the Spanish coast, May–June 1798
Aurora (32; Capt. Henry Digby) captured the *Receviso* (6) off Lisbon on 8 May, and in June burnt a brig and sank a schooner in Curnas Bay, raided Cedeira harbour, driving two brigs on shore, forced a privateer on shore at Baquio, and destroyed the sloop *Egalité* (20) in the Bay of Biscay. (James 2.232; Clowes 4.553, 555, 560)

Aurora v. *Velos Aragonesa*, 16 September 1798
The Spanish frigate *Velos Aragonesa* (30; *en flute*) was captured by *Aurora* (32; Capt. Henry Digby) near the Azores. (Clowes 4.560)

Aurora and *Nigeria* v. *Bremse* and convoy, 6–7 September 1941
A German convoy off northern Norway was attacked by Force K, notably the cruisers *Aurora* and *Nigeria*. The German gunnery training ship *Bremse* was sunk. (Rohwer 93)

Aurora and others v. Italian convoys, November–December 1941
An Italian convoy from Naples to Tripoli was intercepted by the cruisers *Aurora* and *Penelope* and the destroyers *Lance* and *Lively*. Off Sicily all seven freighters in the convoy were sunk, as was the destroyer *Fulmine*; two more destroyers were damaged. The submarine *Upholder* later sank the destroyer *Libeccio* and attacked the covering cruisers *Tulo* and *Trieste*. On 25–26 November an Italian convoy from the Aegean to Benghazi was intercepted by Force K. *Penelope* and *Lively* sank two ships from the convoy and a third ship, sailing independently, was sunk next day. On 1 December Force K searched for an Italian convoy and its escort; two ships were sunk by bombing; the destroyer *Alvise da Mosto* was sunk by gunfire from *Penelope* while rescuing survivors. (Rohwer 113–114, 118, 119)

Aurora and others v. Italian convoys, 1 December 1942
Force Q – the cruisers *Aurora, Sirius,* and *Argent* and two destroyers – encountered an Italian convoy near the Skerki Bank; the destroyer *Folgore* was sunk and *Da Reccio* damaged; four freighters were sunk, and German aircraft later sank the destroyer *Quentin*. (Rohwer 216; Greene and Massignani 279–290)

Australia, East Coast, March 1943
A convoy escorted by Australian warships was attacked off the east coast of Australia by the Japanese submarine *I-177*, which sank two ships of the convoy, including the hospital ship *Centaur*. (Rohwer 239)

Australia v. *Eleanore Woermann*, 6 January 1915
The battle-cruiser *Australia* (Vice-Admiral Sir George Patey) met the German raider supply ship *Eleanore Woermann* near the Falkland Islands, and sank her. (Corbett 2.243)

Avon and *Castilian* v. *Wasp*, 1 September 1814
The sloop *Avon* (18; Cmdr Hon. James Arbuthnot) met the US sloop *Wasp* (20) in the Bay of Biscay. *Wasp*'s first broadside brought down *Avon*'s masts and then *Wasp* fired into *Avon* without serious reply for an hour and a half; *Avon* then agreed to surrender. At that point *Castilian* (18; Cmdr David Braimer) arrived and *Wasp* departed. *Castilian* rescued *Avon*'s people, but the ship sank. (*NC* 5.236–237; James 6.165–166; Clowes 6.164–166)

Avon v. pirates, Perak, Malaya, December 1874–January 1875
The screw gunvessel *Avon* (Cmdr John Patterson) drove away some pirates as they attacked, then located the pirates' homes at the Larut River mouth, took possession of some junks, and burned some houses. (Clowes 7.269)

Azores Islands, 1567–1602
The Azores were Portuguese from the mid-fifteenth century, but the union of Portugal with Spain in 1580 made them enemy territory to the English during the Armada war.

1567 George Fenner raided the islands in his private warship *Castle of Comfort*, but was driven off by a Portuguese squadron. (K.R. Andrews, *Trade, Plunder and Settlement*, Cambridge 1984, 110; Clowes 1.478)

1587 Sir Francis Drake with several English ships captured the Portuguese carrack *San Felipe* at Sao Miguel by a surprise attack. She was loaded with spices from the east. (Rodger 1.252; Clowes 1.489; Andrews 143–144)

1589 The Earl of Cumberland's squadron, including the royal ship *Victory*, raided Horta on Fayal Island, cutting out a 250-ton ship and five smaller ships. He failed to find the *flota*, returned and stormed the town, then attacked Graciosa and other islands unsuccessfully. (Clowes 1.493; Spence 87–90)

1590 An English fleet cruised unsuccessfully, searching for Spanish ships. During the return to England the island of Fayal was attacked, but this had been newly fortified, and the attack failed. (Clowes 1.494)

1591 Lord Thomas Howard with a squadron of seven ships lay in wait at Flores for six months, hoping to intercept the Spanish treasure fleet, but he was warned that a Spanish fleet was on its way from Corunna and sailed off in time. *Revenge* (Sir Richard Grenville) was trapped into a fight with fifty-three Spanish ships. The other English ships attempted to assist, but could not; *Revenge* fought for fifteen hours, sinking two enemy ships, but was beaten into surrender. Grenville died, as did most of his crew; *Revenge* sank in a storm later. This episode was converted from stupidity to heroism in English sea-myth. (Clowes 1.495–497)

1592 An English squadron of ten ships, commanded by Sir John Burgh, intercepted the Portuguese carrack *Madre de Deus* at Flores and, after a long fight, captured her. The squadron, six ships by then, later met several more Portuguese ships, capturing one. (Rodger 1.281; Clowes 1.499–501; Spence 102–106)

1594 The Earl of Cumberland took a privateering squadron to the islands and intercepted and attacked the Spanish carrack *Cinco Chagas*, but it caught fire and blew up; a second carrack was met, but she beat off the English ships. (Clowes 1.503–504; Spence 119–122)

1595 A squadron of three ships sent out by the Earl of Cumberland attacked the Spanish *San Thome*, which escaped. (Spence 129–130)

1597 The Earl of Essex took an expedition to the islands. Fayal was captured, and Graciosa submitted, but the Spanish treasure fleet evaded them. (Clowes 1.521–523)

1602 Sir Richard Leveson, with a squadron of five ships, encountered the Spanish *flota* near Terceira, but, heavily outnumbered, he fought only briefly before withdrawing. (Clowes 1.553)

B

***B-11* v. *Messudiyeh*, 13 December 1914**
The British submarine *B-11* (Lt D.N. Holbrook) navigated the mine-strewn Dardanelles, found, torpedoed, and sank the Turkish cruiser *Messudiyeh*, then returned, virtually blind, to the Aegean. (Corbett 2.72–73; Halpern, *Naval History* 119)

***Babet* v. *Désirée*, 18 June 1798**
Between Martinique and Dominica, *Babet* (20; Capt. Jemmett Mainwaring) and the French schooner *Désirée* were becalmed. *Désirée* attempted to get away under sweeps; *Babet*'s barge and pinnace went in chase. The pinnace arrived first and captured *Désirée* as the barge arrived. (James 3.225–226)

***Bacchante* off Cuba, April–May 1805**
The sloop *Bacchante* (20; Capt. Charles Dashwood) captured the Spanish privateer *Elisabeth* (10) off Havana on 3 April. Two days later two boatloads of sailors from *Bacchante* went into Mariel harbour to cut out privateers, first storming a tower guarding the entrance. The privateers had gone, but the party took out two loaded schooners instead. On 14 May *Bacchante* captured the Spanish privateer *Felix* (6). (James 4.28–29, 360, 512)

***Bacchante* at Santa Marta, Spanish Main, 29 August 1806**
The boats of *Bacchante* (20; Capt. James Dacres) went into the harbour of Santa Marta to attack vessels there; a brig and two feluccas, all armed, were brought out. (James 4.170–171; Clowes 5.389)

***Bacchante* v. *Griffon*, 11 May 1808**
The sloop *Bacchante* (20; Capt. Samuel Inglefield) fought the French brig *Griffon* (16) near Cape San Antonio, Cuba, driving her ever closer to the shore; *Griffon* surrendered just before being wrecked, and was later added to the navy. (James 4.342; Clowes 5.419)

***Bacchante* and *Kennet* at Bodrum, 28 May 1915**
The port of Bodrum sheltered much Turkish shipping. The cruiser *Bacchante* (Capt. Hon. A.D. Boyle) and the destroyer *Kennet* (Lt-Cmdr F.A.H. Russell) bombarded the ships, and attacked the castle and the barracks as well. (Corbett 3.36)

***Bacchus* v. French ship(s), 1808**
The cutter *Bacchus* (10) was captured in the West Indies by one or more French ships. (Colledge 31)

***Badger* v. *Souris*, 26 February 1798**
The gunboat *Badger* (3; Lt Charles Price), with others, captured the French *chasse-marée Souris* off St Marcouf. (James 4.555; Clowes 2.128–130)

Badger and *Sandfly* v. *Flibustie*r 7 May 1798
The gunboat *Badger* (3; Lt Charles Price) and the floating battery *Sandfly* (14) captured the French *Flibustier* off St Marcouf. (James 4.555)

Baker's squadron v. Spanish ship, 16 February 1712
A British squadron under Rear-Admiral John Baker fought a Spanish ship of 66 guns and drove it ashore on the Portuguese coast. A French vessel headed for Martinique was captured at the same time. (Clowes 2.533)

Balasore, Bengal, 29 November 1689
The EIC ship *Defence* (Capt. Heath), during an armed dispute with the Mogul emperor Aurangzeb, landed a force of soldiers and seamen to capture a battery of 30 guns at Balasore. (Low 1.73)

Ballahou v. *Perry*, 29 April 1814
The cutter *Ballahou* (4; Lt Norfolk King) fought the American privateer *Perry* (5), but was captured. (James 6.167–168; Clowes 5.555)

Baltic Sea
1715–1721 In order to protect British merchant ships trading in the Baltic from Swedish privateers, a fleet, usually commanded by Admiral Sir John Norris, cruised in that sea annually for six years. The fleet made no attacks on any of the belligerents (in the 'Great Northern War'). Admiral Sir George Byng was more assertive during his command in 1716: the Swedish frigate *Ilderim* (36) was captured in 1716 and given to the Danes, and *Panther* (50; Capt. Richard Lestock) was one of several vessels detached from the main fleet to suppress Swedish privateers. There was little other fighting since the privateers tended to be using small craft. As an exercise in seapower the regular cruises were effective in protecting the merchantmen and in assisting the combatants towards the conclusion of peace. (Clowes 3.26–29, 40–42, 3.257; Anderson 176)

1809 A squadron under the command of Capt. Sir Thomas Byam Martin, consisting of *Implacable* (74), *Bellerophon* (74; Capt. Samuel Warren), the frigate *Melpomene* (38; Capt. Peter Parker), and the sloop *Prometheus* (18; Cmdr Thomas Forrest), found a convoy sheltering behind rocks and a screen of gunboats at Porcola Point, Finland on 7 July. The boats of the squadron were sent in, and twelve merchant ships laden with powder were captured, as were six of the eight gunboats, but the attack was expensive, seventeen men being killed, and thirty-six wounded; the Russians lost at least sixty-three dead. (James 5.40–41; Clowes 5.441)

Bamburgh, Northumbria
c.623 The king of Dal Riada and overking of Ulster, Fiachnae mac Baetan, made an expedition, partly by sea, to capture Bamburgh. (*NHI* 1.218)

1462 Queen Margaret, wife of King Henry VI, defeated and exiled, collected a squadron in France and sailed to renew the civil war. A landing at Tynemouth failed but she succeeded at Bamburgh on 25 October. Her campaign was only briefly successful, and the queen had to go into exile again. (Clowes 1.388–389; B. Wolffe, *Henry VI*, London 1981, 334)

Banda Islands, Moluccas
1796 A squadron under Rear-Admiral Peter Rainier occupied Amboyna on 16–18 February, and landed troops at Banda Neira on 7 March. Some resistance was encountered, but was soon overcome. A considerable treasury of dollars and a large quantity of spices were captured. (James 1.414–415; Clowes 4.290–294; Parkinson 94)

1810 A squadron sailed from Madras and collected troops at Penang to capture the Dutch Spice Islands, restored to Dutch rule in 1803. The ships – *Caroline* (36; Capt. Christopher Cole), *Piémontaise* (38; Capt. Charles Foote), *Barracouta* (18; Lt Richard Kenah), and *Mandarin*, a Dutch prize, with 140 soldiers – approached the Dutch fortress island of Banda Neira. Taking advantage of a stormy night, Capt. Cole took the troops, plus sailors, to land in the darkness. They captured a battery, then stormed the main Dutch fort, Casteel Belgica, from which the whole north end of the island was dominated. The suddenness of Cole's assault brought the Dutch government of the island to an immediate surrender. The assaulting force was 180 strong; the Dutch forces on the island were ten times that. Amboyna was also retaken. (James 4. 338, 5.194–202; *NC* 5.7; Parkinson 413)

Banka Strait, Dutch East Indies, January 1744
Commodore Curtis Barnet, in command of a squadron of four ships, including *Deptford* (60; Cmdr John Phillipson) and *Preston* (50; Capt. Earl of Northesk), captured three French East Indiamen; later they captured more French ships in the Bay of Bengal. (Clowes 2.108–109; Keay 274–275)

Bann v. slavers, 1816
The sloop *Bann* (20; Cmdr Charles Tyler) captured the Portuguese slaver *San Antonio*, carrying 600 slaves, the Spanish schooner *Rosa* (8), and, after an hour's fight, another Portuguese slaver brig. (Ward 59–60, 112–113)

BANTRY BAY, Ireland
1689 (Battle of BANTRY BAY) A French fleet of twenty-four line-of-battle ships, five frigates, and ten fireships put into Bantry Bay in May with supplies and men for the forces of King James II in Ireland. The fleet was located there by an English fleet of nineteen line-of-battle ships under Admiral Arthur Herbert. The fighting took place in the narrow waters of the bay. The French intention was to land supplies, and they were not seeking a battle, while the English were outnumbered and unable to gain the weather gauge. The French failed to press their advantage and sailed away. The English, considerably damaged, returned to Portsmouth for repairs. (Clowes 2.327–329; Rodger 2.143; Childs 93–94; Tunstall 52)

1796 A French fleet arrived in Bantry Bay in December, intending to land an expeditionary force. It had taken some months for the expedition to get going, and the fleet had sailed in sections. In the bay the decision to land was pre-empted by bad weather and the landing failed to take place. The French ships largely escaped, and the British ships arrived only to interrupt the process of leaving. (James 2.2–7; Clowes 4.296–303)

Baralong v. *U-27*, 19 August 1915

The steamer *Nicosian* was attacked and captured by *U-27* south of Ireland. The process was interrupted by the arrival of the Q-ship *Baralong* (Lt-Cmdr A. Wilmot-Smith), which sank the submarine and then recovered *Nicosian*. Survivors from the U-boat were shot as they tried to board the steamer by men from the *Baralong*. (Corbett 2.131–134; Grant 27)

Baralong v. *U-41*, 23 September 1915

The liner *Urbino* was stopped by *U-41*. The Q-ship *Baralong* (Lt-Cmdr A. Wilmot-Smith) arrived and was signalled to stop by the submarine. Having got within 500 yards, *Baralong*'s guns were unmasked and the submarine was sunk. (Corbett 3.139–140; Grant 28)

Barbadoes and convoy v. French fleet, 8–27 June 1805

A British convoy of fifteen ships, under the escort of the frigate *Barbadoes* (28; Capt. Joseph Nourse) and the brig *Netley* (16; Lt Richard Harward) met a French fleet of twenty line-of-battle ships off Antigua. The merchantmen were captured. The convoy, now escorted by five French frigates, was met near Barbuda by the sloops *Kingfisher* (Cmdr Richard Cribb) and *Osprey* (Cmdr Timothy Clinch). By a ruse, they persuaded the French that a large fleet was approaching. The French frigates fled, but the merchantmen had been burned. (James 3.351–353; Clowes 5.107–108)

Barbadoes and *Goshawk* v. French gun brigs, 6 September 1811

Off Normandy the frigate *Barbadoes* (28; Capt. Edward Rushworth) and the sloop *Goshawk* (16; Cmdr James Lilburne) intercepted seven French gun brigs; one was wrecked, and the others were driven into Calvados. (James 5.216)

Barbadoes v. *James Madison*, 22 August 1812

The frigate *Barbadoes* (28; Capt. Thomas Huskisson) captured the US schooner *James Madison* (10). (James 5.567)

Barbados, West Indies, 1651

The civil war in England extended to Barbados, which was under Royalist control. Admiral Sir George Ayscue sailed to the island with some ships and, after some fighting, secured control of the island for Parliament. The other English islands in the Caribbean then quickly submitted to Parliament. (Clowes 2.139; Capp 72)

Barbara v. *Général Ernouf*, 17 September 1807

The schooner *Barbara* (10; Lt Edward D'Arcey) fought the French privateer *Général Ernouf* (14) near Guadeloupe. *Barbara* was boarded and captured. (James 4.336–337; Clowes 5.402)

Barcelona, Spain

1704 The city of Barcelona was in the control of the forces of Philip V, the Bourbon claimant to the Spanish throne. Admiral Sir George Rooke, in command of a British and Dutch fleet, summoned the city, and when this was ignored landed soldiers and marines on 19 May, bombarded the city on the 20th, then recovered his forces next day. (Francis 106–107; Clowes 2.390)

1705–1706 Admiral Sir Cloudisley Shovell's fleet landed 12,000 men under the Earl of Peterborough at Barcelona, along with the Habsburg claimant to the Spanish throne, Charles III. A naval bombardment assisted in the assault, and the city capitulated. It was soon besieged by the Philippist forces, and the French fleet came out of Toulon to help. A British fleet under Admiral Sir John Leake reached the city in time to break the siege. The French fleet retired but the city was then again besieged by land and blockaded by sea by French ships. The arrival of the Anglo-Dutch fleet under Admirals Sir John Leake and Sir George Byng in April 1706 induced a French withdrawal and the city was relieved. (Clowes 2.407–409; Corbett, *Mediterranean* 2.290–293; Francis 180)

BARFLEUR and LA HOUGUE, 19–24 May 1692

James II and Louis XIV gathered an invasion army in the Cotentin; the Comte de Tourville commanded the French fleet which was to carry the army to England. But the Anglo-Dutch fleet, ninety-nine ships of the line under Admiral Edward Russell, had first to be removed. Tourville had been given peremptory orders to fight but he had only forty-four of the line. The French fleet came up the Channel from Brest, and met the Anglo-Dutch fleet near Cape Barfleur on 19 May. Firing began when the two fleets were fairly close together. The object of the allies was to use their numbers to envelop the French. This was partly achieved, but a fog in the afternoon caused general confusion. The fog intermittently cleared, and fighting took place when the enemy could be seen. Eventually the fog stopped the conflict.

The allied fleet chased the French for the next two days, with many French ships in serious trouble. Three large vessels, including Tourville's flagship *Soleil Royal*, went aground near Cherbourg and were burned by allied fireships; others got into the Bay of La Hougue; half the fleet escaped into St Malo or to the east. Those in the bay were trapped, and Vice-Admiral Sir George Rooke directed their destruction. Fifteen French line-of-battle ships were destroyed, while the allies lost none. The invasion was postponed. (Clowes 2.347–356; Aubrey 95–132; Mahan 189–191; Tunstall 55–56)

Barham v. *U-30*, 28 December 1939

The battleship *Barham* was damaged by a torpedo from *U-30*, which also sank an ASW trawler. (Rohwer 12)

Barham v. *U-331*, 25 November 1941

The British Mediterranean fleet, attempting to assist the campaign in the

Western Desert, was attacked by *U-331*, which sank the battleship *Barham*. (Rohwer 118)

***Basilisk* v. *Audacieux*, 29 October 1762**
The bomb *Basilisk* (8; Lt William Lowfield) was captured by the French privateer *Audacieux*. (James 3.312)

***Basilisk* v. gunboat *436*, 18 December 1803**
The brig *Basilisk* (14; Lt William Shepheard) captured the French gunboat no. *436*. (James 4.556)

***Basilisk* v. Australian Aborigines, 1872**
Some of the crew of the brig *Maria* having been killed by Australian aborigines, the paddle sloop *Basilisk* (Capt. John Moresby) landed a party to exact revenge. On being attacked most of the men of *Basilisk* ran away; one midshipman and one sailor, on the other hand, armed with rifles, killed and wounded sixteen of the Australians. (Clowes 7.232)

***Basilisk* v. *U-38*, May 1918**
The destroyer *Basilisk* and the US yacht *Lydonia* together attacked *U-38* (long thought to be *UB-70*) south of the Balearic Islands, but the submarine survived. (Newbolt 5.411; Grant 131)

Basque Roads, France
1809 (Battle of BASQUE ROADS) A French squadron under Admiral Willaumez left Brest aiming to collect other French squadrons at Lorient and Rochfort. A corresponding gathering of British squadrons finally penned the French ships into the Basque Roads passage between Ile d'Oléron and the Charente estuary on 21 February. Admiral Lord Gambier hesitated to send in his big ships, and it seemed that the French position was too strong for the smaller vessels. The Admiralty ordered the use of fireships, and sent Capt. Lord Cochrane in *Impérieuse* (38) to direct the fire attack. This he did, but he was poorly and only hesitantly supported by Gambier. Most of the French ships ran aground in the confusion of the fireship attack, but many were refloated before another conventional attack was made. *Impérieuse* was gradually supported by other frigates, and eventually by some of the line-of-battle ships, but most of the French ships were able to get into the Charente estuary, where they were safe. The result was the destruction of three French line-of-battle ships and *Calcutta* (*en flute*). Gambier was court-martialled for lack of endeavour, but acquitted. It was certainly a British victory, but in the aftermath of Trafalgar, destruction of the enemy, and not merely defeat, was expected. (James 4.394–430; Clowes 5.254–275; Thomas 146–173)

1810 Three French brigs sheltered below a battery at Pointe de Ché. A boat party of sailors and marines went from *Caledonia* (120; Rear-Admiral Sir Harry Neale), *Valiant* (74; Capt. Robert Oliver), and *Armide* (38; Capt. Richard Dunn) to capture the ships on 28 September. The battery was taken and its guns spiked; then the marines formed up to block the approach from the nearby village, and the brigs were captured. One was burned, the others were taken away. (James 5.101–102; Clowes 5.471; *NC* 4.232–258)

Batabano, Cuba, 30 August 1806
A flotilla of small British warships raided Batabano, Cuba. The schooner *Pike* (4; Lt John Ottley) captured a Spanish *guarda costa* (10) on 30 August. Boat parties from the sloop *Stork* (18; Cmdr George Le Geyt), and the schooners *Superieure* (Cmdr Edward Rushworth) and *Flying Fish* (Lt James Gooding), landed on 2 September and fought their way to the town, capturing a fort and the ships in the harbour (a felucca, one French and three Spanish privateers, and six merchant vessels), all of which were brought out. (James 4.171–172; Clowes 5.389)

Bayano v. *U-20*, 11 March 1915
The AMC *Bayano* (Cmdr H.C. Carr) was sunk by *U-20* in the North Channel; the AMC *Ambrose* was attacked also, but was missed three times. These ships were part of the Northern Patrol. (Corbett 2.277; NRS, *Maritime Blockade* 124)

Bayntun and others v. *U-1279* and *U-1278*, February 1945
The destroyers *Bayntun* and *Braithwaite* and the frigate *Loch Eck* sank *U-1279* north of Shetland on 3 February. Twelve days later *Bayntun* and *Loch Eck* sank *U-1278*. (Rohwer 390)

Bay of Biscay
1342 Sir Walter Mauny took a fleet carrying 1000 archers and 120 men-at-arms to relieve the siege of Hennebont Castle in March. He arrived just as the garrison was about to surrender; he and his companions were rewarded by several kisses from the Countess of Montfort, commanding in the castle during the siege. (Clowes 1.259; Sumption 1.394–395)

In October a French squadron surprised an English naval force of seven ships in a bay near Vannes, which the English were besieging. All seven ships were captured or sunk. (Clowes 1.260)

1696 Raids were made in June by an Anglo-Dutch fleet under Admiral Lord Berkeley on the islands off the French Biscay coast – Groix, Re, Belle Isle – and on Olonne on the mainland. A few ships were captured. (Clowes 2.488–489)

1746 An expedition commanded by General James St Clair and Admiral Richard Lestock landed near Lorient, and laid siege to the city. This was lifted as soon as the defenders displayed some energy. The troops were re-embarked and then landed briefly at Quiberon Bay and on the islands of Houat and Hoedie where the fortifications were destroyed. In November Lestock's squadron drove the French *Ardent* (64) on shore at Quiberon. (Clowes 3.117–119, 283)

1747 A British squadron of five line-of-battle ships and a frigate, commanded by Capt. Thomas Fox in *Kent* (74), intercepted a French West India convoy escorted by three line-of-battle ships and a frigate on 20 June. The escort fled into Brest and fifty ships of the convoy were captured. (Clowes 3.283)

1757 An expedition commanded by Admiral Sir Edward Hawke went to attack the French naval base of Rochefort in the belief that it was vulnerable. A preliminary attack on the fort on the Ile d'Aix on 20 September alerted the French, and an inspection of the defences of Rochefort showed them to be stronger than expected. On the 29th it was decided to risk an attack, but the wind was foul. The expedition returned to port. (Clowes 3.171–172; Syrett, *Howe* 16; NRS, *Hawke*, nos. 155–161)

1780 The British Channel Fleet under Admiral Francis Geary intercepted a French convoy arriving from St Domingue; twelve merchant ships were captured. (Syrett, *European*, 136)

1782 A squadron of twelve line-of-battle ships, commanded by Vice-Admiral Hon. Samuel Barrington, on 20 April intercepted a French convoy taking reinforcements to the Indian Ocean. *Foudroyant* (Capt. John Jervis) fought and captured *Pégase*, and thirteen out of nineteen merchant ships were also captured, as were 1000 soldiers. (Syrett, *European* 154–155; Clowes 3.538–539, 4.80–82)

1800 The frigate squadron commanded by Rear-Admiral Sir John Borlase Warren raided French convoys at St Croix, the Quimper estuary, and Noirmoutier between 10 June and 2 July. (Clowes 4.531)

1940 British and Allied troops were evacuated from St Nazaire and Nantes on 16–18 June, and from Bayonne and St Jean de Luz on 19–25 June; 70,000 troops were taken off. (Rohwer 28–29)

1943 In an operation aimed at intercepting a German blockade runner, the cruisers *Gambia*, *Glasgow*, *Enterprise* (Canadian), and *Penelope*, two French destroyers, and a minelayer encountered the German 8th Destroyer Flotilla (five ships) and the 4th Torpedo Boat Flotilla (six boats) on 28 December. Heavy seas foiled the Allied attack but the destroyers *Z-27*, *T-25*, and *T-26* were sunk and the rest of the German ships scattered, reaching various French ports. In searching for survivors the ships of the British 6th Support Group were attacked by U-boats of the *Borkum* pack. Attacks and counter-attacks all failed. Survivors were rescued by British, Spanish, Irish, and German vessels. (Rohwer 295)

See also: **Aix Roads, Basque Roads, Bay of Bourgneuf, Gironde River, Islands in the Bay of Biscay, La Rochelle, Quiberon Bay, St Nazaire.**

Bay of Bourgneuf, France
An important source of salt, this was the scene of three battles during the Hundred Years' War.

1342 An English fleet, commanded by Robert of Artois, with some 800 soldiers on board, sailed along the south Breton coast in November, and met a Castilian galley squadron on hire to France in the bay. Artois attacked but was driven off with the loss of several of his own large ships. (Sumption 1.404)

1375 An English merchant fleet returning from Bordeaux stopped at the Bay of Bourgneuf to load salt. It was attacked by a squadron of Spanish galleys. Thirty-six of the English vessels were captured or sunk. (Clowes 1.285–286; Rodger 1.110)

1388 The Earl of Arundel led an expedition to raid in the bay. The castle at Noirmoutier was stormed, the town and ships burned, and much loot was collected. An attack on La Rochelle failed. (Sumption 3.653)

Bay of Lebedos, Aegean Sea, 22 March 1916
The minesweeper *Whitby Abbey* raided the Turkish coast in the Bay of Lebedos, landing a party of armed refugees who fought a Turkish patrol and rustled 600 animals. (Halpern, *Mediterranean* 290)

Bay of Naples, 1943–1944
The destroyers *Laforey* and *Lookout* bombarded positions north of the Volturno River in support of army operations on 13 October 1943; *Grenville*, *Tumult*, and *Tyrian* bombarded positions in the Gulf of Gaeta on 8 November. The cruiser *Orion* and three destroyers bombarded positions north of the Garigliano River on 26 November, and in the Minturno area on 1 December. The destroyer *Bicester* bombarded positions near Ardea on 9 May 1944, and the cruiser *Dido* bombarded those in the Gulf of Gaeta on 15 May. (Rohwer 281, 287, 290, 291, 324)

Bazely and others v. *U-636*, 21 April 1945
U-636 was sunk by the destroyers *Bazely*, *Drury*, and *Bentinck* west of Shetland. (Rohwer 406)

BEACHY HEAD, 30 June 1690
A large French fleet, including sixty-eight line-of-battle ships, came out of Brest to establish French domination of the Channel in order that James II could return to his English throne. Commanded by the Comte de Tourville it faced the joint Anglo-Dutch fleet under Arthur Herbert, Earl of Torrington, which, with only fifty-six line-of-battle ships, was substantially weaker. Torrington retreated slowly up the Channel as Tourville advanced, both men fully appreciating that while the allied fleet existed there was no possibility of an invasion. Torrington articulated the concept by using the phrase 'fleet in being', which became the way such a policy was referred to in the future. The government in London was not impressed. Queen Mary II sent Torrington a direct order to fight a battle, and reluctantly he did so. (It may be that the queen was right; so soon after the Revolution of 1688 there were still many in England who wished for James's return; the presence of a superior French fleet acting for him in the Channel might have persuaded them to rise.) The two fleets formed lines of battle, on the allied side with the Dutch ships in the lead. French superiority in numbers allowed Tourville to concentrate a powerful force upon those Dutch ships. Torrington attempted

to help them, but the winds were too light. Fighting ended when calm fell. The French got out boats to pull their ships back into the fight; the allies anchored, and the tide shifted the French out of reach.

No French ship was lost, but the allies lost nine, mainly Dutch ships so badly damaged that they were in danger of being captured in the aftermath; they were run aground and burned. The disparity in allied losses did nothing for the cohesion of the alliance. (Clowes 2.336–344; Aubrey 48–50; Mahan 182–184; Tunstall 53–54)

Beaulieu v. French sloop, 2 December 1794
The frigate *Beaulieu* (40; Capt. Edward Riou) captured a French sloop in the West Indies. (Clowes 4.553)

Beaulieu v. *Marsouin*, March 1796
The frigate *Beaulieu* (40; Capt. Lancelot Skynner) captured the French frigate *Marsouin* (26) in the West Indies. (Clowes 4.554)

Beaulieu, *Uranie*, and *Doris* v. *Chevette*, 20–22 July 1801
The French corvette *Chevette* (20) was in Camaret Bay, Brittany. The frigates *Beaulieu* (40; Capt. Stephen Poyntz) and *Doris* (36; Capt. Charles Brisbane) made an unsuccessful attempt to capture her on the night of 20–21 July. Next day, joined by the frigate *Uranie* (38; Capt. William Gage), ten boats went in to try again. Both sides put as many men as possible into the fight. *Chevette* was boarded, the French sailors were driven below decks, and the ship was sailed out of the bay while the fighting went on. (Clowes 4.539–540; James 3.137–141).

Beaver v. American privateer, 1777
Beaver (14; Cmdr James Jones) captured the rebel American privateer *Oliver Cromwell* (14). (Clowes 4.7; Colledge 39)

Bedford v. *Comete*, 16 March 1761
Bedford (64; Capt. Joseph Deane) captured the French frigate *Comete* (32) near Ushant. (Clowes 3.305)

Bedford and *Speedy* v. *Modeste* and others, Genoa, 17 October 1793
The French frigate *Modeste* (36), in Genoa harbour, was seized and brought out by *Bedford* (74; Capt. Robert Man), while boats from *Speedy* (14; Cmdr Charles Cunningham) captured two armed tartans and brought them out. (Clowes 4.213; James 1.96–97)

Begonia v. U-boat, 6 October 1917
The sloop *Begonia* was sunk in the Atlantic; the cause is not clear; she was probably torpedoed by a U-boat. (Colledge 39)

Beirut and the Lebanese coast, 9 September–10 October 1840
A British and Austrian fleet, under the command of Admiral Hon. Sir Robert Stopford, approached Beirut to induce the Egyptian army to evacuate Syria.

A landing was made north of the city at Jounieh, and Beirut was bombarded from the sea. Further landings were made at Jebail and Batrun and south of the city at Tyre, but an attempted landing at Tortosa failed, with a number of casualties. When Sidon was captured only Beirut was left under Egyptian control. The city, threatened with attack and frequently bombarded, was evacuated on 10 October. (Clowes 6.310–318)
See also: **Acre**

Belfast Lough, Ulster, 1689
Capt. George Rooke, cruising in the Irish Sea in *Deptford* (54), sent a raid into Jacobite-held Carrickfergus in May, as a result of which a provision ship was burned. Later Carrickfergus castle, whose guns threatened the shipping of the Anglo-Dutch army in the lough, was besieged by land and bombarded from the sea until it surrendered.

In August the Anglo-Dutch army of King William III landed at Bangor Bay. The strength of the force – thirteen infantry battalions – ensured that it was not opposed by the local Jacobite forces, and this landing was decisive for the campaign in Ireland. (Powley 221, 259–261; Childs 148–149)

Belize, Central America, 3–15 September 1798
A squadron of Spanish schooners and sloops attacked the British settlements in Honduras. Cmdr John Moss of the sloop *Merlin* gathered up a number of vessels and installed guns in them. The Spaniards had to attack through or over shoals and between keys (islands); the British ships countered these attacks, usually waiting to attack until their enemies got into navigational difficulties. Five separate attacks of this type were defeated. (*NC* 1.205–209; James 2.280–282)

Belleisle, *Bellona*, and *Melampus* v. *Impetueux*, 14 September 1806
The French *Impetueux* (74), badly damaged by a hurricane, encountered *Belleisle* (74; Capt. William Hargood), *Bellona* (74; Capt. John Douglas), and the frigate *Melampus* (36; Capt. Stephens Poyntz) off the coast of Virginia. *Impetueux* was driven ashore, and later burnt by a party from *Melampus*. (James 4.116–117; Clowes 5.196)

Belle Poule v. *Var*, 15 February 1809
The frigate *Belle Poule* (38; Capt. James Brisbane) came up with the French storeship *Var* (22), which was apparently protected by the fort at Valona, Albania, but, when *Belle Poule* opened fire, the fort took no part; *Var* surrendered after a few shots, the crew removing themselves quickly to the shore. (James 5.9–10; Clowes 5.432)

Bellerophon at Hango, Finland, 19 June 1809
Three ships were found by *Bellerophon* (74; Capt. Samuel Warren) amid islands near Hango, Finland, and boats were sent in to capture them, but they were deemed useless and abandoned. A battery overlooking the area had to be captured and destroyed to ensure a safe return for the boats. (James 5.39–40; Clowes 4.532)

Belliqueux and convoy v. French frigates, 4 August 1800
A convoy of Indiamen escorted by *Belliqueux* (64; Capt. Rowley Bulteel) was threatened by three French frigates off the coast of Brazil. *Belliqueux* attacked first, compelling the surrender of *Concorde* (40), and the Indiamen *Bombay Castle* and *Exeter* chased and captured *Medee* (36), whose captain was so annoyed at being captured by merchantmen that he wanted to start the fight again. The third frigate, *Franchise* (36), escaped. (James 3.22–23)

Bellona and *Brilliant* v. *Courageux* and others, 14 August 1761
Bellona (74; Capt. Robert Faulknor) and *Brilliant* (36; Captain James Logie) met *Courageux* (74) and the frigates *Malicieuse* (32) and *Hermione* (32) off Vigo, Spain. The two line-of-battle ships fought each other while *Brilliant* kept the French frigates occupied. *Courageux* was at first successful in disabling *Bellona*, but the latter revived and inflicted such damage that *Courageux*, having suffered 300 casualties, surrendered. (Clowes 3.307)

Bellona and *Alarm* v. Duras and convoy, 8 January 1795
Bellona (74; Capt. George Wilson) and *Alarm* (32; Capt. Charles Carpenter) encountered a French convoy heading for Guadeloupe. *Bellona* captured *Duras* (20) from the escort, but the convoy reached its destination. (James 1.331–332; Clowes 4.280)

Bellona and others v. German convoy, 5 August 1944
The cruiser *Bellona* and four destroyers located and sank the German minesweepers *M-263* and *M-486*, the patrol boat *V-414*, and the launch *Otto*, which were escorting a convoy north of the Ile d'Yeu in the Bay of Biscay. (Rohwer 347)

Belvidera and *Nemesis* v. Danish gunboats, 22 July 1810
Boats from the frigates *Belvidera* (36; Capt. Richard Byron) and *Nemesis* (28; Capt. William Ferris) went into a bay near Studtland, Norway, to attack three Danish gunboats, two of which, *Baldur* and *Thor*, were captured; the third was abandoned and then burnt. (James 5.99; Clowes 5.458; Anderson 343)

Belvidera v. *President*, 23 April 1812
A squadron of three US frigates and two sloops went to intercept the British Jamaican convoy. They met the frigate *Belvidera* (36; Capt. Richard Byron) which led them away from the convoy. The leading US frigate *President* chased *Belvidera* all day, each ship firing at the other without serious effect until *Belvidera* got into Halifax. (James 5.352–362; Clowes 6.30–31)

'Benbow's Last Fight', 19–24 August 1702
Vice-Admiral John Benbow commanded a small squadron based at Jamaica. He heard of the arrival of a French squadron off the Spanish Main and found it near Santa Marta. He formed his six ships into line of battle and made to attack. However most of his ships failed to comply. Benbow, in *Breda* (70; Capt. Christopher Fogg), and *Ruby* (48; Capt. George Walton) were the only ships which came close enough to sustain a fight. The French eventu-

ally sailed away. Benbow was badly hurt, but at Jamaica insisted on courts martial on five of his captains. He died. Two captains were shot, and one was cashiered, imprisoned, and dismissed. (Clowes 2.368–373; Rodger 2.165)

Bencoolen, Sumatra, 3–4 December 1803
A French squadron commanded by Admiral Linois entered the harbour of the EIC station at Bencoolen by a ruse and burnt the warehouses of the EIC factory; two prizes were taken but five other ships were burned by their crews. (James 3.210–211; Parkinson 210–211)

BENGAL, India, December 1756–June 1757.
Vice-Admiral Charles Watson ignored orders to return to Britain in favour of carrying a small force commanded by Lt-Col. Robert Clive from Madras to Bengal, where a war between the EIC and the Nawab of Bengal had begun. He had three line-of-battle ships, *Kent* (70), *Cumberland* (80), and *Tiger* (50), and six other vessels. In the Ganges delta various batteries and forts were taken, including Fort William at Calcutta and the French post at Chandernagore. The Nawab of Bengal, Suraj-ud-Dawla, brought up an army, but this was beaten at the battle of Plassey, in part by the troops brought by Admiral Watson. (Clowes 3.160–164)

Bengal v. *Aikiko Maru* and *Hokoko Maru*, 11 Novermber 1942
The Japanese auxiliary cruisers *Aikiko Maru* and *Hokoko Maru* attacked the Indian minesweeper *Bengal* (Lt-Cmdr W.J. Wilson) and the Dutch tanker *Ondina* in the Indian Ocean. The tanker was damaged and set on fire but *Bengal* drove off the attackers, and *Hokoko Maru* exploded and sank. *Ondina* was saved. (Rohwer 213).

Benin, Nigeria, February 1897
An expedition was mounted against Benin City, consisting of a Naval Brigade and a locally recruited force. A squadron headed by the cruisers *St George* and *Theseus* (Capts George Egerton and Charles Campbell) was brought in. The forces had to fight all the way to the city, which was captured, but then burnt, supposedly by accident. The force suffered about sixty casualties, but was then attacked by fever, which laid low half the naval crews. (Clowes 7.440–444; R. Home, *City of Blood Revisited*, London 1982)

Benjamin Stevenson v. U-boat, 18 August 1917
The trawler *Benjamin Stevenson* was sunk by gunfire from a U-boat in the northern part of the North Sea. (Colledge 42)

Ben Lawer v. *UB-18*, 9 December 1917
The trawler *Ben Lawer*, escorting a coal convoy in the English Channel, rammed and sank *UB-18*; the trawler was badly damaged. (Grant 68)

Ben-My-Chree at Castelorizo, 9 January 1917
The seaplane carrier *Ben-My-Chree* was attacked and sunk by Turkish artil-

lery at Castelorizo Island, off Anatolia. (Halpern, *Mediterranean* 231, *Naval History* 132)

Bergamot v. *U-84*, 15 August 1917
The sloop *Bergamot* (a Q-ship) was torpedoed by *U-84* near Tory Island, but sank too quickly for the usual ploys to succeed. (Newbolt 5.109)

Bergen, Norway
1665 The king of Denmark arranged with the English fleet in the North Sea, commanded by the Earl of Sandwich, to make a joint attack on the Dutch West India fleet which had gone into neutral Bergen and was awaiting an escort. A squadron of fourteen line-of-battle ships under Rear-Admiral Sir Thomas Teddeman went into the harbour on 3 August. The city governor either had not received orders, or disobeyed them, so the English ships were fired on by both Danes and Dutch. After several hours the English withdrew defeated, their ships damaged, having suffered considerable casualties. (Clowes 2.426–428; Anderson 100; Rodger 2.70)

1940 When the German invasion of Norway began, the convoy HN-25 at Bergen (thirty-seven ships) was at first told not to sail by the Admiralty, but put to sea on its own initiative on 9 April, and all the ships reached Britain safely. (Rohwer 18)

Berkeley Castle v. French ship, 25 October 1695
The EIC ship *Berkeley Castle* was captured by a French warship in the English Channel on her homeward voyage. (Low 1.77–78)

Bermuda, 20 June 1780
A British squadron of five line-of-battle ships and a frigate, commanded by Capt. Hon. William Cornwallis, encountered a French troop convoy escorted by seven line-of-battle ships commanded by Commodore de Ternay near Bermuda. The two squadrons manoeuvred and fired at each other, but Cornwallis had heavy odds against him, and Ternay had to protect the troopships. The two forces separated. (Clowes 3.474–477)

Berwick, Anglo-Scots border
1295 King Edward I besieged the town. His fleet attacked the harbour before the army was ready, and three of the ships were burnt by the Scots. The flames and smoke alerted the king, however, and his army then captured the town swiftly. (Rodger 1.209–210; Prestwich 470–471)

1317–1318 The town, held by the English, was besieged by the Scots by land and blockaded by sea by Flemish privateers in the pay of the Scots. (Nicholson 96–97)

1333 The town was besieged by the forces of King Edward III, and blockaded by an English naval force. Attempts by local vessels failed to break the blockade, and relieving vessels arrived with supplies for both parties. When the Scots army was beaten at the battle of Halidon Hill, the town fell, in part by means of an assault from the sea. (Clowes 1.233; Rodger 1.89)

Berwick v. French frigates, 7 March 1795
Berwick (74; Capt. Adam Littlejohn) was the only British ship in Corsican waters when the French Toulon fleet arrived to retake the island. The ship, already under a jury rig, was attacked by the frigates *Alceste, Minerve,* and *Vestale*; Capt. Littlejohn was killed and the ship effectively disabled by the destruction of the rigging; the first lieutenant surrendered her. (James 1.283–284; Clowes 4.267–269)

Berwick and others v. *Amazone*, 24–25 March 1811
Berwick (74; Capt. James Macnamara) chased *Amazone* (40) into a bay near Barfleur. Unable to enter himself, Macnamara summoned *Amelia* (38; Capt. Hon. Frederick Irby), *Goshawk* (16; Cmdr James Lilburne), and *Hawk* (16; Cmdr Henry Bourchier); *Niobe* (38; Capt. Joshua Loring) arrived also. At floodtide the smaller ships went in and bombarded *Amazone*, inflicting and receiving minor damage. Next morning, in the face of another likely attack, *Amazone* was burned. (James 5.211–212)

Berwick and *Euryalus* at Cavaliere Road, Provence, 16 May 1813
A raid in the boats of *Berwick* (74; Capt. Edward Brace) and the frigate *Euryalus* (Capt. Charles Napier) was mounted against a large convoy gathered in Cavaliere road, near Toulon. One party landed and captured two batteries, then took twenty-two ships of the convoy. (James 6.18–19; Clowes 5.527)

Beryl III v. *U-109*, 26 January 1918
The drifter *Beryl III* sank *U-109* near Cap Gris Nez. (Newbolt 5.427; Grant 80)

Betty v. French ship, 14 August 1695
The hired armed ship *Betty* (Capt. John Papwell) was captured by a French ship. (Clowes 2.536)

Bias Bay, China, 1 October 1849
A pirate base was located at Bias Bay, 60 kilometres from Hong Kong. A squadron including *Hastings* (74), *Columbine* (18), and the paddle sloop *Fury*, and the P&O steamer *Canton* attacked the base, destroying twenty-three junks, killing 500 pirates, and capturing 200 guns. (Graham 273)

Bickerton and others v. *U-765*, 6 May 1944
U-765 was depth-charged to the surface by the frigates *Bickerton, Bligh,* and *Aylmer*, and then sunk by air attack from the carrier *Vindex*. (Rohwer 313)

Bienfaisant and *Charon* v. *Comte d'Artois*, 13 August 1780
Comte d'Artois, a large privateer (64), attacked a convoy and was then captured by *Bienfaisant* (64; Capt. John MacBride) and *Charon* (44). (Clowes 4.56–57)

***Birdlip* v. *U-547*, 14 June 1944**
The ASW trawler *Birdlip* and a merchant ship were sunk off Liberia by *U-547*. (Rohwer 326)

***Birmingham* v. *U-15*, 9 August 1914**
The light cruiser *Birmingham* found the submarine *U-15* on the surface near Fair Isle, apparently undergoing repairs. *Birmingham* opened fire then rammed the submarine, which was cut in two and sank at once. (Corbett 1.77; Massie 79; Halpern, *Naval History* 29; Grant 19)

BISMARCK and others, Atlantic Ocean, 20–27 May 1941
The German battleship *Bismarck* and the heavy cruiser *Prinz Eugen* left Bergen in Norway and sailed north round Iceland to reach the Atlantic convoys. Weather ships and supply tankers were already positioned. *Bismarck* and *Prinz Eugen* were seen by the cruisers *Suffolk* and *Norfolk* in the Denmark Strait on 23 May, and next day they met the battleship *Prince of Wales* and the battle-cruiser *Hood*. In a short battle *Hood* blew up and *Prince of Wales* turned away damaged. *Bismarck* was also damaged and began leaking oil. On the night of 24–25 May air attacks from the carrier *Victorious* registered one hit but no damage, and a feint attack by *Bismarck* on the shadowing cruiser *Suffolk* allowed the two German ships to separate. *Bismarck* was located again by a Catalina flying boat on the 26th and the Home Fleet and Force H from Gibraltar closed in. An attack by Swordfish aircraft from the carrier *Ark Royal* damaged *Bismarck*'s rudder, so that the ship was effectively disabled. On 27 May she was sunk by gunfire from the battleships *King George V* and *Rodney* and torpedoes from the cruiser *Dorsetshire*. *Prinz Eugen* refuelled from two of the pre-positioned tankers, but defects were discovered in her engines and she damaged a propeller. She returned to Brest on 1 June. Neither ship succeeded in attacking any of the Atlantic convoys.

One other result of this campaign was the capture of several German ships whose positions were revealed by radio traffic. A weather ship, *August Wriedt*, was sunk on 29 May; the tanker *Belchen* was sunk by the cruisers *Aurora* and *Kenya* in the Davis Strait on 3 June while attempting to refuel U-boats; the tanker *Gedania* was captured by the AMC *Marsdale* on 4 June; the patrol ship *Gonzenheim* was located by aircraft from *Victorious*, found by several ships, scuttled, and finally sunk by the cruiser *Neptune* on 4 June. The supply ship *Lothringen* was found by aircraft from the carrier *Eagle* and captured by the cruiser *Dunedin* on 15 June. Five destroyers from Force H located and sank *U-138* on 16 June; the weather ship *Lauenburg*, located by D/F, was captured on 28 June near Jan Mayen Island, having been set on fire, and Enigma materials were recovered. (Roskill 1.397–415; Rohwer 74–83; David J. Bercuson and Holger H. Herwig, *The Destruction of the Bismarck*, New York 2001)

***Bittern* v. *Hirondelle*, 28 April 1804**
The sloop *Bittern* (18; Cmdr Robert Corbet) captured the French cutter *Hirondelle* (14) in the Mediterranean. (Clowes 5.556)

Bittern v. Chinese pirates, August–September 1855
The brig *Bittern* (12; Cmdr Westby Vansittart) attacked a group of pirate ships off Leotung on 18–19 August, some being burnt; on 18 September Vansittart attacked a group of twenty-two ships off Shenpu, destroying them and their people. (Clowes 6.390)

Bittern at the Corisco Islands, West Africa, January 1872
The screw sloop *Bittern* (Cmdr Hon. Archibald St Clair) operated to suppress pirates coming from the Corisco and Elobey Islands. (Clowes 7.233)

Black Joke v. Rebecca, 27 April 1799
The hired lugger *Black Joke* (10; Lt James Nicholson) captured the chasse-marée *Rebecca* off Ushant. *Rebecca* carried a French naval captain with dispatches for Ireland, which seemed to confirm that the French fleet was heading that way; this was, in fact, a ruse which persuaded the British to guard Ireland and allowed the French fleet to get out of Brest. (James 2.287; Clowes 4.381)

Black Joke v. Mouche, 21 May 1809
The lugger *Black Joke* (10; Lt Moses Cannaday) met the French corvette *Mouche* (16) and exchanged fire; *Mouche* evaded and went into Santander as intended. (James 5.27; Clowes 5.438)

Black Joke v. French ship, 2 March 1811
The lugger *Black Joke* (10; Lt Moses Cannaday) was captured by a French ship in the Channel. (Clowes 5.553)

Black Joke in West Africa, 1829
Black Joke (Lt Henry Downes), a captured and converted slaver, cruised off the coast of West Africa, capturing twenty-one slave ships, including *Providencia* (14), *Vengador* (8), *Presidente* (7), and *Almirante* (14). Four thousand slaves were freed. Downes and his officers were all then promoted. Under Lt William Ramsay, *Black Joke* then captured *Marinerito* (5) off Calabar. (Clowes 6.269; Lloyd 72–73)

Blake's squadron v. Roebuck, 3 November 1650
General-at-Sea Robert Blake, with a squadron of four ships, chased Prince Rupert's Royalist squadron. Off Cape Palos he captured the Royalist *Roebuck*, 'without many blows, except among themselves'. (Powell 105; Clowes 2.132)

Blake's squadron v. French convoy, 4 September 1652
A squadron commanded by General-at-Sea Robert Blake, off Calais, intercepted and destroyed a French convoy heading to relieve the Spanish siege of Dunkirk. Seven of the eight warships of the escort were captured and the transports were scattered. (Capp 71; Clowes 2.159; Powell 165–166)

Blake and *Franchise* at Tarragona, Spain, 27 September 1812
Boats from *Blake* (74) and the frigate *Franchise* (36) raided Tarragona harbour. (Hall 186)

Blanche v. French sloops, 30 December 1793
The frigate *Blanche* (32; Capt. Christopher Parker) captured the sloops *Sans Culotte* (22), *Revolutionnaire* (20), and *Vengeur* (12) in the West Indies. (Clowes 4.552)

Blanche v. *Pique*, 4 January 1795
Blanche (32; Capt. Robert Faulknor) sailed into the harbour of Desirade Island, fired at the fort and troops on shore, and seized a schooner there. On 4 January the French frigate *Pique* (38) was enticed to attack when *Blanche* seized a schooner she had been guarding. The fight began about midnight and continued through the night. *Blanche*'s mizen and mainmast fell, and *Pique* ran up against her and attempted to board. *Blanche*'s crew lashed the two ships together; mutual gunfire soon made the main decks of both ships untenable. About dawn, the French cried for quarter. *Blanche* lost eight men killed and twenty-one wounded; *Pique* had seventy-six killed and 110 wounded. Both captains died; *Pique* became a British ship. (James 1.308–313; Clowes 4.488–490)

Blanche v. *Albion*, 3–4 November 1803
Blanche (Capt. Zachary Mudge) found the French cutter *Albion* (8) on 3 November 1803 at Monte Christi, St Domingue, protected by a battery. A boat attack that afternoon failed. Next day a schooner appeared and was captured. A night attack on the 4th succeeded in capturing *Albion*. Two days later, a party of five men captured another schooner – which had a crew and over thirty soldiers. (James 3.196–201; Clowes 5.329–331)

Blanche v. French ships, October 1804–July 1805
On 21 October 1804 *Blanche* captured the French brig *Gracieuse* (12) near Curacao, and on 10 June 1805 the French schooner privateer *Amitié* near Jamaica. A month later, north of Puerto Rico, *Blanche* was attacked by the French frigate *Topaze* (40) and three corvettes. After a fight in which *Blanche* was largely disabled, she surrendered and sank soon after. (James 4.38–46; Clowes 5.336, 356, 364–365)

Blanche v. *Guerriere*, 18–19 July 1806
The frigate *Blanche* (38; Capt. Sir Thomas Lavie) met the French frigate *Guerrière* near the Faeroe Islands. *Guerrière* had been attacking fishing vessels in the north, and had a large part of her crew sick from scurvy. The two ships fought for an hour; *Guerrière* surrendered. (James 4.160–162; Clowes 5.385–386)

Blandford v. French ship, June 1745
The sloop *Blandford* (20; Capt. Edward Dodd) was captured by a French ship in the West Indies. (Clowes 3.311)

Blandford v. French squadron, 13 August 1755

Blandford (20; Capt. Richard Watkins) met a French squadron off Brest, and was surrounded and captured. It was technically a time of peace, so the French returned the ship. (Clowes 3.289)

Blast v. Spanish ships, 19 October 1745

The bomb *Blast* (8) was captured by a Spanish ship in the West Indies. (Clowes 3.311; Colledge 46)

Blazer and *Brevdrageren* at Cuxhaven, 15–21 March 1813

The brigs *Blazer* (12; Lt Francis Baker) and *Brevdrageren* (12; Lt Thomas Devon) went into the Elbe estuary and took possession of batteries at Cuxhaven; boats from the ships went upriver to Brunsbuttel where two Danish galliots, *Junge Trautman* and *Liebe*, were captured. (James 6.4–6; Anderson 347)

Blean v. *U-443*, 14 December 1942

The destroyer *Blean* was sunk by *U-443* in the western Mediterranean. (Rohwer 216)

Blenheim, *Drake*, and *Swift* v. *Harmonie*, 14 November 1803

Blenheim (74; Rear-Admiral Sir Thomas Graves) sent in parties of seamen and marines to cut out the privateer *Harmonie* from Marin harbour, Martinique. The marines, towed in by the hired cutter *Swift*, captured and destroyed a covering battery; the sloop *Drake* (13; Cmdr William Ferris) towed in the sailors, who captured *Harmonie* after a brisk fight. (James 3.201–202; Clowes 5.331)

Blenheim v. *Curieuse*, 4 March 1804

The French schooner *Curieuse*, at anchor in the harbour of St Pierre, Martinique, was attacked by boat parties from *Blenheim* (74; Capt. William Ferris). The schooner was captured, but grounded, being held fast by chains; the attackers withdrew having lost three dead, three missing, and nineteen wounded (out of fifty). (James 3.255; Clowes 5.339)

Blenheim v. *Marengo* and *Belle Poule*, 6 August 1805

Blenheim (74; Capt. Austin Bissell, with Rear-Admiral Sir Thomas Troubridge on board) was escorting a fleet of ten Indiamen south of Ceylon when *Marengo* (74) and *Belle Poule* (40), commanded by Admiral Linois, attacked the Indiamen. *Blenheim* turned about and the two French ships gave up the attack. Firing at the Indiamen as they passed, they sailed away. (James 4.51–52; Parkinson 269–271; Clowes 5.367)

Blonde at Wilmington, North Carolina, 28 January 1781

A small expedition led by *Blonde* (32; Capt. Andrew Barkley) occupied Wilmington to assist the campaign of Lord Cornwallis. Seven ships were captured. (Clowes 4.61)

Bloody Bay, Tobermory, Mull, 1481
A dispute between John II, Lord of the Isles, and his son Angus Og involved much of the Western Isles of Scotland. The Macleods of Lewis and Harris, Macleans of Duart, and MacNeills of Barra supported John, and Angus had support from the Earls of Atholl and Argyll. The result was a battle at what became known as Bloody Bay between two galley fleets. Angus was victorious. (Rodger 1.166–167; Nicholson 482)

Bloom and *Brighton* v. French ship, 24 February 1797
The tenders *Bloom* (14; Lt Andrew Congalton) and *Brighton* (14) were captured by a French ship near Holyhead. (Clowes 4.549)

Blossom v. *César*, 4 November 1810.
The sloop *Blossom* (8; Cmdr William Stewart) sent its boats to attack *César*, a privateer xebec, off Cape Sicie. *César* was captured after a stiff fight, with some loss. (James 5.128–129; Clowes 5.473)

Bluebell v. *Libau*, 20–21 April 1916
The German auxiliary *Libau* (formerly the British liner *Castro*, disguised as the Norwegian *Aud*) brought a cargo of arms to assist the Sinn Fein rebellion in Ireland. She put into Tralee where *U-19* also brought Sir Roger Casement. But the two did not connect. Casement was arrested by the local police; *Libau* sailed and scuttled herself when intercepted by the sloop *Bluebell*. (Corbett 3.300–301)

Bluebell v. *U-69*, 7 December 1941
U-69 was damaged by depth-charges from the corvette *Bluebell* in the Strait of Gibraltar. (Rohwer 121)

Boadicea in the English Channal, 1799–1801
Boadicea (38; Capt. Richard Keats) captured the privateer *L'Invincible Général Bonaparte* and the sloop *Utile* (16) in April 1799, the French privateer *Gironde* in September 1800, and the gunvessel *Bombarde* in January 1801. (Colledge 53, 160, 424; Clowes 4.557)

Boadicea v. *Duguay-Trouin* and *Guerrière*, 31 August 1803
The French ships *Duguay-Trouin* (74) and *Guerrière* (40) were met in crossing the Atlantic by the frigate *Boadicea* (38; Capt. John Maitland). *Boadicea* fired, but *Duguay-Trouin* proved to be fully armed and manned, so Capt. Maitland avoided action and sailed away. (James 3.187–188; Clowes 5.323)

Boadicea v. *Vautour*, 25 November 1803
The frigate *Boadicea* (38; Capt. John Maitland) captured the French lugger *Vautour* (12) near Finisterre. *Vautour* was carrying dispatches from St Domingue. (Clowes 5.331)

Boadicea v. *Vénus*, 14 September 1810
The frigate *Boadicea* (38; Capt. Josias Rowley) chased the French frigate

Vénus (44), which had just captured *Ceylon*, an Indiaman. *Vénus*, already considerably damaged, surrendered after a brief fight; *Ceylon* was retaken. (James 5.187–190; Clowes 5.468–470)

Boadicea v. slaver, 6 November 1888
The pinnace of the screw corvette *Boadicea* (Capt. Hon. Assheton Curzon-Howe) chased a slave dhow off East Africa for six hours before it was captured, despite strong resistance; forty-one slaves were freed. (Clowes 7.391)

Bolton v. US squadron, 5 April 1776
The brig *Bolton* (12; Lt Edward Sneyd) was captured by a US squadron commanded by Commodore Esek Hopkins. (Clowes 4.109; Syrett, *American* 26)

Bomarsund, Finland, June–August 1854
The paddle steamers *Hecla*, *Odin*, and *Victorious* went to bombard Bomarsund on 21 June, without result. Landings were made by French troops on 8 August and guns were moved to assaulting positions. After a short bombardment by land and from ships of the fleet, the fortress was surrendered on the 10th. (Clowes 6.420, 422–425; NRS, *Misc* V)

Bombay (Mumbai), India, April 1674
A Mogul fleet landed a force at Sion on Bombay Island, but was driven off by the garrison and an EIC frigate; a second landing at Mazagaon was also repelled. (Low 1.62)

Bombay v. *Jaseur*, 10 July 1807
The frigate *Bombay* (38; Capt. William Lye) captured the French sloop *Jaseur* (12) near the Andaman Islands. (Clowes 5.400)

Bonaventure off Iceland, Summer 1696
Bonaventure (50; Capt. James Davidson) guarded the English fishing fleet off Iceland. When four French armed privateers attacked they were driven away. (Clowes 2.491)

Bonbee, Benin River, 28 March 1850
The people of Bonbee attacked a factory at Warree; boats from *Archer* (14; Cmdr James Strange) and the paddle steamer *Jackal* attacked Bonbee in reply, captured and destroyed the town, and did the same to another town nearby. (Clowes 6.393–394)

Bône, North Africa, 23 May 1824
A corsair brig (16 guns) was moored in Bône harbour, protected by the fort. Boats from *Naiad* (40; Capt. Hon. Sir Robert Spencer) went in, captured, and burned her. (Clowes 6.236–237)

Bonetta at Yorktown, 1781
The brig *Bonetta* (14) was captured by the French in the James River during the Yorktown campaign. (Clowes 4.111)

Bonetta v. Nuestra Senora del Carmen, June 1800
The Spanish felucca *Nuestra Senora del Carmen* was sunk by fire from the sloop *Bonetta* (16; Cmdr Henry Vansittart) in the West Indies. (Clowes 4.561)

Bonetta v. slavers, 1838–1840, and 1848
The brig *Bonetta* (3; Lt John Stoll) captured nine slavers while stationed in West Africa, three of them well inside the Congo estuary. In 1848, commanded by Lt Edwyn Forbes, she captured several slavers in quick succession. (Clowes 6.306, 367; Bethell 182)

Bonne Citoyenne v. Furieuse, 5–6 July 1809
The sloop *Bonne Citoyenne* (20; Cmdr William Mounsey) found the French frigate *Furieuse* in mid-Atlantic in the act of taking possession of a prize, and went in chase. The two ships closed and fired at each other for seven hours. At last, almost out of powder, *Bonne Citoyenne* threatened to board, and *Furieuse* surrendered. The British ship had only one man killed and five wounded, but *Furieuse* had thirty-five dead and perhaps fifty wounded. *Bonne Citoyenne* towed her defeated antagonist for twenty-five days to Halifax, Nova Scotia. (James 5.23–27; Clowes 5.436–437)

Bordelaise v. Curieux, 29 January 1801
The corvette *Bordelaise* (24; Capt. Thomas Manby) met three French ships near Barbados; *Bordelaise* closed and attacked *Curieux* (18); the others (*Mutine* (16) and *Esperance* (6)) fled; *Curieux* surrendered after half an hour, but then sank. (James 3.124–125; Clowes 4.536)

Bordentown, New Jersey, 6 May 1778
The *Hussar* galley (Capt. John Henry) rowed up the Delaware River and landed a force at Bordentown. Forty-four vessels were burned and a battery was destroyed. The men were re-embarked without loss. (Clowes 4.13)

Boreas v. Diane, 30 April 1758
Boreas (28; Capt. Robert Boyle) met and captured the French frigate *Diane* (36), off North America. (Clowes 3.298)

Boreas v. Compas, August 1779
The frigate *Boreas* (28; Capt. Charles Thompson) captured the French warship *Compas* (18; *en flute*) with a cargo of sugar, near Jamaica. (Clowes 4.31)

Boscawen's squadron v. Chaffault's squadron, 27–28 October 1758
Returning from the conquest of Louisbourg, Admiral Edward Boscawen, with four line-of-battle ships and three frigates, met a French squadron returning from Québec under the command of Admiral de Chaffault, who had five line-of-battle ships, one frigate, and a prize (the East Indiaman *Carnarvon*). The two squadrons passed on opposite courses and exchanged fire, fruitlessly. Next day, Boscawen found the French squadron again and went in

chase; *Carnarvon* was retaken, but no further fighting took place. (Clowes 3.185–186)

Boston, Massachusetts, 17 March 1776
After the battle of Bunker Hill, the siege of the British force in Boston by the American rebel army under General Washington was unbreakable. Shipping was collected in the harbour to evacuate the British forces and the loyalist inhabitants. They were taken to Halifax which became for a time the main British base. (Clowes 3.371)

Boston v. French ships, 4 January 1695
Boston (24) was captured in the Atlantic by a French force. (Colledge 50)

Boston v. *Embuscade*, 31 July 1793
The frigate *Boston* (32; Capt. George Courtnay) waited outside New York for the French frigate *Embuscade* (36), which had taken refuge there. Courtnay eventually sent in a formal challenge, and the two ships fought for three hours, by which time both were effectively disabled. *Boston* managed to get away, having lost ten men killed, including Courtnay; *Embuscade* may have lost about the same. (James 1.110–114; Clowes 4.478–479)

Boston and others v. *Bronzo*, 12 July 1943
The Italian submarine *Bronzo* surfaced into the midst of a British force – the minesweepers *Boston*, *Poole*, *Cromarty*, and *Seaham* – in the Strait of Messina, and was captured. (Rohwer 262)

Bostonian v. *U-53*, 10 October 1917
The ocean escort ship *Bostonian*, in charge of the convoy HH-25 in the English Channel, was torpedoed by *U-53*, and sank quickly; most of her crew were saved. (Newbolt 5.163)

Botha v. *A-7* and *A-19*, 21 March 1917
The destroyer *Botha* (Cmdr R. Rede), leading a group of French ships, encountered a German destroyer force in the North Sea, which got clear; two German TBs were located: *A-19* was rammed and sunk by *Botha*; *A-7* was engaged by *Botha* and a French ship, which mistook *Botha* for a German ship and torpedoed her. One of the German destroyers was torpedoed by *MB-20* on their return to port. (Newbolt 5.225–227)

Bougie Bay, North Africa, 2 and 8 May 1671
Vice-Admiral Sir Edward Spragge sent a fireship against a group of Algerine ships in the bay, but this failed. An attack six days later broke the boom and *Little Victory*, converted to a fireship, went in. The Algerine ships were all destroyed. The Dey of Algiers was then dethroned; his successor made a new treaty. (Clowes 2.440–441)

Bouncer and *Havock* v. pirates, China, June 1866
The gunboats *Bouncer* (Lt Karl Mainwaring) and *Havock* (Lt Yelverton

O'Keefe) attacked two pirate ships in Starling Inlet; both were destroyed. (Clowes 7.216)

Bouncer v. pirates, China, June 1869
The gunboat *Bouncer* (Lt Rodney Lloyd) and two Chinese gunboats attacked a group of pirate junks. Twenty-one were captured by a landing party. (Clowes 7.227)

Bourbon Island (Reunion), Indian Ocean
1809   A raid was mounted by Capt. Josias Rowley of *Raisonnable* (64) against the harbour of St Paul on 21 September, where the French frigate *Caroline* and her prizes, the EIC ships *Europe* and *Streatham*, were moored. Soldiers were collected from Rodriguez Island, and a landing took place from the frigate *Neréide* (36; Capt. Robert Corbet) to capture the batteries; the ships in the harbour were then attacked from land and sea. *Caroline*, *Europe*, and *Streatham* were all taken, along with several smaller ships. The batteries and magazines in the town were demolished.

1810   A force of soldiers, sailors, and marines commanded by Capt. Josias Rowley was gathered from the squadron blockading Mauritius and from Rodríguez Island and was landed on Bourbon on 6 July. Little resistance was met from the inhabitants. (James 5.58–62, 141–144; Clowes 5.444–445, 457–458; NC 4.319–322; Parkinson 364–367)

Boxer v. *Enterprise*, 5 September 1813
The sloop *Boxer* (14; Cmdr Samuel Blyth) met the US gun brig *Enterprise* (16) off Portland; the *Boxer* was defeated in the fight; both captains were killed. (James 6.75–78; Clowes 6.88–89; NC 5.167–168)

Boyne and *Caledonia* v. *Romulus* and *Adrienne*, 12 February 1814
Part of the French Toulon fleet came out. The Mediterranean fleet attempted to attack, but only *Boyne* (98; Capt. George Burlton) and, more distantly, the flagship *Caledonia* (130) were able to engage with the *Romulus* (74) and the frigate *Adrienne* (40). Despite being badly damaged, *Romulus* returned safely to Toulon, as did *Adrienne*. (James 6.118–119; Clowes 5.306)

Bradford City v. U-boat, 16 August 1917
The decoy ship *Bradford City* was sunk by a U-boat in the Strait of Messina. (Colledge 52)

Braeneil v. *U-93*, 7 January 1918
The steamer *Braeneil* rammed and sank *U-93* off the Lizard. (Grant 115–116)

BREST, Brittany
A village and a castle in the medieval period, Brest later developed as a major naval base, thereby becoming a prime target for the Royal Navy, and subject to blockade.

The Hundred Years' War

1340 The English fleet raided Brest in September. The place was neutral at the time, but several merchant ships, including six Genoese merchant galleys, were taken. (Sumption 1.347)

1342 Brest was besieged by a French force in pursuit of a local succession dispute. An English fleet carrying a small army arrived unexpectedly, and drove eleven Genoese galleys in the French service ashore. The French abandoned the siege and retreated out of western Brittany. (Sumption 1.400)

1373 A large squadron of fifty ships sailed to Brest in July to relieve the besieged English garrison, then returned to England. (Sumption 3.185)

1377 A relieving force sailed from the Thames in December carrying supplies and reinforcements to Brest. A Castilian squadron blockading the harbour was defeated, eight ships being captured. (Sumption 3.309–310)

1386 An expedition commanded by John of Gaunt, Duke of Lancaster, sailed from Plymouth to pursue Gaunt's claim to the throne of Castile. On the way a landing was made to relieve the siege at Brest; the besiegers soon agreed to terms and the fleet sailed on. (Sumption 3.582–583; Clowes 1.298–299)

1388 A fleet under the command of the Earl of Arundel raided the Breton coast, but could only land at Bréhat Island. (Sumption 3.653)
See also: **Bay of Bourgneuf**

Tudor Wars

1512–1513 An English naval force under Lord Edward Howard patrolled off Brest and raided the Breton coast, capturing sixty or more ships. After returning to England for supplies, the fleet met a Breton fleet. The fight was mainly between the English ship *Regent* and the Breton ship *Marie de Cordelière*. *Cordelière* was set on fire and in a great explosion both ships were destroyed; almost a thousand men died.

After a winter break the blockade was resumed in April 1513. French galleys from the Mediterranean fleet were now present. The English attacked but lost one ship wrecked and two to the galleys' great guns. Howard made a frontal attack on the well-prepared French and was killed. The English withdrew to Plymouth. The English fleet raided Blanc Sablon Bay in July. (Clowes 1.452–457; Rodger, 1.169–171; Loades 58–60)

1558 A raid was attempted in July; Le Conquet was attacked, but the attack on Brest failed. (Loades 174; Clowes 1.473)

War of the League of Augsburg

1694 An expedition of nine English and Dutch line-of-battle ships went to attack Brest in June. The expedition had been betrayed and was greeted by a powerful defence. Several hundred troops were landed; perhaps 500 of them were killed or captured. One ship went aground and had to surrender. (Clowes 2.474–476; NRS, *Misc* II)

Brevdrageren and *Algerine* v. Danish brigs, 31 July–1 August 1811
The brig *Brevdrageren* (12; Lt Thomas Devon) and the cutter *Algerine* (10; Lt John Blow) were attacked by the Danish brigs *Langeland* (20), *Lugen* (20), and *Kiel* (16), off the coast of Norway. The two ships separately escaped, then returned to attack the isolated *Langeland*; however, *Brevdrageren* was in turn isolated, eventually escaping when *Algerine* returned. (Anderson 344–345; Clowes 5.483–489)

Bridgewater v. *Affaire* and *Concorde*, 16 May 1707
Bridgewater (32; Capt. Thomas Lawrence) met the French privateers *Affaire* (24) and *Concorde* (12) and their prize off Kinsale. After a long fight the French ships sailed away, but *Bridgewater* reclaimed the prize. (Clowes 2.514)

Bridgewater v. Sallee pirates, 1716
Bridgewater (24) fought two pirate ships out of Sallee (16 guns each) and drove both ashore near that port. (Clowes 3.258)

Bridlington, Yorkshire, February 1643
Queen Henrietta Maria with four ships brought arms and treasure from the Netherlands for the Royalist cause, landing at Bridlington. A Parliamentary squadron under Sir William Batten bombarded the ships and the town, including the house in which the queen was staying. (Clowes 2.78)

Brilliant v. *Regenerée* and *Vertu*, 26 July 1798
The frigate *Brilliant* (28; Capt. Hon. Henry Blackwood) found the French frigates *Regenerée* (36) and *Vertu* (36) at Santa Cruz, Tenerife. They chased her for most of the day, then *Brilliant* bore up and severely damaged *Regenerée* by a sudden broadside, and got clear by a sudden drastic course change in the night. (James 2.250–251; Clowes 4.512)

Briseis and *Bruiser* v. *Coureer*, May 1809
The sloop *Briseis* (10) and the brig *Bruiser* (12) captured the Danish gunboat *Coureer* in the North Sea. (Clowes 5.565)

Briseis v. *Sans Souci*, 14 October 1810
The sloop *Briseis* (10; Lt George Bentham) chased the schooner *Sans Souci* through the North Sea for several hours, then the two ships fought bulwark to bulwark for an hour until *Sans Souci* surrendered. She had nine dead and nineteen wounded out of fifty-five men; and *Briseis* had four dead and eleven wounded. (James 5.103–104; Clowes 5.472–473)

Briseis v. *Urania*, 19 June 1812
The sloop *Briseis* (10; Cmdr John Ross) sent boats into Pillau roads (East Prussia) to take out the captured British merchant ship *Urania*. The French resisted, but the boarding party succeeded. (James 5.327; Clowes 5.511–512)

Brisk v. *Prueba*, 7 March 1831
The sloop *Brisk* (10; Lt Edward Butterfield) chased and captured the slaver *Prueba* off West Africa; 313 slaves were freed as a result. (Clowes 6.270)

Bristol and Cambridge v. Dutch West India Fleet, 22 July 1672
Bristol (48; Capt. Charles Wyld) and *Cambridge* (70; Capt. Arthur Herbert) attacked the returning Dutch West India fleet near Heligoland, but failed to take any of the ships; *Cambridge* was damaged by return fire. (Clowes 2.444)

Bristol and Adventure v. Citron Tree, April 1680
Bristol (48; Capt. John Wyborn) and *Adventure* (40; Capt. William Booth) fought the Algerian corsair *Citron Tree* (32), driving her ashore near Tangier; fifty slaves were rescued. (Clowes 2.454)

Bristol and Chester v. Achille and Gloire, 24 April 1709
Bristol (48; Capt. Henry Gore) was attacked and captured by *Achille* (64) and *Gloire* (38). The Channel Fleet was nearby and chased the French off, retaking *Bristol*. *Chester* (50; Capt. Thomas Mathews) became separated from the fleet and fought and captured *Gloire*. *Bristol*, holed badly, foundered. (Clowes 2.521–522)

Bristol v. Karlsruhe, 6–7 August 1914
The German light cruiser *Karlsruhe* was sailing north past the Bahamas, pursued by the cruiser *Suffolk*, but outpacing her. The light cruiser *Bristol*, heading south, fired at *Karlsruhe* during the night; *Karlsruhe* replied; both missed. *Karlsruhe* evaded both ships next day. (Corbett 1.47–48; Halpern, *Naval History* 78)

Bristol Channel
997 A Viking force which had been raiding in England sailed to the west and raided in Devon and Cornwall, South Wales, and along the River Severn. (Maund 159–160; *ASC* s.a. 997)

1067–1068 The sons of the former king Harold II sailed from Ireland in 1067 with a fleet recruited in Leinster and Dublin to attempt the reconquest of England. They landed at Bristol, in Somerset, and at the Tawe estuary in Devon, but were opposed each time, and returned to Ireland. Next year Godwin, son of Harold II, raided in Cornwall and Devon with another Irish fleet but was defeated and returned to Ireland. (*ASC* s.a. 1067–1068; Hudson 157–160)

1401 Scottish ships came to help Owain Glyn Dwr in his revolt against King Henry IV, but two of the ships were captured by Henry Percy (Hotspur), one near Bardsey Island, the other near Milford Haven. (Clowes 1.357)
See also: **Milford Haven, Irish Sea, South Wales**

Britannia and Nonsuch v. Vengeur and Resolue, 22 January 1794
The EIC ships *Britannia* (Capt. Thomas Cheap) and *Nonsuch* (Capt. John Canning), part of a squadron sent to the Sunda Strait to protect the China trade, chased two French privateers, *Vengeur* (34) and *Resolue* (26). After fighting less than an hour the privateers surrendered, when *William Pitt* and another ship approached. (James 1.218–219; Clowes 4.483; Low 1.205)

Britannia v. *UB-50*, 9 November 1918
The old battleship *Britannia* was torpedoed near Cape Trafalgar by *UB-50*, and sank after three hours – the last British warship sunk in the Great War. (Newbolt 5.359–360; Halpern, *Mediterranean* 586)

British brigs v. *Faaborg*, 15 November 1807
Two British brigs fought the Danish gunboat *Faaborg* (6) in Kallebostrand, Amager, Denmark. One of the brigs retired damaged, but the other forced *Faaborg* ashore. Reinforced, the Danes forced the second brig away. (Anderson 321)

British brig v. Danish gunboats, 26 April 1810
A British brig sent three boats on shore at Amrum Island; the boats were captured by two Danish gunboats. (Anderson 342)

British frigate v. Danish gunboats, 27 April 1810
A British frigate was attacked by four Danish gunboats near Skagen; she was rescued by the arrival of a British line-of-battle ship. (Anderson 342)

British patrol boat v. *UB-23*, 26 July 1917
The submarine *UB-23* was attacked by a patrol boat in the English Channel. The submarine was damaged and finally went into Corunna, where she was interned. (Newbolt 5.130n, 425)

British ships v. German minesweepers, 22 August 1944
The German minesweepers *RA-255* and *RA-259* were sunk by British ships near Genoa, and *RA-251* in the Golfe de Juan. (Rohwer 353)

British Transport v. *U-49*, 11 September 1917
The steamer *British Transport* was attacked several times, by gun and by torpedo, in the North Sea. On the last attack, at night, the torpedo track was seen. After it missed, the ship retraced the track, and found and rammed *U-49*, which sank. (Grant 67)

Briton v. slavers, 1884–1887
The corvette *Briton* (Capt. Rodney Lloyd) captured ten slave dhows during the ship's service in East Africa. (Clowes 7.387)

Brune v. *Oiseau*, 23 October 1762
The frigate *Brune* (32; Capt. George Tonyn) captured the corvette *Oiseau* (20) in an encounter in the Mediterranean. (Clowes 3.309)

Brune v. *Renard*, July 1780
The corvette *Renard* (18) was captured by *Brune* (32; Capt. Francis Hartwell) in the West Indies. (Clowes 4.114)

Brunswick and *Sarah* v. *Marengo* and *Belle Poule*, 11 July 1805
The French *Marengo* (74) and *Belle Poule* (40), commanded by Admiral

Linois, encountered the China ship *Brunswick* and the country ship *Sarah* off Ceylon. *Sarah* ran ashore and was wrecked; *Brunswick* made a nominal resistance and was captured. (James 4.50–51; Parkinson 266–267)

Bucephalus v. *Nymphe* and *Meduse*, 3–5 September 1811
The frigate *Bucephalus* (36; Capt. Charles Pelly) searched for *Nymphe* (40) and *Meduse* (40) recently arrived at Surabaya, Java. Having already sailed, they were followed by *Bucephalus* for nine days. Suddenly they turned to chase the British ship. Shots were exchanged. *Bucephalus*, somewhat damaged, led them towards a shoal, but they escaped that and the British frigate as well. (James 5.305–307; Clowes 5.300–301)

Buckingham v. *Florissant*, 3 November 1758
The French *Florissant* (74), with two frigates, was escorting a French convoy off St Eustatius in the Windward Islands, and was attacked by *Buckingham* (70; Capt. Richard Tyrell). The frigates were quickly driven away, but the two big ships fought until dark, and *Florissant* sailed off during the night. *Buckingham* was badly damaged. (Clowes 3.300)

Bulldog at Ancona, Italy, 27 February 1801
As the French captured Ancona, the bomb *Bulldog* (18; Cmdr Barrington Dacres) was also captured, having entered the harbour unawares. (Clowes 4.551)

Bulldog at Cap Haitien, Haiti, 23 October 1865
The paddle sloop *Bulldog* (Capt. Charles Wake) went into Cap Haitien seeking reparations for the sacking of the British consulate; in the fighting that followed, *Bulldog* destroyed several batteries and two warships and set the town on fire. She then ran aground, and was abandoned and blown up. The forts of the town were then bombarded to destruction by the screw frigate *Galatea* (Capt. Rochfort Maguire) and the screw gunvessel *Lily* (Cmdr Algernon Heneage). (Clowes 7.212–214)

Bullen and others v. *U-775*, 6 December 1944
North of Scotland *U-775* sank the destroyer *Bullen*, and was then attacked and damaged by the frigate *Loch Insh* and the destroyer *Goodall*. (Rohwer 373)

Bunker Hill, Boston, 17 June 1775
Glasgow (20; Capt. William Maltby) cannonaded rebel positions during the battle on Bunker Hill; her red-hot shot set fire to the houses in Charlestown. (Clowes 4.3)

Burburata, Spanish Main, 1567–1568
A joint Franco-Scots force took and sacked the town of Burburata on the Spanish Main. Next year it was coerced into trading by Sir John Hawkins. (Rodger 1.239; Williamson 81–82)

BURMA (Myanmar)

1824–1826 (First Burmese War)   The campaign of conquest in southern Burma was a river war, where the naval forces were involved in a series of small raids and river campaigns. Initial success in the bombardment and capture of Rangoon on 11 May involved *Larne* (20; Cmdr Frederick Marryat), *Liffey* (50; Capt. Charles Grant), and *Slaney* (20; Cmdr Charles Mitchell). Expeditions were also sent against Cheduba Island, Negrais, and Tenasserim. Having lost Rangoon, the Burmese counter-attacked by land and river, sending fire rafts against the ships. The ships went upriver to bombard Burmese palisaded camps. A river expedition was mounted against the capital Ava: a landing at Danabyu was defeated, but a second succeeded. Another expedition worked its way up the Bassein River, capturing the ports at the seaward end of the Delta. In 1825 the same sort of fighting occurred, but this time along the middle Irrawaddy River. A considerable number of small ships were again used to target and bombard Burmese positions. The Burmese did not defend their towns, but fought hard otherwise, suffering heavy casualties. At last, with British forces close to Ava, the king agreed to a treaty by which he gave an indemnity and surrendered Arakan and Tenasserim. (James 6.302–354; Clowes 6.237–250; Low 1.410–473)

1852–1854 (Second Burmese War)   Another river campaign, but the British now used screw steamships and rifles, so the Burmese were killed at a greater rate. No Burmese vessels were able to confront such ships as the screw frigate *Fox*, the paddle sloops *Hermes*, *Salamander*, and *Serpent*, and the screw sloop *Rattler*, together with EIC steamers *Phlegethon* and *Proserpine*. Once the British forces began to occupy territory Burmese guerrilla tactics had some effect. Unable to bring the king to negotiate, the British simply announced the annexation of the southern third of the country (Pegu) and campaigned to suppress the resistance – now described as robbers and brigands. (Clowes 6.372–386)

1885 (Third Burmese War)   This war involved only minor naval action. The British aim was to capture Mandalay, which was reached by another river voyage in which only the gunvessel *Woodlark* was needed, though it was reinforced by other vessels later. The city taken, the king was deposed and the country annexed. For the next two years *Ranger* (Cmdr John Pipon) was employed in Upper Burma in anti-bandit patrols, enduring several skirmishes. (Clowes 7.375–385; A.T.Q. Stewart, *The Pagoda War*, London 1972)

1942   Burma was invaded and conquered with ease by the Japanese in 1942, a process in which the navy had little part, though 3500 people were evacuated from Rangoon on 7–8 March. The submarine *Truant* sank two Japanese army transports on 1 April. (Rohwer 150, 156)

1944–1945   The British campaign of reconquest began in 1944. In the coastal area, Arakan, there were landings and raids. A British task force of Australian destroyers, British minesweepers, and Indian MTB flotillas bombarded Japanese positions near St Martin's Island between 11 and 24 December to support the land campaign. On 24 January 1945 a task force – RAN destroyers *Napier* and *Nepal*, the sloop *Shoreham*, and motor launches

– landed a commando force on the Akyab peninsula and this, with the Indian sloops *Narbada* and *Jumna* and two motor launches in support, brought the 74th Indian Brigade from the mainland. *Napier, Narbada,* and *Jumna* and motor launches landed part of a British commando brigade below Akyab and Ramree on 12 January. Further landings took place on Ramree Island, preceded by a bombardment by the battleship *Queen Elizabeth,* the cruiser *Phoebe,* and destroyers and sloops, on 16 January 1945, and on 22 January a commando force was landed at Kangaw by *Jumna, Narbad*a, and four motor launches. On 24–25 January landings took place on Cheduba Island, on the 30th on Sagu Island, and on 16 February the sloops *Flamingo* and *Narbada* supported an assault on Rangwa. The destroyers *Eskimo* and *Roebuck* and the Indian sloops *Cauveri* and *Jumna* supported an attack on Lalpan on 13 March 1945.

A divisional strength landing in the south on 1 May used several landing ships and 150 smaller craft, covered by six Indian Navy sloops, four escort carriers, and several destroyers. There was no resistance and Rangoon was occupied on 3 May. The covering force carried out air attacks on Martaban on 1 May, and a Japanese convoy of nine ships was destroyed in the process. Raids were also made on Japanese bases further south on the Kra Isthmus on 5 and 6 May. (Rohwer 377, 382, 386, 387, 394, 395, 399, 412)
See also: **Indian Ocean**

Bustard v. *Minerve,* 17 May 1810
The sloop *Bustard* (16; Cmdr John Markland) captured the French sloop *Minerve* (18). (Clowes 5.560)

Bustard at Chuchi, China, 29 June 1868
Supplies for the screw gunboat *Bustard* (Lt Cecil Johnson) were captured by pirates out of Chuchi near Swatow. Johnson went to Chuchi, obtained the co-operation of the local people and mandarins, and together they attacked the town several times over the next days, finally capturing and destroying it. (Clowes 7.223)

Busum, Holstein, 3 September 1813
A force of seven Danish gunboats defeated sixteen British gunboats and ships' boats in the Elbe estuary. (Anderson 347–348)

Bute and Arran, Scotland, September 1335
A fleet of fifty ships carried an army of 1500 men from Ireland to raid the Isles of Bute and Arran in the campaign to compel Robert the Steward to submit to Edward III. (Nicholson 132)

Bute, 1502–1504
Men of the Western Isles raided the Isle of Bute in retaliation for an assertion of royal authority by the Earl of Huntly; the damage was so great that royal tenants were excused payment of rent for the next three years. (MacDougall 181)

Buttercup and *PC-56* v. *U-87*, 29 December 1917
The sloop *Buttercup* and the patrol boat *PC-56* attended a sinking ship. *Buttercup* on its way rammed *U-87*; later *PC-56* depth-charged, shelled, and rammed the submarine, and *Buttercup* fired as well; unsurprisingly, *U-87* sank. (Grant 68–69)

Buzzard's Bay, Massachusetts, September 1778
The British squadron under Rear-Admiral Lord Howe raided the shores of Buzzard's Bay, attacking Martha's Vineyard and New Bedford. (Syrett, *Howe* 87)

Buzzard v. slavers, 1835–1836
The brig *Buzzard* (10; Lt Jeremiah McNamara) fought and captured the slaver *Formidable* early in 1835; 400 slaves were freed, but 300 others had already died on the passage. On 22 July 1836 *Buzzard* sent a party of five men against the slaver *Joven Carolina*, which had a crew of thirty-three. They captured the ship and freed 422 slaves. (Clowes 6.275–277)

Buzzard v. *Eagle* and *Clara*, 1839
The brig *Buzzard* captured the slavers *Eagle* and *Clara* and took them into New York harbour. There followed a complicated dispute over their nationality. (Lloyd 55)

Byng's Squadron v. *Auguste*, 13 January 1705
Auguste (54), one of the ships of Duguay-Trouin's command, blundered into Sir George Byng's squadron in the Channel and was captured by *Chatham* (48; Capt. Robert Bokenham) after a fight. There was much pleasure on the English side at the capture of one of his ships; it was added to the navy. (Clowes 2.508)

Byng's Fleet v. *Thetis* and privateers, 1705
The Channel Fleet, commanded by Admiral Sir George Byng, captured the French warship, *Thetis* (44), and twelve privateers during a cruise. (Clowes 2.508)

C

C-7 v. UB-10, 5 April 1917
The British submarine *C-7* met and attacked *UB-10* in the southern North Sea, without success. (Grant 60)

C-15 v. UC-65, 3 November 1917
The submarine *C-15* torpedoed and sank *UC-65* in the eastern part of the English Channel. (Newbolt 5.426; Grant 48)

C-34 v. U-52, 20 July 1917
The submarine *C-34* was sunk off the north coast of Ireland by *U-52*. (Colledge 62)

Cabinda and Abriza, West Africa, 1841
Cmdr H.J. Matson, with men from the sloop *Waterwitch* and from *Madagascar* (46), raided slave bases at Cabinda and Abriza, liberating over 1300 slaves. (Lloyd 96)

Cachalot v. U-51, 20 August 1940
The submarine *Cachalot* sank *U-51* in the Bay of Biscay. (Rohwer 35)

Cachalot v. Papa, 30 July 1941
The Italian TB *Papa* fought the British submarine *Cachalot* by gunfire, then rammed her, whereupon the submarine surrendered, but later sank. (Rohwer 89)

CADIZ, Spain
The main Spanish naval base, the landfall of the treasure galleons, and close to Gibraltar, Cadiz was an inevitable target and concern for the Royal Navy.

1587 An English fleet of thirty to forty ships commanded by Sir Francis Drake raided Cadiz to disrupt Spanish preparations for the Armada. Sailing directly into Cadiz harbour on 19 April Drake achieved complete surprise. Almost thirty ships were sunk in the next days, and a large quantity of supplies intended for the Armada was destroyed. The English suffered few losses. (Rodger 1.251; Clowes 1.488; Andrews 139–140; Williamson 295–298)

1596 A joint Anglo-Dutch expedition sailed from Plymouth to attack Spanish ships reported to be preparing for another Armada-style attack. The fleet, sailing well clear of land and seizing any ships which might alert the Spaniards, succeeded in surprising Cadiz on 21 June. The city was captured and ships in the outer harbour destroyed. A *flota* of ships in the inner harbour was burnt by the crews. The city was held for a fortnight, then the allies withdrew. (Rodger 1.284–285; Clowes 1.508–518; Loades 263–266)

1625 A poorly organized and badly led expedition went to attack Cadiz. The commander, Viscount Wimbledon, was indecisive and his officers largely inexperienced. The possibility of a surprise attack was forfeited by delay, the landing was disorderly, and the soldiers quickly found wine and became drunk. Re-embarkation was just as messy. (Rodger 1.357–359; Corbett 159–160)

1656 Capt. Richard Stayner, on blockade duty off Cadiz, intercepted the Spanish treasure *flota* as it approached. Two ships were captured, one was burned, and two went ashore. Only a fraction of the treasure was taken, most of which was annexed by the English sailors. (Corbett, *Mediterranean* 332–333; Capp 98; Clowes 2.213–214; Powell 287–288; Rodger 2.25–26)

1702 A force of 7000 men landed near Rota, which was captured, and ships of the fleet under Rear-Admiral Sir Stafford Fairborne bombarded nearby forts. An advance on Cadiz failed to capture the defending forts; the troops were re-embarked. (Owen 77–79; Clowes 2.377–380; Francis 43–51; Rodger 2.165–166)

1797 The bomb *Thunder* (Lt John Gourly), covered by gunboats from the Mediterranean fleet, bombarded Cadiz for a short time on 3 July. The covering force, with Commodore Horatio Nelson in command, was attacked by Spanish gunboats and Nelson survived a hand-to-hand fight. Two days later a second bombardment, using three bomb vessels, *Thunder*, *Terror*, and *Strombolo*, took place. (James 2.60–62; Clowes 4.321)

1810–1812 The city of Cadiz was besieged by French forces from 1810. British ships based at Gibraltar assisted the resistance by landing troops and naval forces, bombarding French positions, raiding, and bringing in supplies. The siege lasted nearly three years, with constant small actions, and preoccupied a large French army. The French, unable to take the city, withdrew in August 1812, mainly as a result of the victories of the allies elsewhere in Spain. (Hall 149–161; Morriss 77–82; Gordon 168–221)

Caesar and squadron v. *Italienne* and others, 24 February 1809
The French 40-gun frigates *Italienne*, *Calypso*, and *Cybèle* came out of Lorient. They were driven into Sables d'Olonne and there bombarded to wrecks by *Caesar* (80; Rear-Admiral Hon. Robert Stopford), *Defence* (74), *Donegal* (74), and other ships. (Clowes 5.254)

Cagliari, Sardinia, 1 August 1708
The British Mediterranean fleet under Admiral Sir John Leake bombarded Cagliari. The town's surrender was secured. (Clowes 2.412; Corbett, *Mediterranean* 303)

Cairndale v. *Marconi*, 30 May 1941
In the course of an attempt to attack Force H west of Gibraltar the Italian submarine *Marconi* sank the fleet tanker *Cairndale*. (Rohwer 76)

Caithness, Scotland, c.900

Jarl Sigurd the Mighty of Orkney and Thorstein the Red of the Hebrides joined forces to invade northern Scotland; they fought Maelbrigte Tusk, the local Pictish ruler, and won, but Sigurd died of blood poisoning soon after, when Maelbrigte's 'tusk' – a large protruding tooth – scratched him. The date of this is unclear. (Thompson 13; *Orkneyinga Saga* 5)

Calabria, Italy, July 1806

A small army of British troops commanded by General Sir John Stuart was transported from Sicily to Calabria, and, escorted by the squadron of Rear-Admiral Sir Sidney Smith, landed in the Bay of St Eufemia. Attacked by a French army almost double their size, the army was victorious at the battle of Maida. British forces were then withdrawn. One detachment, conveyed on the frigate *Amphion* (Capt. William Hoste), assaulted and captured the town of Crotone. (James 4.124–125; Clowes 5.199–200)

Calcutta v. French squadron, 26 September 1805

Calcutta (50; Capt. Daniel Woodriff), an Indiaman converted to a cruiser, escorting a homeward-bound Indian convoy, encountered the French Rochefort squadron under Rear-Admiral Allemand near Finisterre. An attack by the frigate *Armide* (40) was driven off. *Calcutta* ordered the convoy to scatter, drew the French ships away, and turned to attack the foremost French line-of-battle ship, *Magnanime* (74). They fought for an hour until *Calcutta* was disabled, and surrendered. The convoy was then largely away (and Allemand in the process missed yet another convoy). (James 4.46–50; Clowes 5.371)

Sir Robert CALDER'S ACTION, 22 July 1805

The Franco-Spanish Combined Fleet under Admiral Villeneuve, heading for Ferrol, met the British blockading force off Cape Finisterre; the Combined Fleet had twenty line-of-battle ships, the British fifteen. The encounter was confused by foggy weather. Two Spanish ships were captured, *Firme* (74) and *San Rafael* (80); one British ship, *Windsor Castle* (98), was disabled. Next day the two fleets watched each other until the Combined Fleet turned away and sailed south for Corunna. (James 3.357–370; Clowes 5.112–117; *NC* 3.151–171; Tunstall 245–247)

Calder and *Bentinck* v. *U-774*, 8 April 1945

U-774 was sunk by the destroyers *Calder* and *Bentinck* west of Ireland. (Rohwer 406)

Calgarian v. *U-19*, 1 March 1918

The AMC *Calgarian* was sunk by *U-19*. (Newbolt 5.227)

Calicut, India, November–December 1780

Covered by *Sartine* (32; Capt. Robert Simonton), raids were made against the ships of Hyder Ali, the Raja of Mysore, in Calicut harbour. One ship was cut out and one driven ashore; but *Sartine* struck a rock and sank. (Clowes 4.58–59)

Callao, Peru, 19 June 1593
Richard Hawkins, in *Dainty*, reached the Pacific by the Strait of Magellan, intending to raid the Spanish coast of South America. He was attacked and captured by warships from Callao. (Rodger 1.281)

***Calliope* v. *Comtesse d'Hambourg*, 25 October 1810**
The sloop *Calliope* (10; Cmdr John McKerlie) chased the privateer schooner *Comtesse d'Hambourg* (14) for three hours in the North Sea, finally coming close enough to fire with effect. The privateer lost her foremast and surrendered. (James 5.104; Clowes 5.473)

***Calvia* and *Vanessa* v. *UB-107*, 27 July 1918**
The trawler *Calvia* and the destroyer *Vanessa* fought and sank *UB-107* in the southern part of the North Sea. (Newbolt 5.418; Grant 128)

***Calypso* v. *Diligente*, 13 April 1800**
A boat from the sloop *Calypso* (16; Cmdr Joseph Baker) found the French schooner *Diligente* (6) close to shore off Cape Tiburon, St Domingue, and captured her by boarding, ten men defeating thirty-nine. (James 3.14; Clowes 4.557)

***Calyx* v. U-boat, 10 July 1916**
The AMC *Calyx* was sunk by a U-boat. (Colledge 65)

Camaret Bay, Brittany, 22 August 1805
The French fleet, twenty-one line-of-battle ships under Admiral Ganteaume, came out of Brest and anchored in the entrance to the Goulet, beside Camaret Bay. The British blockading fleet, seventeen line-of-battle ships under Admiral Sir William Cornwallis, approached with the intention of attacking. The French, under rigid instructions from Napoleon, withdrew. An action took place between the foremost British and French ships, who were assisted by shore batteries, without result. (James 3.311–314; Clowes 5.122–123)

***Cambrian* and *Fishguard* v. *Dragon*, 5 May 1800**
The French *Dragon* (14) was captured by the frigates *Cambrian* (40) and *Fishguard* (44) in the English Channel. (Clowes 4.557)

***Cambrian* v. privateers, 13 June–7 July 1805**
The frigate *Cambrian* (40; Capt. John Beresford), south of Bermuda, sent boats to attack the Spanish privateer *Maria*, which was captured after a tough fight. A second privateer, *Matilda*, was pursued into shoal water several days later and then captured. On 6 July boats were sent up St Mary's River, Florida, where, after overcoming considerable resistance, a privateer brig and her prizes, *Golden Grove* and *Ceres*, were captured. (James 4.36–37; Clowes 5.363)

Camel and Rattlesnake v. Preneuse, 20–21 September 1799

Camel, an armed storeship, and the sloop *Rattlesnake* (16; Cmdr Samuel Gooch) were at anchor in Algoa Bay, South Africa (both captains being ashore), when the French frigate *Preneuse* (36) arrived. *Preneuse* edged close enough for the two British ships to fire. Fighting continued for some hours, by which time *Camel* was leaking badly, but then *Preneuse* suddenly sailed away. (James 2.390–392; Clowes 4.524–525)

Cameleon v. Dutch ship, 14 August 1781

The sloop *Cameleon* (16; Cmdr Thomas Drury) fought a Dutch dogger (18) in the North Sea. After a short fight the Dutch ship blew up. (Clowes 4.73–74)

Cameleon v. pirates, Aegean Sea, 1825–1827

The sloop *Cameleon* (10) campaigned to suppress Greek piracy. This had emerged as a side blow of the Greek war of independence against the Ottoman Empire, but the pirates did not confine their attentions to enemy shipping. On at least seventeen occasions, *Cameleon* fought and defeated parties of pirates at sea and on land. (NRS, *Piracy, passim*)

Cameronia v. U-33, 15 March 1917

The troopship *Cameronia* was sunk by *U-33* east of Malta; 170 men died. (Halpern, *Naval History* 339; Newbolt 4.286)

Cameronian v. U-boat, 2 June 1917

The transport *Cameronian*, carrying mules to Egypt, was sunk by a U-boat's torpedo. (Newbolt 4.311–312)

Camito v. U-97, 6 May 1941

The ocean boarding ship *Camito* was sunk by *U-97*, as was the *Sangro*, an Italian tanker which had been captured. (Rohwer 71)

Campanula v. UB-66, 18 January 1918

UB-66 attacked a convoy off Cape Bon, and was herself then attacked by the sloop *Campanula*, which successfully depth-charged her. (Grant 131)

CAMPERDOWN, North Sea, 11 October 1797

The Dutch fleet, eleven line-of-battle and eight smaller ships, came out of the Texel on 8 October. The British North Sea Fleet, under Admiral Adam Duncan, came out of Great Yarmouth next day. The British fleet had fourteen line-of-battle and three smaller ships. The Dutch deliberately sought battle, which was hard-fought on both sides, centring above all on the fight between the two flagships *Vryheit* (74) and *Venerable* (74). Two Dutch ships had been compelled to surrender when *Vryheit*, reduced to a hulk and under no control, gave in. Eleven Dutch ships were captured all together, and others had pulled out when faced by stronger opponents. The battle differed from other contemporary encounters in that both sides fired at their opponents' hulls, not, as the French did, at the masts and rigging. The British ships were all badly damaged and casualties were heavy: over a thousand on the British side, more on the Dutch. (James 2.75–89; *NC* 1.224–232; Clowes 4.325–333; Tunstall 219–224)

Canada v. *Santa Leocadia*, 1 May 1781
Canada (74; Capt. Sir George Collier) chased the Spanish frigate *Santa Leocadia* (34) from a convoy. The pursuit lasted all day and the subsequent fight took place during the night. Despite the disparity in force the Spanish ship fought until, disabled, she surrendered. (Clowes 4.64)

Canada v. *Coquille*, 13 October 1798
Canada (74; Capt Sir John Borlase Warren) fought the frigate *Coquille* (36) in a confused action off Tory Island which frustrated a French attempt to land troops in Ireland. *Coquille* was heavily outmatched and surrendered after resisting for some time. (James 2.146)

Cancale Bay, Normandy, 13 May 1779
A small French force of *Danae* (26), *Diane* (26), and three smaller ships out of St Malo twice attempted to land on Jersey; they were attacked by *Experiment* (50; Capt. Sir James Wallace), *Pallas* (38), *Unicorn* (20), *Richmond* (32), and ten smaller vessels. The French ships were driven on shore in Cancale Bay near Coutances, and a defending battery was silenced by gunfire. Three ships were set on fire; *Danae* and two others were captured. (Clowes 4.25)

Candytuft v. *U-59*, 18 November 1917
The sloop *Candytuft* was sunk by *U-39* off Bougie, Algeria. (Colledge 67)

Cannanore, Malabar, India, 1790
A force of the Bombay EIC army was landed by the BM to assault and capture Cannanore during the Second Mysore War. (Low 1.184)

Canton River, China
1637 Capt. John Weddell, with four ships of Courteen's Association (a competitor of the EIC), sailed to Macao to trade. Prevented by the Portuguese from landing, he entered the Canton River in order to try direct trade with the Chinese. The Chinese strengthened a fort there and on 12 August fired on one of Weddell's ships; he bombarded it in reply. On 10 September the Chinese attacked with two fireships. Weddell replied by destroying a local village, but then retired to Lintin Island. The Portuguese on Macao assisted in brokering a settlement, and Weddell sailed away. (Foster 326–328)

1816 *Alceste* (46; Capt. Murray Maxwell) wished to sail up the Canton River to Whampoa for repairs. Maxwell's request for a pass was refused. He sailed nevertheless, on 13 November, being three times fired at. He returned fire in a minimal way, and reached his destination without harm. (Clowes 6.231–232)

1833–1834 The frigates *Andromache* (28; Capt. Henry Chads) and *Imogene* (28; Capt. Hon. Price Blackwood) forced their way past the fortifications of the Canton estuary at Bocca Tigris in September. The Chinese gunnery from the forts was wild and ineffective; the ships' gunnery was all too accurate in reply. Next year, again making their way up the Canton River, they were bombarded on 7 September by some junks and two forts. The Chinese shooting was just as erratic and inaccurate. The ships were able to get past by bombarding the forts into ruin. (Clowes 6.273–275; Graham 56–57)

1841 (CANTON RIVER battle) A campaign by a naval squadron and army forces pushed up the Canton River in stages, alternating advances with negotiations. On 7 January Chuenpen fort was bombarded from the river, assaulted by land and captured; next day the Bogue forts were attacked but negotiations stopped the fighting. A treaty was made but broke down quickly, and the British attack, led by the iron paddle frigate *Nemesis* (Master, William Hall), resumed on 20 February when two forts protecting a chain across the passage were bombarded, then captured by landing parties; by 27 February Whampoa and its forts had been taken. After more fruitless negotiations the advance resumed. Between 7 and 18 March all the fortifications below Canton city were captured or destroyed, largely by *Nemesis*'s fire. In May Canton itself was attacked, the way being opened by *Nemesis*, and a landing was made near the city. The Chinese gave in just as the assault on the city was about to begin. *Nemesis* had borne the brunt of the fighting, her iron hull and screw drive were the campaign winners. (Hall was commissioned into the Royal Navy and received accelerated promotion to captain by 1844.) Later Chinese refortifications of the banks of the river were attacked by *Herald* (Capt. Joseph Nias), but the work was resumed once Nias had withdrawn. (Clowes 6.264–295; Graham 147–163; Low 2.141–142)

1856–1857 The British China squadron moved up various channels of the Canton River, alternately bombarding places into destruction and sending letters demanding submission to the province's High Commissioner. Several forts before the city were captured with little resistance, though once they were taken the British found that they could do no more. The Chinese harried the British forces during the winter, and the British retreated.

In the spring of 1857 several ships, notably *Hornet*, *Samson*, *Sybille*, and *Nankin*, raided and burnt junks which were suspected to be pirate vessels. In March seventeen vessels were destroyed by *Hornet*, on 6 April thirteen by *Hornet* and *Samson*. In December, landings were made near Canton from the ships of the British and French squadrons. The forces captured outlying positions and gained control of the city. A week later raiding parties seized the city's High Commissioner and Chinese commanding generals. (Clowes 7.93–102, 113–116; Graham 301–310, 336–337)

Cape Bon, Tunisia, 10–12 April 1941
An Italian convoy from Palermo to Tripoli was attacked repeatedly by the British submarines *Upholder*, *Tetrarch*, *Ursula*, and *Unique*; *Tetrarch* sank a tanker; the others all missed. (Rohwer 68)

Cape de Gata, Spain, 28 February 1758
A British squadron commanded by Admiral Henry Osborn blockaded Cartagena. A French force approached, intending either to break the blockade

or to enter the port, but was detected. The French ships separated, so the fighting was between individual ships on each side. *Revenge* (64; Capt. John Storr) took the *Orphée* (64) assisted by *Berwick* (64), though Storr was killed. *Monmouth* (64; Capt. Arthur Gardiner) chased and fought *Foudroyant* (84) – Gardiner was killed. Despite the great disparity in force, *Foudroyant*'s guns were silenced; *Swiftsure* (70; Capt. Thomas Stanhope) arrived, and finally forced *Foudroyant*'s surrender. *Oriflamme* (50) was driven ashore by *Monarch* (74; Capt. John Montagu) and *Montagu* (64; Capt. Joshua Rowley). One French ship, *Pléiade* (28), got away. (Clowes 3.189–190)

Cape Finisterre, Spain
1712 A British squadron under Admiral Sir Thomas Hardy encountered a French squadron near Cape Finisterre in August. The French ships *Griffon* (44), *Aventure* (12), *Incomparable* (10), and *Rubis* were captured, and *St Esprit* (36) blew up. It was later judged that hostilities had been suspended by the time this fight took place. (Clowes 2.532)

1747 (First Battle of CAPE FINISTERRE) A French East Indies convoy was met by the British Channel Fleet under Rear-Admiral George Anson off Cape Finisterre on 3 May. Admiral de la Jonquiere attempted to shield the convoy by forming his biggest ships in a line of battle, but the British fleet was far too strong. All the French line-of-battle ships were taken, as were nine of the convoy. (This battle is referred to as 'Cape Ortegal' in France.) (Clowes 3.124–126; Tunstall 92–97)

1747 (Second Battle of CAPE FINISTERRE) A French convoy of 252 merchantmen for the West Indies, escorted by nine line-of-battle ships under the command of Commodore Herière de l'Etenduere, was intercepted off Cape Finisterre on 14 October by a British fleet commanded by Rear-Admiral Edward Hawke. L'Etenduere formed his ships in a line of battle and sent the convoy's ships away with one ship to guard them. Hawke ordered a general chase, so the fighting was mainly between individual ships. Six of the French line-of-battle ships were taken, and two escaped. The British ships suffered sufficient damage that it was decided not to chase the convoy. The French ships had therefore performed the protective task with which they were entrusted. (Clowes 3.126–129; Mahan 271–273; Tunstall 98–99)

1780 The British fleet commanded by Vice-Admiral Sir George Rodney was carrying supplies for Gibraltar. Off Finisterre on 7 January an enemy fleet was seen and seven Spanish warships, including a 64, were captured, as were fifteen merchantmen carrying naval stores and supplies to Cadiz. Those supplies were added to those for Gibraltar. (Clowes 3.448–449)

CAPE HENRY, Virginia, 16 March 1781
The French squadron at Narragansett, under Commodore des Touches, sailed for the Chesapeake; Vice-Admiral Marriot Arbuthnot followed from Long Island with a British squadron. They met off Cape Henry, roughly equal in strength, but des Touches outmanoeuvred Arbuthnot; three of the eight

British ships were so badly damaged as to be unmanageable. (Clowes 3.488–493; Syrett, *American* 167–170; Tunstall 168–169)

Capel and *Affleck* v. *U-486*, 26 December 1944
The destroyers *Capel* and *Affleck* were torpedoed by *U-486* off Cherbourg; *Capel* was sunk and *Affleck* was not repairable. (Rohwer 373)

CAPE OF GOOD HOPE, South Africa
1795 An expeditionary force of three 74s, two 64s, and two sloops commanded by Vice-Admiral Sir George Elphinstone landed the 74th Foot commanded by Major General Craig at Simonstown. The Dutch resisted. Reinforced by sailors and marines from the ships, the army attacked. *America* (64; Capt. John Blankett), *Stately* (64; Capt. Billy Douglas), and *Echo* (16; Capt. Temple Hardy) assisted by bombardments. More troops arrived on 3 September and Cape Town was attacked both by land and from the sea. On 14 September the Dutch governor surrendered the colony. (James 1.333–336; *NC* 1.139–140)

1796 A Dutch squadron arrived at Saldanha Bay, north of Cape Town, intending to retake the Dutch colony. On 12 August the British squadron commanded by Vice-Admiral Sir George Elphinstone anchored in line within gunshot of the Dutch ships. The Dutch force consisted of two 66s, one 54, three frigates, and a sloop; the British had two 74s, five 64s, one 50, one frigate, and five sloops. The Dutch admiral, invited to surrender, did so. (James 1.415–417)

1806 A convoy of transports carrying 5000 troops, escorted by a small squadron under the command of Capt. Sir Home Popham, landed at two places north of Cape Town; in a short campaign they secured possession of the colony. (James 4.186–189; NRS, *Misc* III 140–141; *NC* 3.261–288)

CAPE PASSARO, Sicily, 11 August 1718
Admiral Sir George Byng with twenty line-of-battle ships met the Spanish fleet of eleven line-of-battle ships and twenty smaller vessels off Cape Passaro, Sicily. Byng aimed to relieve the siege of Messina, the Spaniards to assist in the siege. The Spanish fleet was unprepared, for no declaration of war had been made, yet it was clear that the British fleet was intent on assisting the city, and battle began when some Spanish ships fired on the approaching British fleet. The British replied with an annihilating attack; six Spanish line-of-battle ships were captured, one was burnt, and five escaped, taking refuge at Malta; most of the smaller ships were taken or burnt. It was a battle which scarcely deserved the name, in which the battle-hardened British had numbers and skills and size on their side against an outnumbered and inexperienced enemy, but it settled the fate of Sicily. (Clowes 3.30–38; Mahan 237–239; Tunstall 68–69)

Cape Roxo, St Domingue, 6 April 1797
A group of vessels captured by privateers had accumulated at the port of Cape Roxo. A squadron of frigates under Capt. William Ricketts of *Magicienne* (32)

sent in boats to remove or destroy them. Thirteen vessels and two batteries were taken or destroyed. On the return voyage *Magicienne* and *Regulus* (44; *en flute*; Capt. William Carthew) bombarded a fort at Irois and captured ships in the harbour. (James 2.114–115; Clowes 4.335)

Cape St Nicolas, St Domingue, 4 August 1746
A squadron of four line-of-battle ships, a frigate, and a sloop commanded by Capt. Cornelius Mitchell met a French squadron of four sail of the line near Cape St Nicolas. Mitchell at first aimed to attack, but then changed his mind. The French, commanded by Admiral de Conflans, thereupon chased the British squadron. *Lenox* (64; Capt. Peter Lawrence) was attacked, but the rest avoided action; the squadrons separated during the night. Mitchell was tried by court-martial, convicted of cowardice and neglect of duty, and dismissed the service. (Clowes 3.123)

Cape St Vincent, Spain
1545 Robert Reneger, a Southampton merchant, was granted letters of marque to recover losses made in trading in Portuguese colonial lands; he captured the Spanish treasure ship *San Salvador* from Hispaniola in March, claiming that his own ships were detained unlawfully in San Lucar. (Loades 135–136)

1780 (MOONLIGHT BATTLE) A squadron of eighteen line-of-battle ships under Admiral Sir George Rodney came up with a Spanish squadron of eleven line-of-battle ships under Admiral Don Juan de Langara off Cape St Vincent on 16 January. The British ships chased the Spaniards, fighting each ship as they came up to them. The fighting lasted twelve hours, ending about 2 a.m., earning it the name of the Moonlight Battle. One Spanish ship was destroyed, five were captured (of which two were soon wrecked), and five escaped. (Syrett, *European* 86–89; Clowes 3.449–450; Tunstall 164–165)

1780 A large British convoy of sixty-three vessels escorted by five warships was intercepted off Cape St Vincent on 10 November by a squadron of thirty-two French and Spanish line-of-battle ships out of Cadiz. The escorting warships escaped capture, but the entire merchant convoy, including the 90th Regiment, was captured. (Syrett, *European* 136–137)

1797 (Battle of CAPE ST VINCENT) The British Mediterranean fleet, commanded by Admiral Sir John Jervis, based at Lisbon, on 14 February met the Spanish main fleet, which was attempting to reach Cadiz. The British fleet consisted of fifteen line-of-battle ships and four frigates; the Spanish fleet included twenty-three line-of-battle ships and twelve frigates, including one ship of 130 guns and six of 112. The British had two of 100 guns.

The British fleet formed in a line of battle, but the Spaniards, who for some time were under the impression that the British ships were a convoy, and later that they were only nine in number, were less organized, and formed into two groups, seventeen line-of-battle ships around the flagship *Santissima Trinidad* (130) and five, with a convoy, some way behind. Jervis directed his fleet into the gap, where the British ships turned mainly to attack the larger Spanish force. The Spaniards were mutually supporting and seemed to be getting away until Capt. Horatio Nelson in *Captain* (74) turned out of the line to assault the Spanish centre, near the *Santissima Trinidad*. The battle then became a mêlée, in which ships fired at whatever enemy ship came within range. Above all, the Spaniards were disconcerted by the sheer frequency and ferocity of the fire from the British ships.

Excellent (74; Capt. Cuthbert Collingwood) forced *Salvador del Mondo* (112) to surrender and then *San Ysidro* (74); then she sailed between *Captain*, which was somewhat damaged, and two Spanish ships, both of which suffered from her broadsides as she passed. These two then collided. Nelson brought *Captain* to lie beside *San Nicolas*, and led a boarding party to seize her. The other Spanish ship, *San Jose* (112), threatened to retake *San Nicolas*, but Nelson pre-empted that by leading his party in another boarding attack, and *San Jose* surrendered as soon as Nelson arrived. These Spanish ships had suffered something like a quarter of their complement as casualties, and the arrival of the boarding party was the final straw.

Salvador del Mundo re-hoisted her colours but was battered into a second submission by *Orion* (74; Capt. Sir James Saumarez). The British ships tended to concentrate on the great *Santissima Trinidad*, which was forced to surrender, but at that moment Jervis called off his whole fleet. There was no time to secure the captures. Four Spanish ships were taken, and four more, including *Santissima Trinidad*, were so damaged as to be floating wrecks. Next morning the Spanish Admiral Córdoba threatened to renew the fight (he still had sixteen line-of-battle ships) but then withdrew when Jervis brought his fleet to line of battle, seeming to accept the challenge. British casualties were 300 killed and wounded, Spanish about 1500. (James 2.34–59; Colin White, *1797, Nelson's Year of Destiny*, Stroud 1998; Tunstall 216–219)

Cape Sicie, Provence, 5 November 1813
The French Toulon fleet came out on an exercising cruise. A sudden change in the wind gave the British blockading fleet under Admiral Sir Edward Pellew a chance to attack, but little was accomplished besides some superficial damage to a few ships. (James 6.2–4; Clowes 5.305)

Cape Spada, Crete, 19 July 1940
Two Italian cruisers, *Giovanni delle Banda Nere* and *Bartolemeo Colleoni*, were intercepted by the cruiser HMAS *Sydney* with five destroyers. *Colleoni* was disabled and sunk; *Sydney* was damaged. (Rohwer 33; Greene and Massignani 82–86)

CAPE SPARTEL, Spain
1705 The French fleet under Baron de Pointis assisted in the Spanish siege of Gibraltar. Admiral Sir John Leake with a fleet of English, Dutch, and Portuguese ships escorted a convoy towards Gibraltar. Part of the French fleet came out of the bay to intercept, and five of their ships were destroyed. The convoy was safely delivered, the blockade raised, and, as a result, the siege was also lifted. (Corbett 2.282; Clowes 2.406–407; Rodger 2.171)

1741 Three British ships under the command of Capt. Curtis Barnet in *Dragon* (60) encountered three ships off Cape Spartel on 24 July in the dark. Barnet did not believe the statement that the ships were French (and so neutral) and a fight followed. Yet they really were French. This cost almost fifty men their lives. Barnet apologised only to the French commander, not to the sailors. (Clowes 3.270–271)

CAPE SPARTIVENTO, Sardinia, 27 November 1940
A convoy from Gibraltar to Alexandria was to be escorted first by Force H from Gibraltar (Admiral Somerville, with the carrier *Ark Royal*, battleship *Renown*, two cruisers, and destroyers), and then from Sicily eastwards by part of the Mediterranean fleet (battleship *Ramillies* and two cruisers). The Italian fleet (two battleships, six cruisers and destroyers) came from Naples to intercept. Force H located the Italian fleet south of Sardinia by air reconnaissance and turned to attack, joined by the Mediterranean fleet. The Italian cruisers retired to draw the British on to their battleships; the British cruisers did the same; air attacks from *Ark Royal* failed, as did Italian submarine attacks; the cruiser *Berwick* and the Italian destroyer *Lanciere* were damaged. (Roskill 1.301–303; Greene and Massignani 116–123)

Capetown v. *MAS-213*, 6 April 1941
The Italian MTB *MAS-213* torpedoed the cruiser *Capetown* off Port Sudan. (Rohwer 66)

Cape Verde Islands, 1582
William Hawkins led a small fleet intending to trade (or raid) in Portuguese Brazil. He was strongly resisted when he attempted a landing in the Cape Verde Islands. (Andrews 107)

Cap François, St Domingue
1757 A French convoy was collected at Cap François. Three British line-of-battle ships intercepted it on 21 October. The French escort consisted of four line-of-battle ships and three frigates. The British nevertheless attacked, and damaged one French ship, at which the French withdrew. The British ships, all damaged, had to go to Jamaica for repairs. The French convoy then sailed without interference. (Clowes 3.164–166)

1780 A British squadron commanded by Capt. Hon. William Cornwallis in *Lion* (64), with *Bristol* (50; Capt. Toby Caulfield) and *Janus* (44; Capt. Bonovrier Glover), encountered a French convoy off Cap François on 20 March. The convoy went into port and its escort turned to fight. The French, with two 74s and one 64, were substantially the stronger, and *Janus* suffered serious damage. Three more British ships came up, including a 64, and the French broke off the fighting. (Clowes 3.473–474)

Captain v. *Foudroyant*, 1758
The French ship *Foudroyant* (22), attempting to reach Louisbourg, was intercepted by the British blockading force. *Captain* (64) captured her and the valuable stores. (Clowes 3.182)

Captain v. Imperieuse, 12 October 1793
Captain (74; Capt. Samuel Reeve) found the French frigate *Impérieuse* in La Spezia, and approached to board. The crew abandoned and scuttled the frigate, but she was saved, brought out, and added to the navy as *Unite*. (Clowes 4.213)

Caradoc and squadron v. Spartak and Avtroil, 26 December 1919
The British squadron in the Baltic, headed by the cruiser *Caradoc*, with four destroyers, intercepted a Soviet force off Estonia. The destroyers *Spartak* and *Avtroil* were captured with little fighting. The rest of the Soviet ships retired. (Bennett 41–43)

Carinthia v. U-46, 6 June 1940
The AMC *Carinthia* was sunk by *U-46* off Brittany; the submarine was part of the first successful use of pack tactics. (Rohwer 25)

Carlingford Lough, Ulster, 853
The Norse who had settled at Dublin were driven out by an attack by Danes in 851; two years later a battle in Carlingford Lough between the two groups resulted in the comprehensive defeat of the Norsemen. The battle lasted three days; at the end the Norse, who had begun with 160 ships, abandoned them. (D.O. Croinin, *Early Medieval Ireland*, Harlow 1995, 250)

Carmania v. Cap Trafalgar, 14 September 1914
The German AMC *Cap Trafalgar* was at Trinidad Island in the South Atlantic when the British AMC *Carmania* (Capt. N. Grant) arrived to examine the island. The two ships fought and each set the other on fire, but *Cap Trafalgar* was also holed below the waterline. She got away, but soon sank. (Corbett 1.305–309)

Carnarvon Castle v. Thor, 5 December 1940
The AMC *Carnarvon Castle* encountered the German AMC *Thor* off the Brazilian coast. In the battle *Carnarvon Castle* was damaged, but escaped. (Rohwer 57; Hore 255)

Carnatian v. Palinure, 3 October 1808
The sloop *Carnatian* (18; Cmdr Charles Gregory) fought the French brig *Palinure* (16) northeast of Martinique. All the *Carnation*'s officers were killed, and *Palinure* boarded and captured her. (James 4.331–334; Clowes 5.426–427)

Caroline v. Pandore, 1 December 1795
The frigate *Caroline* (36; Capt. William Luke) captured *Pandore* (14) in the North Sea. (Clowes 4.554)

Caroline v. Haasje, 2 August 1803
The frigate *Caroline* (36; Capt. Benjamin Page) captured the Dutch ship *Haasje* (6) off the Cape of Good Hope. (Clowes 5.564)

Caroline v. *Zeerob* and *Maria Reijgersbergen*, 18 October 1806
The frigate *Caroline* (42; Capt. Peter Rainier) captured the brig *Zeerop* (16) off Java, then went on to attack and capture the frigate *Maria Reijgersbergen* (40). (James 4.179–180; Clowes 5.592)

Carrickfergus, Ulster
1513   War having begun between England and Scotland, the Scots fleet, consisting of the great ship *Michael* and nine (or eleven) other ships commanded by the Earl of Arran, sailed round the north of Scotland in August, raided Carrickfergus, then sailed on to Brest. The intended joint Franco-Scots operation in the Channel was prevented by a gale, and the Scots defeat at Flodden Field removed Scotland from the war. (Rodger 1.171–172; Nicholson 599–600; MacDougall 268)

1760   A French frigate squadron carrying 1300 soldiers left Dunkirk and sailed in stages northabout to Ireland, refreshing at Gothenburg, Bergen, the Faeroes, and Islay on the way. A landing was made in Carrickfergus on 11 February, and the town was captured. The alarm reached three British frigates at Kinsale and they sailed to intervene, catching the remaining three French frigates as they sailed on 28 February. *Aeolus* (32; Capt. John Elliot) captured *Marechal de Belleisle* (44), and *Pallas* (36; Capt. Michael Clements) and *Brilliant* (36; Capt. James Logie) forced the surrender of *Blonde* (36) and *Terpsichore* (24). (Clowes 3.229–231)

Carrigan Head v. U-boat, 8 September 1916
Carrigan Head, a Q-ship, fought a U-boat off the southern Irish coast, but was defeated; both ships survived. (Newbolt 4.336)

Cartagena, Spain
1650   General-at-Sea Robert Blake, with a squadron of four ships, came up with a scattered group of Royalist ships of Prince Rupert's squadron. One of those ships, *Black Prince*, was harried into running aground on 4 November and then destroyed; the others, including *Royal Charles* and *Mary* and two prizes, ran into Cartagena harbour. Blake demanded that they be handed over, but before anything could be done, next day a sudden squall drove them ashore, and partially wrecked them. (Powell 104–105; Corbett, *Mediterranean* 1.219; Capp 65; Clowes 2.132)

1706   The English Mediterranean fleet assisted in the capture of the city on 1 June. (Clowes 2.409)

Cartagena, Spanish Main
1586   Cartagena was captured on 10 February and looted by the fleet under Sir Francis Drake. (Rodger 1.249; Andrews 122–125; Loades 235)

1697   A French fleet under Admiral de Pointis raided Cartagena, and was met by an Anglo-Dutch fleet under Vice-Admiral John Neville from Jamaica. Neville's ships followed the French for several days, during which two of the French ships were captured, but the fleet as a whole escaped. (Clowes 2.492–493)

1706 An English squadron of five ships under Commodore Charles Wager intercepted a Spanish convoy near Cartagena on 28 May. Wager's ship, *Expedition* (20; Cmdr Henry Long), succeeded in destroying the *San Josef* and capturing another ship; a third was run aground and burned by her crew. Two English captains who avoided action were court-martialled and dismissed the service. (Clowes 2.373–376)

1711 The British West Indies squadron based at Jamaica, commanded by Commodore James Littleton, went to Cartagena on information that a French squadron was there. On 27 July a Spanish galleon and another ship were captured. (Clowes 2.530)

1741 Admiral Edward Vernon, commanding a fleet of twenty-nine line-of-battle ships, brought an army of 12,000 men to attack Cartagena. An initial landing was successful, as was the bombardment of defensive batteries and forts. Three Spanish ships, each of 60 guns, were scuttled, and one of 70 captured. The army suffered much sickness and a shortage of supplies, and Vernon failed co-operation, then refused to land seamen to assist in further attacks. The army commanders voted to withdraw. (Clowes 3.68–75)

Cartagena, Colombia, February

1842 The warlord ruling Cartagena seized two British ships and imprisoned their crews. In February *Charybdis* (10; Lt Michael de Courcy) went to demand their release and, on being refused, entered the harbour, forced a corvette and two schooners to surrender, and sank a brig. She then anchored in the port to secure the release of the prisoners. (Clowes 6.307–308)

Carysfort v. *Castor*, 29 May 1794

The frigate *Carysfort* (28; Capt. Francis Laforey) met the French frigate *Castor* (32), formerly British, southwest of Ireland. *Castor* was forced to surrender. (James 1.228–230; Clowes 4.485)

Carysfort v. *Alerte*, 19 August 1796

Alerte, a privateer schooner, scouting for a French frigate squadron off Coromandel, India, was captured by *Carysfort* (28; Capt. James Alexander), whom the privateer mistook for an Indiaman. Papers on board revealed French plans. (James 1.389; Parkinson 101)

Carysfort, Canterbury, and others v. German destroyers, 23 July 1916

A German destroyer flotilla (six ships) was intercepted separately by two British forces led respectively by the light cruisers *Carysfort* and *Canterbury*. No damage was received on either side, but the German ships were deterred from attacking vessels crossing to the Hook of Holland. (Newbolt 4.27–30)

Casilha Bay, China, August 1840

In retaliation for an assault on a clergyman, a raid was made into Casilha

Bay, near Macao, by five ships, which landed 400 soldiers, marines, and sailors, and destroyed fortifications and junks. (Clowes 6.283)

Castelorizo Island, Anatolia, 25–27 February 1941
A party of commandos and sailors was landed on the Italian island of Castelorizo from a small squadron on 25 February. Next day, however, an Italian force arrived, and drove the British ships away. The survivors were evacuated on 27 February. (Rohwer 61)

Castlehaven, Ireland, 6 December 1601
A Spanish force was landed at Castlehaven to support the Irish in their war with England. The ships were attacked by an English squadron under Sir Richard Leveson, which forced its way into the harbour and destroyed most of the Spanish ships either by grounding or by sinking. (Rodger 1.291; Silke 127, 130–135)

***Castor* and *Crescent* v. *Gloire* and *Friponne*, 20 June 1781**
The frigates *Castor* (36) and *Crescent* (34) were chased, attacked, and captured by the French frigates *Gloire* (32) and *Friponne* (32) off Cadiz. *Flora* (32), which was also present, escaped. (Clowes 4.69)

***Castor* v. *Patriote*, May 1794**
The frigate *Castor* (32; Capt. Sir Thomas Troubridge) had charge of a Newfoundland convoy. The French *Patriote* (74) met the convoy, forced *Castor* into surrender, and captured much of the convoy. (James 1.142; Clowes 4.485)

***Castor* v. *L'Hereux*, January 1814**
The frigate *Castor* (32) captured the privateer *Heureux* out of Barcelona. (Hall 191)

Castro Urdiales, Spain, May 1813
The Spanish forces in Castro Urdiales were evacuated to safety in the face of a strong French attack. The commander of the operation was Capt. Sir George Collier, in the frigate *Surveillante*. Collier's squadron then blockaded Castro Urdiales and forced the French to leave. (James 6.15–16; Hall 208)

***Cato* and *Magic* v. German human torpedoes, 6 July 1944**
The minesweepers *Cato* and *Magic* were sunk by attacks by twenty-six German human torpedoes; ten of those human torpedoes were lost. (Rohwer 340)

Cattaro, Dalmatia, October 1813–January 1814
Bacchante (38), *Saracen* (18), and three gunboats launched an attack on Cattaro, a port city at the head of an intricate system of fjords, where the local population had risen against the French garrison. Capt. William Hoste in *Bacchante* collected a force of soldiers from Curzola, and captured the outpost at Castello Nuova and the fort on San Giorgio Island, handing the

guns over to the insurgents. He then sailed away, though *Saracen* remained. When Hoste returned on 12 December, Cattaro was still holding out. He organised the occupation and fortification of some of the surrounding hills, after which two weeks' bombardment and the explosion of the powder magazine brought the French garrison to surrender on 8 January 1814. (James 6.34, 119; T. Pocock, *Remember Nelson*, London 1977, ch. 9; Clowes 5.306; Hore, *Seapower* 47–49)

Cavendish's squadron in South America, 1587
Thomas Cavendish with three ships (*Desire, Content,* and *Hugh Gallant*) reached the Pacific by way of the Strait of Magellan and sailed north along the American coast. He raided Quintero near Valparaiso, Arica, and Puna in the Bay of Guayaquil, where he captured a Spanish ship. He burnt the town of Gualulco in Mexico, and off Baja California captured the ship *Santa Ana*, with a rich cargo. He then sailed on to circumnavigate. (Clowes 1.636–638; Foster 118–119)

Cayenne, Guiana, January 1809
The French colony of Cayenne was attacked by a force composed mainly of Portuguese troops from Brazil, commanded by Capt. James Yeo of the sloop *Confiance*. The troops were transported up the river towards the main town in canoes. Preliminary forts were taken with little fighting, and on 14 January the whole colony capitulated. (James 5.73–77; *NC* 4.220–224)

***Censeur* v. French squadron, 7 October 1795**
Censeur (74; *en flute*) was part of a convoy escort which was attacked by the French squadron of Rear-Admiral Richery. *Censeur* lost her mainmast before the action even began, and was wholly dismasted during it. She surrendered. (Clowes 4.278)

***Centaur* v. *Ste Anne*, 5 June 1761**
Centaur (74; Capt. Arthur Forrest) captured *Ste Anne*, a French merchantman of 40 guns, in the West Indies. (Clowes 3.306)

***Centaur* and *Cormorant* v. *Guadalupe*, 16 March 1799**
The Spanish frigate *Guadalupe* (34) was attacked and driven on shore by *Centaur* (74) and *Cormorant* (20) near Cape Oropesa, Spain. (Clowes 4.560)

***Centaur* and others v. *Courageuse* and others, 19 June 1799**
The advanced division of the Mediterranean fleet, the 74s *Centaur, Captain,* and *Bellona*, with the frigates *Emerald* and *Santa Teresa*, captured the French frigates *Junon, Alceste,* and *Courageuse*, and the brigs *Salamine* and *Alerte*, off Cape Sicie, Provence. (James 2.294–295)

***Centaur* v. *Curieux*, 4 February 1804**
Under the orders of Commodore Samuel Hood, *Centaur* (74) sent in four boats to cut out the brig *Curieux* (16) at Port Royal, Martinique. This was

accomplished despite extensive French defences and strong resistance. (Clowes 5.334; James 3.297)

Centurion v. Spanish galleys, 1592
Centurion (Capt. Robert Bradshaw), a Turkey ship returning from the Levant, was attacked by five Spanish galleys near Gibraltar; they were driven off with just a few casualties. (Clowes 1.498)

Centurion v. French privateer, July 1692
Centurion (48; Capt. Francis Wyvill) met three French privateers in the Channel; two of them quickly sailed away, but the other fought for three hours before being captured. (Clowes 2.468–469)

Centurion and Kingfisher v. French privateers, September 1692
Centurion (48; Capt. John Bridges) encountered a squadron of six French privateers off the east coast of Scotland. *Kingfisher* (46) helped in the fight; between them they captured three of the privateers. (Clowes 2.469)

Centurion v. French privateers, 24 February 1694
Centurion (48; Capt. John Price) fought four privateers out of Dunkirk; one of the privateers was captured; the others got away. (Clowes 2.479)

Centurion and Defiance v. French warships, 1710
Two French warships were fought by *Centurion* (48; Capt. John Mehell) and *Defiance* (64; Capt. John Evans) off southeast Spain. All parties suffered considerable casualties and the fight was inconclusive. (Clowes 2.524–525)

Centurion v. Nuestra Senora de Covadonga, 20 June 1743
Centurion (60), Commodore George Anson's flagship in his great voyage of circumnavigation, by 1743 was the only ship he had left. One of his objects was to capture the Spanish annual galleon which operated between Manila in the Philippines and Acapulco in Mexico. He had failed at Acapulco, but succeeded across the Pacific. *Nuestra Senora de Covadonga* fought for an hour or so, but then surrendered. The prize was valued at between £300,000 and £400,000; Anson received £91,000 prize money, ordinary seamen £300. (G. Williams, *The Prize of All the Oceans*, London 1999; Clowes 3.320–324)

Centurion v. Marengo, Semillante, and Atalante, 15 September 1804
Centurion (50; Lt James Phillips) was at anchor in Vizagapatam road, India, with two Indiamen. A French squadron – *Marengo* (74) and two frigates, *Semillante* and *Atalante*, commanded by Admiral Linois – attacked. One Indiaman, *Barnaby*, ran itself ashore, and the other, *Princess Charlotte*, surrendered at once. But *Centurion* stayed in the shoals out of *Marengo*'s reach. The French squadron then retired. (James 3.282–286; Parkinson 244–245)

Ceram, Banda Islands, 2 February 1617
The EIC vessel *Swan* (Capt. John Davis) watered at Ceram in defiance of

Dutch objections and of his commander's prohibition. *Swan* was attacked by a Dutch ship and captured. (Foster 268)

Cerberus v. Grana, 25 February 1781
Cerberus (28; Capt. Robert Man) chased and captured the Spanish frigate *Grana* off Finisterre. (Clowes 4.62)

Cerberus v. Duc d'Estissac, 6 June 1781
The frigate *Cerberus* (32) captured the French privateer *Duc d'Estissac*, which was taken into the navy. (Colledge 117)

Cerberus and Santa Margarita v. Jean Bart, 29 March 1795
The frigates *Cerberus* (32) and *Santa Margarita* (36) captured the French ship *Jean Bart* (18) in the English Channel. (Clowes 4.491)

Cerberus v. French privateers, 12–14 November 1797
The frigate *Cerberus* (32; Capt. John Drew) captured the privateers *Epervier* (16) and *Renard* (18), and chased the privateer *Buonaparte* so determinedly that she jettisoned her guns and stores to escape. (James 2.101)

Cerberus v. Spanish convoy frigates, 20 October 1799
The frigate *Cerberus* (32; Capt. James Macnamara) met a Spanish convoy escorted by five frigates off Cape Ortegal. One of the frigates was attacked and beaten, but the rest attacked *Cerberus* from two sides. She escaped, having captured one brig from the convoy. (James 2.404–405; Clowes 4.526–527)

Cerberus v. Chameau, 21 January 1804
The frigate *Cerberus* (32) captured *Chameau* (4) off La Hougue in the English Channel. (Clowes 5.556)

Ceres v. Iphigénie, 17 December 1778
Ceres (18; Cmdr Richard Dacres) was escorting a convoy near St Lucia when the French frigate *Iphigénie* (32) attacked. *Ceres* was able to fight until the convoy got away, but was then compelled to surrender. (Clowes 4.22)

Cestrian v. UB-42, 24 June 1917
The transport *Cestrian*, carrying horses and troops, was sunk by *UB-42* in the Aegean; most of the men were saved. (Newbolt 4.312)

Ceylon (Sri Lanka)
1795–1796 An expeditionary force commanded by Capt. Peter Rainier sailed from Madras to take the Dutch posts in Ceylon. A landing was made near Trincomalee, which, after a bombardment, surrendered. *Centurion* (50; Capt. Samuel Osborn) captured Jaffna in September and *Hobart* (18; Lt Benjamin Page) took Muletive in October, in each case by landing troops. In February 1796 a force from the Cape of Good Hope, escorted by the frigate *Heroine* (32; Capt. Alan Hyde Gardner), two sloops, and five Indiamen,

landed at the fort of Negombo; Colombo was taken on the 15th. (James 1.337–338, 413–414; Low 1.206; Clowes 4.282, 294; Parkinson 78–80)

1942 The Japanese 1st Carrier Fleet made an air attack on Colombo on 4–5 April. The auxiliary cruiser *Hector* and the destroyer *Tenedos* were sunk in the harbour; at sea the cruisers *Cornwall* and *Dorsetshire* were sunk by dive bombers. Trincomalee was bombed on 9 April. Japanese dive bombers found and sank the carrier *Hermes*, the destroyer *Vampire*, the corvette *Hollyhock*, and two tankers as they sailed south from Trincomalee. The main British Eastern Fleet, however, was not found. The Japanese fleet then withdrew eastwards. (P. Willmott, *Empires in the Balance*, London 1982, 441–445)
See also: **Providien, Trincomalee**

Ceylon and others v. French squadron, 3 July 1810
Three Indiamen, *Ceylon*, *Astell*, and *Windham*, were accosted in the Mozambique Channel by three French ships, the frigates *Bellone* and *Minerve*, and the sloop *Jéna*. The subsequent fight lasted several hours. *Ceylon* and *Windham* were compelled to surrender; *Astell* escaped in the darkness. (James 5.132–137; Clowes 5.456–457)

Cezimbra Roads, Portugal, 3 June 1602
An English squadron under Sir Richard Leveson sailed into Cezimbra Roads and captured the Portuguese carrack *Sao Valentinho*, despite a strong defence by galleys (two were sunk) and the shore batteries. (Rodger 1.292; Clowes 1.533–535)

Chagford v. *U-44*, 5 August 1917
The Q-ship *Chagford*, northwest of Ireland, was torpedoed by *U-44*. When the submarine surfaced *Chagford* fired on it, but caused no damage, and *Chagford* was then hit by two more torpedoes. The crew were saved but *Chagford* sank. (Newbolt 5.107; Grant 62)

Chagres, Panamá, 22–24 March 1740
Admiral Edward Vernon took part of his squadron to the port of Chagres, Panamá, and spent three days bombarding the place. The arrival of the rest of his ships persuaded the Spanish commander to surrender. Considerable booty was obtained. (Clowes 3.61–62)

Challenger v. French frigate, 12 March 1811
The gun brig *Challenger* (16; Cmdr Goddard Blennerhasset) was captured by a French frigate off Mauritius. (James 5.447; Clowes 5.553)

Champion v. *Bulldog*, 16 September 1801
Bulldog (18) was captured by *Champion* (24; Capt. Lord William Stuart) near Gallipoli. (Clowes 4.558)

Channel Islands
These islands remained under English control after the conquest of mainland Normandy by the French.

1548–1549   An attack by French galleys on the Channel Islands during August 1548 was blocked by an English squadron under William Winter, which defeated the French force near Jersey. Next year Sark was captured by a French galley squadron; a second squadron was attacked by an English force under William Winter in August; one French galley was captured. (Rodger 1.187; Clowes 1.469; Loades 148)

1651   Royalists controlling the islands were attacked by a Parliamentary squadron under the command of General-at-Sea Robert Blake. He forced a landing on Guernsey covered by a heavy bombardment in October. The islands were under Parliament's control by the end of the year. (Capp 67; Clowes 2.140; Powell 121–133)

1794   A British frigate squadron – *Arethusa* (38), *Flora* (36), *Melampus* (36), *Concorde* (36), and *Nymphe* (36) – under Capt. Sir John Borlase Warren met a French frigate squadron – *Engageante* (36), *Pomone* (44), *Resolue* (36), and the corvette *Babet* (20) – near the Channel Islands on 23 April. The two forces formed lines of battle and fought, the British overtaking the French line. *Flora* tackled the French ships in succession, and was badly damaged in the rigging; *Arethusa* came up with *Melampus* and engaged *Babet* and *Pomone*; *Babet*, much damaged, surrendered to *Flora*; *Engageante* and *Resolue* got away. *Pomone* fought *Melampus* and *Arethusa* for some time, then surrendered. *Concorde* and *Melampus* chased the other French ships, but only *Concorde* was able to reach them. A long fight ensued until *Concorde* forced *Engageante* to surrender. *Resolue* escaped. All three captures were taken into the navy, *Pomone* being especially admired for its strong construction. On 8 June a frigate squadron commanded by Capt. Sir James Saumarez – *Crescent* (36), *Druid* (32), and *Eurydice* (24) – met a French force of two cut-down 74s, two 36-gun frigates, and a brig (14). Watched by a large crowd from his home island (Guernsey), Saumarez kept the French ships occupied until the slow *Eurydice* reached safety, then escaped himself. (James 1.222–226, 230–231; Clowes 4.483–484)

Champion and convoy v. *Vétéran*, 10 August 1806

The French *Vétéran* (74), with Prince Jerome Bonaparte in nominal command, met a Québec convoy in mid-Atlantic. The escorting ship, *Champion* (22; Capt. Robert Bromley), tried to draw *Vétéran* away but failed, and six out of the convoy (of sixteen ships) were burnt. (James 4.112; Clowes 5.194–195)

Chapoo, China, 18 May 1842

An expeditionary force went to attack the city of Chapoo. Three forces were landed, and found they had to fight hard against a small but determined garrison of Manchu soldiers. Ships in the river assisted by bombarding the city. Of the 350 defenders, only sixty survived. (Clowes 6.297–298; Graham 213–214)

Charity, Korea, 1952

The destroyer *Charity* exchanged fire with shore-based artillery off the east coast of Korea, and bombarded shore installations. (Wettern 69)

Charles and others v. Portuguese carrack, 5 August 1616
A squadron of four EIC ships, *Charles, Unicorn, James,* and *Globe,* encountered a Portuguese carrack of great size near the Comoro Islands in the Mozambique Passage. The four English ships battered the carrack in turn, and eventually the Portuguese drove their ship on shore and burnt her. (Low 1.25–30; Clowes 2.36–37)

Charles and *Constant Warwick* v. *Charles*, 25 April 1649
The Parliamentary ships *Charles* (Capt. Alexander Popham) and *Constant Warwick* encountered the Royalist *Charles* (formerly *Guinea*) near the Scilly Islands. The Royalists fought for an hour, but then surrendered. (Powell 81)

Charles and *James* v. Algerine warship, 28 October 1677
The galleys *Charles* (32; Capt. Thomas Hamilton) and *James* (30; Capt. George Canning) came out of Tangier to intercept an Algerine vessel being chased by *Portsmouth* (48). A hard fight followed, in which Canning was killed, before the Algerine ship was captured. (Clowes 2.452)

Charles and *Mary* v. French privateers, July 1691
The galleys *Charles* (32; Capt. James Buck) and *Mary* (32; Capt. James Wishart), escorting a convoy to Denmark, were attacked by four French privateers. These were driven off and their prizes, including *Tiger* (34), were retaken. (Clowes 2.466)

Charles v. French convoy, November 1695
The *Charles* galley (13; Capt. Stephen Elliott) fought the escort of a French convoy off Le Havre. Two ships were captured; others were driven ashore. (Clowes 2.485)

Charleston, South Carolina, 1776 and 1780
A fleet was sent from Britain to the southern rebel American colonies. An attack was made on Charleston on 23 June 1776, centring on a bombardment of Fort Moultrie in the harbour. This failed, at a cost of considerable casualties, and left *Bristol* (50; Capt. John Morris) and *Experiment* (50; Capt. Alexander Scott) very seriously damaged. Four years later a new expedition went from New York to reinforce the British military presence in the southern colonies. Charleston was captured on 25 May 1780. (Clowes 3.372–379, 472; Syrett, *American* 23–39, 135–140)

Charlestown and others v. *Astrée* and *Hermione*, 21 July 1781
Charlestown (28) and four smaller ships were escorting a convoy off Cape Breton Island when the French 32-gun frigates *Astrée* and *Hermione* attacked. The British ships formed a line of battle to protect the convoy. One ship, *Jack* (14), was captured, but the rest got away, and *Astrée* was too damaged to pursue. (Clowes 4.71)

Charlotte v. Angria's squadron, April 1720
The EIC ship *Charlotte* was attacked by a squadron of four grabs and ten

galivats; the ship was captured after a long defence when her powder was exhausted. (Low 1.100)

Charlotte v. French ship, February 1799
The schooner *Charlotte* (8; Lt John Thicknesse) was captured by a French ship off Cap François, St Domingue. (Clowes 4.550)

Charybdis v. *Tamega*, June 1834
The slaver *Tamega*, heading for Brazil with 440 slaves, was captured by the sloop *Charybdis* (10) off Lagos. (Bethell 126)

Chaser v. *Bellone*, 25 February 1782
Chaser (18; Cmdr Thomas Parr) was captured by the French frigate *Bellone* (32) in the Bay of Bengal, after a short fight. (Clowes 4.77)

Chatham v. *Connetable*, 14 January 1705
Chatham (48; Capt. Robert Bokenham) met and captured the St Malo privateer *Connetable* (30). (Clowes 2.507)

Chatham v. *Magicienne*, September 1781
Chatham (50; Cmdr Andrew Douglas) chased *Magicienne* (32) near Boston; unable to get away *Magicienne* turned to fight, but was captured, having suffered a third of her men casualties. Soon after *Chatham* captured the rebel American privateer *General Washington*, which was then taken into the navy as *General Monck* (20). (Clowes 4.74; Colledge 158)

Cherokee v. *Aimable Nelly*, 11 January 1810
The sloop *Cherokee* (10; Capt. Richard Arthur) entered Dieppe harbour at night, having seen that there were seven luggers there. One of these, *Aimable Nelly* (16), was captured and brought out. (James 5.86)

CHESAPEAKE, 9 September 1781
In 1781 a small British army was in occupation of the tobacco port of Yorktown in Virginia. Lieutenant-General Earl Cornwallis, its commander, requested supply and reinforcement from New York, and a fleet sailed from New York under Rear-Admiral Thomas Graves, the naval Commander-in-Chief in North America. He knew that Admiral Comte de Grasse with a French fleet was on his way north from the West Indies. American and French armies under General Washington and Comte Rochambeau were marching south to besiege Cornwallis. The crucial strategic point for the fleets was the entrance to Chesapeake Bay. Cornwallis could escape if the British fleet arrived first; but, if the French fleet beat Graves to it, Cornwallis was trapped.

Grasse arrived first, with the larger fleet. Graves's arrival brought Grasse out, and a battle developed in which the French fleet of twenty-four line-of-battle ships was attacked by nineteen British. The British approach was mishandled; only part of the fleet took part, the rear scarcely being involved. Five British ships were badly damaged and effectively put out of action – one was soon abandoned and burnt. None of the French ships were seriously damaged.

For the next three days Grasse sailed slowly south, with Graves following. During the night of 10/11 September Grasse turned north once more; the British did not discover this until the morning, by which time Grasse had a clear lead. and was able to reoccupy Chesapeake Bay, denying entrance to Graves's ships. Grasse was joined by another French naval force from Newport, Rhode Island, under Admiral Barras (eight line-of-battle ships), carrying the French siege train, with which Cornwallis and his army were battered into surrender. Graves's fleet, outnumbered by almost two to one, was wholly unable to affect matters; he took the fleet back to New York, where he made preparations to sail once more in the hope of assisting Cornwallis. All his efforts were in vain; on 18 October Cornwallis and his army surrendered.

Rear-Admiral Hood, who had commanded the rear in the battle, vehemently criticised Graves for his conduct of the battle, both to his face and in letters to the Admiralty, but Graves was faced with a task far beyond both his ability and his strength. The French had occupied Chesapeake Bay before his arrival, so it was impossible for him to force an entrance into the estuary and survive. His primary task was to preserve his fleet more or less intact, and it was already in poor condition. Grasse's tactics were eminently sensible. He only had to avoid defeat in order to secure a strategic victory, whereas Graves had to destroy a superior enemy and drive him from the position he had seized. Graves could only win by fighting a Trafalgar-style battle of annihilation, and this was beyond his strength; Hood's criticism was quite misconceived. The surrender of Cornwallis's army finally persuaded the British government that the war was lost. (F.E. Chadwick, *The Graves Papers*, New York 1916; Mahan 386–390; J.D. Grainger, *The Battle of Yorktown, 1781: A Reassessment*, London 2005; Mackesy, *America*; Clowes 3.494–502; Syrett, *American* 190–204; Tunstall 172–177)

Chesapeake Bay
1813 A squadron of British ships commanded by Rear-Admiral George Cockburn collected in Chesapeake Bay. Boats were sent to capture any enemy ships located: on 8 February the schooner *Lottery* was captured, and on 16 March four more schooners. Raids were made on Frenchtown, Havre de Grace, Specucie Island, and other places. On 22 June the squadron made a raid against Norfolk, the US naval base, but the boat parties did not even get ashore; one group could not get away from the landing point; the other's boats grounded on a shoal directly before a US battery. Another raid was mounted on Hampton, Virginia; 2000 men were landed, covered by the sloop *Mohawk* (Cmdr Hon. Henry Byng), and captured the town with little difficulty. (James 6.83–95; Clowes 6.96)

1814 The British squadron in Chesapeake Bay, commanded by Rear-Admiral George Cockburn, conducted a series of landings and raids along the shores and tributaries of the bay, facing only occasional opposition. A US flotilla of sixteen vessels was attacked in May; they were burnt by the crews.

A force of 4000 soldiers landed at Upper Marlborough in September and marched to Washington, which was captured and the public buildings burnt. Other ships raided Alexandria and attacked Baltimore. (James 6.168–193; Morriss 89–110; *NC* 5.177–184)

Cheshire v. *U-137*, October 1940
The AMC *Cheshire* was sunk by *U-137*. (Rohwer 43)

Chester v. French privateer, April 1694
Chester (42; Capt. William Jenkins) drove a privateer (18) on shore at Dominica, West Indies; the ship caught fire and blew up. (Clowes 2.481)

Chester v. *Glorieux*, 14 May 1709
Chester (50; Capt. Thomas Mathews) captured the French *Glorieux*. (Clowes 2.515)

Chester and *Sunderland* v. *Eléphant*, 20 February 1745
The French ship *Eléphant* (20) was returning to France from the Mississippi when she was chased and captured by *Chester* (50; Capt. Francis Geary) and *Sunderland* (60; Capt. John Brett) in the approaches to the Channel. (Clowes 3.278)

Childers at Brest, 2 January 1793
The sloop *Childers* (14; Cmdr Robert Barlow) was fired on by the forts at Brest harbour, indicating that France was preparing for war with Britain. *Childers* was hit by one ball. The declaration came a month later. (James 1.50; *NC* 1.3–4; Clowes 4.475)

Childers v. *Vigilante*, 3 September 1795
The French cutter *Vigilante* was captured by *Childers* (14; Cmdr Richard Dacres) near St Brieux, Brittany. (Clowes 4.554)

Childers v. *Lougen*, 14 March 1808
The sloop *Childers* (14; Cmdr William Dillon) in Norwegian waters sent her boats to capture a Danish galliot. She was then challenged by the Danish brig *Lougen* (20), and the fight lasted for several hours. *Lougen* finally sailed away; *Childers* had to return to Leith for repairs. (James 4.315 –318; Anderson 322–323; Clowes 5.410–411)

China, 1900
The blockade and siege of the legation quarter in Peking by the 'Boxers' was resisted by, amongst others, a party of British sailors and marines, and the first relief attempt was entirely naval in composition, half the men involved being from British ships in Chinese waters. In the assault on the Taku forts, the sloop *Algerine* was prominently used in the bombardment, and 600 sailors took part in the attack. Sailors also took part in the defence of Tientsin, and a Naval Brigade was part of the relief force which reached Peking on 15 August. (Clowes 7.520–561; Hore, *Seapower* 174–179)

Chingkiang, China, July 1842

An expedition sailed up the Yangzi River to Chingkiang, the southern terminus of the Grand Canal. Landings were made on either side of the city, but the British forces – 9000 soldiers reinforced by sailors – had to fight hard against determined opposition by Manchu soldiers before they could reach the city gates, and fighting continued inside the city. When defeat was obvious the Manchu garrison and their families committed suicide. Control of the entrance to the canal persuaded the imperial government to agree to terms. (Clowes 6.298–303)

Chinhai and Ningpo, China, 1841–1842

A British squadron with a strong army contingent attacked a strong defensive position before the city of Chinhai. A joint attack on 10 October 1841 took the position, and the city was taken; Ningpo, upriver and abandoned, was captured three days later. Chinese counter-attacks on both cities followed. At Ningpo the attackers succeeded in entering the city before being defeated. Several ships of the British squadron patrolled the river, sinking fire rafts, and bombarding formed bodies of troops. (Clowes 6.295–296; Low 2.146–149; Graham 185–186)

Chinsura, Bengal, 24 November 1759

A Dutch East India squadron from Batavia sailed to attack the EIC post at Chinsura. It was defeated by forces under Colonel Robert Clive and a squadron of British EIC ships under Captain Wilson of *Calcutta*; several Dutch ships were captured. (Clowes 3.201)

Christ v. Turkish ship, 1515

Christ, a ship purchased to add to Henry VIII's navy, was captured by a Turkish force. (Colledge 80)

Christian VII and *Armide* v. French convoys, January–February 1810

Boats from *Christian VII* (80; Capt. Sir Joseph Yorke) and the frigate *Armide* (38; Capt. Lucius Hardyman) attacked French convoys between Ile d'Aix and La Rochelle. Twelve enemy ships of various sorts were destroyed. (James 5.95–97)

Chusan, China, 1840–1842

A British squadron led by *Wellesley* (74; Capt. Thomas Maitland) and commanded by Commodore Sir James Bremer occupied Chusan harbour, but was resisted. The fort at Tinghai was bombarded and junks were driven ashore or wrecked. The fort was taken, then evacuated, but a new attack had to be made in October 1841. The ships of the squadron menaced a long line of batteries while landing parties took them in flank, and Tinghai city was captured and garrisoned. The steamers *Nemesis* and *Phlegethon* sailed around Chusan to intercept escapees. In April 1842 an attack by fire rafts was launched by the Chinese against the British squadron, but boats were successful in deflecting or sinking the rafts. (Clowes 6.282–283, 295, 297; Graham 126–128, 184; Low 2.140–141)

Circe v. Lijnx and Perseus, 9 October 1799
The Dutch ships *Lijnx* (12) and *Perseus* (8) were captured by *Circe* (28; Capt. Robert Winthrop) in the Ems estuary. (Clowes 4.559)

Circe in the West Indies, 1805–1808
Circe (32; Capt. Hugh Pigot) captured the French schooner *Constance* (10) on 21 June 1805, the French gunboat *Créole* (1) off Caracas, Spanish Main, on 2 January 1807, the French privateer *Austerlitz* on 5 April 1807 – taken into the navy as the sloop *Pultusk* (16) – and on 31 October 1808 chased, attacked, and captured the French brig *Palinure* (16) near Diamond Rock, Martinique. (James 4.332; Clowes 5.427, 558; Colledge 248, 323)

Clayoquot v. U-806, 24 December 1944
U-806 sank the Canadian minesweeper *Clayoquot* in the Gulf of St Lawrence. (Rohwer 373)

Cleopatra v. Aurore, April 1796
The frigate *Cleopatra* (32; Capt. Charles Rowley) captured the French brig *Aurore* (10) in American waters. (Clowes 4.554)

Cleopatra and Leander v. Ville de Milan, 16–23 February 1805
The frigate *Cleopatra* (32; Capt. Sir Robert Lawrie) encountered the French frigate *Ville de Milan* (40) in the Atlantic, and chased her for a day and a half. When they fought, *Ville de Milan* dismasted *Cleopatra* and she was boarded and taken. On the way to France, however, the two ships were found by *Leander* (50; Capt. John Talbot) which quickly compelled both badly damaged ships to surrender. (James 4.20–26; Clowes 5.357–359)

Cleopatra and others v. Topaze, 22 January 1809
The French frigate *Topaze* (40) took shelter under a battery in Guadeloupe against attack by the frigate *Cleopatra* (32; Capt. Samuel Pechell). Anchored and with springs on their cables the two ships fired broadsides at each other until one of *Topaze*'s springs was cut and she swung round so that *Cleopatra* had a virtually free shot. The sloop *Hazard* (18; Cmdr Hugh Cameron) bombarded the covering battery, and when the frigate *Jason* (38; Capt. William Maude) joined in the attack *Topaze* surrendered. (James 5.3–4; Clowes 5.43)

Cleopatra v. Segundo Rosario, 27 January 1841
Cleopatra (26; Capt. Alexander Milne), in the West Indies, captured the slaver *Segundo Rosario*, freeing 294 slaves. (Clowes 6.396)

Cleopatra v. Progresso, 1843
The frigate *Cleopatra* (26; Capt. Christopher Wyvill) chased the slaver *Progresso* off Mozambique; when captured, she was carrying 447 slaves; half of them died before they could be landed. (Lloyd 221–222)

Cleopatra and others v. *Gavriil*, 18 May 1919
The cruiser *Cleopatra*, accompanied by three smaller vessels, compelled the Soviet destroyer *Gavriil*, which had been protecting minelayers, to retreat to Kronstadt. (Bennett 110–111)

Cleopatra and others v. *Petropavlovs*k and *Azard*, 30 May 1919
The British squadron in the Baltic, commanded by Rear-Admiral Walter Cowan in the cruiser *Cleopatra*, with destroyers and smaller ships, confronted the Soviet battleship *Petropavlovsk*, the destroyer *Azard*, and six minesweepers in the Gulf of Finland. The Soviet ships turned away when confronted. (Bennett 116–117)

Clio in Piumas Islands, Brazil, 12 May 1841
A party from the sloop *Clio* (18) searched in the Piumas Islands for slavers; one was found and boarded, but local inhabitants recovered it. When the boat crew landed at Santos nearby they were arrested as pirates. (Bethell 205)

Clontarf, Ireland, 1014
A great alliance of Norse rulers was formed to join in a war between Irish kings. Jarl Sigurd the Stout of Orkney and Jarl Gilli of the Hebrides mounted a large seaborne expedition to Dublin to join King Sitric of that city. Sigurd died at the climactic battle of Clontarf. (Thompson 41–42)

Clyde v. *Vestale*, 20 August 1799
The frigate *Clyde* (38; Capt. Charles Cunningham) met two French ships off Rochefort which separated. *Clyde* caught up with the larger, the frigate *Vestale* (32), which was boarded after two hours' fighting and surrendered. (James 2.384–387; Clowes 4.523)

Clyde v. *Veloz*, 20 August 1800
The frigate *Clyde* (38; Capt. Charles Cunningham) captured the Spanish gunboat *Veloz* (4) in the English Channel. (Clowes 4.561)

Clyde v. a coaster, 25 August 1807
The frigate *Clyde* (38; Capt. Edward Owen) sent boats to intercept a coasting sloop near Fécamp. The sloop ran ashore and the crew fought hard, but a boat party refloated and brought her out, somewhat damaged. (James 4.265; Clowes 5.402)

Clyde v. *Gneisenau*, 20 June 1940
The German battle-cruiser *Gneisenau* was damaged by a torpedo from the submarine *Clyde* off Trondheim. (Rohwer 29)

Clyde v. three U-boats, 27–28 September 1941
Alerted by decrypted intelligence, the submarine *Clyde* was sent to ambush the German U-boats *U-111*, *U-68*, and *U-67* when they were refuelling at

the Cape Verde Islands; the ambush failed, and all torpedoes missed. (Sebag-Montefiore 196–200; Rohwer 102)

Cnut's expeditions to Denmark and Norway, 1019–1028

King Cnut in 1019, with just nine ships, sailed to Denmark and secured the kingship there. In 1025 he took a larger fleet to defend his Danish kingship against a coalition of local Danes and the Swedish king. His army of Danes and English was defeated in battle at the Holy River, with heavy casualties, but he held onto the kingdom. In 1028 he sailed to Norway with a fleet of fifty ships manned by Danes and English, defeated and drove out the local king Olaf, and ruled as king until his death. (*ASC* s.a. 1019–1020, 1025, 1028–1029)

Cochrane at Pechenga Bay, May 1918

The cruiser *Cochrane* landed Russian troops and Royal Marines at Pechenga Bay on 3 May in the face of a possible attack by Finnish forces, which were driven off on 12 May. (Newbolt 5.315)

Colaba, India, 1722–1740

Colaba was a strong coastal fort near Bombay, controlled in the early eighteenth century by members of the Angria family, Mahratta viceroys of the coast, often regarded by the EIC at Bombay as pirates. In 1722 Anglo-Portuguese forces besieged Colaba, and a small naval force of royal ships under Capt. Matthews blockaded it. The attack failed. In 1740, an alliance was made with Manaji Angria of Colaba, which was being attacked by Samboji Angria's forces from Suvarnadrug. A force of EIC ships relieved the siege and Samboji's ships retired. (Low 1.100–101, 109; Keay 262–268)

Colchester and *Lyme* v. *Aquilon* and *Fidele*, Rochefort, 17 May 1756

The French ships *Aquilon* (50) and *Fidele* (26), escorting a convoy towards Rochefort, were chased and attacked by *Colchester* (50; Capt. Lucius O'Brien) and *Lyme* (28; Capt. Edward Vernon). Sending the convoy into port, the French ships fought, the ships pairing off. All four ships were badly damaged. (Clowes 3.291)

Col de Balaguer, Catalonia, Spain, 3–7 June 1813

A force of British troops was landed from a squadron headed by *Invincible* (Capt. Charles Adam) to assist in the capture of a French fort at the Col de Balaguer. The bombardment exploded a magazine, at which the French surrendered. (Hall 188)

Colonia, Rio de la Plata, January 1763

A small private expedition sailed from Britain, commanded by the former Royal Navy Capt. Macnamara, to attack Spanish positions in the River Plate. A first attack on Colonia failed. In the second, on 6 January, the expedition's main ship, *Lord Clive* (50), caught fire and burned out. Macnamara was killed; the survivors retired. (Clowes 3.251–252)

Colossus v. *Vanneau*, 6 June 1793
The brig *Vanneau* (6) was captured by *Colossus* (74) in the Bay of Biscay. (Colledge 426)

Colpoys at Aviles, Spain, 21 March 1806
The brig *Colpoys* (16; Lt Thomas Ussher) sent two boats into Aviles harbour. Three Spanish luggers, two of them loaded with flax and steel, the third in ballast, were captured; that in ballast was released with the captured sailors. (James 4.132; Clowes 5.374)

Colpoys and *Attack* at Douillan, 19 April 1806
The brigs *Colpoys* (16; Lt Thomas Ussher) and *Attack* (Lt Thomas Swain) landed a party in the Douillan estuary, Brittany. A battery was stormed, a signal post destroyed, and three *chasse-marées* captured. (James 4.132–133)

Columbia and others v. *A-2* and *A-6*, 1 May 1915
Four trawlers searched for a submarine in the southern North Sea. Two German TBs, *A-2* and *A-6*, found them. The trawler *Columbia* was sunk. The other trawlers fought back, and when four destroyers out of Harwich arrived the TBs were quickly sunk. (Corbett 2.401–402)

Columbine v. three slavers, 1840
The sloop *Columbine* (18) captured three slave ships off the Congo. (Bethell 182)

Columbine v. Chinese pirates, 28–29 September 1849
The sloop *Columbine* (18) chased a fleet of pirate junks; three were damaged and abandoned, another was blown up by her crew; *Columbine* had ten casualties, three of them fatal. Next day *Columbine* and the steamer *Fury* (6) attacked and destroyed twenty-three pirate ships. (Clowes 6.356–357; Graham 273)

Columbine v. slavers, East Africa, 1871
The screw sloop *Columbine* (Cmdr John Tucker) cruised against the slave-trade dhows off East Africa, capturing eleven of them and freeing 412 slaves. (Clowes 7.234; Howell 146)

Comet v. French ship, 10 October 1706
The bomb vessel *Comet* was captured by a French ship. (Clowes 2.537)

Comet v. *Sylphe*, 11 August 1808
The sloop *Comet* (Cmdr Cuthbert Daly) encountered three French corvettes. Two sailed clear, but *Comet* was able to capture the third, *Sylphe*. (James 4.371–372; Clowes 5.424)

Comet v. submarine, 6 August 1918
The destroyer *Comet* was sunk by an Austrian submarine in the Mediterranean. (Colledge 86)

Commendah, Gold Coast, 28 May 1781
Campion (32) attacked the Dutch fort at Commendah, but failed to have any real effect. (Clowes 4.69)

Comus in the Canary Islands, March–May 1807
Comus (22; Capt. Conway Shipley) sent boats into Puerto de Haz to cut out ships from the harbour. On 8 May the boats went into Grand Canaria for the same purpose; this was more difficult, but still successful. (James 4.244–245; Clowes 5.398)

Comus v. Frederickscoarn, 14 August 1807
The Danish frigate *Frederickscoarn* sailed for Norway when a British attack on Denmark was imminent. *Comus* (22; Capt. Edmund Heywood) and *Defence* (74; Capt. Charles Ekins) went in chase. *Comus* caught up after a long chase and disabled and boarded *Frederickscoarn*. (James 4.203–204; Clowes 5.211–212)

Comus at Selangor, Malaya, 1955
The destroyer *Comus* bombarded communist insurgents in a swamp area of Selangor where a final group of communist insurgents had taken refuge; she was part of a combined operation by all three services; the cruiser *Newcastle* joined in later. (Wettern 106)

Concord v. Dutch squadron, March 1672
Concord (Capt. Francis Willshaw) was escorting a convoy near Portugal when she met a Dutch squadron; she fought her way through the Dutch ships; the convoy was scattered by a gale and largely avoided capture. (Clowes 2.443)

Concorde v. Bravoure, 27 January 1801
The frigate *Concorde* (36; Capt. Robert Barton) discovered a squadron of the French Brest fleet at sea off Finisterre, and set off to carry the news to England. She was chased by the frigate *Bravoure* and the ships fought until *Bravoure* returned to the shelter of her squadron. (James 3.69–71; Clowes 4.48)

Confiance v. Reitrada, 18 August 1807
The sloop *Confiance* (Capt. James Yeo) sent boats into the harbour of Guardia, Portugal, to cut out the Spanish privateer *Reitrada*. (James 4.264–265; Clowes 5.401)

Confiance v. Gun Vessel no. 1, 13 February 1808
Confiance (20; Capt. James Yeo) found the French *Gun Vessel no. 1* in the Tagus estuary; two boat parties captured her without loss. (James 4.306–307; Clowes 5.407)

Congo River
1852 The merchant brig *Mary Adeline* ran aground in the Congo estuary, and was rescued by the brigantine *Dolphin* (Lt Henry Temple) on 19–22

June. The local people were attempting to plunder her and had to be driven off. (Clowes 6.394)

1868 The screw gunvessels *Myrmidon* (Cmdr Henry Johnstone), *Pandora* (Cmdr John Burgess), and *Plover* (Cmdr James Poland) attacked pirates at Maletta Creek in the estuary of the river. (Clowes 7.224)

1870 The screw gunvessel *Growler* (Cmdr Edward Seymour) went to the rescue of the schooner *Loango*, which had been boarded and looted by pirates in the Congo estuary. The ship was recovered. In the subsequent search for missing seamen several villages were attacked and destroyed. (Clowes 7.228–229)

1875 An expedition went into the Congo estuary to combat pirates after the stranded schooner *Geraldine* was attacked. The paddle sloop *Spiteful* (Cmdr Mervyn Medlycott) reconnoitred, and then boats from *Spiteful*, the screw corvette *Active* (Capt. Sir William Hewett), and *Encounter* (Capt. Richard Bradshaw) captured and destroyed several villages and towns. (Clowes 7.275–277)

1877 A grounded ship was attacked. The screw gunvessel *Avon* (Cmdr Leicester Keppel) went into the estuary and burnt several villages. (Clowes 7.284–285)

Conn v. *U-905*, 23 March 1945
U-905 was sunk in the Minches by the destroyer *Conn*. (Rohwer 397)

Connecticut River, Connecticut, 7 April 1814
Boats from the British blockading squadron, commanded by Capt. Hon. Thomas Capel of *Hogue* (74), raided into the Connecticut River. They penetrated 14 miles up the river to Pettipague Point. After a short skirmish, twenty-seven vessels were captured and destroyed. (James 6.196)

Consort and *Mounts Bay* v. Chinese artillery, September 1952
The destroyer *Consort* and the frigate *Mounts Bay* were fired on by Chinese guns near Hong Kong; they returned fire. (Wettern 69)

Constance v. *Druides*, 8 June 1801
The Spanish cutter *Druides* (8) was captured by *Constance* (22; Capt. Zachary Mudge) off Vigo. (Clowes 4.561)

Constance and others v. *Salamandre*, 12 October 1806
Constance (22; Capt. Alexander Burrowes) and the brigs *Sharpshooter* (14) and *Strenuous* (14) chased the French *Salamandre* (26; *en flute*) carrying ship timber by Cape Fréhel. *Salamandre* got away, but *Constance* and companions found her again and bombarded her into surrender. *Constance* went aground and was lost. (Clowes 5.389–390)

Constant Warwick v. Portuguese Indiaman, 19 August 1650
Off the Rock of Lisbon *Constant Warwick* (Capt. Moulton) fought and sank

a Portuguese Indiaman. The fight lasted five hours; most of the crew were rescued, but the rich cargo was lost. (Powell 100)

Constant Warwick v. *Royal James*, March 1654
Royal James (42; Capt. Beach), a notorious privateer operating out of Brest, was caught by *Constant Warwick* (42) and forced to surrender after a stiff fight. Beach had with him several other privateer captains; their capture went a long way to suppress their activities. (Clowes 2.202)

Constant Warwick v. Dutch warship, March 1667
Constant Warwick (42; Capt. Robert Ensom) fought a large Dutch warship off the Tagus estuary; the arrival of *Little Victory* (28) persuaded the Dutch to leave. *Constant Warwick* suffered serious damage to its masts and yards. Ensom was killed. (Clowes 2.435)

Constant Warwick v. Dutch privateer, February 1673
Constant Warwick (42; Capt. Thomas Hamilton) met and fought a Dutch privateer off the Lizard, but suffered considerable damage; the privateer got away. (Clowes 2.447)

Constant Warwick and others v. French squadron, 12 July 1691
In the West Indies, *Constant Warwick* (42; Capt. James Moody), *Mary Rose* (48; Capt. John Bounty), and the ketch *Talbot* (15) were captured by the local French squadron. Bounty was killed. (Clowes 2.465)

Constitution v. two French cutters, 9 January 1801
The hired cutter *Constitution* (Lt William Faulknor) was captured by two French cutters, but was retaken later that day. (Clowes 4.551)

Content v. Spanish squadron, Cape Corrientes, Cuba, 1591
The barque *Content* (Capt. Nicholas Liste) and two other English ships fought a Spanish squadron. The other English ships soon left, but *Content* fought on for a full day and eventually got away. She had no casualties. (Clowes 1.497)

Contest and *Mohawk* v. *Asp* and *Scorpion*, 11 July 1813
The brigs *Contest* (12; Cmdr James Rattray) and *Mohawk* (10; Cmdr Hon. Henry Byng) chased two US gunvessels into the Yeocomico River, capturing *Asp*, after a fight; the other, *Scorpion*, escaped. (James 6.96)

Contest v. slaver, May 1850
The brig *Contest* (12) captured a schooner belonging to New Calabar which was carrying 152 slaves. (Dike 132)

Contest v. U-boat, 18 September 1917
The sloop *Contest* was sunk by a U-boat off Ushant. (Colledge 89)

Copenhagen, Denmark

1700 A joint Anglo-Dutch fleet, the English part commanded by Admiral Sir George Rooke, sailed to the Sound to compel the Danes to make peace with Sweden; a Swedish fleet joined them. After considerable manoeuvring and consultation and a bombardment of Copenhagen, a Swedish force landed near the city, at which the Danes made peace. (Anderson 134–136; Clowes 2.365–366)

1801 (Battle of COPENHAGEN)   A British fleet of eighteen line-of-battle ships and as many smaller vessels was sent to enforce British demands on Denmark. The commander was Admiral Sir Hyde Parker, but it was his second, Vice-Admiral Lord Nelson, who led the attack. The Danish fleet, a miscellany of ships of from 20 to 74 guns, mainly fairly old, was moored before the city in a very strong defensive position. Nelson led his division of ten line-of-battle ships, plus frigates, sloops, and bombs, into the channel between the Danish line and a sandbank called the Middle Ground, advancing from the south so that the ships could bombard the Danes as they passed. Parker with a smaller part of the fleet moved in from the north blocking the exit, but as he was moving against the wind he did so only slowly.

The firing lasted about three hours, ceasing about 2 p.m., when Nelson arranged a truce with the Danish Crown Prince. Of the eighteen Danish ships in the line, only three escaped, and one of these sank later. The British casualties were over 900 men, but none of their ships were more than damaged.

The purpose of the action on the British side was not simply to destroy an aged fleet, but to destroy an alliance of the northern naval powers, Denmark, Sweden, and Russia. As an intimidator the action was very effective. Nelson went into the Baltic. The Swedish fleet retired into the Karlskrona, and Nelson had only to appear at Reval for the Russians to retreat into Kronstadt. The message to all Europe was clear: Britain was prepared to fight all and sundry, and would send Nelson to do it, a promise to chill the blood of any enemy. (James 3.42–64; Clowes 4.427–44; Dudley Pope, *The Great Gamble*, London 1972; Warner 103–147; Anderson 303–310; *NC* 2.149–190; Tunstall 231–234)

1807 (Second battle of COPENHAGEN)   The British government feared Napoleon would gain control of the fleets of the Baltic states. The surrender of the nearest, that of Denmark, was demanded, but refused. A fleet of twenty-five line-of-battle ships and twice as many smaller vessels, under the command of Admiral Lord Gambier, sailed to enforce the demand. Denmark's fleet was in the harbour of Copenhagen which was surrounded by the city, and the British therefore landed troops, a process hindered by attacks by Danish gunboats, then bombarded the city, much of which was set on fire. The result was a Danish capitulation, the surrender of the Danish fleet – fifteen line-of-battle ships, ten frigates, fourteen smaller ships, and twenty-five gunboats – and an abiding Danish hostility for the rest of the Napoleonic war; 250 Danish troops were casualties; in the city the civilian casualties were ten times that. (James 4.200–212; Anderson 315–319; Clowes 5.212–217; *NC* 4.39–49, 80–81, 86–90; NRS, *Misc* III, IV)

Coreopsis v. UB-85, 30 April 1918
The drifter *Coreopsis* sank *UB-85* in the North Channel. (Newbolt 5.427; Grant 113)

Corfu Channel, 1946
Albania, newly independent, objected to the channel between the Greek island of Corfu and the Albanian coast being regarded as the open sea and a passage for ships. Two British ships taking the channel were shelled in May, and in October the destroyers *Saumarez* and *Volage* ran into a new minefield in attempting the passage. A major minesweeping operation involving the Mediterranean fleet removed the minefield in November. (L. Gardiner, *The Eagle Spreads his Claws*, London 1966; Cable 224)

Cork, Ireland
1013 The fleet of King Olaf Sitricsson of Norse Dublin raided the Viking settlement at Cork, and went on to raid Cape Clear. (Hudson 95)

1689–1690 Capt. George Rooke, with an Irish Sea squadron, sent four ketches into Cork harbour, then under Jacobite control, in September 1689. The crews rustled cattle from the island, and seized and brought out a pink loaded with sugar. Next year an expedition was sent from England under the joint commands of Admirals Haddock, Killigrew, and Ashby, carrying 500 troops commanded by the Earl of Marlborough. The landing was effected on 23 September, after a battery at the entrance had been bombarded into silence. The city was captured on 29 September. (Powley 296; Clowes 2.331, 462–463)

Cormorant v. French fleet, 24 August 1781
Cormorant (14; Cmdr Robert McEvoy) was captured by the fleet of Admiral de Grasse off Charleston. (Clowes 4.110)

Cormorant v. Téméraire, 30 July 1782
Cormorant (12; Cmdr John Melcombe) captured the sloop *Téméraire* (10) off Brest, together with *Temeraire*'s dispatches. (Clowes 4.84)

Cormorant v. Alerte, March 1796
The French *Alerte* (14) was captured by *Cormorant* (18; Cmdr Joseph Bingham) in the West Indies. (Clowes 4.554)

Cormorant v. Valiente, 2 January 1799
The packet *Valiente* (12) was captured by *Cormorant* (20; Capt. Lord Mark Kerr) off Malaga. (Clowes 4.560)

Cormorant v. Vencejo, 19 March 1799
The Spanish ship *Vencejo* (18) was captured by *Cormorant* (20; Capt. Lord Mark Kerr) in the Mediterranean. (Clowes 4.560)

Cormorant v. slavers, Brazil, 1850–1851
The paddle sloop *Cormorant* (Capt. Herbert Schomberg) captured the slaver

Santa Cruz near Rio de Janeiro on 5 January 1850; the ship's condition induced Capt. Schomberg to burn it. He captured the slaver *Paulina* near Rio de Janeiro a week later; she was sent to St Helena for adjudication. A boat party was sent to capture the slaver *Rival* in a river near Cabo Frio, Brazil, on 26 June. This was done, despite local hostility and threats from the fort at the mouth of the river. Next year *Cormorant* went into the Rio Paranagua to attack a group of slave ships. One was scuttled, and three were brought out. The guard fort and *Cormorant* exchanged fire. In 1851 *Cormorant* sank the Brazilian steam tug *Sarah* which was carrying slaving equipment to the *Valarozo*. (Lloyd 144–145; Bethell 310, 330, 355; Clowes 6.392)

Cormorant IV and *Young Fred* v. *UB-63*, 14 January 1918
The trawler *Cormorant IV* and the drifter *Young Fred*, north of Ireland, attacked and sank a submarine which may have been *UB-63*; it certainly did not return from its last cruise. (Grant 109–111)

Cornwall v. *Pinguin*, 8 May 1941
The cruiser *Cornwall* encountered and sank the German AMC *Pinguin* near the Seychelles Islands. (Rohwer 72; Hore 256–258)

Cornwallis's Retreat, 8–17 June 1795
A squadron commanded by Vice-Admiral Hon. William Cornwallis encountered a French squadron under Rear-Admiral Vence near the Penmarcks. The French ships took refuge behind Belle Isle, and Cornwallis escorted some prizes to an English port. Vence's squadron was reinforced by a larger fleet under Admiral Villaret-Joyeuse and met Cornwallis's ships returning. The French fleet divided into two parts, intending to attack the British from two sides, but Cornwallis led a fighting retreat, bringing his flagship *Royal Sovereign* (98; Capt. John Whitby) to the aid of other ships in danger, notably *Triumph* (74) and *Mars* (74). Despite its great superiority the French fleet withdrew after a day's fighting. (James 1.262–270; *NC* 1.120–124; Clowes 255–259; Tunstall 211–212)

Cornwallis v. *Margaretta*, 1 March 1810
Cornwallis (44; Capt. William Montagu) near Amboyna chased the Dutch brig *Margaretta* (8), which took refuge in a bay which the light winds made inaccessible to *Cornwallis*. Montagu sent in boarding parties in boats, which captured *Margaretta* in the face of grape shot, musketry, pikes, and swords. (James 5.194)

Cornwallis v. *U-32*, 9 January 1917
Cornwallis, an old battleship, was torpedoed and sunk by *U-32* off Malta. (Halpern, *Mediterranean* 325)

Coro, Spanish Main, 1659
Capt. Christopher Myngs, the senior English naval officer in the Caribbean, led a raid on Coro; a considerable treasure was seized, mostly kept by Myngs and the sailors. (Capp 96)

CORONEL, Chile, 1 November 1914

The German East Asiatic squadron under Admiral von Spee, having crossed the Pacific, encountered a British squadron under Admiral Craddock off Coronel, Chile. The two squadrons manoeuvred for an hour or so, and then fought briefly. The cruisers *Good Hope* and *Monmouth* were sunk; two other ships, the light cruiser *Glasgow* and the AMC *Otranto*, escaped. (Corbett 1.341–351)

Corsica

1794 The British fleet in the Mediterranean commanded by Admiral Lord Hood landed a force at San Fiorenzo on 7 February. The tower of Mortella was attacked by *Fortitude* (74) and *Juno* (32). The town and the frigate *Minerve* were taken on the 18th. (*Minerve* was taken into the navy as *San Fiorenzo* (36); the tower at Mortella provided a model for the later Martello towers on the British coast.) Hood went on to attack Bastia with his whole fleet, and the city fell on 21 May. The islanders agreed to a declaration of independence from republican France, and with army reinforcements the last republican fort at Calvi was taken on 10 August. One of the French vessels taken from Toulon, the frigate *Proselyte*, was lost at Bastia; at Calvi two frigates were captured, one of which, *Melpomène* (38), was taken into the navy. Corsica was retaken by a French republican force in 1796. (James 1.207–213; NRS, *Misc* IV; Clowes 4.243–245; Hore, *Seapower* 55–57)

1813 A squadron which included *America* (74; Capt. Josias Rowley) and *Leviathan* (74; Capt. Patrick Campbell) raided shipping along the Corsican coast, notably at Langueglia on 9 May and Alassio on 27 June. (Clowes 5.505–509)

Corso v. Corvesse, 27 May 1801

Corso (18; Cmdr William Ricketts) captured the French dispatch vessel *Corvesse* in the Mediterranean. (Clowes 4.558)

Corunna, Spain

1386 An Anglo-Portuguese fleet sailed from Plymouth carrying an English army under John of Gaunt. The army landed at Corunna in July, achieving complete surprise. The English ships at once returned home. (Sumption 3.594)

1589 An English expedition of eighty ships and several thousand soldiers led by Sir Francis Drake raided Corunna. The fleet occupied the harbour and the soldiers captured the lower town, but not the well-fortified upper town. The Spaniards burnt their own ships in the harbour to prevent capture. A Spanish relieving force was defeated, but the English then evacuated the town. (Clowes 1.490–491; Andrews 163–164)

1809 (Battle of CORUNNA) Corunna was the evacuation point for the British expeditionary force under Major-General Sir John Moore which was retreating before the larger French army under Marshal Soult. A battle was fought to block the French advance and the navy brought a fleet of warships and transports which evacuated the whole of the British forces, 26,000 men. (Hall 67–74; *NC* 4.207–212)

Cossack v. Mouche, August 1808
The French schooner *Mouche* was captured by the sloop *Cossack* (22; Capt. George Digby) in the English Channel. (Clowes 5.558)

Cossack v. Altmark, 16 February 1940
The destroyer *Cossack* violated Norwegian territorial waters to release 300 captive British sailors from the German auxiliary ship *Altmark* in Jossingfjord. (Rohwer 15)

Coulan, China, 26 August–3 September 1858
The paddle frigate *Magicienne* (Capt. Nicholas Vansittart), together with a set of gunboats, attacked the pirate town of Coulan, which was taken and destroyed, together with about 100 ships and boats. (Clowes 7.122)

Countess of Scarborough v. Pallas, 23 September 1779
Countess of Scarborough (20; Cmdr Thomas Piercy), part of an escort for a Baltic convoy, was threatened by the rebel American squadron commanded by John Paul Jones. She fought *Pallas* (32), and was forced to surrender, heavily damaged, after two hours. (Clowes 4.39)

Courageous v. U-29, 17 September 1939
The aircraft carrier *Courageous* was attacked by *U-29* in the Western Approaches. *Courageous* had only two destroyers as escort and was sunk by two torpedoes; 518 men died. *U-29* survived a retaliatory attack by the destroyers. (Terraine 221–222; Rohwer 3)

Courageux v. Minerve, 4 January 1781
The French frigate *Minerve* (32) fought *Courageux* (74; Capt. Constantine Phipps) for some time, despite the odds, only surrendering when another 74, *Valiant*, came up; *Minerve* had a quarter of her people casualties. She had been the British *Minerva*, and now rejoined as *Recovery*. (Clowes 4.60–61)

Coureur v. American privateers, October 1780
The schooner *Coureur* (16; Lt Christopher Major) was captured by two rebel American privateers off Newfoundland. (Clowes 4.110)

Courier v. Ribotteur and another, 12–13 May 1799
The cutter *Courier* (10; Lt Thomas Searle) intercepted a French privateer in the act of capturing a ship and drove it off; next day *Courier* found and captured without resistance another privateer, *Ribotteur*. (James 2.379–380)

Courier v. Guerrier, 22 November 1799
The cutter *Courier* (10; Lt Thomas Searle) chased the privateer *Guerrier*; they fought off Lowestoft and *Guerrier* was beaten into surrender. (James 2.413–414)

Coventry v. French warship, 24 July 1704

Coventry (48; Capt. Henry Lawrence) was captured off the Scilly Isles by a French ship captained by Duguay-Trouin; Capt. Lawrence was judged not to have made a good fight and was imprisoned and dismissed the service. (Clowes 2.506)

Coventry v. Bellone, 12 August 1782

Coventry (28; Capt. Andrew Mitchell) met the French frigate *Bellone* (32) off southern India. The two ships fought for two hours with no result other than considerable damage and casualties. (Clowes 4.85)

Coventry v. French squadron, 10 January 1783

Coventry (28; Capt. William Wolseley) was captured by a French squadron off the coast of Orissa, India. (Clowes 4.77; Colledge 93)

Cowslip v. UB-105, 18 April 1918

The sloop *Cowslip* was sunk near Cape Spartel by *UB-105*. (Colledge 93)

Crafty v. three privateers, 9 March 1807

The schooner *Crafty* (12; Lt Richard Spencer) was captured by three privateers south of Gibraltar. (Clowes 5.551; James 4.467)

Crash off the Dutch coast, 26 August 1798

The gun brig *Crash* (12; Lt Buckley Praed) was captured by the Dutch off the coast of Holland. (Clowes 4.550; James 2.469)

Creole and Astraea v. Sultane and Etoile, 23 January 1814

The frigates *Creole* and *Astraea* (Capts George McKenzie and John Eveleigh) discovered the French frigates *Sultane* and *Etoile* at anchor at Mayo Island in the Cape Verde Islands. The two pairs of frigates fought each other until the afternoon, when both *Creole* and *Astraea* were dismasted and defeated. (James 6.124–128)

Crescent v. Berkeley, 13 August 1759

The French ship *Berkeley* (20) was captured by *Crescent* (32). (Clowes 3.313)

Crescent v. Réunion, 20 October 1793

The frigate *Crescent* (36; Capt. James Saumarez) lay in wait off Cape Barfleur for the French frigate *Réunion* (40) which raided British shipping in the Channel at night. The two ships met at dawn as *Réunion* returned and in the fight both ships received damage to their masts and rigging. Saumarez suddenly swung his ship round to bring his unengaged side to bear and this compelled *Réunion* to surrender. Saumarez was knighted for his achievement on his return to Portsmouth. He had no casualties; *Réunion* may have had 120 men killed or wounded. (James 1.114–117; Clowes 4.479)

Crescent and Calypso v. Spanish squadron, 15 November 1799

The frigate *Crescent* (36; Capt. William Lobb) and the sloop *Calypso* (Cmdr

Joseph Baker) were escorting a convoy towards Jamaica when a Spanish squadron, consisting of *Asia* (64), the frigate *Amfitrite*, and the corvette *Galgo*, appeared. By manoeuvring carefully *Crescent* secured the convoy from attack, while *Calypso* remained as an escort and *Galgo* was captured. (James 2.462–463; Clowes 4.528)

Crescent v. *Diligente*, June 1800
The frigate *Crescent* (36; Capt. William Lobb) captured the French ship *Diligente* (12) in the West Indies. (Clowes 4.557)

Crete
1760 A French squadron from Toulon was pursued by a British squadron headed by *Shrewsbury* (74; Capt. Hugh Palliser) and took refuge at a Cretan port in June. It was blockaded there for a time, but emerged once the British squadron withdrew. (Clowes 3.229)

1897–1898 An international naval force intervened in a civil war in Crete, protecting Turkish forces from the Greek insurgents. The main naval incident came when *Camperdown* shelled an insurgent group at Fort Izzedin, which was then occupied by a marine detachment. (Clowes 7.444–448)

1941 (Battle of CRETE) The German invasion of Crete began on 20 May. It was mainly a land and air operation, but naval activity was constant. One German troop convoy was scattered by a cruiser and destroyer force, most of the men being saved by the Italian TB *Lupo*; an attack on a second convoy had only minor success, and the cruisers *Naiad* and *Carlisle* were damaged. Air attacks sank the cruisers *Gloucester* and *Fiji*, the sloop *Grimsby*, the destroyers *Juno*, *Greyhound*, *Kashmir*, and *Kelly*, and four MTBs. Many other ships were damaged. Defeated on land, the British forces were evacuated on 27 May–1 June; 17,000 soldiers were taken out; the destroyers *Imperial* and *Hereward* and the AA cruiser *Calcutta* were sunk during the evacuation, and many other ships damaged. The net result was a serious weakening of the Mediterranean fleet. (Rohwer 75)

Crocodile v. *Mercedita*, 1839
Crocodile (26; Capt. Alexander Milne), in the West Indies, captured the slaver *Mercedita*. (Clowes 6.305)

Crocus v. *U-353*, 6 October 1942
In mid-Atlantic *U-353* fought a gun duel with the corvette *Crocus*; both ships were damaged. (Rohwer 200)

Croome v. *Baracca*, 8 September 1941
West of Gibraltar, the Italian submarine *Baracca* was depth-charged to the surface and sunk by ramming by the destroyer *Croome*. (Rohwer 93)

Crown and *Nightingale* v. Dutch squadron, 8 June 1673
Crown (42; Cmdr Richard Carter) and *Nightingale* (18; Capt. Joseph Harris) met three Dutch warships in the North Sea. The English ships attacked,

despite the Dutch having twice their number of guns; the Dutch broke off the fight after three hours. (Clowes 2.447–448)

Cruizer v. Contre Amiral Magon, 16 October 1804

The privateer *Contre Amiral Magon* (17), having captured several ships, was chased for nine hours in the North Sea by the sloop *Cruizer* (18), reputed to be the only ship fast enough to capture her. Both ships lost masts and sails in the chase, but *Magon* surrendered as soon as *Cruizer* came up. (*NC* 3.56–57; Clowes 5.352)

Cruizer v. Jéna, 6 January 1807

The sloop *Cruizer* (18) captured the French privateer *Jéna* in the North Sea; *Jéna* was taken into the navy as the sloop *Grenada* (16). (Colledge 168)

Cruizer v. Danish gunvessels, 1 October 1808

The sloop *Cruizer* (18; Lt Thomas Wells) encountered a group of twenty Danish armed vessels of various types near Gothenburg, and fought them off, capturing one. (James 4.369; Anderson 327)

Cruizer v. Christianborg, 31 May 1809

The sloop *Cruizer* (18; Cmdr Thomas Toker) captured the Danish ship *Christianborg* (6) off Bornholm. (Clowes 5.438)

Cuba, August–September 1739

Capt. Charles Brown took the Jamaica squadron on a cruise around Cuba. Off Havana *Shoreham* (24; Cmdr Hon. Edward Boscawen) sank two sloops and captured one, and burnt stores at Porto Maria; *Diamond* (50; Capt. Charles Knowles) captured two ships, and destroyed a fort. (Clowes 3.266–267)

Cubugua, West Indies, 1602

An English privateering fleet under William Parker captured the town of La Rancheria, but then ransomed it. (Clowes 1.531)

CUDDALORE, India

1758 (First battle) A French squadron commanded by the Comte d'Ache met a British squadron under Vice-Admiral George Pocock off Cuddalore on 29 April in a fight between roughly equal forces. The French eventually broke off the fight and retired to Pondicherry; one of their ships was wrecked on the coast because it had lost its anchors in the battle. (Clowes 3.174–176; Mahan 307; Tunstall 112–113)

1783 (Second battle) A British force laid siege to Cuddalore, assisted by a fleet of eight line-of-battle ships under Vice-Admiral Sir Edward Hughes. The French fleet, fifteen ships under Vice-Admiral Pierre Suffren, intervened on behalf of the besieged on 20 June. In the battle the British were driven away and Hughes took his fleet to Madras. Suffren thus relieved the siege. (Clowes 3.561–564; Mahan 462–463; Tunstall 186–187)

Culloden and others near Toulon, 7 June 1759
Culloden (74; Capt. Smith Callis), *Conqueror* (70; Capt. William Lloyd), and *Jersey* (60; Capt. John Barker) pursued two French frigates which had taken shelter in a bay near Toulon. The British ships entered the bay, but were becalmed and bombarded for two hours, then recalled. (Clowes 3.211)

Culloden and *Minotaur* at Rome, September 1799
Minotaur (74; Capt. Thomas Louis) and *Culloden* (74; Capt. Thomas Troubridge) were sent by Rear-Admiral Nelson to gain control of the city of Civitavecchia, which was done. The terms of surrender included other places nearby, including Rome. Capt. Louis was rowed in his barge up the Tiber and hoisted the British flag on the Capitol. (James 2.317)

Culloden v. *Duguay-Trouin* and *Guerriere*, 2 September 1803
Duguay-Trouin (74) and the frigate *Guerriere* encountered a British squadron near Corunna. *Culloden* (74; Capt. Barrington Dacres) attacked both ships but they got into Corunna. (James 3.188)

Culloden v. *Emilieu*, 25 September 1806
The French sloop *Emilieu* was captured by *Culloden* (74; Rear-Admiral Sir Edward Pellew) in the East Indies. (Clowes 5.558)

Cumberland's squadron v. *Hare*, 1587
The Earl of Cumberland, in his second privateering voyage, captured a Dunkirk ship, *Hare*, in the Channel. (Spence 81–82)

Cumberland and others v. French squadron, 1707
A large convoy of 130 ships, escorted by five warships, sailed from Plymouth on 9 October. Next day it was attacked by a squadron of fifteen French warships under the joint command of Duguay-Trouin and the Chevalier de Forbin off the Lizard. Most of the merchantmen got away, but *Cumberland* (80; Commodore Richard Edwards), *Chester* (58; Capt. John Balchen), and *Ruby* (50; Capt. Hon. Peregrine Bertie) surrendered to their French attackers, respectively *Lys* (70), *Jason* (54), and *Amazone* (40). *Devonshire* (80; Capt. John Watkins) fought on against five attackers, and then blew up. *Royal Oak* (76; Captain Baron Wylde) got away, badly damaged. Bertie and Watkins died; Wylde was cashiered. (Clowes 2.512–513; Owen 220–235; Tunstall 77)

Cumberland v. *Duc de Chartres*, 1781
Cumberland (74) captured the French privateer *Duc de Chartres* off North America. (Colledge 117)

Cumbria
913 A fleet from Ireland, composed of Irish Vikings and Irishmen, raided Cumbria, but was defeated by the Norsemen already settled there. (Hudson 22)

1042 Jarl Thorfinn of Orkney gathered a great army and fleet from the

Norse of Orkney, Scotland, and Ireland, and raided northwest England. (Thompson 50; *Orkneyinga Saga* 23–24)

Curacao, West Indies
1800 The Dutch island of Curacao was attacked by a force of French privateers. The arrival of the frigate *Nereide* (Capt. Frederick Watkins) allowed the governor to place his colony under British protection; Watkins thereupon landed his marines and the privateers left. (Duffy 317–318; *NC* 2.119; Clowes 4.425)

1803–1804 Curacao was summoned to surrender by Cmdr Robert Tucker of the sloop *Surinam* in July 1803, but he and his ship were captured instead. A British squadron under Capt. John Bligh in *Theseus* (74) landed a force of sailors and marines on 31 January 1804, with guns from the ships. A fort was captured, but other forts and the town proved invulnerable. The landing force was evacuated on 25 February. (James 3.290–296; Clowes 5.80–82)

1807 A squadron of frigates under Capt. Charles Brisbane of *Arethusa*, with *Latona* (Lt Charles Wood), *Anson* (Capt. Charles Lydiard), and *Fisguard* (Capt. William Bolton), sailed into the harbour of St Ann, Curacao, at dawn on 1 January. The frigate *Halstaar* and the corvette *Surinam* were seized in the harbour, then the main forts were attacked. All this was done suddenly, violently, and successfully; the island had capitulated by 10 a.m., with very few casualties. (James 4.275–279; Clowes 5.238–239)

Curieux **v.** *Dame Ernouf*, **8 February 1805**
The sloop *Curieux* (16; Cmdr George Bettesworth), near Barbados, chased the privateer *Dame Ernouf* all day; coming close the two ships pounded each other until *Dame Ernouf*, partly dismasted and her decks no longer habitable, surrendered; *Curieux* had five killed; *Dame Ernouf* thirty, with forty wounded. (James 4.17–18; Clowes 5.355)

Curieux **v.** *Revanche*, **3 December 1807**
The sloop *Curieux* (16; Cmdr John Sherriff) was attacked by the privateer *Revanche* (25) while east of Martinique. Badly damaged by the first firing, *Curieux* then repelled two attempts to board, and *Revanche* sailed off. (James 4.271–272; Clowes 5.404)

Curlew **v.** *Panda*, **6 June 1833.**
Curlew (10; Cmdr Henry Trotter) located the pirate schooner *Panda* near Principe Island, West Africa, and pursued it into an estuary. Three boats went in and captured the ship, though the crew got ashore. (Clowes 6.272–273)

Curlew **v. slaver, 1834**
The brig *Curlew* (Lt Hon. Joseph Denman) captured a slaver off Brazil, but the court in Rio de Janeiro denied it had jurisdiction; the ship went back to West Africa, where the court in Sierra Leone also refused to deal with it, and sent her once more to Brazil. (Lloyd 93)

Curlew v. *Dous Amigos*, June 1843
The sloop *Curlew* detained the slaver *Dous Amigos* as it left Rio de Janeiro; the ship was later released as having been taken inside territorial waters. (Bethell 211)

Cuxhaven, Germany
1809 A squadron of small craft led by *Mosquito* (18; Cmdr William Goate) captured the town of Cuxhaven from the Dutch on 8 June. Batteries were destroyed. (Clowes 5.442; *NC* 4.262)

1914 Three seaplane carriers, *Engadine*, *Riviera*, and *Empress*, covered by cruisers and destroyers and submarines, sent seven seaplanes to bomb the ships, airship yards, and sheds at Cuxhaven on Christmas Day. Fog over the target meant none of the planes could locate the sheds. Five of the seaplanes were lost. (Corbett 2.51–53; Massie 361–373)

Cyane v. *Hortense* and *Hermione*, 12 May 1805
The sloop *Cyane* (18; Cmdr Hon. George Cadogan) was captured by the French frigates *Hortense* and *Hermione*. (Clowes 5.550)

Cyane and *Espoir* v. *Cerere* and *Fama*, 25–26 June 1809
The sloops *Cyane* (22; Capt. Thomas Staines) and *Espoir* (18; Cmdr Robert Mitford), with some gunboats, screened an expedition taking possession of the islands of Ischia and Procida. They were attacked by the Neapolitan frigate *Cerere*, the corvette *Fama*, and gunboats from Pozzuoli, and then by more gunboats from Gaeta, of which eighteen were captured and four sunk. *Cyane* and *Espoir* sent a party into Pozzuoli Bay to destroy a battery. *Cerere* and *Fama* sailed for Naples and *Cyane* and *Cerere* fought each other almost to the entrance to the harbour; *Cerere* got into the harbour; *Cyane* was so badly damaged she had to be towed out by *Espoir*. (James 5.32–55; Clowes 5.440–441)

Cyane and *Laurel* v. *Constitution*, 20 February 1815
The US frigate *Constitution* encountered the sloops *Cyane* (22; Capt. Gordon Falcon) and *Levant* (20; Capt. Hon. George Douglas) near Madeira. By keeping her distance *Constitution* was able to defeat each vessel with ease and in succession; both surrendered. (James 6.248–252; Clowes 6.169–171)

Cyclamen v. *UB-69*, January 1918
The sloop *Cyclamen* sank *UB-69* off Cap Bon. (Newbolt 5.411; Halpern, *Mediterranean* 453; Grant 130–131)

Cyclops v. *Railleur*, 11 January 1783
The French brig *Railleur* (14), damaged in an earlier fight, was captured near the United States coast by *Cyclops* (28). (Clowes 4.92)

Cygnet v. French ships, 20 September 1693
The fireship *Cygnet* (6; Capt. John Perry), in the West Indies, was captured

by the French. Perry was court-martialled and dismissed as a result. (Clowes 2.472)

Cygnet v. Imperiale, 24 May 1806
The French schooner *Imperiale* was captured by *Cygnet* (18; Cmdr Robert Campbell) near Dominica. (Clowes 5.557)

Cygnet v. Galianna, November 1841
The brig *Cygnet* (8) captured the slaver *Galianna* in the Bight of Benin. (Bethell 194)

Cyrenaica, North Africa, 1940–1942
1940 (June–October)   Tobruk was bombarded on 12 June by the cruisers *Gloucester* and *Liverpool* and four destroyers; the Italian minesweeper *Giovanni Berta* was sunk; the Italian submarine *Bagnolini* sank the cruiser *Calypso*. The British submarine *Parthian* bombarded Tobruk on 19 June, missing the Italian cruiser *San Giorgio* in the harbour, but sinking the submarine *Diamante*. Bardia was bombarded on 20–21 June by an Anglo-French squadron and on 6 July the cruiser *Capetown* and four destroyers repeated the bombardment. Planes from the carrier *Eagle* raided Tobruk on 5 July and sank the destroyer *Zeffiro* and a freighter; the destroyer *Euro* and two ships in the harbour ran aground. *Eagle*'s planes raided Tobruk again on 20 July and sank the Italian destroyers *Nembo* and *Ostro* and a freighter. The Mediterranean fleet bombarded Bardia and Fort Capuzzo on 17 August, and on the night of the 23rd the gunboat *Ladybird* raided the harbour. On 22 August planes from the carrier *Eagle* sank the Italian submarine *Iride* and a depot ship near Tobruk, and four destroyers raided the area next day. Bardia was raided again, by aircraft from *Eagle*, on 24 August. Next month Benghazi was raided by the Mediterranean fleet, sinking the Italian destroyer *Borea* and three other ships; Bardia, Sollum, and Sidi Barrani were also bombarded; the cruiser *Kent* was damaged. Sidi Barrani was bombed and bombarded on 24 and 25 September and again on 25 October. (Rohwer 27, 28, 31, 33, 36, 37, 29, 32, 41; Greene and Massignani 54)

1940–1941 (December–April)   Destroyers and gunboats bombarded the Italian positions on the Cyrenaican coast in support of the land campaign in the winter of 1940–1941. The cruiser *Coventry* was damaged by torpedo attacks by the Italian submarine *Neghelli* on 13 December; next day the Italian submarine *Naiade* was sunk by the destroyers *Hereward* and *Hyperion*. Tripoli was raided on 20–21 December, Bardia was bombarded on 2–3 January 1941, and Tobruk on 21 January. Between 9 and 20 April, the Cyrenaican coastal towns were bombarded by naval forces as the British land forces retreated. (Rohwer 51–54, 56, 68)

1941 (April–December)   Tobruk, under siege, was periodically supplied, usually by night, by naval forces, the vessels employed usually being destroyers or smaller, and often coming under attack by enemy aircraft. In August, the Australian government insisted that the Australian division in the town be relieved, so a squadron of minelayers and destroyers took 6000 reinforcements into Tobruk and evacuated 5000 of the Australians. The minelayers *Abdiel* and *Latona*, with destroyers, took 6300 troops and supplies into Tobruk on 12–22 September; later they evacuated 6000 soldiers. A slow convoy carried troops and arms from Alexandria to Tobruk on 18–23 November escorted by the RAN sloops *Parramatta* and *Avon Vale*. On 27 November *U-559* sank *Parramatta*, and the destroyers *Kipling* and *Jackal* bombarded the Halfaya Pass area. (Rohwer 92, 99, 116)

1942 (December–September)   Bardia was bombarded by the 7th Destroyer Flotilla led by RAN *Napier* on 31 December 1941; the gunboat *Aphis* bombarded Halfaya Pass between 8 and 13 January 1942. British cruisers and destroyers bombarded the Cyrenaican coast road at various places, notably Mersa Matruh, between 11 and 22 July. On 19 July they were attacked by German S-boats, but neither side suffered damage. On 14 September the cruiser *Dido* and four destroyers bombarded the Daba area of Egypt. (Rohwer 128, 134, 180, 181, 196)

A combined naval, army, and air force raid on Tobruk was a total failure. The AA cruiser *Coventry*, the destroyers *Sikh* and *Zulu*, and five MTBs were sunk and one MTB captured. Over 500 men were made prisoner and code and cypher equipment was captured. (Rohwer 196)

Cyrene v. *Aurora* and *Hypolite*, West Africa, 23 October 1822

The sloop *Cyrene* (20; Cmdr Percy Grace) chased, intercepted, and captured the Dutch slaver *Aurora* and the French slaver *Hypolite*, though neither was carrying slaves at the time. (Ward 91–92)

D

D-2 v. German patrol, 25 November 1914
The submarine *D-2* was sunk off Wester Eems by a German patrol. (Colledge 100)

D-4 v. UB-72, 12 May 1918
The German submarine *UB-72* was sunk by the British submarine *D-4* in Lyme Bay. (Newbolt 5.280; Grant 118)

D-6 v. UB-73, 28 June 1918
The submarine *D-6* was sunk off the north Irish coast by *UB-73*. (Colledge 100)

D-7 v. U-45, 12 September 1917
The British submarine *D-7* torpedoed and sank *U-45* west of Shetland. (Newbolt 5.425; Grant 61)

Daedalus v. Prudente, 9 February 1799
The frigate *Daedalus* (Capt. Henry Ball) met the French frigate *Prudente* with its prize off Natal. The prize escaped, but the *Prudente* was battered into surrender in an hour; the ship was so badly damaged that it was not worth repairing. (James 2.357–359; Clowes 4.520)

Daedalus and Fox at Kosseir, Egypt, 14–17 August 1799
The frigates *Daedalus* and *Fox* (Capt. Henry Ball and Cmdr Henry Stuart) bombarded the fort at Kosseir on the Egyptian Red Sea coast for three days, and attempted several times to land a force, but were always beaten off by the French garrison. (James 2.338–339; Clowes 4.406; Parkinson 152)

Daedalus and others v. Dutch brig, 21 August 1800
The frigate *Daedalus* (Capt. Henry Ball), along with three other ships, captured a Dutch brig (16) in the East Indies. (Clowes 4.560)

Dainty and others v. Italian submarines, 27–29 June 1940
Five British destroyers, *Dainty*, *Defender*, *Ilex*, *Decoy*, and *Voyager*, searched for Italian submarines in the area of Crete, sinking *Lilizzi*, *Uebi Scelebi*, *Argonauta*, and *Robina*, while *Sulpa* was damaged. (Rohwer 30)

DAKAR, West Africa, July–September 1940
A British attack on the French ships in Dakar on 7–8 July 1940 damaged the battleship *Richelieu*. An expedition of a substantial British force of ships and troops was sent to land Free French forces at Dakar (September). The Vichy French governor and garrison resisted, first fighting back against a

heavy bombardment and then beating off an attempted landing. The battleships *Resolution* and *Barham* and the destroyers *Inglefield* and *Foresight* were damaged by shellfire and torpedoes. The Vichy submarine *Pensee* was sunk, and the destroyer *L'Audacieux* driven ashore by fire from the cruiser HMAS *Australia*. The operation was marked by general incompetence at all command levels. (A. Marder, *Operation Menace and the Dudley North Affair*, Oxford 1976; Rohwer 32, 42)

Dal Riada (Argyll), Scotland
719 The first recorded battle at sea in British waters was between two rivals for the kingship of Dal Riada on 6 October. Neither the size of the forces involved nor the result are known. (J. Bannerman, *Studies in the History of Dalriada*, Edinburgh 1974, 152–154; J. Haywood, *Dark Age Naval Power*, 2nd edn, Hockwold-cum-Wilton 1999, 91)

986–989 Godfrey Haraldsson, king of the Isles, raided Dal Riada, was defeated, and went on to sack the monastery at Iona. Three years later, he was killed while again raiding in the kingdom. (Hudson 62; Maund 158)

Damaon, India, 7–8 October 1625
A Portuguese squadron blockaded two EIC ships at Surat. Three more EIC ships arrived, but sheered off and were attacked near Damaon; all survived, but damaged. One, *Lion*, had been boarded and could only get rid of the boarders on the poop by blowing up that part of the ship. The others, *Palsgrave* and *Dolphin*, escaped. (Clowes 2.45)

Danae v. *Sans Quartier*, 4 April 1799
The brig *Sans Quartier* (14) was captured by *Danae* (20) off the coast of France. (Clowes 4.556)

Danzig, Prussia, April–May 1806
The French siege of Danzig attracted a group of British sloops which could operate in the shallow waters. The sloop *Sally* (Cmdr Edward Chetham) sailed up the Vistula River to bombard French troops on Holm Island to assist the besieged city beyond, but was driven back by fire from French troops on the island. A month later, the sloop *Dauntless* (Cmdr Christopher Strachey) attempted to run a supply of powder into the city, but a change of wind trapped her, and the ship was run aground and surrendered. (James 4.196–198)

Daphne v. French ships, 22 December 1794
The sloop *Daphne* (20; Capt. William Cracraft) was captured in the Bay of Biscay by two French ships, part of the main French fleet. She was retaken two days later. (James 1.261–262; Clowes 1.261–262)

Daphne and others v. Danish convoy, 23 April 1808
A Danish convoy off Fladstrand, Denmark, was attacked by boats from *Daphne* (22; Capt. Francis Mason), *Tartarus* (18; Cmdr William Russell), and

Forward (12; Lt David Shiels). The ships of the convoy were captured, despite heavy fire from the shore. (James 4.320–321; Clowes 5.413)

Daphne v. *Acertif*, August 1808
The sloop *Daphne* (22) captured the Dutch brig *Acertif* (8) in the Baltic. (Clowes 5.565)

Daphne v. slave dhow, 1874
The screw sloop *Daphne* captured a slave dhow in the Indian Ocean; of 300 slaves on board when the dhow left Zanzibar only fifty were still alive. (Lloyd 194)

DARDANELLES
1807   A squadron of eight line-of-battle ships, two frigates, and two bombs, commanded by Vice-Admiral Sir John Duckworth, was sent to enforce British and Russian demands on the Ottoman Empire. In running the Dardanelles on 19 February the fleet was fired at from the forts and was challenged by an Ottoman squadron of one line-of-battle ship, three frigates, and four corvettes. Most of these were destroyed by a detached force of three line-of-battle ships and a frigate commanded by Rear-Admiral Sir Sidney Smith; a party landed to storm a fort. Even with the British squadron in the Sea of Marmara the Turks proved defiant, and it returned through the Dardanelles on 3 March, again being bombarded. Casualties in the fleet were almost fifty killed and nearly 300 wounded. One ship, *Ajax* (74; Capt. Hon. Henry Blackwood), was destroyed by an accidental fire. (James 4.216–321; Clowes 5.219–230)

1914–1916 (DARDANELLES Expedition)   An Allied squadron blockading the Dardanelles bombarded the Turkish forts guarding the entrance to the Strait on 3 November 1914. A campaign for a major naval force to break through the Dardanelles to Constantinople began with the bombardment of the forts on both sides of the Strait, and landings to complete the destruction of forts and batteries. The Turks used mobile artillery to reply, notably against the minesweeping trawlers; as a result the minefields remained largely intact. The naval bombardment was intermittent, as battleships retired to re-arm or the weather prevented action, and the Turks recovered in these intervals. Landings on 4 March at places on both coasts showed that the defences were still strong and active.

A new plan was formed, to force a way through with eighteen battleships and battle-cruisers, British and French. The forts and batteries were to be battered into submission, and the minefields were to be swept. The first part of the Strait was swept clear during the night before the attack, but a new minefield was laid. During the assault on 18 March four of the big ships struck mines, first the French *Bouvet*, then the battle-cruisers *Inflexible* and *Irresistible* and the battleship *Ocean*. All four were lost. The naval force was then withdrawn. On 25 April landings were made on the southern and western shores of the Gallipoli Peninsula, covered by units of the French and British fleets. The delay since the naval attack enabled the Turks to organise their defences, and the landings were opposed very strongly. They were successful in getting the troops on shore, but then became stuck on or near the beaches. A new landing was made by British forces at Suvla, covered by naval forces, but again the advance inland was quickly blocked. The failure to advance finally persuaded the commanders to order evacuation. All three bridgeheads were successfully evacuated, largely as a result of careful naval planning; on 19–20 December at the Suvla and Anzac areas, and on 8–9 January 1916 at Cape Helles. Casualties in the evacuation were nil. (Corbett 1.363–364, 2.140–183, 213–258, 3.84–100; Halpern, *Naval History* 64, 109–124; Massie 426–502)

Dar-es-Salaam, Tanganyika
1914 The light cruiser *Astraea* came out of Zanzibar and bombarded the German radio station at Dar-es-Salaam on 5 August; the Germans sank a floating dock to block the entrance to the port. To prevent replenishment of the German light cruiser *Königsberg*, which was in the Rufiji delta, small craft at Dar-es-Salaam were destroyed by the battleship *Goliath* and the cruiser *Fox* on 28 November. The German governor's residence was shelled. (Corbett 1.154, 2.236–237)

1964 A mutiny of the Tanganyika Rifles in January was put down by British troops and sailors; the carrier *Centaur* sent aircraft to attack them, and laid down gunfire as a diversion. (Wettern 230)

Darién, Panama, 1698–1700
A Scottish expedition went to establish a colony and free trade centre at Darien on the Isthmus of Panama. Much of the liquid wealth of Scotland was invested in the venture, organised by the Company of Scotland. The first settlers soon gave up, and a second group was driven off by a Spanish force led by the governor of Cartagena. No support was available from King William III, as he had made quite clear from the start. (J. Prebble, *The Darien Disaster*, London 1968)

***Daring* v. *Rubis*, 27 January 1813**
Daring (12) encountered *Rubis* (40) off West Africa, ran aground in escaping, and was burnt by her crew to prevent her capture. (Clowes 5.519)

***Daring* v. *U-23*, 18 February 1940**
The convoy HN-13 (Britain to Norway) survived an attack by U-boats, but the destroyer *Daring* was sunk by *U-23*. (Rohwer 15)

***Darkdale* v. *U-68*, 22 October 1941**
The naval tanker *Darkdale* was sunk by *U-68* near Ascension Island. (Rohwer 108)

***Dart* and others v. Dutch gunboats, October 1799**
A group of five ships and brigs headed by *Dart* (28) cut out four gunboats and three vessels on the Dutch coast. (Clowes 4.560)

Dart and Wolverine v. Mary, 1–2 December 1806
The Liverpool slaver *Mary* (24) was attacked by *Dart* (28; Cmdr Joseph Spear) and *Wolverine* (18; Cmdr Francis Collier) by mistake. The fighting lasted seven hours and only when *Mary* was boarded was she discovered to be a British ship. Most of the casualties were slaves on *Mary*. (Clowes 5.394)

Dartmouth v. French warships, 4 February 1695
The frigate *Dartmouth* (40; Capt. Roger Vaughan) was beaten into surrender by two French ships, each of which was equal to her in strength. (Clowes 2.484)

Dartmouth and others v. Demir Hissar, 16 April 1915
The Turkish TB *Demir Hissar* attempted to sink the troop transport *Minstrel* near Skyros, and was then chased by the cruiser *Dartmouth* (Capt. J. D'Arcy) and the destroyers *Kennet* and *Wear*. Between them they trapped the TB in the Chios Channel; she went ashore and was wrecked. (Corbett 2.300–301)

Dartmouth and Weymouth v. Austrian squadron, 29 December 1915
The light cruisers *Dartmouth* and *Weymouth* were part of an Allied force which attempted to intercept an Austrian force which had raided Durazzo. The Austrians escaped during a long chase. (Newbolt 4.106–119; Halpern, *Naval History* 156–157)

Darwin, Australia, 20 January 1942
The Japanese submarine *I-124* was sunk by the Australian minesweepers *Deloraine*, *Lithgow*, and *Katoomba* and the US destroyer *Edsall*. (Rohwer 135)

Deale Castle v. French ship, 3 July 1706
Deale Castle (24) was captured by a French ship off Dunkirk. (Clowes 2.537)

Decouverte v. French schooners, 7–9 February 1808
The schooner *Decouverte* (8; Lt. Colin Campbell), off St Domingue, chased two schooners with their prize. One schooner turned away and escaped; the second and the prize went ashore, and the prize was burnt. Two days later a third schooner, *Dorade*, was chased and captured. (James 4.305–306; Clowes 5.405)

Decoy v. French ship, 22 May 1814
The brig *Decoy* (10) was captured by a French ship in the English Channel. (Clowes 5.555)

Dedeagatch, Bulgaria, 21 October 1915
Monitors bombarded the railway, barracks, and bridges at the Bulgarian port of Dedeagatch. (Corbett 3.173–174)

Deerness, Scotland, c.1030
Jarl Thorfinn of Orkney with a small fleet was attacked at Deerness by a

larger fleet led by his enemy Karl Hundisson. Thorfinn had the victory in a hard-fought battle. (*Orkneyinga Saga* 20)

Defiance v. Embuscade, 12 April 1746
Defiance (69) captured the French *Embuscade* (40). (Clowes 3.315)

Defiance v. Venganza and Marte, 28 May 1762
Defiance (69) captured the Spanish shops *Venganza* (26) and *Marte* (18) at Mariel, Cuba. (Clowes 3.317)

Defiance v. Dutch brig, 1782
The brig *Defiance* (12) captured a Dutch brig in the North Sea. (Clowes 3.116)

Delaware River, September–November 1777
A British expedition against Philadelphia was delayed by obstructions placed in the Delaware River and fortifications on both banks. A squadron under Capt. Andrew Hamond steadily worked to remove both. An attack by land and sea on Fort Mifflin on 22 October led to *Augusta* (64; Capt. Francis Reynolds) and *Merlin* (16; Cmdr Samuel Reeve) running aground, where *Augusta* blew up and *Merlin* was burnt. In November *Vigilant* (20; Lt Hugh Christian) towed a floating battery past the fort, which was then evacuated by the Americans and the river opened to British use. A rebel vessel of 28 guns was captured and renamed *Delaware*. (Clowes 3.391–392)

Delight at Reggio, 30 January 1808
The sloop *Delight* (Capt. Philip Handfield) attempted to recover four Sicilian gunboats taken by the French and grounded under the batteries at Reggio in Calabria. *Delight* was unsuccessful, the captain was killed, and the ship was destroyed by its crew before it could be captured. (James 4.294; Clowes 5.245)

Demerara v. Grand Décide, 14 July 1804
Demerara (6) was captured by the privateer *Grand Décide* in the West Indies. (Clowes 5.549)

Denia, Spain, August–October 1812
The British ship *Fame* bombarded the fort at Denia, then evacuated the inhabitants of nearby Xabia to escape French reprisals. Denia was attacked again in October, but the attempt to take the fort failed. (Hall 185)

Deptford v. two French ships, 4 February 1667
Deptford (10; Capt. Marle Pearce) met four French ships in the Channel; two left at once; of the others a large merchantman (6) was captured, and *Deptford* forced the fourth, a warship (8), away in a fight lasting some time. (Clowes 2.433)

Deptford v. French privateers, October–November 1692
Deptford (50; Capt. William Kerr) captured a French privateer (22) in

November 1691, the *Fortune* privateer (24) in the Channel in October 1692, and in November, with *Portsmouth* (32; Capt. Charles Britiff), the *Hyacinthe* privateer. (Clowes 2.466, 469)

Derby v. Angria's squadron, 1735
The EIC Indiaman *Derby*, with a cargo of treasure and military stores, was captured without resistance by four grabs out of Suvarnadrug. (Keay 264)

Derry (Londonderry), North Ireland
1212–1214   Ruari, son of Ranald, and Thomas of Galloway raided Derry by sea for plunder. In 1214 Thomas raided Derry again, and then constructed a castle at Coleraine to control the local area. This was all part of the English extension of control in north Ireland. (MacDonald 150; Oram 116–117)

1600   Sir Henry Docwra took a small squadron and a force of soldiers to land at Derry on 15 May. The garrison threatened the rebellious province, and a force of ships disputed control of the local waters with the galleys of Ulster and the Isles. (Rodger 1.291)

1689   Londonderry was threatened by the forces of King James II. In April *Swallow* (Capt. Woolfran Cornwall) escorted a dozen transports carrying two regiments to reinforce the garrison, but the city's governor, Lt-Col. Lundy, decided the city would fall and ordered the ships to retire; he went with them. *Greyhound* (16; Capt. Thomas Gwilliam) sailed into Lough Foyle to investigate the situation. Off Culmore she exchanged bombardments with the fort, with some success, but ran aground on retiring, and was heavily bombarded from the shore, suffering considerable damage, before getting out of the lough next day. The city held out, and on 28 July a relieving squadron broke the Jacobite boom in an evening attack. While *Dartmouth* (Capt. John Leake) bombarded the fort, *Mountjoy* (Master, Micaiah Browning) broke the boom and, along with two victualling ships, reached the city. (Powley 92–94, 221–223, 246–250; Clowes 2.331; Childs 74–75, 113–114, 133–135)

Desirade Island, Guadeloupe, 22 February 1692
The English West Indies squadron, five line-of-battle ships and two armed merchantmen commanded by Capt. Ralph Wrenn, escorting a convoy from Barbados to Jamaica, was attacked by a French force of eighteen line-of-battle ships under Capt. Comte de la Roche-Courbon-Blenac; Wrenn conducted such a good defence that he lost neither warships nor any of the convoy. (Clowes 2.466–468)

Desiree and others in the Elbe, November 1813–January 1814
The frigate *Desiree* (36; Capt. Arthur Farquhar) headed a group of smaller vessels based at Heligoland in operations in the Elbe, Ems, and Weser rivers, in co-operation with Russian and Swedish forces, particularly at Cuxhaven and Gluckstadt. (James 6.6; *NC* 5.175–176)

Despatch v. *Présidente*, 27 September 1806
The French frigate *Présidente* (40) met a squadron commanded by Rear-

Admiral Sir Thomas Louis, which set out in chase. The sloop *Despatch* (Capt. Edward Hawkins) maintained a running fight with *Présidente* for an hour until the rest of the squadron came up, whereupon *Présidente* surrendered. (James 4.178–179; Clowes 5.391)

Déterminée v. French corvette, 25 July 1801
The sloop *Déterminée* captured a French corvette off Alexandria. (Clowes 4.558)

Devonshire v. Etoile, 21 June 1747
The French *Etoile* (46), escorting five merchantmen, was driven ashore at Cape Finisterre, Spain, by *Devonshire* (66; Rear-Admiral Peter Warren), and burnt. (Clowes 3.283; NRS, *Rodney* 1.211)

Devonshire v. Atlantis, 22 November 1941
Guided by radio intercept, the cruiser *Devonshire* surprised and sank the German auxiliary cruiser *Atlantis* near Ascension Island. The crew were rescued by *U-126*. (Rohwer 117; Hore 259; Sebag-Montefiore 202–204)

Dexterous v. Gunboat no. 4, 11 October 1805
Dexterous (4) captured the Spanish *Gunboat no. 4* off Gibraltar. (Clowes 5.562)

Diadem v. Arrogante, 30 July 1806
Diadem (64; Capt. Sir Home Popham) captured the Spanish *Arrogante* off Montevideo. (Clowes 5.563)

Diadem and others v. Speerbrecher 7, 12 August 1944
The cruiser *Diadem*, with two destroyers, attacked and sank *Speerbrecher 7* near La Rochelle in the Bay of Biscay. (Rohwer 347)

Diadem and Mauritius v. German destroyer squadron, 28 January 1945
The cruisers *Diadem* and *Mauritius* attacked three German destroyers off Bergen, Norway; one of the destroyers was damaged. (Rohwer 391)

Diamond and Cygnet v. French squadron, 20 September 1693
Diamond (48; Capt. Henry Wickham) was defeated and captured by the French squadron in the West Indies, together with *Cygnet* (8); Capt. Wickham was punished for his conduct with imprisonment for life. (Clowes 2.448, 535)

Diamond v. two storeships, 23 October 1740
Diamond (40) captured two Spanish storeships in the West Indies. (Clowes 3.314)

Diamond v. Amaranthe, 31 December 1796
Diamond (38; Capt. Sir Richard Strachan) captured the sloop *Amaranthe* near Alderney. (Clowes 4.555)

Diamond v. Infanta Don Carlos, December 1804
Diamond (38) captured the Spanish sloop *Infanta Don Carlos* (16). (Clowes 5.562)

Diamond Rock, Martinique, January 1804
Diamond Rock overlooks the passage to Martinique and dominates Marin Bay. Capt. Samuel Hood arranged a landing on the rock, and despite its height and steep sides had guns, ammunition, and supplies placed on its summit, which was then garrisoned. The rock was then registered as the sloop HMS *Diamond Rock*. (James 3.244–245; Clowes 5.332–333; *NC* 3.144–150)

Diana and Pique v. Diligencia, December 1804
Diana (38) and *Pique* (40) captured the Spanish ship *Diligencia* (28) near Altavela. (Clowes 5.562)

Diana v. Vlieg and Zephyr, August–September 1809
The brig *Diana* (10; Lt William Kempthorne) captured the Dutch brig *Vlieg* (6) near Java on 6 August; on 10–11 September she manoeuvred for two days to bring the Dutch brig *Zephyr* (14) to action, and finally, near the fort of Monado in Celebes, succeeded. After an hour's fighting, and when she was about to receive assistance from some gunboats, under threat of being boarded, *Zephyr* surrendered. (James 5.43–45)

Diana, Niobe, and others v. Amazone and Eliza, 12–28 November 1810
The French frigates *Amazone* and *Eliza* sailed from Cherbourg and were followed by the frigates *Diana* (Capt. Charles Grant) and *Niobe* (Capt. John Loring). The French ships took refuge under battery protection at La Hougue, but *Eliza* was damaged. *Diana* attacked *Amazone* without effect. *Donegal* (74; Capt. Pulteney Malcolm) and *Revenge* (74; Capt. Hon. Charles Paget) were brought in by *Niobe*, but an attack by all four ships, and a rocket attack, failed. *Amazone* got away to Le Havre; *Eliza* was refloated and avoided a bomb attack, but on 23 December a boat party sent from *Diana* destroyed her. (James 5.106–108)

Dictator and others v. Nayaden and others, 6 July 1812
Off Mardoe, Norway, *Dictator* (64; Capt. James Stewart), with the sloops *Calypso* (Cmdr Henry Weir) and *Podargus* (Cmdr William Robilliard) and the brig *Flamer* (Lt Thomas England), chased a Danish flotilla, consisting of the frigate *Nayaden*, three brigs, and several gunboats, into Lyngoe Creek. The British ships followed and battered *Nayaden* to a wreck; two brigs, *Laaland* (20) and *Kiel* (18), were captured, but were driven aground by Danish gunboats on the way out. (James 5.325–327; Clowes 5.510–511; Anderson 346)

Dictator v. Danish lugger, August 1812
Dictator (64) captured the Danish *Lugger no. 28* in a boat attack. (Clowes 5.566)

Dido v. Téméraire, March 1795
Dido (28) captured the French cutter *Téméraire* (20) in the Mediterranean. (Clowes 4.553)

Dido and Lowestoffe v. Minerve and Artémise, 24 June 1795
The frigates *Dido* (28; Capt. George Towry) and *Lowestoffe* (32; Capt. Robert Middleton) encountered two French frigates, *Minerve* (40) and *Artémise* (36), near Minorca. At first the French ships sailed away, but they then turned to fight. *Dido* was attacked by *Minerve*; after they fired at each other, *Minerve* attempted to ram, but her attempts to board were thwarted. They resumed firing until another collision disabled *Dido*. *Lowestoffe* joined in and brought down *Minerve*'s masts. *Artémise* took little part and was chased away by *Lowestoffe*, which returned to batter *Minerve* to surrender. (James 1.321–324; Clowes 4.492–493)

Dido v. Borneo pirates, May 1843
Dido (18; Capt. Hon. Henry Keppel), in alliance with the locally powerful James Brooke, raided settlements in Borneo identified as pirate bases; at least three towns were destroyed. (Clowes 6.323–324)

Dido and others at Assab, 10 June 1941
An Indian battalion was landed at the port of Assab in Eritrea by the cruiser *Dido*, the AMC *Charleston*, and two sloops. This had been the last Italian-controlled harbour on the Red Sea. (Roskill 1.426; Rohwer 78)

Digby's squadron v. French convoy, 23 March 1780
A squadron of fifteen line-of-battle ships under Rear-Admiral Hon. Robert Digby, returning from Gibraltar, encountered a French convoy off Brittany; the French warship *Protée* (64) was forced to surrender by *Resolution* (74) and *Bedford* (74) after a hard fight. The convoy scattered, but three of the transports were captured; a large sum of money was taken in *Protée*. (Syrett, *European*, 92–93; Mackesy, *America* 323; Clowes 4.50)

Diligent at Machias, Maine, 15 July 1775
The schooner *Diligent* (Lt John Knight) was seized by the people of Machias while visiting the town. (Clowes 4.3)

Diligent v. Providence, 7 May 1779
Diligent (12; Lt Thomas Walbeoff) fought the rebel American brig *Providence* (14). The contest was very uneven, but *Diligent* fought for three hours; she gave in when half her crew were casualties. (Clowes 4.26)

Diomede and Québec v. South Carolina, 20 December 1782
The rebel American frigate *South Carolina* (40) was chased by three British ships, of which *Diomede* (54; Capt. Thomas Frederick) came close enough to fight her; *South Carolina* eventually surrendered when the other British ships came up. (Clowes 4.91)

***Dispatch* v. *Tyrannicide*, 12 July 1776**
The sloop *Dispatch* was captured by the rebel American privateer *Tyrannicide*. (Colledge 108)

Dodecanese Islands, Aegean Sea
1940 Two British cruisers and two destroyers shelled Scarpanto on 3–4 September 1940; the Italian TB *MAS-537* was sunk by the destroyer *Ilex*. The cruiser *Orion* shelled Padagia, and Stamphalia was shelled on 2 October. Planes from the carriers *Eagle* and *Illustrious* bombed Leros on 13–14 October; the cruiser *Liverpool* was damaged by an Italian aircraft. Rhodes and Leros were raided from *Illustrious* on 26 November, and Rhodes and Stamphalia on 16 December. (Rohwer 38, 43, 50, 52)

1942–1943 A British force shelled Rhodes on 15 March 1942. The German TB *TA-12* was damaged by the destroyer *Eclipse* off Rhodes on 22 August 1943, and later destroyed by an air attack. (Rohwer 153, 267)

1943 After the surrender of Italy on 1 September German forces seized Rhodes, while British troops took control of Kos, Samos, and other islands, and were then attacked by German forces, who were well supported from the air. German troops captured Kos on 3 October, but another force coming to the island was annihilated by the cruisers *Sirius* and *Penelope* and the destroyers *Faulknor* and *Fury* on 5 October. The submarine *Unruly* sank the German minelayer *Bulgaria*. The destroyers *Intrepid* and *Panther* were sunk, and the cruiser *Carlisle* badly damaged in air attacks. The destroyers *Echo* and *Intrepid* sank the submarine chaser *UJ-2104*, and the destroyer *Eclipse* damaged the TB *TA-10*, later scuttled. The British and Italian forces on Leros were attacked by the German 22nd Infantry Division who landed on 10 November. British destroyers shelled targets on Leros, but the German attack succeeded and the Allied forces surrendered on 16 November. The destroyers *Hursley* and *Miaoulis* (Greek) sank the submarine chaser *UJ-2109* on 16–17 October. The cruiser *Aurora* bombarded Rhodes on 20 October. In attempts to supply Leros the destroyers *Hurworth* and *Eclipse* were mined and sunk on 22 and 24 October. The destroyers *Penn* and *Pathfinder* sank the submarine-trap *GA-45* on 7 November, but the destroyer *Dulverton* was sunk and *Rockwood* badly damaged. Samos and the other islands surrendered soon after. (S. Roskill, *Churchill and the Admirals*, London 1977, 218–221; Rohwer 273, 278, 281)

1944–1945 The cruiser *Ajax* shelled Rhodes on 2–3 May 1944 and the destroyer *Kimberley* bombarded Alimnia on 12 November; the cruiser *Aurora* and three destroyers bombarded Rhodes on 4 December. The destroyer *Liddesdale* supported landings on the island of Piscopi on 2 March 1945. The destroyers *Kimberley* and *Catterick* and the Greek destroyer *Kriti* bombarded Rhodes. (Rohwer 322, 372, 396)

Dogger Bank, North Sea
1665 A convoy of merchant ships laden with naval stores and escorted

by an English warship was captured entire by the Dutch fleet on 20 May. (Clowes 2.258; Rodger 2.71)

1781 (Battle of DOGGER BANK) A Dutch convoy out of the Texel, escorted by eight warships, met a British convoy heading for the Baltic escorted by seven ships commanded by Admiral Hyde Parker. The escorts battered at each other at point-blank range for nearly four hours on 5 August; one Dutch ship sank next day. Each side claimed victory. Since the Dutch ships returned to the Texel and the British convoy went on to its destination, the advantage was to the British. (Syrett, *European* 130–131; Clowes 3.504–509; Tunstall 152–154)

1915 (Battle of DOGGER BANK) The German battle-cruiser squadron was intercepted by British battle-cruisers under Admiral David Beatty in an elaborate trap on 24 January. The British knew of the German sortie from intercepted radio messages. The German cruiser *Kolberg* exchanged shots with the cruiser *Aurora*, and the whole German force turned for home. Beatty's squadron chased, and having a higher speed, caught up with and began shelling the German ships. The German cruiser *Blucher* was sunk; one battle-cruiser on each side was badly damaged, *Seydlitz* and *Lion*. The Germans otherwise escaped the British trap. (Corbett 2.82–102; Halpern, *Naval History* 44–47; Massie 375–410)

Dolphin v. Barbary pirates, Sardinia, 22 January 1617
The armed merchantman *Dolphin* (Capt. Edward Nicholls) was attacked by five Barbary ships one at a time. Three times boarded, *Dolphin* each time fought off her attackers, who eventually retired defeated. (Clowes 2.49–50)

Dolphin v. French privateer, July 1693
Dolphin (26; Capt. Thomas Kercher) defeated a French privateer of 24 guns, and recovered its prize. (Clowes 2.472)

Dolphin v. French privateer, August 1757
Dolphin (24) captured a French privateer (12), which was taken into the navy and renamed *Dolphin's Prize*. (Colledge 113)

Dolphin v. *Incomprehensivel*, December 1836
The brigantine *Dolphin* (3) captured the Brazilian slaver *Incomprehensivel* in mid-Atlantic. (Bethell 127)

Dolphin v. *Firme*, 30 May 1841
Two boats from the brigantine *Dolphin* (3; Lt Edward Littlehales) went to cut out the slaver *Firme* near Whydah, West Africa. The sailors rowed for over two hours and then boarded the ship against opposition, but successfully. (Clowes 6.305)

Dolphin v. *Maria Teresa*, December 1843
The brigantine *Dolphin* (3) captured the Brazilian slaver *Maria Teresa* off Brazil. (Bethell 211)

Dominica, West Indies, June 1761
The British fleet in the West Indies, with troops brought from North America, attacked and captured Dominica; it surrendered on 8 June. (Clowes 3.233)

Dominica v. Manette, Dauphin, and Chiffonne, 2–4 October 1806
Boats from the brig *Dominica* (14) cut out the sloops *Manette* and *Dauphin* at St Pierre, Martinique on 2 October, and captured the schooner *Chiffonne* two days later. (Clowes 5.558)

Dominica v. Decatur, 5 August 1813
The schooner *Dominica* (Cmdr George Barrete) was boarded and captured by the privateer *Decatur* off the southern United States. *Dominica* lost eighteen men killed (including Barrete) and forty-seven wounded out of a crew of seventy-six. (James 6.74–75)

Doris v. Cygne, 7 May 1796
The frigate *Doris* (36) captured the cutter *Cygne* off the Scilly Isles. (Clowes 4.554)

Doris and others v. Ville de Lorient, 7 January 1797
The frigates *Doris*, *Unicorn*, and *Druid* captured the French frigate *Ville de Lorient* (36; *en flute*) off Ireland. (Clowes 4.558)

Doris v. Affronteur, 18 May 1803
On the first day of the new war, the frigate *Doris* (36; Capt. Richard Pearson) chased and captured the lugger *Affronteur* (14) off Ushant; *Affronteur* put up a very stubborn resistance, a quarter of her crew becoming casualties. (James 3.179; Clowes 5.314–315)

Doris v. Gunboat no. 360, 29 April 1804
The French *Gunboat no. 360* was captured by a boat party from the frigate *Doris* (36) in Audierne Bay. (Clowes 5.556)

Doris on the Syrian coast, December 1914–January 1915
The cruiser *Doris* raided and bombarded along the coast of Syria, paying particular attention to the railways in Cilicia. (Corbett 2.74–77; Halpern, *Naval History* 107)

Dorothy Gray and Garry v. U-18, 23 November 1914
The trawler *Dorothy Gray* saw *U-18* off Hoxa, Orkney Islands, and forced her to dive so hurriedly that she was damaged; later the submarine surfaced and the crew surrendered to the destroyer *Garry*. (Corbett 2.15)

Dorsetshire v. Raisonnable, 29 May 1758
Dorsetshire (70; Capt. Peter Denis) went in chase of *Raisonnable* (64) and had battered her into a wreck when *Achilles* (60; Capt. Hon. Samuel Barrington) came up; this persuaded the French ship to surrender. (Clowes 3.299)

Dorsetshire v. *Python*, 1 December 1941
The cruiser *Dorsetshire*, guided by an Ultra intercept, surprised the U-boat supply ship *Python* in the South Atlantic. *Python* was scuttled, and the crew were rescued by *U-A* (which attacked *Dorsetshire* unsuccessfully) and *U-68*, and later by five other submarines. (Rohwer 120; Sebag-Montefiore 204–206)

Douglas and others v. *U-732*, 31 October 1943
U-732 was sunk by the destroyer *Douglas* and the trawlers *Imperialist* and *Loch Osaig* near Gibraltar. (Rohwer 284)

Dove v. Rochefort squadron, 5 August 1805
The cutter *Dove* (6) was captured by a French squadron from Rochefort. (Clowes 5.550)

Dover v. *Lion Eveille*, January 1693
Dover (48; Capt. Edward Whitaker) captured the privateer *Lion Eveille*. (Clowes 2.472)

Dover v. *Comte de Toulouse*, January 1703
Dover (50; Capt. Nicholas Trevanion) met, fought, and captured the privateer *Comte de Toulouse* off Scilly. The fight lasted six hours; the privateer carried 300 French soldiers, many of whom were casualties. (Clowes 2.504)

Dover v. *Bien Aimé*, 1707
Dover (48; Capt. Thomas Mathews) captured the French warship *Bien Aimé* (26). (Clowes 2.515)

Dover v. *Renommee*, 13 September 1747
Dover (50) met *Renommée*, already badly damaged after a fight with *Amazon*, and captured her. (Clowes 3.284)

Dover v. *Los Magellanes*, 12 March 1797
Dover (44) captured the Spanish ship *Los Magellanes* (4) off the Portuguese coast. (Clowes 4.560)

Dover v. *Rembang* and *Hoop*, 6 February 1810
Dover (8) captured the Dutch ships *Rembang* (18) and *Hoop* (10) in the East Indies. (Clowes 5.564)

Dover Castle and *Karapara* v. *UC-67*, 26 May 1916
The hospital ships *Dover Castle* and *Karapara* were attacked by *UC-67* off Algeria. *Dover Castle* was sunk, though the patients were mostly saved. The U-boat commander was tried after the war for this war crime, but was acquitted when he pleaded superior orders. (Halpern, *Mediterranean* 318; Newbolt 4.309–310)

Downpatrick, North Ireland, 941
A raid was made on Downpatrick by a group of Vikings, evidently from the Hebrides. (Oram 9)

Dragon v. Algerines, May 1671
Dragon (38; Capt. Arthur Herbert) met and fought two Algerine ships. The fighting lasted for three days, but the Algerines finally escaped. (Clowes 2.440)

Dragon v. privateers, 25 September 1672
Dragon (38; Capt. Thomas Chamberlayne) was attacked by two privateers near Berry Head, Devon. The first was disabled by broadsides at the beginning of the fight; the second was sunk. (Clowes 2.445)

Dragon and *Endymion* v. *Colombe*, 18 June 1803
The French corvette *Colombe*, without guns, was captured by *Dragon* (74) and *Endymion* (44) off Ushant. (Clowes 5.316)

Drake in South America, 1578
Having traversed the Strait of Magellan, Francis Drake in *Pelican* raided along the South American coast. Valparaiso was plundered and a ship captured, and ships were taken at Arica and Callao. Off Cape San Francisco he captured *Nuestra Senora de la Concepcion*, alias *Cacafuega*, carrying 26 tons of silver; the silver was taken and the ship and crew released; *Pelican* was renamed *Golden Hind*. The town of Gualulco in Mexico was raided and burnt. Drake sailed on to California and to his circumnavigation. English investors in the voyage were paid a dividend of 4700 per cent. (Rodger 1.243–245; Clowes 1.631–632; Williamson 188–190)

Drake v. *Ranger*, 24 April 1778
The rebel American ship *Ranger* (18; Capt. John Paul Jones) met *Drake* (20; Capt. George, Burdon) at the entrance to Belfast Lough. *Ranger* deliberately waited for *Drake* to come out into open water, and as *Drake* closed, Jones identified himself and opened fire, mainly at *Drake*'s masts and sails, hoping to capture the ship. The fighting lasted about an hour, then *Drake* surrendered, having lost almost all its sails and masts. Jury-rigged that night, she was taken to Brest as prize. (S.E. Morison, *John Paul Jones*, New York 1959, 156–163; Clowes 4.12–13)

Drake at Trinite, Martinique, 19–24 February 1804
The sloop *Drake* (Lt William King) sent boats in to attack two brigs and a schooner under a fort at Trinite, Martinique. The ships were taken, but only the schooner could be brought out; five days later King took in a party which captured the fort and spiked its guns. On 14 March *Drake* attacked a French schooner and her prize near Guadeloupe; the prize ran aground and the schooner escaped. A second prize ship appeared and was retaken; her boats then seized the first prize, which blew up. (James 3.254–255, 257; Clowes 4.339–340)

Drake v. *U-79*, 2 October 1917
The cruiser *Drake*, returning to port after escorting a convoy, was torpedoed by *U-79* off Rathlin Island. Despite receiving much assistance, the ship eventually capsized and sank. (Newbolt 5.162)

Dreadnaught and *Grampus* v. *Medée*, 27 April 1744
Medée (26), off the Portuguese coast, was captured by *Dreadnaught* (50; Capt. Hon. Edward Boscawen) and *Grampus* (40). (Clowes 3.274)

Dreadnaught v. French sloop, 1748
Dreadnaught (50) captured a French sloop which was renamed *Dreadnought Prize* when taken into the navy. (Colledge 116)

Dreadnaught and *Assistance* v. *Palmier*, 2 September 1758
Dreadnaught (60; Capt. Maurice Suckling) came up with *Palmier* (74), but was dismasted in the fight before *Assistance* (50; Capt. John Wellard) could reach her. *Palmier* sailed away. (Clowes 3.300)

Dreadnaught at Ushant, 7 September 1810
Vice-Admiral Thomas Sotheby in *Dreadnaught* (98; Capt. Valentine Collard) sent in boats to capture the Spanish ship *Maria Antonia*, a French prize at Ushant. Having taken the ship, however, the captors were attacked from the cliff above the harbour by heavy fire, suffering over forty casualties. (James 5.102–103; Clowes 5.470–471)

Dreadnaught v. *U-29*, 18 March 1915
U-29 launched an attack on the Grand Fleet off the Orkney Islands; in reply the battleship *Dreadnaught* (Capt. W.J.S. Alderson) rammed and sank her. (Corbett 2.281; Grant 23)

Druid v. *Raleigh*, 4 September 1777
Druid (14; Cmdr Peter Carteret), one of the escort of a British convoy from the Leeward Islands, was attacked by surprise by the rebel American frigate *Raleigh* (32). *Druid* was very badly damaged (and Carteret killed), but other warships with the convoy turned to her assistance, and *Raleigh* fled. (Clowes 4.7–8)

Druid v. *Basque*, 13 November 1809
Druid (32; Capt. Sir William Bolton) captured the French sloop *Basque* (16). (Clowes 5.559)

Druid v. *Destimado*, March 1831
The frigate *Druid* (46) captured the Portuguese slaver *Destimado*, but it was released because the Anglo-Brazilian court had no jurisdiction. (Bethell 135)

Dryad v. *Abeille*, 2 May 1796
The frigate *Dryad* (36; Capt. John Pulling) captured the French corvette *Abeille* (14). (Clowes 4.498)

Dryad v. *Proserpine*, 13 June 1796
The frigate *Dryad* (36; Capt. Lord Amelius Beauclerk) met, chased, and fought the French frigate *Proserpine* (40), which surrendered. (James 1.369–370; Clowes 4.499; *NC* 1.11)

Dryad v. French brig, 23 December 1812
The frigate *Dryad* (36; Capt. Edward Galway) attacked a French brig (22) off the Ile d'Yeu and drove her on shore. (Clowes 5.561)

Duala, German Cameroon, September 1914
The Cameroon River estuary leading to Duala was surveyed and cleared of obstacles by the gunboat *Dwarf*. A landing was made on 26 September on a branch of the estuary, and next day the town and its environs were surrendered. The light cruisers *Cumberland* and *Challenger* had covered operations. (Corbett 1.267–277)

Duala, French Cameroons, 7–9 October 1940
A small force was landed at Duala in order to establish a Free French regime there. (Rohwer 43)

Dublin, Ireland
875 Halfdan, one of the Danish Great Army leaders in England, attacked Dublin; Eystein, king in the city, died in the fighting, but Halfdan was soon driven out again. (Smyth, *Warlords* 194)

1036 Echmarach, king of Galloway and Man, captured Dublin in alliance with Domchad, king of Munster. Presumably he arrived by sea. (Hudson 134–135)

1091 Godred Crovan, king of the Isles and Man, led a fleet into the Liffey and captured Dublin. (Hudson 178)

1102 King Magnus of Norway, Orkney, and the Isles made a second expedition into the Irish Sea and seized control of Dublin. (Hudson 194)

Dublin Bay
1405 A Scottish privateering force led by Thomas MacCulloch raided ports in Ulster. The ships were cornered and defeated in Dublin Bay. (R.C. Patterson, *My Wound is Deep*, Edinburgh 1997, 36)

1690 A squadron of ships under Sir Cloudisley Shovell raided the French ships in Dublin Bay on 17 April and seized or destroyed them; later *Fripon* (18) was captured. (Clowes 2.463; Aubrey 46)

Dublin v. U-4, 9 June 1915
The cruiser *Dublin*, with a strong destroyer escort, on a high-speed search for Austrian surface craft in the Adriatic, was torpedoed by the Austrian submarine *U-4*. *Dublin* survived, though badly damaged. (Halpern *Mediteranean* 146)

Duc de Chartres v. Aigle, 1 September 1782
The *Duc de Chartres* (18; Cmdr John Child Purvis) captured *Aigle* (22) off the American coast. (Clowes 4.86; Gordon 3–4)

Duckworth v. U-339 and U-1169, 26 and 29 March 1945
The destroyer *Duckworth* sank *U-339* and *U-1169* off the Lizard. (Rohwer 397)

Dudley's fleet v. Breton pirates, 21 August 1537.
Two Breton ships, hovering off St Helen's awaiting English ships to capture, were instead themselves captured by English ships of the royal fleet under John Dudley. (Loades 118)

***Duke* v. Spanish galleys, St Tropez, June 1742**
Five Spanish galleys were blockaded in the French port of St Tropez by *Oxford* (50; Capt. Richard Norris) and the fireship *Duke* (Cmdr Smith Callis). The galleys fired on the British ships, so Norris sent *Duke* in to destroy them; all five galleys were burnt. (Clowes 3.273)

***Duke of Albany* v. *UB-27*, 26 August 1916**
The armed boarding steamer *Duke of Albany* was sunk by *UB-27* in the North Sea. (Colledge 118)

***Duke of York* and others v. German convoys, 4 October 1944**
The Home Fleet, headed by the battleship *Duke of York*, and including a US contingent, raided two German convoys at Bodo in Norway; eleven ships were sunk or damaged. (Rohwer 280)

***Dumbarton Castle* v. French privateers, 1705**
The Scots Navy ship *Dumbarton Castle* captured several small French privateers during its patrol off western Scotland. (Lavery 25)

***Dumbarton Castle* v. French privateers, 26 April 1708**
The former Scots (now Royal) Navy ship *Dumbarton Castle* (28; Capt. Campbell) was captured by French privateers off Waterford, Ireland. (Lavery 70; Colledge 118)

Dunamonde fort, Gulf of Riga, 15 October 1919
The fort at Dunamonde, occupied by German forces, was bombarded by the destroyer *Abdiel* and stormed by local Lettish forces. (Bennett 176–180)

Dunaverty, Scotland, summer 1306
Believing that the fugitive King Robert Bruce was at Dunaverty, Kintyre, an English force sailed there and laid siege to the castle. Bruce was no longer there, and the besiegers found the local population hostile. The castle was taken in September. (Barrow, *Robert Bruce*, 232; Rodger 1.86; MacDonald 173)

Dunaverty, Scotland, 1494
King James IV of Scots, using a new fleet built in the Firth of Clyde, captured Dunaverty castle from the MacDonalds of Islay. They retook it almost at once. (Rodger 1.167; Nicholson 543; MacDougall 104–105)

Duncan's squadron v. *Suffisante* and *Victorieuse*, 31 August 1795
The French sloops *Suffisante* and *Victorieuse*, cruising off the Texel, were captured by Admiral Duncan's squadron. (Clowes 4.93)

Duncan v. Hypolite, September 1805
The frigate *Duncan* (38; Lt Clement Sneyd) drove the French brig *Hypolite* (4) ashore. (Clowes 5.557)

Dunedin v. U-124, 24 November 1941
The cruiser *Dunedin* encountered *U-124* in the South Atlantic, and was sunk. (Rohwer 118; S. Gill, *Blood in the Sea: HMS Dunedin and the Enigma Code*, London 2003)

DUNGENESS, 30 November 1652
A great Dutch fleet, commanded by Admiral Tromp, escorting a huge convoy, was attacked by the English fleet under Robert Blake off Dungeness. The English were heavily outnumbered, though only a section of each fleet was engaged. Five English ships were lost, but only one Dutch, and the Dutch convoy ran through the Channel in safety. (Clowes 2.172–174; Powell 185–190; Rodger 2.15)

Dunivaig, Scotland, 1614
A royal expedition was mounted to suppress the operations of the MacDonalds of Islay. Some of the MacDonalds' galleys were destroyed; Dunivaig Castle was taken. (Rodger 1.350)

Dunkirk v. Le Hocquart, 15 November 1705
Dunkirk (48) captured the French privateer *Le Hocquart*, which became the Royal Navy ship *Dunkirk Prize* (24). (Colledge 119)

Dunkirk Prize v. French ship, 18 October 1708
Dunkirk Prize (24; Cmdr George Purvis) chased a French 14-gun ship, but ran aground on the coast of St Domingue. Even then, with his ship a wreck, Purvis captured his opponent. (Clowes 2.518)

Dunraven v. UC-71, 8 August 1917
The Q-ship *Dunraven* (Cmdr Campbell) was attacked by *UC-71* west of Ushant. The submarine was very wary, and was able to so damage *Dunraven* that the ship had to be abandoned. (Newbolt 5.107–109)

Dunvegan Castle v. U-46, 28 August 1940
The AMC *Dunvegan Castle* was sunk by *U-46* west of Ireland. (Rohwer 35)

Durazzo, Albania, 2 October 1918
Durazzo, under Austrian occupation, was bombarded by an Allied force of Italian, British, Australian, and US ships. Some houses were damaged and a merchant ship sunk; the three Austrian destroyers in the harbour were not seriously damaged. The cruiser *Weymouth* was torpedoed by *U-31*. For entirely separate reasons, Durazzo was evacuated by the Austrians nine days later. (Halpern, *Naval History* 175–176; Halpern, *Mediterranean* 556–566)

Dursley Galley v. Spanish *guarda costa*, 1728
A Spanish *guarda costa* on the Spanish Main demanded to search the *Dursley Galley*, and when ignored, fired. The British ship replied, and after a short fight the Spanish ship surrendered. It was soon released. (Clowes 3.263)

Dutch East Indies (Indonesia), 1942–1945
The Dutch East Indies were invaded by the Japanese in 1942. The Japanese submarine *I-60* was sunk by the destroyer *Jupiter* in the Sunda Strait on 17 January. Refugee convoys from Singapore were attacked by Japanese forces in February, and the gunboat *Scorpion* and several transports were sunk. At the Japanese invasion of Palembang the RAN cruiser *Hobart* was damaged and the gunboats *Dragonfly* and *Grasshopper* were sunk. The destroyer *Stronghold* was sunk by a Japanese force of a cruiser and two destroyers in a one-hour fight near Java on 2 March.

British forces returned to the attack in 1944. The Eastern Fleet raided on Surabaya on 17 May, and the carriers *Illustrious* and *Atheling* raided Sabang on 10–13 June and 15 July, sinking a minelayer and a ship, and Port Blair in the Andaman Islands on 19 June. The submarine *Terrapin* shelled Japanese positions on Nias Island, near Sumatra. The Eastern Fleet raided Padang on 24 August, Sigli on Sumatra on 17 September, and other Sumatran targets on 20 November. A British task force of two carriers, three cruisers, and seven destroyers attacked sites in Sumatra by air attack on 17 and 20 December and 4 January 1945.

The new British Pacific Fleet, on its way from Trincomalee to Fremantle, raided Sumatran targets on 24 and 29 January 1945. The Eastern Fleet shelled Sabang and mounted air attacks and reconnaissance over Sumatran and Malayan ports. The cruiser *Ashigara* and the destroyer *Kamikaze*, sailing from Singapore to Batavia, fought the British submarines *Trenchant* and *Stygian* on 8 June. *Trenchant* sank *Ashigara*; *Kamikaze* survived. Naval air attacks were made on airfields in North Sumatra on 10 July and the Kra Isthmus on 24 July. The carrier *Ameer* was damaged by a kamikaze attack on 26 July, and the minesweeper *Vestal* sunk.

Australian ships were the scenes of the surrender of the various Japanese forces in the Dutch East Indies between 9 and 21 September.
See also: **Java Sea, Strait of Malacca**

Dutch Guiana, 22 April–2 May 1796
Demerara, Essiquibo, and Berbice were taken by an expedition led by *Malabar* (54; Capt. Thomas Parr) with 1200 soldiers. A Dutch ship, *Thetis* (24), and a cutter were captured, as were several laden merchantmen. (James 1.409–410; Clowes 4.291)

Dwarf at Ubean Island, East Indies, December 1868
Pirates from Ubean island, Sulu Sea, attacked a schooner, killing three of the crew. *Dwarf* (Lt Charles Walker) retaliated by burning their villages. (Clowes 7.224)

E

E-1 v. *Aachen*, 1 July 1915
The submarine *E-1* sank the German auxiliary ship *Aachen* off Gotland in the Baltic. (Corbett 3.63)

E-1 v. *Moltke*, 19 August 1915
The submarine *E-1* torpedoed the German battle-cruiser *Moltke*, which was attempting to penetrate the defences of the Gulf of Riga. The expedition was abandoned, the Germans having had many other ships damaged by other means. (Corbett 3.136–137)

E-3 v. *U-27*, 18 October 1914
The submarine *E-3*, on patrol off the Ems estuary, was sunk by a torpedo from *U-27*. (Corbett 1.212)

E-7 in the Sea of Marmara, 15–22 June 1915
The submarine *E-7* bombarded shore installations in the Sea of Marmara, including trains, powder mills, and railway tracks. (Corbett 3.76–8)

E-7 v. *UB-14*, 5 September 1915
The submarine *E-7* was caught in nets in the Dardanelles, and was then destroyed by *UB-14*. (Colledge 121)

E-8 v. *Prinz Adalbert*, 22 October 1916
The submarine *E-8* (Lt-Cmdr F.H.H. Goodhart), off Libau, torpedoed and sank the German cruiser *Prinz Adalbert*. (Newbolt 4.95–6)

E-9 v. *Hela*, 12 September 1914
The submarine *E-9* (Lt-Cmdr Max Horton) sank the German light cruiser *Hela* south of Heligoland. (Corbett 1.165–6)

E-9 v. *S-116*, 6 October 1914
The submarine *E-9* (Lt-Cmdr Max Horton) sank the German destroyer *S-116* off the Ems estuary. (Corbett 1.191)

E-9 v. German convoy, May–June 1915
The submarine *E-9* attacked a convoy escorted by cruisers and destroyers off Libau, sinking one transport ship. On 4 June she sank a collier and damaged the destroyer *S-148* as she was refuelling off Dagerort. On 2 July she was in the path of a German squadron near Libau and torpedoed the cruiser *Prinz Adalbert*, which was damaged. (Corbett 3.61–63)

E-11 in the Sea of Marmara, 23 May–7 June 1915
The submarine *E-11*, in the Sea of Marmara, sank a gunboat and sank or

drove ashore seven other ships transporting troops or ammunition for the Turkish army. (Corbett 3.32–5)

E-11, *E-14*, and *E-2* in the Sea of Marmara, August–September 1915
The Turkish gunboat *Berc-i-Satvet* was chased by the submarine *E-11* for some distance on 6 August, and was then torpedoed, going ashore at Silivri. *E-11* and *E-14* then lay in wait off Bulair, and shelled Turkish troops on the coast road on 7 and 8 August. This did not stop the soldiers, and the submarines were soon driven to submerge by return fire from a field gun. *E-11* sank the Turkish battleship *Barbarossa Khair-ed-din*, conveying munitions to the Gallipoli peninsula, with considerable losses of Turkish troops. From 9 August to 12 September *E-11* and *E-2* crossed and recrossed the Sea of Marmara, bombarding targets on shore and sinking ships where they could be found. (Corbett 3.100–101, 114–119)

E-11 v. *Yar Hissar*, 3 December 1915
The submarine *E-11* in the Sea of Marmara torpedoed and sank the Turkish destroyer *Yar Hissar*. (Corbett 3.217–218)

E-12 in the Sea of Marmara, June–September 1915
The submarine *E-12* in the Sea of Marmara stopped a Turkish steamer on 6 June, which had a concealed gun. The steamer was sunk in the subsequent fight. In September *E-12* shelled shore installations and sank ships; one gunboat was attacked but escaped. (Corbett 3.75–76, 167–168)

E-13 v. *G-132*, 19 August 1915
The submarine *E-13* ran immovably aground on Saltholm Island, Denmark. Despite the presence of Danish gunboats, the German destroyer *G-132* torpedoed the submarine and fired at the escaping submariners, until prevented by a Danish ship. (Corbett 3.135–136)

E-14 in the Sea of Marmara, 27 April–1 May 1915
The submarine *E-14* passed through the Dardanelles on 27 April, attacking a gunboat on the way. In the Sea of Marmara she damaged a transport and sank another gunboat. On 10 May she torpedoed the transport *Gul Djemal*, carrying artillery and 6000 Turkish soldiers. The transport may have sunk. (Corbett 2.375, 3.27)

E-14 and *Ben-My-Chree* v. Turkish transport, 8 and 11 August 1915
A large Turkish transport was torpedoed by the submarine *E-14* and ran itself on shore at Bulair. Four days later the seaplane carrier *Ben-My-Chree* sent a seaplane against the transport, which succeeded in striking the ship with a torpedo. This was the first successful aerial torpedo attack. (Corbett 3.101–102)

E-15 v. Turkish destroyer, 17 April 1915
The submarine *E-15* attempted to run the Dardanelles, but went aground and was shelled by a Turkish destroyer. Two boats from the battleships *Triumph*

and *Majestic* finally succeeded in destroying the submarine. (Corbett 2.302–305)

E-16 v. *V-188* and others, 25–26 July 1915
The British submarine *E-16* (Cmdr C.P. Talbot) was caught in a trap off Borkum Island and, as she struggled to get free, was bombed from a Zeppelin. Having freed herself she met three German destroyers, one of which, *V-188*, was sunk; attacks on the others failed. (Corbett 2.60)

E-16 v. *U-6*, 15 September 1915
U-6 was attacking ships off Stavanger, Norway; she was sunk by the submarine *E-16*. (Corbett 3.128)

E-16 v. German auxiliary, 22 December 1915
The submarine *E-16* sank a German naval auxiliary ship in the German Bight. (Corbett 3.263)

E-19 v. *Undine*, 7 November 1916
The submarine *E-19* (Lt-Cmdr F.N. Cromie) encountered the German cruiser *Undine*, with a single destroyer as escort, in the western Baltic. The cruiser was torpedoed and sunk. (Newbolt 4.97–98)

E-20 v. *UB-14*, 5 November 1915
E-20 (Lt-Cmdr C.H. Warren) in the Sea of Marmara had arranged a rendezvous with the French submarine *Turquoise*, but that boat had been captured and the rendezvous revealed. *UB-14* torpedoed *E-20* while on the surface. (Corbett 3.179, 205–206)

E-22 v. *UB-18*, 25 April 1916
The submarine *E-22* (Lt Herbert) was attacked and sunk by *UB-18* in the North Sea. (Corbett 3.309n)

E-23 v. *Westfalen*, 19 August 1916
The German High Seas Fleet, returning to harbour after an abortive cruise in the North Sea, was shadowed by the submarine *E-23* (Lt-Cmdr R.R. Turner), which torpedoed the battleship *Westfalen*, though the ship survived. (Newbolt 4.37)

E-34 v. *UB-16*, 10 May 1918
The submarine *E-34* sank *UB-16* in the North Sea. (Newbolt 5.428; Grant 122)

E-35 v. *U-154*, 11 May 1918
The submarine *E-35* sank *U-154* in the Atlantic Ocean. (Newbolt 5.428; Grant 119)

E-38 v. *München*, 19 October 1916
The British submarine *E-38* (Lt-Cmdr J. de B. Jessop) encountered the

German High Seas Fleet in the North Sea; the light cruiser *München* was torpedoed. (Newbolt 4.50–51)

E-40 and *Watchman* v. *Pantera*, 24 July 1919

The Soviet Russian submarine *Pantera* attacked the British submarine *E-40* outside Kronstadt; its torpedoes missed, as did those of *E-40* in retaliation. The destroyer *Watchman* attacked with depth-charges; *Pantera* survived and returned to Kronstadt. (Bennett 131–132)

E-42 v. *Moltke*, 24 April 1918

The German High Seas Fleet was attacked by the submarine *E-42*, which torpedoed the battleship *Moltke*, though she did not sink. (Newbolt 5.238)

E-45 v. *UC-62*, 19 October 1917

The submarine *E-45* sank *UC-62* in the southern North Sea. (Newbolt 5.426)

E-52 v. *UC-63*, 1 November 1917

The submarine *E-52* torpedoed and sank *UC-63* near Dover. (Newbolt 5.426)

E-54 v. *UC-10*, 21 August 1916

UC-10, returning from a cruise, was torpedoed and sunk by *E-54* at the Schouwen Bank in the North Sea. (Grant 37)

E-54 v. *U-81*, 1 May 1917

The submarine *E-54* sank *U-81* in the eastern Atlantic. (Newbolt 5.424; Grant 48)

Eagle in the Western Channel, 1746–1747

Eagle (60; Capt. George Rodney) cruised in the Western Channel against privateers, capturing ten in the course of the year, sometimes in company with other British ships. (NRS, *Rodney* 1.15–16)

Eagle v. *Duc d'Aquitaine*, 31 May 1757

Eagle (60; Capt. Hugh Palliser) met and fought the French Indiaman *Duc d'Aquitaine* (50) in the Bay of Biscay; the French ship was reduced to a near wreck before she surrendered. (Clowes 3.295)

Eagle v. Italian squadron, 2 April 1941

Aircraft from the carrier *Eagle* attacked an Italian squadron of four destroyers off Port Sudan, Red Sea, sinking *Manin* and *Sauro*. The others were scattered. (Rohwer 66)

Eaglet v. French squadron, Jersey, June 1666

The ketch *Eaglet* (Capt. Stephen Sartaine) was chased by six French warships and took refuge under the batteries on Jersey, where she fought off a cutting-out attack by boats. (Clowes 2.428)

Earls Godwine and Harold return, 1052
Earl Godwine and his son Earl Harold were driven into exile, the first to Flanders, the second to Dublin. They returned, each with a fleet. Godwine was driven away from Sussex by a combination of a storm and a threatening royal fleet. Harold landed at Porlock in Somerset. Both earls then joined up at the Isle of Wight. The royal fleet had been withdrawn to London, and Godwine took the joint fleet there. Just as a fight in the Pool of London was in prospect, King Edward the Confessor gave in, agreeing to restore the earls to all their positions. (*ASC* s.a. 1052)

Earnest v. *Fire Bredre* and *Makrel*, May 1809
Earnest (14) captured *Fire Bredre* (4) and *Makrel* (2), possibly privateers, in Wingo Sound, the Baltic. (Clowes 5.566)

Echo v. *Buonaparte*, 14–17 October 1799
The sloop *Echo* (Cmdr Robert Philpot) chased the brig *Buonaparte* into Langadille Bay, Puerto Rico. Next day boats went in to cut the ship out, but failed, though a Spanish ship was taken. Next night a second attempt succeeded. (James 2.400–401)

Echo v. *Hasard*, 1 October 1804
The sloop *Echo* captured the French sloop *Hasard* off Curacao. (Clowes 5.556)

Eclair v. *Grand Decide* and *Rose*, February–March 1804
The schooner *Eclair* (12; Lt William Carr) met the privateer *Grand Décide* (22) near Tortola. The two ships fired at each other for an hour, and then the privateer sailed away. A month later *Eclair*'s cutter attacked the privateer *Rose*, anchored under batteries off Guadeloupe. The twelve men in the cutter stormed the privateer and defeated the forty-nine men of the crew. (James 3.248–249; Clowes 5.335–336, 339–340)

King Edgar on the River Dee, 973
King Edgar of England loaded a collection of subject kings from around the Irish Sea on his ship on the River Dee at Chester; it is said that the kings rowed and Edgar was steersman and captain, but the story may be only a symbolic representation of Edgar's overlordship. (*ASC* s.a. 973; J. Pullen-Appleby, *English Sea Power c.871 to 1100*, Hockwold-cum-Wilton 2005, 58–60)

Edinburgh and others v. *Bellone*, 1747
Edinburgh, *Eagle*, and *Nottingham* encountered *Bellone* (36) out of Nantes. *Bellone* was captured and taken into the navy as *Bellona*. (Clowes 3.284)

Egeria v. *Aalborg*, 2 March 1809
The sloop *Egeria* captured the Danish sloop *Aalborg* (6). (Clowes 5.565)

Egersund, Norway, 13–14 October 1940
A British destroyer force attacked German shipping at Egersund. The German netlayer *Genua* was sunk. (Rohwer 30)

Egmont v. Wild Cat, 14 July 1779
The schooner *Egmont* (10; Lt John Gardiner), on the Grand Banks of Newfoundland, was captured by the rebel American brig *Wild Cat* (14) by boarding. (Clowes 4.27–28)

Egmont v. Nemesis and Sardine, 9 March 1796
The French ships *Nemesis* (28) and *Sardine* (22) were captured by *Egmont* (74) off Tunis. (Clowes 4.554)

Egypt, July–September 1882
After the occupation of Alexandria, a Naval Brigade was formed from ships of the Mediterranean fleet, and operated to keep the Egyptian army away from the city. Ships of the fleet, with another Naval Brigade, gained control of the Suez Canal and assisted in the campaign which led to the capture of Cairo. (Clowes 7.337–346)

Egyptienne v. Epervier, 27 July 1803
The frigate *Egyptienne* (40) captured the French brig *Epervier* (16) in the Atlantic. (Clowes 5.324)

Egyptienne v. Acteon, 2 October 1805
The frigate *Egyptienne* (40) captured the French brig *Actéon* (16) off Rochefort. (Clowes 5.557)

Egyptienne v. Libre, 24 December 1805
The frigate *Egyptienne* (40; Lt Philip Handfield) encountered the French frigate *Libre* off Rochefort, and chased her, assisted by the frigate *Loire* (Capt. Frederick Maitland). *Egyptienne* ran close to the French ship and soon forced its surrender. (James 4.76–77; Clowes 5.372)

Egyptienne v. Alcide, 8 March 1806
The frigate *Egyptienne* (40; Capt. Hon. Charles Paget) sent boats into Muros, Spain, to attack the privateer *Alcide*, which was moored there. This was executed successfully. (James 4.129; Clowes 5.373)

EIC first voyage, 1602
Under James Lancaster four ships were dispatched to India and the east. During the voyage one Portuguese ship was captured and looted; otherwise the voyage was peaceful. All four ships returned successfully. (Foster 156–157)

EIC convoy v. Pourvoyeuse, 9 September 1782
The French brig *Pourvoyeuse* (14) attacked a fleet of merchantmen, which

included four Indiamen, in the Strait of Malacca, but was driven off. (Clowes 4.89)

EIC fleet v. Mogul ships, 1688–1690
The governor of Bombay, Sir John Child, embarked on a war with the Mogul Empire. The EIC fleet captured Mogul ships in the Persian Gulf, at Bombay, and at sea. In reply the Mogul army landed at Bombay Island, captured the town, and besieged the castle. The EIC eventually submitted to the emperor Aurangzeb, under humiliating conditions. (Low 1.73–77; Keay 144–147)

Elba
1797 Capt. Horatio Nelson oversaw the evacuation of troops and stores from Porto Ferraio, Elba on 27 January 1797. (James 1.344–345; Hore, *Seapower* 57–59)

1944 A fleet of small craft collected in Corsica landed a force on Elba on 17 June, which captured the island. (Rohwer 336–337; Roskill 3.2.79–82)

Electra **v.** *Diligente,* **December 1838–March 1839**
The sloop *Electra* (18) captured the slavers *Diligente*, *Carolina*, and *Especulador*. (Bethell 149)

Elephant **v.** *Duguay-Trouin* **and** *Guerrière,* **24 July 1803**
Duguay-Trouin (74) and the frigate *Guerrière* came out of Cap François, St Domingue, to try to reach Europe. *Elephant* (74; Capt. George Dundas) chased, but failed to catch *Duguay-Trouin*, and suffered some damage; the presence of *Guerrière* deterred further attempts. (James 3.185–187; Clowes 5.321–323)

Eliza **v.** *Diableto* **and** *Firme Union,* **22 December 1822**
The Spanish schooner *Diableto*, accompanied by the felucca *Firme Union*, came into conflict with the British sloop *Eliza* at Guajara, Cuba. *Diableto* and *Eliza* fought, then *Firme Union* intervened, but was boarded and taken by *Eliza*'s crew. The schooner, a pirate, escaped. (James 6.269–270; Clowes 6.234)

Elizabeth **and** *Nonsuch* **v. Dutch ship, July 1649**
A Dutch ship of 30 guns, laden with silk, was captured by the Parliamentary ships *Elizabeth* and *Nonsuch*. (Powell 84)

Elizabeth **v. French squadron, Arabian Sea, 11 October 1692**
The EIC ship *Elizabeth* was intercepted by a squadron of four French ships on its way to Bombay, and was captured. (Low 1.77)

Elizabeth **and** *Chatham* **v.** *Jason* **and others, 12 November 1704**
Elizabeth (70; Capt. William Cross) and *Chatham* (48; Capt. Robert Bokenham) were attacked by *Jason* (54), *Auguste* (54), and *Valeur* (26); *Chatham* fought off the attack by *Auguste*, but *Elizabeth* did not fight well

against *Jason*, and was taken. Cross was dismissed the service. (Clowes 2.506–507; Owen 120)

Eltham and *Lively* v. Spanish squadron, 12 October 1742

Eltham (40; Capt. Edward Smith) and *Lively* (20; Cmdr Henry Stewart) met the survivors of a Spanish squadron carrying reinforcements to Cartagena which had been damaged by a hurricane. Badly battered in the fight which followed, the three Spanish ships got away to Puerto Rico. They suffered 600 casualties. (Clowes 3.272–273)

Emden, Germany, March 1758

The city of Emden was besieged by French and Austrian forces. The siege was raised in part by the actions of *Seahorse* (24) and the fireship *Strombolo* (8) sent in by Commodore Charles Holmes. (Clowes 3.190)

Emerald and *Flora* v. *Havfru*, 24 December 1799

The frigates *Emerald* (32) and *Flora* (36) tried to inspect a Danish convoy in the Strait of Gibraltar but *Havfru* (40) fired on the boats, so preventing the inspection. (Anderson 301; Clowes 4.427)

Emerald v. *Enfant Prodigue*, 24 June 1803

The sloop *Enfant Prodigue* was captured by *Emerald* (36) off St Lucia, West Indies. (Clowes 5.555)

Emerald v. *Mosambique*, 13 March 1804

The frigate *Emerald* (Capt. James O'Bryen) found the French schooner *Mosambique* at anchor off the Pearl Rock, Martinique. The sloop *Fort Diamond* was sent in and captured the schooner. (James 3.255–256; Clowes 5.340)

Emerald v. *Apropos*, 13 March 1808

The frigate *Emerald* (Capt. Frederick Maitland) sent boats into Vivero harbour, Spain, in quest of the large French schooner *Apropos*. It was necessary first to attack two forts, one of which was captured, by which time *Apropos* had been run aground; it was set on fire, and soon exploded, causing nine deaths and fifteen wounded amongst the British attackers. (James 4.311–312)

Emerald v. *Incomparable* and *Fanfaron*, October 1809

The French brig *Incomparable* (8) was captured off Ireland by the frigate *Emerald* (36), which, a month later, also captured the French sloop *Fanfaron* (16) near Guadeloupe. (Clowes 5.559)

Empress of Britain v. *U-32*, 26–28 October 1940

The luxury liner *Empress of Britain*, used as a troop transport, was located by a German Condor aircraft northwest of Ireland, and hit by two bombs. Set ablaze, the liner did not sink. *U-32* was directed to the site when the ship was being towed, under escort of two destroyers, and sank her with two torpedoes. *U-32* was itself sunk two days later in an encounter with the destroyers *Harvester* and *Highlander*. (Terraine 269; Rohwer 46)

Enchantress v. Corallo, 13 December 1942
The Italian submarine *Corallo* was sunk by the sloop *Enchantress*. (Rohwer 216)

Endymion v. San Antonio, May 1798
The Spanish packet *San Antonio* was captured by the frigate *Endymion* off Ireland. (Clowes 4.560)

Endymion v. Bacchante and Adour, June–July 1803
The frigate *Endymion* (Capt. Hon. Charles Paget) met, chased, fought, and captured the corvette *Bacchante*, and on 16 June she captured the French sloop *Adour* (22), in the Atlantic. (James 3.180; Clowes 5.556)

Endymion and Loire at Corcubion, Spain, 9 April 1809
The frigate *Loire* brought muskets for the use of Spanish guerrillas, and was joined by *Endymion* in landing them at Corcubion, Galicia. When French forces attacked the town, *Endymion* went into the harbour to assist the defence. She was trapped by a change in the wind, and only just escaped before the French assault. (Hall 139–140)

Endymion v. Prince de Neufchatel, 9 October 1814
The frigate *Endymion* (Capt. Henry Hope) sent boats to attack the US privateer *Prince de Neufchatel* off Nantucket. The privateer resisted fiercely, inflicting and receiving heavy casualties, and capturing the launch and its crew. (James 6.237–238; Clowes 6.157)

Endymion v. President, 15 January 1815
The US frigate *President* came out of New York and encountered the British blockading squadron. The frigate *Endymion* (Capt. Henry Hope) chased and fought her. The two separated, *Endymion* to repair sails and rigging. *President* surrendered when two other ships, *Tenedos* and *Pomone*, arrived. (James 6.238–246; Clowes 6.166–169; *NC* 5.267–272)

ENGLISH CHANNEL

King Athelstan
In 939, in support of his protégé Louis d'Outremer as king of the Franks, Athelstan sent his fleet to ravage the French coast. (*ASC* s.a. 939)

The Norman Invasion, 1066
The campaign which brought William the Conqueror to the English throne began with a Channel crossing. Harold II held his fleet together on the English side as long as possible, and William had to wait for a change in the wind before he could cross from Dieppe to land at Pevensey. By that time Harold's fleet had dispersed and he was fighting in Yorkshire. (*ASC*, s.a. 1066)

The Norman Succession, 1088–1105
1088 Robert of Normandy claimed the English kingship and attempted to

invade the country with a scratch fleet. This was blocked by English ships mobilised by William II, and Robert failed to make a landing in England. (F. Barlow, *William Rufus*, London 1983, 74–75, 80)

1100 Robert claimed the English kingship, which had been seized by his brother Henry I. He collected a fleet at Treport, and, evading Henry's ships at Pevensey, landed at Portsmouth. He marched to Winchester but was outwitted by Henry in the subsequent negotiations

1105 Five years later Robert broke his agreement with Henry I, who took his army across the Channel, landing near Bayeux, and defeated Robert at Tinchebrai, after which the Norman Empire was reunited. Robert was imprisoned at Cardiff until his death. (D. Carpenter, *The Struggle for Mastery*, London 2003, 134–138)

The English Succession, 1137–1139
1137 King Stephen, having seized the English throne, sailed to Normandy to claim the duchy as well. He landed without opposition, and gained control of much of Normandy, though with some awkward exceptions, but he was unable to maintain his hold

1139 Stephen's rival for the kingship, the Empress Matilda, landed at Arundel with noble supporters and 140 knights. This was intended to be the beginning of the easy capture of the throne from Stephen, but the king soon compelled her to move to Bristol (in rebellion against him). (R.H.C. Davis, *King Stephen*, 2nd edn, London 1977, 27–29, 39–40)

Brittany, 1156
The exiled Count of Brittany, Conan IV, sailed from England to recover his county from his stepfather Eudo of Porhoet. Conan was probably supported in his expedition by King Henry II, along with English soldiers. It was successful. (J. Le Patourel, *The Norman Empire*, Oxford 1976, 111n)

The War for Normandy, 1212–1230
1212 King John's naval commander, Geoffrey de Lucy, raided French shipping in the Seine estuary and at Fecamp, then burnt Dieppe

1230 King Henry III sent an expedition which landed at St Malo, with the aim of recapturing Normandy and Poitou. The campaign failed. (Clowes 1.179, 194)

The Early Hundred Years' War, 1326–1346
1326 A preliminary period of tension between England and France led to an English fleet patrolling the Channel; many Norman ships were captured; Cherbourg was raided in September. (Clowes 1.228; Rodger 1.91)

1339 A large French galley fleet sailed to raid the Cinque Ports. Part of the force landed at Rye in July, but an English fleet immediately attacked the grounded ships, and the French Channel fleet across the Channel. Off Wissant a confrontation ended when the French ships got into harbour. An English fleet then raided along the French Channel coast at Ault, Treport, and Mers, then sailed round to attack Poitevin harbours. (Sumption 1.265–266; Clowes 1.247; Rodger 1.97)

1342 A small expedition commanded by Sir Walter Mauny landed near Brest in May. They raided the manor house at Trégonatec and captured several local lords. (Sumption 1.393–394; Clowes 1.259)

The Crecy War, 1346–1360

1346 King Edward III brought his fleet to make a landing at St Vaast-la-Hougue on 12 July, the beginning of the campaign which led to the victory at Crecy and the siege of Calais. There was no resistance to the English landing except for a brief attack by a small French force. Eleven ships were captured and burned on the beach. (Sumption 1.500–501; Clowes 1.263)

1356 An English fleet including several of the king's ships anchored off the Isle of Wight. It was attacked by a squadron of French galleys, and several of the English ships were captured and carried off. In reply on 2 and 18 June an expeditionary force commanded by Henry, Duke of Lancaster, landed at St Vaast. About 1300 men landed, and were joined by more from Brittany. All were mounted and campaigned through Normandy for the next month. (Clowes 1.236, 275; Sumption 1.164, 2.219–222)

1360 A French fleet raided Winchelsea, and in defence an English fleet was gathered, and drove the French off; then the English fleet landed an invasion force at Leure on the Seine estuary, where an old fort was quickly captured. An attack on Harfleur failed and the local population rallied and drove the invaders back to the river. The fighting was then stopped by news of peace. The ships evacuated both the raiders and the main English army. (Sumption 2.445, 448)

The Revived War, 1369–1379

1369 In July a squadron detached from the main English fleet at Sandwich investigated French invasion preparations and attacked several French ships in the Somme estuary and St Denis. Another English squadron went from Rye to assist a land campaign by John of Gaunt in October. The coasts of Picardy and northern Normandy were raided.

1373 The advanced force of an English expedition commanded by the Earl of Salisbury landed at St Malo in April; seven Castilian ships were captured and their crews killed. Raiding parties went to ports on the coast nearby, but a rapid French conquest of Brittany forced a cancellation of the main expedition; the advanced force was recalled.

1377 In June and September raids by a large French force under Jean de Vienne out of Harfleur resulted in the defeat of a small English force off Rottingdean. Rye, Lewes, Folkstone, Portsmouth, Dartmouth, Plymouth, Poole, and Hastings were raided or burnt; the French were repelled at Southampton, Dover, and Winchelsea.

1378 An English squadron under the Earls of Arundel and Salisbury sailed from Southampton. An attack on Harfleur failed against the strong walls and determined resistance of the town. Cherbourg was captured from its Navarrese garrison, but the French fleet under Jean de Vienne then blockaded the town and intercepted Arundel and his fleet as he came out. The French were victorious but the English ships escaped.

In August another English expedition, under John of Gaunt, sailed from the Solent to St Malo, achieving complete surprise. Several ships were captured. The army landed and besieged the town, which was relieved by French pressure. The English army re-embarked in September. Seamen from the Cinque Ports raided the French coast near Fecamp; one group found and recovered the bells of Rye church which had been taken in a French raid a year before. (Sumption 3.36–37, 42, 316, 324–325; Clowes 1.285–290; Rodger 1.111)

1379 An English fleet carried John de Montfort, exiled Duke of Brittany, to St Malo in July. A fleet of Castilian and French galleys came out to dispute a landing, but were forced back and took refuge in the harbour. This is one of the first sea battles in which ship-borne cannon were widely used; the galleys were beaten in part because the English had large ships and those ships had the wind and sea room for manoeuvre. (Sumption 3.362; Clowes 1.292; Rodger 1.112)

Henry IV's War, 1403–1407
1403 An English force cruised off Brittany in July, possibly trying to interrupt French communications with Wales during the revolt of Owain Glyn Dwr; it was attacked by a Breton naval force, which forced the surrender of forty English ships. In November an English squadron took an army of 6000 men to Brittany, burnt St Mathieu, and defeated a Breton force; the fleet scoured the Breton coast, destroying all the ships it could find.

1404 An English fleet raided along the coasts of Brittany and Picardy.

1406 A Spanish galley fleet raided the English coast, then was attacked off Calais by a superior English force, and took refuge in Gravelines until the English left.

1407 Henry IV threatened to take an army to France. An English fleet was met by a French fleet, and they fought; one French ship was captured. The king did not invade after all.

1408 The Earl of Kent took a force to Brittany, attacking the castle on Brehat Island. The castle was captured; Kent was killed. (Clowes 1.358–360, 366–368)

The Agincourt War, 1415–1417
1415–1416 Henry V gathered a fleet of 1400 ships to transport his army to France. The troops landed near Harfleur on 14 September, and laid siege to the town, while the ships blockaded the harbour; the town fell on the 22nd. The French replied with their own siege. An English fleet under the Duke of Bedford sent to attempt its relief met a French fleet, including eight Genoese carracks and eight galleys, in the Seine estuary. A day-long battle resulted in an English victory, with considerable loss to the French fleet.

1417 A large English fleet under the Earl of Huntingdon sailed from Southampton to attack French ships threatening Harfleur; on 25 July off Cap de la Heve, Normandy, four of the galleys of the Franco-Genoese fleet were captured. Henry V's army landed at Touques nearby a few days later. The Earl of Huntingdon commanded a squadron which patrolled in the Channel, and captured five Genoese carracks after a fight lasting several hours. (Clowes 1.373–380; Rodger 1.143–144; Rose 86–87; A. Byrne, *The Agincourt War*, London 1956, 36–47, 104–109; Barker 9)

The French Reconquest, 1436–1450

1440 Harfleur was under English siege; an English squadron blockaded the port and defeated French attempts at relief by sea. The town capitulated after four months

1450 The castle of Cherbourg was the last place in Normandy held by the English of the Hundred Years' War; its evacuation marked the extinction of the attempt to conquer France begun by Henry V in 1415. (Barker 284–286, 398–400; Clowes 1.383–384)

Henry VIII's Wars, 1522–1524, 1545–1546

1522–1523 The Earl of Surrey, commanding a joint English-Imperial fleet, raided Cherbourg and Morlaix, burning the latter town and seventeen ships. Next year the English fleet under Sir William FitzWilliam raided Treport, burning part of the town and some ships in the harbour, but was then driven off by local forces. (Loades 105–107; Clowes 1.444)

1544–1546 A French fleet of 150 ships and twenty-five galleys crossed the Channel in July 1545, raided Brighton, and sailed into the Solent. The English fleet of eighty ships retreated into Portsmouth harbour. No battle resulted though both sides made threats. The *Mary Rose*, one of the largest of the English ships, capsized and sank when caught by a fluke of the wind. The French and English fleets fought briefly off Shoreham on 15 August, without result. The English fleet raided Treport. Next year an English squadron of eight ships met a similar French squadron on 15 May; the French galley *Blanchard* was captured. (Rodger 1.182–185; Clowes 1.462–466; Loades 128–134, 137; M. Rule, 'The Sinking of the *Mary Rose*', *History Today* 32, 1982)

Queen Mary's War, 1557–1558

An English fleet under Lord William Howard met a squadron of four French ships off Dieppe in June 1557; two of the French ships were captured, seven more ships came out and the English were chased into Boulogne. When Elizabeth succeeded to the throne an English force of 7000 men was sent to France. It landed at Le Conquet near Brest in July, and burnt the village. It was then almost at once evacuated. (Loades 170–174; Rodger 1.192–194; Clowes 1.472–473)

Queen Elizabeth's First War, 1562–1563

English ships based at Le Havre sailed up the Seine in October 1562 to bring supplies to Huguenots besieged in Rouen. The galley *Brigandine* was lost in breaking the boom – though the supplies were landed – and the galley *Flower de Luce* was lost when the city fell. In 1563 the Huguenot party in France offered Le Havre and Dieppe to Elizabeth I in exchange for her help in the French civil war; these towns were occupied by English soldiers in October, but Dieppe was soon abandoned. The Huguenots were defeated and Le Havre was taken by the French in July 1563. (Rodger 1.198; Clowes 1.476–477; Loades 214–215; T. Glasgow, 'The Navy in the Le Havre Campaign, 1562–1564', *MM* 54, 1968)

The Spanish War, 1585–1604 (the Armada War)
See also: **Spanish Armada**

1591 An English expedition under Sir John Norris landed in Brittany in May to contest Spanish power. At first allied with a French Royalist force, it was soon withdrawn

1592 An English expedition assisted in the defence of Rouen against a Spanish attack, and four English pinnaces operated in the Seine, but Rouen fell to the Spanish attack

1594 A Spanish fort on the headland of Roscanvel, Brittany, threatened to block Brest and control its harbour, so providing a powerful Spanish base which would control the western approaches to the Channel. A force of English troops was landed on 7 November to co-operate with a French force. The English squadron bombarded the fort from the sea. The fort was then stormed and destroyed. (Rodger 1.275; Clowes 1.502–503; W. MacCaffrey, *Elizabeth I*, London 1993, 254–255)

Dutch Wars
See also: **Dungeness, Four Days' Fight, Portland**

War of the League of Augsburg, 1689–1697
1693 An expedition commanded by Capt. John Benbow bombarded St Malo from the sea. On 19 November a fireship was exploded by the town wall. A landing destroyed some of the defences and captured some prisoners.

1694 The Anglo-Dutch Channel fleet bombarded Le Havre from 16 to 19 June. The town was set on fire by bombs; the bomb vessel *Granado* (Capt. Thomas Willshaw) was hit by a shell from the shore and blew up. The fleet bombarded Dieppe between 9 and 14 July; an explosive fireship was sent against the pier. Some damage was caused, but neither the bombardment nor the French reply had much effect.

1695 An attack was made on St Malo using bomb vessels on 7 July, without success; one bomb, *Dreadful* (Capt. John Carleton), had to be burnt. An Anglo-Dutch fleet bombarded Granville next day, and the town was set on fire.

1696 At Calais on 17 August the ketch *Aldborough* (Capt. Robert Osbourne), bombarding the town, was sunk by French return fire. (Clowes 2.471–472, 476–478, 481–482, 487, 536)
See also: **Beachy Head, Barfleur and La Hougue, Torbay**

The Seven Years' War, 1756–1763
1756 Capt. Hon. Richard Howe in *Dunkirk* (60), commanding a squadron

in the Channel Islands, raided Grande Ile, off Granville, hoping to use it as a raiding base, but abandoned the idea as impractical. (Syrett, *Howe* 13)

1758 A series of raids was made on the French Channel coast in June, against St Malo – but the town was too well protected to be attacked – and Le Havre and Cherbourg. On 6 August an expedition commanded by Lt-General Thomas Bligh and Capt. Lord Howe landed 10,000 troops on the Cotentin Peninsula. Cherbourg was captured and military installations there were destroyed. The troops were then successfully re-embarked by the 16th. In September another landing was made near St Malo, and the landing force was attacked as it re-embarked. In the midst of all this *Renown* (32) captured the frigate *Guirlande* (22)

1759 A small squadron under Rear-Admiral George Rodney attacked boats gathered at Le Havre for an invasion of England. The town and the harbour were shelled and bombed for over two days, destroying many of the boats and much property. (Syrett, *Howe* 22; Clowes 3.192–195, 215–216; NRS, *Rodney* 1.567–571)

The Franco-Spanish fleet in the Channel, 1779–1782

1779 The Spanish fleet from Cadiz and the French fleet from Brest joined off Cape Finisterre on 27 June, and sailed for the Channel. The British Channel Fleet awaited their arrival near the Scilly Isles. The allied fleet came as far as the waters off Plymouth. The Channel Fleet, commanded by Admiral Sir Charles Hardy, was unable to reach them, but by the end of August the allied fleet had exhausted its supplies and went into Brest. *Ardent* (64) was captured when she blundered into the allied fleet, and the cutter *Active* (12) was captured by *Mutine* on 18 August

1781 The allied Franco-Spanish fleet, nineteen French and thirty Spanish ships, arrived again at the western end of the Channel, much to the surprise of the Admiralty. It had approached from the Atlantic to avoid detection. The ships were reported off the Scilly Islands to the British Channel Fleet under Vice-Admiral George Darby, who took his thirty ships into Torbay. The allied fleet soon turned away, unable to move up the Channel in the face of the awaiting British fleet, and returned to its bases

1782 For the third time in four years, the Franco-Spanish fleet, twenty-seven Spanish and five French line-of-battle ships, reached the western end of the Chanel. The aim was for eighteen Dutch ships to join as well. The Dutch did not move, but eight more French ships joined from Brest. On the way, the allied fleet captured a British convoy heading for Canada. The allies were confronted by the British Channel Fleet under Admiral Lord Howe, with twenty-five ships. He escaped their view by sailing west between the Scilly Isles and Land's End, and the allies' ignorance of his position paralysed them; then a gale drove the ships away. (Syrett, *European* 70–78; Clowes 3.443–447, 504, 539–540, 4.29–31; Mahan 402–403, 408; Tunstall 142)
See also: **Ushant**

The French Revolutionary War, 1793–1801
1795–1796 *Diamond* (38; Capt. Sir Sidney Smith) was active in harassing

French shipping in the Channel. On 2 September 1795 the French brig *Assemblé Nationale* was driven onto rocks on the Breton coast; on 18 March 1796 the port of Erqui was raided and eight ships burnt; on 17 April, in the Seine estuary, Smith took a boat party to capture the privateer lugger *Vengeur*. The captured lugger was attacked by boats from the shore and was retaken. Smith was captured in her, with about twenty of his men. (James 1.358–361; Clowes 4.493–496)

1798 The islands of St Marcouf, off the mouth of the Isigny River in Normandy, were garrisoned by the British to interrupt coastal trade. In April a squadron of French flatboats was intercepted while approaching these islands, and was driven back by the frigates *Diamond* and *Hydra* (Capts Sir Richard Strachan and Sir Francis Laforey). A larger force made a second attempt in May, but was beaten off by the guns of the islands' redoubts. (James 2.128–131; Clowes 4.339–341)

The invasion threat, 1803–1805
1803 The frigate *Immortalité* (Capt. Edward Owen), accompanied by three bombs, bombarded Dieppe harbour for several hours, aiming at the boats and the batteries. Part of the town was set on fire. *Immortalité*, with three bombs, then bombarded St Valéry harbour, where gunvessels were under construction. The frigate *Cerberus* (Capt. William Selby) and several smaller vessels, under the command of Rear-Admiral Sir James Saumarez, bombarded the town of Granville three times on 14 and 15 September 1803; a group of French gunboats was driven off when they attacked the briefly grounded *Cerberus*. (Clowes 5.50–51; James 3.230)

1804 A squadron of small ships commanded by Capt. Robert Oliver of the frigate *Melpomene* bombarded Le Havre in July and August to disrupt the gunboats gathered there; part of the town was set on fire. On 25 September, off the Seine estuary, the cutter *Georgiana* (Lt Joshua Kneeshaw) was burnt to avoid being captured. (Clowes 5.67, 550; James 3.227)

1805 The brig *Archer* (14; Lt William Price) captured two Dutch gunboats off Cap Gris Nez. The frigate *Chiffonne* (36; Capt. Charles Adam) chased a group of gunboats coming from Le Havre to Fecamp on 19 June. *Chiffonne* was assisted by the sloop *Falcon* (14; Capt. George Sanders) and the brig *Clinker* (12; Lt Nisbet Glen). The firing continued with breaks from 9.30 a.m. to 4.30 p.m. until the flotilla reached Fecamp. Some damage was given and received. On 16 July the brigs *Plumper* (12; Lt James Garrety) and *Teazer* (12; Lt George Ker) were becalmed off Granville. A flotilla of gunboats came out of the port and bombarded and captured both ships. (Clowes 5.177, 5.564; James 3.316–318)

Hitler's War, 1940–1945
1940
Convoys Dispersed in the western approaches by a storm, convoy OA-90 lost two ships to an attack by *U-55* on 30 January; the submarine was then hunted by the destroyers *Fowey* and *Whitshed* and a Sunderland of Coastal Command, until it was scuttled. (Roskill 1.129; Rohwer 34)

Evacuations Boulogne was evacuated by sea on 23–24 May. The destroyers *Vesper* and *Wanderer* bombarded the road south of Abbeville on 8 June. St Valéry was evacuated on 10–11 June, 3300 men being taken off; 11,000 troops were taken off from Le Havre on 10–13 June, where the transport *Bruges* was sunk. Cherbourg was evacuated on 15–18 June, 30,000 troops being collected, and St Malo and Brest were evacuated on 16–17 June with 54,000 troops taken off. The Channel Islands were also evacuated – 26,000 troops and civilians were taken off. (Rohwer 24–30)

Invasion threat The cruiser *Aurora* bombarded a collection of invasion barges in the harbour at Boulogne on 8 September, and British MTBs sank a German freighter in a convoy off Boulogne on the 9th. The monitor *Erebus* and two destroyers bombarded invasion barges in Calais on 30 September. *MTB-22*, *MTB-31*, and *MTB-32* sank two German trawlers off Calais on 11 October. Cherbourg was bombarded by the battleship *Revenge*, the 5th Destroyer Flotilla, and the 3rd MTB Flotilla on the same day. A flotilla of five German S-boats raided the seas near the Isle of Wight on 11–12 October 1940, sinking two trawlers and two French submarine chasers. German S-boats sank three freighters off the southeast coast on 17–18 October 1940. A squadron of four German destroyers, aiming to attack convoys, was intercepted off the Bristol Channel by a British squadron. Fire was exchanged, but no hits were achieved by either side. (Rohwer 39, 43, 44, 45)

1940–1942
Convoy raids *U-26* attacked convoy OA-175 on 1 July 1940; one ship was sunk and another damaged; the submarine was then sunk by the corvette *Gladiolus*. Convoy OA-178 was attacked by air on 14 July; the AA ship *Foyle Bank* and four freighters were sunk; nine ships were damaged. Attacked by dive-bombers and then by S-boats on 25–26 July, convoy CW-8 lost five ships sunk, five damaged, and two destroyers damaged. The destroyer *Delight* was sunk in an air attack off Portland three days later. Three German destroyers raided shipping off Plymouth on 25 November; on a second raid on 28 November they were intercepted by a British destroyer force; in each case two merchant ships were sunk, and in the second attack the destroyer *Javelin* was torpedoed. Convoy FN-366 was attacked by the 3rd S-boat Flotilla on 23 December; a freighter and a trawler were sunk

1942
The 'Channel Dash' The battle-cruisers *Scharnhorst* and *Gneisenau* and the cruiser *Prinz Eugen* with a destroyer and aircraft escort sailed from Brest for Wilhelmshafen on 12 February, under constant attack from coastal batteries, planes, destroyers, and MTBs. Both battle-cruisers were damaged by mines, and a German patrol vessel was sunk; two TBs were damaged. The destroyer *Worcester* was badly damaged. (Rohwer 143; Sebag-Montefiore 208–210)

Convoys and raids The 2nd S-boat Flotilla attacked a convoy on 11 March, sinking one ship. The German auxiliary cruiser *Michel* and the 5th S-boat Flotilla fought a force of British MTBs and destroyers while on passage to Le Havre on 13–14 March; two British destroyers, *Fernie* and *Walpole*, were damaged. The German auxiliary cruiser *Stier*, escorted by the 5th S-boat Flotilla, sailed from Rotterdam for the Gironde on 12 May and was bombarded by British coastal artillery in the Strait of Dover, and attacked by British MTBs; *Iltis* and *Seeadler* were sunk, as was one British MTB; the minesweeper *M-26* was damaged by air attack off Cap de la Hague. *Stier* reached the Gironde undamaged on 15 May. (Rohwer 151, 165)

A German convoy was attacked by the destroyer *Albrighton* and three gunboats on 18 June; one ship was sunk from the convoy, but the gunboat *SGB-7* was lost. Convoy WP-183 was attacked by the 2nd S-boat Flotilla in Lyme Bay on 9 July; six ships were sunk. The German patrol vessel *V-202* was sunk by British destroyers off Cap de la Hague on 28 July. The German 10th Motor Minesweeper Flotilla was attacked by five British MTBs on 16 August; all the boats involved were damaged; *MTB-330* sank the minesweeper *R-184* by ramming. *MGB-35* was captured by the 2nd S-boat Flotilla on 10 September. The 5th S-boat Flotilla attacked a convoy off Eddystone on 2 October; one tanker was sunk. (Rohwer 174, 178, 183, 189, 200)

Dieppe raid A landing in division strength was made at Dieppe from landing craft escorted by destroyers and minesweepers on 19 August. Badly planned and using out-of-date intelligence, surprise was lost when a German convoy was encountered during the approach – one gunboat was set on fire and a submarine chaser sunk. The landing was defeated with heavy loss. The destroyer *Berkeley* was sunk, and three others were damaged; thirty-three other craft were lost. Casualties were over 4000, mainly Canadian. (Rohwer 190)

1942–1944
Convoys and raids A British force of five destroyers and eight MTBs attacked a German convoy on 13–14 October 1942; the auxiliary cruiser *Komet*, escorted by the 3rd S-boat Flotilla, was sunk by torpedoes from *MTB-256*. The 5th S-boat Flotilla (six boats) sank the trawler *Ullswater* and three ships from a convoy south of Plymouth on 19 November. *S-81* sank the trawler *Jasper* on 1 December, and the 5th S-boat Flotilla (four boats) sank a freighter in a convoy on 3 December; *S-115* sank the destroyer *Penylan*. The German *Beijerland* was sunk by attacks by six destroyers on 12 December. (Rohwer 202, 214, 216–218)

The 5th S-boat Flotilla attacked a convoy in Lyme Bay on 26–27 February 1943, sinking a ship, one LCT, and two trawlers. British coastal artillery hit the freighter *Penthièvre*, which was escorted by four German patrol vessels. German S-boats attacked a convoy off Start Point twice between 6 and 8 March; the Polish destroyer *Kwakowiak* frustrated the first attack, and the second was prevented by the destroyer *Mackay* and three MGBs; two S-boats were sunk. The German 8th Destroyer Flotilla (four ships) ran through from the North Sea to Le Havre on 5–6 March, and on to Bordeaux by the 8th. British coastal artillery and MTBs attacked the flotilla but failed to damage it. (Rohwer 234–236)

Three British MTBs attacked a German convoy off Boulogne on 11–12 March, without success. Four British MTBs fought a German minesweeper and two patrol vessels off Dieppe on 25 March, without result other than minor damage. British MTBs attacked a German convoy on 12–13 April, without success. Next night the 5th S-boat Flotilla attacked the British convoy PW-323 off the Lizard; the Norwegian destroyer *Eskdale* was sunk by hits from *S-90*, *S-112*, and *S-65*, and a freighter was sunk. Three British boats clashed with German submarine chasers and patrol boats off Cap de la Hague; the gunboat *Grey Shark* and *V-1525* were damaged. Seven British MTBs sank the German patrol boat *V-1409* off the mouth of the Somme on 17–18 April. (Rohwer 237, 240, 245)

The destroyers *Goathland* and *Albrighton* sank the submarine chaser *UJ-1402* in an attack on a German convoy off Ushant on 27–28 April. MTBs on a mining operation fought the 13th and 14th Patrol Boat Flotillas; one MTB was sunk and two damaged. On 19 June British MTBs sank the German minesweeper *R-41*. A German convoy escorted by S-boats and minesweepers was attacked by the destroyers *Melbreak*, *Wensleydale*, and *Glaisdale* on 9–10 July; *M-153* was sunk and *Melbreak* damaged. (Rohwer 247, 249, 257)

British and Dutch MTBs attacked a German convoy escorted by patrol boats and minesweepers on 26–27 September, sinking *V-1501*, *M-534*, and a freighter. The 4th S-boat Flotilla (five boats) fought five British destroyers off the Sept Iles on 3–4 October. The cruiser *Charybdis* and four destroyers fought the 4th S-boat Flotilla (five boats) off Brittany on 23 October; *Charybdis* was sunk by *T-23* and *T-26*; the destroyer *Limbourne* was sunk by *T-22*. The 5th S-boat Flotilla (nine boats) attacked the convoy CW-221 off Hastings on 2–3 November; three ships from the convoy were sunk. (Rohwer 278, 279, 282, 284, 286)

The 5th S-boat Flotilla attacked a convoy off Beachy Head on 1–2 December, sinking one trawler. The flotilla encountered a British convoy's escorts on 23 December, but neither side had any success. With seven boats the flotilla attacked the convoy WS-457 on 5–6 January 1944, sinking three ships and the trawler *Wallasea*, and attacked another convoy off the Lizard on 16–17 January, though the boats were driven off by the convoy's escort. It attacked convoy CW-243 near Beachy Head on 31 January, sinking the trawler *Pine* and two ships from the convoy. (Rohwer 291, 294, 297, 301, 303)

Four British destroyers engaged three German S-boats off Brittany on 5 February; *M-156* was badly damaged and later destroyed by air attack. *U-413* sank the destroyer *Warwick* on 25 February. Two days later two British MTBs attacked a German convoy south of Jersey; the minesweeper *M-4618* was damaged. The 2nd and 9th S-boat Flotillas sailed to attack convoy WP-492 off Land's End, but encountered a strong British force; in the action *S-143* was damaged. (Rohwer 303, 304, 308, 309, 311–312)

The 5th S-boat Flotilla laid mines off the Isle of Wight on 18–19 April, and had to fight the destroyer *Middleton* and some MTBs. Next night the 5th and 9th S-boat Flotillas attacked a convoy and were driven off by the destroyers *Middleton* and *La Combattante*. The two flotillas attacked a convoy off Dungeness on 21–22 April and were driven off by the destroyers *Middleton* and *Volunteer* and several MGBs. The 5th S-boat Flotilla raided a convoy near Dungeness on 23–24 April, sinking one tug, and clashed with MTBs near Cap Barfleur; one MTB was sunk. The 9th S-boat Flotilla fought four destroyers, MGBs, and MTBs near Hastings. (Rohwer 317)

The 4th TB Flotilla was engaged by a cruiser and four destroyers on 25–26 April; *T-27* and *T-24* were damaged, and *T-29* was sunk by the Canadian destroyer *Haida*. On the same night, the 5th and 9th S-boat Flotillas fought the destroyers *Rowley* and *La Combattante* near the Isle of Wight; *S-147* was sunk. The S-boats *T-24* and *T-27* encountered the Canadian destroyers *Athabascan* and *Haida* off St Brieux on 22–23 April; *Athabascan* was sunk; *T-27* was further damaged and later destroyed. The 5th and 9th S-boat Flotillas fought an Allied force off Selsey Bill in May; *S-141* was sunk and two other S-boats were damaged; two LSTs were sunk and almost 700 men died. *V-211* was sunk by *MTB-90* near Guernsey on 19–20 May, and *M-39* and *M-4623* were also sunk by MTBs. (Rohwer 318, 324)

D-Day and after, 6–14 June 1944

Operation Neptune took place on 6 June, in which landings were made on a five-division front in Normandy. The operation required preliminary minesweeping by 102 minesweepers, and the landings were made from over 2750 landing craft of various types, which put over 132,000 troops on shore on the first day. The escorts and fire support and bombardment ships were mainly US or British, but also included significant Canadian, Dutch, Norwegian, French, and Polish forces. The British naval force included three battleships, nineteen cruisers, seventy-five destroyers, three headquarters ships, two monitors, twenty-six corvettes, and fourteen frigates, sloops, and trawlers. MTBs and MGBs were deployed as more distant protection.

German naval reaction was largely limited to sorties of S-boats and submarines. S-boats sank two LSTs off St Vaast on the first day, but otherwise they were generally without much success. The 8th Destroyer Flotilla (four ships) came out from Brest on 8–9 June, and was intercepted by the British 10th Destroyer Flotilla (eight ships); in the subsequent engagement north of Ile de Bas *Z-81* was sunk by *Ashanti* and *Z-32* by *Haida*; *Huron* was damaged and beached, and *Tartar* was damaged. S-boats came out each night from Cherbourg, Le Havre, and Boulogne, usually attempting to lay mines. Almost always intercepted by Allied forces, they usually succeeded in deploying their mines and escaping their enemies. Casualties were relatively few, though several ships were damaged. Three freighters from a convoy were sunk on 10–11 June, and one S-boat and three MTBs. Air attacks were more successful in destroying the German ships.

Thirty-six U-boats came out from several ports to attack the expedition. Five were sunk and five damaged by air attack as they approached. Only boats equipped with the new schnorkel apparatus were able to get close enough to fire, but all their attacks failed. (Rohwer 330–334; Roskill 3.2.5–53)

The German retreat, 1944

U-boats at last reached the Normandy forces on 15 June. *U-621* sank a landing ship, *U-767* the frigate *Mourne*, and *U-764* damaged the destroyer *Blackwood*. *U-767* was sunk on 18 June by the destroyers *Fame*, *Inconstant*, and *Havelock*, and *U-763* was damaged and then sunk in air attacks. *U-971* was sunk by the destroyers *Eskimo* and *Haida*, *U-269* by the destroyer *Bickerton*.

U-984 damaged the destroyer *Goodson. U-719* was sunk by the destroyer *Bulldog* on 26 June. *U-988* sank the corvette *Pink* and two merchant ships, and was itself sunk by air attack, the frigates *Essington* and *Duckworth*, and the destroyers *Domett* and *Cooke*.

The S-boats from Cherbourg made attacks on 15–18 June, but were driven off by British gunboats. The Canadian 65th MTB Flotilla attacked a German convoy off the Cotentin Peninsula, sinking the minesweeper *M-133*. A second attack along with British MTBs sank the supply ship *Hydra* on 22–23 June; *S-190* was damaged and abandoned. Several ships in an evacuation convoy from Cherbourg were sunk by MTBs on 23–24 June. *S-145* was damaged by the Canadian destroyers *Gatineau* and *Chaudiere* on 25–26 June. The next night the trawler *M-4620* was sunk by MTBs, and on the 28th *M-4611* was sunk by the Canadian destroyers *Eskimo* and *Huron*. Allied ships bombarded positions on shore near Cherbourg on 25 June and near Caen next day, and on demand throughout July.

The group of German one-man torpedoes out of Villers-sur-Mer sank the minesweepers *Magic* and *Cato* on 5–6 July, and damaged the destroyer *Trollope*; a second attack on 8–9 July sank the destroyer *Pylades*. The patrol vessels *V-208* and *V-210* were sunk by MTBs off St Malo on 4 July. One MTB and one German patrol vessel were sunk in a fight on 8–9 July; other fights in July produced little result. A German minesweeper was sunk off Fecamp on 1–2 July. Off Brittany the Canadian 65th MTB Flotilla sank the supply ship *Minotaure* and two patrol boats; another was sunk off Brest on 5 July. The 10th Destroyer Flotilla sank two minesweepers on 7–8 July and two submarine chasers on 14–15 July.

German S-boats were attacked whenever they came out. The frigate *Trollope* was beached and destroyed in one of these fights. *U-390* sank the ASW trawler *Ganilly* and a tanker from a convoy on 5 July; she was then sunk by the destroyer *Wanderer* and the frigate *Tavy. U-678* attacked a convoy off Beachy Head on 6 July, but was sunk by the Canadian destroyers *Ottawa* and *Kootenay. U-672* was damaged by the destroyer *Balfour* on 18 July and later scuttled. *U-212* was sunk by the destroyers *Curzon* and *Ekins* on 21 July. *U-621* sank the landing ship *Prince Leopold* and damaged the troop transport *Ascania* in late July. (Rohwer 338, 340)

U-671 was sunk by the destroyers *Stayner* and *Wensleydale* on 4 August. *U-214* was sunk by the frigate *Cooke* on 26 July, *U-333* by the sloop *Starling* and the frigate *Loch Killin* on 31 July, and *Loch Killin* sank *U-736* on 6 August. *U-608* was sunk by the corvette *Wren* and air attack on 9 August. *U-584*, damaged by air attack, was sunk by *Starling. U-618*, also damaged by air attack, was sunk by the frigates *Duckworth* and *Essington* on 14 August. *U-667* sank the Canadian corvette *Regina*, two landing ships, and a transport between 8 and 14 August. *U-741* was sunk by the corvette *Orchis* on 15 August near Brighton. *U-621* was sunk by the Canadian destroyers *Ottawa*, *Kootenay*, and *Chaudiere* on 18 August; the same ships sank *U-984* two days later. *U-413* was sunk by the destroyers *Wensleydale, Forester*, and *Vidette* on 20 August. *U-480* sank the Canadian corvette *Alberni*, the minesweeper *Loyalty*, and two merchant ships on 22 August. (Rohwer 342)

The battleship *Rodney* bombarded Alderney on 12 August, *Warspite* Brest on 25 August, *Malaya* the Ile de Cezebre near St Malo on 1 September, the monitor *Erebus* Harfleur on 9 September. There were engagements between German minesweepers and MTBs and Patrol Torpedo boats off Brittany and off Le Havre in August with little result. *Warspite* and the monitor *Erebus* bombarded Le Havre on 5 and 8 September. The German 15th Patrol Boat Flotilla withdrew from Le Havre to Dieppe on 23–24 August, attacked on the way by destroyers and MTBs; next night it withdrew to Boulogne. Several of the ships were sunk. (Rohwer 346–347, 352)

1944–1945
Final U-boat attacks   *U-978* sank two ships in early November. *U-1200* was sunk by the corvettes *Pevensey Castle* and *Kenilworth Castle*. *U-1018* sank a ship on 11 February 1945, but was then sunk by the frigate *Loch Fada* off the Lizard on 27 February. *U-1004* sank the Canadian corvette *Trentonian* and another ship on 22 February. *U-480* sank three ships under convoy on 24 February but was then sunk by the frigates *Duckworth* and *Rowley*. *U-1195* sank a ship from convoy TBC-102 in the Channel on 21 March 1945; on 6 March she sank the troop transport *Cuba*, but was then herself sunk by the escort destroyer *Watchman*. (Rohwer 360, 382, 391, 397)
See also: **North Sea, Strait of Dover**

English squadron v. *Lindorm*, May 1695
The Danish ship *Lindorm* (50) and a Swedish frigate, in the Channel with a convoy, failed to salute English ships and were attacked. They beat off their attackers. (Anderson 132)

***Enquiry* v. French ships, 13 October 1691**
The sloop *Enquiry* was captured by French ships. (Clowes 2.535)

***Entreprenante* v. privateers, 12 December 1810**
The cutter *Entreprenante* (8; Lt Peter Williams) was attacked by four French privateers while becalmed off Faro, Spain. Much of *Entreprenante*'s rigging was destroyed, but three attempts to board were repelled. Well-aimed and well-timed broadsides so damaged two of the privateers that their fellows towed them to port. (James 5.110–111; Clowes 5.476)

***Enterprise* v. American ship, 1778**
The tender *Enterprise* (10) was captured and burned by a rebel American ship. (Clowes 4.109)

***Epervier* v. *Peacock*, 29 April 1814**
The sloop *Epervier* (Cmdr Richard Wales) was escorting a convoy from Jamaica when she met the US sloop *Peacock*. In a fight lasting an hour *Epervier* was soundly beaten, virtually dismasted, and many of its guns were made unusable. (James 6.158–161; Clowes 6.159–161)

***Eridge* and *Aldenham* v. *MAS 228*, 29 August 1942**
The destroyers *Eridge* and *Aldenham*, having bombarded the Daba area of

the Western Desert on 25–29 August, were attacked by the Italian TB *MAS 228*; *Eridge* was damaged and later sank. (Rohwer 191)

Erne and others v. *U-213*, 19 October 1941
U-213 was sunk by the sloops *Erne*, *Rochester*, and *Sandwich* west of the Bay of Biscay. (Rohwer 182)

Escape Creek, Canton Delta, 25 May 1857
A squadron of small steamers and gunboats attacked a squadron of Chinese junks in Escape Creek. After considerable resistance the Chinese line broke, and the retreating vessels were pursued by the British ships and eventually by boats. Twenty-seven out of forty-one Chinese ships were captured or burnt. The rest escaped. (Clowes 7.102–103; Graham 315–316)

Escort v. *Marconi*, 11 July 1940
The Italian submarine *Marconi*, positioned before the start of the war, sank the destroyer *Escort*, part of Force H, east of Gibraltar. (Rohwer 32)

Esk v. *Netuno*, 14 March 1826
The Brazilian slaver *Netuno* was captured by *Esk* (20) in the Benin River, West Africa; *Netuno*, with a prize crew of six men from *Esk*, was attacked later by a pirate vessel but fought off the attack successfully. (Ward 116–118)

'L'Espagnols sur Mer', 29 August 1350
A convoy of twenty-four Castilian ships sailing along the Channel from Flanders was attacked by an English fleet off Winchelsea. The casualties caused on the English side were heavy as the ships approached, but the Castilian ships were mostly captured, and their crews killed. The victory was clear, but Castilian hostility virtually closed the Channel to English ships for the next several months. (Sumption 2.66–68; Clowes 1.268–272)

Espion v. French frigates, November 1794
The sloop *Espion* (formerly a French privateer) was captured by three French frigates. It was retaken next year. (Clowes 4.548; Colledge 133)

Espoir in Spanish waters, August 1798–February 1799
The sloop *Espoir* (14; Cmdr Loftus Bland) was escorting a convoy in from Oran to Gibraltar when the Genoese pirate *Liguria* (26) attempted to seize one of the ships. *Espoir* challenged and eventually beat *Liguria*, despite the disparity in firepower. On 20 October 1798 *Espoir* captured the French cutter *Fulminante* (8). On 22 February 1799 *Espoir*, now under Cmdr James Sanders, encountered a group of Spanish ships off Marbella, Spain, and tackled one of them, the xebec *Africa* (14). After firing at each other for an hour the British sailors boarded the brig, which was captured after a twenty-minute fight. (James 2.256–258, 264–265; Clowes 4.513, 520, 556)

Esquimault v. *U-190*, 16 April 1945
U-190 sank the Canadian minesweeper *Esquimault* off Halifax, Nova Scotia. (Rohwer 407)

Essex, England, 992
A Norse fleet was off the Essex coast, and an English fleet was collected in London to challenge it. Either the enemy was warned, as the *Chronicle* claims, or the battle was largely avoided; one Danish ship was captured. (*ASC* s.a. 992)

Essex v. French ship, 16 July 1694
Essex (70) captured a French ship, which was then taken into the navy as the sloop *Essex Prize* (16). (Colledge 133)

Essex and Pluto v. Galatée, 7 April 1758
The French sloop *Galatée* (22) was captured by *Essex* (64) and the fireship *Pluto* (8). (Clowes 3.313; NRS, *Hawke* 174)

Ethalion v. Bellone, 12 October 1798
The frigate *Ethalion* (38; Capt. George Countess) fought the French frigate *Bellone* for several hours near Tory Island, Ireland. *Ethalion* suffered little damage; *Bellone* was virtually dismasted and almost sinking when she surrendered. (James 2.146–147; Clowes 4,348)

Ethalion v. Indefatigable, April 1799
Ethalion (38) captured the French privateer *Indefatigable*, which was taken into the navy as the sloop *Dispatch* (14). (Colledge 108)

Eupatoria, Crimea, 14 September 1854
The Franco-British fleet in the Black Sea transported their forces from Varna to Eupatoria in the Crimea. Russian troops at Katcha were shelled from the sea to deter interference with the landing. Otherwise it was unopposed. (Clowes 6.411–413; Lambert 120–122)

Eurotas v. Clorinde, 25–26 February 1814
The frigate *Eurotas* (Capt. John Phillimore) met the French frigate *Clorinde* near Brest. The two ships fired broadsides at each other until both were dismasted. *Clorinde* got away slowly. Next day *Eurotas*, having repaired much of the damage, was catching up when *Clorinde* met the frigate *Dryad*, which received her surrender. (James 6.132–142; Clowes 5.541–542)

Euryalus and Cruizer v. Danish convoy, 16 June 1808
The frigate *Euryalus* (36; Capt. Hon. George Dundas) and the sloop *Cruizer* (18; Cmdr George Mackenzie) sent in boats against a group of Danish ships in the River Naskon in the Great Belt. A gunvessel was captured and two ships burned. (James 4.367; Anderson 325)

Euryalus v. Etoile, November 1809
The French sloop *Etoile* (14) was captured off Cherbourg by *Euryalus* (36). (Clowes 5.559)

***Euryalus* v. *Baleine*, 2 December 1813**
The French storeship *Baleine* (22) was driven ashore on Corsica by *Euryalus* (36). (Clowes 5.561)

***Euryalus* and others v. German patrol vessels, 15–21 October 1944**
A British squadron, headed by the cruiser *Euryalus*, and including two escort carriers, carried out raids on several places in Norway, during which the German patrol vessels *V-1605*, *V-5716*, *V-6801*, *V-5560*, and several steamships were sunk. (Rohwer 352)

***Eurydice* v. *Saméa*, 14 October 1782**
Eurydice (24; Capt. George Courtenay) captured the French gun brig *Saméa* (14). (Clowes 4.89)

***Excellent* v. *Aréthuse*, 13 September 1799**
Excellent (74) captured the French corvette *Aréthuse* (18) off Lorient after a long chase. (Clowes 4.525)

***Excellent* v. *Arc*, 29 February 1801**
The French cutter *Arc* was captured by a boat party from *Excellent* (74) in Quiberon Bay. (Clowes 4.558)

***Exertion* v. Danish gunboats, 1 July 1808**
The brig *Exertion* (12) ran aground in the Great Belt and was attacked by a Danish schooner and two gunboats, but drove them off. (Anderson 326; Clowes 5.420)

Exeter, Devon, August 1643
The Parliamentary fleet under the Earl of Warwick attempted to disrupt the Royalist siege of Exeter. Three ships were lost through going aground. (Clowes 2.78)

***Exmoor* and others v. *U-450*, 10 March 1944**
The destroyers *Exmoor*, *Blankney*, *Blencathra*, and *Broom*, with the US destroyer *Madison*, sank *U-450* off Anzio, Italy. (Rohwer 311)

***Exmouth* v. *U-22*, 21 January 1940**
The destroyer *Exmouth* was sunk by *U-22* in the Moray Firth. (Rohwer 14)

***Expedition* and *Society* v. French ships, 32 August 1697**
Expedition (70; Capt. James Stewart) was attacked by two French ships, of 60 and 50 guns, southwest of Scilly; when they failed in an attempt to board the French turned to attack *Society*, a hospital ship, but were then driven off. (Clowes 2.496)

***Experiment* v. *Télémaque*, 1757**
Experiment (24; Capt. John Strachan) captured the French privateer *Teélémaque* (26). (Clowes 3.296)

Experiment and *Unicorn* v. *Raleigh*, 26 September 1778
Experiment (50; Capt. Sir James Wallace) and *Unicorn* (20; Cmdr Matthew Squire) came up with the rebel American frigate *Raleigh* (32) near Boston. *Unicorn* brought down part of *Raleigh*'s masts, and *Raleigh* was then run aground by her crew. *Experiment* came up and with *Unicorn* captured the grounded ship and most of the crew. *Raleigh* was refloated and added to the navy. (Clowes 4.20–21)

Experiment v. French squadron, 24 September 1779
Experiment (50; Capt. Sir James Wallace), escorting a convoy, was dismasted in a storm and then captured after a brief resistance by a French force of three larger ships; two of the convoy were also captured. (Clowes 4.32)

Experiment v. Spanish ships, 2 October 1796
The lugger *Experiment* (10) was captured by Spanish ships in the Mediterranean. (Clowes 4.549; Colledge 136)

F

Fair Rosamond v. slavers, 1828–1832
Fair Rosamond was a captured slaver used by the navy as an anti-slavery ship; she captured several slavers. (Lloyd 72–73)

Fairy v. French privateer, 9 January 1781
Fairy (6; Lt Joseph Browne) was captured by a large French privateer off the Scilly Isles. (Clowes 4.61)

Fairy and Fox v. Epervier, 14 November 1797
The sloop *Fairy* (16; Cmdr Joshua Horton), accompanied by the armed cutter *Fox*, captured the privateer *Epervier* in the Western Channel. (James 2.101–102)

Fairy v. UC-75, 31 May 1918
The destroyer *Fairy* rammed and sank *UC-75* in the North Sea. (Newbolt 5.428; Grant 123)

Falcon v. French ship, 1 May 1694
Falcon (36) was captured by a French ship in the Mediterranean. (Colledge 139)

Falcon v. French ship, 12 August 1745
The sloop *Falcon* (14) was captured by a French ship off St Malo; she was retaken a year later. (Colledge 138)

Falcon in the Great Belt, 29 April–7 May 1808
The sloop *Falcon* (16; Lt John Price) destroyed eight boats off Endelau, and six at Thuno, Denmark. A schooner was chased into port, and two boats carrying supplies to the fort at Kyholm were captured. (James 4.321; Anderson 324; Clowes 5.416)

Falkland Islands, South Atlantic
1764–1771 A dispute developed over possession of the Falkland Islands between France, Spain, and Britain, during which a force of five Spanish frigates fired on the only British ship in the islands, *Favourite* (16; Cmdr William Maltby). The French withdrew their settlers and refused to support Spain, so when Britain mobilised a fleet Spain backed down and evacuated the settlement. (Clowes 4.3–5)

1832 The sloop *Clio* (18; Cmdr John Onslow) was dispatched to recover the Falkland Islands from a small expedition sent from Buenos Aires. The garrison and its schooner were removed in December. (Clowes 6.272)

1914 (Battle of the FALKLANDS) The German Far Eastern squadron sailed around the southern end of South America after its victory at Coronel. The British had sent reinforcements to the Falklands under Vice-Admiral Sir Doveton Sturdee, notably the battle-cruisers *Invincible* and *Inflexible*, so when the German squadron arrived on 8 December it was received by an overwhelming British force. The battle was essentially a chase. Four German cruisers, *Gneisenau*, *Scharnhorst*, *Nürnberg*, and *Leipzig*, were sunk, as were two colliers. The light cruiser *Dresden* escaped. (Corbett 1.400–436; Halpern, *Naval History* 97–99)

1982 (The 'Falklands War') An Argentinian expedition seized the Falkland Islands and proclaimed their annexation to Argentina. A seaborne expedition went from Britain to recover the islands. The destroyers *Coventry* and *Sheffield* and two frigates, *Antelope* and *Antrim*, were sunk. A landing took place at San Carlos. An apparent threat from the Argentine carrier *25 de Mayo* and the cruiser *General Belgrano* was blocked when the latter was sunk by the nuclear submarine *Conqueror*. The landing ship *Sir Galahad* was sunk by air attack with substantial casualties. By 2 June the islands had been recovered. (M. Hastings and S. Jenkins, *The Battle for the Falklands*, London 1983; M. Middlebrook, *Task Force: The Falklands War 1982*, rev. edn, Harmondsworth 1987; J. Burns, *The Land that Lost Its Heroes*, London 1987)

Falkland and others v. *Seyne*, 13 July 1704
A small squadron, including *Falkland* (50; Capt. John Underdown), met the French *Seyne* (54); *Falkland* took the leading part in forcing its surrender, and the ship was added to the navy. (Clowes 2.506; Owen 107–108)

Falmouth, Maine, 18 October 1776
A small British squadron of four ships called at Falmouth and required the surrender of arms. When refused, the commander, Capt. Henry Mowatt, ordered the town to be bombarded and burnt. (Clowes 4.4; Syrett, *American* 7–8)

Falmouth v. French warship, 18 May 1709
Falmouth (50; Capt. Walter Riddell) was escorting a convoy from New England when it was attacked by a French 64-gun ship. Thwarting a series of attempts to board, Riddell also protected his convoy successfully, but at the cost of nearly seventy casualties. (Clowes 2.522)

Falmouth and *Mary* v. French ships, 11 March 1712
Falmouth (50; Capt. Walter Riddell) and *Mary* galley (26; Lt. William Mabbott) met and fought two stronger French warships off the coast of Guinea, with indeterminate results. (Clowes 2.533)

Falmouth v. *U-66* and *U-63*, 19 August 1916
The light cruiser *Falmouth* was hit by torpedoes from *U-66*; the ship was being towed to the Humber when she was also torpedoed by *U-63*, and then sank. (Newbolt 4.45–46)

Fame and Lion v. Ecureil, 23 October 1762
The French ship *Ecureil* (10) was captured by *Fame* (74) and *Lion* (60). (Clowes 3.314)

Fantome v. Josephine, 30 April 1841
The slaver *Josephine* was chased for twenty-four hours by the sloop *Fantome* (Capt. E.W. Butterfield), and finally caught and forced to surrender; 200 slaves were freed. (Lloyd 91–92)

Fantome v. Moorish pirates, 12 May 1846
The brig *Ruth* was captured and run ashore by pirates at Cape Treforcas, Morocco. *Fantome* (16; Cmdr Sir Frederick Nicholson) was sent to rescue her. This was done despite a large pirate force on shore. (Clowes 6.360–361)

Farnborough and Biddeford v. Malicieuse and Opale, 4 April 1760
The French frigates *Malicieuse* (32) and *Opale* (32) were aiming to intercept a convoy from Lisbon, but met *Farnborough* (20; Capt. Archibald Kennedy) and *Biddeford* (20; Capt. Lancelot Skynner) who harassed the two French ships until they sailed off. The convoy arrived safely. (Clowes 3.302)

Farnborough v. U-68, 22 March 1916
U-68 fired a torpedo at the Q-ship *Farnborough*, whose crew feigned abandonment. When the submarine approached she was hit by shells several times and then depth-charged and sunk. (Grant 31)

Farnborough v. U-83, 17 February 1917
The Q-ship *Farnborough* was torpedoed by *U-83* off southwest Ireland. The submarine was then sunk by gunfire from *Farnborough* when it surfaced. *Farnborough* herself was saved. (Newbolt 4.357–359; Grant 64)

Farndale v. Caracciolo, 11 December 1941
The Italian submarine *Caracciolo*, transporting supplies to North Africa, was detected by the destroyer *Farndale* which was escorting a convoy, and sunk. (Rohwer 119)

Fatshan Creek, Canton Delta, China, 1 June 1857
A group of armed junks had gathered in Fatshan Creek. The China Squadron, commanded by Rear-Admiral Sir Michael Seymour, made an attack on them, first capturing two small forts, then boarding the junks one by one. The fighting was hard, with vigorous Chinese resistance which inflicted many British casualties. The captured ships (almost eighty in number) were burnt. (Clowes 7.104–109; Graham 316–370)

Faulknor and others v. U-138, 18 June 1941
U-138 was detected near Gibraltar by the destroyer screen of Force H, and sunk. (Rohwer 77)

Favourite v. French squadron, 6 January 1806
The sloop *Favourite* (16; Cmdr John Davie) encountered a marauding French

squadron under Commodore L'Hermitte off West Africa, and was captured. (James 4.178; *NC* 5.214)

Fearless v. Stralsund, 11 August 1914
The light cruiser *Fearless* was sighted by the German cruiser *Stralsund* in the North Sea. The ships with *Fearless* turned away, but *Fearless* became engaged with *Stralsund*, and called in reinforcements. After an hour *Stralsund* turned away. *Fearless* followed but could not find the enemy again. (Corbett 1.85)

Fearless and Brazen v. U-49, 15 April 1940
The destroyers *Fearless* and *Brazen*, escorting the troop convoy NP-1 to Norway, discovered and sank *U-49* in the convoy's path. A document giving the disposition of all U-boats in northern waters was found. The troop convoy arrived safely on 19 April. (Rohwer 20; Sebag-Montefiore 81–82)

Feilding's squadron v. Dutch convoy, 1 January 1780
A British squadron under Capt. Charles Feilding was sent into the Channel to intercept and inspect a Dutch convoy heading for French ports. The Dutch commander, Capt. Graaf van Bylandt, refused to allow an inspection and, when British boats were sent to begin doing so, fired on the British ships. When the British replied, the Dutch ships hauled down their colours, and nine Dutch merchant ships were confiscated as carrying contraband of war. (Syrett, *European* 115–117; Clowes 4.47)

Ferret v. French ship, 25 February 1706
The sloop *Ferret* (10) was captured by the French near Dunkirk. (Clowes 2.537; Colledge 141)

Ferret v. Spanish ship, 1 September 1718
The sloop *Ferret* (10) was captured by Spaniards in Cadiz Bay. (Colledge 141)

Ferret v. Spanish privateer, 5 October 1799
The schooner *Ferret* (Lt Michael Fitton) intercepted a large Spanish privateer east of Jamaica, and drove it into Santiago de Cuba. (James 2.398–399)

Ferreter v. Dutch gunboats, 31 March 1807
The sloop *Ferreter* was captured by a group of seven Dutch gunboats in the Ems River. (Clowes 5.554)

Ferrol, Spain, 25 August 1800
A force of about 8000 British soldiers was landed near Ferrol from a fleet of transports escorted by a squadron under Rear-Admiral Sir John Borlase Warren. The warships bombarded a fort into silence, and the landing force drove back the defenders. The force was re-embarked later in the day, the army commander having decided the Spanish defences were too strong to be attacked. (James 2.450–451; Clowes 4.424–425)

Fiji, August 1868
A dispute over land and crops in Fiji brought the bombardment of a hill village by *Challenger* (18; Capt. Rowley Lambert). The effect was minimal. (Clowes 7.223; R.A. Derrick, *A History of Fiji*, rev. edn, Suva 1950, 185–186)

Firebrand and others in the Danube estuary, June–July 1854
The paddle vessel *Firebrand* (Capt. Hyde Parker) and the paddle sloops *Vesuvius* (Cmdr Richard Powell) and *Fury* bombarded Russian military positions in the Sulima mouth of the Danube and captured batteries there. (Clowes 6.405; Lambert 111)

Firedrake v. *UC-51*, 13 November 1917
The destroyer *Firedrake* sank the submarine *UC-51* in the North Sea. (Newbolt 5.426; Grant 58)

Firedrake and *Wrestler* v. *Durbo*, 18 October 1940
The destroyers *Firedrake* and *Wrestler*, assisted by two flying boats, sank the Italian submarine *Durbo* east of Gibraltar; ciphers were captured. (Rohwer 45)

FIRST OF JUNE, 1794
The French Brest fleet sailed to cover the arrival of a large and rich convoy from America. The British Channel Fleet, under Admiral Lord Howe, lay in wait to intercept either the fleet or the convoy. On 28 May the two fleets were in contact, and the rearward French ships were harassed by the forward British: *Revolutionnaire* (110) endured attacks from several ships, and she and *Audacious* (74; Capt. William Parker) were seriously damaged; both ships left for port. The two fleets continued on parallel courses and the British again attempted to reach a position from which to attack, but the only result was considerable damage to some ships, above all to the flagship *Queen Charlotte* (100; Capt. Roger Curtis) and *Queen* (98; Capt. John Hutt). Howe attempted to break the French line with *Queen Charlotte*, but only two ships followed him, and the French fleet evaded.

On 31 May the British tried once more to get to grips, but failed again. During the night, with a fresh breeze, the French attempted to get away. This, however, was predictable, and they gained only a few miles. Next morning Howe was able to mount an attack at last. The French had twenty-six line-of-battle ships and six frigates and corvettes, the British twenty-five line-of-battle ships and seven frigates. Howe aimed to strike the French line in the centre so allowing the full British weight to be concentrated on half of the French fleet. This plan scarcely worked, and in the general fighting half the ships in each fleet ended up dismasted. Several of the French ships in this state were rescued by the French flagship *Montagne* under Admiral Villaret-Joyeuse. The undamaged French ships and those with the admiral escaped. Seven French ships were captured, though one sank almost at once. The convoy reached port on 12 June. The British took to referring to the battle as the 'Glorious First of June', with scant justification. (James 1.138–202; *NC* 1.89–110; Clowes 4.214–216; Tunstall 208–210)

Firth of Clyde, Scotland, summer 1544
The Earl of Lennox, a Scottish ally of Henry VIII, raided Arran, Bute, and Argyll with a fleet of a dozen ships, probably mainly from Bristol. (Loades 127)
See also: **Arran, Bute, Kintyre, Rothesay**

Firth of Forth, Scotland
This was always the main target of every English naval expedition against Scotland.

1303 Edward I invaded Scotland, and arranged for a squadron of thirty ships to convey three prefabricated pontoon bridges to enable his army to cross the Forth below Stirling. (Nicholson 66)

1335 An English fleet, 180 ships, operated in the firth, ravaging the coast. A detachment captured Dunottar Castle after an opposed landing. (Clowes 1.234; Rodger 1.90; Sumption 1.158)

1356 King Edward III invaded Lothian in January, and a squadron of his ships landed a raiding force which attacked the shrine at Whitekirk; next month adverse winds scattered the ships, sinking some. The Scots, of course, assumed that this was God's revenge. (Nicholson 162)

1381 An English squadron under Lord John Howard raided the shores of the firth in the spring, and again in July–August, capturing eight ships, and burned Blackness and a ship there. (Nicholson 490–491; MacDougall 225)

1409–1410 Sir Robert Umfravill, Vice-Admiral of England, raided in the firth, burning ships and boats; he took fourteen ships laden with a variety of goods which were sold in English markets, so relieving a momentary shortage there. (Clowes 1.369; Nicholson 231)

1482 An English fleet commanded by Sir Robert Radcliff blockaded the firth from a position off Inchkeith, but landings were generally repulsed by the alerted local population. (Nicholson 493; MacDougall 235; C. Ross, *Edward IV*, London 1974, 282)

1489–1490 A substantial English naval force under Lord Willoughby de Broke threatened the firth. It is not clear that any hostilities took place, but James IV did expel the pretender Perkin Warbeck from Scotland. Next year the Scots sea commander Sir Andrew Wood captured five English privateers in the firth; he was then attacked by three English ships commanded by Stephen Bull who had been preying on Scottish fishing vessels. Wood was victorious in a considerable fight. (Clowes 1.444, 446; Nicholson 549; MacDougall 226; Loades 43–56)

1552 An English squadron of seven ships under William Sabyn raided shipping in the firth, attacking Leith and Kinghorn. (Clowes 1.458; Rodger 1.174)

1544 A large English fleet sailed from Newcastle in May, carrying an invasion army. Boats were seized and a landing was made west of Leith. A hastily gathered Scots army was defeated at Leith and the town was occupied and looted. Edinburgh was assaulted and burned, but the castle proved impregnable. The fleet ravaged lands on both sides of the firth almost as far as Stirling. (Phillips 161–162; Rodger 1.181–182; Clowes 1.460; Loades 127; NRS, *Misc* VII)

1547–1549 An English fleet of eighty ships accompanied an invading army commanded by Lord Clinton; Leith and Blackness were bombarded. The fleet resupplied the army when it arrived in September 1547. At the battle of Pinkie Cleugh the Scots army was bombarded from the sea, a considerable contribution to the English victory. In July 1548 an English fleet under Lord Clinton, thirty-eight strong, sailed to the firth. An attack by eight French galleys was beaten off – two galleys were sunk – and twelve French ships were destroyed at Burntisland. The shores of the firth were raided until September. The English fleet returned in June 1549. The Bass Rock fort was bombarded but held out. Raids were made on the shores and Inchkeith Island was occupied. The fleet then withdrew; French and Scottish forces retook the island in the face of stiff resistance. (Rodger 1.186; Phillips 194, 200, 234–255, 248–249; Clowes 1.467; Loades 142–143, 146)

1551 The English fleet under William Winter sailed to the firth and attacked the French fleet there, with only minor success. (Rodger 1.188)

1558–1560 In September 1558 the English fleet attempted a landing at St Monans, but were defeated by local forces, losing 300 killed or captured. Next year William Winter, with a fleet of thirty-four ships, arrived in the firth to combat French influence in Scotland. Scotland was in the midst of the crisis over the adoption of Protestantism, and Winter was able to intervene on the rebels' side by capturing two French galleys and assisting in the (unsuccessful) siege of Leith. The French and English agreed on a mutual withdrawal of their forces, and Winter carried the French troops home. The Protestant cause succeeded. (Phillips 241–242; Clowes 1.468; Rodger 1.197–198; Loades 210–212)

1639 and 1640 During the brief Bishops' Wars between Charles I and the Scottish revolutionaries, the English navy imposed a blockade on the firth. The ships were not really suitable for the task, but in the second war at least the blockade was becoming effective when the two sides made peace. (Rodger 1.412–413)

1650 A parliamentary squadron bombarded Leith to assist in the advance of the army in the Scottish campaign. (Capp 67)

1692 Bass Rock, in the firth, held by Jacobites, was bombarded by *Sheerness* (52) on 12 April, with little success. (Lavery 21)

1709 An expedition to Scotland on behalf of the Old Pretender sailed from Dunkirk under the command of the Chevalier de Forbin. The British North Sea Fleet under Admiral Sir George Byng searched for it. Forbin failed to land his forces in the firth, and Byng's arrival forced the French expedition to move away northwards. In the pursuit, the French ship *Salisbury* (52) was captured near Buchan Ness by *Leopard* (50; Capt. Thomas Gordon) after other ships had engaged her. Three other French ships were also lost during the expedition. (Clowes 2.516–518; Owen 253–258; Rodger 2.173–174)

1715 As rebellion spread in 1715, Hanoverian ships patrolled the firth, but were unable to prevent several ships with 1600 or so Jacobite soldiers crossing from Fife to land at North Berwick and other ports. (Lavery 38–39)

1746 The sloop *Vulture* sailed up the Forth as far as Kincardine in January, trying to cut Jacobite communications. Twice the ship fought the Jacobites, but neither could claim the victory. (Lavery 55–56)

Firth of Tay, Scotland, 1547–1548
The castle of Broughty Crag, near Dundee, was surrendered to an English fleet commanded by Lord Dudley on 20 September 1547. From this base the English dominated the shores of the Tay. The Scots replied by besieging the castle. The squadron bombarded Dundee into surrender, supplied the castle's garrison, and raided the shores of the firth several times. English soldiers from Broughty Castle were landed at Dundee by the fleet, and drove out the inhabitants. They were counter-attacked, but held onto the town. The castle was retaken by the Scots in February 1550. (Phillips 203–254; Rodger 1.185; Loades 143–145)

Fishguard v. *Immortalité*, **20 October 1798**
The frigate *Fishguard* (Capt. Thomas Byam Martín) chased and fought the French frigate *Immortalité*, returning to Brest after the failure of the French landing in Ireland. A first fight reduced *Fishguard* to helplessness, but a second brought *Immortalité* to a sinking condition, though *Fishguard* was little better. (James 2.159–161; Clowes 4.350)

Fishguard v. *Vivo*, **30 September 1800**
The frigate *Fishguard* captured the Spanish ship *Vivo* (4) off the coast of Spain. (Clowes 4.561)

Fishguard, Diamond, and *Boadicea* v. *Neptuno* and others, **20 August 1801**
Boats from the frigates *Fishguard, Diamond,* and *Boadicea,* commanded by Lt Philip Pinon, went in to Coruna to cut out the *Neptuno* (20), a gunboat, and merchantmen; this was achieved without any loss. (James 3.142–143)

Fiskerton v. **Indonesian sampan, November 1964**
The minesweeper *Fiskerton* was attacked by three Indonesians in a sampan who threw grenades; the three men were all killed. (Wettern 241)

Fitzroy and others v. *U-722*, **27 March 1945**
U-722 sank a ship from convoy RU-156 on 16 March off the Hebrides, but was then sunk by the destroyers *Fitzroy, Redmill,* and *Byron*. (Rohwer 397)

Fitzroy and *Byron* v. *U-1001*, 8 April 1945
U-1001 was sunk by the destroyers *Fitzroy* and *Byron* southwest of Ireland. (Rohwer 406)

Fladstrand, Denmark, 5 April 1809
An English sloop went into Fladstrand and began lowering its boats to seize some ships there; local gunboats drove them away. (Anderson 338)

Flamborough v. *Jason*, 10 October 1705
Flamborough (24) was captured by Duguay-Trouin's ship *Jason* (54) off Cape Spartel. (Clowes 2.537; Colledge 144; Owen 206)

Flamborough v. *Général Lally*, 1757
Flamborough (22) captured the French privateer *Général Lally*, which was taken into the navy as the sloop *Flamborough Prize*. (Colledge 144)

Flamborough Head, Yorkshire, 30 March 1405
Prince James, son of King Robert III of Scots, was sailing to France in a Hamburg ship for his safety and to complete his education. The ship was captured by an outlaw, Prendergast of Great Yarmouth, who delivered the prince to King Henry IV; he stayed in an English prison for the next eighteen years. This in effect makes Prendergast's exploit official. (Clowes 1.362)

Fleetwood and *Mignonette* v. *U-528*, 11 May 1943
U-528 was attacked by a Halifax aircraft of 58 Squadron and damaged; she was then sunk by a depth-charge attack by the sloop *Fleetwood* and the corvette *Mignonette*. (Rohwer 250)

Flora v. *Nymphe*, 10 August 1780
Flora (36; Capt. William Williams) encountered *Nymphe* (32) near Ushant. The ships clashed and a French boarding attempt was repelled; *Flora* retaliated and captured *Nymphe*, which had almost half her company casualties. (Clowes 4.55–56)

Flora, *Crescent*, and *Castor* off Gibraltar, May–June 1781
Flora (36; Capt. William Williams) and *Crescent* (28; Capt. Hon Thomas Pakenham) off southeastern Spain were chased by a Spanish squadron on 23 May, but escaped after a short fight. A week later they intercepted the Dutch frigates *Castor* (36) and *Briel* (36) off Gibraltar. *Flora* defeated *Castor* in a two-hour fight, both ships suffering heavy casualties; *Briel* defeated *Crescent*, but *Flora* prevented *Crescent* being taken. On 19 June 1781 two French frigates came upon *Flora*, *Crescent*, and the prize *Castor*, which were all badly damaged and undermanned. *Crescent* and *Castor* were captured; *Flora* got away. (Clowes 4.66–69)

Flora v. *Vipère*, 23 January 1794
Vipère, a French privateer (16), was captured by *Flora* (36) in the English Channel. (Colledge 433)

Flora v. *Corcyre*, 2 May 1798
The frigate *Flora* (36) captured the French brig *Corcyre* (12) near Sardinia. (Clowes 4.510)

Flora v. *Mondovi*, 13 May 1798
The frigate *Flora* (36; Capt. Robert Middleton) chased the corvette *Mondovi* into Cerigo harbour. Boats were sent in and captured her in the face of heavy fire. (James 2.249–250; Clowes 5.510)

Flora v. *Cortez*, 22 June 1800
The Spanish ship *Cortez* (4) was captured off Lisbon by *Flora* (56). (Clowes 4.561)

Fly v. French ship, 1781
The cutter *Fly* (14) was captured by the French in American waters. (Colledge 146)

Fly at Vingorla, India, 1800
The BM brig *Fly* (10; Cmdr John Hayes) attacked the pirate base of Vingorla, where a battery was destroyed and captured material was surrendered. (Low 1.203–204)

Fly v. *Fortune*, 1803
The EIC brig *Fly* (10; Lt Mainwaring) was captured in the Persian Gulf by the privateer *Fortune*. (Low 1.222–223)

Flying Fish v. French schooners, 16 June 1795
The schooner *Flying Fish* was captured in the West Indies by two French schooners. (Colledge 147)

Folkstone v. *Surveillante*, 24 June 1778
The cutter *Folkstone* (8; Lt William Smith) encountered five French frigates and was captured by *Surveillante*. (Clowes 4.16)

Force K v. Italian convoys, 8–20 January 1943
The Italian navy evacuated its ships from Tripoli, and was attacked by Force K from Malta. The destroyers *Kelvin* and *Nubian* sank a steamship, *Pakenham* and *Javelin* an auxiliary, *Pakenham* and *Nubian* a transport, and *Kelvin* and *Javelin* seven minesweepers and three other ships. Five British submarines also sank fifteen ships between them. The Italian submarine *Narvalo* was sunk by *Pakenham* and *Husky*, and *Santarosa* by *MTB-260*. (Rohwer 220)

Foresight and *Mordaunt* v. French squadron, 4 October 1689
Foresight (48; Capt. Daniel Jones) and *Mordaunt* (48; Capt. John Tyrrel) met a squadron of twelve French warships west of the Scilly Isles. In the fighting which followed, an accompanying ship, the *Lively Prize* (Capt. William Tichborne), was captured by the French. (Clowes 2.462)

Foresight and others v. French convoy, May 1694
Foresight (48; Capt. Isaac Townsend), along with another warship and four privateers, attacked a French convoy in the Channel, which was guarded by seven French warships. *Foresight*'s squadron captured or destroyed ten or eleven of the merchantmen in the convoy. (Clowes 2.479)

Formidable v. *U-24*, 31 December 1914
The battleship *Formidable* (Capt A.N. Loxley), returning from firing exercises off Portland Bill after dark, was torpedoed by *U-24*, and sank two hours later. Casualties were almost 550 men. (Corbett 2.57–60; Halpern, *Naval History* 44)

Formosa (Taiwan), 25–26 November 1868
In pursuance of a dispute over a commercial monopoly *Algerine* (Lt Thornhaugh Gordon) attacked a position on Taiwan. A party was landed at night and carried the position by surprise. (Clowes 7.222)

Fort Beausejour, Nova Scotia, June 1755
An expedition of ships and men from New England and Halifax attacked French posts in Nova Scotia, under the joint command of Capt. John Rous and Lt-Col. Monckton. Fort Beausejour and several smaller posts were captured. (Clowes 3.141)

Fort Gustafvard, Hango Head, Finland, 22 May 1854
The paddle frigate *Dragon* (Capt. James Wilcox) was sent to bombard the fort; the garrison soon found the range and replied; *Dragon*, damaged, was recalled. (Clowes 4.418; Lambert 164)

Fortitude and convoy v. French squadron, 7 October 1795
A squadron of ships from the Mediterranean fleet under the command of Capt. Thomas Taylor in *Fortitude* (74), with *Bedford* (74; Capt. Augustus Montgomery) and the jury-rigged prize *Censeur*, met a squadron from the French Toulon fleet under Rear-Admiral Richery with four 74s and three frigates near Cape St Vincent. The British ships, escorting a convoy, were unable to resist the French assault. *Censeur* was recaptured, the rest escaped; all but one of the thirty-one ships in the convoy were captured. (James 1.302–305; Clowes 4.278)

Fort Royal, Martinique, 18 December 1779
A French convoy was attacked by the British squadron from St Lucia; half the ships were captured or forced ashore. A French squadron came out from Martinique and the two forces clashed near Fort Royal, with no result. (Clowes 3.452–453)

Fort Schlosser, New York, 29 December 1837
A US steamer, *Carolina*, which had assisted rebels in Canada, was cut out by a party led by Cmdr Andrew Drew, set on fire, and sent over Niagara Falls. (Clowes 6.277)

Fortune v. Dutch ships, 1652
Fortune was captured in a fight with a Dutch ship or ships; it was felt that the surrender had been made far too quickly. (Clowes 2.160)

Fortune v. French privateer, 1757
The sloop *Fortune* (Cmdr William Hotham) captured a French privateer of 26 guns. (Clowes 3.296)

Fortune v. *Iphigénie* and *Gentille*, 26 April 1780
Fortune (18; Cmdr Lewis Robertson) was captured by the French frigates *Iphigénie* and *Gentille* in the West Indies. (Clowes 4.51)

Fortune and *Dame de Grace* v. *Salamine*, 8 May 1798
The British polacca *Fortune* (10) and the gunboat *Dame de Grace* were attacked by the French brig *Salamine* (18) off the coast of Syria. *Dame de Grace* was sunk; *Fortune* surrendered when three French frigates arrived. (Clowes 4.522; James 2.378–379)

Fortune and *Fortescue* v. *U-27*, 20 September 1939
U-27 attacked British trawlers, and ten destroyers and some aircraft went to attack her; *Fortune* and *Fortescue* succeeded; the crew were captured, and the boat sunk. (Terraine 231; Rohwer 24)

Forward and convoy v. Danish brigs, Skaggerak, 9 July 1810
A British convoy was attacked by five Danish brigs; the escorting brig *Forward* escaped, but forty-eight ships were captured. (Anderson 343)

FOUR DAYS' FIGHT, 1–4 June 1666
The English fleet under the Duke of Albemarle, off the Downs, was attacked by the Dutch fleet and Admiral de Ruijter. The English were heavily outnumbered but another part of their fleet, under Prince Rupert, was off the Isle of Wight. Albemarle retreated down-Channel to link up with Rupert's squadron, which took three days. Fighting began each day with the fleets in good order, but quickly became confused. Rupert's division joined in at the end of the third day. The Dutch preponderance in numbers was partly offset by better English seamanship and discipline. The Dutch lost seven or eight ships; the English lost perhaps twenty; human casualties were proportionate. (Clowes 2.269–278; Rodger 2.72–75; Mahan 116–126; Tunstall 26–27)

Fowey v. French ships, 1 August 1704
The frigate *Fowey* (32) was captured by a French ship near the Scilly Isles. (Colledge 150)

Fowey v. French ships, April 1709
Fowey (32; Capt. Richard Lestock) was captured by French ships off the Portuguese coast. (Clowes 2.523; Colledge 150)

Fowey v. *Ventura*, **October 1762**
Fowey (24) twice in two days met and fought the Spanish *Ventura* (26) off St Domingue; *Ventura*, having lost forty men killed, at last surrendered. (Clowes 3.308)

Fowey v. *Washington*, **5 December 1776**
Fowey (24; Capt. George Montagu) captured the rebel American brig *Washington* (10). (Clowes 4.4)

Fox v. **Algerine ship, February 1666**
Fox (14; Capt. Henry Osgood) attacked a larger Algerine ship at Argilla, and after a day-long fight, cut her out, suffering only one casualty. (Clowes 2.428)

Fox v. *Hancock* and *Boston*, **7 June 1777**
Fox (28; Capt. Patrick Fotheringham) was attacked by the rebel American ship *Hancock* (32) and was partly dismasted; *Boston* (30) came up and both ships then battered at *Fox* for another hour until she surrendered. (Clowes 4.5–6)

Fox v. *Junon*, **10 September 1778**
Fox (28; Capt. Hon. Thomas Windsor) chased two vessels off Brest, but was intercepted by the frigate *Junon* (32). In the fight *Fox* was dismasted and most of her guns silenced. With a quarter of her crew casualties she surrendered. (Clowes 4.20)

Fox v. *Santa Catalina*, **16 March 1782**
The Spanish ship *Santa Catalina* (22) was captured by *Fox* (32) near Jamaica. (Clowes 4.115)

Fox v. *Modeste*, **March 1797**
The French *Modeste* (20) was captured by the frigate *Fox* (32) off Vizagapatam, India. (Clowes 4.555)

Franchise v. *Raposa*, **6 January 1806**
The frigate *Franchise* (Capt. Charles Dashwood) sent in three boats against vessels in the harbour of Campeche, Mexico; despite being detected well in advance, they captured the brig *Raposa* (20), and defended it against a considerable counter-attack. (James 4.127–129; Clowes 5.372–373)

Francis v. *Trompeuse*, **1 August 1683**
Francis (20; Capt. Charles Carlile) was sent by Sir William Stapleton, governor of the Leeward Islands, to hunt down *Trompeuse*, a notorious pirate ship. She was found protected by the guns of a fort at St Thomas. Carlile sent boats in after dark and burned *Trompeuse* and two other ships. (Clowes 2.458)

Franconia v. *UB-47*, **4 October 1916**
The troopship *Franconia*, empty at the time, was torpedoed and sunk by *UB-47* east of Malta. (Halpern, *Mediterranean* 253)

Freija at Guadeloupe, 17 January 1810
The frigate *Freija* (Capt. John Hayes) captured a schooner, and learned from its log of two other ships in Mahaut Bay, Guadeloupe. Four boats went in that night, captured a brig, and stormed and destroyed two batteries on the shore in the face of considerable fire. The two ships were destroyed. (James 5.87–90; Clowes 5.450)

Frolic v. *Wasp*, 18 October 1812
The British sloop *Frolic* (Capt. Thomas Whinyates), escorting a convoy in the Caribbean, was attacked by the US sloop *Wasp*. *Frolic*, already damaged and undermanned, was captured by boarding. (James 5.383–393; Clowes 6.38–41)

Frolic v. *Vencedora*, September 1843
A boat party from the sloop *Frolic* captured the Brazilian slaver *Vencedora*. (Bethell 210)

Frolic at the Gold Coast, 31 June 1885
In reprisal for attacks on British subjects, the screw gunvessel *Frolic* (Cmdr Alfred Parr) sent a party on shore and burnt a town. (Clowes 7.375)

Furieuse at Santa Marinella, Latium, 14 October 1813
The frigate *Furieuse* (Capt. William Mounsey) sent a force of marines against the fort at Santa Marinella, which was taken; the French garrison retired to a stronger fort overlooking the harbour. Sixteen ships were taken out by *Furieuse*, though two sank on the way. (James 6.35; Clowes 5.537–538)

Furness, Lancashire, 4 June 1487
Lambert Simnel, the pretended Edward VI, sailed from Dublin with a small army mainly of German mercenaries, and landed unopposed at Furness. After a short campaign he was defeated at Newark by Henry VII. (Loades 98–99)

Fury v. *Eliza*, 18 October 1796
The French ship *Eliza* (10) was captured by *Fury* (16) in the West Indies. (Clowes 4.554)

Fury v. pirates, 1808
The EIC cruiser *Fury* (6) was attacked by pirate ships while carrying dispatches from Basra to Bombay, but drove off her attackers. (Low 1.320)

Fury and *Phlegethon* v. Chinese pirates, 18–20 October 1849
A large pirate fleet commanded by 'Shap'n'gtzui' was pursued by the paddle sloop *Fury* (Cmdr James Williams) and the Indian paddle gunvessel *Phlegethon* (Cmdr G.T. Niblett). With Chinese co-operation, the pirate fleet was found in the Red River and in a series of actions almost sixty ships were destroyed. (Clowes 6.357–359; Graham 273–274)

G

G-2 v. U-78, 28 October 1918
The British submarine *G-2* torpedoed and sank *U-78* in the North Sea. (Newbolt 5.429; Grant 138)

G-13 v. UC-43, 8 March 1917
The British submarine *G-13* located and sank the submarine *UC-43* off Muckle Flugga, Shetland. (Newbolt 4.360; Grant 59)

GABBARD, 2–3 June 1653
The Dutch fleet under Admiral Tromp came out seeking battle, and on 2 June found the English fleet north of North Foreland in the Thames estuary. The fighting continued through that day and the next. It is claimed that the English adopted a line-ahead formation, but the fighting soon became much less organised than that implies. The battle was much affected by mist, and by changes in wind direction and strength. By late on 3 June the Dutch fleet was in confusion and withdrew into the Dutch harbours. This was a comprehensive English victory; they lost no ships. The Dutch lost eleven ships captured, six sunk, and two others destroyed. (Clowes 2.185–191; Powell 234–238; Rodger 2.17; Tunstall 19–21)

Gabes, Tunisia, 22 March 1943
The gunboat *Aphis* bombarded Gabes in Tunisia in support of the advance of the Eighth Army. (Rohwer 231)

Gabon, West Africa, 7 November 1940
The Vichy French submarine *Poncelet* attacked the sloop *Milford* during a landing by Free French forces; the submarine was forced to the surface and then scuttled. (Rohwer 48)

Gaeta and Capri, Italy, April 1806
The kingdom of Naples was invaded by French forces. Only the fortress of Gaeta held out, under siege. A British squadron under Rear-Admiral Sir Sidney Smith revictualled the place and assisted in its defence. The island of Capri was invaded by a force of seamen and marines landed by *Eagle* (74; Capt. Charles Rowley), which drove the French garrison to surrender. (James 4.123–124; Clowes 5.199; NC 3.324–328)

Galatea and Sylph v. Andromaque, 22–23 August 1796
The frigate *Galatea* (32; Capt. Richard Keats) chased the French frigate *Andromaque* (36) until, with the approach of other British ships, she went aground. The crew either got to shore or were taken off by boats from *Galatea* and *Sylph* (18; Cmdr John White); *Sylph* later set fire to *Andromaque*. (James 1.381–384; Clowes 4.502)

Galatea v. Venturier, 14 October 1797
The frigate *Galatea* (32) captured the French sloop *Venturier* off Brest. (Clowes 4.555)

Galatea v. Général Ernouf, 12–13 August 1804
The frigate *Galatea* (32; Capt. Henry Heathcote) twice sent in boats to take the sloop *Général Ernouf* at the Saintes. Both attempts failed, costing sixty-five men killed or wounded. (James 3.279–282; Clowes 5.347–348)

Galatea on the Spanish Main, August 1806–January 1807
The frigate *Galatea* (32; Capt. George Sayer) chased a privateer schooner upriver near Puerto Cabello, Spanish Main, and, having captured it on 21 August, blew it up. A second schooner was found three days later, driven ashore, and destroyed. On 11 October *Galatea*'s barge went into the harbour of Barcelona to cut out three schooners. This was done in the face of heavy fire, without casualties. On 12 November *Galatea* chased the French schooner *Réunion*. Being becalmed, boats were sent against it and the schooner surrendered as they arrived. On 21 January 1807 *Galatea* sent six boats to chase the French brig *Lynx*. After seven hours at the oars, and being repelled in attempts to board twice, *Lynx* was finally carried, but with heavy casualties. (James 4.168–169, 239–242; Clowes 5.387–388, 396–397)

Galatea v. U-557, 15 December 1941
The cruiser *Galatea* was sunk by *U-557* off Alexandria. (Rohwer 125)

Gallant and others v. Lafole, 20 October 1940
The Italian netlayer *Lafole* was sunk by the destroyers *Gallant*, *Griffin*, and *Hotspur* east of Gibraltar. (Rohwer 45)

Gallinas River, West Africa, 1840
The Gallinas River was the main centre of slave exporting by 1840. Capt. Hon. Joseph Denman, the commander of the West African Slave Patrol, blockaded the river with the sloops *Wanderer*, *Rolla*, and *Saracen*, then went in to rescue some enslaved British subjects. In the process he liberated 841 slaves and destroyed the barracoons. (Lloyd 94–96)

Galloway, Scotland, 1153
The sons of King Harald of Man, having conquered Man, sailed to invade Galloway, but were heavily defeated. (Oram 69)

Gambia, West Africa, 1891–1892
The paddle vessel *Alecto* (Lt Frederick McInstry), the screw sloop *Swallow* (Cmdr Frank Finnis), and the screw gunboat *Widgeon* (Lt George Bennett) campaigned against the local ruler Fodeh Cabbah, who objected to a boundary commission passing through his territory. A first campaign failed, so a Naval Brigade of almost 200 men was formed, and was briefly successful. A third

attack drove the chief into French territory. In the process several towns and villages were destroyed.

Two years later, in another attack by a Naval Brigade on the territory of Fodeh Sillah, some stockaded villages were captured. The attackers were stopped by an ambush, but a second attack succeeded. Losses on both sides were considerable. (Clowes 7.402–403, 426–427)

Gamla Carleby, Finland, 7 June 1854
A boat attack was mounted on Gamla Carleby in the Gulf of Bothnia. The paddle steamers *Odin* (Capt. Francis Scott) and *Vulture* (Capt. Frederic Glass) contributed boats and men. They were fired on as they approached; having suffered heavy casualties, the attackers withdrew. (Clowes 6.416–417)

Ganges and *Montagu* v. *Jacobin*, 30 October 1794
Ganges (74) and *Montagu* (74), part of the West Indies squadron, captured *Jacobin* (24). (Clowes 4.553)

Gannet v. pirates, 8 April 1827
The sloop *Gannet* (Cmdr F. Brace) chased a pirate mistico into a Cretan bay and sank her. (NRS, *Piracy* 96–97)

Garland v. Dutch ships, 1624
Garland (Capt. Thomas Best) intervened between a Dutch force and a Dunkirker, driving the Dutch away. (Clowes 2.60–64)

Garland and *Nonsuch* v. *Santa Teresa*, July 1649
Santa Teresa (Capt. Francis Darcy), a Royalist cruiser operating in the Channel, was captured by the Parliamentary ships *Garland* (34) and *Nonsuch* (34). (Clowes 2.120)

Garland and *Francis* at Sallee, September–October 1668
Garland (30; Capt. Richard Booth) and *Francis* (14; Capt. William Bustow) blockaded Sallee, the corsair port in Morocco, and drove four Sallee ships and their prizes ashore. For the moment this crippled Sallee's activities. (Clowes 2.437)

Garland and others v. French convoy, 15–17 January 1801
A convoy of coasters, escorted by a schooner, was attacked by the schooner *Garland* and boats from other ships near Guadeloupe; one vessel was captured. Two days later the boats of *Garland* succeeded in cutting out the escort schooner *Eclair* at Trois Rivieres. (James 3.120–121; Clowes 4.534)

Garry and *ML-263* v. *UB-110*, 19 July 1918
The destroyer *Garry* and *ML-263* combined to sink *UB-110* off the Yorkshire coast. (Newbolt 5.428; Grant 124–125)

Gaspé in captivity, 1775–1776
The brig *Gaspé* (6) was seized by insurgent Americans on 1 January 1775, but was recaptured in April next year. (Colledge 157)

Gate *Pa*, New Zealand, 29 April 1864

A Naval Brigade was part of a strong British force which attacked the Maori fortification Gate *Pa*. An initial assault on the *pa* was defeated with the cost of over 100 casualties. That night the *pa* was evacuated without the British noticing. (Clowes 7.183–185; Belich 178–180)

Gaza, Palestine, 30 October–9 November 1917

The monitors *M-31*, *M-32*, and *Raglan*, the cruiser *Grafton*, the destroyers *Comet* and *Staunch*, and the seaplane carrier *City of Oxford* bombarded positions in and around Gaza as part of the assault on the Turkish line. Several French vessels also took part. (Newbolt 5.77–80)

Gemaizeh, Sudan, 20 December 1888

The Mahdist camp at Gemaizeh was shelled by the screw gunvessel *Racer* (Cmdr Henry May); a Naval Brigade, formed from the crews of *Racer* and the screw gunboat *Starling* (Lt Alfred Paget), assisted in the land attacks, which resulted in defeat for the Mahdists. (Clowes 7.390)

General Monk v. *Hyder Ali*, 8 April 1782

General Monk (18; Cmdr Josias Rogers) in Delaware Bay, assisted by a privateer, captured a brig (14) and drove another (16) on shore. She was then attacked by the American ship *Hyder Ali* (8), which fired from a distance at which *General Monk*'s carronades had no effect; she was compelled to surrender. (Clowes 4.80)

Genista v. *U-57*, 23 October 1916

The sloop *Genista* was sunk by *U-57* in the Atlantic. (Colledge 158)

Genoa, Italy

1795 (Battle of Cape Noli) The British Mediterranean fleet commanded by Vice-Admiral William Hotham came up with the French Toulon fleet which was heading back to France from Corsica. For two days (11–12 March) occasional conflicts ensued, but neither side could bring its full force to bear. Two French ships, *Ça-Ira* (80) and *Censeur* (74), were captured. *Illustrious* (74; Capt. Thomas Frederick) was damaged in a gale following the fight, went aground, and was abandoned and burnt. (James 1.285–292; Clowes 4.269–272; Gordon 47–52)

1800 The frigate *Aurora* (Lt Philip Beaver) and a group of gunboats and mortars bombarded the French army which was under Austrian siege in the city during May. A galley, *Prima*, blocked the harbour entrance effectively. On the night of 21 May *Prima* was stormed by the men from ten boats from the blockading fleet. (James 2.432–436; NC 2.79–80; Clowes 4.416–417)

1814 A squadron of vessels and Sicilian gunboats under Capt. Josias Rowley, with a detachment of British troops, captured Genoa and the newly built line-of-battle ship *Brilliant* (74). (James 6.119; Clowes 5.306–307; NC 5.224)

1941 The city and harbour of Genoa were shelled by the battleships *Renown* and *Malaya* and the cruiser *Sheffield* on 9 February; five ships were sunk in the harbour. (Rohwer 58)

Genoese Coast and Corsica, November 1745
Genoa joined Spain and France in the Austrian Succession War. Commodore Thomas Cooper, from the British Mediterranean fleet, bombarded the Genoese towns of San Remo and Savona. The Corsicans, Genoese subjects, rebelled. Cooper bombarded Bastia, the main town of the island, for some days, then withdrew, but his bombardment caused such damage that the city fell easily to the rebels who soon arrived. (Clowes 3.116)

***George and Molly* v. American privateer, 16 April 1781**
George and Molly (8; Lt Richard Saunders) captured a rebel American privateer in the Channel. (Clowes 4.63)

***George* v. Spanish privateers, 3 January 1798**
The sloop *George* was captured by two Spanish privateers in the West Indies. (Clowes 4.549)

***Germaine* v. American ships, 1781**
The armed ship *Germaine* (20; Lt George Keppel) was captured by rebel American ships. (Clowes 4.121)

Gheriah, India
Gheriah, one of Kanhoji Angria's towns, twelve hours' sailing south of Bombay, was a frequent enemy of the Bombay EIC.

1718 After the capture by Angria of the EIC ship *Success*, an expedition in April seized control of the outer harbour of Gheriah, but the castle was too well fortified. The besiegers withdrew with some loss. (Low 1.97–98)

1721 An attack made by EIC troops and ships out of Bombay failed. (Keay 261)

1756 The arrival of a Royal Navy force under Rear-Admiral Charles Watson and an alliance with the Mahrattas provided the power needed to attack Gheriah fort. Six naval and ten BM ships attacked from the sea; an artillery detachment under Lt-Col. Robert Clive landed to bombard the fort; in the face of such strength resistance was slight. (Low 1.135–136; Keay 269; Clowes 3.142–144)

Gibraltar
1704–1705 The English Mediterranean fleet bombarded the Spanish fort at Gibraltar and a landing was made on the mole. The governor capitulated. This was the beginning of the British occupation of the Rock, though it was originally undertaken on behalf of the claimant to the Spanish throne, Charles III. The garrison, commanded by the Prince of Hesse, was besieged by a joint French and Spanish force, and the bomb vessel *Terror* (4; Cmdr Isaac Cooke) was captured by the French fleet in Gibraltar Bay. However,

as an assault by land and sea was about to be launched, a British squadron under Admiral Sir John Leake arrived. Six French frigates in the bay were captured or burned; the assault was scotched. Leake remained in the bay for the winter, harassing the besiegers. Next year a French squadron under Baron de Pointis occupied Gibraltar Bay, but was then scattered by a storm. An Anglo-Dutch squadron under Admiral Leake arrived with reinforcements before the French could recover; of the five French ships still in the bay one surrendered, two were captured by boarding, and two were driven ashore and burned. (This is sometimes called the battle of Marbella.) Soon afterwards the siege was finally abandoned. (Corbett, *Mediterranean* 256–261, 280–285; Owen 90–92; Clowes 2.393–396, 404–407; Francis 109–115, 129–131, 142–146; Rodger 2.169–170; Mahan 211–212; Tunstall 67)

1727 A Spanish siege of Gibraltar began in February. A British squadron under Vice-Admiral Sir Charles Wager assisted in the defence by bombarding Spanish positions and batteries, and by intercepting Spanish shipping. The siege was lifted in June. (Clowes 3.46–47)

1781–1782 The British Channel Fleet escorted a victualling convoy from Cork to besieged Gibraltar in 1781. The Spanish fleet remained in harbour at Cadiz and Spanish ships and guns in and around Gibraltar Bay failed to prevent the landing of supplies. Next year, the fleet under Admiral Lord Howe escorted victuallers to the Strait of Gibraltar on 9 October. The Franco-Spanish fleet stayed in Cadiz as British ships were blown through the Strait, then an east wind brought the British back and the supplies were landed at Gibraltar. The rival fleets met on 19 October in the Strait and fired at each other without result (battle of Cape Spartel). (Clowes 3.502–503, 540–542; Syrett, *European* 140–142, 160–162; Mahan 407–408)

1941 Three human torpedo teams were launched from the Italian submarine *Scire* and penetrated into Gibraltar harbour, where three ships were sunk, including the naval tanker *Denbydale*. (Rohwer 101; Greene and Massignani 181)

Gibraltar v. French privateer, February 1757
Gibraltar (20) captured a French privateer, which was taken into the navy as the *Gibraltar Prize*. (Colledge 159)

Gibraltar v. Spanish ship, July 1781
The brig *Gibraltar* (14; Lt W. Anderson), originally captured from rebel Americans, was captured by the Spanish off Gibraltar. (Clowes 4.111)

Gipsy v. Quidproquo, 8 October 1800
The schooner *Gipsy* (Lt Coryndon Boger) met and fought the French sloop *Quidproquo* (8) near Guadeloupe. Keeping far enough off to avoid the heavy musket fire from the sloop, which was carrying about ninety soldiers, *Gipsy* bombarded it into surrender. (James 3.30)

Gipsy v. schooner, 21 January 1805
The schooner *Gipsy* (10; Lt Michael Fitton) was threatened by five privateers while on station off Cape Antonio, Jamaica. In the chase which followed, one of the privateers, a schooner, became separated from the rest; *Gipsy* turned and attacked, and the enemy schooner was driven onto the rocks and wrecked. (James 4.13; Clowes 5.352)

Gironde River, France
1294 A naval expedition sailed from Portsmouth to the Gironde, where Gascony had been occupied by the French king's forces. The fleet sailed up the Gironde River, past Bordeaux, and captured several towns, including Bourg and Blaye on the way. (Rodger 1.18)

1338 A large convoy from England carrying food for Gascony was attacked in the river by a French galley force of eighteen ships out of La Rochelle on 23 August; two ships were taken. (Sumption 1.233)

1806 A large complement of boats from ships of Capt. Sir Samuel Hood's squadron went into the Gironde estuary on 4 July to attack a large convoy there. The corvette *César* (18) was captured but the rest of the convoy moved upriver to safety. (James 4.157–159; Clowes 5.385)

1811 The frigates *Diana* (38; Capt. William Ferris) and *Semiramis* (36) bluffed their way into the Gironde estuary in August, where a convoy was seized by boats, *Teazer* captured by boarding, and the corvette *Pluvier* driven on shore. (James 5.213–215; Clowes 5.491)

1814 On 27 March a squadron of ships commanded by Rear-Admiral Charles Penrose sailed into the Gironde, ignored shore battery fire, and pursued *Regulus* (74) and three smaller vessels up the river, though without catching them. On 2 April *Porcupine* (24; Capt. John Coode) chased a flotilla of gunboats in the Gironde River until they ran ashore; defending troops were driven off, twelve vessels were captured, and four destroyed. On 7 April, in the face of an imminent attack, the French burnt their ships. The fort at Blaye blocked the Gironde below Bordeaux. *Porcupine* and the bomb *Vesuvius* (8) made several attacks on it. The frigate *Belle Poule* (38; Capt. George Harris) sent marines and sailors on shore, who destroyed a series of five batteries. The fort held out until the news arrived of Napoleon's abdication. (Hall 229–232; James 6.120–121; Clowes 5.216–217)

Glasgow and Tryall v. Bien Trouvé, 22 June 1746
Bien Trouvé was searching to rescue Prince Charles Edward when she was seen by *Glasgow* (24) and driven into Loch Broom. The sloop *Tryall* went into the loch, and when *Bien Trouvé* came out *Glasgow* forced her surrender. (Lavery 64)

Glasgow v. American squadron, 6 April 1776
Glasgow (20; Capt. Tyringham Howe) fought a squadron of five rebel American ships, escaping after two hours. (Clowes 4.3–4; Syrett, *American* 267)

Glatton v. French squadron, 15 July 1796
Glatton (56; Capt. Henry Trollope), a former Indiaman, encountered a squadron of six French ships close to the Flemish coast. By sailing very close its 68-pounder broadsides proved deadly, and all the French ships were driven off, badly damaged; *Glatton* was badly damaged aloft. The French ships are supposed to have been, in effect, three frigates and two corvettes and a brig. (James 1.372–377; Clowes 4.501)

Glatton and Hirondelle v. Turkish corvette, 1 March 1807
The brig *Hirondelle* (14; Lt George Skinner) and boats from *Glatton* (50; Capt. Thomas Seccombe) seized a Turkish corvette, supposedly a treasure ship, in the port of Signi, Lesbos, at a cost of four men killed. (James 4.244; Clowes 5.398)

Gleaner v. U-33, 12 February 1940
U-33, heading for the Firth of Clyde to lay mines, was depth-charged into surrender by the minesweeper *Gleaner*; three Enigma code wheels were found on one of the crew. (D. Kahn, *Seizing the Enigma*, London 1991, 107–111; Rohwer 15; Sebag-Montefiore 67–77)

Glen v. UB-39, 14 May 1917
The destroyer *Glen* sank *UB-39* in the English Channel. (Newbolt 5.424; Grant 46)

Glenmore and Aimable v. Siréne and Bergère, 17 December 1799
Glenmore (36; Capt. George Duff) and *Aimable* (32; Capt. Henry Raper), escorting a convoy near Madeira, met three ships which proved to be the French *Siréne* (36), *Bergère* (18), and *Calcutta*, a captured Indiaman. The two British ships made chase. *Calcutta* was recaptured by *Glenmore*, but *Aimable* could not separate the two French ships, and returned to the convoy. (James 2.417–419; Clowes 4.529)

Glorious and others v. Scharnhorst and Gneisenau, 8 June 1940
An attempt to intercept British troop convoys from Norway was made by the German battle fleet and brought the battle-cruisers *Gneisenau* and *Scharnhorst* into contact with the carrier *Glorious*, the destroyers *Acasta* and *Ardent*, the transport *Orama*, the tanker *Oil Pioneer*, and the trawler *Juniper*. All these ships were sunk, though the convoys all arrived safely at Scapa Flow. (Rohwer 26)

Glory, Korea, May 1951–May 1952
The carrier *Glory* raided communications and positions as required in North Korea. (Wettern 53)

Gloucester v. Dutch fleet, May 1672
Gloucester (50; Capt. William Coleman) was patrolling along the Dutch coast when she was attacked by a fleet of about thirty ships; by conducting a careful fighting retreat the ship escaped. (Clowes 2.444)

Gloucester and Hampshire v. Achille, 26 October 1709
Gloucester (60; Capt. John Balchen) and *Hampshire* (50) escorted a convoy sailing off Ireland. They were attacked by Duguay-Trouin's ship *Achille* (64). Both warships were badly damaged, and *Gloucester* was captured. (Clowes 2.522)

Gloucester and others v. Aventurier, 25 February 1746
Gloucester (Capt. Charles Saunders), with three other ships, found the French *Aventurier* off Peterhead, having landed men there. *Aventurier* was driven on shore in Cruden Bay. (Lavery 59)

Gloucester v. Breslau, 7 August 1914
The light cruiser *Gloucester* followed the German battle-cruiser *Goeben* and the cruiser *Breslau* in the Ionian Sea. *Breslau* made repeated attempts to shake off the pursuit; eventually *Gloucester* opened fire, hoping *Goeben* would turn back to assist *Breslau* and so be delayed. This she did, but neither ship hit the other. *Gloucester* was ordered to rejoin the Mediterranean fleet, and the German ships went into the Aegean and on to Constantinople. (Corbett 1.66; Halpern, *Naval History* 56; Massie 41–45)

Gloucester v. Macedonia, 28 March 1915
The German AMC *Macedonia* was captured by the light cruiser *Gloucester* in the West Indies. She was immediately made prize and used in the hunt for *Kronprinz Wilhelm*. (Corbett 2.256)

Glowworm v. Admiral Hipper, 8 April 1940
The destroyer *Glowworm* fought the German destroyer *Bernd von Arnim* in the Norwegian Sea; the cruiser *Admiral Hipper* intervened; *Glowworm* was sunk in ramming *Admiral Hipper*, which was badly damaged. (Rohwer 17)

Gnat v. U-79, 21 October 1941
U-79 torpedoed the gunboat *Gnat* near Bardia. *Gnat* was run aground but could not be salved. (Rohwer 105)

Gold Coast (Ghana), February–March 1782
Leander (50; Capt. Thomas Shirley) and *Alligator* (14; Cmdr John Frodsham) attacked the Dutch forts on the Gold Coast. The attack on Elmina was unsuccessful, but Mourree, Commendah, Baraccoe, and Accra were all captured. (Clowes 4.79)

Goldfinch v. Mouche, 17 May 1809
The sloop *Goldfinch* (10; Cmdr FitzOwen Skinner) chased the corvette *Mouche* (16), which stayed clear until forced to return fire; *Goldfinch* was then so damaged that *Mouche* got away. (James 5.27; Clowes 5.438)

Goliath v. Torride, 18 March 1798
The French ketch *Torride* (7) was cut out by boats from *Goliath* (74) at Aboukir, Egypt. *Torride* was recaptured by the French on 11 March next year and re-recaptured at once. (James 2.216; Clowes 4.376, 550, 556)

Goliath v. *Mignonne*, 28 June 1803
Goliath (74; Capt. Charles Brisbane), off St Domingue, chased the corvette *Mignonne* and captured her after only a brief exchange of fire. (James 3.181; Clowes 5.370)

Goliath and *Camilla* v. *Faune*, 16 August 1805
The French sloop *Faune* (16) was met by *Goliath* (74) and *Camilla* (20) west of Rochefort and captured. (Clowes 5.365)

Goliath v. *Muavenet-i-Miliet*, 13 May 1915
The battleship *Goliath*, in Morto Bay, Gallipoli Peninsula, provided flanking fire for the troops on land. The destroyer *Muavinet-i-Miliet* came out of the Dardanelles and with three torpedoes sank her. The destroyer got away. (Corbett 2.407–408; Halpern, *Naval History* 117)

Good Hope v. Dutch squadron, May 1665
Good Hope (34; Capt. Anthony Archer), part of a convoy escort from Hamburg towards England, was captured in an attack by a Dutch squadron out of the Texel. (Clowes 2.425)

Goodwin, Kent, 1512
Andrew Barton, a Scots seaman commanding two ships, captured several ships by piracy, but he was attacked by ships commanded by Lords Thomas and Edward Howard. One ship was captured, one sunk. (Clowes 1.449; Nicholson 595–596; MacDougall 240–242; Loades 55–56)

Goodwin v. French privateer, 23 February 1695
Goodwin (6), originally a French ship captured in 1691, was sunk by a French privateer off Dover. (Colledge 164)

Gorée, West Africa, January–March 1804
The British post at Gorée was captured by a French force on 17 January. On 7 March the frigate *Inconstant* (Capt. Edward Dickson) arrived and landed a force from boats. The French garrison surrendered next morning. (James 3.298–299; Clowes 5.84; NC 3.34–35)

Gosport v. *Jason* and others, 1706
Gosport (32) was captured by *Jason* (Duguay-Trouin) and other French ships. (Clowes 2.537; Owen 206)

Grabusa, Crete, 31 January 1828
Grabusa, an island west of Crete, a pirate base, was attacked by a squadron of British, French, and Greek ships, led by *Isis* (50; Capt. Sir Thomas Staines). There was no opposition; the ships in the port were destroyed. (Clowes 6.261–262; NRS, *Piracy* 246–255)

Gracieuse at Santo Domingo, 8–9 April 1805
The schooner *Gracieuse* (Midshipman John B. Smith) captured a large

Spanish schooner in Santo Domingo. Next day she attacked a French sloop, but it got away. Later *Gracieuse* was attacked by another Spanish schooner, which was driven ashore and wrecked. (James 4.29–30; Clowes 5.360)

Gramont at St John's, June 1762
Gramont (18; Cmdr Patrick Mouat) was captured when a small French expedition took St John's, Newfoundland. (Clowes 8.312)

Grampus v. Italian TBs, 16 June 1940
The submarine *Grampus* was sunk by the Italian TBs *Cirie*, *Clio*, and *Polluce* off Augusta, Sicily. (Rohwer 27)

Grand Banks of Newfoundland, 8 June 1755
A French fleet taking troops to Canada was to be intercepted by a British fleet commanded by Rear-Admiral Edward Boscawen. He found only a group of three ships which had become separated from the rest. Two of these were captured, and the third escaped. (Clowes 3.141)

Grasshopper and *Rapid* v. Spanish convoy, 23 April 1808
The sloop *Grasshopper* (18; Cmdr Thomas Searle) and the brig *Rapid* (Lt Henry Baugh) encountered a Spanish convoy of two ships escorted by four gunboats off Faro, Portugal. The convoy anchored below a battery, but this was beaten down; two of the gunboats were run ashore, the other two surrendered. The ships, with a joint cargo worth £60,000, were then captured. (James 4.329–330; Clowes 5.415–416)

Grasshopper at Texel, 25 December 1811
Grasshopper (18; Cmdr Henry Fanshaw) was blown by a storm (in which *Hero* (74; Capt. James Newman) was wrecked) into the Nieuwe Diep, where she was compelled to surrender. (Clowes 5.498)

Grasshopper v. pirates, 23 November 1865
The screw gunboat *Grasshopper* (Lt George Morant) chased three pirate vessels near Amoy, China. They were penned into a bay and shelled. One blew up, and the other two were captured by boarding. (Clowes 7.211)

Great Yarmouth, 7 March 1547
A Scottish squadron, carrying supplies and reinforcements to Scotland from France, was captured by an English squadron. (Rodger 1.184)

Grecian v. slavers, 1839–1841
The brig *Grecian* captured the slavers *Ganges* and *Leal* off Cape Frio, Brazil, in April 1839, and *Maria Carlota* and *Recuperador* in May. Two years later she captured the slaver *Costante* in Rio de Janeiro harbour, being fired on by the Santa Cruz fortress as *Costante* was being towed out. (Bethell 149, 168, 204)

Grecian v. *Bella Miquelina*, 1848
The brig *Grecian* captured the slaver *Bella Miquelina*, carrying about 500

slaves, off Bahia, Brazil, and had to defeat an attempt from the shore to rescue the ship. (Bethell 288)

Greece, March–May 1941
A series of convoys from Alexandria transported British forces to Greece during March 1941, landing mainly at the port of Piraeus. The Italian submarine *Amfitrite* was sunk by the destroyer *Greyhound* while attacking a convoy on 6 March. An attack by one-man Italian explosive motorboats at Suda Bay, Crete, launched from the destroyers *Crispi* and *Sella* on 26 March, resulted in the cruiser *York* being disabled and a tanker sunk. The cruiser *Bonaventure* was sunk by the Italian submarine *Ambra* on 31 March. Evacuation of British troops from Greece took place on 24–29 April and resulted in the sinking of the destroyers *Diamond* and *Wryneck* and several transports; 50,000 troops were taken to Crete and Egypt. (Rohwer 62, 70)

Greenwich v. *Diademe* and others, 16–18 March 1757
Greenwich (50; Capt. Robert Roddam) was chased by a French squadron. *Diademe* (74), *Eveille* (64), and a frigate fired and surrounded her; Roddam was forced to surrender. (Clowes 3.293)

Grenaa, Denmark, 7 July 1810
Boats from *Edgar* (74) and *Dictator* (74) cut out three Danish armed luggers from this small port. (Anderson 343)

Grenada, West Indies
1762 The French garrison on Grenada was summoned to surrender by a small British force on 3 March. The governor refused, but two days later the inhabitants insisted. (Clowes 3.244)

1779 (Battle of GRENADA) Admiral Comte d'Estaing sailed from Martinique to capture St Vincent and Grenada. Vice-Admiral Hon. John Byron, with the British West Indies fleet, sailed to find the French. The British attacked in poor order on 6 July; several ships suffered badly, though none were captured. (Clowes 3.433–440; Mackesy, *America* 272–273; Mahan 367–370; Tunstall 162–164)

1796 A landing by British forces on Grenada was covered by the frigate *Mermaid* (32; Capt. Robert Otway) and two sloops. (James 1.412)

Greyhound v. Spanish *guarda costas*, 15 April 1722
Greyhound (20) was captured by Spanish *guarda costas*, but then quickly returned. (Clowes 3.310)

Greyhound v. *Hunter*, 1775
The sloop *Hunter* (10) was captured by a rebel American privateer off Boston in November 1775; it was soon after recaptured by *Greyhound* (28). (Colledge 190)

Greyhound and *Harrier* v. Dutch ships, July 1806
The frigate *Greyhound* (Capt. Charles Elphinstone) and a sloop *Harrier*

(Cmdr Edward Troubridge) captured the Dutch brig *Belgica* (12) in the East Indies on 6 July. On the 26th they found a squadron of Dutch vessels (the frigate *Pallas*, two Dutch EIC ships, *Vittoria* and *Batavia*, and the corvette *William*) south of Celebes (Sulawesi). The British ships combined to attack *Pallas*, which surrendered, then *Harrier* attacked and took *Vittoria*, and *Greyhound* captured *Batavia*. *William* escaped. (James 4.162–164; Clowes 5.386–387, 564)

Greyhound v. *Neghelli*, 19 January 1941
The Italian submarine *Neghelli* was sunk by the destroyer *Greyhound* after sinking a transport from a Piraeus convoy. (Rohwer 56)

Griffin v. *Polares*, 26 April 1940
The destroyer *Griffin* captured the German Q-ship *Polares* near Andalsnes, Norway; intelligence material was recovered. (Sebag-Montefiore 83–86; Rohwer 21)

Griffon v. slaver, 17 October 1888
The cutter of the gunvessel *Griffon* (Cmdr John Blaxland) chased the slave dhow off East Africa, which resisted until driven on shore and captured. Seventy-four slaves were rescued. (Clowes 7.390–391; Howell 194–195)

Grindall and *Keats* v. *U-285*, 15 April 1945
U-285 was sunk by the destroyers *Grindall* and *Keats* in the Bay of Biscay. (Rohwer 406)

Grinder v. Danish gunboats, 15 April 1810
The gunboat *Grinder* was captured near Anholt Island by four Danish gunboats. (Anderson 342)

Grive v. U-boat, 8 December 1917
The hired royal fleet auxiliary *Grive* was torpedoed in the North Sea and sank four days later. (Colledge 170)

Grove v. *U-77*, 12 June 1942
U-77 sank the destroyer *Grove*. (Rohwer 176)

Growler v. *Espiègle* and *Ruse*, 27 December 1797
The gun brig *Growler* (12; Lt John Hollingsworth) was boarded and captured at night by men from the luggers *Espiègle* and *Ruse* off Dungeness. Hollingsworth died. (James 2.105)

Growler v. slaver, 12 January 1845
A boat from the paddle sloop *Growler* (Cmdr Claude Buckle), commanded by Lt John Lodwick, challenged a slaving felucca off West Africa, but was fired on. Two men were killed and the boat damaged. The felucca got away. (Clowes 6.364)

Guadalcanal, Solomon Islands, 1942
Australian and New Zealand ships were part of the fleet covering the US landings at Guadalcanal on 7–9 August 1942; the RAN cruiser *Canberra* was heavily damaged on 9 August by Japanese fire. The RNZS minesweeper *Matai* and the corvette *Kiwi* were active in the fighting on 11 November. The RNZS cruiser *Achilles* was damaged by air attack on 4–5 January 1943, and the corvette *Moa* sunk by air attack on 7 April. (Rohwer 185, 210, 223, 244)

Guadeloupe, West Indies
1690 An expedition was organised at Barbados to attempt the conquest of Guadeloupe. Mariegalante Island was captured first, and the landing made on the main island on 21 April. The approach of a French squadron compelled the landing force to be withdrawn. (Clowes 2.465)

1703 Capt. Hovenden Walker, commanding a British squadron, raided Guadeloupe. (Clowes 4.503)

1759 A squadron under Capt. John Moore, using eight line-of-battle ships, bombarded and subdued forts protecting Basse Terre, and bombarded the town from four bomb vessels. The army was landed there and later at Fort Louis as well. French resistance continued in the interior until 1 May. (Clowes 3.202–203)

1794 A landing was made at Gosier on 10 April, covered by bombardment from the frigate *Winchelsea* (32; Capt. Lord Garlies). On the 20th another landing was made at Petit Bourg in Basse Terre, and these successes led to the capitulation of the island. On 3 June a French expedition retook the island, and the British fleet returned. A new landing was made, but the French prevailed. The last British holding, Fort Matilda, was evacuated on 10 December. (James 1.246–250; Duffy 93–95; Clowes 4.248–250; *NC* 1.83–86)

1809 Two French frigates *en flute*, *Loire* and *Seine*, took refuge in the harbour of Anse la Barque when their entry into Point-a-Pitre was prevented. British ships mounted a raid into the refuge. One battery was stormed by a party from the sloop *Ringdove* (16; Cmdr William Dowers). The frigates *Blonde* (36; Capt. Volant Ballard) and *Thetis* (38; Capt. George Miller) bombarded the French ships until first one and then the other exploded. A fort which had fired at the British ships was then stormed. (Clowes 5.447–448; James 5.58–63)

1810 Transported by the navy, a force of soldiers landed on Guadeloupe on 27 January. Within a week the French troops had been defeated; the island capitulated. (James 5.119–191)

1815 The governor of Guadeloupe, Comte Linois, adhered to Napoleon on his return from Elba; a landing was made on the island by a British force, the ships being commanded by Rear-Admiral Sir Philip Durham. The island capitulated after a short fight. (James 6.229)

Guadeloupe and *Loyalist* v. *Glorieux* and *Diligente*, 30 July 1781
Loyalist (16; Cmdr Morgan Laugharne) was captured after being chased by

Glorieux (74) and *Diligente* (26), which were part of the fleet of Admiral de Grasse; *Guadeloupe* (28; Capt. Hugh Robinson) was able to get away. (Clowes 4.72)

Guadeloupe v. *Tactique* and *Guèpe*, 27 June 1811
The sloop *Guadeloupe* (16; Cmdr Joseph Tetley) fought the corvette *Tactique* and the xebec *Guèpe* (8) off northeast Spain for two hours before the French ships got away into harbour. (James 5.253–254)

Guardian and others v. Angria's squadron, 1749
Guardian (28; Cmdr William James), with *Bombay* (28) and *Drake* (bomb), escorting a convoy from Bombay, were attacked by Angria's fleet of sixteen grabs and galivats; James sent the convoy on to Tellicherry and stood off the attacks, sinking one galivat and damaging several others. (Low 1.127)

Guernsey v. *White Horse*, 19 January 1678
Guernsey (32; Capt. James Harman) fought the Algerine warship *White Horse* (50). Several boarding attempts were repelled, and eventually the Algerine broke away. Harman was killed. (Clowes 2.453)

Guerrière v. *Peraty*, 17 July 1808
The frigate *Guerrière* (Capt. Alexander Skene) encountered and captured the schooner *Peraty* (10) near Florida. (James 4.337)

Guerrière v. *Constitution*, 19 August 1812
The frigate *Guerrière* (Capt. James Dacres) was intercepted off Nova Scotia by the US frigate *Constitution*. After a fight lasting two hours *Guerriere* was reduced to unmanageability and surrendered. (James 5.372–389; Clowes 6.134–137; *NC* 5.112–117)

Gulf of Bothnia, June–July 1855
Raids were made by a British squadron along the shores of the gulf. On 22 June the screw sloop *Harrier* (Cmdr Henry Story) raided shipping at Nystadt, destroying forty-seven sailing vessels. On 2 July the paddle sloop *Driver* (Cmdr Alan Gardner) and *Harrier* raided Raumo, bombarding the town without effect. *Harrier*, the paddle packet *Cuckoo*, and the paddle survey vessel *Firefly* attacked Brandon, where the British were driven off. Attacks were also made at Bjorneborg and other places. (Clowes 6.485–486, 490–491, 499)

Gulf of Finland, June–July 1855
Several ships raided the coasts of the gulf. On 6–7 June the paddle frigate *Magicienne* (Capt. Nicholas Vansittart) sent gunboats into Kansiala Bay and drove away some Russian forces. On 9 June five ships went close to Kronstadt to reconnoitre. The French corvette *D'Asass*, the paddle survey vessel *Firefly* (Capt. Henry Otter), and the paddle packet *Merlin* struck mines, though all three survived. On 20 June the screw frigate *Arrogant* (Capt. Hastings Yelverton), *Magicienne*, and the screw gunboat *Ruby* (Lt Henry Hale)

attacked and destroyed a fort at Rotchensalm. On 27 June *Firefly* and *Driver* (Cmdr Alan Gardner) bombarded and destroyed two masked but unarmed batteries at Christenestad. On 30 July *Ruby* and boats from *Magicienne* raided Werolax Bay, destroying twenty-nine ships. In July *Arrogant*, *Magicienne*, and *Ruby* attacked Loviso, Transsund, and other places. Joined by the screw corvette *Cossack* (Capt. Edward Fanshawe) they bombarded Frederikshamn on 21 July, and on 26 July Kotka; guard houses, workshops, and military stores were destroyed by a marine landing party. (Clowes 6.482–486, 488; Lambert 276–277)

Gulf of Riga, July–August 1855
The screw sloops *Archer* (Capt. Edward Heathcote) and *Desperate* (Cmdr Richard White) seized control of Arensburg Island, and raided in the gulf. More ships joined in, raiding along the coast. (Clowes 6.489–490, 496–499; Lambert 292)

Gulf of St Lawrence, July–August 1758
A British squadron of seven line-of-battle ships commanded by Rear-Admiral Sir Charles Hardy sailed along the coast of the Gulf, destroying French settlements, and took possession of Ile St Jean, which was renamed Prince Edward Island. (Clowes 3.184–185)

Gulf of Smyrna, Anatolia, May 1916
Long Island in the Gulf of Smyrna was occupied as a means of blockading the gulf, but the monitor *M-30* was bombarded and sunk on 13 May by fire from Turkish shore guns, so the island was evacuated on 27 May. (Halpern, *Mediterranean* 289)

Gulf of Thailand, June–August 1945
The submarine *Statesman* damaged the Japanese submarine depot ship *Kamahashi* in the gulf in June 1945, and *Taciturn* sank the submarine chaser *Cha-105* on 1 June. *Solent* and *Sea Scout* each sank a patrol boat on 1 August, and *Thorough* and *Taciturn* bombarded shore targets in the Bueleng Roads on that day. *Trump* and *Tiptoe* sank a freighter and the patrol boat *109* in a convoy on 3 August. (Rohwer 419, 422, 426)

Gurkha v. *U-8*, 4 March 1915
U-8, moving down the English Channel, was seen and attacked more than once on the journey. Eventually she was sunk by the destroyer *Gurkha*. (Corbett 2.276; Grant 22)

Gurkha v. *U-53*, 23 February 1940
The destroyer *Gurkha* met and sank *U-53* near the Faeroe Islands. (Rohwer 14)

Guthfrith on the Lancashire coast, 927
King Guthfrith of Dublin claimed the kingship of York, and when King Sitric died in 927 he gathered ships from Dublin and Anagassan and landed

somewhere on the coast of Lancashire, possibly at Heysham. His attempt to become king failed in the face of King Athelstan's determination to block him. (Smyth, *Dublin* 22–23)

Guysborough v. *U-868*, 17 March 1945
U-868 sank the Canadian minesweeper *Guysborough*. (Rohwer 397)

H

H-4 v. UB-52, May 1918
The British submarine *H-4* sank *UB-52* south of Cattaro. (Newbolt 5.411; Halpern, *Mediterranean* 454; Grant 132)

H-5 v. U-51, 14 June 1916
U-51, returning from a patrol, was torpedoed in the Ems estuary by the British submarine *H-5*. (Grant 36)

H-31 v. UJ-126, 18 July 1940
The submarine *H-31* sank the German submarine chaser *UJ-126* off Terschelling. (Rohwer 33)

H-49 v. German submarine chasers, 18 October 1940
The British submarine *H-49* was sunk by a flotilla of German submarine chasers off Terschelling. (Rohwer 45)

Haarlem v. American flotilla, 16 July 1779
Haarlem (14; Lt Josias Rogers) was chased by a rebel American flotilla and forced on shore, where it was captured. (Clowes 4.27)

Haddock v. Génie, 30 January 1809
The schooner *Haddock* (4) was captured by the French sloop *Génie* in the English Channel. (Clowes 5.552)

Halcyon v. Neptuno, 13 December 1806
The sloop *Halcyon* (Cmdr Henry Pearse) came up with three Spanish vessels, the corvette *Neptuno*, a brig, and a xebec, off Denia in Spain; five settees were also visible nearby. *Halcyon* concentrated on attacking *Neptuno*, which finally surrendered; meanwhile the brig, the xebec, and the settees got away. (James 4.185–186; Clowes 5.394–395)

Halcyon, Lively, and Leopard v. German squadron, 3 November 1914
A powerful German squadron, four battle-cruisers and four light cruisers, crossed the North Sea to lay mines and bombard the English coast in the area of Gorleston. The torpedo gunboat *Halcyon* challenged them and was shelled; she was assisted by the destroyers *Lively* and *Leopard*; all three were hit but not seriously. (Corbett 1.250–251)

Halcyon v. UB-27, 29 July 1917
The torpedo gunboat *Halcyon* attacked and rammed *UB-27* in the southern North Sea. The submarine submerged and was then destroyed by depth-charges. (Newbolt 5.130n, 425; Grant 62)

Hamadryad v. *Abigail*, 12 December 1812
The Danish ship *Abigail* was captured by the frigate *Hamadryad* (36; Capt. Edward Chetham). (Clowes 5.566)

Hampshire v. *Galgo*, April 1742
Hampshire (50) captured the Spanish sloop *Galgo* in the English Channel. (Colledge 155)

Hampshire and others v. *Sirene* and convoy, 16–18 October 1760
A squadron of four French frigates and a sloop left Cap François, St Domingue, and was chased by a British squadron commanded by Capt. Coningsby Norbury in *Hampshire* (50). The chase devolved into individual fights. *Boreas* (28; Capt. Samuel Uvedale) twice fought *Sirene*, finally forcing her surrender; *Lively* (20; Capt. Hon. Frederick Maitland) captured *Valeur* (20). *Prince Edward* (a French 32) was forced on shore; *Fleur de Lys* (32) was abandoned and burnt by her crew. One frigate, *Duc de Choiseul* (32), got into Port de Paix safely. (Clowes 3.225–226)

Hampshire near Orkney, 5 June 1916
The cruiser *Hampshire* (Capt. Savill), carrying Lord Kitchener to Russia, struck a mine off Marwick Head, Orkney, and sank in a few minutes; there were very few survivors. (Newbolt 4.20–22; Halpern, *Naval History* 329)

Hampton Court and others v. *Toulouse*, December 1711
Hampton Court (70; Capt. James Mighells) with a squadron of British ships encountered *Toulouse* (62) and *Trident* (56) near Port Mahon. *Hampton Court* fought *Toulouse*, which surrendered when also attacked by *Stirling Castle* (70). (Clowes 2.531)

Hampton Court v. *Nymphe*, 1757
Hampton Court (64) fought *Nymphe* (56) and drove her ashore on Majorca. (Clowes 3.295)

Han River, Korea, July 1951
The frigates *Cardigan Bay*, *Mounts Bay*, and *Morecambe Bay*, with four other frigates, operated in the Han River, Korea, fighting shore-based artillery and assisting land forces. (Wettern 54)

Hango Head, Finland, June 1855
Cossack (20; Capt. Edward Fanshawe) sent boats into Hango Head in a bungled attempt to land prisoners and obtain supplies. Fighting broke out and *Cossack* bombarded the town. (Clowes 6.481–482; Lambert 276)

Hannah v. Spanish privateer, 25 October 1806
The gunboat *Hannah* was captured near Algeciras by a Spanish privateer. (Clowes 5.551)

Hannibal v. *Necker*, 26 October 1781
Near the Cape of Good Hope, *Hannibal* (50; Capt. Alexander Christie) captured *Necker* (28), which was escorting a French convoy. (Clowes 4.76)

Hannibal v. *Héros* and *Artésien*, 18 January 1782
Hannibal (50; Capt. Alexander Christie) was chased and captured by *Héros* (74) and *Artésien* (64), part of the French fleet in the Indian Ocean. (Clowes 3.549, 4.77)

Hannibal and *Astraea* v. *Gloire* and *Gentille*, 10 April 1795
A British squadron cruising to the west of Brest met three French frigates, which turned away and separated. *Hannibal* (74; Capt. John Markham) captured *Gentille* (36); *Astraea* (52; Capt. Lord Henry Paulet) chased, fought, and captured *Gloire* (36). (James 1.315–316; Clowes 4.491)

Hannibal v. *Sultane*, 22 March 1814
The French frigate *Sultane*, already under a jury rig after an earlier fight with *Creole*, was chased by *Hannibal* (74; Capt. Sir Michael Seymour). When *Hannibal* caught up, *Sultane* was unable to fight, and quickly surrendered. (James 6.128–131; Clowes 5.547)

Happy Return v. French privateers, 4 November 1691
Happy Return (54; Capt. Peter Pickard) fought a group of French privateers near Dunkirk, and was captured. (Clowes 2.455)

Harlow's squadron v. French fleet, 14–17 August 1697
The French West Indian fleet under Admiral de Pointis, returning to Europe, encountered an English squadron under Capt. Thomas Harlow southwest of the Scilly Isles. A running fight lasting three days followed, until the French fleet was out of sight. (Clowes 2.494)

Harpy, Fairy, and others v. *Pallas*, 5 February 1800
The sloops *Fairy* and *Harpy* (Cmdrs Joshua Horton and Henry Bazely) fought the French frigate *Pallas* (46) off Cape Frehel. The sloops suffered serious damage to masts and rigging which had to be repaired. They then chased *Pallas*, which also met the frigate *Loire* (Capt. James Newman) and the sloops *Danae* (Capt. Lord Proby) and *Railleur* (Cmdr William Torquand). *Pallas* eventually succumbed. (James 3.3–8; Clowes 4.429–430)

Harpy v. *Penriche*, 12 March 1804
The French ship *Penriche* (2) was captured by *Harpy* (18; Cmdr Edmund Heywood) near Calais. (Clowes 5.556)

Harrier v. Malay pirates, 1834
Harrier (18; Cmdr Spencer Vassall) attacked pirate bases at Pulo Arroa and Pulo Sujee in the Strait of Malacca; both were destroyed. (Clowes 6.275)

Harrington and others v. Angria's fleet, 9–10 January 1739
Harrington (Capt. Robert Jenkins), *Pulteney*, *Ceres*, and *Halifax*, EIC Indiamen, were attacked by Angria's fleet, six grabs and nine smaller vessels. The fighting lasted two days, the Angrians concentrating on *Harrington*, which

finally beat off the attackers, but suffered considerable damage. (Low 1.108; Keay 284)

Hart v. Dutch ships, 1652
Hart (12) fought three Dutch ships and was forced to surrender. (Clowes 2.160)

Hart v. Coetquen, 9 June 1692
The ketch *Hart* (10; Capt. David Condon), escorting a convoy, was captured by the French privateer *Coetquen* (18), along with a second warship and five of the convoy. Condon was killed. (Clowes 2.468)

Harvester and Highlander v. U-32, 15 October 1940
U-32 was attacked and sunk by the destroyers *Harvester* and *Highlander* while itself aiming to attack a convoy. (Terraine 217; Rohwer 46)

Harvester and Hesperus v. U-208, 11 December 1941
The destroyers *Harvester* and *Hesperus* sank *U-208* west of Gibraltar. (Rohwer 121)

Hasty and Havock v. Berillo, 2 October 1940
The Italian submarine *Berillo* was sunk by the destroyers *Hasty* and *Havock* off Benghazi. (Rohwer 43)

Hasty and Hotspur v. U-79, 23 December 1941
A British convoy off Cyrenaica was attacked by *U-79* which sank one ship; the submarine was then itself sunk by the destroyers *Hasty* and *Hotspur*. (Rohwer 128)

Havana, Cuba
1748 A British convoy was threatened by a Spanish squadron of seven ships on 1 October; the escorting ship, *Lenox* (70; Capt. Charles Holmes), led the Spaniards towards a British squadron of seven vessels commanded by Rear-Admiral Charles Knowles, while the convoy dispersed. The two squadrons hesitantly approached each other and the fight was conducted at a discreet distance. Two Spanish ships and one British were badly damaged, allowing the British to claim a victory. Knowles was court-martialled on his return to Britain, and found guilty of 'negligence'. (Clowes 3.135–137; Tunstall 101–103)

1762 An expedition from Britain with forces collected in the West Indies attacked Havana. Vice-Admiral Sir George Pocock, commanding twenty-six line-of-battle ships and fifteen frigates, took the Bahamas Strait passage, and put the expeditionary force, 15,000 soldiers under General the Earl of Albemarle, on shore on 7 June. The attack on the city turned on the siege of Moro Castle, in which the navy assisted by bombardment. The castle was taken on 30 July and the city capitulated a fortnight later. Treasure of £3 million was secured and eight line-of-battle ships captured. Two smaller ships, *Thetis* (22) and the storeship *Fenix*, had been captured on the approach by *Alarm* (32; Cmdr James Almes). (Clowes 3.344–349)

Havelock v. *Faa di Bruno*, 8 November 1940
The Italian submarine *Faa di Bruno* was sunk by the destroyer *Havelock* near Rockall. (Rohwer 48)

Havock v. *Iride*, 31 August 1938
The destroyer *Havock* was attacked by the Italian submarine *Iride*. This was one incident in an Italian submarine campaign against ships conveying supplies to the Republicans in Spain. *Havock* spent several hours chasing and depth-charging *Iride* after the attack. Both ships survived. (H. Thomas, *The Spanish Civil War*, London 1961, 604–606)

Havock v. *Aradam*, 5 April 1942
The Italian submarine *Aradam* destroyed the destroyer *Havock*, which had run aground at Kelibia, by gunfire. (Rohwer 152)

Hawk v. French ship, November 1759
The sloop *Hawk* (10) was captured off Cape Clear by a French ship. (Clowes 3.311)

Hawk v. French convoy, 19 August 1811
The sloop *Hawk* (Cmdr Henry Bourchier) chased a convoy near the St Marcouf Islands off Normandy. The convoy escorts defended their charges, and *Hawk* drove most of the convoy and the escorts aground, then went aground herself. After getting free, under constant fire, boats were sent in against the convoy, of which the *Heron* (10) and three merchantmen were captured. (James 5.215–216; Clowes 5.490)

Hawke v. *U-9*, 15 October 1914
The light cruiser *Hawke*, part of a patrol in the North Sea east of Peterhead, was torpedoed by *U-9* and sank at once; about 500 men died. (Corbett 1.207–208; Halpern, *Naval History* 33)

Hazard v. *Renommée*, 24 November 1745
The sloop *Hazard* was captured in Montrose harbour by the French frigate *Renommée* and by fire from the shore. (Lavery 53–54)

Hazard v. *Musette*, 2 December 1796
The sloop *Hazard* (18; Cmdr Alexander Ruddach), after a brief fight, captured the French privateer *Musette*. (James 2.93)

Hazard v. *Hardi*, 1 April 1797
The sloop *Hazard* (18; Cmdr Alexander Ruddach) met the French privateer *Hardi* (18) off western Ireland, and chased and captured her. (James 2.92–93)

Hazard v. *Neptune*, 12 August 1798
The sloop *Hazard* (18; Cmdr William Butterfield) met the French armed ship *Neptune* (10), which was carrying 270 soldiers. They fought for two hours, until *Neptune* surrendered. (James 2.259; Clowes 4.513)

Hazard and *Pelorus* v. French schooner, 17 October 1809

The sloops *Hazard* (18; Cmdr Hugh Cameron) and *Pelorus* (Cmdr Thomas Huskisson) sent boats to attack a privateer schooner protected by a Guadeloupe battery. The schooner was captured, but was blown up; the attack cost the lives of six men; seven were wounded. (James 5.45; Clowes 5.445)

Hazard and *Speedy* v. German Destroyer Flotilla, 17 December 1941

The minesweepers *Hazard* and *Speedy* were attacked off the Kola coast, northern Russia, by the four ships of the German 8th Destroyer Flotilla; *Speedy* was damaged. (Rohwer 127)

Hebrides, Scotland (the Western Isles)

580 An expedition from northern Ireland and from Dal Riada attacked the Hebrides. This was clearly a naval exploit, but its precise size and purpose are not known. (*NHI* 1.216)

941 A force of 'foreigners', probably from Orkney, conquered the Western Isles. In reply Muirchertach mac Niell, king of Ailech in north Ireland, mounted an expedition against the Norse in those islands. (Oram 9)

1108 King Lagman of the Isles accompanied his overlord, King Sigurd of Norway, on crusade to the Holy Land; Lagman died on the way. Some of his men will have completed the journey and returned home. (Hudson 198–199)

1111 Donmall mac Taidc, having a claim to the kingship of the Isles, led a fleet there from Ireland on hearing of the death of King Lagman on crusade. His rule lasted only two years before he was expelled by the Islesmen. (Hudson 199–200)

1156 Somerled, ruler of Argyll, attempted to gain control of the Isles, but was challenged in this by King Godfrey of Man and the Isles. Somerled's fleet of eighty galleys and ships, including some from Dublin, defeated Godfrey's galleys, and he gained control of the islands south of Ardnamurchan; Godfrey retained Man and the islands north of Ardnamurchan. (MacDonald 54–56)

1221 Thomas of Galloway, commanding a fleet from Galloway, encountered and defeated a fleet commanded by Diarmait ua Conchobair from Ireland. (Oram 122)

1230 Half of a Norwegian fleet sailed on an expedition to the Hebrides, made up of ships provided by Jarl Jon of Orkney. (Thompson 80)

1495 An expedition led by King James IV in May asserted Scots royal authority in the Hebrides. The king based himself at Mingary, Ardnamurchan, and secured some control over Islay, Kintyre, and Tiree. (Nicholson 543; MacDougall 115–116)

1504 A squadron of ships commanded by the Earl of Arran sailed to the Western Isles, and bombarded Cairn-na-Burgh Castle in the Treshnish Islands. This effective demonstration of artillery power induced several recalcitrant chiefs to submit to the king in the next years. (Nicholson 546; MacDougall 185–186)

1506 An expedition from Dumbarton under the Earl of Huntly bombarded and took Stornoway Castle to capture Donald Dubh, a claimant to the lordship of the Isles. (Nicholson 546; MacDougall 189)

1719 A small expedition led by the Earl Marischal brought 300 Spanish troops to Stornoway, Isle of Lewis, where it was joined by Jacobite lords from France. (The Spanish expedition had been much larger, but was scattered by a storm.) The expedition landed at Loch Alsh, and seized Eilean Donan Castle. A Royal Naval squadron isolated the castle, which was held by just forty-five Spanish soldiers. Three ships, *Worcester*, *Enterprise*, and *Flamborough*, under the command of Capt. Charles Boyle, bombarded the castle, which quickly surrendered. (Clowes 3.39–40; Lavery 43–44)
See also: **Man, King Magnus's Expedition**

Hebrus and *Swallow* v. *Etoile*, 26–28 March 1814
The French frigate *Etoile* was chased by the frigate *Hebrus* (Capt. Edward Palmer) and the sloop *Swallow* (16; Cmdr Francis Loch) into waters close to Alderney. *Swallow* had been damaged already, but *Hebrus* caught up with *Etoile*, and for two hours the two ships fought until both were partly dismasted; *Etoile* surrendered. (James 8.128–131; Clowes 5.545–546)

Hecla v. *U-515*, 12 November 1942
The submarine depot ship *Hecla* was torpedoed by *U-515* west of Gibraltar. (Rohwer 212)

Hector v. *Aigle* and *Gloire*, 4 September 1782
Hector (74; Capt. John Bourchier), a French ship captured by Admiral Rodney and with only a prize crew, was part of a convoy sailing to Britain. She fell astern due to battle damage and was attacked by *Aigle* (40) and *Gloire* (32). The attack failed. *Hector*'s prize crew, after a very unpleasant time, were rescued by a British privateer. *Hector* sank. (Clowes 4.86–88)

The HELDER, Netherlands, 1799
An expedition was organised to take advantage of perceived anti-French sentiment in the Batavian Republic. British and Russian forces were to invade North Holland, hoping for an uprising to assist them; other offensives would take place in Switzerland and Italy, and perhaps Germany.

The expedition from Britain landed at the Helder on 27 August. The naval forces were commanded by Admiral Lord Duncan, but tactical command lay with Vice-Admiral Andrew Mitchell. He was successful early on in securing the surrender of a group of Dutch ships. The main Dutch fleet had been moved into the Zuider Zee, but Mitchell got his own ships to follow, trapped the Dutch, and induced Admiral Story to surrender. Ten line-of-battle ships, nine frigates, and four smaller vessels were captured.

The army was unable to advance against increasing enemy forces. On 7 October the Franco-Bavarian forces won the battle of Egmond, and the Russo-British retreated. A truce was followed by evacuation, over the same beaches where the invaders had landed. (James 2.343–351; Clowes 4.407–412; P. Mackesy, *The Strategy of Overthrow*, London 1974; *NC* 2.47–63)

Helena v. *Sensible*, September 1778
The brig *Helena* (14) was captured by the French frigate *Sensible*. (Clowes 4.207n)

Helena v. Spanish gunboats, 7 August 1781
Helena (14; Cmdr Francis Roberts) was attacked by fourteen Spanish gunboats at the approaches to Gibraltar; she survived, being eventually rescued by two British gunboats. (Clowes 4.73)

Helena v. *Leocadia*, 5 June 1805
The sloop *Helena* captured the Spanish sloop *Leocadia* in the Atlantic. (Colledge 226)

Helena v. *Jason*, 1 September 1809
The French brig *Jason* (10) was captured by *Helena* (18; Cmdr James Worth) off the Irish coast. (Clowes 5.559)

Helena v. *Revanche*, 13 November 1809
The French sloop *Revanche* (18) was captured by *Helena* (18; Cmdr James Worth). (Clowes 5.559)

Helga at Dublin, April 1916
The gunboat *Helga* bombarded nationalist positions in Dublin during the rebellion of Easter 1916. (R. Kee, *The Bold Fenian Men*, London 1976, 273)

Helgoland v. two U-boats, 8 September 1916
The armed brig *Helgoland* fought two German submarines off the Lizard; all involved survived. (Newbolt 4.336)

Heligoland Bight
1914 An elaborate trap was laid for the German patrols in the Heligoland Bight on 28 August, but fog and confusion resulted in a general free-for-all between British and German forces. The decisive action was the intervention, originally not intended, of the British battle-cruisers. Three German cruisers, *Mainz*, *Ariadne*, and *Köln*, were sunk, as was one German destroyer, *V-187*; two British light cruisers, *Arethusa* and *Fearless*, were badly damaged. (Corbett 1.98–120; Halpern, *Naval History* 30–32; Massie 97–121; Bennett 128–134)

1917 The British 1st Battle Cruiser Squadron planned to attack German minesweepers and so compel the larger German escorting ships to come to action (16 November). In the end one of the minesweepers was sunk and the bigger ships exchanged fire without serious result; the battle-cruiser *Repulse* was damaged, as was the light cruiser *Königsberg*. (Newbolt 5.164–177; Halpern, *Naval History* 377–378)

Heligoland Island, 5 September 1807
Heligoland, Danish territory, was captured by the frigate *Québec* (32; Capt. Viscount Falkland), escorted by *Majestic* (74). The island was annexed by Britain at the peace. (Anderson 320; Clowes 5.217; James 4.213; *NC* 4.49)

Herbert v. French squadron, 1690
The EIC ship *Herbert* was attacked by a French squadron on its way to India, and captured after a stubborn defence. (Low 1.77)

Hercule v. Poursuivante, 28 June 1803
Hercule (74; Lt John Hills) chased the frigate *Poursuivante* off St Domingue, but mismanaged the chase; the frigate escaped into Cap Nicolas Mole. (James 3.181–182; Clowes 5.317–318)

Hercules v. Souverain, 10 October 1759
Souverain (74), a survivor of a scattered French fleet, met *Hercules* (74; Capt. Jervis Porter) near the Canary Islands. The two ships fought an indecisive battle until *Hercules* was disabled; *Souverain* got away. (Clowes 3.302)

Hermes v. U-27, 31 October 1914
The cruiser/seaplane carrier *Hermes*, off Calais, was torpedoed and sunk by *U-27*; most of the crew were rescued. (Corbett 1.234; Halpern, *Naval History* 35)

Hermione at Puerto Rico, 22–23 March 1797
A Spanish brig and other vessels were sheltering under the guns of a fort in Puerto Rico. Boats from *Hermione* (32; Capt. Hugh Pigot) went to capture or destroy them; two were burnt, the rest brought out. Next day the guns were captured and spiked. (James 2.111–112; Clowes 4.334n)

Hermione v. Tambien, 1 August 1941
The cruiser *Hermione* rammed and sank the Italian submarine *Tembien* near Tunis. (Rohwer 89)

Hero and Venus v. Bertin, 3 April 1761
Bertin, *en flute*, a French East Indiaman carrying soldiers for India, was captured by *Hero* (74; Capt. William Fortescue) and *Venus* (36; Capt. Thomas Harrison). (Clowes 3.306)

Hero, Hurworth, and Eridge v. U-568, 28 May 1942
U-568 was sunk by the destroyers *Hero*, *Hurworth*, and *Eridge* off Sollum after a long chase. (Rohwer 166)

Heureux v. Egypt, 28 May 1801
Heureux (22; Capt. Loftus Bland) captured the French ship *Egypt* (16) near Barbados. (Clowes 4.558)

Heureux at Mahaut, 28–29 November 1808
The sloop *Heureux* (16; Cmdr William Coombe) sent boats into Mahaut, Guadeloupe, to cut out some of the ships there. The guns of one battery were spiked, and two ships were secured. The attackers were then driven off by artillery fire; the two captured ships grounded on the way out and could not be taken further. (James 4.334–335; Clowes 5.429)

Heythrop v. *U-652*, 20 March 1942
The destroyer *Heythrop* was attacked and damaged by *U-652* off Sollum; she was later sunk by the destroyer *Eridge*. (Rohwer 152)

Highflyer v. *President*, 23 September 1813
The US frigate *President* (48) captured the schooner *Highflyer* (5; Lt William Hutchinson) off Nantucket. (James 6.73; Clowes 5.554)

Highflyer v. *Kaiser Wilhelm der Grosse*, 26 August 1914
The AMC *Kaiser Wilhelm der Grosse* was found while coaling inside Spanish waters off Rio de Oro, West Africa, by the light cruiser *Highflyer*; the AMC was sunk, though the crew reached the shore. (Corbett 1.134–135; Halpern, Na*val History* 81)

Hilary v. *U-88*, 25 May 1917
The AMC *Hilary*, part of the Northern Patrol, was sunk by *U-88* west of Shetland. (NRS, *Maritime Blockade* no. 349)

Hinchinbrooke v. American privateers, 1778
The armed ship *Hinchinbrooke* (12) was captured by rebel American privateers. (Clowes 4.109)

Hind v. Sallee pirates, 1716
Hind (20; Capt. Arthur Delgarno) captured a pirate ship out of Sallee in May and another in October. (Clowes 3.258)

Hind v. *Reina Luisa*, January 1801
Hind (28; Capt. Thomas Larcom) captured *Reina Luisa* (2) near Jamaica. (Clowes 4.561)

Hippomenes v. *Egyptienne*, 25 May 1804
The sloop *Hippomenes* (14; Cmdr Conway Shipley) encountered the French privateer frigate *Egyptienne* (36), already damaged, which turned away; *Hippomenes* chased for three days, and then fought on the run for three hours; when *Hippomenes* closed, *Egyptienne* surrendered. (James 3.258–259; Clowes 5.342)

Hippomenes v. *Bonaparte*, 21 June 1804
The sloop *Hippomenes* (14; Capt. Kenneth McKenzie) near Antigua encountered the privateer *Bonaparte* (18). The two ships fought each other until Capt. McKenzie led a party to board the privateer, but only a few men

followed him (the rest, foreigners, refused). The privateers rallied and retook their ship. (James 3.272–275; Clowes 5.345)

Hispaniola, 27 December 1740
A detachment of four British line-of-battle ships encountered four French ships off Hispaniola. The British affected to believe that they were really Spanish ships sailing on false colours. (Britain was at war with Spain, but not with France.) The British fired, the French returned fire. The senior British officer, Capt. Lord Aubrey Beauclerk, finally sent an officer to establish just who it was he was fighting. The French were justifiably annoyed. (Clowes 3.64–65)

Holmes's 'Bonefire', 8 August 1666
Rear-Admiral Sir Robert Holmes, with nine warships, five fireships, and seven ketches, raided the Dutch anchorage and stores at Terschelling Island. About 170 merchant ships and some guardships were burned. Landing parties partly destroyed storehouses on the island. (Clowes 2.283–285; Rodger 2.76)

Holmes's squadron v. Smyrna fleet, 12–13 March 1672
The Dutch Smyrna fleet was attacked in the Channel by a squadron under Admiral Sir Robert Holmes. The Dutch were prepared, and the fight lasted two days. Half a dozen of the ships were taken. The Dutch declared war. (Clowes 2.441–443)

***Holmes* v. Sallee corsairs, October 1670**
Holmes (24; Capt. Henry Clarke) fought a series of Sallee raiders, driving one on shore, and burning another. (Clowes 2.439)

Holstock's cruise against the pirates, 1574
A small squadron commanded by the Controller of the Navy, William Holstock, cruised in the Channel in 1574 to discourage piracy. Twenty ships were taken and fifteen merchant ships were released. (Clowes 1.480)

Hong Kong, China
1941 In the Japanese conquest of Hong Kong, completed by 25 December 1941, the destroyer *Thracian*, the minelayer *Redstart*, four gunboats, and eight MTBs were sunk or scuttled. (Rohwer 127)

1945 A large British expedition reached Hong Kong on 30 August. It was threatened by some explosive motor boats; the boats were destroyed and their base shelled. The Japanese forces in the city surrendered on 16 September. (Rohwer 429)

***Hope* v. American privateer, January 1779**
The sloop *Hope* (16; Cmdr Michael Hindman) was captured by rebel American privateers. (Colledge 127)

Hope v. French ships, May 1781
The cutter *Hope* (14; Lt Lewis Vickers) was captured by French ships in American waters; Vickers was killed. (Clowes 4.111)

Horatio and others v. *Junon*, 8–10 February 1809
The French frigate *Junon*, south of the Virgin Islands, was pursued by a series of British frigates and sloops. The frigate *Horatio* (58; Capt. George Scott) did the main fighting, until her masts and rigging were heavily damaged. The sloop *Supérieure* (14; Cmdr William Ferrie) did most of the chasing, and the frigate *Latona* (38; Capt. Hugh Pigot) and the sloop *Driver* (18; Cmdr Charles Claridge) also took part. The chase and the fight lasted over two days. (James 5.4–9; Clowes 5.431–432)

Horatio v. *Necessité*, 21 February 1810
The frigate *Horatio* (38; Capt. George Scott) in mid-Atlantic met the French storeship *Necessité* (28), chased her for some hours, and fought for another hour; the storeship surrendered. (James 5.97; Clowes 5.451)

Horatio v. Danish ships, 2 August 1812
The frigate *Horatio* (38; Capt. Lord George Stuart) sent boats to attack Danish *Cutter no. 79* near Tromso in northern Norway. When found it was in company with *Schooner no. 114* and an American prize; the Danes resisted attack fiercely, and by the time the ships had been taken both sides had heavy casualties. (James 5.328–329; Anderson 346; Clowes 5.512)

Horatio v. *S-58*, January 1943
The German 3rd S-boat Flotilla sortied into Algerian waters; *S-58* sank the ASW trawler *Horatio*. (Rohwer 223)

Hornet v. French ships, December 1746
The sloop *Hornet* was captured by the French, but was soon retaken. (Clowes 3.311)

Hornet v. *Vencedora*, March 1836
The brigantine *Hornet* captured the slaver *Vencedora* off Brazil, but not having the necessary warrant had to release her. (Bethell 142)

Hound v. *Seine* and *Galatée*, 17 July 1794
The sloop *Hound* (16; Cmdr Richard Piercy) was captured west of the Scilly Isles by the French frigates *Seine* (40) and *Galatée* (36). (Clowes 4.488)

Hoyer, Germany, 24 March 1916
A raid by five seaplanes from the seaplane carrier *Vindex* against the Zeppelin base on Hoyer failed, since there was no such base. The covering destroyers sank two German armed trawlers but the destroyer *Medusa* was damaged in a collision and had to be abandoned. The destroyer *Cleopatra* met and rammed the German destroyer *G-194*, which sank, but *Cleopatra* then

collided with *Undaunted*, which was badly damaged. (Corbett 8.290–296; Halpern, *Naval History* 311)

Hudson River, New York, October 1777
In an attempt to assist the expedition of General Burgoyne from Canada, a river flotilla commanded by General Sir Henry Clinton sailed up the Hudson River, capturing American forts and batteries and burning ships. It was a good example of army–navy co-operation – but Burgoyne surrendered at Saratoga. (Clowes 3.392–393; Mackesy, *America* 138–140)

Hudson's Bay, Canada
1696–1697 An expedition was sent to recover control of Company posts captured by the French. *Bonaventure* (48; Capt. William Allin) and *Seaford* (20; Capt. John Grange) helped regain York fort and other posts. On their way out, on 24 August, they met a French vessel, the formerly English *Mary Rose* (50), which fought off their attack; Allin was killed. Next year *Hampshire* (48; Capt. John Fletcher), escorting a convoy in Hudson's Bay, was attacked on 26 August by the French *Pelican* (50) and other ships; *Hampshire* was sunk and the French squadron captured Fort Nelson. (Clowes 2.491, 495)

1782 A French squadron commanded by Captain Comte de la Perouse raided the Hudson's Bay Company posts at Forts Churchill and York; a Company ship just avoided being taken. The posts surrendered with neither resistance nor casualties. (Clowes 4.84–85)

Hull, Yorkshire, 1642–1643
Under siege by Royalist forces, Hull was relieved by Parliamentary ships in June 1642 and October 1643. (Rodger 1.416)

***Hunter* v. privateers, 23 November 1775**
The sloop *Hunter* was captured by two American privateers off Boston, as was an accompanying British brig; both were soon retaken. (Clowes 4.3)

***Hussar* and *Dolphin* v. *Alcion*, 23 November 1757**
Hussar (28; Capt. John Elliott) and *Dolphin* (24; Capt. Benjamin Marlow) met and fought the French ship *Alcion* (50) in a night action. *Alcion* was so badly damaged that she sank. (Clowes 3.297)

***Hussar* v. *Nuestra Senora de la Buen Confeso*, 19 November 1779**
Hussar (28; Capt. Elliott Salter) was detached from a convoy to chase *Nuestra Senora de la Buen Confeso* (28), which surrendered after a day's chase and a short fight. (Clowes 4.46)

***Hussar* v. *Sybille*, 22 January 1783**
The French frigate *Sybille* (32), partly dismasted and badly damaged after a fight with *Magicienne*, had jettisoned several guns and now had only twenty. *Hussar* (28; Capt. Thomas Russell) attacked her several times, and *Centurion*

(50) joined in. *Sybille* jettisoned even more guns, but then surrendered when her magazine was flooded. (Clowes 4.93)

Hyacinth, Termagent, and *Basilisk* at Nerja and Almunecar, 20–27 May 1812

Hyacinth (20; Capt. Thomas Ussher) along with *Termagent* (16; Capt. William Gawen) and *Basilisk* (6; Lt George French) bombarded the castle at Nerja in southern Spain, which was then occupied by guerrillas from inland. The ships then bombarded Almunecar, carried a group of guerrillas there, and the French retired to Granada. (James 5.337–538; Hall 127–128; Clowes 5.506–507)

Hyacinth v. slaver, 13 August 1844

A gig with men from the sloop *Hyacinth* (18; Cmdr Francis Scott) drove ashore a large slave brig at Fish Bay, West Africa. The gig commander, Mate John Tottenham, was made lieutenant for this action. (Clowes 6.363)

Hyacinth v. *Perla,* 9 July 1942

The corvette *Hyacinth* sank the Italian submarine *Perla* off Beirut. (Rohwer 179)

Hyacinth v. *Fisalia,* 28 September 1942

The corvette *Hyacinth* sank the Italian submarine *Fisalia* off Haifa. (Rohwer 102)

Hyaena v. *Concorde,* 27 May 1793

Hyaena (24; Capt. William Hargood) was chased by *Concorde* (14), the advance frigate of a French squadron, off Cape Tiburon, St Domingue. Unable to escape, *Hyaena* fired token shots at *Concorde,* and surrendered. *Hyaena*, as *Hyène*, was retaken in 1797. (James 1.105–106; Clowes 4.476)

Hyderabad, Sind, February 1843

Several vessels of the BM took part in the fighting around Hyderabad which resulted in the annexation of Sind. (Low 2.172–178)

Hydra and others v. *Confiante* and others, 30–31 May 1798

The frigate *Hydra* (Capt. Sir Francis Laforey), the bomb *Vesuvius* (8), and the cutter *Trial* (12) encountered three French ships near the mouth of the Orne River in Normandy. The frigate *Confiante* was driven ashore by *Hydra*, which next day sent in boat parties to burn her; the corvette *Vésuve* was driven ashore, but later took refuge in the Orne. (James 2.133–137; Clowes 4.342–343)

Hydra v. *Favori,* 1 August 1803

The frigate *Hydra* (Capt. George Mundy) sent in boats to secure the French lugger *Favori* (4) anchored near Le Havre; it was brought out in the face of considerable flanking fire. (James 3.171–172; Clowes 5.50)

Hydra v. *Furet*, 27 February 1806
The frigate *Hydra* (Capt. George Mundy) followed a French squadron of four frigates and the corvette *Furet* out of Cadiz. The corvette lagged behind the rest, and was captured without resistance; the frigates sailed on. (James 4.120; Clowes 4.198)

Hydra v. *Argonauta*, 12 April 1806
The Spanish brig *Argonauta* (12) was captured by the frigate *Hydra* (Capt. George Mundy) off the coast of Spain. (Clowes 5.563)

Hydra at Bagur, Catalonia, 6 August 1807
In order to seize ships in the harbour of Bagur, Capt. George Mundy anchored his frigate *Hydra* in the harbour entrance and bombarded the forts. A party was landed to capture the fort commanding the harbour, then the three ships in the harbour were taken. (James 4.263–264; Clowes 5.401)

Hydra v. *Unaio*, 1849
Hydra (Cmdr Grey Skipwith), off the southeast of America, captured the armed slaver *Unaio*. (Clowes 6.367)

Hyères Islands, Provence
1710 A French ship from Scanderoon was discovered in Hyères road. A party sent in by Admiral Sir John Norris to take the ship first captured the fort. The ship was boarded, then blew up. (Clowes 2.525)

1795 The British Mediterranean fleet commanded by Vice-Admiral William Hotham came up with the French Toulon fleet, which was trying to get back to Toulon. The forward British ships fought the rearward French, and *Alcide* (74) was taken. The wind changed, giving the French the weather gauge, while the British were becalmed. *Alcide* took fire and exploded soon after the action ended. (James 1.296–302; Clowes 4.274–277; *NC* 1.144–154)

Hyperion v. *Serpente*, 21–22 December 1940
The destroyer Hyperion was torpedoed by the Italian submarine *Serpente* in the Sicilian Channel and later sank. (Rohwer 52)

Hythe v. *U-371*, 11 September 1943
U-371 sank the minesweeper *Hythe* off the Algerian coast. (Rohwer 275)

I

Ibiza and Majorca, Balearic Islands, 1706
The islands were surrendered to the English Mediterranean fleet commanded by Sir John Leake. (Clowes 2.409)

***Immortalité* v. *Invention*, 27 July 1801**
The frigate *Immortalité* (Capt. Henry Hotham) captured the French privateer *Invention*, an experimental ship with four masts. (James 3.141–142; NC 2.235)

***Immortalité* and others v. *Inabordable* and *Commode*, 14 June 1803**
The frigate *Immortalité* (Capt. Edward Owen), with the sloops *Cruizer* and *Jalouse* (Cmdrs John Hancock and Christopher Strachey), chased the schooner *Inabordable* (4) and the brig *Commode* (4) until they went on shore at Cap Blanc Nez. *Cruizer* and *Jalouse* bombarded the battery above the ships, then went in and brought both ships off. (James 3.171; Clowes 5.49–50)

***Impérieuse* on the Catalonian and Languedoc coasts, February–September 1808**
The frigate *Impérieuse* (36; Capt. Lord Cochrane) raided the Catalonian and Balearic coasts, sinking gunboats and destroying forts; after the Spanish uprising Cochrane operated to assist Spanish forces. On 31 July marines were landed at Mongat, north of Barcelona, to assist Spanish militia besieging the castle; it was taken and demolished. Cochrane then repeatedly landed along the coast of Languedoc, destroying six telegraphs, fourteen barracks, a battery, and a fortified tower. (James 4.384–385; Clowes 5.405–407; Thomas 124–137; Hall 49–50)

***Impérieuse* v. *Gauloise* and *Julie*, 30 December 1808**
Impérieuse (36; Capt. Lord Cochrane) sank *Gauloise* (7) and *Julie* (5) in Caldagues Bay, Catalonia, and captured eleven ships laden with supplies. (Clowes 5.430; Hall 54)

***Impérieuse* on the Italian coast, October–November 1811**
The frigate *Impérieuse* (Capt. Hon. Henry Duncan) raided Positano harbour on 11 October. A party landed first to capture the town's fortress which was partly demolished; two gunboats were taken out and one sunk. *Impérieuse* and the frigate *Thames* (Capt. Charles Napier) raided a convoy near Palinuro, Calabria, taking away ten laden polacres. On 1 November the soldiers of the 62nd Foot from Sicily were landed at Palinuro itself, and a combined land and sea action captured the fort. Two gunboats were sunk and more captured; two batteries and a signal tower were destroyed; twenty-two laden feluccas were taken off. (James 5.258–260; Clowes 5.494–495)

Impetueux and *Sylph* v. *Sainte Famille*, 5 April 1798
Impetueux (74) and *Sylph* (16) captured the French *chasse-marée Sainte Famille*. (Clowes 4.555)

Impetueux v. *Insolente*, 6 June 1800
Boats from *Impetueux* (74; Capt. Sir Edward Pellew) burnt *Insolente* (18) in Quiberon Bay, Brittany. (Clowes 4.415)

Implacable and *Centaur* v. *Sewolod*, 26 August 1808
Implacable (74; Capt. Byam Martin) and *Centaur* (74; Capt. William Webley), the flagship of Rear-Admiral Sir Samuel Hood, attached to the Swedish fleet in the Baltic, followed the retiring Russian fleet, where one Russian ship, *Sewolod* (74), lagged behind. *Implacable* and *Sewolod* fought; the latter signalled surrender, but the approach of the Russian fleet compelled Hood to recall *Implacable*. *Sewolod* was recovered by the Russians, but grounded off Rogerswick; *Centaur* came up to make good the earlier surrender. A new fight followed, until *Implacable* arrived and *Sewolod* finally surrendered. She had grounded again, and so was burned. (James 4.300–302; Anderson 331–333; Clowes 5.248–250; NC 4.187–188)

Ina Williams v. *U-35*, 5 June 1915
The armed trawler *Ina Williams* fought *U-35* off Mizen Head, Ireland, though neither ship was damaged. (Corbett 3.46)

Incendiary v. *Indivisible* and *Créole*, 29 January 1801
The fireship *Incendiary* (16; Cmdr Richard Dunn) was captured and destroyed by the French *Indivisible* (80) and the frigate *Créole* off Cape Spartel. (James 3.71; Clowes 4.448)

Inch Island, Lough Swilly, Ireland, 9–10 July 1698
The island was occupied by several hundred soldiers landed from ships of the Derry relieving force. A redoubt was built and communications established with besieged Derry. (Powley 233–235)

Inconstant v. *Curieux*, 3 June 1793
The frigate *Inconstant* (56; Capt. Augustus Montgomery) captured the French brig *Curieux* (14) in the West Indies. (Clowes 4.552)

Inconstant v. *Speedy*, March 1795
The French brig *Speedy* was captured by the frigate *Inconstant* (36; Capt. Charles Fremantle) in the Mediterranean. (Clowes 4.553)

Inconstant v. *Unité*, 28 April 1796
The French corvette *Unité* was cut out of the (neutral) harbour of Rona by the frigate *Inconstant* (36; Capt. Thomas Fremantle). (Clowes 4.496)

Indefatigable v. *Virginie*, 20–21 April 1796
The frigate *Indefatigable* (58; Capt. Sir Edward Pellew) chased the French

frigate *Virginie* (40) near Ushant. The chase lasted fifteen hours and the subsequent fight two hours. The arrival of two more frigates finally brought *Virginie* to surrender. (James 1.361–362; Clowes 4.496–497)

Indefatigable and *Amazon* v. *Droits de l'Homme*, 13–14 January 1797

Droits de l'Homme (74), carrying troops intended to be landed in Ireland, was sighted by *Indefatigable* (38; Capt. Sir Edward Pellew) and *Amazon* (36; Capt. Robert Reynolds) west of Ushant. In a storm, the French ship, hampered by being unable to open her lower-deck gunports for long, fought against her antagonists for almost twelve hours in one of the most renowned engagements of the time. *Droits de l'Homme* was badly damaged, and lost at least one mast, while the British ships more than once broke off the fight to make emergency repairs. Soon after 4 a.m. on the 14th, all three ships were close to the Penmarcks rocks. *Indefatigable* was able to get clear, but *Amazon* and *Droits de l'Homme* were both wrecked. Most of the crew of *Amazon* got ashore (to be made prisoners); most of those on *Droits de l'Homme* perished, the few survivors being rescued after four days. (James 2.12–22; Clowes 4.302–304; *NC* 1.166–170)

Indefatigable v. *Ranger* and *Hyène*, 14 October 1797

The frigate *Indefatigable* (38; Capt. Sir Edward Pellew) captured the French *Ranger* (14) near the Canary Islands. On 25 October the French privateer *Hyène* (24), assuming *Indefatigable* was an Indiaman, proposed to attack. *Indefatigable* chased her for eight hours and compelled her to surrender. (James 2.101–102; Clowes 4.508)

Indefatigable v. *Vaillante*, 7 August 1798

The frigate *Indefatigable* (38; Capt. Sir Edward Pellew) chased and captured the corvette *Vaillante* (20) off the Ile de Re. (James 2.258; Clowes 4.513)

Indefatigable and *Fishguard* v. *Vénus*, 22 October 1800

The French corvette *Vénus* (28) was captured by the frigates *Indefatigable* (38) and *Fishguard* (38) off the Portuguese coast. (Clowes 4.534)

Indefatigable and others v. Spanish treasure ships, 3 October 1804

Britain and Spain were at peace. A large treasure was expected at Cadiz from America. In London it was believed to be destined for France. The frigates *Indefatigable* (38; Capt. Graham Moore), *Medusa* (32; Capt. John Gore), *Amphion* (32; Capt. Samuel Sutton), and *Lively* (38; Capt. Graham Hamond) were sent to intercept the four frigates carrying the treasure. The interception degenerated into a fight. One frigate, *Mercedes* (34), soon blew up; the other three, *Medea* (40), *Clara* (34), and *Fama* (34), were forced to surrender. The value of the prize was put at £1 million; the result was a Spanish declaration of war, and considerable detestation of British methods both at home and abroad. (James 3.386–390; Clowes 5.350–352; *NC* 3.71–77)

Indefatigable and others v. *Tirpitz*, 22 August 1944

An attack by aircraft from the carriers *Indefatigable*, *Formidable*, and *Furious* on the German battleship *Tirpitz* in Kaa Fjord, Norway, damaged the ship slightly. Later *U-354* sank the frigate *Bickerton* and damaged the carrier *Nabob*, but was itself sunk in retaliation. (Schofield 200–201; Rohwer 350)

India, 1857–1858
During the Indian mutiny a Naval Brigade was formed from the crew of the screw frigate *Shannon*. Commanded most of the time by Capt. William Peel, the brigade took part in fighting near Cawnpore (Kanpur) and Lucknow (Laknau). Peel, badly wounded, died. Another Naval Brigade, from the crew of the screw corvette *Pearl*, under the command of Capt. Edmund Sotheby, operated along the Ganges and the Nepal frontier. (Clowes 7.138–149)

***India* v. *U-22*, 8 August 1915**
The AMC *India* was sunk by *U-22* off Norway. (Colledge 194)

Indian Ocean Convoys, 1943–1944

PA-44, 5 July 1943
One ship was sunk from this convoy by the Japanese submarine *I-27*. (Rohwer 243)

BC-2, 1 August 1943
One ship was sunk from this convoy by *U-198*. (Rohwer 243)

CB-21, 2 August 1943
One ship was sunk from this convoy by *U-196*. (Rohwer 243)

AP-47, 5 October 1943
The Japanese submarine *I-10* sank a tanker from this convoy. (Rohwer 273)

KR-8, 12 February 1944
This convoy was attacked by the Japanese submarine *I-27* while passing through the Maldive Islands; a troop transport was sunk with heavy loss of life. The destroyer *Petard* forced the submarine to the surface and then sank her by torpedo; the destroyer *Paladin* was badly damaged during the fight. (Rohwer 406)

PA-69, 23 February 1944
U-510 sank a ship from this convoy. (Rohwer 299)

***Industry* v. U-boat, 19 October 1918**
The Q-ship *Industry* (also operating as *Tay* or *Tyne*) was torpedoed, but survived and reached harbour. (Colledge 195)

***Inflexible* v. Chinese pirates, 30 May 1849**
The paddle sloop *Inflexible* (Cmdr John Hoseason) attacked a pirate base in the Lemma Islands near Hong Kong. A boat party cut out eight junks; others were damaged or destroyed by fire from the ship. (Clowes 6.353)

Inis Cathaig, River Shannon, Ireland, 974
In a dispute between Viking kings, Magnus Haraldsson of the Isles fought

Olaf of Anglesey and Ivar of Limerick at Inis Cathaig in the River Shannon. Magnus won after circumnavigating Ireland during the campaign. The monastery on Inis Cathaig, now Scattery Island, was raided by a force commanded by Magnus, who was accompanied by 'the Lawman' of the Isles. (Hudson 59; Oram 10)

Inishowen, Ireland, 1154
Toirrdelbach ua Conchobair, king of Connaught, made a raid by sea on Tir Connaill and Inishowen in northeast Ireland. Muirchertach mac Lochlainn, king of Cenel nEoghan, gathered ships from Kintyre, Arran, Galloway, and Man; in the battle the Connaught fleet was victorious, causing great casualties to the enemy. (Oram 73)

Intrepid and *Chichester* v. *Sirène*, August 1794
The French *Sirène* (16) was captured by *Intrepid* (64) and *Chichester* (44) off St Domingue. (Clowes 4.553)

Intrepid v. *Percante*, 21 April 1796
Intrepid (64; Capt. Hon. Charles Carpenter) captured *Percante* (26) in the West Indies. (Clowes 4.554)

Inverlyon v. *UB-40*, August 1915
The sailing smack *Inverlyon*, armed with a small gun, patrolled to protect other fishing vessels off Lowestoft; when *UB-4* approached she sank the submarine. (Corbett 3.129; Grant 27)

Invincible v. *Argo*, 16 February 1783
Invincible (74; Capt. Charles Saxton) recaptured *Argo* (44), which had been taken by the French three days before. (Clowes 4.94)

Ionian Islands, Greece, October 1809
The lesser Ionian Islands were taken from the French by British expeditions: Cerigo by the frigate *Spartan* (Capt. Jahleel Brenton) and troops of the 35th Foot; Ithaca by the sloop *Philomel* (Cmdr George Crawley) and some soldiers; Zante and Cephalonia by *Warrior* (74; Capt. John Spranger) and soldiers. No resistance was encountered. (James 4.449; Mackesy, *Mediterranean* 351–355)

Iphigenia v. *Actif* and *Espiègle*, 16 March 1794
The frigate *Iphigenia* (32; Capt. Patrick Sinclair) captured *Actif* (16) and *Espiègle* (12) in the West Indies. (Clowes 4.552)

Iphigenia at the Bonny River, West Africa, 15 April 1822
Boats from *Iphigenia* rowed into the Bonny River, West Africa, and were fired on by slavers, two Spanish schooners and three French brigs. These they rapidly boarded and captured; over 1400 slaves were freed. (Ward 108–109)

Ipswich and *Revenge* v. *San Isidro*, Ajaccio, 1743
The Spanish ship *San Isidro* (70), anchored in the Bay of Ajaccio, Corsica,

was attacked by a cutting-out expedition from *Ipswich* (70; Capt. William Martin) and *Revenge* (70; Capt. George Berkeley). Unable either to surrender or fight, the captain fired *San Isidro*, which blew up with many casualties. (Clowes 3.273)

Ireland

962 A Viking fleet from Anglesey led by Sihtric Camm, a claimant to the Dublin kingship, raided the island of Ireland's Eye, the mainland near Lusk, County Down, and in Munster. (Hudson 41, 60)

1169–1171 The exiled king of Leinster, Dermot mac Morrough, appealed for assistance in recovering his kingdom to Richard Strongbow, Earl of Pembroke, Robert FitzStephen, and Maurice FitzGerald. The latter two collected a force of about 500 men, landed at Bannow, and soon captured Wexford. Strongbow followed, having gained permission from Henry II, landing at Waterford. King Henry himself came in 1171, also landing at Waterford, in order to ensure that none of his subjects became too powerful. (D. O'Croinin, *Early Medieval Ireland 400–1200*, Harlow 1995, 285–287; R. Frame, *The Political Development of the British Isles, 1100–1400*, Oxford 1990, 35–39)

1313–1315 Edward Bruce, with a Scottish army, landed in Belfast Lough and campaigned against the English in Ireland, causing great destruction and decisively weakening English power. (Barrow 434–436)

1545 Donald Dubh invaded Ireland with a fleet of 150 galleys recruited in the Western Isles, but soon died at Drogheda. (Rodger 1.184)

1796–1797 A French expedition set out from several ports to land an army in Ireland, but it was scattered by a storm. The rendezvous, Bantry Bay, was missed by most ships; some were damaged and returned to France; others were wrecked on the Irish coast; still others were captured by British patrols. Of the warships lost, the frigates *Impatiente* and *Surveillante* were wrecked; the frigate *Tortue* was captured by *Polyphemus* (64), and the corvette *Atalante* was also captured. (James 2.3–12; Clowes 4.297–302)

Iris v. *Hermione*, 6 June 1780
The frigate *Iris* (32; Capt. James Hawker) fought the French frigate *Hermione* (32) in the West Indies. The two ships, equal in force, broke off the fight, apparently by mutual consent, after an hour. (Clowes 4.52)

Iris v. *Trumbull*, 8 August 1781
Trumbull (32), a rebel American frigate damaged in a gale, and with a weak crew, was captured after a short fight by *Iris* (32; Capt. George Dawson). A month later *Iris* and *Richmond* (32; Capt. Charles Hudson), in Chesapeake Bay, were captured by the squadron of Admiral de Barras. (Clowes 4.72–73, 75)

Iris v. *Citoyenne Française*, 13 May 1793
The frigate *Iris* (32) chased the French privateer *Citoyenne Française*. They

fought for a time until *Citoyenne Française* managed to get clear. *Iris*'s mast fell, the French ship sailed away. (James 1.101–103; Clowes 4.475–476)

Irish Sea
1035 Echmarcach was expelled from Dublin; his successor, Imart mac Arailt, pursued him by sea as far as the North Channel and Rathlin Island. (Oram 60)

1058 The exiled Earl of Mercia, Aelfgar, recruited fleets and allies around the Irish Sea, including Magnus, son of the king of Norway, who had forces from Orkney, the Isles, and Dublin under his command. The course of the fighting is unknown, but Aelfgar was reinstated as earl. (Hudson 148–149; *ASC* s.a. 1058)

Irresistible **and** *Emerald* **v.** *Ninfa* **and** *Santa Elena*, **26 April 1797**
Irresistible (74; Capt. George Martin) and the frigate *Emerald* (36; Capt. Velters Berkeley) followed two Spanish frigates, *Ninfa* (34) and *Santa Elena* (34), into Conil Bay near Trafalgar. Both Spanish ships were captured, though *Santa Elena* was wrecked. The frigates had landed the treasure they had carried by means of fishing boats the night before. (James 2.93–94; Clowes 4.507)

Ischia and Procida, Bay of Naples, 24–25 June 1809
An expedition under the command of Rear-Admiral George Martin took control of the islands of Ischia and Procida. Procida was occupied without opposition; a castle on Ischia held out for a few days. (James 5.52–53; Clowes 5.440)

Isis **v.** *Escarboucle*, **1757**
Isis (50) captured the French sloop *Escarboucle*. (Clowes 3.313)

Isis **v.** *Rhinocéros*, **September 1758**
Isis (50) captured and burnt the French frigate *Rhinocéros* (36). (Clowes 3.313)

Isis **and** *Aeolus* **v.** *Blonde* **and** *Mignonne*, **19 March 1759**
Isis (50; Capt. Edward Wheeler) and *Aeolus* (32; Capt. John Elliot) met a French convoy off Ile d'Yeu in the Bay of Biscay. Two of the escort fought: *Blonde* (32) escaped; *Mignonne* (20) was captured. (Clowes 3.301)

Isis **v.** *Oriflamme*, **1 April 1761**
Isis (50; Capt. Edward Wheeler) fought and captured *Oriflamme* (40) in the Mediterranean; Wheeler was killed. (Clowes 3.306)

Isis **v.** *César*, **16 August 1778**
Isis (50; Capt. John Raynor) was attacked by *César* (74), but replied by bombarding *César* on the side where it was not prepared for battle. The two ships effectively disabled each other. (Clowes 4.17–18)

Isis and *Warwick* v. *Rotterdam*, December 1780
Isis (50; Capt. Evelyn Sutton) attacked *Rotterdam* (50) in the English Channel, but *Isis*'s crew were raw and untrained, so *Rotterdam* got away without difficulty. She had already escaped from another line-of-battle ship and six days later met *Warwick* (50; Capt. Hon. George Elphinstone) to which she was surrendered at once. (Clowes 4.59–60)

Islands in the Bay of Biscay
Belle Isle
1413 An English squadron commanded by Sir John Colville stopped two Prussian hulks near Belle Isle, demanding to investigate their cargoes; the Prussians refused and attacked, but were captured and taken into Southampton and Poole. (Clowes 1.370–371)

1761 A British expedition of 7000 men, fifteen line-of-battle ships, and eight frigates sailed to attack Belle Isle. A first attempt at landing on 8 April was a failure; a second on 22 April succeeded, but it took until 8 June to capture the whole island. (Clowes 3.235–236)

Ile d'Aix
1758 Admiral Sir Edward Hawke, in command of seven line-of-battle ships and three frigates, located a French convoy of forty merchantmen escorted by five line-of-battle ships and seven frigates off Ile d'Aix on 4 April. By threatening to attack, the British forced the French ships to try to escape; many went aground. There was little fighting, except by a group of marines who were landed on the island to destroy the defences; the convoy, which had 3000 troops on board, was prevented from sailing to Canada. (Clowes 3.190–191)

1761 A squadron under Capt. Peter Parker, detached from the main fleet off Belle Isle on 21 June, attacked and destroyed the fortifications on Ile d'Aix. (Clowes 3.237)

Ile de Ré
1462 A large English fleet under the Earl of Kent raided Le Conquet in Brittany in September. A force was landed and ravaged the Ile de Ré, capturing ships and booty. (Clowes 1.388)

1627 The Duke of Buckingham led an expeditionary force, carried in 100 ships, against France. The intention had been to join with Huguenots at La Rochelle, who were in rebellion, but the French Royalists blocked the harbour. Buckingham landed his forces on the Ile de Ré, but was unable to take St Martin Castle, and withdrew in October. (Rodger 1.360; Clowes 3.66–70)

Ile d'Yeu, October 1795
The island was taken by Capt. Sir John Borlase Warren; a substantial French Royalist garrison was installed, but was evacuated in December. (James 1.280; Clowes 4.267)

Ile Groix

1760 Capt. Hon. Augustus Hervey in *Dragon* (74) was fired at from a fort on Ile Groix on 12 July. He landed a force in boats, and captured and dismantled the fort. (Clowes 3.303)

1795 The British Channel Fleet under Admiral Lord Bridport was covering the British landing force heading for Quiberon. On 22 June the French fleet under Admiral Villaret-Joyeuse came out from behind Belle Isle where it had been sheltering from a storm, and turned for Brest. Bridport ordered a chase, but only the most advanced British ships reached the enemy, and only the most rearward of the French were attacked. Three French ships, *Formidable*, *Alexandre*, and *Tigre* (all 74s), were taken, and Bridport then discontinued the action. The French ships took shelter behind Ile Groix. (James 1.270–278; Clowes 4.260–266)
See also: **Bay of Biscay, Gironde River**

Islay v. *Scire*, 11 August 1942

The Italian submarine *Scire* was sunk by the ASW trawler *Islay*. (Rohwer 183)

Isle of Pines, Cuba, 1 March 1596

An English squadron which had raided in the West Indies and was now commanded by Sir Thomas Baskerville was intercepted by a Spanish squadron near the Isle of Pines. In the fight which followed neither side suffered serious damage, and the English got away. (Rodger 1.284; Clowes 1.507–508; Andrews 203)

Itchen and *J-2* v. *U-99*, 6–7 July 1917

U-99 torpedoed the destroyer *Itchen* in the Norwegian Sea on 6 July; the submarine was sunk next day by the British submarine *J-2*. (Grant 60–61)

Ivernia v. *UB-47*, 1 January 1917

The troopship *Ivernia* was torpedoed and sunk off Cape Matapan by *UB-47*; 125 men died. (Halpern, *Mediterranean* 325)

J

***J-1* v. *Grosser Kurfürst* and *Kronprinz*, 3 November 1916**
Four German battleships came out to rescue two stranded U-boats. The British submarine *J-1* fired torpedoes which damaged both *Grosser Kurfürst* and *Kronprinz*. (Newbolt 4.67–68)

***Jacinth* v. *UC-41*, 21 August 1917**
UC-41 fouled one of its own mines in the Tay estuary; then the armed trawler *Jacinth* finished her off with depth-charges. (Newbolt 5.103, 425; Grant 70–71)

***Jackal* v. *Deane*, 11 April 1782**
The cutter *Jackal* (20; Lt Gustavus Logie) was captured by the rebel American frigate *Deane* (32) in the West Indies. (Clowes 4.18)

***Jackal* v. *Sylph*, October 1782**
The cutter *Jackal* (14; Lt. Daniel Dobree) captured the French lugger *Sylph*. (Clowes 4.89)

***Jackal* v. French schooner, 27 September 1803**
The gun brig *Jackal* (2; Lt Charles Leaver) captured a French schooner off Nieuport. (Clowes 5.556)

***Jackdaw* v. Spanish ship, January 1807**
The schooner *Jackdaw* (4; Lt Nathaniel Brice) was captured off the Cape Verde Islands by a small Spanish boat, and was retaken a month later by the frigate *Minerva*. (James 4.336)

***Jaguar* v. *U-652*, 26 March 1942**
U-652 sank the destroyer *Jaguar* off Tobruk. (Rohwer 151)

Jakarta, Java, 1618
Sir Thomas Dale, in command of a squadron of six EIC ships, defeated a Dutch squadron near Jakarta. He then landed to attack the Dutch fort, unsuccessfully. (Clowes 2.39)

Jamaica
1643 A squadron of ships commanded by Capt. William Jackson was sent to the Caribbean by Parliament; he seized control of Jamaica for a short time. (Rodger 1.415)

1655 A landing was made by troops from the fleet of William Penn, who led the landing in the *Martin* galley, from which the Spanish fort was bombarded. There were few Spanish forces on the island, and they soon capitulated. (Clowes 2.207; Rodger 2.23)

Jamaica v. North Korean MTBs, July 1950
The cruiser *Jamaica* was part of a joint US-British force which sank five North Korean MTBs off the east coast of South Korea. On 6 July she was damaged by fire from a North Korean shore battery. (Wettern 34–35)

James Fletcher v. UC-6, 11 January 1916
The armed yacht *James Fletcher* rammed the submarine *UC-6* near the Goodwin Sands. The submarine was damaged, but survived and returned to Zeebrugge. (Corbett 3.277)

Janet and Pelican v. French frigates, 10 July 1689
Two Scots Navy ships, *Pelican* (18; Capt. William Hamilton) and *Janet* (12; Capt. John Brown), were attacked by three French frigates, *Lutine* (36), *Jolie* (30), and *Tempête* (28), off the Mull of Kintyre. Both Scots ships were captured, after suffering very heavy casualties. (Powley 240–243; Rodger 2.144; Lavery 18–19)

Janus v. Moorish pirates, 17–19 September 1851
After two ships were taken by Moroccan pirates, the paddle sloop *Janus* (Lt Richard Powell) went in search of them. Both ships were found ashore and looted, but the pirates were in too great a strength to risk further action. (Clowes 6.362)

Japan, July–September 1945
The British Pacific Fleet joined in the air raids on Tokyo and Yokohama on 17–18 July, and other Japanese targets, along with a US task force. Planes from the carriers *Formidable*, *Indefatigable*, and *Victorious* damaged the carrier *Kaiyo*, and numerous other ships were sunk or damaged. Harbour and city installations were shelled on 24–30 July. Attacks were resumed on 9 August until 15 August.

A British naval force was included in the predominantly US fleet which arrived in Sagami Bay on 27 August to receive Japan's official surrender; an Australian contingent arrived on 31 August. The official surrender took place on the USS battleship *Missouri* on 2 September. (Roskill 3.2.321–385; Rohwer 422, 424, 426, 428–429)

Jason v. Marie, 21 November 1797
Jason (38) captured the brig *Marie* (14). (Colledge 248)

Jason and Naiad v. Arrogante, 19 April 1798
The French gunboat *Arrogante* (6) was captured by the frigates *Jason* and *Naiad* off Brest. (Clowes 4.511)

Jason v. Naiade, 13 October 1805
The frigate *Jason* (Capt. William Champain) encountered the French corvette

Naiade east of Barbados, and after a nine-hour chase and a short fight, compelled her surrender. (James 4.76)

Jason v. *Favourite* and *Argus*, 27 January 1807
The frigate *Jason* (Capt. Thomas Cochrane), off Guyana, chased the French sloop *Favourite* (18) and the corvette *Argus* (16). *Favourite* was forced to surrender after a short action; *Argus* got away. (James 4.242; Clowes 5.347)

Jasper v. pirates, August 1827
The sloop *Jasper* (10; Lt Adam Duncan) escorted a convoy from Malta to Greece, and in Greek waters two pirate ships were seized. (NRS, *Piracy* 164–165)

JAVA, July–August 1811
An expedition of 11,000 soldiers was transported in several divisions from India to capture the Dutch island of Java. A raid by two boats from *Minden* (74; Capt. Edward Hoare) on Fort Marrack on 27 July aimed at distracting the Dutch defenders of Java from the intended attack; the fort, taken by surprise, was captured, the guns spiked, and the raiders then withdrew.

The main landing took place in August, and in a swift campaign the city of Batavia was captured and the main Dutch point of resistance, an entrenched camp north of the city, was taken. The naval force involved consisted of four line-of-battle ships, fourteen frigates, seven sloops, and eight Company cruisers; Rear-Admiral Hon. Robert Stopford commanded. Other landings were made at Semarap on Madura, Cheribon, and Taggal. (James 5.298–310; Low 1.237–252; *NC* 5.65, 75–78; Clowes 5.297–300; Parkinson 410–417)

JAVA SEA, 27 February 1942
Japanese invasion forces heading for Java attacked an Allied force of British, Dutch, US, and Australian ships which sailed to prevent a landing. One Dutch destroyer was sunk in a torpedo attack, and the British cruiser *Exeter* was badly damaged. Three British destroyers covered *Exeter*'s withdrawal; *Electra* was sunk by the destroyer *Asigamo*, and the destroyer *Jupiter* struck a mine and sank. In a night action two Dutch cruisers were also sunk. The Allied force was now reduced to two cruisers and a few destroyers, while only two Japanese vessels had been damaged. *Exeter*, in attempting to get away, was caught between two Japanese forces south of Borneo and sunk, as was the attendant destroyer *Encounter*. (Rohwer 147–148)

Java v. *Constitution*, 29 December 1812
The frigate *Java* (38; Capt. Henry Lambert) met the US frigate *Constitution* (44) off the coast of Brazil. During a fight lasting four hours *Java* was dismasted and battered into submission. (James 5.408–423)

Jeddah, Arabia, June–July 1858
Rioting in Jeddah cause the death of, amongst others, the British vice-consul. The paddle frigate *Cyclops* (Capt. William Pullen) evacuated those under

Jersey v. French convoy, 15 September 1666
Jersey (40; Capt. Hon. Francis Digby) met a small convoy of four French ships and their escort in the Channel. All the ships were driven ashore and parties went in to burn them. (Clowes 2.430)

Jersey v. French squadron, 18 December 1691
Jersey (48; Capt. John Bomstead) was captured by a French squadron off Dominica. (Clowes 3.465)

Jersey v. *St Esprit*, 1745
Jersey (60; Capt. Charles Hardy) met the French *St Esprit* (74) near Cadiz. Both ships were extensively damaged in the subsequent fight. (Clowes 3.280)

Jervis and others v. *Lupo*, 2 December 1942
The Italian TB *Lupo*, rescuing sailors from an earlier sinking, was sunk by four destroyers of Force K out of Malta – *Jervis, Javelin, Janus*, and *Kelvin* – near Kerkennah. (Rohwer 218)

Jessamine v. *U-104*, 25 April 1918
The destroyer *Jessamine* sank *U-104* in the North Channel. (Newbolt 5.427; Grant 112)

John Gillman and others v. *UB-30*, 13 August 1918
UB-30 was seen and attacked by the trawler *John Gillman* near Whitby; other trawlers – *John Broome, Viola, Floria* – attacked as well with depth-charges. After ten hours it was clear that the submarine was sunk. (Newbolt 3.429; Grant 128)

Juno v. *Entreprenant*, February 1793
The merchantman *Glory* was captured by the French privateer *Entreprenant*; shortly afterwards the frigate *Juno* (32; Capt. Samuel Hood) took both *Entreprenant* and *Glory*. *Glory*'s captain complained of ill-treatment by the privateer's men. (*NC* 1.11–12)

Juno at Toulon, 11 January 1794
The frigate *Juno* (52; Capt. Samuel Hood) sailed from Malta to Toulon. Not having heard that the port had reverted to hostile French control, Hood took his ship into the harbour. *Juno* grounded. A French boat arrived and an officer announced that the British were prisoners. A sudden wind allowed the ship to escape with the Frenchmen now themselves prisoners, fired at by the guns of all the forts around. She escaped with damage to her masts and rigging but no casualties. (James 1.216–218; Clowes 4.482; *NC* 1.47–49)

Juno and others v. *Egeo*, 24 April 1941
The British 14th Destroyer Flotilla, searching for an Italian convoy running

from Naples to Tripoli, instead found the steamship *Egeo*, which was sunk by the destroyer *Juno* after a hard fight. (Rohwer 69)

Junon v. *Renommée*, *Clorinde*, and others, 13 December 1809
The frigate *Junon* (58; Capt. John Shortland) challenged a French squadron of two frigates, *Renommée* (40) and *Clorinde* (40), and two frigates *en flûte*, *Loire* and *Seine*, carrying troops and supplies to Guadeloupe. Deceived at first by the French ships flying Spanish colours, *Junon* was soon having to fight all four ships at once, and was overwhelmed, being so damaged that her captors burnt her. Her companion, the sloop *Observateur* (16; Cmdr Frederick Weatherall), could do nothing to help. (James 5.47–50; Clowes 5.446)

Junon and *Barossa* v. US gunboats, 18 June 1813
The frigate *Junon* (38; Capt. James Sanders), at the entrance to the James River, Virginia, was attacked by a force of fifteen gunboats out of Norfolk; the two sides fired at each other without result for some time. Then the frigate *Barossa* (36; Capt. James Shirreff) arrived and the gunboats fled. (James 6.90–91; Clowes 6.95)

Junon and *Martin* v. US gunboats, 29 July 1813
The frigate *Junon* (38; Capt. James Sanders) and the sloop *Martin* (18; Cmdr Humphrey Senhouse) were in Delaware Bay when *Martin* grounded on a shoal on the ebb tide. Ten gunboats came out to attack, but *Martin* was defended vigorously. One of the gunboats was captured by boats from both ships. The rest retired. (James 6.96–97; Clowes 6.96)

Jupiter and *Medea* v. *Triton*, 20 October 1778
Near Finisterre *Jupiter* (50; Capt. Francis Reynolds) and *Medea* (28; Capt. James Montagu) encountered the French *Triton* (64). By attacking together on both sides of *Triton* the British ships successfully harassed her. *Triton* got clear in the darkness. (Clowes 4.21–22)

Jupiter v. *Blanche*, 21 May 1779
Jupiter (50; Capt. Francis Reynolds) encountered a French convoy off Finisterre. Aiming to discover the convoy's destination Reynolds took his ship into the middle of the convoy, where he was attacked by the frigate *Blanche*, but captured a merchantman. *Jupiter* then withdrew but had to abandon her prize. (Clowes 4.26–27)

Jupiter and *Apollo* v. *Mutine* and *Pilote*, 2 October 1779
The French cutters *Mutine* (14) and *Pilote* (14) were captured by a small British squadron; *Jupiter* (50; Capt. Francis Reynolds) took *Pilote*, and *Apollo* (32; Capt. Philemon Pownoll) took *Mutine*. (Clowes 4.39–40)

Jupiter v. *Preneuse*, 10–11 October 1799
Jupiter (50; Capt. William Granger) chased the frigate *Preneuse*, damaged in a fight at Algoa Bay, South Africa. The rough sea prevented *Jupiter* using her

main guns; *Preneuse* succeeded in disabling *Jupiter*'s masts and rigging, and so got away. (James 2.392–394; Clowes 4.525)

JUTLAND, 31 May–1 June 1916

The British Grand Fleet and the German High Seas Fleet were at sea in the early hours of 31 May and encountered each other, each determined to fight, off the Jutland peninsula early in the afternoon. Admiral Jellicoe had twenty-four dreadnoughts, three battle-cruisers, twenty cruisers, and fifty-one destroyers, and in addition Admiral Beatty had four dreadnoughts, six battle-cruisers, fourteen cruisers and twenty-seven destroyers. Admiral Scheer had sixteen dreadnoughts, six older battleships, five battle-cruisers, nine cruisers, and sixty-one destroyers.

The advanced battle-cruiser squadrons of Beatty and Admiral Hipper met first; Hipper turned south to bring Beatty's force onto the High Seas Fleet. The squadrons fired at each other, and the battle-cruisers *Indefatigable* and *Queen Mary* blew up, while the battle-cruiser *Lion* was badly damaged. Each commander then ordered a destroyer attack in which two British (*Nestor* and *Nomad*) and two German (*V-27* and *V-29*) destroyers were sunk. This 'run to the south' brought Beatty's ships to the High Seas Fleet, and he turned north to bring it onto the Grand Fleet. Several of the German ships were badly battered at this stage. Scouting cruisers met, and *Chester* was badly damaged, while *Wiesbaden* was disabled. Another British destroyer, *Shark*, was sunk.

The Grand Fleet was deployed into battle formation just as the High Seas Fleet arrived. The two fleets fired at each other for about twenty minutes. The battle-cruiser *Invincible* blew up and sank. Scheer turned the High Seas Fleet right round in an unexpected manoeuvre and got away. The two fleets clashed again and Scheer once more turned his fleet around, covered by a torpedo attack by destroyers from which the Grand Fleet turned away. The two fleets thus separated. During the night both fleets ran to the south. Several clashes occurred in the darkness: the British lost a cruiser and five destroyers; the Germans lost the old battleship *Pommern*, three cruisers, and two destroyers. The battle-cruiser *Lutzow*, already disabled, was sunk by a German destroyer. By morning the High Seas Fleet was behind a minefield and close to home. The Grand Fleet returned to port.

The casualties of the battle were mainly on the British side, notably in the loss of three battle-cruisers. Losses of smaller ships were much the same on each side. The main results were strategic. Admiral Jellicoe reported the Grand Fleet next day ready for action; Admiral Scheer, however, was unable to move his fleet far from the German bases, and many of the ships required extensive repair. The High Seas Fleet never risked another fight on the same scale. (Corbett 3.313–442, 4.1–18; Halpern, *Naval History* 310–329; Massie 553–684)

K

Kagoshima, Japan, 15 August 1863
A British squadron of seven ships in Kagoshima Bay seized three vessels belonging to the *daimyo* of Satsuma, and came under fire from shore batteries. The squadron burnt the captured ships and moved along the coast bombarding each battery into silence, set the town on fire in places, and destroyed the arsenal and its storehouses. The ships survived a typhoon and were withdrawn to Yokohama two days later, enabling Satsuma to claim a victory. The ships suffered more than sixty casualties and sustained considerable damage. (Clowes 7.196–200)
See also: **Shimonoseki**

***Kandahar* and others v. *Torricelli*, 23 June 1940**
Off Perim Island, the Italian submarine *Torricelli* was sunk in a gun duel with the destroyers *Kandahar*, *Khartoum*, and *Kingston* and the sloop *Shoreham*; *Khartoum* was set on fire and sank after an explosion; *Shoreham* was damaged. (Rohwer 27)

***Kangaroo* and *Speedy* at Oropesa, Spain, 9 June 1801**
The sloops *Kangaroo* (Cmdr George Pulling) and *Speedy* (Cmdr Lord Cochrane) found a xebec and gunboats beneath a battery at Oropesa; attacking, the British vessels overcame the Spaniards, defeated Spanish reinforcements, and finally silenced the battery. The xebec was sunk; three brigs were captured. (James 3.134–135; Clowes 4.539)

Karachi, Sind, 2–3 February 1839
In conjunction with EIC forces inland, *Wellesley* (74; Capt. Thomas Maitland) and *Algerine* (10; Cmdr Sidney Thomas) were deployed by Rear-Admiral Sir Frederick Maitland to assist in the capture of Karachi. (Clowes 6.279; Low 2.101–104)

Karada, Turkey, 3–5 June 1916
A raid was made on Karada on the Aegean Turkish coast. A Turkish patrol was defeated and some animals removed. (Halpern, *Mediterranean* 292)

Karakisi, Turkey, 20 July 1916
A raid from Samos was made on Karakisi Bay on the Turkish coast. (Halpern, *Mediterranean* 292)

Kathiawar, India, 1803–1811
Pirates operated from various ports in Kathiawar. In 1803, *Fox* and two EIC ships, *Ternate* and *Teignmouth*, attacked Beyt; in 1808 the schooner *Lively*

blockaded Beyt and Poshtra; in 1811 the 65th Foot and a squadron of cruisers attacked Fort Nurasier. (Low 1.273–275)

KATWIJK, Netherlands, 29 July 1653
The English fleet, commanded by General-at-Sea George Monck, blockaded the Dutch coast, but Admiral Tromp came out of the Maas with part of the Dutch fleet. The other half was in the Texel under Admiral de With, and Tromp manoeuvred to draw the English to him so as to allow the Texel division to come out to join in. He tried to avoid action for the present, but the English caught up with him and fighting ensued until dark. The Dutch lost two ships sunk. (Clowes 2.193–194)

Kelly v. *S-31*, 10 May 1940
The destroyer *Kelly* was torpedoed by *S-31* in the North Sea. (Rohwer 13)

Kempenfelt's squadron v. French convoy, 12 December 1781
Rear-Admiral Richard Kempenfelt, with a squadron of twelve line-of-battle ships, encountered a large French convoy carrying troops to the West Indies under the escort of a French squadron of nineteen line-of-battle ships commanded by Admiral Comte de Guichen. The two squadrons clashed briefly near Ushant, but Kempenfelt took his squadron very skilfully between the French warships and the convoy, and captured fourteen ships and 1000 soldiers. (Syrett, *European* 148–150; Clowes 3.509–510)

Kennet v. German destroyer, 23 August 1914
The destroyer *Kennet* was part of the force blockading the German colony of Tsingtao in China. A German destroyer was seen approaching the port and *Kennet* attempted to intercept, but failed and was badly damaged in the encounter. (Corbett 1.149)

Kent, England, May 1471
The Bastard of Fauconberg, an adherent of Henry VI, in command of a fleet, collected soldiers from Calais and landed in Kent. His army marched to London, and the fleet sailed up the Thames. Their joint attacks on the city failed, however, and the fleet retired to Sandwich and Calais. (Gillingham 208–213; Clowes 1.390)

Kent and others v. French convoy, July 1703
Kent (70) was the flagship of Rear-Admiral Thomas Dilkes, which, with a number of smaller vessels, he took on a cruise to Norman waters. Off Granville in July he attacked a convoy of forty-five ships, and in the first attack captured or destroyed twenty-four of them; two days later, penetrating upriver to Avranches, almost all the rest were destroyed. (Clowes 2.505)

Kent and others v. *Porta Coeli* and others, 12 March 1704
Admiral Thomas Dilkes, with *Kent* (70; Capt. Jonas Hanway), *Bedford* (70; Capt. Sir Thomas Hardy), and *Antelope* (50; Cmdr Thomas Legge), chased a Spanish squadron consisting of *Porta Coeli* (60), *Santa Teresa* (60), and a

merchantman, *San Nicolas* (24), all of which were captured; they were laden with ordnance and military stores. (Clowes 2.506)

Kent and others v. *Superbe* and convoy, 30 July 1710
Kent (70; Cmdr Robert Johnson), *Assurance* (70), and *York* (62) chased a French convoy bound for the West Indies off the Lizard. *Superbe* (56) was captured by *Kent*, though *Concorde* (30) got away, and only one ship of the convoy was captured. (Clowes 2.524)

Kent v. *Confiance*, 9 October 1800
The Indiaman *Kent* was attacked off the Sandheads of Bengal by the privateer *Confiance*; after a sturdy resistance, she was boarded and captured. (James 3.31; Parkinson 162)

Kent and *Wizard* v. French convoy, 1 August 1808
Kent (74; Capt. Thomas Rogers) and *Wizard* (18; Capt. William Ferris) sent in boats against a convoy anchored near the shore at Noli, Italy. A battery was stormed, a force of soldiers driven way, and the gunboat *Vigilante* captured. Then the convoy of seven ships was captured. (James 4.383–384; Clowes 5.424)

Kent and *Glasgow* v. *Dresden*, 14 March 1915
The German light cruiser *Dresden* hid in the fjords of southern Chile after the battle of the Falkland Islands, but was finally expelled, and went to a rendezvous to coal. She was found and chased by the cruiser *Kent*, got away, then was found again at Mas a Tierra Island by *Kent*, the light cruiser *Glasgow* (Capt. J. Luce), and the AMC *Orama*, and sunk. (Corbett 2.239–251; Halpern, *Naval History* 100)

Kent and others at Kristiansand, Norway, 10 August 1944
Aircraft from the carriers *Indefatigable*, *Trumpeter*, and *Nabob*, in a squadron headed by the cruiser *Kent*, raided Gossen airfield near Kristiansand, Norway. The German minesweeper *R-89* was destroyed at Letsoe. (Rohwer 349)

Kent and others v. German convoy, 12–13 November 1944
The cruisers *Kent* and *Bellona* and four destroyers attacked a German convoy off Listerfjord, Norway. Four ships in the convoy were sunk, as were the minesweepers *M-427* and *M-416* and three submarine chasers. (Rohwer 371)

KENTISH KNOCK, 20 September 1652
The Dutch fleet commanded by Witte de With sought out the English fleet, which took some time to assemble. The divisions under Robert Blake and William Penn were caught between sections of the Dutch fleet in the shallows of the Kentish Knock, where several of the larger ships grounded for a time. Despite this the Dutch attack was defeated, first by the resistance of Blake's and Penn's ships, then by the intervention of the third English division under Nehemiah Bourne. The fighting lasted all day. Next morning a

third of the Dutch fleet had moved out of range and refused to rejoin. De With wished to fight again but his deputies demurred. Late on the 29th the Dutch withdrew. Casualties were relatively slight. Two Dutch ships were captured. (Clowes 2.168–170; Powell 171–179; Rodger 2.14)

Kerkennah Island, Gulf of Sirte, 16 April 1941
Off Kerkennah Island the destroyers *Jervis*, *Nubian*, *Mohawk*, and *Janus* intercepted and sank a German troop convoy escorted by Italian destroyers; five freighters and three destroyers were sunk; in reply the Italian destroyer *Tarigo* sank *Mohawk*. (Rohwer 69)

Kertch, Crimea, 24 May 1855
A large fleet sailed to begin operations in the Sea of Azov. As a preliminary the forts and towns on either side of the Kertch Strait had to be captured. The expedition, thirty-three ships and about 16,000 men, landed at the southern end of the strait, taking the Russians by surprise. The garrisons evacuated, blowing up the forts and destroying stores. The strait was secured with little fighting. (Clowes 6.453; Lambert 224–234)

Kestrel in Malaya, August 1879
The screw gunvessel *Kestrel* (Cmdr Frederick Edwards) attacked the village of Tarrebas in reprisal for pirate attacks. (Clowes 7.312–313)

Khanderi, Bay of Bombay
1679 The EIC at Bombay aimed to occupy the island of Khanderi. This was disputed by the Mahrattas. Both sides put soldiers on shore and supported them with ships. A skirmish between the fleets in September resulted in several Mahratta and two English ships being lost. Next month intervention by the Mogul Admiral Sidi distracted the Mahrattas, but in the end Khanderi remained theirs. (Low 1.66–70)

1718 An expedition was sent from Bombay in October to attack Khanderi, held by Kanhoji Angria. The attack failed, Angria having had advance warning. (Low 1.98–99)

Kimberley and others v. *U-74*, 27 May 1916
The submarine *U-74*, on a mission to lay mines off the Scottish coast, was sunk in an action with armed trawlers; *Kimberley* fired the fatal shots. (Corbett 3.323; Grant 35)

Kimberley v. *U-77*, 12 January 1942
The destroyer *Kimberley* was torpedoed by *U-77* but was towed to Alexandria. (Rohwer 134)

Kinburn, Russia, 17–18 October 1855
The fortress of Kinburn was bombarded by the joint British and French fleets; after a day the Russian commander surrendered. (Clowes 6.649–674; Lambert 256–261)

Kingfish v. privateer, January 1808
The schooner *Kingfish* (6; Lt Charles Hunter) was captured by a French privateer in the West Indies. (Clowes 5.552)

Kingfisher v. Algerine squadron, 22 May 1681
Kingfisher (46; Capt. Morgan Kempthorne) was attacked by four Algerine vessels in succession. Kempthorne was killed and his lieutenant Ralph Wrenn continued the fight. The Algerine admiral came close, and the others bombarded from a distance. The fighting lasted for twelve hours, until the Algerine ships withdrew. (Clowes 2.456)

Kingfisher v. Sallee corsair, October 1681
Kingfisher (46; Capt. Francis Wheler) fought and sank a large Sallee ship. (Clowes 2.457)

Kingfisher at Ellengreg, June 1685
The Earl of Argyll landed from the Netherlands in May, aiming to raise a rebellion against the new king, James VII and II. He stored weaponry at Ellengreg Castle. *Kingfisher* (46; Capt. Thomas Hamilton), with some smaller vessels, landed, seized the castle, and captured Argyll's three ships, so contributing significantly to the defeat of the rebellion. (Clowes 2.459)

Kingfisher and others v. *U-35*, 29 November 1939
The destroyers *Kingfisher*, *Kashmir*, and *Icarus* encountered and sank *U-35* east of Shetland. (Rohwer 4)

King George, Dartmouth, Russell, and others v. *Glorioso*, 6–8 October 1747
The Spanish treasure ship *Glorioso* (74) met a group of British privateers off Lagos Bay, and was chased. Only *King George* (32; Capt. George Walker) was able to catch her, and attacked, despite the disparity in power. *Glorioso* broke off the fight when other privateers arrived, but then met and fought *Dartmouth* (50; Capt. James Hamilton), which blew up after a brief fight. *Russell* (80; Capt. Matthew Buckle) now arrived. Despite having a reduced crew, *Russell* succeeded in forcing *Glorioso* to surrender. She had already landed her treasure cargo. (Clowes 3.285–286)

Kinghorn, Fife, August 1332
Edward Balliol and 'the disinherited' – men whose loyalty to English kings had resulted in their expulsion from Scotland – sailed from the Humber and landed at Kinghorn, Fife. Balliol had a small army, enough to win a battle and seize the throne, but only briefly. (Nicholson 125–126; Clowes 1.231)

King Magnus's expedition, 1098
King Magnus of Norway conquered Orkney with a fleet from Norway. He recruited ships from Orkney and seized control of the Isles. With a fleet from all three states he conquered Man. He completed this campaign with a raid on Anglesey; here he fought and defeated the Norman Earls of Chester

and Shrewsbury. He had thus reconstituted the kingdom of the Isles. He died in a raid into Ulster in 1102. (Hudson 189–193; *NHI* 1.909–910)

King Stephen v. *G-41*, 25 April 1916
The trawler *King Stephen* was sunk by the German destroyer *G-41* during the German Lowestoft raid. (Colledge 217)

Kingstonian v. U-boat, 11 April 1918
The troop transport *Kingstonian*, carrying part of the 52nd Division from Alexandria to France, was torpedoed south of Sardinia. Most of the men were saved when the ship was run aground. (Newbolt 5.284)

Kinsale, Ireland
1380 A French squadron attacked Kinsale in July, but was driven off by joint Anglo-Irish resistance. A number of English vessels were captured, and four French vessels were taken. (Clowes 1.294)

1601–1602 A Spanish force of 3000 men landed at Kinsale in support of Irish forces fighting the English conquest. The ships immediately sailed away, and the landing force was besieged by an English army under Lord Mountjoy. An English squadron commanded by Sir Richard Leveson brought English reinforcements. The Spaniards surrendered on 6 January. (Clowes 1.550; Rodger 1.291–292; Silke 108–152)

1649 Prince Rupert with a Royalist squadron was based at Kinsale from January. In April a Parliamentary squadron blockaded him in the port. One ship, *Santa Teresa* (9; Capt. d'Arcy), came out in July but was chased and captured by *Nonsuch* (34); she yielded prominent Royalist prisoners and dispatches. By October the Royalists were under threat by land, and seized the opportunity of the absence of the Parliamentary squadron through bad weather to escape. (Capp 61–63; Clowes 2.120–121; Powell 81–87)

1689 The exiled King James II landed at Kinsale from a French squadron of twenty-five ships, in his attempt to regain his thrones. (Powley 47–48; Clowes 2.327)

Kintyre and Arran, Scotland, September 1558
A squadron of nine ships sailed to Dublin under Sir Thomas Cotton, and collected a force of soldiers. The aim was to attack the MacDonald position in the Isles, but all that was achieved was a raid on Kintyre and Arran. (Rodger 1.194; Loades 175)

Kintyre, Scotland, May 1689
Capt. George Rooke, cruising in the Irish Sea, helped to drive off a Scottish rebel force which had gathered on Gigha Island. (Powley 221)

Kipling v. *U-75*, 28 December 1941
U-75 was sunk by the destroyer *Kipling* on 28 December near Mersa Matruh. (Rohwer 128)

Kirkenes and Petsamo, Norway/Russia, 26 July–4 August 1941
Aircraft from the carriers *Victorious* and *Furious* raided Kirkenes and Petsamo on 30 July; a minelaying cruiser with supplies went into Murmansk, another raid was mounted on Petsamo, and on 4 August Tromso was raided. (Rohwer 88)

Kismayu, Somaliland, 1893
A complex of disputes centred on Kismayu produced a bombardment by the screw gunboat *Widgeon* and a landing by the crew of the cruiser *Blanche* (Capt. George Lindley). (Clowes 7.408–410)

Kiunga, East Africa, 1873
In a fight on shore a British officer from the screw sloop *Daphne* (Cmdr Richard Bateman) was killed by the people of Kiunga. A boat raided the village to recover the body. With the screw corvette *Briton* (Lt Arthur Philpotts) another attack damaged the village further. (Clowes 7.234)

Kuphorisi, Crete, 16 April 1942
The destroyers *Kelvin* and *Kipling* landed a party of Royal Marines to raid a German radio station. (Rohwer 159)

Kut el-Amara, Mesopotamia (Iraq), 24 April 1916
The Mesopotamian expeditionary force, under siege at Kut el-Amara, was close to surrender. The armed river steamer *Julnar* attempted to bring in supplies, running the gauntlet of increasingly effective fire from the shores. A cable stretched across the river finely stopped her; she drifted to the shore and was captured. Five days later the besieged force surrendered. (Newbolt 4.90–91)

***Kuttabal* v. Japanese midget submarines, 31 May 1942**
The accommodation ship *Kuttabal* in Sydney harbour was sunk by Japanese midget submarines launched from *I-22*, *I-24*, and *I-27*. (Rohwer 164)

L

L-10 v. S-33, 3 October 1918
The submarine *L-10* was sunk by the German destroyer *S-33* and others off Texel. (Colledge 219)

L-12 v. UB-90, 16 October 1918
The British submarine *L-12* torpedoed and sank *UB-90* in the Skagerrak. (Newbolt 5.429; Grant 106–107)

L-55 v. Gavriil, 4 June 1919
The submarine *L-55*, attempting an attack, was seen by the Soviet destroyer *Gavriil*, which sank her. (Bennett 119)

Lacedemonian v. French ships, 17 May 1797
Lacedemonian (12; Cmdr Matthew Wrench) was captured by French ships in the West Indies. (Clowes 4.549; James 2.462)

Laconia v. U-50, 25 February 1917
The Cunard liner *Laconia*, which had been hired as an AMC earlier in the war, but was no longer, was sunk by *U-50* west of Fastnet Rock. Several Americans died; this was one of the incidents propelling the USA into belligerency. (Halpern, *Naval History* 341)

Laconia v. U-156, 12–17 September 1942
U-156 sank *Laconia*, which was carrying 1800 Italian prisoners of war, on 12 September; French, German, British, and US ships participated in the rescue, but US planes attacked the U-boats. Admiral Donitz afterwards issued the '*Laconia* order', which insisted that U-boats should not rescue survivors. (Rohwer 195)

Lady Nelson v. French privateers, 21 December 1799
The cutter *Lady Nelson* was captured by French privateers off Gibraltar; boats from ships in the bay went out to rescue her, which was accomplished by men from *Queen Charlotte*. (James 2.419)

Lady Olive v. UC-18, 19 February 1917
The Q-ship *Lady Olive* was attacked by *UC-18* in the English Channel. Though sinking, *Lady Olive* was able to fire at the submarine as it approached, and sink it. (Grant 64)

Lady Patricia v. U-46, 28 May 1917
The cargo ship *Lady Patricia*, operating as the Q-ship *Paxton*, was sunk by *U-46* in the Atlantic. (Colledge 220)

Lady Somers v. U-boat, 15 July 1941
The ocean boarding vessel *Lady Somers* was sunk by a U-boat in the Atlantic. (Colledge 20)

Laertes v. U-201, July 1942
The ASW trawler *Laertes* was sunk by *U-201* off West Africa. (Rohwer 191)

Lagos, Nigeria, 25 November–29 December 1851
Kosoko, king of Lagos, refused to stop his people trading in slaves. An attack by boats from six ships was made on 25 November and repelled by a strong defence. Capt. Henry Bruce organised a new attack beginning on 24 December, which also failed, in part because two of the ships went to ground, but also because of the fierce resistance of the people of the city. A third attack by rocket set many of the houses on fire, and exploded a magazine. Kosoko fled; a former king, Akitoye, was reinstalled. Casualties were considerable on the British side – about 100 killed and wounded. The African casualties were never counted. (Clowes 6.367–371; Ward 205–215; Lloyd 156–160)

LAGOS BAY, Portugal, 18–19 August 1759
The French fleet out of Toulon was detected as it passed Gibraltar. Half the ships went into Cadiz; the other half were chased by the British Mediterranean fleet under Admiral Edward Boscawen. Only part of the British fleet reached the French but there were effectively fifteen British ships against seven French. Two French ships were destroyed, and three were captured; two escaped. (Clowes 3.211–215; Tunstall 113–115)

La Guayra, Spanish Main, 18 February 1743
A British squadron under the command of Capt. Charles Knowles attacked La Guayra on the Spanish Main. The Spaniards knew an attack was intended and made preparations to resist, so the British attack was beaten off. Many ships were disabled, and many casualties were incurred. (Clowes 3.85–86)

Laigueglia and Alassio, Liguria, May 1812
A British squadron consisting of *Leviathan* (74; Capt. Patrick Campbell), *America* (74; Capt. Josias Rowley), and *Eclair* (18; Cmdr John Bellamy) attacked the port of Laigueglia on 9 May, capturing two forts and sixteen settees, and destroying two settees. A day or two later, marines landed at Alassio to attack a second convoy. An early French attack was defeated but other French troops held on to their positions within houses, and it was impossible to reach the French ships. (James 5.343–344; Clowes 5.509)

Lake Borgne, Louisiana, 13–14 December 1814
To clear the way for a British landing near New Orleans, the US gunboats dominating Lake Borgne had to be defeated. The six US ships and gunboats were either captured or destroyed by an expedition of launches commanded by Cmdr Nicolas Lockyer. Eighteen men died and seventy-seven were

wounded. Landings were thereafter made close to the city. (James 6.232–234; Clowes 8.148–150)

Lake Champlain, New England
1776 American forces under Benedict Arnold and British forces under Sir Guy Carleton, governor of Canada, competitively built ships aiming to gain control of Lake Champlain, the key to the route between Canada and the Hudson Valley. Arnold built galleys and 'gondolas', but the British built *Inflexible* (18) and two schooners, *Maria* and *Carleton*. The two forces fought on 11 October, after which the Americans retreated – or escaped – during the night. The British pursued and the American vessels were gradually sunk or abandoned. (Clowes 3.358–368; Mackesy, *America* 94–96)

1813 Two US sloops, *Eagle* and *Growler*, attacked the British post at the north end of the lake; they were defeated and captured by three gunboats and soldiers on shore on 3 June 1813. The flotilla of British gunboats took a force to raid the US shores; the town of Plattsburg was captured on 1 August, and then the towns of Burlington and Swanton, Vermont. In each case public buildings were destroyed. (James 6.115; Clowes 6.115)

1814 A squadron of British ships and gunboats advanced in concert with the army, as far as a position north of Plattsburg. It was met by the US squadron on 11 September, but not supported, as had been promised, by the army. The British ships were defeated and captured. The accompanying gunboats escaped. (James 6.114–115, 212–223; Clowes 6.131–141; *NC* 5.250–254)

Lake Erie, North America
1813 A small British squadron challenged a larger US force for control of Lake Erie on 10 September. Although one of the US ships was forced to surrender, the overall result was a comprehensive British defeat, in which all the ships of the squadron were captured. (James 6.109–140; Clowes 6.120–128; *NC* 5.201–203)

1814 Three US schooners near Fort Erie at the mouth of the Niagara River were attacked by a party from the storeship *Charwell* and *Netley* (12) on 12 August. Two schooners, *Somers* and *Ohio*, were boarded and captured; the third, *Porcupine*, escaped. (James 6.210–211; Clowes 6.129–130; *NC* 5.243)

Lake Huron, North America, August–September 1814
The North-West Company's schooner *Nancy* was destroyed by a US raid on the company's base at Narrawassa, but the people, commanded by Lt Miller Worsley, survived. Worsley, with reinforcements from Michilimackinac, replied by boarding and capturing in succession the US schooners *Tigress* and *Scorpion*, giving him command of the whole lake. (James 6.208–210; Clowes 6.128–130)

Lake Nyasa, Central Africa, 1893
In pursuit of a dispute with Makanjira, a slaving chieftain, three small steamers were constructed in Britain, shipped out, and reassembled on Lake

Nyasa. They were then used to destroy villages belonging to the chieftain. (Clowes 7.410–412)

Lake Ontario, North America
1813 A small squadron of sloops and schooners based at Kingston, Ontario, and commanded by Capt. Sir James Yeo, raided the US naval base at Sackett's Harbor. After some dithering, a force was landed on 29 May and some installations were burnt. Other US posts on the south coast of the lake were raided in June. (James 6.105; Clowes 6.112–114; *NC* 5.198–199)

A US squadron of fourteen vessels met a British squadron of eight ships near Port Niagara, Lake Ontario on 8 August. For two days they manoeuvred until on the 10th a fair wind allowed the British squadron, under Captain Sir James Yeo, to attack. The US squadron precipitately retired, though two of its schooners were captured. More manoeuvring between the forces followed until the end of September. (James 6.105–109)

1814 A squadron of ships sailed from Kingston, Ontario, to attack the US logistics base which had been developed at Oswego, Lake Ontario. A preliminary reconnaissance located the US position, and a landing on 5 May resulted in the removal and destruction of artillery and stores. On 30 May a raid by boats was made into Big Sandy Creek, near Sackett's Harbor, New York State, but this was defeated by the US garrison with some loss. (James 6.204–207)

Lake Tanganyika, Central Africa, December 1916–February 1917
Two motor boats shipped from Britain to Cape Town were transported by train, traction engine, and river to Lake Tanganyika, until then controlled by German vessels. A harbour at Kalemi was constructed, and on 26 December 1916 one German ship, the wooden gunboat *Kingani*, was located, chased, and captured by the motorboats, which were named *Mimi* and *Tou-tou*. *Kingani* was repaired, renamed *Fifi*, and the three ships met and sank the second German vessel, *Hedwig von Wissmann*, on 9 February 1917. The remaining German vessels on the lake were destroyed by their officers. (Newbolt 4.80–85)

***Lancaster* at Denia, Spain, July 1707**
Denia was under siege. *Lancaster* (80; Capt. James Moodie) landed marines to assist in the defeat of a major assault. (Francis 248; Clowes 2.516)

***Lancaster* and *Dunkirk* v. *Comte de Gramont* and *Merlin*, 1757**
The French privateer *Comte de Gramont* (36) was captured by *Lancaster* (66; Capt. Hon. George Edgecumbe) and *Dunkirk* (60; Capt. Hon. Richard Howe). Later they recaptured *Merlin* (10; Cmdr John Cleland), which had been captured by a French ship off Brest on 19 April. (Clowes 3.296, 311, 312)

***Lance* and *Landrail* v. *Königin Luise*, 5 August 1914**
The German AMC *Königin Luise* laid mines off Harwich. A trawler reported this to the destroyers *Lance* and *Landrail*, patrolling with the cruiser

Amphion. The destroyers searched for, chased, and sank the minelayer by gunfire. *Amphion*, however, ran on to the mines, and sank. (Corbett 1.38–39; Halpern, *Naval History* 27)

Landguard Fort, Suffolk, 2 July 1667
The Dutch fleet which had just raided the Medway landed 3000 men to attack the Landguard Fort. They were defeated in two assaults by the marine garrison under Capt. Nathaniel Darrel, and then driven to re-embark by the local trained bands and a force of infantry from Harwich. (Clowes 2.295)

Landrail v. Syren, 12 July 1814
The cutter *Landrail* (Lt Robert Lancaster) was chased by the US privateer *Syren* and badly damaged before surrendering. (James 6.167)

Landrail v. U-29, 13 December 1916
The destroyer *Landrail* sank *UB-29* with a depth-charge attack. (Grant 39)

Langa, Macasser, Sulawesi, May 1815
The village of Langa was a pirate base. The EIC ship *Teignmouth* (Capt. Sealy) carried a force of soldiers there, but an attempt to storm the stockaded village failed. (Low 1.265)

Languedoc, France, July 1710
Admiral Sir John Norris, with troops from the Mediterranean fleet, landed in Languedoc and captured Cette and Agde. They were abandoned when French land forces approached. (Clowes 2.15; Francis 305)

Lanzarote, Canary Islands, April 1598
The Earl of Cumberland, commanding a large privateering fleet, landed on the island of Lanzarote, collected plunder, and sailed on. (Clowes 1.526–527)

Lapwing v. Decius and Vaillante, 26 November 1796
Capt. Robert Barton of *Lapwing* (28) heard at St Kitts that a French raid was aimed at Anguilla, and sailed to prevent it. He failed to do so, but attacked the French ships *Decius* (20) and *Vaillante* (6). *Decius* was pounded into striking her colours; *Vaillante*, which escaped at first, ran aground and was there destroyed. (James 1.401; Clowes 4.504)

Largs, Scotland, 1263
King Haakon of Norway with a large fleet sailed to Scotland in pursuance of a quarrel with the king of Scots over their spheres of control in the Hebrides. The arrival of the fleet brought most Hebrideans back to loyalty to Haakon. Joined by forces from Orkney, Argyll, and Man, he came to the Clyde estuary and began negotiations. Fighting broke out when a storm drove one of his ships on shore near Largs. The fighting was fairly minor, but effectively ended the negotiations. The season being late, Haakon returned to Orkney, where he died in December; the Hebridean Islands returned permanently to the Scots king. The 'battle' of Largs was thus only a minor military-naval event,

but one with major political consequences. (Thompson 86–88; MacDonald 106–114)

Lark v. privateers, 21–25 April 1800
The hired lugger *Lark* (16; Lt Thomas Wilson) chased a privateer near Texel, which ran ashore and could not be reached. Then *Lark* met the notorious privateer *Imprenable*, and drove her ashore also. This time boats were able to take the privateer off, the crew having escaped ashore. (James 3.14–15)

Lark v. Esperanza, 13 September 1801
The sloop *Lark* (16; Lt James Johnstone) chased the Spanish privateer *Esperanza* into reefs off Cuba; boats were sent in; after a stiff fight the schooner was taken. (James 3.148–149)

Lark v. Spanish ships, 26 January–1 February 1807
The sloop *Lark* (16; Cmdr Robert Nicholas) encountered and captured the Spanish *guarda costas Postillon* and *Carmen* off the Spanish Main. On 1 February *Lark* encountered a convoy of boats escorted by a schooner and two gunboats. These escorts were chased up the river; one gunboat was boarded and captured, the others got away. The *guarda costas* ran ashore, and had to be destroyed. (James 4.243; Clowes 5.397)

Lark and Ferret v. Mosquito, 23 August 1807
The Spanish brig *Mosquito* (8) was captured by *Lark* (16) and *Ferret* (18) off Jamaica. (Clowes 5.558)

Larne, Ireland, 1017
Jarl Einar Wry-mouth of Orkney raided into the north of Ireland, but was defeated by the Irish at Larne. He returned to Orkney with just one ship out of his fleet. (Thompson 50)

Larne v. Izabel, May 1844
The paddle gunship *Larne* captured the slaver *Izabel*. (Bethell 197)

La Rochelle, Bay of Biscay, France
1206 King John collected a fleet and army at Yarmouth, Isle of Wight, and landed at La Rochelle, whence he campaigned into Anjou. (Clowes 1.179)

1214 King John collected his navel forces at the Isle of Wight and sailed with an expedition to La Rochelle, intending to campaign in Poitou. He had no success. (Clowes 1.183)

1242 La Rochelle, a French base, was placed under an intermittent blockade by ships called up by Henry III from local ports. The ships were galleys, so it is unlikely that the blockade was in any way continuous. (Rose 31; M. Weir, 'English Naval Activities 1242–1243', *MM* 58, 1972, 85–92)

1372 An English convoy under the Earl of Pembroke, carrying £20,000 to La Rochelle, was intercepted by a Castilian fleet. The fleets fought for two days, on 22–23 June. The English squadron was reinforced by four barges from La Rochelle during the night, but the ships were sunk or captured, and the treasure also captured. (Clowes 1.282–283; Rodger 1.110; Sumption 3.138–141)

1405 An English force attempted an attack on La Rochelle, but was foiled. (Clowes 1.362)

1563 A skirmish took place between English and French ships near La Rochelle. (Rodger 1.199)

1628 The city was held by Huguenots and besieged by French Royalist forces. An English fleet was sent to convey relief, but was unable to break the Royalist blockade. One fleet under the Earl of Denbigh tried in May, and a second under Lord Lindsey failed again in September. The city fell in October. (Rodger 1.360–361; Clowes 2.70–71)

Las Palmas, Canary Islands, September 1595
The joint fleet of Sir Francis Drake and Sir John Hawkins made an attempt to raid the town of Las Palmas, but the landing force was driven off by gunfire. (Andrews 191–192)

La Spezia, Italy, March 1814
A squadron under Capt. Sir Josias Rowley, including a division of Sicilian gunboats, transported a detachment of British troops from Sicily to take possession of the port of La Spezia. (James 6.119; Clowes 5.306)

***Latona* v. *Tigre* and *Blonde*, November 1793**
The frigate *Latona* (38; Capt. Edward Thornborough) followed a French squadron and fired at the rearmost French frigate; two 74s came to chase her off. *Tigre* fired, *Latona* replied, then they parted. Nine days later *Latona* and *Phaeton* (38) captured the French corvette *Blonde* off Ushant. (Clowes 4.201–202, 552; James 1.66, 493)

***Latona* v. *Felicité*, 14–17 June 1809**
The French frigate *Felicité* sailed from Guadeloupe with a cargo of colonial produce. Chased by the frigate *Latona* (Capt. Hugh Pigot), she surrendered as soon as *Latona* came up after only a brief fight. (James 5.23; Clowes 5.436)

***Laura* v. *Diligent*, 8 September 1812**
The schooner *Laura* (12; Lt Charles Hunter), operating near the Delaware, met the French privateer *Diligent* (18), which defeated, boarded, and captured her. (James 5.424; Clowes 5.515)

***Laurel* v. *Canonnière*, 12 September 1808**
Laurel (22; Cmdr John Woolcombe), on blockade duty at Mauritius, came to a fight with the newly arrived French frigate *Canonnière* (48); *Laurel* was battered into surrender. (James 4.363–366; Clowes 5.425)

Laurentic and *Patroclus* v. *U-99*, 3 November 1940
The AMCs *Laurentic* and *Patroclus* were attacked by *U-99* west of Ireland. The submarine fired several torpedoes at each ship; both were sunk. (Rohwer 46)

Lavender v. *UC-75*, 5 May 1917
The sloop *Lavender* was sunk by *UC-75* in the English Channel. (Colledge 224)

Leander v. unknown ship, 19 January 1783
Leander (52; Capt. John Payne) encountered a 74-gun ship, which was attacked. *Leander* was badly damaged, but repelled several boarding attempts, and put out several fires. The victorious ship's identity is not known; Payne thought she was Spanish. (Clowes 4.92–93)

Leander v. *Généreux*, 18 August 1798
Leander (52; Capt. Thomas Thompson) was intercepted by *Généreux* (74) while on the way from the battle of the Nile with dispatches. Outmatched, *Leander* fought for six hours until dismasted and ungovernable, with a third of her crew killed or wounded. (James 2.259–269; Clowes 4.513–516)

Leander v. *Rattlesnake*, 22 June 1814
The US sloop *Rattlesnake* (16) was captured by *Leander* (50; Capt. Sir George Collier). (Clowes 5.567)

Leander and others v. *Constitution* and prizes, 11 March 1815
The US frigate *Constitution* was at Porto Praya, Cape Verde Islands, when *Leander* (50; Capt. Sir George Collier), *Newcastle* (50; Capt. Lord George Stuart), and *Acasta* (40; Capt. Alexander Kerr) arrived. *Constitution* and her prizes *Cyane* and *Levant* at once sailed. The British ships closed, *Cyane* tacked away and escaped, *Levant* turned away to return to Porto Praya, and all three British ships followed her. *Constitution* thus escaped. *Levant*, despite being in a neutral port, was attacked by the British ships when they came in. (James 6.252–261; Clowes 6.171–173)

Leander and convoy v. Italian squadron, 20–21 October 1940
Four Italian destroyers attacked convoy BN-7 in the Red Sea, but they were driven off by the escort, the RNZS cruiser *Leander*, a destroyer, three sloops, and two minesweepers. The Italian destroyer *Nulla* was later beached at Massawa; the British destroyer *Kimberley* was damaged. (Rohwer 46)

Leander v. *RAMB-1*, 27 February 1941
The Italian auxiliary cruiser *RAMB-1* broke out of Massawa, Eritrea, but was located by the cruiser *Leander* west of the Maldive Islands and blew up after a short fight. (Hore 255–256; Rohwer 59)

Leasowe Castle v. U-boat, 26 May 1918
The troop transport *Leasowe Castle* was sunk in the Mediterranean by a U-boat. (Newbolt 5.292)

Leda v. Eclair, 9 June 1793
The French sloop *Eclair* (22) was captured in the Mediterranean by *Leda* (36; Capt. George Campbell). (Clowes 4.552)

Leeward Islands, 1801
On the news of the outbreak of war with Denmark and Sweden, Rear-Admiral John Duckworth forced the capitulation of the islands of St Bartholomew and St Martin (Swedish), St Thomas, St John, and Santa Cruz (Danish). The Dutch island of Saba was taken by *Arab* (20; Capt. John Perkins) and a party of soldiers. (James 3.150; NC 2.191–197)

Leghorn (Livorno), Italy
1651 Capt. Edmund Hall chased two French ships into Leghorn, a neutral port. He then complained that his arrival had not been greeted by the usual salute. The Grand Duke of Tuscany in turn complained of his very arrival. (Capp 72)

1652 *Phoenix* (38), captured by a Dutch force, was taken into Leghorn. Choosing a night (11 November) following a Dutch celebration during which the prize crew drank plenty of wine, Capt. Edward Cox boarded the ship and sailed it out of the harbour through the Dutch blockading squadron. Fighting on board went on for two hours, and two Dutch frigates chased her, but Cox's men won the fight on board and the frigates were outsailed. (Corbett, *Mediterranean* 268; Clowes 2.164–165)

1653 An English squadron was blockaded in several ports, including Leghorn, by the Dutch fleet of Admiral Johann van Galen. On 28 February Capt. Richard Badiley brought out the ships which were in Porto Ferraio, but Capt. Henry Appleton delayed coming out from Leghorn until 4 March. The Dutch caught him in the harbour entrance and only one of Appleton's six ships joined Badiley's squadron. Van Galen died of wounds; Badiley took his whole fleet to England. (Corbett, *Mediterranean* 264–268; Clowes 2.176–177)

1796 The British residents of Leghorn and their property were evacuated on 27 June on the approach of the French army, by *Inconstant* (36; Capt. Thomas Fremantle) and three storeships. Almost forty ships were also taken. (Capt. Fremantle soon married one of the refugees.) (James 1.344; Clowes 4.265)

1940 Aircraft from the carrier *Ark Royal* raided Livorno and the harbour at La Spezia on 9 February. (Rohwer 58)

Leinster, Ireland, 984
The fleets of the Haraldssons, kings of Man, raided along the coast of Leinster in alliance with Brian Boru, king of Munster. (Hudson 60–61)

Lenox, Kent, and Orford v. Princesa, 8 April 1740
The Spanish *Princesa* (64) was chased and attacked by *Lenox* (70; Capt. Coville Mayne), *Kent* (70; Capt. Thomas Durell), and *Orford* (70; Capt. Lord

Augustus Fitzroy) off the Spanish coast. *Princesa* fought stubbornly all day, and drove *Orford* out of the fight for a time; when she returned, however, *Princesa* surrendered. (Clowes 3.267–268)

Lenox and squadron v. French convoy, 31 October 1745
A French convoy for Martinique, escorted by *Magnanime* (74) and other ships, was intercepted by a squadron under Vice-Admiral Isaac Townsend in *Lenox* (70), with *Dreadnought* (60) and *Ipswich* (70). Some of the merchant ships were captured and others wrecked, but most of them got away. (Clowes 3.280)

Léogane, St Domingue, September 1694
Three English ships, *Advice* (42), *Hampshire* (46), and *Experiment* (32), bombarded Léogane, with little result other than that the captain of *Advice*, William Harman, was killed by return fire. (Clowes 2.481)

Leopard v. *Chesapeake*, 21 February 1807
Leopard (50; Capt. Salusbury Humphreys) was under instructions to recover deserters from British ships on board the US frigate *Chesapeake*. Being refused, he fired several broadsides into the ship, which struck her colours. Four men thought to be deserters were taken out – though only one proved to be British. The incident evoked profuse apologies from the British government. The admiral giving the instructions was dismissed. (James 4.245–254; Clowes 6.17–19; *NC* 4.52–54)

Leopoldville v. *U-486*, 24 December 1944
U-486 sank the troop transport *Leopoldville*; 819 men died. (Rohwer 373)

Levant v. *Vigilant*, June 1777
Levant (28) encountered and captured the rebel American privateer *Vigilant* (14) in the Mediterranean, after a short fight. (Clowes 4.4)

Leveret at Mozambique, September 1836
The sloop *Leveret* (10; Lt Charles Bosanquet) took the lead in combating a rebellion in Portuguese Mozambique by landing a force, gathering support, and occupying a fort and government offices. (Clowes 6.276)

Leveret v. *Diogenes*, December 1836
The sloop *Leveret* (10; Lt Charles Bosanquet) chased the slaver *Diogenes* for 800 miles along the East African coast, captured her, and released the slaves on board. (Clowes 6.276)

Leviathan and *Emerald* v. *Fiorentina*, *Carmen*, and convoy, 5–7 April 1800
Leviathan (74; Capt. James Carpenter, with Vice-Admiral John Duckworth) and *Emerald* (36; Capt. Thomas Waller) chased a Spanish convoy off Cadiz for two days. The Spanish escort mistook the British ships for stragglers from the convoy until it was too late. *Emerald* did most of the fighting. The

escorting frigates *Fiorentina* (34) and *Carmen* (32) surrendered after a short fight. Ten of the convoy escaped, as did one of the escorting frigates. (James 3.12–14; Clowes 4.531)

Leviathan and *Undaunted* at Agay, Provence, 29 April 1812
Boats from *Leviathan* (74; Capt. Patrick Campbell) and the frigate *Undaunted* (Capt. Richard Thomas) went into the port of Agay and took out four merchantmen, but could not move a privateer; it was set on fire, but saved by the people. (James 5.342; Clowes 5.503)

Libau, Gulf of Riga
1854   The city of Libau was briefly captured by the screw frigate *Amphion* (Capt. Astley Cooper Key) and the screw sloop *Conflict* (Capt. Arthur Cumming) on 10 May. They seized ships there, then blockaded the gulf. (Clowes 6.416)

1919   German attacks on Lettish forces at Libau were countered by fire from British cruisers and destroyers in the harbour, and later by the monitor *Erebus*. The final German attack on 14 November in considerable strength was decisively beaten. (Bennett 189–191)

Liberty v. *UC-46*, 8 February 1917
The destroyer *Liberty* located, rammed, and sank the submarine *UC-46* at the northern entrance to the Strait of Dover. (Newbolt 4.457n; Grant 44)

Lichfield v. *Tigre*, January 1696
Lichfield (42; Capt. Lord Archibald Hamilton) captured the French privateer *Tigre* (24) in the Channel. (Clowes 2.489)

Lichfield v. *Sunn Prize*, 1704
Lichfield (50; Capt. Rupert Billingsley) captured the French *Sunn Prize* (22), which was retained by the navy but retaken by a French privateer later. (Clowes 2.507; Colledge 388)

Lichfield and *Norwich* v. *Chariot Royal*, March 1756
The French frigate *Chariot Royal* (36), attempting to reach Louisburg in Nova Scotia with supplies, was intersected and captured by *Lichfield* (50) and *Norwich* (50). (Clowes 3.293)

Lightning v. French ship, 24 November 1705
The fireship *Lightning* (Cmdr Archibald Hamilton) was captured by the French. (Clowes 2.553)

Lightning v. *Hoop*, 8 October 1808
Lightning (16; Cmdr Bentinck Doyle) captured the Dutch armed transport *Hoop*. (Clowes 5.564)

Lightning v. *S-55*, 8 March 1943
S-55, a German TB, sank the destroyer *Lightning*. (Rohwer 231)

Lily v. Draak, 1 March 1804
Lily (18; Cmdr William Lyall) captured the Dutch schooner *Draak* (5) near Bermuda. (Clowes 5.564)

Lily v. Dame Ambert, 15 July 1804
The sloop *Lily* (Cmdr William Compton) was attacked by the privateer *Dame Ambert* off Cape Roman, USA. *Dame Ambert* had guns of greater range, and destroyed *Lily*'s rigging; she then made repeated attempts to board, succeeding at the ninth. Compton was killed. (James 3.276–277; Clowes 5.346–347)

Lily v. Confidencia, 1843
The brig *Lily* captured the Brazilian slaver *Confidencia* off Quelimane, Mozambique. (Bethell 196)

Limerick Vikings, Ireland, 922–937
A large Viking fleet, led by 'Tamar mac Ailche', seized Kings Island in Limerick harbour, developed a permanent base there, then immediately sailed to raid the shores of Loughs Derg and Ree; and in 924, led by their king Kolli Bardarsson they raided into Lough Ree again. In 928, led by Tamar mac Ailche, they took their ships overland to Lough Neagh and raided the islands and shores there. Next year they took their ships to Lough Corrib in Galway and from there raided the surrounding lands; they were eventually driven out by the local Irish.

In 936, led by Olaf Guthfrithsson, they raided the lands along the River Shannon and into Lough Erne, portaging their ships on the way; but in 937, Olaf, now king of the Dublin Vikings, attacked the Limerick Vikings as they raided in Lough Ree, capturing and destroying their ships and carrying off their leaders; the next king of Limerick was a member of Olaf's family. (Smyth, *Dublin* 21, 24–25, 32, 34)

Linnet v. Courier, 10 January 1808
The brig *Linnet* (14; Lt John Tracey) challenged the French lugger *Courier*, which was chasing two British merchant vessels in the English Channel. *Linnet* and *Courier* fought each other for nearly three hours, until *Courier*, almost sinking, surrendered. (James 4.305)

Linnet v. Gloire, 25 January 1813
The packet *Linnet* (14; Lt John Tracey) met the French frigate *Gloire* in the western Channel. The unequal fight ended with *Linnet*'s surrender. (Clowes 5.517; James 6.8–9)

Linnet v. Bellona and another, 30 April 1853
The packet brig *Linnet* (Cmdr Henry Need) sent boats into the Pongos River, West Africa; the slaver *Bellona* and a slaver schooner were captured. (Clowes 6.394)

Lion v. Mary Antrim, February 1649
Lion (Capt. William Penn) met and fought the Royalist *Mary Antrim*. Both ships suffered damage and casualties. (Clowes 2.120)

Lion v. Elizabeth, 9 July 1745
The French ship *Elizabeth* (64) escorted *Dentelle*, which was carrying Prince Charles Edward to Scotland. The two met *Lion* (60; Capt. Piercy Brett) in the Bay of Biscay and the two big ships fought each other, inflicting mutual damage with 400 casualties. Meanwhile *Dentelle* got away and landed the prince in Scotland. (Clowes 3.110–111; NRS, *Misc* III; Lavery 46)

Lion v. Zephyr, 1 September 1762
Lion (60) met and captured the French *Zephyr* (32) which was attempting to carry troops to Newfoundland. (Clowes 3.308–309)

Lion v. Santa Dorotea, 17 July 1798
Lion (64; Capt. Manley Dixon) encountered four Spanish frigates near Cartagena. The rearmost of the Spaniards, *Santa Dorotea*, was attacked; the other three made ineffective attempts at rescue; *Santa Dorotea* eventually surrendered when the others left. (James 2.254–255; Clowes 4.511–512)

Lion v. French corvette, 27 April 1799
Lion (64; Capt. Manley Dixon) captured a French corvette in the Mediterranean. (Clowes 4.556)

Lion, Foudroyant, and Penelope v. Guillaume Tell, 31 March 1800
Guillaume Tell (80) sailed from Valetta, Malta, at night, but was seen and harassed by *Penelope* (36; Capt. Hon. Henry Blackwood). *Lion* (64; Capt. Manley Dixon) took up the fight, but was so badly damaged she had to retreat; the fighting devolved upon *Foudroyant* (80; Capt. Sir Edward Berry). After eight hours' fighting, *Guillaume Tell*, partly dismasted, at last surrendered, having reduced two British line-of-battle ships to near wrecks; the surrender was taken by *Penelope*. (Clowes 4.420–422)

Lisbon, Portugal
1147 A seaborne expedition of Englishmen, Flemings, and Frisians, on their way to Palestine on the Second Crusade, stopped to assist the Portuguese siege of the Muslim city of Lisbon, which was captured after a four-month siege. (S. Runciman, *History of the Crusades*, vol. 2, London 1952, 258–259; J. Philips, *The Second Crusade*, New Haven 2007, ch. 8)

1589 An English expeditionary force landed at Peniche on 6 May and marched to attack Lisbon. The fleet, under Sir Francis Drake, sailed on to take Cascais at the mouth of the Tagus River. Lisbon was defended with determination, and the attempt was given up after only two days. The army re-embarked at Cascais, where sixty Hanseatic ships were seized. An attack by a squadron of twenty Lisbon galleys was driven off, and the fleet sailed away. (Clowes 1.492–493; Rodger 1.273–274; Andrews 164–165)

1602 Sir William Monson, in command of a squadron, captured a caravel in the roadstead at Cezimbra. He sailed into the mouth of the Tagus, but soon found himself amid a whole Spanish fleet and had to fight his way out, though without much difficulty. (Clowes 1.557)

1650 A Royalist squadron commanded by Prince Rupert took refuge in Lisbon. It was blockaded there by the Republican fleet commanded by General-at-Sea Robert Blake. The Royalists were joined by two French ships, and the Portuguese king indicated his support. Blake was reinforced by nine merchant ships which had been hired by the Portuguese as part of a Brazil convoy but which joined Blake when they came out. Twice the Royalists attempted to leave, and each time avoided a fight – Blake's and Rupert's flagships fired at each other on one occasion. Blake intercepted the arriving Portuguese fleet, sank one ship and took seven, then left. The king then compelled the Royalists to leave Lisbon. (Corbett, *Mediterranean* 206–216; Clowes 2.124–131; Capp 64–65; Powell 91–102; Rodger 2.4)

1807 A squadron under Rear-Admiral Sir Sidney Smith went to Lisbon on news of the French threat to Portugal, giving refuge to the British ambassador, Lord Strangford. The Portuguese government was persuaded that evacuation of the government and the royal family to Brazil was preferable to submitting to French authority. The Portuguese fleet carried 18,000 Portuguese out of the city the day before French troops entered Lisbon. Smith escorted the Portuguese fleet towards Brazil, then returned to Lisbon to find that a Russian squadron had arrived; this was then blockaded. (James 4.235–259; Clowes 5.232–233; *NC* 4.183–197; Hall 14–15)

Lissa, Adriatic Sea, 13 March 1811
A squadron of French frigates, four of 44 and two of 32 guns, two sloops, and two smaller ships, commanded by Capt. Dubordieu, came out of Ancona aiming to attack the British naval base on the island of Lissa, where Capt. William Hoste had three frigates and a sloop. The two squadrons met, the French attacking in two parallel lines, aiming to break the British line, but they couldn't achieve this. Hoste sailed close to the coast, and succeeded in getting the leading French ship, *Favourite*, to strike on the rocks. After three hours, the frigates *Flore* and *Bellona* struck to Hoste's ship *Amphion*; *Corona* surrendered to *Active* and *Cerberus*. *Flore* later got away, and *Favourite*, on shore, was set on fire and blew up. (James 5.233–245; Clowes 5.478–481; T. Pocock, *Remember Nelson*, London 1977, 164–179; *NC* 5.17–18)

Little Belt v. *President*, 16 May 1811
The sloop *Little Belt* (18; Cmdr Arthur Bingham) was accosted by the US frigate *President* (44) off Cape Hatteras, and fired at. *Little Belt* replied, but was heavily overmatched. This was an incident in the ongoing quarrel over the British practice of removing men ('deserters') from US ships. (James 5.273–282; *NC* 5.19–20)

Lively v. *Curieuse* and *Iphigenie*, 9 July 1778
Lively (20; Capt. Robert Biggs) encountered the French fleet near Brest. The

cutter *Curieuse* (10) attempted to take *Lively* and failed; when *Iphigénie* (32) arrived, *Lively* fired one broadside, then surrendered. (Clowes 4.16)

Lively v. Espion and Tourterelle, March 1795
The frigate *Lively* (32; Cmdr George Burlton) captured *Espion* (18) off Brest on 2 March. On the 13th *Lively* met and fought the French corvette *Tourterelle* (28) near Ushant. *Tourterelle* fought until dismasted. (James 1.313–315; Clowes 4.490–491, 553)

Lively v. pirates, 1808
The EIC schooner *Lively* (Lt MacDonald) was attacked by four dhows off the Gujerati coast; they were driven off. (Low 1.319)

Lively Prize v. French squadron, 4 October 1689
Lively Prize (30; Capt. William Tichborne) was captured by a French squadron off the Scilly Isles. (Clowes 2.462)

The Lizard, 12 June 1652
An English squadron commanded by Sir George Ayscue attacked a Dutch convoy near the Lizard, capturing several ships, though most escaped. (Clowes 2.152–153)

Lizard v. Calypso, 12 September 1758
Lizard (28; Cmdr Brodrick Hartwell), part of a squadron cruising off Brest, found a French convoy near the coast. *Lizard* was the only ship able to get amongst the convoy, and drove *Calypso* ashore in Audierne Bay. On 2 October *Lizard* captured the French privateer *Duc d'Hanovre* (14). (Clowes 3.299)

Lizard v. Espion, 1782
The French *Espion* (16) was captured by *Lizard* (28; Capt. Edmund Dod) near St Kitts. (Clowes 4.115)

Loch Glendhu v. U-1024, 7–13 April 1944
U-1024 had sunk ships on 7 and 12 April in the Irish Sea; she was herself sunk on 13 April by the frigate *Loch Glendhu*; valuable intelligence material was found on board. (Rohwer 406)

Loch nan Uamh, Scotland, 1746
Two French privateers, *Mars* (56) and *Bellone* (36), brought gold and arms to assist the rebellion in Scotland, and hoped to bring out Prince Charles Edward, who was on the run after his defeat at Culloden. The ships anchored in Loch nan Uamh, a small inlet off the Sound of Arisaig, western Scotland, on 30 April, and unloaded their cargo. On 2 May *Greyhound* (24; Capt. Thomas Noel) and the sloops *Terror* and *Baltimore* entered the bay and attacked. Fighting continued for six hours or so. The British were badly damaged about the masts and sails and had to withdraw. Both French ships, also damaged, returned to France next day. (Lavery 63; Syrett, *Howe* 4; J.S. Gilson, *Ships of the '45*, London 1967)

Loch Scavaig **and others v.** *U-1014*, **4 February 1945**
U-1014 was sunk by the 23rd Escort Group, the frigates *Loch Scavaig, Loch Shin, Nyasaland*, and *Papua*, in the North Channel. (Rohwer 391)

Lofoten Islands, Norway, 26–27 December 1941
A cruiser and destroyers landed two Commando groups to destroy fish oil plants in the Lofoten Islands. This was achieved before the Germans reacted; 225 prisoners were taken, and over 300 Norwegians were evacuated by their own request. Meanwhile the destroyer *Somali* captured the armed trawler *Krebs* and seized its codes and its Enigma machine. The collection of refugees and destruction of fishery equipment successfully hid from the Germans the loss of their codes. (D. Howarth, *The Shetland Bus*, London 1951, 65–70; Sebag-Montefiore 132–135)

Loire **v.** *Venteux*, **27 June 1803**
The frigate *Loire* (38; Capt. Frederick Maitland) sent boats in to the Ile de Batz, near Brest; they captured the brig *Venteux*, which was accomplished after a severe fight. (James 3.180–181; Clowes 4.317)

Loire **v.** *Blonde*, **17–18 August 1804**
The frigate *Loire* (38; Capt. Frederick Maitland) met the French privateer *Blonde*, chased her for a day, and forced her surrender after a short fight. (James 3.282; Clowes 5.348)

Loire **v.** *Esperanza* **and** *Confiance*, **1–4 June 1805**
The frigate *Loire* (38; Capt. Frederick Maitland) sent boats in to Camarinas Bay, northwest Spain, to cut out the Spanish privateer *Esperanza*. This and another ship were quickly taken, as were some merchant ships. A day later they attacked the French privateer *Confiance* at Muros: two forts were stormed, *Confiance* and a brig were captured, and Capt. Maitland persuaded the townspeople to hand over the cargoes of both ships. (James 4.32–36; Clowes 5.362–363; *NC* 3.137–140)

Loire **v.** *Hebe*, **5 January 1809**
The frigate *Loire* (Capt. Alexander Schomberg) met the French corvette *Hebe*, which had just captured two British merchant ships; *Hebe* was chased for a time, fought, and was captured. (James 5.2–3; Clowes 5.430–431)

London **and** *Torbay* **v.** *Scipion* **and** *Sybille*, **17–18 October 1782**
London (98; Capt. James Kempthorne) and *Torbay* (74; Capt. John Gidoin) chased *Scipion* (74) and *Sybille* (40) near St Domingue. *Scipion* evaded the British attacks, but then went into Samara Bay, struck a rock, and sank. *Sybille* got away. (Clowes 4.89–90)

London **and** *Amazon* **v.** *Marengo* **and** *Belle Poule*, **13 March 1806**
Marengo (74) and *Belle Poule* (40) were intercepted north of the Cape Verde Islands by a British squadron commanded by Vice-Admiral Sir John Borlase Warren. *London* (98; Capt. Sir Harry Neale) fought *Marengo*, with *Belle*

Poule intervening; *Belle Poule* was tackled by *Amazon* (38; Capt. William Parker). Fighting continued for five hours until *Foudroyant* (80; Capt. John Chambers White) approached, and both French ships surrendered. (James 4.129–132; Clowes 5.373–374)

London v. slavers, 3 December 1881
The pinnace of *London*, the guardship at Zanzibar, challenged a slave dhow. Capt. Charles Brownrigg and several of his men were killed in the fighting which followed; the dhow got away. (Clowes 7.386–387)

Lookout and others on the Riviera, 27 April 1945
The destroyer *Lookout* was part of an Allied force which shelled German bases on the Italian Riviera on 23 April. (Rohwer 411)

Lord Eldon v. Spanish gunboats, 12 November 1804
The hired ship *Lord Eldon* (16; Cmdr Francis Newcombe) was captured by Spanish gunboats. (Clowes 5.550)

Lord Nelson v. *Bellone* and others, 14–26 August 1803
The Indiaman *Lord Nelson* (Capt. Robert Spottiswood) was attacked near Spain by the privateer *Bellone* and forced to submit after a two-hour fight. The prize crew took *Lord Nelson* towards Corunna; on the 20th she was chased by a British frigate, which instead went after *Bellone*; on the 23rd a British privateer attacked, and on the 25th the sloop *Seagull* – both were driven off. Finally on the 26th a squadron of line-of-battle ships under Capt. Sir Edward Pellew compelled the Indiaman's surrender. (James 3.191; Clowes 5.325–326)

Lorna v. *UB-74*, 26 May 1918
The armed yacht *Lorna* sank *UB-74* with depth-charges in Lyme Bay. (Newbolt 5.428; Grant 119–120)

Louis v. *U-445*, 24 August 1944
U-445 was sunk by the destroyer *Louis* while on passage to Germany through the Bay of Biscay. (Rohwer 349)

Louisburg, Cape Breton Island
1745 An expedition was organised in New England to attack the French fortress at Louisburg. A squadron of ships from the West Indies commanded by Commodore Peter Warren came to assist; the two forces joined at Casco, and landed near Louisburg on 30 April. The French frigate *Renommée* (32) attempted to intercept the expedition but was driven off; a second French ship, *Vigilante* (64), was captured by Warren's ships. Louisburg fell on 28 June. A French attempt to recover it next year collapsed. The fort was returned to France at the peace. (Clowes 3.113–115; Mahan 269)

1755 Commodore Richard Spry, commanding the naval forces at Halifax, Nova Scotia, instituted a loose blockade of Louisburg, attempting to intercept or deter French activity. In July he had encounters with groups of French ships, including a fight with one of them

1758 (Siege of LOUISBURG)   Louisburg was attacked by a British invasion force. The ships, commanded by Admiral Edward Boscawen, landed troops on 8 July, covering the landing with a bombardment; marines from the ships assisted in the siege. In the harbour were three French line-of-battle ships which took fire and were destroyed; two others were attacked by seamen, *Prudente* (74) was grounded and burnt, and *Bienfaisant* (64) cut out. A new seaborne attack by six British line-of-battle ships was only forestalled by the fortress's surrender. (Clowes 3.144–145, 182–184; Mahan 294)

Louvain v. *UC-22*, **20 January 1918**
The armed boarding steamer *Louvain*, carrying a large amount of mail, was sunk by *UC-22* in the eastern Mediterranean. (Halpern, *Mediterranean* 379)

Lowestoft, Suffolk
1665 (Battle of LOWESTOFT)   The English and Dutch fleets, each 100 strong, met off Lowestoft on 3 July. They were commanded respectively by the Duke of York and Jacob van Wassenaes, lord of Opdam. The fleets first passed each other on opposite courses, then reversed to repeat the process. Soon they became intermingled and the battle was between individual ships. Opdam died when his flagship blew up, by which time some Dutch ships were already retreating. The English lost one or two ships captured; the Dutch had fifteen ships destroyed, and fourteen captured. (Clowes 2.259–265; Rodger 2.69–70)

1916   The German High Seas Fleet came out to bombard Lowestoft on 24 April, in co-ordination with the Republican rebellion in Ireland. The intervention of Commodore Tyrwhitt's Harwich force deflected the fleet from an attack on Yarmouth. During the operation the light cruiser *Conquest* and the destroyers *Laertes* and *Penelope* were damaged; the German battle-cruiser *Seydlitz* was damaged, and the submarines *UB-13* and *UC-5* were sunk, all on mines. (Corbett 3.301–309)

Ludlow v. *Adroit*, **16 January 1703**
Ludlow (32; Capt. William Cock) was captured by the French *Adroit* (40) off Gorée, West Africa. (Clowes 2.536)

Ludlow Castle v. *Nightingale* and *Squirrel*, **30 December 1707**
Ludlow Castle (40; Capt. Nicholas Haddock) met the French privateers *Nightingale* and *Squirrel*. *Ludlow Castle*, though outgunned, forced *Nightingale* to surrender. The captain, a renegade English naval officer called Thomas Smith, was hanged. *Squirrel* got away. (Clowes 2.514)

Lurat River, Perak, Malaya, September 1873
A group of pirates from a stockaded town on the Lurat River was attacked by men from the screw corvette *Thalia* (Capt. Henry Woollcombe) and the screw gunvessel *Midge* (Cmdr John Grant) with assistance from the local

raja. After a stiff fight two stockades were captured, together with five large junks. (Clowes 7.237–238)

Lusitania v. *U-20*, 7 May 1915
The liner *Lusitania*, from New York, was torpedoed off Kinsale, Ireland, by *U-20*. The liner sank quickly, and 1200 people died. This was one of the events which caused such violent US protests that Germany suspended its unrestricted submarine campaign for a time. (Corbett 2.392–394; Halpern, *Naval History* 298–302)

Lychnis v. *U-64*, 17 June 1918
The sloop *Lychnis*, escorting a convoy, was attacked by *U-64* between Sicily and Sardinia, and rammed and sank her. (Newbolt 5.411; Halpern, *Mediterranean* 457; Grant 132)

Lyme, Dorset
1644   The Parliamentary fleet under the Earl of Warwick relieved the siege of Lyme in May. (Clowes 2.78)

1685   The Duke of Monmouth landed at Lyme on 11 June aiming to raise a Protestant rebellion against the new King James II and VII. *Soldadoes* (16; Capt. Richard Trevanion) arrived and captured the duke's ships. (Clowes 2.456)

Lyme v. French privateer, 15 January 1704
Lyme (32; Capt. Edward Lechmere) and a French privateer of 46 guns fought each other, to mutual ruin; Lechmere was killed. (Clowes 2.505–506)

Lynx and *Monkey* v. Danish gunboats, 12 August 1809
Lynx (18; Cmdr James Marshall) and the brig *Monkey* (14; Lt Thomas Fitzgerald) attacked three armed Danish luggers at Issehoved, Denmark. *Monkey* fired broadsides into the anchored luggers and they ran aground; they were then refloated and brought out. (James 5.42–43; Clowes 5.443)

Lynx v. *Simpathia*, July 1843
The brig *Lynx* captured the Brazilian slaver *Simpathia* off West Africa. (Bethell 177)

Lynx and *Assaye* at Zanzibar, 14 October 1860
Men from the screw gunvessel *Lynx* and the Indian Navy's ship *Assaye* assisted the Sultan of Zanzibar against rebels. (Howell 16–17; Lloyd 237–238)

Lyra v. slavers, 1860–1861
The screw sloop *Lyra* (Cmdr R.B. Oldfield) captured the slaving brig *Vaga* in 1860, and four slaving dhows in 1861, freeing over 250 slaves; another dhow was taken at Zanzibar, where *Lyra* was attacked by other dhows, unsuccessfully. Three more dhows were captured next day. (Howell 22–23)

M

Macedonian v. *United States*, 25 October 1812
The frigate *Macedonian* (38; Capt. John Carden) met the US frigate *United States* (55) in the western Atlantic. *United States*'s firing dismounted many of *Macedonian*'s guns and gradually dismasted the ship. The fight lasted three hours, then *Macedonian* surrendered. She remained a US ship for the next century. (James 5.394–406; Clowes 6.41–47; J.T. de Kay, *Chronicles of the Frigate Macedonian*, New York 1995; *NC* 5.110)

Madagascar
1796 The frigates *Crescent* (36; Capt. John Spranger), *Braave* (40), and *Syphax* (20) destroyed the French settlement at Foul Point, capturing five merchant ships. (James 1.417; Clowes 4.296)

1811 A detachment of troops, carried in the brig *Eclipse*, occupied the Malagasy town of Tamatave, landing on 12 February. The intention was to deny the place to French ships but later that year three French 40-gun frigates, *Renommée*, *Néréide*, and *Clorinde*, called for provisions. They were attacked by a British frigate squadron, *Astraea* (Capt. Charles Schomberg), *Phoebe* (Capt. James Hillyar), and *Galatea* (Capt. Woodley Losack) with the sloop *Racehorse* (Cmdr James de Rippe). The British ships suffered badly from the French fire, but *Renommée* was forced to surrender; *Clorinde* got away, and *Néréide* was captured later in Tamatave. (James 5.282–295; Clowes 5.486*; *NC* 5.49–59)

1845 A landing was made by British and French forces at Tamatave on 15 June in an attempt to compel the Malagasy queen to accept their dictation. Batteries and a small fort were captured and the town was bombarded, but the allies quarrelled, and a stronger fort defied attack. The allies withdrew, defeated, having suffered over seventy casualties. (Clowes 6.345–346)

1942 Madagascar, governed by Vichy authorities, was likely to be used by Japanese ships as their base. A landing by British forces at Courrieur Bay near Diego Suarez in the north on 5 May was preceded by air attacks from the carrier *Illustrious* which sank the auxiliary cruiser *Bougainville* and the submarine *Bevéziers*; the corvette *Auricula* was mined in the operation. French resistance was successful until the destroyer *Anthony* went into Diego Suarez by night and landed a force of marines who captured important central installations and caused widespread confusion. The gunboat *D'Entrecasteaux* ran aground, and the Vichy French submarines *Genista* and *Monge* were sunk attempting attacks on the British fleet. Resistance in the north ceased on 8 May. On 30 May the battleship *Ramillies* and a tanker were torpedoed by Japanese midget submarines launched from the submarines *I-16* and *I-20*. Landings were made by British forces at four different points on the Madagascar coast in September; the campaign was completed by the French surrender on 5 November. (C. Buckley, *Five Ventures*, London 1954, 165–210; Rohwer 161, 169–170, 195)

Madeira
1801 The Portuguese island of Madeira was seized on 23 July by a party of British troops on the news that Portugal had agreed, as part of the treaty of peace with Spain, to exclude British ships from her ports. (James 3.150)

1807 Portugal's invasion by the French prompted the British to take control of Madeira again, on 24 December. An unopposed landing was made by troops escorted by the squadron of Rear-Admiral Sir Samuel Hood. (James 4.275)

Mafia Island, Tanganyika, 10 January 1915
Mafia, off the mouth of the Rufiji River, was occupied by a force carried by the light cruiser *Fox* and AMC *Kinfauns Castle*. (Corbett 2.237–238)

***Magicienne* v. *Sybille*, 2 January 1783**
Magicienne (32; Capt. Thomas Graves), near St Domingue, chased a French convoy escorted by *Sybille* (32), and the two ships fought fiercely, side by side. *Magicienne* lost her foremast, then the rest of her masts. *Sybille* sailed away as other ships arrived to assist *Magicienne*. (Clowes 4.91–92)

***Magicienne* v. *Cerf Volant*, 1 November 1796**
The French corvette *Cerf Volant* (18) was captured by *Magicienne* (32; Capt. William Ricketts) near St Domingue. (Clowes 4.554)

***Magicienne* v. *Carmen*, 29 January 1806**
The Spanish ship *Carmen* (14) was captured in the Mona Passage by *Magicienne* (32; Capt. Adam McKenzie). (Clowes 5.563)

***Magicienne* in Malaya, 1832**
Magicienne (24; Capt. James Plumridge) sent boat parties upriver in Malaya to blockade the Raja of Nanning, at war with the EIC. (Clowes 6.270)

***Magnanime* and *Naiad* v. *Decade*, 24 August 1798**
The French frigate *Decade* was captured off Finisterre by *Magnanime* (44) and *Naiad* (38). (Clowes 4.556)

***Magnificent* and others v. *Fortunée*, *Blanche*, and *Elise*, 21–22 December 1779**
A British squadron consisting of *Magnificent* (74), *Suffolk* (74), *Vengeance* (74), and *Stirling Castle* (64), commanded by Rear-Admiral Joshua Rowley, flying French colours, came close to the French frigates *Fortunée* (32), *Blanche* (32), and *Elise* (28) near Guadeloupe. The French ships attempted to escape, but *Fortunée* was quickly captured, and the others were taken next day. (Clowes 4.47)

Magpie v. **French ship, 19 February 1807**
Magpie (4; Lt Edward Johnson) was driven into Perros, Brittany, and captured. (Clowes 5.551)

Mahé, India, February 1761
The French port of Mahé was besieged by the EIC army and blockaded by a small squadron under Rear-Admiral Sir Samuel Cornish. It surrendered on 10 February. (Clowes 3.232)

Maidstone v. *Lion*, **3 November 1778**
Maidstone (28; Capt. Alan Gardner) fought the French *Lion* (40), a royal ship hired out as a privateer. *Lion* drove *Maidstone* off at first, but had to surrender to a second attack. (Clowes 4.22)

Maidstone v. *Arabe*, **14 June 1803**
The frigate *Maidstone* (32; Capt. Richard Moubray) captured the French *Arabe* (8) in the Mediterranean. (Clowes 5.555)

Maidstone v. *Principe de Guinea*, **September 1826**
Maidstone (36) captured the slaver *Principe de Guinea* off West Africa; 600 slaves were freed. (Ward 115)

Majestic and others v. *Suffren*, **8 January 1797**
Suffren (44; a storeship) was sunk by *Majestic* (74), *Daedalus* (32), and *Incendiary* (14) off Ushant. (Clowes 4.555)

Majestic v. *Bolador*, **14 November 1797**
Majestic (74; Capt. George Westcott) captured the Spanish *Bolador* (14) off the Portuguese coast. (Clowes 4.560)

Majestic v. *Eddercop*, **May 1809**
The boats of *Majestic* (74) in the Baltic captured the Danish gunboat *Eddercop* (2). (Clowes 5.565)

Majestic v. *Atalante* and *Terpsichore*, **3 February 1814**
Majestic (74; Capt. John Hayes) met the French frigates *Atalante* and *Terpsichore* with two prizes near the Azores. *Majestic* chased for ten hours and forced *Terpsichore* to surrender, but the other ships got away. One of the prizes, the Spanish *San Juan de Baptista*, was taken later. (James 6.144–147; Clowes 5.547–548)

Majestic v. *U-21*, **27 May 1915**
The battleship *Majestic* (Capt. Talbot), off Cape Helles, even though protected by nets and transport ships, was successfully torpedoed by *U-21*. (Corbett 8.30–31)

Majorca, Balearic Islands, February 1655
A squadron of four English ships patrolled in the area of the Balearic Islands

in search of French ships. One frigate was captured and, after a complicated series of actions, *Pensee* (30) was driven ashore on Majorca. (Corbett, *Mediterranean* 1.302–303)

Makaronia, Turkey, 12 May 1916
The destroyer *Chelmer*, the minesweeper *Whitby Abbey*, and several smaller vessels raided the Anatolian coast south of Makaronia, carrying off over 200 animals. (Halpern, *Mediterranean* 391–392)

Malabar, India, 1768
In the First Mysore War, the BM captured several ports on the Malabar coast which had been held by Hyder Ali's forces – Onore, Fortified Island, and Mangalore. As soon as the ships departed, Hyder Ali recaptured the ports. (Low 1.153–154)

Malacca, Malaya, 17 August 1795
An expeditionary force from India sailed for the Dutch city of Malacca, which quickly surrendered. (James 1.336)

Malaga, Spain
1656 Four frigates were sent into Malaga under Capt. Eustace Smith; a fireship burned two ships, a galley, and several smaller vessels; Smith then landed a force on the mole, drove the Spanish guard away, and spiked the guns of the battery. (Corbett, *Mediterranean* 1.331; Capp 98; Powell 285)

1704 (Battle of MALAGA) The English Mediterranean fleet under Admiral Sir George Rooke met and fought the French Toulon fleet under Admiral Comte de Tourville. The two fleets were approximately equal in numbers, and both suffered considerable damage before the fighting ended at darkness. Neither fleet was willing to renew the battle in the next days. The French aim to recover control of Gibraltar had been thwarted. (Corbett, *Mediterranean* 2.271–276; Clowes 2.376–404; Owen 93–97; Francis 116–117; Rodger 2.169–170; Mahan 211–212; Tunstall 66–67)

Malaya
1941 The battleship *Prince of Wales* and the battle-cruiser *Repulse*, with four destroyers, commanded by Admiral Tom Phillips, sailed from Singapore to attack the Japanese invasion fleet approaching from Indo-China on 8 December. Several submarine attacks on the ships failed, but air attacks during the night succeeded, and both big ships were sunk. (Rohwer 123)

1949 Ships of the East Indies Squadron repeatedly bombarded positions held by communist insurgents in Malaya. (Wettern 16)

Malta, September–October 1798
French rule in Malta proved unpopular with the Maltese, who rose against the garrison and drove the French troops into Valetta. Nelson's fleet landed arms and marines, the nearby island of Gozo was captured, and the Maltese

were assisted in the siege of the city, finally taken in 1800. (James 2.211–213; Clowes 4.374–375; *NC* 1.290, 2.80–83)

MALTA CONVOYS, 1940–1943

The Axis air assault on Malta began soon after the Italian declaration of war, and could only be combated by regular reinforcements of aircraft and the delivery of supplies. The convoys are numbered with the prefix M-, but are often better known by their operational names. Most convoys were combined with other operations. (The dates are those of naval action.) For general accounts see: Roskill 1–3 *passim*; Ernle Bradford, *Siege: Malta, 1940–1943*, London 1985; David A. Thomas, *Malta Convoys 1940–1942*, London 1999

MA-3, 27–30 June 1940

This convoy sailing from Alexandria to Malta met a rival Italian convoy sailing from Taranto to Tobruk. In the battle the Italian destroyer *Espero* was sunk by HMAS *Sydney*. Most of the Italian convoy reached Libya safely. (Rohwer 30)

'Hurry', 2 August 1940

Force H from Gibraltar raided Cagliari in Sardinia and flew Hurricanes into Malta. The submarine *Oswald* was rammed and sunk by the Italian destroyer *Vivaldi* on 1 August off Cape Spartivento, Sardinia. (Rohwer 34)

'Hats', 31 August–4 September 1940

Force F from Alexandria combined with Force H from Gibraltar to run a convoy to Malta and then on to Alexandria. Aircraft from the carrier *Ark Royal* bombed Port Elmas in Sardinia. Various Italian forces attempted attacks but usually could not find the British ships. In a subsidiary operation Scarpanto Island was shelled, and when two Italian torpedo boats attacked, one was sunk by the destroyer *Ilex*. (Rohwer 37–38)

MB-5, 28 September–3 October 1940

The cruisers *Gloucester* and *Liverpool* sailed from Alexandria with 1200 soldiers for Malta; despite attacks by Italian aircraft, the ships got through; the British covering fleet was undamaged. (Rohwer 42–43)

MB-6, 8–14 October 1940

Covered by bad weather this convoy reached Malta (from Alexandria) undiscovered. In an attempted ambush by the Italian 1st Torpedo Boat Flotilla on the convoy's return, the cruiser *Ajax* sank the TBs *Ariel* and *Airone*. The Italian 11th Destroyer Flotilla arrived to assist the TBs: the destroyer *Artigliere* was damaged by *Ajax* and later sank. (Rohwer 44)

MB-8 and 'Coat', 4–14 November 1940

Convoys from Egypt and from Gibraltar moved simultaneously. Having escorted one convoy to Suda Bay in Crete, the Mediterranean fleet took MB-8 on to Malta. Force H from Gibraltar launched an air raid on Cagliari and then collected the 'Coat' convoy and delivered it to the island. Force H returned to Gibraltar; the escort of the Malta convoy took empty vessels back to Suda Bay. Several air and submarine attacks were made by Italian forces, but all failed. (Rohwer 47)

'White', 15–20 November 1940
A fleet from Gibraltar sent five aircraft into Malta, and the cruiser *Newcastle* delivered personnel to the island. (Rohwer 49)

'Collar', 24–29 November 1940
This convoy of two ships for Malta and one for Egypt was menaced by the Italian fleet coming south from Naples. The convoy went on. Force H challenged the Italian fleet and fought the battle of Cape Spartivento. (Rohwer 49–50)

MC-2, 16–24 December 1940
Operations in the Dodecanese Islands and the Strait of Otranto were combined with a convoy of eight ships for Malta and westwards. The destroyer *Hyperion* was sunk by the submarine *Serpente*; aircraft from the carrier *Illustrious* sank two ships from an Italian convoy. (Rohwer 52)

'Excess', 6–13 January 1941
This convoy from Gibraltar for Piraeus in Greece was subjected to TB and air attacks on 9–11 January on its passage between Malta and Crete. The Italian TB *Vega* was sunk; the carrier *Illustrious* was damaged by bombs and the cruiser *Southampton* was sunk. (Rohwer 54–55)

MD-3, 18–23 April 1941
The Mediterranean fleet escorted the transport *Breconshire* to Malta, and as a subsidiary and a distraction Tripoli was bombarded by three battleships, in which six freighters and the TB *Partenope* were hit. (Rohwer 69)

'Dunlop', 24–28 April 1941
Force H took Hurricane aircraft and reinforcements for Malta and more ships to join the Mediterranean fleet; several empty transports were taken on to Alexandria. (Rohwer 70)

'Tiger', 5–12 May 1941
Convoys from Gibraltar and Alexandria were run through to Malta, each covered by a heavy escort. As a subsidiary operation Benghazi was shelled. Both convoys were subjected to several air attacks, but only one of the escorts, the destroyer *Fortune*, was damaged; one transport sank after hitting a mine. (Rohwer 72)

'Substance', 21–27 July 1941
Force H escorted six freighters from Gibraltar to Malta, and was attacked by air and by TBs: the cruiser *Manchester* and the destroyer *Fearless* were sunk; one transport was damaged; a tanker was sunk on the return journey. (Rohwer 88)

'Style', 31 July–4 August 1941
Five ships carried troops and supplies from Gibraltar to Malta covered by Force H. Alghero harbour and airfield in Sardinia were bombarded by the destroyers *Cossack* and *Maori* and bombed by aircraft from *Ark Royal*; the cruiser *Hermione* rammed and sank the Italian submarine *Tembien* near Tunis. (Rohwer 89)

'Halberd', 24–30 September 1941
A convoy of nine freighters, escorted by a large force, was run through from Gibraltar to Malta. The Italian fleet came out to intercept but neither side was able to find the other. The battleship *Nelson* was damaged by air attack and one freighter was sunk. The Italian submarine *Adua* was sunk by the destroyers *Gurkha* and *Legion*. (Rohwer 103–107; Greene and Massignani 181–191)

'Perpetual', 10–14 November 1941
Forty aircraft were flown off carriers to Malta. Force H was attacked by two U-boats. *U-81* sank the carrier *Ark Royal*. (Rohwer 114)

MF-1, 15–18 December 1941 (FIRST battle of SIRTE)
The transport *Breconshire* was escorted from Alexandria to Malta, at first by Force B from Alexandria, then by Force K from Malta; she reached Malta safely. Force B then met the Italian escort of a convoy from Taranto to Tripoli, covered by three battleships with heavy cruisers and destroyers. Neither side had any success in the manoeuvring which followed, being mainly concerned to protect their convoys. The British cruiser *Neptune* and the destroyer *Kandahar* were sunk in an Italian minefield on the return journey, and the cruisers *Aurora* and *Penelope* were damaged. (Rohwer 125; Greene and Massignani 200–202)

MS-3, 16–20 January 1942
This convoy set sail from Alexandria for Malta; one freighter was sunk, as was the destroyer *Gurkha* (by *U-133*); three of the transports reached Malta. (Rohwer 136)

MF-5, 12–16 February 1942
An exchange of transports between Alexandria and Malta came under heavy attack. The destroyer *Maori* was sunk, as were two of the transports, while one was badly damaged. The Italian main fleet failed to locate the convoys and the destroyer *Carabiniere* was torpedoed by the submarine *P-36* off Taranto on the fleet's return. (Rohwer 143)

MW-10, 26 March 1942 (SECOND battle of SIRTE)
A group of four transports escorted by a large force of cruisers and destroyers sailed from Alexandria for Malta. Italian forces came out of Messina and Taranto to intercept, and German and Italian aircraft attacked. Admiral Philip Vian, in command of the escort, established a rolling smokescreen which confused the Italian gunnery, and a storm finally forced the engagement to be broken off. Several British ships were damaged. On retiring the Italian destroyers *Lanciere* and *Scirocco* sank in the storm. The convoy arrived late at Malta and three of the transports were sunk by bombing almost at once; the destroyer *Legion* was badly damaged and later destroyed. Many ships on both sides suffered storm damage. The submarine *P-39* was sunk. (Rohwer 152–153; Greene and Massignani 217–222)

'Harpoon' and 'Vigorous', 12–16 June 1942
Simultaneous convoys from Alexandria and Gibraltar headed for Malta; both were heavily escorted by strong covering forces, and both were attacked by

air, by submarine, and by surface ships. Casualties were heavy; seven of the nineteen freighters were sunk and one damaged; the cruiser *Hermione* was sunk by *U-205* and the destroyers *Hasty, Bedouin*, and *Nestor* were sunk; eleven other warships were damaged. On the Italian side the battleship *Vittorio Veneto* was twice hit by bombs from British aircraft, and the cruiser *Trento* was damaged by an aerial torpedo and then sunk by the submarine *Umbra*. Twelve of the freighters reached Malta. (Rohwer 173–174; Greene and Massignani 235–238)

'Pinpoint', 14–16 July 8, 1942

Part of Force H sailed from Gibraltar to fly off aircraft for Malta from the carrier *Eagle*; the minelayer *Welshman* went on alone with supplies, successfully evading both air and submarine attacks. (Rohwer 181)

'PEDESTAL', 10–15 August 1942

A convoy of thirteen freighters and the tanker *Ohio*, under heavy escort and covered by a force which included four carriers, sailed from Gibraltar on 10 August; two empty transports set out from Malta on the opposite journey; the escorts of these two clashed briefly with an Italian destroyer off Cape Bon. The carrier *Furious* flew off thirty-seven Spitfires for Malta, then returned to Gibraltar with an escort of five destroyers; an attack by Italian submarines resulted in *Dagabur* being rammed by the destroyer *Wolverine*, and *Giada* was bombed and damaged.

In the main body the carrier *Eagle* was sunk by *U-73*. A flight of British fighters attacked Italian bases in Sardinia. Several air attacks were made on the convoy; one transport was damaged and left behind; submarine attacks were repeatedly blocked by the destroyers of the escort. The carrier *Indomitable* was badly damaged in an attack. The destroyer *Foresight* was damaged and later sunk. The Italian submarines *Dessie* and *Axum* each scored torpedo hits, on the cruisers *Cairo* (later abandoned) and *Nigeria*. The tanker *Ohio* was torpedoed, but was able to continue.

Another air attack sank two transports and immobilised a third. An attack by the submarine *Alagi* damaged the cruiser *Kenya* and another transport. Italian TBs made fifteen successive attacks in which the cruiser *Manchester* was hit and later abandoned, and four of the transports were hit, three of which sank. On 14 August there were continuous air attacks: three transports and *Ohio* were hit. A force of minesweepers came out from Malta to escort the remaining three transports to the island. One other transport arrived later. The tanker *Ohio* arrived later still, escorted, even physically supported, by four destroyers. The people of Malta lined the Great Harbour to cheer her in; it was one of the great emotional moments of the war.

In subsidiary and later operations the Italian main fleet came out, but without air support could not attack; the submarine *Unbroken* torpedoed the cruisers *Atendolo* and *Bolzano*. Cruisers and destroyers in the Mediterranean fleet bombarded Rhodes in an attempt to distract Italian attention from the convoy. The convoy's escorting ships – now only two cruisers and five destroyers – were attacked repeatedly on their return to Gibraltar by a submarine, a TB, and large numbers of aircraft, all without success. This proved to be the decisive convoy battle of the Mediterranean war. (Rohwer 186–187; Greene and Massignani 224–226)

'Stone Age', 17–20 November 1942
Four freighters, escorted by three cruisers and ten destroyers, sailed from Alexandria to Malta. The cruiser *Arethusa* was badly damaged by air attack, but all four freighters reached Malta safely. (Rohwer 213)

Mamora, Morocco, 12 June 1685
A raiding party in boats from *Bonaventure* (48; Lt Stafford Fairborne), *Greyhound* (16; Capt. Randall McDonald), and *Lark* (18; Capt. Thomas Leighton) went into the harbour of Mamora and burned two Sallee pirate ships. (Clowes 2.459)

Man, Irish Sea
The Isle of Man occupied a strategic position in the Irish Sea which made it a target for any sea power.

577–578 Expeditions were launched by King Baetan mac Cairill of Dal Fiatach in Ireland against Man. The island appears to have been conquered, but the Irish were driven out in 582. (*NHI* 1.216)

c.630 King Edwin of Northumbria's seaborne expedition took Man from the Ulster King Eiachnae mac Baetan, who had presumably recovered his father's control. (*NHI* 1.218)

914 Ragnall, king of York, won a sea battle near Man against Barid son of Oitir; as a result Ragnall went on to capture Waterford. (Oram 2; *NHI* 1.854–855)

987–989 Jarl Sigurd the Stout of Orkney and Jarl Gilli of the Hebrides attacked Man in 987, acquiring loot. Godfrey Haraldsson, king of the Isles, then led a fleet to conquer Man. Another attack by Sigurd in 989 resulted in the death of King Godfrey and the conquest of the island. (Thompson 37; Oram 11; Hudson 62)

995 The island was raided by a Viking force under Swegn son of Harald. (Maund 159)

1000 King Aethelred II's fleet ravaged the island – the intention had been to attack Cumbria, but the weather prevented the fleet reaching there. (*ASC* s.a. 1000)

1061 Murchad, king of Dublin, raided the island, and by taking a tax from the inhabitants established his overlordship. He presumably defeated the king, Echmarcach, to do this. (Hudson 145; *NHI* 1.879)

1073 A fleet from Ireland led by Sitric, brother of the king of Dublin, and two descendants of Brian Boru, attacked Man but were defeated by Fingal, king of Man and the Isles. (Hudson 172)

1079 After two failed attempts, Godred Crovan, king of the Isles, succeeded in invading Man. He landed at Ramsey by night and ambushed and defeated the Manxmen next day. (Hudson 172; MacDonald 33–34)

1087 An attempt to conquer Man was made by a joint Viking-Irish fleet but was defeated by King Godred Crovan. (Hudson 174)

1096 Man was attacked by Olaf mac Taidc after the death of King Godred Crovan; the attack was defeated by Godred's son Lagman. (Hudson 188)

1098 See: **King Magnus's expedition**

1153 Three nephews of King Olaf of Man invaded Man from Dublin, and killed Olaf himself. Each nephew took over part of the island. Godred, Olaf's son, sailed from Norway and was accepted as king in the Isles. With support from there he sailed on to Man to dispute possession with the murderers of his father, whose local support was very poor. Godred was successful. His enemies were killed or blinded in revenge. (MacDonald 32; Oram 69–70)

1157–1158 Somerled of the Isles launched an attack on Godred of Man, and the two rulers fought a battle at sea near the island on 5–6 January 1157; neither could claim the victory, and this led to a peace treaty dividing the islands between them. Next year Somerled, commanding a fleet of fifty-three ships, defeated Godred, who fled to Norway. Somerled reigned as king of the Isles and Man. (MacDonald 56–57; Oram 76)

1210 Man was ravaged by King John's mercenary captain Faulkes de Breaute as part of the king's expedition to Ireland. (Oram 124)

1224 Olaf, ruler in Lewis, attacked his brother Ragnvald, king of Man, with a fleet of thirty-two ships, and forced a share-out of territory between them. (MacDonald 85)

1228–1230 The exiled king of Man, Ragnvald, in alliance with Alan of Galloway, invaded, devastated, and repossessed Man, but was soon expelled. He returned in 1229 with five ships to attempt to recover the kingship. At Peel he captured and burnt the ships of King Olaf, but was defeated and killed at Tinwald in February. Alan of Galloway, allied with two Hebridean chiefs, invaded in 1230. King Olaf fled to Norway, where he persuaded King Haakon IV to assist him. The expedition failed, and Olaf sailed to recover Man himself. He defeated a fleet recruited in the island and succeeded in recovering the kingship. (MacDonald 86; Oram 127–129)

1250 The island was invaded by Ewen, exiled king of the Isles, while King Harald of Man was in Norway. Ewen landed at Ronaldsway and held the island briefly; he was driven out by c.1252. (MacDonald 104)

1275 Scottish control of Man was disputed by Godfred, son of the last king, who led a rebellion against Scottish rule. King Alexander III sent an expedition to recover control, consisting of some knights and men from the Isles and Galloway, in a fleet of ninety galleys. They landed at Ronaldsway, and a battle next day returned Man to Scottish rule. (MacDonald 137)

1310 King Robert Bruce of Scots mounted a naval expedition from the Isles to gain control of Man, apparently successfully. (MacDonald 195–197)

1313 King Robert Bruce of Scots sailed with a fleet to Man, landing at Ramsey on 1 May. He besieged and took Rushen Castle, and presumably thereby gained control of the island. (Barrow 279–281; MacDonald 197; Duncan 102)

1315 John of Argyll, in the service of King Edward II, invaded Man from Dublin with a fleet of twelve ships and returned the island to English rule. (MacDonald 198; Duncan 103; Nicholson 94)

1533 A Scots raid on the island in July resulted in the capture of the English ship *Mary Willoughby* which had been sent to suppress piracy. (Phillips 146)

1651 The Earl and Countess of Derby held the island for the king, but a Parliamentary force landed in October and compelled an early surrender. (Clowes 2.139–140)

Mangalore, India, 8 December 1781
A small British squadron under Rear-Admiral Sir Edward Hughes cruised along the Malabar coast. Boats from the squadron went in to Mangalore and captured and burned several of Hyder Ali's ships in the harbour, including one of 28 and one of 26 guns. (Clowes 3.545)

Manila, Philippines, September 1761
An expedition was sent from India to capture Manila from Spain. It consisted of eight line-of-battle ships and three frigates commanded by Rear-Admiral Samuel Cornish, and 79th Foot, and artillery. Surprise was achieved and the landing was made on 24 September. On 5 October the city surrendered and all the Philippine Islands with it. (Clowes 3.239–242)

Manistee v. *U-107*, 24 February 1941
The ocean boarding vessel *Manistee* was sunk by *U-107* in the North Atlantic. (Rohwer 57)

Manly v. Dutch force, January 1806
Manly (12; Cmdr Martin White) was captured by Dutch forces in the Ems River; she was retaken in 1809. (Clowes 5.430)

Manly and *Chanticleer* v. three Danish brigs, 2 September 1811
The sloop *Chanticleer* (10; Cmdr Richard Spear) and the brig *Manly* (12; Lt Richard Simonds) were attacked by three Danish brigs. In the subsequent fight *Chanticleer* failed to assist *Manly*, which had to surrender. (James 5.229–230; Anderson 345; Clowes 5.492)

Manners and others v. *U-1051*, 26 January 1945
In the Irish Sea *U-1051* torpedoed the destroyer *Manners* and was then hunted and sunk by ships of two Escort Groups, *Aylmer*, *Bentinck*, and *Calder*. (Rohwer 384)

Manxman v. *U-375*, 1 December 1942
The minelayer *Manxman* was sunk by *U-375* in the western Mediterranean. (Rohwer 216)

Maria v. Département des Landes, 29 September 1808
The brig *Maria* (12; Lt James Bennett) challenged the French corvette *Département des Landes* (22) near Guadeloupe; *Maria* was sinking when she finally surrendered; Bennett was killed. (James 4.374–375; Clowes 5.426)

Mariamne v. Caridad Perfecta, 12 August 1805
The schooner *Mariamne* (Lt James Smith) attacked and captured the Spanish *guarda costa Caridad Perfecta* in the harbour of Truxillo, Honduras. (James 4.75; Clowes 5.370)

Mariegalante and Desirade Islands, West Indies, March 1808
A party of sailors and marines from the frigates *Cerberus* (Capt. William Selby) and *Circe* (Capt. Hugh Pigot) and the sloop *Camilla* (Capt. John Bowen) landed on the island of Mariegalante. After only minimal fighting, the principal town surrendered; a similar landing from the same ships on Desirade Island had equal success. (James 4.387–388; NC 4.142)

Marigold v. U-433, 16 November 1941
U-433 attacked a British convoy near Gibraltar, but was detected and sunk by the corvette *Marigold*. (Rohwer 113)

Marlborough and Bellona v. Prinses Carolina, 30 December 1780
The Dutch *Prinses Carolina* (54) was intercepted in the English Channel by *Marlborough* (74; Capt. Taylor Penny) and *Bellona* (74; Capt. Richard Onslow) and forced to surrender after a short fight. (Clowes 4.59)

Marmaduke v. Constant Reformation and Conventive, 6 November 1650
Princes Rupert and Maurice in the Royalist ships *Constant Reformation* and *Conventive* met and chased a large merchant ship, the *Marmaduke* of London. *Marmaduke* fought back but had to surrender when she lost her mainmast. (Clowes 2.132)

Marmora v. UB-64, 23 July 1918
The AMC *Marmora* was sunk by *UB-64* south of Ireland. (Colledge 249)

Marne, Milbrook, and Pigeon v. UB-124, 20 July 1918
The drifters *Marne*, *Milbrook*, and *Pigeon* combined to attack and sink *UB-124* in the waters north of Ireland. (Newbolt 5.428; Grant 113)

Maron v. U-81, 14 November 1942
The ocean boarding vessel *Maron* was sunk by *U-81* off Bougie, Algeria. (Rohwer 209)

Marquette v. U-35, 23 October 1915
The troop transport *Marquette* in the Gulf of Salonica was torpedoed and sunk by *U-35*. (Halpern, *Mediterranean* 178)

Mars and *Oxford* v. *Anemone* and *Sardoine*, 1761
Mars (74) and *Oxford* (50) captured the French ships *Anemone* (14) and *Sardoine* (14) in the Bay of Biscay. (Clowes 3.313)

Mars v. *Hercule*, 21 April 1798
The French *Hercule* (74) was chased by *Mars* (74; Capt. Alexander Hood) for several hours, until she anchored in the Passage de Raz. *Mars* also anchored, and they fought side-by-side. *Hercule* twice attempted to board but failed, and with almost half her company casualties, she surrendered. Hood was killed. (James 2.120–123; Clowes 4.336–337)

Mars v. *Matilda*, June 1805
The privateer *Mars* from Liverpool captured the Spanish treasure galleon *Matilda*, but both were then taken by the French fleet of Admiral Villeneuve. *Mars* was burnt. (James 3.353)

Mars v. *Rhin*, 27–28 July 1806
The frigate *Rhin* was one of a squadron of four which were chased by *Mars* (74; Capt. Robert Oliver). When *Mars* came close, *Rhin* was left to her fate, and she surrendered at the first shot. (James 4.164; Clowes 5.387)

Martin v. French privateers, 29 August 1702
The ketch *Martin* (10; Capt. Thomas Warren) was captured by three French privateers off Jersey. (Clowes 2.556; Colledge 250)

Martinique, West Indies
1667 Rear-Admiral Sir John Harman's squadron bombarded the French forts into silence on 24 June, and next day burned or captured most of the ships in the harbour. (Clowes 2.432–433; Rodger 2.78)

1693 An expedition commanded by Rear-Admiral Sir Francis Wheler landed forces on the island and caused destruction, but when the army expedition under General Codrington arrived the invasion was called off. (Clowes 2.470)

1759 A landing was made on Martinique by a squadron commanded by Commodore John Moore on 16 January. Outnumbered by the defending French forces, it was then withdrawn. A second attempt, in which *Ripon* (60; Capt. Edward Jekyll) bombarded a fort at St Pierre, was also called off. (Clowes 3.201–202)

1762 An expeditionary force of seventeen line-of-battle ships and fifteen frigates, commanded by Rear-Admiral George Rodney, landed at St Anne's Bay, but this was too far from Fort Royal to be effective. On 16 January a new landing was made close to Fort Royal. The fort was taken by 4 February, and the whole island was in British possession by 16 February. (Clowes 3.242–244)

1780 (Battle of MARTINIQUE)   The British and French West Indian fleets met near Martinique on 17 April. The British fleet, commanded by Admiral

Sir George Rodney, manoeuvred with the intention of making a decisive attack on the French, commanded by Comte de Guichen. The French had twenty-two line-of-battle ships; the British twenty. Rodney's flagship, *Sandwich* (90), battered its way through the French line. This may not have been his intention, but its effect was to make the French turn away. Rodney complained afterwards at the conduct of a number of his captains in not closing with the enemy. The fleets manoeuvred for several days to gain advantage, and on 29 April, when the British had the weather gauge, Rodney at once ordered an attack. The wind changed, and the fleets passed each other on opposite courses, without result. Manoeuvres for another nine days produced another clash, after which the fleets separated to seek repairs and supplies. The French appear to have suffered more severely than the British. (Clowes 3.453–468; NRS, *Rodney* 2.701, 857–861; Tunstall 165–168)

1781 (Battle of MARTINIQUE) A French fleet of twenty line-of-battle ships under Admiral Comte de Grasse brought a convoy to Martinique; the British fleet of seventeen line-of-battle ships under Rear-Admiral Sir Samuel Hood awaited them. Each fleet was reinforced, giving the French an even greater advantage of twenty-four to eighteen ships. Despite several attempts Hood could not manoeuvre his fleet close to the enemy. When one of his ships was badly damaged, he broke off the fight. (Clowes 3.482–487; Mahan 383–384; Tunstall 171–172)

1793–1794 Persuaded by Royalists that there was little Republican support in Martinique, a British force landed from Barbados on 14 April 1793, but on the march towards the fort at St Pierre it was routed; the troops, and 2000 refugees, were re-embarked on the 21st. Next year a new expedition of 7000 troops from Barbados landed at three separate places. A party from the flagship *Boyne* (98) entered the harbour to capture the frigate *Bienvenue* (32). The sloop *Zebra* (Capt. Robert Faulknor) made a swift assault on Fort Louis, and boats from other ships seized Fort Royal. At this the governor, General Rochambeau, surrendered. (James 1.127–128, 239–245; Duffy 35–37, 64–88; Clowes 4.213–214, 247–248; *NC* 1.67–83)

1808 A squadron of French ships approached St Pierre and was attacked by a group of British ships on 12 December. One French schooner went ashore below a battery, which was silenced by bombardment from the sloop *Stork* (Cmdr George Le Geyt), the frigate *Circe* (Cmdr Francis Collier), and the brig *Morne Fortunée* (Lt John Bowen). Other French ships, protected by another battery, were attacked by boats from *Stork*, *Circe*, and the schooner *Express* (Cmdr William Dowers), but French fire sank one, disabled another, and captured the third. A new attack by boats from *Stork*, *Circe*, and the sloop *Amaranthe* (Cmdr Edward Brenton) next morning resulted in the capture of the corvette *Cigne*, which was destroyed. (James 4.376–382)

1809 A force of 10,000 soldiers, escorted and transported by a squadron under Rear-Admiral Hon. Sir Alexander Cochrane, captured the Islet de Ramiers, commanding the entrance to Fort Royal harbour. Three French ships there were burned. The army then captured the main point of resistance, Fort Desaix, at which point the island capitulated. (James 5.69–73; Clowes 5.283–284; *NC* 4.224–225; Morriss 61–63)

Martin's squadron v. French squadron, 23–25 October 1809
Three French line-of-battle ships and two frigates, escorting a convoy for Barcelona, were chased by a squadron under Rear-Admiral George Martin in *Canopus* (80) with five other line-of-battle ships. After two days two French ships, *Robuste* (80) and *Lion* (74), were run on shore. Their crews landed and the ships were dismantled and burnt; *Borée* (74) and the frigate *Pauline* escaped into the harbour at Cette. (James 4.445–447; Clowes 5.278–280; *NC* 4.299–304)

***Mary* and *Rupert* v. Algerine ship, 1 March 1678**
Mary (60; Capt. Sir Roger Stickland) and *Rupert* (64; Capt. Arthur Herbert) fought an Algerine ship of 40 guns. *Rupert* fought first, and all the officers on board were killed or wounded. When *Mary* came up the Algerine surrendered. (Clowes 2.453–454)

***Mary* v. *Real Carlos*, 27 December 1780**
The Indiaman *Mary* (22; Capt. M. Stewards) was attacked by the Spanish *Real Carlos* in the Atlantic, but beat off her attacker. *Mary*, partly disabled, was later captured by *Pilgrim*, an American privateer. (Clowes 4.59)

***Maryton* and *Puncheston* v. Indonesian landing craft, 28 March 1965**
The minesweepers *Maryton* and *Puncheston* intercepted and sank an Indonesian landing craft attempting to land a raiding party in Malaya. (Wettern 253)

Maasnah, Gulf of Oman, March 1874
The screw gunvessels *Philomel* (Cmdr Edward Garforth) and *Nimble* (Cmdr Henry Best) and the BM screw gunboat *Hugh Rose* bombarded the fort at Maasnah. (Clowes 7.277–278)

Massawa, Eritrea, February–March 1941
Aircraft from the carrier *Formidable* raided Massawa on 13 and 21 February and 1 March. The Italian auxiliary cruiser *RAMB 1* and a German supply ship broke out. (Rohwer 59)

***Master Standfast* v. *V-1606*, 2 November 1943**
The British *MTB-508* (*Master Standfast*) was captured by the German patrol trawler *V-1606* off Lysekil. She was recommissioned into the German navy. (Rohwer 288)

Masulipatam, India, 21 August 1673
A Dutch East India fleet attacked an English convoy of ten armed merchantmen off Masulipatam; three were captured. (Clowes 2.446)

***Matane* and *Swansea* v. *U-311*, 22 April 1944**
U-311 was sunk by the Canadian frigates *Matane* and *Swansea*. (Rohwer 313)

MATAPAN, 28–29 March 1941

An Italian fleet consisting of the battleship *Vittorio Veneto*, eight cruisers, and attendant destroyers came out from various ports with the intention of interrupting the British convoys between Alexandria and Greece. Admiral A.B. Cunningham in command of the British Mediterranean fleet was warned of this move by decrypted Enigma signals, and laid an ambush for the Italian ships. He had one aircraft carrier, *Formidable*, three battleships, and four cruisers with destroyers. The fleets met south of Crete on 28 March in the morning; the Italian fleet turned back and a series of air attacks from *Formidable* and Crete resulted in hits on *Vittorio Veneto* and the cruiser *Pola*. The battleship, slightly slowed, was able to continue; *Pola* remained at a standstill and was attended by other ships. These were located after nightfall. British radar (the Italians had none) allowed a close approach in the dark. The battleships quickly sank the cruisers *Fiume* and *Zara* and the destroyers *Alfieri* and *Carducci*. One destroyer was damaged; one escaped. *Pola* was sunk later. (Roskill 1.427–431; S.W.C. Pack, *The Battle of Matapan*, London 1961; Greene and Massignani 141–160; Sebag-Montefiore 123–127)

Matilda v. French schooner, 13 February 1797

Matilda (28; Capt. Henry Mitford) captured a French schooner off Barbados. (Clowes 4.555)

Mauritius, Indian Ocean (Ile de France), 1810

The frigate *Nereide* (Capt. Nesbit Willoughby) sent a raiding party into the Jacolet anchorage on 30 April. The local militia and a party of regulars were defeated, a battery's guns were spiked, and the schooner *Estafette* was taken out. In July the frigate *Sirius* (Capt. Samuel Pym) found a French schooner nearly ashore and a boat party destroyed it.

The frigates *Sirius* and *Iphigenia* (Capt. Henry Lambert) sent in boats on 30 August to attack the fort on the Ile de la Passe, which commanded the south entrance to Grand Port. The fort was successfully stormed and from there *Nereide* raided along the coast during the next few days. Two French frigates, *Bellone* and *Minerve*, and the sloop *Victor* arrived; they got past the fort into the main harbour despite being fired on. *Nereide*, joined by *Iphigenia*, *Magicienne* (Capt. Lucius Curtis), and *Sirius*, went into the harbour to attack the French ships. *Sirius* and *Magicienne* both ran aground; *Nereide* managed to get close to the French ships; *Iphigenia* stayed clear. In the fight, *Nereide* was battered into ruin and surrendered, her crew almost entirely killed or wounded. *Sirius* and *Magicienne* were abandoned and destroyed. On 27 August, the French frigates *Venus*, *Astree*, and *Manche* arrived, and *Iphigenia* and the fort had to surrender.

The frigate *Africaine* (38; Capt. Robert Corbet) attacked the French schooner *Aviso no. 25* moored close to the beach on 11 September. Corbet sent in ship's boats with sailors and marines, who boarded the schooner and tried to sink her. French soldiers fired from the shore; two men were killed and seventeen wounded. The schooner was soon refloated. Next day *Africaine* fought the French frigates *Iphigenie* (36) and *Astree* (36) close to Ile Reunion, hoping to prevent them from reaching safety at the island, so that

Boadicea (38; Capt. Josias Rowley) which was nearby would be able to assist. Corbet was soon wounded, and *Africaine* was compelled to surrender with 160 casualties out of almost 300 crew. Corbet died of his wounds. *Africaine* was recaptured by *Boadicea* soon after.

On 17 September the frigate *Ceylon* (32; Capt. Charles Gordon) looked into Grand Port and was chased as she left by the frigate *Venus* and the corvette *Victor* (18). A long fight followed between the two frigates, and when *Victor* caught up, *Ceylon* surrendered. *Venus* and *Ceylon* were virtually disabled by that time.

On 29 November an expedition of 10,000 soldiers from India, escorted and transported by *Illustrious* (74), twelve frigates, nine smaller warships, and many transports, landed on Mauritius. After several minor fights, the island capitulated on 3 December. Much military equipment was captured, also four frigates, three British Indiamen which had become prizes, and twenty-four French merchantmen. (James 5.138–140, 144–145, 149–180, 183, 203–205; Parkinson 386–411; Clowes 5.293–295, 418, 459–467; NC 4.352–356; S. Taylor, *Storm and Conquest*, London 2007; Low 1.229–231)

Mauritius and others v. German squadron, August 1944

The cruiser *Mauritius* and two destroyers fought a German force consisting of a TB, the aircraft repair ship *Richthofen*, *Speerbrecher 157*, and two minesweepers in the Sables d'Olonne, Bay of Biscay, on 14 August. *Speerbrecher 157* was sunk; the minesweepers were damaged and ran aground. A week later the British ships located and sank a force of German patrol boats off Audierne. (Rohwer 347)

Mechanician v. *UB-35*, 20 January 1918

The escort vessel *Mechanician* was sunk by *U-35* in the English Channel. (Colledge 253)

Medea v. *Belisarius*, 7 August 1781

The rebel American ship *Belisarius* (24) was captured by *Medea* (28). (Colledge 40)

Medea in the Bay of Bengal, January 1783

The French sloop *Chasseur* (20) was captured by *Medea* (28; Capt. Erasmus Gower) on 16 January. On the 30th *Medea*'s boats were sent in to Cuddalore against the Dutch ship *Vrijheid* (50), despite firing from guns on shore. *Vrijheid* was captured, but was wrecked soon after. (Clowes 4.94, 115)

Mediator v. French convoy, 12 December 1782

Mediator (44; Capt. Hon. John Luttrell) attacked a convoy of French and American ships escorted by French warships, capturing *Alexandre* (24) and two storeships. (Clowes 4.91)

Medusa and *Donegal* v. *Matilda* and *Amfitrite*, 25 November 1804

The frigate *Medusa* (38; Capt. John Gore) and *Donegal* (74; Capt. Sir Richard Strachan) captured the Spanish frigates *Matilda* (34) and *Amfitrite* (40) off Cadiz. (Clowes 5.562)

MEDWAY Estuary, 9–13 June 1667
A Dutch fleet sailed into the Thames estuary and forced its way up the River Medway. Sheerness was captured and ships further upstream, *Royal Charles* (100) and the frigate *Unity*, were captured or burned. The English sank other ships to block access channels. The English lost at least a dozen ships. At the same time a blockade of the Thames was enforced by the Dutch fleet, causing instant distress in London. (Clowes 2.289–295; P.G. Rogers, *The Dutch in the Medway*, Oxford 1970; Rodger 2.76–77; Mahan 132)

Medway v. *Pontchartrain*, 28 April 1697
Medway (60; Capt. William Clevland) met and fought the French privateer *Pontchartrain* (50) off Ireland. *Medway* resisted *Pontchartrain*'s attempt to board, then chased her for several hours before *Pontchartrain* surrendered with nearly 100 casualties; *Medway* had less than twenty. (Clowes 2.496)

Medway v. *Hind*, 21 September 1709
Medway (60) captured the sloop *Hind*, which was taken into the navy. (Colledge 185)

Medway v. *Favorette*, January 1744
The French ship *Favorette* was captured by *Medway* (60) in the East Indies, and was taken into the navy as *Medway's Prize*. (Colledge 254)

Medway v. *Siren*, 2 July 1814
Medway (74; Capt. Augustus Brine) captured the US sloop *Siren*. (Clowes 5.567)

Medway v. *U-372*, 30 June 1942
The submarine depot ship *Medway*, moving from Alexandria to Haifa, was sunk by *U-372* off Port Said. (Rohwer 174)

Megas Islands, Spain, August 1811
Undaunted (38; Capt. Richard Thomas) and two sloops seized control of the Megas Islands off Catalonia and fortified them, thereby partly blocking the French coastal supply route. (Hall 179)

Melampus and squadron v. French convoys, May–October 1795
A French convoy, chased by a squadron commanded by Capt. Sir Richard Strachan, took shelter close to shore at Cape Carteret. Boats from the frigates *Melampus* (38; Capt. Strachan), *Diamond* (38), *Hebe* (38), *Niger* (32), and *Syren* (32) went in and captured the whole convoy of thirteen vessels and two gunvessels, *Eclair* (3) and *Crache-feu* (3). On 3 July *Melampus* and *Hebe* (38; Capt. Sir Sidney Smith) captured the brig *Vesuve* (4) and six ships out of thirteen in another convoy, carrying military stores, and on 15 October *Melampus* and *Latona* (32; Capt. Arthur Legge) chased the frigates *Tortue* (40) and *Nereide* (36) towards Rochefort. *Latona* managed to exchange shots with one of them, but they reached Rochefort safely. (James 1.317–318, 329–330)

***Melampus* and *Childers* v. *Etna*, 13 September 1795**
The frigate *Melampus* (36; Capt. Graham Moore) and the sloop *Childers* (14) captured *Etna* (18) off the French coast. (Clowes 4.554)

***Melampus* v. *Resolue*, 30 October 1798**
The frigate *Melampus* (36; Capt. Graham Moore) came up with the French frigate *Resolue* off Donegal. *Resolue*, one of the ships intended to land French forces in Ireland, was unprepared and unfit for battle; after two or three broadsides she surrendered. (James 2.152–153)

***Melampus* v. *Colibri*, 16 January 1809**
The frigate *Melampus* (Capt. Edward Hawker) captured the French brig *Colibri* (16) near Barbuda. (Clowes 5.431)

***Meleager* v. Spanish privateers, February 1808**
The frigate *Meleager* (36; Capt. John Broughton) sent boats into Santiago de Cuba to capture the privateer *Renard* on 8 February, which was achieved without loss; the Spanish privateer *Antilope* was captured on 19 February. (James 4.306; Clowes 5.407)

***Meleager* v. *Béarnais*, 14 December 1809**
The frigate *Meleager* (Capt. Edward Hawker) chased the corvette *Béarnais* near Guadeloupe. The corvette resisted, but was eventually captured. (James 5.46)

***Melpomene* and *Childers* v. *Aventurier*, 3 August 1798**
Aventurier (14) was in Coregou harbour, Brittany. Boats from the frigate *Melpomene* (38; Capt. Sir Charles Hamilton) and the sloop *Childers* (Cmdr James O'Bryen) went in, covered by a thunderstorm, and cut her out. (James 2.255–256; Clowes 4.512–513)

***Melpomene* v. *Sénégal*, 3 January 1801**
Boats from the frigate *Melpomene* (38; Capt. Sir Charles Hamilton) entered the estuary of the Senegal River to attempt the capture of the French corvette *Sénégal* and a schooner. The corvette was seized, with some loss, but could not be taken out across the bar and was abandoned. The schooner escaped to the shelter of a battery. (James 3.118–119; Clowes 4.535)

***Melpomene* off Denmark, May 1809**
The frigate *Melpomene* (38; Capt. Peter Parker) sent boats into the harbour of Huilbo on 11 May to seize a cutter which had taken refuge there. The ship gave covering fire while the cutter was destroyed. Two weeks later *Melpomene* was attacked while at anchor in the Great Belt by twenty-four Danish gunboats; she eventually got away, badly damaged and with thirty-four casualties; she was decommissioned a few months later as a result. (James 4.38–39; Anderson 338; Clowes 5.438)

***Menai* v. slavers, 1821–1822**
The frigate *Menai* (26; Capt. Fairfax Moresby) captured the French slaver

Industry in the Indian Ocean, though the ship was later released. Next year *Menai* captured the French slaver *Camilla* in the harbour of Zanzibar, despite a threat of bombardment by the fort's governor. (Lloyd 204)

Menelaus v. St Joseph, 29 February 1812
The French storeship *St Joseph* was captured by the boats from the frigate *Menelaus* (38) near Fréjus. (Clowes 5.561)

Menelaus on the Tuscan coast, August–September 1812
Boats from the frigate *Menelaus* (58; Capt. Sir Peter Parker) attacked Porto San Stefano on 13 August; marines captured a covering battery, and the seamen took a brig and destroyed several other vessels. On 2 September boats were sent into the mouth of the Mignone River near Civitavecchia and captured the privateer *St Esprit*; next day three sloops were driven into Porto Ercole; on the 4th the storeship *Fidèle* was seized near Orbetello. (James 5.348–350; Clowes 5.512–515)

Mentor and others v. German destroyers, 17 August 1915
The British 10th Destroyer Flotilla escorted the minelayer *Princess Margaret* to lay mines in the German Bight. The German 2nd Torpedo Boat Flotilla attacked, and the destroyer *Mentor* was damaged by a torpedo. (Corbett 3.127)

Mercian v. U-38, 3 November 1915
The troop transport *Mercian* was attacked near Alboran Island by the submarine *U-38*. Despite problems with the crew, *Mercian* avoided most of *U-38*'s shells. Troops on board retaliated successfully with their machine guns. (Corbett 3.225–226; Halpern, *Mediterranean* 223)

Mercury v. French ship, 1745
Mercury (14) was captured by the French. (Clowes 3.311)

Mercury v. French convoys, January 1801
The frigate *Mercury* (28; Capt. Thomas Rogers) intercepted a convoy of twenty vessels in the Gulf of Lions on 6 January, capturing fifteen ships; the escorting gunboats fled. Two weeks later *Mercury* chased and captured the corvette *Sans-Pareille* off Sardinia; the corvette was loaded with military stores intended for the French army in Egypt. (James 3.119–120; Clowes 4.535)

Mercury v. Bulldog, May 1801
Bulldog, captured at Ancona in February, was still there in May. *Mercury* (28; Capt. Thomas Rogers) sent in boats to retake her. The raiders seized the ship and cut the cables, but the alarm was raised. A breeze carried the ship out of the harbour and then died away. Several boats came out in pursuit, and induced the raiders to abandon their prize. (*Bulldog* was retaken a few months later by *Mercury* and *Santa Dorotea*.) (James 3.135–136; Clowes 4.539–540)

Mercury and Corso v. Tigre, 23 June 1801
The pirate ship *Tigre* was attacked by boats from *Mercury* and the sloop *Corso* (Cmdr William Ricketts) at Tremiti in the Gulf of Venice; the ship was seized along with its plunder. (James 3.137; Clowes 4.542)

Mercury v. Fuerte de Gibraltar, 4 February 1805
Mercury (28; Capt. Duncombe Bouverie) captured *Fuerte de Gibraltar* (4). (Clowes 5.562)

Merion v. UB-8, 30 May 1915
The steamer *Merion*, part of the Special Service squadron, had been disguised as the battle-cruiser *Tiger*; it was sunk off Mudros by *UB-8*. (Halpern, *Mediterranean* 116)

Merlin v. Dutch squadron, 13 October 1665
Merlin (14; Capt. Charles Haward), escorting a convoy to Tangier, was attacked by five Dutch warships. Haward placed the ship between the attackers and their prey, fighting all five of the enemy, until *Merlin* was captured. Three of the convoy had been taken at the start, but *Merlin*'s defence allowed the rest to get to safety. (Clowes 2.425–426)

Merlin v. Machault, 19 April 1757
Merlin (10; Cmdr John Cleland) was attacked by the privateer *Machault* (30) during a near gale. *Merlin* was effectively unable to defend herself, and surrendered. She was retaken five months later. (Clowes 3.294)

Merlin and Shannon in the Isigny estuary, 10–16 December 1803
The frigate *Shannon* (36; Capt. Edward Leveson Gower) and the sloop *Merlin* (16; Cmdr Edward Brenton) were driven into the Isigny estuary by a gale; *Shannon* went on shore and was wrecked; *Merlin* just avoided the same fate; six days later *Merlin* returned and burnt the wreck. (James 3.202–203; Clowes 5.330)

Mermaid in Delaware Bay, 2 July 1778
Mermaid (28; Capt. James Hawker) was driven ashore in Delaware Bay by the French fleet, and surrendered to a passing US ship. (Clowes 4.16)

Mermaid v. Brutus and Républicaine, 10–13 October 1795
The frigate *Mermaid* (32; Capt. Henry Warre) drove the French corvettes *Républicaine* (18) and *Brutus* (10) into the Bay of Requain, Grenada; *Brutus* was captured, and taken to St George's. *Mermaid* met *Républicaine* again three days later; the French ship fought back, but was forced to surrender. (James 1.328–329; Clowes 4.494)

Mermaid v. Vengeance, 8 August 1796
The frigate *Mermaid* (32; Capt. Robert Otway) came up with the French frigate *Vengeance* (44) near Guadeloupe. The two ships fought for almost four hours, *Vengeance* attempting to get away, *Mermaid* attempting to attack.

None of the people on *Mermaid* were hurt; *Vengeance* had twelve killed and twice as many wounded. (James 1.378–380; Clowes 4.501–502)

Mermaid v. *Général Leveau*, 10 December 1796
The French ship *Général Leveau* was captured by *Mermaid* (32) and *Resource* (28) near St Domingue. (Clowes 4.555)

Mermaid and *Kangaroo* v. *Loire*, 16 October 1798
The frigate *Loire* (40) was part of a French squadron attempting to land troops in Ireland. The squadron dispersed, and *Loire* met the frigate *Mermaid* (32; Capt. James Newman) and the sloop *Kangaroo* (Cmdr Edward Brace). *Loire* fought the two ships separately, and damaged both so badly that they had to retreat. (James 2.154–157; Clowes 4.349–350; NC 1.288–289)

Mermaid v. *Cruelle*, 1 June 1800
The French cutter *Cruelle* (16) was captured off Toulon by the frigate *Mermaid* (32; Capt. Robert Oliver). (Clowes 4.557)

Mersa Matruh, Cyrenaica, 7 December 1915
A contingent of troops, 4500 strong, was landed at Mersa Matruh to combat the hostility of the Sennussi. (Corbett 3.226)

MERS-EL-KEBIR (ORAN), Algeria, 3 July 1940
In doubt as to the fate of the French fleet after France's surrender to Germany, the British government ordered that the concentration of French battleships at Mers-el-Kebir should be either surrendered or made inoperable. This resulted in the British Force H from Gibraltar bombarding the ships. The battleships *Dunquerque*, *Provence*, and *Bretagne* were destroyed or badly damaged; *Strasbourg* escaped, though chased for a time by *Hood*. There were no British casualties or damage. Three days later aircraft from *Ark Royal* damaged *Dunquerque* further and sank the auxiliary *Terre Neuve*. (Rohwer 31; E.M. Gates, *The End of the Affair*, London 1981, 352–369; Greene and Massignani 57–61)

Mesopotamia (Iraq), 31 May–4 June 1915
The sloops *Espiègle*, *Clio*, and *Odin*, with the Indian Navy ship *Lawrence* and the armed tug *Comet*, co-operated with the army's advance along the Euphrates as far as Kut el-Amara. (Corbett 3.17–23)

Meteor and others, Liguria, Italy, 7–12 April 1944
The destroyers *Meteor* and *Musketeer* were part of an Allied force bombarding German positions in Liguria on 7–12 April; the cruiser *Orion* shelled San Remo on the 12th. (Rohwer 408, 409)

Meteor and *Lookout* v. German TBs, 18 March 1945
The German 10th Torpedo Boat Flotilla, laying mines in the Gulf of Genoa, was attacked by the British destroyers *Meteor* and *Lookout*; the TBs *TA-24* and *TA-29* were sunk. (Rohwer 401)

Michael v. *U-110*, 15 March 1918
The trawler *Michael* sank *U-110* north of Ireland by depth-charges and gunfire. (Newbolt 5.427; Grant 111)

Milbrook v. *Bellone*, 13 November 1800
The schooner *Milbrook* (16; Lt Matthew Smith), in Oporto roads with several vessels under her protection, went out to attack the threatening French privateer *Bellone* (30). *Milbrook*'s guns were mounted to fire without recoil, and managed eleven broadsides while *Bellone* fired three. The two ships reduced each other to near wrecks; *Bellone* struck, but *Milbrook* could not board to secure possession. When a breeze came, *Bellone* sailed away. (James 3.34–35; Clowes 4.534)

Milford v. French ship, 1 December 1693
Milford (52; Capt. Roger Vaughan) was captured by the French in the North Sea. (Clowes 2.535)

Milford v. French privateers, 7 January 1697
Milford (32) was captured by two French privateers in the North Sea. (Colledge 260)

Milford v. *Gloire*, 7 March 1762
Milford (28; Capt. Robert Mann) fought and captured the French privateer *Gloire*; Mann and his first lieutenant were killed. (Clowes 3.308)

Milford v. *Cabot*, 26 March 1777
Milford (28; Capt. John Burr) drove the rebel American brig *Cabot* (14) on shore at Nova Scotia and captured her. (Clowes 4.4)

Milford and *America* v. *Licorne*, 17–18 June 1778
Licorne (32), one of the French squadron cruising in the Channel before war began, was chased by *Milford* (28; Capt. Sir William Burnaby). *Licorne*'s captain was persuaded to attend on Admiral Keppel, but there *Licorne*, perhaps out of patience, fired a broadside at Keppel's flagship *America* (64), and then immediately surrendered. (Clowes 4.14; Syrett, *European* 36–38)

Milford Haven, Wales
1405 A large French force landed at Milford Haven in August to assist the rebellion of Owain Glyn Dwr. Fifteen French ships were cut off and burnt by an English squadron under Lord Berkeley, and fourteen more were captured in another action. (Clowes 1.363–364)

1485 Henry, Earl of Richmond, landed on 7 August with a force of 2000 French and Breton soldiers transported from Harfleur in a fleet of French ships. He went on to defeat Richard III at Bosworth and became King Henry VII. (Gillingham 237–238; Clowes 1.392–393)

Milne v. *UC-26*, 9 May 1917
The destroyer *Milne* attacked and sank *UC-26* in the southern North Sea. (Newbolt 5.424–426)

***Milne* v. *U-289*, 31 May 1944**
The destroyer *Milne* sank *U-289* near Bear Island. (Rohwer 330)

***Minerva* v. *Warwick*, 24 January 1761**
Minerva (32; Capt. Alexander Hood) met the French *Warwick* (34) in the Mediterranean. The ships fought. Both suffered dismasting. In the end *Warwick* surrendered. (Clowes 3.304–305)

***Minerva* v. *Concorde*, 22 August 1778**
Minerva (32; Capt. John Stott) met the French frigate *Concorde* (32) in the West Indies. Unaware that war with France had begun, *Minerva* was soon forced to surrender when *Concorde* opened fire. Stott was killed. (Clowes 4.18–19)

***Minerva* and *Melampus* v. *Etonnant*, 13 November 1796**
The sloop *Etonnant*, off Barfleur, was destroyed by fire from *Minerva* (38) and *Melampus* (36). (Clowes 4.554)

***Minerva* at Finisterre Bay, Spain, 22–23 June 1806**
Minerva (32; Capt. George Collier) sent two boats to attack some Spanish luggers. The boat parties captured a fort, then seized five luggers in the harbour with their cargoes of wine. (James 4.154)

***Minerva* v. *Buena Dicha*, 11 July 1806**
Boats from *Minerva* (Capt. George Collier) captured the privateer *Buena Dicha* off the Portuguese coast. (James 4.155)

***Minerva* v. *Gunboat no. 4*, 2 October 1806**
Minerva's cutter was challenged by Spanish *Gunboat no. 4* in the Bay of Rocks, but the gunboat found itself attacked instead and was captured. (Clowes 5.384)

***Minerva* v. *Amethyste*, October 1809**
The frigate *Minerva* (32; Capt. Richard Hawkins) captured the French brig *Amethyste*. (Clowes 5.559)

***Minerve* and *Blanche* v. *Sabina* and *Ceres*, 17 December 1796**
Minerve (38; Capt. George Cockburn), carrying Commodore Horatio Nelson, in company with *Blanche* (32; Capt. D'Arcy Preston), met two Spanish frigates off Cartagena. *Minerve* fought *Sabina* (40), which was disabled and surrendered after two hours; *Blanche* similarly fought *Ceres* (40) and secured her surrender. The arrival of three more Spanish ships resulted in their recapture. (James 1.406–408; Clowes 4.505–506; Morriss 29–31)

***Minerve*, *Pomone*, and *Phoenix* v. *Bravoure* and *Succès*, 2 September 1801**
Two French frigates, *Bravoure* and *Succès*, expected to attack the frigate *Phoenix* (36; Capt. Lawrence Halstead) at Porto Ferraia, Elba, but found *Minerve* (32; Capt. George Cockburn) and *Pomone* (44; Capt. Edward

Leveson Gower) there as well. Both French frigates were driven on shore; *Succes* was recovered, and *Bravoure* destroyed. (James 3.79–80; Clowes 4.45; Morriss 51–52)

Minerve at Cherbourg, 2 July 1803
The frigate *Minerve* (32; Capt. Jahleel Brenton) ran aground at the entrance to the harbour of Cherbourg; for ten hours, under fire, the crew fought enemy ships and struggled to refloat her. This proved to be impossible, and Brenton surrendered. (James 3.182–185; Clowes 5.318–320)

Minorca, Balearic Islands
1756 (Battle of MINORCA)   A French force landed on Minorca and laid siege to Port Mahon, protected by a French fleet of twelve line-of-battle ships and five frigates. A British fleet was sent, rather tardily, from Britain to relieve the siege. It eventually included thirteen line-of-battle ships and five smaller vessels, all commanded by Vice-Admiral John Byng. After some manoeuvres, Byng ordered an attack on 20 May, but did not press it home. The French aim was only to prevent the British reaching and relieving Minorca, but the British had to comprehensively defeat the French fleet. The result of the fighting – several British ships were disabled – was considered by a council of senior naval officers, whose decision was to return to Gibraltar. Six weeks later Port Mahon surrendered to the French siege. Byng was recalled and court-martialled, in effect for not trying hard enough. It is clear that conviction on this count was correct, but he was sentenced to death, and the sentence was carried out, which was unexpected. (Clowes 3.147–160; Mahan 285–291; Tunstall 107–111)

1798   A British squadron sent to recapture Minorca landed troops at Addaya Creek. They drove off a counter-attack and marched to Port Mahon which quickly surrendered. The squadron, commanded by Commodore John Duckworth, then drove off a Spanish squadron, and recaptured a British sloop taken the day before. No casualties were incurred in any of these operations. (James 2.211–223; Clowes 4.377–378)

Minorca v. *Furieuse*, 10 February 1801
The xebec *Furieuse* (6) was captured in the Mediterranean by *Minorca* (16; Cmdr George Miller). (Clowes 4.558)

Minotaur and *Niger* raid Barcelona, 3 September 1800
Boats from the frigate *Niger* (*en flute*; Capt. James Hillyar) and *Minotaur* (74; Capt. Thomas Louis) rowed into Barcelona roads, and seized a Swedish galliot entering the port. The boats hooked on, then, once inside the harbour, they boarded and took two Spanish corvettes, *Esmeralda* and *Paz* (both 22), despite very heavy fire from the shore and other ships. (James 3.27–29; Clowes 4.536)

Minotaur v. *Franchise*, 28 May 1803
The French frigate *Franchise* was chased and captured by *Minotaur* (74;

Capt. Charles Mansfield) near Brest, probably before receiving news of the outbreak of war. (James 3.118; Clowes 5.315–316)

Minstrel v. Ortenzia, 16 July 1808
The Venetian ship *Ortenzia* (10) was captured by *Minstrel* (18; Cmdr John Hollingsworth). (Clowes 5.558)

Minstrel at Valencia, 29 September 1812
The sloop *Minstrel* (18; Capt. John Peyton) sent in boats to cut out six ships laden with shells; despite an active defence, four were captured. (James 5.349; Clowes 5.516)

Minx and Kite v. Danish gunboats, 3 September 1808
The brigs *Minx* (12) and *Kite* (16) were attacked by twenty-one Danish gunboats in the Great Belt; *Minx* escaped, but *Kite* was badly damaged. (Anderson 326; Clowes 5.425)

Minx v. Danish gunboats, 2 September 1809
The gun brig *Minx* (12; Lt George Le Blanc), acting as a lightship near Skagen, was attacked by six Danish gunboats. After a fight lasting all day *Minx* surrendered. (Anderson 339; Clowes 5.553)

Minx at Old Town, Old Calabar, 1855
The British consul in the Niger Delta area, Lynslager, instigated the destruction of Calabar Old Town by the screw gunboat *Minx* on the pretext of punishing the inhabitants for indulging in human sacrifice; others, however, regarded the action as one designed to intimidate other local trading towns. (Dike 118)

Mitchell v. U-boat, 19 December 1917
The sailing ship *Mitchell*, off North Devon, having a disguised armament, met a German submarine; they fired at each other, but without result. (Newbolt 5.199)

ML-413 v. UB-71, 17 April 1918
Motor launch *413* sank *UB-71* west of Gibraltar. (Newbolt 5.411; Grant 131)

Mobile, Alabama, 15 September 1814
An attempted landing at Mobile from a British squadron was defeated by the resistance of the fort, with the loss of *Hermes* (20; Cmdr Hon. William Percy). (James 6.230–231; Clowes 6.150)

Mocha, Yemen
1610 The EIC ship *Trades Increase* went aground off Mocha. The cargo was landed to help refloat her, but then plundered by local people, with the connivance of the governor. In reply Capt. Sir Henry Middleton with *Peppercorn* and *Darling* blockaded the port until the ship and its cargo were released. (Clowes 2.32)

1820 The frigate *Topaze* (46; Capt. John Lumley) an EIC ship, went to Mocha to exact recompense from the Imam of Sana for injuries to British subjects. An attack on one fort was repulsed, but after negotiations failed, it was bombarded to destruction. Further negotiations failing, another fort was then destroyed. Successful negotiations followed. (Clowes 6.233; Low 1.299–309)

Moderate and *Gloucester* v. *Auguste* and *Jason*, 5 August 1704
A set of privateers under Duguay-Trouin, principally *Auguste* and *Jason*, were surprised in the act of taking possession of a prize by the arrival of *Moderate* (Capt. Henry Lumley) and *Gloucester* (Capt. Thomas Meads). A confused action followed in which all involved suffered serious damage and had to return to port for repairs. (Owen 114–150)

Modeste v. *Jena*, 8 October 1808
The frigate *Modeste* (36; Capt. Hon. George Elliott) chased, fought, and captured the French corvette *Jena* (18) in the Bay of Bengal. (James 4.366–367; Clowes 5.427)

Modeste and *Barracouta* v. *Tuijncelaar*, 12 July 1809
The Dutch brig *Tuijncelaar* (8) was cut out at the Sunda Strait by boat parties from *Modeste* (36) and *Barracouta* (16). (Clowes 5.564)

Modeste v. two slavers, February 1840
The sloop *Modeste* (18) captured two slave ships carrying almost 1000 slaves between them, off the east coast of Africa. (Bethell 182)

Moldavia v. *UB-57*, 23 May 1918
The AMC *Moldavia* was sunk by *UB-57* in the English Channel. (Colledge 265)

Molly v. *Semillante*, October 1782
Molly (18) was captured near Madeira by the French corvette *Semillante* (18). (Clowes 4.90)

Mombasa, East Africa, 17 January 1874
The castle at Mombasa was seized by rebels against the Sultan of Zanzibar. A British force commanded by Capt. George Sulivan was carried there in the screw gunvessels *Nassau* (Lt Francis Grey) and *Riflemen* (Cmdr Stratford Tuke). The castle was bombarded for five hours, then occupied and returned to the Sultan. (Clowes 7.263–264)

Mona Passage, Caribbean Sea, 19 April 1782
Rear-Admiral Sir Samuel Hood, with ten line-of-battle ships, chased French ships retiring from the battle of the Saintes, capturing two 64s, a frigate, and a sloop. (Clowes 3.537)

Monarch and others v. *Mars*, 4 February 1781
The Dutch ship *Mars* (60), escorting a convoy from the West Indies to

Europe, was attacked by *Monarch* (74; Capt. Francis Reynolds). When the convoy's commander, Rear-Admiral Willem Crul, was killed, Dutch resistance ended. *Panther* (60) and *Sibyl* (28) accompanied *Monarch*; all thirty ships of the convoy were captured. (Clowes 4.61–62)

Monarch and others v. French squadron, 25 September 1806
A squadron of five French frigates and two sloops in the Bay of Biscay was chased by a squadron commanded by Commodore Samuel Hood – *Centaur*, *Monarch*, and *Mars*. *Monarch* reached the French first and the others came up later. Four of the frigates were taken – *Gloire* (46), *Indefatigable*, *Minerve*, and *Armide* (all 44). (*NC* 3.332–333)

Monck and *Chatham* v. French West Indiamen, 1693
Monck (52; Capt. Stafford Fairborne) and *Chatham* (44; Capt. John Leader) captured two French West Indiamen, each of which had 50 guns and some troops on board. (Clowes 2.472)

Monck v. *Salamandre* and *Comte de Giraldin*, April 1712
Monck (60; Capt. George Camocke) captured the privateer *Salamandre* near Ireland, and retook its prize. Camocke fortified Crookhaven to deter other privateers, and captured another, *Comte de Giraldin* (40), after a two-hour fight. (Clowes 2.552–533)

Mondego Bay, Portugal, August 1808
The British army was landed to support Portuguese efforts to drive out the French forces. (Hall 29–33)

Monitors in the Adriatic, Italy, May and November 1917
The monitors *Sir Thomas Picton* and *Earl of Peterborough* bombarded the Austrian airfield at Prosecco in the Gulf of Trieste on 24 May. In November, after the great Italian defeat at Caporetto, the monitors assisted in the defence of Venice. (Halpern, *Mediterranean* 366, 400)

Monkey v. slavers, April–June 1829
The schooner *Monkey* (Lt Joseph Sherer), in the West Indies, captured *Josepha*, a slaver, in April 1829; on 27 June, near Florida, *Midas*, another slaver, was captured after a short fight. Over 600 slaves were freed. (Clowes 6.268; Ward 137)

Monmouth and others v. *Jersey* and convoy, 10 May 1694
Monmouth (66; Capt. Peter Pickard), *Resolution* (70; Capt. John Baker), and the fireship *Roebuck* (6; Capt. Robert Kirton) found a large French convoy in Blanc Sablon Bay, Brittany. *Monmouth* chased the escorting warship, *Jersey* (48), and boats attacked the merchant ships. *Jersey* was driven ashore and burned, and two French sloops close by took fire when she exploded. Over forty of the merchant ships were captured or destroyed. (Clowes 2.473)

Monmouth and *Lyme* v. *Rose*, 1758
The French frigate *Rose* (36) met *Monmouth* (64) and *Lyme* (28) near Malta, and was driven ashore and wrecked. (Clowes 3.298)

Montagu v. French privateer, 2 January 1691
Montagu (60; Capt. John Layton) fought a small French privateer near Ushant. The privateer was captured, having suffered forty casualties; Layton was killed. (Clowes 2.465)

Montague and *Warwick* v. Angria's fleet, 1743
The EIC ships *Montague* and *Warwick*, escorting a convoy, were attacked by seven grabs and eight galivats of Samboji Angria's fleet. The Indiamen stood off the attack, but six of the convoy were captured. (Low 1.119)

Montagu's squadron v. *Marie Guiton*, 15 May 1794
The corvette *Marie Guiton* (20), sailing towards France in charge of ten ships of a captured Newfoundland convoy, met a squadron of British ships under Rear-Admiral Montagu – six 74s and two frigates. *Marie Guiton* was captured, and the convoy's ships were released. (James 1.142)

Monte Christo, Corsica, 27–28 August 1652
A Dutch squadron under Admiral Johan van Galen intercepted the English Smyrna convoy commanded by Capt. Badiley off Monte Christo on the east coast of Corsica. A preliminary fight on 27 August had no result. The convoy went on, and two English ships fought off another Dutch attack on the 28th, but *Phoenix* (36) was captured, and one Dutch ship sank. The convoy reached Leghorn safely. (Corbett, *Mediterranean* 1.250–253; Clowes 2.161–164)

Montevideo, River Plate, 2 August 1845
The Argentine fleet blockading Montevideo was ordered by the British and French commanders of the observing squadron to surrender all foreign nationals on the ships, which would have effectively crippled the Argentine force; Admiral Guillermo Brown took his ships away, but was compelled to surrender after a short fight. The ships were handed over to the besieged in Montevideo and placed under the command of Giuseppe Garibaldi. (Clowes 6.385; D. McLean, *War, Diplomacy and Informal Empire*, London 1995, 73)

Montréal, Canada, July–September 1760
British expeditions moved from Québec and Crown Point to attack Montréal. The Québec force moved up the St Lawrence, fighting French batteries and ambushes. The second, smaller force drove the French ahead of it. The two reached Montréal almost together on 11 August. Montréal was put under siege and surrendered on 8 September. In the process three small French warships and a number of privateers were taken and destroyed on the St Lawrence. (Clowes 3.227–228)

Montréal v. *Bourgogne* and *Victoire*, 1 May 1779
The frigates *Montréal* (32; Capt. Stair Douglas) and *Thetis* (32; Capt. John

Gell) met the French 64s *Bourgogne* and *Victoire* in the Strait of Gibraltar. *Thetis* got away, but *Montréal* had to surrender. (Clowes 4.25–26)

Montrose, Scotland

1548 The English fleet attempted to make a landing by night near the town in September, but was beaten off by the local forces. (Phillips 242; Clowes 1.468)

1709 The leaders of the Jacobite rising, including the Old Pretender ('James III and VIII'), left Scotland on 6 February from Montrose in the *Marie-Thérèse*, a small boat of Dieppe, landing at Calais six days later. (Lavery 30–31)

1745 The French ship *Fine* sailed from Dunkirk with materials to assist the Jacobites in their rebellion. She ran aground at Montrose and was there attacked on 26 February by *Milford* (50), which was unable to capture her. (Lavery 52, 54)

Montrose's last campaign, 9 April 1650

The Earl of Montrose made an attempt to recover Scotland for the Royalist cause, recruiting a number of Orkneymen. From Orkney the expedition invaded Scotland, but was defeated at Carbisdale. (Thompson 183)

Moonstone v. *Galilei*, 19 June 1940

The Italian submarine *Galilei* in the Red Sea was compelled to surrender by the ASW trawler *Moonstone*. (Rohwer 27)

Morea Castle, Greece, 1828

The last Turkish forces in Greece were besieged in Morea Castle by a French army. Sailors from *Blonde* (40; Capt. Edward Lyons) and *Talbot* (28; Capt. Hon. Frederick Spencer) formed a Naval Brigade which assisted in the siege. (Clowes 8.262)

Morecambe Bay, Korea, 1951

The frigate *Morecambe Bay* systematically bombarded a railway on the Korean coast for two weeks, wrecking track, trains, and tunnels. (Wettern 55)

Morgiou, Provence, 31 March and 2 May 1813

The frigates *Undaunted* (38; Capt. Thomas Ussher) and *Volontaire* (38; Capt. Hon. George Waldegrave) and the sloop *Redwing* (Cmdr Sir John Sinclair) raided the harbour of Morgiou. Landing nearby, the party marched to capture the batteries overlooking the harbour. Once this was done, eleven ships were taken out, and others destroyed. A month later, reinforced by *Repulse* (74; Capt. Richard Moubrey), another raid went in to destroy the replacement batteries and capture six more vessels. (James 6.17–18; *NC* 5.186–187)

Morib, Malaya, 9 September 1945

A landing by 100,000 British and Indian troops took place at Morib in Malaya, even though the war with Japan was officially over. (Rohwer 429)

***Morning Star* v. Angria's squadron, 1717**
The EIC ship *Morning Star* was intercepted by two of Kanhoji's squadrons, in all seven ships carrying 2000 men; despite such heavy odds, the ship survived attempts at boarding. (Low 1.101)

***Mornington* v. *Eugénie*, 1801**
The EIC sloop *Mornington* (24; Capt. Frost), disguised as a merchantman, attacked the privateer *Eugénie* in the Bay of Bengal. *Eugénie* was partly dismasted at the first shot, and was forced to surrender after a three-hour chase. (Low 1.231–234)

***Moselle* at Toulon, 7 January 1794**
The sloop *Moselle* (24; Cmdr Richard Bennet) entered Toulon believing it was in British control; Bennet was wrong and the ship was captured. (Clowes 4.548)

***Moselle* v. *Beau Narcisse*, 28 May 1809**
The French *Beau Narcisse* (8) was captured by the sloop *Moselle* (18; Cmdr Henry Boys) in the West Indies. (Clowes 5.559)

***Mosquito* v. Spanish ship, February 1798**
The schooner *Mosquito* (6; Lt Thomas White) was captured off Cuba by a Spanish ship. (Clowes 4.550)

***Mosquito* v. slavers, 1817–1818**
The sloop *Mosquito* captured the slavers *Petite Armée*, *St Joseph*, and *Zephir*, freeing all together 290 slaves. (Lloyd 18)

***MTB-345* at Bergen, 27 July 1943**
MTB-345 was grounded near Bergen and captured by the Germans; the crew were murdered by the Gestapo. (Rohwer 264)

MTBs v. Italian convoy, 1 April 1943
Three ships of a convoy from Sicily to Tunis were sunk by *MTB-266* and *MTB-315*, which sank one each, and by air. (Rohwer 241)

MTBs v. *Sagittario* and convoy, 28 April 1943
Three British MTBs (*633*, *637*, and *639*) attacked an Italian convoy carrying supplies to Tunis; *MTB-639* was sunk by the Italian TB *Sagittario*. (Rohwer 241; Greene and Massignani 279)

MTBs v. *Juminda*, 23 October 1943
A squadron of British MTBs sank the German minelayer *Juminda* off San Stefano. (Rohwer 262)

MTBs v. *R-192*, 8 April 1944
A squadron of MTBs sank the German minesweeper *R-192* off Cecina. (Rohwer 316)

MTBs v. *UJ-2207*, 20 November 1944
British MTBs attacked a German convoy off the Ligurian coast, sinking the submarine chaser *UJ-2207*. (Rohwer 374)

MTBs v. *Paris*, 12 March 1945
The German minesweeper depot ship *Paris* was sunk by MTBs off Haugesund, Norway. (Rohwer 399)

MTBs v. *TA-45*, 13 April 1945
MTBs *670* and *697* sank the German torpedo boat *TA-45* in the Morlacca Channel on 13 April. (Rohwer 409)

Muckee, Sumatra, 1803
A squadron of EIC ships under Commodore John Hayes blockaded the Dutch fort at Muckee, landed a force, and captured and destroyed batteries, seizing ordnance and other stores. (Low 1.221)

Mull v. *U-343*, 10 March 1944
The ASW trawler *Mull* sank *U-343* off Cagliari, Sardinia. (Rohwer 311)

Munster, Ireland
857 An expedition by 'Gall-Gaidhil' into Munster, probably led by Ketil Flatnose, who had made himself Jarl of the Hebrides, was defeated by Olaf the White, king of Dublin. (Smyth, *Warlords* 156–158)

962 A fleet from the Isles (Hebrides), led by a pretender to the Dublin Viking kingship, raided in Munster. (Hudson 40)

Mutine v. *Invincible*, 17 April 1813
The brig *Mutine* (Cmdr Nevinson de Courcy) chased and attacked the French privateer *Invincible* in the Bay of Biscay. The two ships fought for nine hours before *Invincible* surrendered. (James 6.9; Clowes 5.525)

Mwele, East Africa, 1895–1896
The ruler of Mwele, M'buruk ibn Rashid, was attacked by forces from the local ships, the Zanzibari army, and Sudanese and Askari troops. The town was captured and burnt; after Malindi was destroyed in revenge, another expedition captured and destroyed several other towns, including Mwele once more. (Clowes 7.432–433)

Myrmidon v. *Bella Dura*, December 1819
Myrmidon (20) sent a boat to capture the slaver *Bella Dura*. Once taken, it was attacked by all the slavers in the Gallinas River before getting out to sea. (Ward 111–112)

Myrmidon v. Spanish slavers, August 1821
Myrmidon (20; Capt. Leeke) sent boats into the Bonny River, where Spanish

slavers were loading slaves. Two attempts by boat parties failed to capture the slavers, so Leeke took his ship into the river, whereupon the slavers surrendered. (Ward 105–107)

N

Naiad and others v. Santa Brigida and Thetis, 15 October 1799
The frigate *Naiad* (38; Capt. William Pierrepont), near Cape Finisterre, chased two Spanish frigates. The frigate *Ethalion* (38; Capt. James Young) and two other frigates joined in. The Spaniards separated; *Ethalion* captured *Thetis* after an hour's fighting. *Naiad*, *Triton* (32; Capt. John Gore), and *Alcmene* (32; Capt. Henry Digby) chased *Santa Brigida* into rocks near Vigo, and captured her there. The Spanish frigates were carrying specie from Mexico to the value of about £700,000; each captain received £40,000 in prize money; each seaman £180. (James 2.402–404; Clowes 4.525–526)

Naiad and Phaeton v. Alcudia and Raposo, 16 May 1801
Boats from *Naiad* (38) and *Phaeton* (38) cut out *Alcudia* and *Raposo* near Pontevedra, Spain. (Clowes 4.561)

Naiad v. Impatiente and Providence, May–July 1803
The frigate *Naiad* (38; Capt. James Wallis) captured the French corvette *Impatiente* after a chase in the Bay of Biscay on 28 May, and on 4 July sent boats among the islands near Brest to capture the schooner *Providence*, laden with guns and ship timber. (James 3.185; Clowes 5.316, 320)

Naiad and others v. gunboats, 20–21 September 1811
In honour of a visit of inspection by Napoleon, a flotilla of gunboats came out of Boulogne to attack the frigate *Naiad* (38; Capt. Philip Carteret); neither side received any damage. This was repeated next day, when *Naiad* was accompanied by three sloops and a cutter, and this time the French *Ville de Lyon* was captured after strong resistance. (James 5.219–222)

Naiad and Cameleon v. Tripoli, 31 January 1824
Capt. Hon. Sir Robert Spencer in *Naiad* (40) with *Cameleon* (12; Cmdr James Burton) was sent to remonstrate with the Dey of Algiers over brigandage by his subjects. He failed to gain redress but met and fought the Algerine ship *Tripoli* (20) as he left the port. *Tripoli* was disabled by fire from *Naiad*, and then boarded by men from *Cameleon*. (James 6.274–275; Clowes 6.236)

Naiad v. U-565, 11 March 1942
The cruiser *Naiad* was sunk by *U-565* north of Sollum. (Rohwer 151)

Nailaka Island, Banda Islands, March 1618
The EIC ships *Solomon* and *Attendant* sailed to bring relief to an English fort established on Nailaka Island, but were captured by four Dutch ships before they could do so. (Foster 275)

Namtao, China, 11 August 1858
The town of Namtao was identified as the source of an attack on a party of seamen from the screw gunboat *Starling* (Lt Arthur Villiers). The squadron covered a landing at the town, which was captured and partly burnt. (Clowes 7.120)

***Namur* v. *Mercure*, 4 August 1846**
The French ship *Mercure* (*en flute*) was captured by *Namur* (90). (Clowes 3.312)

***Nankin* at Sailau, China, 14–15 December 1856**
A boat party went ashore at Sailau from the screw gunboat *Banterer*, but was attacked and driven away by the people of Sailau, five men being killed. *Nankin* (50) bombarded the town on the 15th in reprisal. (Clowes 7.111–112)

Nanking, China, November 1858
The city of Nanking had been occupied by the Taiping rebels. They fired on the British screw gunboat *Lee* (Lt William Jones); the whole British squadron returned fire, and later more exchanges took place. This was all largely due to misunderstandings on both sides. (Clowes 7.120–121)

***Narcissus* v. *Alcion*, 8 July 1803**
Narcissus (32; Capt. Ross Donnelly) pursued *Alcion* (16) near Sardinia; she surrendered when *Narcissus* came close. (Clowes 5.323)

***Narcissus*, *Seahorse*, and *Maidstone* v. settees, 11 July 1804**
Boats from the frigates *Narcissus* (32; Capt. Ross Donnelly), *Seahorse* (38; Capt. Hon. Courtney Boyle), and *Maidstone* (32; Capt. Hon. George Elliott) went into the Bay of Hyères to attack twelve settees there. Almost all of these were burnt or captured, at the cost of four men killed and twenty-one wounded. (James 3.275; Clowes 5.345–346)

***Narcissus* v. *Cautela*, 18 August 1807**
The Spanish schooner *Cautela* (12) was captured in the Bay of Biscay by *Narcissus* (32; Capt. Charles Malcolm). (Clowes 5.401)

***Narcissus* v. *Viper*, 17 January 1813**
The US sloop *Viper* (12) was captured by the frigate *Narcissus* (32; Capt. John Lumley). (Clowes 5.567)

***Narcissus* v. *Surveyor*, 12 June 1813**
Boats from the frigate *Narcissus* (32; Capt. John Lumley) were sent up the York River against the US schooner *Surveyor*, which was captured in a fierce little fight. (James 6.90)

Narragansett Bay, Rhode Island, May 1778
The frigate *Flora* (32; Capt. John Brisbane) covered a landing by troops

and sailors at Narragansett Bay; rebel American vessels were destroyed and several guns taken. (Clowes 4.13)

Narva, Estonia, 4 January 1919
The cruisers *Caradoc* and *Calypso* and the destroyer *Wakeful*, of the Baltic squadron, bombarded Soviet lines in a confrontation between Soviet and Estonian forces. The Soviet forces retreated. (Bennett 46)

Narvik, Norway
1940 The 2nd Destroyer Flotilla under Capt. Warburton-Lee (five ships) sailed into Ofotfjord on 10 April and sank two German destroyers, the *Wilhelm Heidcamp* and *Anton Schmitt*, damaged two others, and sank several freighters and a supply ship; two British destroyers, *Hardy* and *Hunter*, were sunk and two others damaged. A second raid on Narvik on 13 April, led by the battleship *Warspite*, sank or forced the scuttling of eight German destroyers and *U-64*. Narvik was shelled by a naval force on 24 April. A landing by British and French forces was made, but they were evacuated on 4–8 June – 25,000 troops were taken off. (Rohwer 19–21, 26)

1945 A British force of three escort carriers, two cruisers, and three destroyers raided German shipping in and near Narvik on 4 May, sinking *U-711*, the depot ship *Black Watch*, and a trawler. (Rohwer 415)

***Narwhal* and others v. *U-63*, 25 February 1940**
Convoy HN-14 (Britain to Norway) was attacked by *U-63*; the submarine was seen by the British submarine *Narwhal* and sunk by the destroyers *Escort*, *Imogen*, and *Inglefield*. (Rohwer 16)

***Nassau* v. *Jean Bart*, 1 September 1809**
Nassau (64) captured *Jean Bart* (4) off Start Point. (Clowes 5.559)

***Nassau* at Sulu, East Indies, May 1872**
A party from the screw gunvessel *Nassau* (Cmdr William Chimmo) landed to survey an island in the Sulu Sea, and were attacked by local people, described as pirates, who were punished by the destruction of their village. (Clowes 7.232–233)

***Natal* and *Wivern* v. *U-714*, 14 March 1945**
U-714, having already sunk the Norwegian minesweeping trawler *Nordhav II* and another ship, was sunk by the South African frigate *Natal* and the destroyer *Wivern*. (Rohwer 396)

***Nautilus* v. *Peacock*, 3 June 1815**
The US sloop *Peacock*, in the Sunda Strait, despite being assured that peace had been agreed, attacked and captured the brig *Nautilus*. (James 5.266–269; Clowes 6.176)

NAVARINO, Greece, 20 October 1827
A developing dispute over Turkish methods used to combat the Greek rebel-

lion brought several fleets into confrontation in Navarino Bay, southwest Greece. On one side, fighting for their Ottoman suzerains, was an Egyptian fleet of between sixty-five and ninety ships, including five line-of-battle ships and fifteen large frigates. On the other side were squadrons of British, French, and Russian ships, all together twelve line-of-battle ships and six large frigates. The combined fleet, commanded by Vice-Admiral Sir Edward Codrington, compelled the Egyptian fleet to move into Navarino Bay after several agreements had failed. On 20 October the allied fleet went into the bay as well. The Egyptian fleet was moored in a wide semi-circle, and the allies moored ship to ship inside the Egyptian line. This could only be interpreted by the Egyptians as a direct threat, and before the allied ships were in position firing had begun. The battle lasted about four hours, with some hesitation on the Egyptian side giving the allies a distinct advantage. Sixty of the Egyptian ships were destroyed, many set on fire by their crews as they abandoned ship. Most of the rest were damaged. Four thousand of the Egyptian forces died. The allies lost no ships, but had 180 men killed and almost 500 wounded. The destruction of the Egyptian fleet eventually impelled the Ottoman government to accept Greek independence. (Clowes 6.252–261)

NEGAPATAM, India – three battles
1746 The governor of Ile de France (Mauritius), La Bourdonnais, gathered a naval force and sailed to Indian waters. Near Negapatam on 25 June he met Commodore Edward Peyton with an approximately equal force. Peyton kept his distance, while La Bourdonnais hoped to close to board; one ship on each side was damaged badly; the squadrons separated. (Clowes 3.119–120; Tunstall 92)

1758 A British squadron commanded by Vice-Admiral George Pocock manoeuvred to attack a French squadron under Comte d'Ache. The fight, on 3 August, was marked by several French accidents, and resulted in their withdrawing, even fleeing, from the battle; d'Ache soon after left Indian waters for Ile de France. (Clowes 3.178–181; Tunstall 113)

1782 British and French fleets in the Bay of Bengal, under Vice-Admirals Hughes and Suffren respectively, each with eleven line-of-battle ships, fought near Negapatam on 6 July. A sudden change in wind direction pushed the fleets apart after several hours' fighting, although two French ships and four British continued fighting between the main fleets until the French were rescued by their fellows. Casualties were heavy, particularly on the French side. (Clowes 3.555–557; Tunstall 185–186)

Nemesis **v. two French warships, Smyrna, 9 December 1795**
Nemesis (28; Capt. Samuel Linzee) was captured by two French warships in Smyrna harbour. (Clowes 4.548)

Nemesis **and others v.** *Freija* **and convoy, 25 July 1800**
The Danish frigate *Freija* (40), escorting a small convoy, refused to allow inspection by a British squadron under Capt. Thomas Baker in *Nemesis* (28). A fight followed, *Freija* against four ships, until she surrendered. This

was the proximate cause of the war between Britain and Denmark. (Clowes 4.426–427; James 3.41–42; *NC* 2.92–93; Anderson 301–302; O. Feldbaek, *Denmark and the Armed Neutrality 1800–1801*, Copenhagen 1981, 48–49)

Nereide v. *Vengeance*, 1–2 March 1800
The frigate *Nereide* (Capt. Frederick Watkins) encountered a group of five privateers off the Penmarcks, who scattered as she came up; next day *Nereide* caught up with and captured one of them, *Vengeance*. (James 3.8)

Nereide v. *Veloz*, 20 November 1806
The frigate *Nereide* (36; Capt. Robert Corbet) captured the Spanish brig *Veloz* in the Atlantic. (Clowes 5.563)

Nestor v. *U-127*, 19 October 1941
U-127 was sunk by the Australian destroyer *Nestor*, one of a hunter group. (Rohwer 126)

Netley v. *Légère*, 31 May 1800
The schooner *Netley* (18; Lt Francis Bond) captured the lugger *Légère* (3) in the Mediterranean. (Clowes 4.557)

Netley v. *San Miguel*, 7 November 1800
The schooner *Netley* (18; Lt Francis Bond) heard of the Spanish privateer *San Miguel* lurking near Lisbon. Locating her in the night, she was boarded and captured along with her prize. (James 3.36)

Netley v. two French cruisers, 17 December 1806
The schooner *Netley* (14; Lt William Carr) was captured by two French cruisers in the West Indies. (Clowes 5.551)

Nevis, West Indies, 4 May 1667
The French and Dutch gathered ships to attack Nevis. Before they could do so, Capt. John Berry of *Coronation* (56), with ten or so other ships, attacked them, and the allies were driven into shelter. (Clowes 2.431–432; Rodger 2.78)

New Britain, Melanesia, 11–15 September 1914
Landings by Australian forces were made at two places in the German colony of New Britain. The radio station was attacked and destroyed. The governor surrendered on the 15th, a capitulation which included all of the local German possessions. The cruiser *Melbourne* captured the German patrol yacht *Nusa*. (Corbett 1.263–267)

Newcastle v. French expedition, 10 July 1711
Newcastle (15; Capt. Sampson Bourne), off Martinique, attacked a French force of two warships, several privateers, and other ships, which was aiming to attack Antigua. The French ships were driven into St Pierre much damaged. (Clowes 2.530)

Newcastle at Kota Tinggi, Malaya, December 1957
The cruiser *Newcastle* bombarded communist insurgents from the Kota Tinggi River, Malaya. (Wettern 143)

New England, 1618
Governor Argall of Virginia heard that a French settlement had been made on the coast of New England. He took an expedition there, seized a ship, and took and destroyed a small fort. (Clowes 2.56)

Newfoundland, 1707 and 1710
An English squadron on the Newfoundland Station, *Falkland* (58; Capt. John Underdown), *Nonsuch* (48; Capt. John Carleton), and *Medway's Prize* (Cmdr Thomas Hughes), raided the French settlements in Newfoundland, destroying fishing plant and ships. Three years later another squadron, *Rochester* (15; Capt. John Aldred), *Severn* (50; Capt. Humphrey Pudner), *Portland* (50; Capt. George Purvis), and *Valeur* (18; Cmdr John Hare), campaigned in Newfoundland waters, again destroying French fishing establishments and ships. At least five substantial armed vessels were taken during the year. (Clowes 2.515, 527)

Newfoundland v. Domiat, 31 October 1956
The cruiser *Newfoundland* met and fought the Egyptian frigate *Domiat* south of Suez; *Domiat* fired first, but was sunk very quickly. (Wettern 130)

New Glasgow and others v. U-1003, 20 March 1945
U-1003 collided with the Canadian frigate *New Glasgow*, was hunted by the 26th Escort Group, and later scuttled. (Rohwer 397)

New Guinea
1942 A Japanese force landed at Milne Bay on 24 August but met such determined resistance from US and Australian forces that evacuation was soon ordered. The RAN destroyer *Arunta* sank the submarine *Ro-33*. A battalion-sized assault team landed on Goodenough Island from two Australian destroyers on 22–23 October. (Rohwer 191, 205)

1944 Two Australian cruisers and two destroyers participated in the landing near Sador on 2–5 January. The Australian cruisers *Australia* and *Shropshire* and the destroyers *Arunta* and *Warramunga* were part of the covering force for landings at Hollandia and Aitape on 22 April, and bombarded Japanese troops near Aitape, and assisted in the landing at Biak on 27 May. Australian destroyers bombarded Japanese positions on the north coast several times between April and June, and Australian gunboats damaged the Japanese submarine *I-365* in an attack on Biak Island on 13 August. Two Australian cruisers and four destroyers covered the landing on Morotai Island on 15 September, and the British minelayer *Ariadne* took part in landings on Pegun Island in the Mapia group north of New Guinea on 15 November to establish a radio station. (Rohwer 297, 320, 328, 343, 349, 358, 373)

1945 An Australian naval force and the British cruiser *Newfoundland* supported the army at Wewak, shelling Japanese positions on the island and covering a landing at Dove Bay on 11 May. Australian naval forces with the carrier *Glory* accepted Japanese surrenders at New Guinea and the Solomon Islands on 6 September, Bougainville on 9 September, Wewak on 13 September, and New Ireland on 19 September. (Rohwer 417, 431)

Newport v. French ship, 5 July 1696
Newport (24; Capt. Wentworth Paxton) was captured by the French in the Bay of Fundy. (Clowes 2.538)

New York
1664 Commodore Robert Holmes and Sir Robert Carr with a small English squadron captured Manhattan from the Dutch in August. The colony of New Amsterdam was occupied and renamed New York. (Clowes 2.423)

1776 Landings were made on Staten Island on 3 July and on Long Island on 22 August from the British fleet under Admiral Lord Howe, which had sailed from Halifax. The rebel American army evacuated Long Island on 29 August and on 15 September another landing was made on Manhattan Island. New York was progressively occupied by the British from then on, with little fighting. (Clowes 3.379–386; Syrett, *American* 54–55)

New Zealand, 1845–1846
Parties from several ships fought in the 'Northern War' from March to July 1845. The British forces attacked Maori *pas* (forts) and in every fight were defeated. *Hazard* (18), *Osprey* (12), and *North Star* (26) supplied men, and all suffered casualties. Next year seamen and marines from *Calliope* (26) assisted in the campaign in western New Zealand (the 'Taranaki War'). (Clowes 6.347–349; J. Belich, *The New Zealand Wars*, Auckland 1986, 36–54)

Nicaragua, Central America, February 1846
A small expedition of men from *Alarm* (28; Capt. Granville Loch) and the paddle sloop *Vixen* (Cmdr Alfred Ryder) went upriver from Bluefields to attack, capture, and destroy a fort held by Colonel Salas, who is said to have kidnapped two British subjects. (Clowes 6.349–351)

Nicobar Islands, Bay of Bengal, July 1867
An expedition by the screw sloop *Wasp* (Capt. Norman Redingfield) and the screw corvette *Satellite* (Capt. Joseph Edge) went to the Nicobar Islands to exact reprisal for actions by the islanders. (Clowes 7.217)

Niger River, West Africa
1861 In revenge for attacks on trading ships the screw gunship *Espoir* entered the Niger Delta and destroyed towns held to be responsible. (Dike 1798)

1876–1877 An expedition to open the river to navigation, commanded by Commodore Sir William Hewett, with the screw gunboat *Cygnet* (Lt Robert Hammick), the gunboat *Ariel* (Lt Orford Churchill), and the armed steamer

Sultan of Sokoto, sailed upriver and destroyed the towns of Akado, Sabogrega, and Agberi. A year later a second expedition, led by Capt. John Purvis in the paddle vessel *Pioneer*, with the screw gunvessels *Avon* and *Boxer*, enforced the conditions imposed by the first; the town of Emblana and several villages were destroyed. (Clowes 7.281–282, 284)

1879 The paddle vessel *Pioneer* (Lt John Burr) sailed up the Niger as far as Nupe, and attacked Onitsha and another town on its return, in revenge for attacks on British traders. (Clowes 7.312)

1883 A dispute between the British and some of the towns along the Niger resulted in the towns of Ibah and Anoh being destroyed by bombardment from the screw corvette *Opal* (Capt. Arthur Brooke) and the paddle gunvessel *Alecto* (Lt Frank Harston). (Clowes 7.349)

1886 The paddle vessel *Alecto* (Lt George Izat), accompanied by two small Niger Company steamers carrying sailors from naval ships, commanded by Capt. George Hand, attacked and burned Patani and several nearby villages. (Clowes 7.386)

1894 A cutter from the paddle gunvessel *Alecto* (Lt John Heugh) was ambushed. Two successive expeditions by sailors from *Alecto* and the cruiser *Phoebe* (Capt. Francis Powell) and *Philomel* (Capt. Charles Campbell) were needed to capture Nanna's Town. It was empty when taken, and was burned. (Clowes 4.428–429)

1895 A factory of the Royal Niger Company was looted; an expedition from the cruiser *St George* (Capt. William Forsyth) and other ships attacked the towns of Nimbi and Fishtown, which were captured and burnt. (Clowes 7.431)

Niger v. *Epreuve*, 1760
Niger (32; Capt. John Bentinck) captured the French sloop *Epreuve* (14). (Clowes 3.313)

Niger v. *Ecureuil*, 27 April 1796
The French armed lugger *Ecureuil* (18) took refuge among the Penmarcks rocks. *Niger* (32; Capt. Edward Foote) fired at her without effect. A party in boats went in and burnt her. (James 1.382–383; Clowes 4.497)

Niger v. *Virgen del Carmen*, 2 May 1806
The Spanish schooner *Virgen del Carmen* (4) was captured by *Niger* (32; Capt. James Hillyar) off the coast of Spain. (Clowes 5.563)

Niger and *Tagus* v. *Ceres*, 5–6 January 1814
The frigates *Niger* and *Tagus* (Capts Peter Rainier and Philip Pipon) chased the French frigate *Ceres* near the Cape Verde Islands. At first *Niger* was in the lead, and then *Tagus* overtook her. Both fired at *Ceres*, which was eventually forced to surrender when both enemy frigates came close at the same time. (James 8.131–132)

Nightingale v. French galleys, 25 August 1707

Nightingale (24; Capt. Seth Jermy), escorting a convoy off Harwich, was attacked by a squadron of six galleys out of Dunkirk. *Nightingale* fought hard, and the convoy escaped, but the ship itself was captured. (Clowes 2.514)

Nightingale v. Danish gunboats, 25 October 1807

The brig *Nightingale* (16) was attacked by three Danish gunboats near Fredericksvaern, Norway, but escaped after a short engagement. (Anderson 321)

THE NILE, 1 August 1798

A large French expeditionary force under General Napoleon Bonaparte sailed for Egypt, capturing Malta on the way. The British fleet under Vice-Admiral Sir Horatio Nelson searched for the French fleet without success for some time. The French were finally found in Aboukir Bay, after the troops had been disembarked.

The French fleet was anchored in a line close to the shore. It consisted of one 120-gun ship, *Orient*, twelve other line-of-battle ships, four frigates, and some smaller ships. The British force consisted of thirteen line-of-battle ships and one of 50 guns. The first British ships to approach, *Goliath*, *Zealous*, *Orion*, *Theseus*, and *Audacious*, passed the head to the enemy line or went between the land and the ships; the later ships, *Vanguard* (Nelson's flagship), *Minotaur*, *Defence*, *Bellerophon*, *Majestic*, and *Leander*, attacked from the seaward side. Some of the ships in the French van were thus attacked from two sides. The battle went on late into the night and the ships in the French van were overwhelmed by about 9.30. Half an hour later *Orient* blew up, having been on fire for an hour.

The explosion stopped the fighting for a time. The rear half of the French line had not yet been attacked, and ships had shifted away from *Orient* before the explosion. In the morning several more French ships, damaged or aground, or perhaps only shocked, were taken. Four French ships escaped; nine were captured, one was sunk, and three were burnt. Several British ships were damaged, but only *Bellerophon* badly.

The geo-strategic result was to establish British maritime supremacy in the Mediterranean for the next century and a half; the immediate strategic effect was to isolate Napoleon in Egypt for a year; tactically Nelson had annihilated the French fleet and established his reputation above all his contemporaries. His presence on the field of battle henceforth chilled the blood of all opponents. (*NC* 1.240–283; James 2.166–211; Clowes 4.351–374; Warner 27–76; Tunstall 224–227)

Nile and others v. Réolaise, 17 November 1800

The French corvette *Réolaise* (20), attacked by the cutter *Nile* (Lt George Argeles), was forced aground off Morbihan. She was later refloated but was captured and destroyed. (James 3.36–57; Clowes 5.534–535)

Nile and Lurcher at Quiberon, 7 December 1800

The cutters *Nile* and *Lurcher* (Lts George Argeles and Robert Forbes) attacked a group of vessels in Quiberon Bay, capturing nine out of sixteen. (James 3.37)

Nimble v. *Gallito*, November 1829

The schooner *Nimble* (Lt Joseph Sherer) captured the slaver *Gallito* in the West Indies, freeing 136 slaves. For this, and his work in *Monkey*, Sherer was promoted to commander. (Clowes 6.268; Ward 137)

Nimble v. *Joaquina* and others, 1833

The schooner *Nimble* (Lt Charles Bolton), in the West Indies, fought the slaver *Joaquina* and reduced it to a sinking condition. *Nimble* took five other slavers during this year, freeing 1900 slaves. (Clowes 6.273)

Ningpo River, China, December 1841

The EIC steam vessels *Nemesis*, *Phlegethon*, and *Sesostris* attacked and destroyed fortifications and batteries along the Ningpo River. (Clowes 6.298; Graham 210–211)

Niobe v. *Néarque*, 28 March 1806

The French corvette *Néarque* (16) was one of four ships out of Lorient intended to cruise in northern waters against the British whale fishery; she was the rearmost of the four and was captured after a chase by the frigate *Niobe* (Capt. John Loring). (James 4.159; Clowes 5.376)

Nogu Island, Solomon Islands, October 1880

A party from the schooner *Sandfly* were attacked while bathing at Nogu Island, and all but one man killed. An attempt at retribution failed, and later the screw corvette *Emerald* (Cmdr Henry Maxwell) destroyed any villages which were deemed guilty. (Clowes 7.392)

Nombre de Dios, Panamá

1571–1573 Francis Drake, with a single ship, raided the coast of Panamá and all vessels he found there in 1571. Next year he attempted to capture Nombre de Dios, but failed. In 1573 he made two attacks on the Spanish silver transport route across the Panamá peninsula. The first, in January, was beaten off by the Spaniards. He then allied with the local *cimarrones* (escaped slaves) and a French force under Guillaume le Testu, and made a successful ambush. This was followed by a successful Spanish counter-attack, but the English got away with a substantial quantity of the silver. (Rodger 1.243; Clowes 1.621–623; Andrews 44–51)

1595 Sir Francis Drake led an expedition which captured Nombre de Dios and aimed to take Panamá, but the Spaniards had received warning and blocked the English approach at a mountain pass. (Rodger 1.283; Clowes 1.506; Andrews 200–202)

Nonpareil v. *Canonniere*, 10 May 1810

The schooner *Nonpareil* (14; Lt James Dickinson) captured *Canonniere* (3) off the Vilaine estuary. (Clowes 5.513)

Nonsuch v. Dutch warship, November 1653
Nonsuch (34) met a Dutch warship while cruising off the Lizard, and was much damaged in the subsequent fight. (Clowes 2.200)

Nonsuch and Tyger v. Railleuse and Serpente, May 1689
Nonsuch (36; Capt. Thomas Roomcoyle) attacked a French Newfoundland convoy of twenty merchantmen guarded by *Railleuse* (24) and *Serpente* (16), off the Casquets. Roomcoyle and *Nonsuch*'s master were killed; the boatswain Robert Sincocke took command. Both French ships were captured. *Tyger* (32) came up and joined in the attack on the merchantmen. Sincocke was rewarded with command of *Nonsuch*. The French captains were imprisoned in Plymouth, but soon escaped, both of them to great seafaring careers. (Powley 151; Clowes 2.462)

Nonsuch v. Français, 3–4 January 1695
Nonsuch (40; Capt. Thomas Taylor), escorting a convoy from New England, was attacked by *Français* (48; Capt. Duguay-Trouin) west of Scilly. Two ships were quickly captured and a third, *Falcon* (36), badly damaged. *Français* attacked *Nonsuch*, which at first drove her off but was dismasted; Taylor was killed. *Falcon* and *Nonsuch* surrendered. (Clowes 2.483)

Nonsuch v. Hussard, Belle Poule, and Légère, July 1780
Nonsuch (64; Capt. Sir James Wallace) forced *Hussard* (18) to surrender near Ushant. Six days later she fought the frigate *Belle Poule* (32) through the night, inflicting heavy casualties; in danger of sinking, the frigate surrendered. Later that month *Légère* (32) was driven ashore and destroyed by *Nonsuch*. (Clowes 4.53–54, 134)

Nonsuch v. Actif, 14 May 1781
Nonsuch (64; Capt. Sir James Wallace) chased and fought the French *Actif* (74). *Nonsuch* was badly damaged and withdrew, but then resumed the action, with similar results. *Actif* successfully got into Brest. (Clowes 4.65)

Norfolk and others v. German convoy, 11–12 January 1945
A British squadron – the cruisers *Norfolk* and *Bellona* and three destroyers – attacked a German convoy off Egersund, Norway; two merchant ships and the minesweeper *M-273* were sunk. (Rohwer 385)

North Africa, 8–17 November 1942 (Operation 'Torch')
Landings of troops were made on 8 November at Casablanca (three US divisions), Oran, and Algiers (three US divisions and one British). British squadrons formed the naval escorts for the Oran and Algiers forces. The landings were generally successful, but ships were attacked by German and Italian submarines and aircraft, and French ships and shore batteries resisted. The destroyer *Martin* was sunk by *U-431* on the 10th, and the sloop *Stork* by *U-77* on the 12th. The AA ship *Tynwald* was sunk, probably by an Italian submarine, and the Italian submarine *Ascianghi* sank the minesweeper *Algerine*. Eight transport ships were also sunk. The Italian submarine *Emo* was

sunk by the trawler *Lord Nuffield*, and *U-660* by the corvettes *Lotus* and *Starwort*.

British ships entered Oran and Algiers harbours to attempt to prevent French ships from being scuttled. This failed; the destroyer *Broke* was sunk by the coastal artillery, and the sloops *Walney* and *Hartland* by fire from French destroyers. The cruiser *Aurora* and the destroyer *Brilliant* sank five French vessels and four submarines which attempted to attack. The destroyers *Westcott* and *Achates* were attacked by the French submarines *Actéon* and *Argonaute*, which were sunk. In the Atlantic sector the destroyer *Wrestler* sank *U-98*. (Rohwer 208–210)

North African convoys, 1943
Once Malta was relieved and North Africa invaded, convoys along the coast became established, and became targets.

TE-13, 17 January 1943
The RCN Corvette *Ville de Québec*, defending this convoy, sank *U-224*. (Rohwer 223)

MKS-6, 19 January 1943
This convoy was attacked off Bougie by the Italian submarine *Tritone*, which was sunk by the RCN corvette *Port Arthur*. (Rohwer 223)

TE-14, 30 January 1943
The Italian submarine *Platino* attacked this convoy and sank the RCN corvette *Samphire*. (Rohwer 223)

MKS-7, 6–7 February 1943
This convoy was attacked from the air – the RCN corvette *Louisbourg* was sunk – and by submarine, which sank a landing craft; a freighter was damaged by *U-596*. Two more ships were sunk by *U-77* after the escort left. (Rohwer 230)

UGS-7, 20 April 1943
U-565 sank two ships from this convoy. (Rohwer 244)

UGS-8/KMS-14, 18 May 1943
U-414 sank one ship from this convoy. (Rohwer 244)

CTX-1, 25 May 1943
U-414 damaged one ship in an attack on this convoy, and was then sunk by the corvette *Vetch*. (Rohwer 244)

KMS-18B, 4–5 June 1943
Three ships of this troop convoy were sunk by *U-375* and *U-593* off the Algerian coast. (Rohwer 262)

MWS-36, 6 July 1943
U-435 sank one ship from this convoy off Bone. (Rohwer 262)

UGS-17, 26–30 September 1943
Off the Algerian coast *U-410* sank one ship from this convoy and another two four days later. (Rohwer 275)

KMS-34, 11–13 December 1943
This convoy was attacked off Algeria. *U-223* torpedoed the frigate *Cuckmere*, and *U-593* sank the destroyers *Tynedale* and *Holcombe*; the convoy was not damaged. (Rohwer 288)

SNG-17, 17 March 1944
U-371 sank the transport *Dampo* and a freighter from this convoy off Algiers. (Rohwer 311)

GUS-39, 14–15 May 1944
U-616 sank two ships from this convoy, but was then hunted by British and US ships and aircraft until she was sunk by the US destroyers. (Rohwer 325)

North Borneo
1845–1846   A squadron commanded by Rear-Admiral Sir Thomas Cochrane attacked a chieftain, Osman, who was based inland of Mullanda Bay, Brunei. Only when a formidable boom across the river was broken was the town taken and destroyed. In 1846 similar expeditions attacked the Sultan of Brunei and other chieftains with similar results and difficulties. The ships involved in this fighting included *Phlegethon*, *Pluto*, and *Nemesis*, all steamers. (Clowes 6.330–335)

1848   Cmdr Arthur Farquhar in *Albatross* (16), with *Royalist*, *Nemesis*, and *Ranee*, was sent to suppress pirates on the north coast of Borneo. Eighty *praus* were destroyed in the attack, and more in the next days. (Clowes 6.362–363)

1852   To punish an apparent pirate base at Sulu, the EIC steam gunships *Cleopatra*, *Saumarez*, and *Pluto* were sent from Singapore. After much confusion the guilty village was reached and destroyed. (Low 2.292–293)

1898   The gunboats *Plover* and *Swift* assisted in the search for Si Tallah, a local disturber of the peace in Brunei. (Clowes 7.451)

1945   Australian ships were part of the force covering the landing of Allied forces at Tarakan on 27 April–1 May 1945. The cruiser *Hobart*, the destroyer *Warramunga*, and three other RAN destroyers were in the escort. *Hobart* and the destroyer *Arunta* were part of the force at the landing at Brunei on 8–9 June 1945; the destroyers *Hawkesbury*, *Barcoo*, and *Lachlan* were in the escort. (Rohwer 420)

1962   Pirate attacks on ships and villages in North Borneo were combated by the minesweepers *Chawton* and *Maryton*, the destroyer *Caesar*, and the frigate *Loch Insh*. (Wettern 208)

Northern Rover v. U-59, October 1939
The trawler *Northern Rover*, operating as an armed boarding vessel, was sunk by *U-59* north of Scotland. (Colledge 283)

Northern Spain
1812   Rear-Admiral Sir Home Popham commanded a squadron which raided

along the north coast of Spain between June and September, capturing forts and batteries; guns were landed to attack the fort at Lequetio; its batteries were destroyed and the town of Castor was liberated. French troops in Santander were forced to evacuate. In September several attempts to capture the harbour at Guetaria were made, without success. (James 5.334–337; Hall 202–205; Clowes 5.508–512)

1837 A squadron headed by *Castor* (36; Capt. Lord John Hay) and *Pique* (36; Capt. Hon. Henry Ross) operated in support of the Spanish government against Carlist rebels, notably at San Sebastian and Bilbao. Actions included shelling Carlist positions, blockading the coast, and having a force operating on shore. (Clowes 6.276)

North Ronaldsay, Orkney, c.900
Halfdan, fleeing from the murderers of his father in Norway, seized control of Orkney from his brother Torf-Einar, the first Jarl of Orkney; the latter returned next year and recovered the islands after winning a battle at sea; Halfdan died. (Thompson 13)

NORTH SEA
Damme, Flanders, 1213
A fleet commanded by the Earl of Salisbury, seeking to support Flemings who were being attacked by King Philip of France, encountered at Damme a French fleet aiming to invade England. A large part of the French fleet anchored outside the harbour, and the English caught them by surprise; 300 French cargo ships were captured and 100 burnt. Salisbury landed troops to pursue the fugitives, but they were defeated by the French army. The surviving French ships were burnt by their king, and the French abandoned their invasions of Flanders and England. (Clowes 1.181–182; Rose 28–29)

The Hundred Years' War
1337 Sir Walter Mauny took an advanced force of English troops to Flanders in November. He failed to capture Sluys, but then seized the island of Cadzand. When the Sluys garrison came out it was defeated, and Mauny secured several valuable captures. (Sumption 1.216; Clowes 1.241)

1338 King Edward III sailed to Flanders with a fleet; his ships were anchored in Arnemuiden when they were attacked and captured by a French naval force on 21 September. Five royal ships, including the *Cog Edward* and *Christopher*, were captured after a stiff fight, and their crews murdered. (Sumption 1.247; Rose 64; Clowes 1.245)

1339 An English fleet carrying supplies and reinforcements to the king in Flanders in April met and chased a French convoy into Sluys harbour; the convoy – along with many neutral ships – was looted. (Sumption 1.3264; Rodger 1.97)

1340 (Battle of SLUYS) The French government collected a Great Army of the Sea in 213 ships at the mouth of the Zwyn to block any English landing. King Edward III, despite strong opposition from many of his advisers, gathered a smaller fleet (perhaps 150 ships) at the Orwell, and sailed on 20 June. The French ships were anchored in three lines, the biggest in the front line. The English had freedom of manoeuvre and concentrated all their vessels on part of the French fleet. The fighting consisted of grappling, bombarding the enemy crews with arrows (English longbows against Genoese crossbows), and boarding. The battle began about 3 p.m. and went on until dark, with Flemings joining in on the English side as the result became clear. No quarter was given. French casualties were between 16,000 and 18,000 dead; 190 of their ships were captured. (Sumption 1.324–328; Clowes 1.250–256; Rodger 1.98–99)

1385 An English expedition of eighty ships and 2000 soldiers sailed to attack the French fleet at Sluys, which was intended to invade England. Several ships were captured, but a fireship attack on the invasion fleet was fended off. The French succeeded in sending an expeditionary force to Scotland when the English withdrew. (Sumption 3.542–543)

1405 An English fleet commanded by Thomas, the second son of Henry IV, raided Sluys in June, burned four ships, and attacked the castle, withdrawing when a relieving force approached. On the return voyage three Genoese carracks were captured, and the Norman coast raided. (Clowes 1.363)

1409–1410 The Vice-Admiral of England, Sir Robert Umfraville, raided the east coast of Scotland with ten ships. He captured a dozen or so merchant ships. (Clowes 1.369)
See also: **Firth of Forth**

Wars of the Roses
1460 A large carrack sailed past Calais in September, heading for Sluys. It was chased by six balingers out of Calais, commanded by the Earl of Warwick, who attacked the carrack, but were unable to cope with the size and height of their victim. After a day's fighting, the carrack got away. (Clowes 1.378–379; Rose 87)

1470 The Earl of Warwick raided Sluys in May, where a Burgundian fleet was being collected against him. (Gillingham 180)

Tudor Wars
1492 Philip van Cleve-Ravenstein, in rebellion against the Emperor, controlled Sluys. Henry VII sent a squadron of twelve ships under Sir Edward Poynings to help suppress Ravenstein's piracy. Poynings blockaded the port and broke a bridge of boats preventing entry to the harbour, at which the town surrendered. (Clowes 1.445; Loades 44)

1523 Rival Scots and English squadrons were active off the east coast. The English squadron under Christopher Coo captured seven Scots ships. (Rodger 1.174)

1547 An English squadron under Andrew Dudley captured the French ship *Lion*. (Loades 141–142)

1558 An English squadron under Captain John Malen assisted an Imperial army in a battle on the shore at Dunkirk on 13 July by bombarding the French from the sea, contributing materially to the Imperial victory. (Clowes 1.473; Rodger 1.193; Loades 174)

1576 A small English squadron under William Holstock cruised in the North Sea to repress Dutch piracy. Several ships were taken and 200 Dutch seamen jailed. (Clowes 1.481)
See also: **Firth of Forth**

English Revolutionary War
1657 A French attack on Mardyke, Flanders (held by Spain), was assisted by an English squadron offshore under General Edward Mountagu. After the town was taken seamen were landed to help defend it, and the ships bombarded a Spanish counter-attack, which thereby failed. (Capp 101)

1658 A Royalist force gathered in Flanders to be taken to England in five Dutch hired merchantmen. The ships were intercepted by William Goodson on 28 February and three were captured; the invasion did not take place. Later a French and English attack on Dunkirk was helped by a bombardment of the seaward defences by the fleet commanded by Edward Mountagu and William Goodson. The town was captured in June and handed over to English possession. (Capp 101)

Dutch Wars – see: **Gabbard, Katwijk, Kentish Knock, Lowestoft, Medway, Schooneveld**

War of the League of Augsburg
1694–1695 The Anglo-Dutch Channel Fleet under Sir Cloudisley Shovell went to attack Dunkirk on 11–12 September 1694. The harbour approach was difficult and two explosive fireships failed to reach their target. The joint fleet attacked Dunkirk again on 1 August 1695. The defences were as strong as ever and again the explosive fireships failed to get close enough to cause any damage; three galleys were sunk by bombs. (Clowes 2.477–478, 482)

1706 The town of Ostend was besieged by the allied army. A squadron under Vice-Admiral Sir Stafford Fairborne blockaded and bombarded it in May–June. The town capitulated on 25 June. Nine Spanish warships and forty merchant ships were captured as a result. (Clowes 2.510)

French Revolutionary and Napoleonic Wars
1793 The frigate *Québec* (32) and another frigate and the floating battery *Redoubt* assisted the British army on 31 October in driving the French from Ostend and Nieuport. (James 1.99)

1798 A force of small ships under the command of Capt. Home Popham on 14 May put ashore 1100 soldiers to attack a lock on the Bruges Canal; the ships meanwhile bombarded Ostend. The sea became too rough to re-embark the soldiers, who were captured on 28 May. (James 2.131–133; Clowes 4.341–342)

1800 Four French frigates blockaded in Dunkirk harbour were the object of a raid on 7 July by a group of gunboats and assault craft, including fireships, led by the sloop *Dart* (Cmdr Patrick Campbell). Only one ship, *Désirée*, was brought out. (James 3.17–20)

1804 The French cutter *Colombe* was cut out of Sluys on 8 March by boat parties from the sloops *Cruizer* (18) and *Rattler* (16). On 23 October a squadron of ships under Cmdr John Hancock in *Cruizer* located a flotilla of armed schuyts coming from Ostend. The two groups fired at each other without effect for over an hour. The brig *Conflict* ran aground and was captured. (James 3.235; Clowes 5.71–72, 556)

The Great War

1914 The retreat of the British army through Belgium brought alarm in the Admiralty for the Belgian ports. A force of barely trained marines, 4000 strong, was landed at Ostend on 27–28 August. A change of plan followed; the force was evacuated a few days later. A British flotilla of monitors and destroyers, commanded by Rear-Admiral Horace Hood, shelled the seaward flank of German forces attacking Belgian positions near Nieuport on 18 October, and was credited with blocking part of the German advance. More ships were brought in on the 20th and eventually the battleship *Venerable* was also used. The flotilla's fire, mainly directed against artillery positions, was eventually countered by the German artillery; the destroyers *Amazon* and *Falcon* were hit from the shore and put out of action. The battleships *Russell* and *Exmouth*, with destroyers and minesweeping trawlers, bombarded Zeebrugge on 23 November with the aim of damaging the German submarine base. (Corbett 1.94–98, 122–124, 220–234, 2.12–13)

1915 The monitors *Lord Clive*, *Prince Rupert*, and *Sir John Moore*, protected by a large escort, bombarded the U-boat base at Zeebrugge on 22 August for two hours; the results were minor. A bombardment of Ostend by five monitors was organised in September. The Germans replied with fire from the Tirpitz battery, which had the greater range. The battleship *Redoubtable* and two gunvessels were also used. The contest between the battery and the monitors was repeated three more times, with no better results. The drifter *Great Heart* and the yacht *Sanda* were sunk. (Corbett 3.148–153)

1916 The monitors of the Dover Patrol, five in all, protected by the drifters of the same patrol, bombarded German positions in Flanders on 28 January, without reply, and with unknown results. (Corbett 3.277)

1917 The German 6th Destroyer Flotilla was moving towards Zeebrugge on 23 January. A large British force out of Harwich was deployed in several sections to intercept. A number of separate fights took place, in which the German flotilla leader *V-69* was badly damaged, and the British destroyer *Simoom* was sunk. The rest of the German flotilla reached Zeebrugge.

An air raid on Zeebrugge on 7 March persuaded the German destroyers to anchor outside the port, where they were attacked by four British coastal motor boats. One destroyer, *G-88*, was badly damaged. An expedition to lay anti-submarine mines and nets off Zeebrugge on 24 April was attacked by German seaplanes, coastal batteries, and destroyers. The destroyer *Melpomene* was damaged but survived. On 12 May the monitors *Terror*, *Marshall Soult*, and *Erebus*, protected by a large fleet of smaller vessels, bombarded the canal gates of the Bruges Canal in Zeebrugge for two hours, but did not succeed in their aims. Two monitors, protected by a force of destroyers and other ships, bombarded the docks at Ostend on 5 June. Damage was caused to the dock installations, a submarine, and three destroyers. Part of the covering force clashed with two German destroyers: *S-20* was sunk. (Corbett 3.299–300; Newbolt 4.73–79, 371–372, 5.46–47; Halpern, *Naval History* 347)

1918 The monitor *Erebus* bombarded Ostend on 19 January. An attack was made to sink blockships in the harbours at Zeebrugge and Ostend on 23 April. German reaction was furious, with the result that none of the stated objectives were achieved, though three blockships were sunk at Zeebrugge. The Ostend raid never took place. The Germans were able to go on using both ports, but the spectacular nature of the raid was a great morale booster for the Allies. The failure of the Zeebrugge raid was to be made good by a new raid on Ostend on 10 May. This was only partly successful, but the Germans ceased to use Ostend anyway. (Newbolt 5.62–66, 206, 266–274; Halpern, *Naval History* 411–415

Hitler's War

1939–June 1940 *U-13* was sunk by the sloop *Weston* in an attack on convoy FN-184 off Lowestoft on 31 May. (Rohwer 24; Sebag-Montefiore 94–96)

DUNKIRK, May–June 1940 'Dunkirk' is the popular name for the evacuation of the British and French forces from Flanders. The evacuation took place between 28 May and 4 June. In evacuating the army and Allied forces the destroyers *Wakeful*, *Grenade*, and *Grafton* were sunk (by *S-30*, bombs, and *U-62* respectively) on 29 May; the destroyers *Keith*, *Basilisk*, and *Havant*, the minesweeper *Skipjack*, the gunboat *Mosquito*, and the transports *British Queen* and *Scotia* were sunk by bombing on 1 June; many other ships were damaged; over 330,000 Allied troops were evacuated. (Rohwer 24, 25)

1940 From mid-1940 onwards, the war in the North Sea was mainly between British MTBs and German S-boats (which the British called E-boats). The aim of each side was to disrupt seaborne convoys which sailed along the British and continental coasts. In this the Germans had many more targets than the British.

On 14–15 August the destroyers *Malcolm* and *Verity* attacked a German convoy off the Texel, sinking two ships. On 4 September S-boats raided a convoy off Great Yarmouth, in which seven ships were sunk. Three days later two S-boats attacked convoy FS-273 off Lowestoft; one ship was sunk. Also that night the 1st S-boat Flotilla attacked a convoy off the Norfolk coast and sank two ships. Off Terschelling between 24 and 27 September the British submarine *H-49* sank a ship from a German convoy. (Rohwer 36, 39, 42)

Between 15 and 18 October German submarine chasers off Terschelling sank the British submarine *H-47*. On the night of 19–20 November the 3rd S-boat Flotilla raided towards Lowestoft but was intercepted by British destroyers and lost *S-38* in sinking one ship. (Rohwer 45, 49)

On the night of 15–16 December *S-58* attacked a convoy off Great Yarmouth, sinking one ship, while two nights later MTBs sank one ship off the Scheldt. On the night of 23–24 December the 1st and 2nd S-boat Flotillas attacked convoy FN-366; two ships were sunk. (Rohwer 52, 53)

1941 The 2nd S-boat Flotilla on the night of 5–6 February sank a ship off the east coast. The 1st S-boat Flotilla raided the Thames estuary on 19 February and sank one ship. On the 25th *S-30* sank the destroyer *Exmoor* off Lowestoft and the 1st S-boat Flotilla sank a ship near Cromer. (Rohwer 56, 60, 61)

On the night of 7–8 March the 1st and 3rd S-boat Flotillas attacked convoys FN-26 and FN-39, sinking seven ships. On 12 March *S-28* sank one ship from convoy FS-32 off Orford Ness, but next night an attack on convoy FS-37 was driven off by the destroyer *Worcester*; next night escorts drove off an attack on convoy FS-35; an attack on convoy FN-33 on the 17th was driven off by the escorts, but on the 18th the 1st S-boat Flotilla off the Humber sank one ship from convoy FN-34. (Rohwer 62, 63, 64)

On 17 April the 2nd S-boat Flotilla attacked a convoy near Great Yarmouth; two ships were sunk. On the 29th the 1st S-boat Flotilla attacked a convoy off Cromer, and sank one ship. (Rohwer 69, 70)

Raids resumed in August. On the 20th the 4th S-boat Flotilla sank two ships from a convoy off Cromer, on 7 September two off Norfolk, and on the 17th two more from a convoy off Cromer. On 12 October the 2nd S-boat Flotilla sank two ships from another convoy off Cromer, but a week later an S-boat was sunk in attacking a convoy off Great Yarmouth, which lost three ships. On 24 November the 4th S-boat Flotilla sank three ships from a convoy off Orford Ness, and on the 29th three from a convoy off Cromer. (Rohwer 93, 98, 101, 107, 116, 118, 119)

1942 On 15 March, in an attack on convoy FS-749, *S-104* sank the destroyer *Vortigern*, but *S-111* was sunk. (Rohwer 152)

On 10 September five MTBs raided a German convoy off the Texel; one MTB was captured. On the night of 30 September–1 October MTBs sank a ship and a destroyer from a convoy off Terschelling, but one MGB and four MTBs were lost. On 14 October the 2nd S-boat Flotilla sank two ships from a convoy off Cromer, and on 9 November a ship from a convoy off Lowestoft. The 4th S-boat Flotilla attacked convoy FN-889 off Lowestoft on 12 December, sinking five ships. (Rohwer 195, 202, 212, 218)

1943 On the night of 24–25 January the 2nd, 4th, and 6th S-boat Flotillas jointly raided a convoy off Lowestoft, but were driven off by the destroyers *Mendip* and *Windsor*. On the night of 17–18 February they were conducting a mining operation off Lowestoft and Great Yarmouth when they were attacked by the destroyers *Montrose* and *Garth* and the corvette *Kittiwake*; *S-71* was sunk. Ten days later MTBs attacked a convoy off Ijmuiden during which *MTB-79* was sunk. (Rohwer 228, 233, 234)

On the night of 4–5 March the 2nd, 4th, and 6th S-boat Flotillas were driven off near Lowestoft and Great Yarmouth by the destroyers *Windsor* and *Southdown* and the corvette *Sheldrake*, losing *S-70* and *S-75*. Three MTBs attacked minesweepers operating off Terschelling on 9 March; *MTB-622* was sunk. On the night of 15–16 March two MTBs attacked a convoy, also off Terschelling, sinking two ships. On the night of 28–29 March the 2nd S-boat Flotilla attacked convoy FS-1074 at Smith's Knoll but was driven off by the destroyers *Windsor* and *Blencathra* and MTBs, losing *S-28*.

On 1 April MTBs attacked a German patrol off Terschelling; *V-1241* was sunk. On the night of 14–15 April the 2nd, 4th, and 6th S-boat Flotillas, raiding near Lowestoft, were driven off by MTBs, the destroyer *Westminster*, and the corvette *Widgeon*. (Rohwer 236, 237, 241, 242, 245)

On 18 April three MTBs attacked a convoy off Scheveningen and on 1 May the 31st and 17th MTB Flotillas fought the German 12th Patrol Boat Flotilla. On the night of 13–14 May four MTBs attacked German minesweepers off the Hook of Holland; the minesweeper *M-8* was sunk. (Rohwer 248, 251)

On the night of 24–25 July MTBs and MGBs attacked S-boats off Dunkirk; *S-77* was sunk. On the night of 4–5 August four S-boat flotillas raided near Harwich; the trawler *Redgauntlet* was sunk. On the night of 24–25 September those four flotillas conducted a mining operation off East Anglia; the trawler *Franctireur* and *S-96* were sunk. A month later the 2nd, 4th, 6th, and 8th S-boat Flotillas again joined forces to attack convoy FN-1160 off Cromer, but were driven off by the escorts; the trawler *William Sugden* and *S-63* and *S-88* were sunk. The 6th S-boat Flotilla, laying mines off Cromer on the night of 4–5 November, attacked convoy FN-1170; two ships from the convoy and *S-74* were sunk. (Rohwer 248, 266, 277, 283, 286)

1944 On the night of 4–5 February, the 8th S-boat Flotilla laid mines near the Humber, during which the trawler *Cap d'Antifer* was sunk. On the night of 12–13 February the 2nd and 8th S-boat Flotillas and the 34th Minesweeping Flotilla laid mines near Great Yarmouth; in the process they fought two corvettes and five MTBs; the minesweeper *M-3411* was sunk. On the night of 22–23 February the 2nd and 8th S-boat Flotillas attempted to attack a convoy at Smith's Knoll but were driven off by the destroyers *Garth* and *Southdown* and two MTBs; *S-94* and *S-128* were sunk. Two nights later the same flotillas laid mines near Great Yarmouth and attacked convoy FS-1371; they sank one ship and were driven off by the destroyers *Vivien* and *Eglinton*. Next night they attacked another convoy in the same area, but were unsuccessful. (Rohwer 306, 308)

On the night of 6–7 March four MTBs attacked a German convoy near the Hook of Holland; the patrol boat *V-1304* was sunk. On the night of 25–26 March the 2nd and 8th S-boat Flotillas attacked a convoy near Hearty Knoll, without success. On the night of 29–30 March rival raids clashed near the Dutch coast; *MTB-241* was sunk. (Rohwer 310, 312)

On the night of 10–11 April four MTBs attacked a convoy near the Dutch coast, but were driven off by the escorts. The 8th S-boat Flotilla made a mining expedition on 18 April and was intercepted by the destroyer *Whitshed* and MTBs. On 11 May MTBs raided the Hook of Holland, sinking the patrol boat *V-1311*. (Rohwer 370, 323)

On 10 June MTBs raided a convoy near the Helder; *MTB-681* was sunk as were three patrol craft – *V-1314*, *V-2020*, and *V-2021*. At the same time another MTB raid fought the German 11th Minesweeping Flotilla near the Hook of Holland. (Rohwer 332)

On 4 and 5 July separate MTB raids attacked convoys near the Dutch coast near Vlieland, in which *M-469* was sunk by *MTB-458*. On the 8th MTBs raided the Ijmuiden area, sinking *V-1411* and the minesweeper *R-111*. Next night they raided near the Hook of Holland and sank *V-1308* and *V-1412*; three of the MTBs were damaged. (Rohwer 340, 342, 343)

On the night of 13–14 August the 10th S-boat Flotilla, raiding near Orford Ness, was driven off by the destroyer *Walpole*. MTBs raided the Scheldt on the 26th, sinking *V-2009*. The 10th S-boat Flotilla attempted to supply the German garrison in Dunkirk on 18 September, but was attacked by the frigate *Stayner*: two MTBs and *S-183*, *S-200*, and *S-702* were sunk. On the night of 30 September–1 October the 11th MTB Flotilla attacked a convoy near Ijmuiden; they were driven off by the escort; *MTB-360* and *MTB-347* were sunk. (Rohwer 346, 353, 359, 362)

On the night of 8–9 October the 4th MTB Flotilla fought a German patrol group near the Hook of Holland, and again a week later; *V-1303* and *V-2016* were sunk. On 2 November the 9th S-boat Flotilla raided in the Ostend area; the trawler *Colsay* was sunk. The flotilla laid mines in the Scheldt on the night of the 15th–16th; they were intercepted by the frigates *Retalick* and *Thornborough*. (Rohwer 362, 372)

On the night of 22–23 December the 6th, 8th, 9th, and 10th S-boat Flotillas laid mines in the Thames estuary; they were attacked by the destroyer *Walpole*, the frigates *Torrington* and *Curzon*, and the corvette *Kittywake*; *S-132* was sunk. Two nights later the 8th S-boat Flotilla attacked a convoy in the southern North Sea but was driven off by the destroyers *Ekins* and *Thornborough*, the frigate *Caicos*, and the corvette *Shearwater*. Between 22 and 27 December German midget submarines made attacks in the Scheldt. One ship was sunk, but the attacks were mainly prevented by MTBs. (Rohwer 379)

1945 On the night of 14–15 January the 5th S-boat Flotilla raided the Humber area, but was driven off by the destroyer *Farndale*, the 6th and 9th S-boat Flotillas raided the Scheldt, but were driven off by the destroyers *Seymour*, *Curzon*, and *Cotswold*, and the 8th S-boat Flotilla attacked Margate, where it was fought by the corvette *Guillemot*. On the night of 21–22 February the 2nd and 5th S-boat Flotillas attacked convoy FS-1134, sinking two ships, and the 8th S-boat Flotilla raided in the Thames estuary, where a landing ship and *S-193* were sunk. Next night the 9th S-boat Flotilla attacked a convoy off Dunkirk, sinking one ship; the 6th S-boat Flotilla raided the Ostend area and was driven off by MTBs; and the 8th S-boat Flotilla attacked a convoy off the North Foreland, being driven away by the destroyer *Seymour*, the corvette *Guillemot*, and MTBs; *S-701* was sunk. (Rohwer 386, 388)

Between 5 and 26 February midget submarines were used in attacks in the Strait of Dover; four ships, the destroyer *La Combattante*, and the cable ship *Alert* were sunk. On the night of 1–2 March the 4th S-boat Flotilla was intercepted by the destroyer *Seymour* and *S-228* was sunk. On the night of 18–19 March the 6th S-boat Flotilla attacked convoy FS-1759 off Lowestoft, sinking two ships; a week later the 4th and 6th S-boat Flotillas, mining the

Thames–Scheldt route, were driven away by the destroyers *Arundel* (Norwegian), *Kwakowiak* (Polish), and *Rion*. (Rohwer 392, 394, 401)

On the night of 6–7 April the 2nd S-boat Flotilla mined the Humber estuary; two S-boats, *S-76* and *S-177*, and two MTBs, *MTB-494* and *MTB-5001*, were sunk. The 4th and 6th S-boat Flotillas mined the Thames estuary; *S-202*, *S-203*, and *S-223* were sunk. Midget submarines were sent against the convoy TBC-123 off East Anglia on the night of 9–10 April. Several of the submarines were sunk, as was the cable ship *Monarch*. On 12 April, the 4th, 6th, and 9th S-boat Flotillas, when mining, were engaged by the destroyer *Ekins* and MTBs. Convoy FS-1784 was attacked by *U-1274* in the Firth of Forth on the 16th; one ship was sunk, and then the destroyer *Viceroy* sank the submarine. *U-245* attacked convoy TAM-142, sinking two ships. On the 23rd *U-2329* sank a ship off Lowestoft. The last raid was by *U-2336* in the Firth of Forth on 7 May, when two ships were sunk. (Rohwer 406, 407, 409)

Northumberland v. French squadron, 8 May 1744

Northumberland (17; Capt. Thomas Watson) chased three French ships (*Content* (64), *Mars* (64), and *Vénus* (26)) near the Tagus estuary. Capt. Watson was killed early in the fighting; the master (the lieutenants being below) precipitately surrendered the ship. (Clowes 3.274–275)

Northumberland v. *Ariane*, *Andromaque*, and *Mamelouck*, 22 May 1812

The French frigates *Ariane* and *Andromaque* and the corvette *Mamelouck* arrived off Lorient to find *Northumberland* (74; Capt. Hon. Henry Hotham) blocking their way. All three ran aground on a ridge of rock. The brig *Growler* (Lt John Weeks) blocked any rescue efforts from the shore. The three French ships were bombarded, keeled over as the tide fell, and were successively set alight and blew up. (James 5.319–324; Clowes 5.499–500; *NC* 5.89–91)

Northumbrian raid on Ireland, 684

King Ecgfrith of the Northumbrians sent an expedition against Ireland, under the command of Beorht; it ravaged Meath and returned home with captives. (*ASC* s.a. 684)

North Wales

c.630 King Edwin of Northumbria sent fleets into the Irish Sea and conquered Anglesey and the Isle of Man; the exact date is not known. (L. Alcock, *Arthur's Britain*, London 1971, 138–139)

852 The first recorded Viking attack on Wales was by a group of Norseman who had been driven from Dublin. (Maund 156)

961 The sons of Amlaibh (Olaf) raided the region. This may be the same force as raided Tywyn c.963. (Maund 157)

969–987 Viking armies, probably based in Ireland, repeatedly raided parts of North Wales: in c.968 Aberffraw in Anglesey; in 969 Macht Haraldsson and his brother Godfred invaded Anglesey; Godfred invaded again in 962, taking up a large plunder. A Viking force commanded by Gwrmid (otherwise unknown) raided the Llyn area in 978, and next year a Viking force, probably driven from Dublin by the Irish conquest of the city, raided North Wales, capturing the refugee king of Gwynnedd, Iago ap Idwal Foel. He returned once more in 980 in alliance with Custennin ap Iago and a Viking army; Custennin was soon killed by Hywel ap Ieuaf. In 987 Godfred ravaged Anglesey, defeated Maredudd, king of Gwynnedd, and carried off many captives. The survivors were taken to Ceredigion and Dyfed by Maredudd ap Owain. (Hudson 62; Maund 12, 55, 157–159; Oram 10)

1030 A joint raid by the fleets of King Cnut of England and King Sihtric of Dublin was made into North Wales. (Hudson 120)

1042 The exiled king of Gwynnedd fled to Dublin and returned with a fleet from that city; he captured the usurping king Gruffydd, who was then rescued by a Welsh counter-attack. (Hudson 136; Maund 163)

1063 St David's and Bangor, both cathedral towns, were raided by a Viking force. Perhaps in association, a combined land and sea attack on Wales was made by Earl Harold Godwinesson and his brother Tostig. Tostig invaded North Wales from his Northumbrian earldom; Harold gathered a fleet at Bristol and sailed 'round Wales'. King Gruffydd of Gwynnedd was killed by his own people, and peace resulted. (Maund 167; *ASC* s.a. 1063)

1098 Anglesey was invaded by the Norman army of the Earls of Chester and Shrewsbury. The Welsh hired a Dublin fleet to fight them, but it quickly changed sides. As the invaders were gathering loot and terrorising the inhabitants, a Norwegian fleet led by King Magnus arrived from the Isle of Man, defeated the Normans, and then looted their loot. (R.R. Davies, *The Age of Conquest*, Oxford 1987, 10; Maund 143)
See also: **King Magnus's Expedition**

1198 Ragnvald, king of Man, assisted Rhodri ab Owain to recover control of Anglesey. (MacDonald 136)

1277–1295 King Edward I campaigned against the princes of Gwynnedd along the coast of North Wales three times. In each case he sent a fleet to capture Anglesey, the main source of food for the Welsh. In 1277 a squad of reapers was included to collect the harvest, though the invading army was quickly evacuated. In 1282 a bridge was constructed across the Menai Strait to facilitate an invasion of the mainland, but the English crossed prematurely and were defeated. The invasion was repeated in 1295, using a fleet of 140 ships, aimed at suppressing the revolt of the conquered Welsh. (Prestwich 180, 190–192, 223; Rodger 1.75–78; J.E. Morris, *The Welsh Wars of Edward I*, Oxford 1901)

1315 Thomas Dun, commanding four Flemish ships in the service of the king of Scots, attacked Holyhead in September and captured an English ship. (Nicholson 94; MacDonald 197)

1401 The revolt of Owain Glyn Dwr gained a boost by the capture of Conwy Castle, in which he was assisted by Scots ships which had taken control of the Menai Strait. (Rodger 1.115)

Norway
1194 Jarl Harald Maddadsson of Orkney sent an expedition across to Norway to intervene in a civil war. The ships were attacked before dawn just before Easter in 1194 at Florvag, north of Bergen; they and the crews were totally destroyed. (Thompson 73)

1940 Landings by British and French forces were made at several Norwegian ports from 13 April onwards – Namsos, Harstad, Stavanger, Trondheim, Andalsnes, Narvik, and others; they were all evacuated after German victories in May and June. (For more details see under these names.) (Rohwer 19–21)

Norwich and convoy v. French squadron, 5 May 1697
A convoy for the West Indies escorted by a squadron headed by *Norwich* (50; Capt. George Symonds) was attacked by a French squadron in the western Channel. *Norwich* and *Chatham* (48; Capt. Samuel Whittaker) were badly mauled and *Seaford* (20; Capt. George Walton) and the fireship *Blaze* (Capt. John Wooden) were captured. *Sheerness* (32; Capt. Valentine Bowles) survived. *Seaford* was burned. Symonds and Bowles were court-martialled and dismissed the service. (Clowes 2.495)

Nottingham v. *Mars*, 11 October 1746
The French ship *Mars* (64) was returning to France from Martinique when she met *Nottingham* (60; Capt. Philip Saumarez). *Mars* was undermanned and her crew was sickly but she fought for two hours before surrendering. (Clowes 3.281–282)

Nottingham and *Portland* v. *Magnanime*, 31 January 1748
The French ship *Magnanime* (64) sailed for the East Indies, but was dismasted in a gale and was then chased and attacked by *Nottingham* (60; Capt. Robert Harland) assisted by *Portland* (50; Capt. Charles Steevens). *Magnanime* lost a quarter of her crew in the fighting, which lasted six hours, ending in her surrender. (Clowes 3.287)

Nottingham v. *U-52*, 19 August 1916
As the British Grand Fleet came south from Scapa Flow, on the news that the German High Seas Fleet was at sea, the cruiser *Nottingham* was torpedoed by *U-52* and sank. (Newbolt 4.35)

Nubian, *Paladin*, and *Petard* v. Tunisian convoys, 3–4 May 1943
The destroyers *Nubian* and *Paladin* and the submarine *Petard* sank the Italian TB *Perseo* and transports carrying supplies to Tunisia. (Rohwer 248)

Nuestra Señora de la Dolores v. *Santa Maria*, 23 January 1801
The felucca *Nuestra Señora de la Dolores* (Lt Michael Fitton), manned by men from the frigate *Abergavenny*, chased a Spanish *guarda costa Santa Maria* near Cartagena, Spanish Main. *Dolores* had only one gun to the *guarda costa*'s six, but *Santa Maria* was driven ashore. Lt Fitton took *Dolores*

ashore, stormed the enemy ship, and took from her equipment needed for *Dolores*; then he burned *Santa Maria*. (James 3.121–123; Clowes 4.535)

Nyasaland v. U-400, 17 December 1944
U-400 was sunk by the frigate *Nyasaland* west of Ireland. (Rohwer 373)

Nyborg, Denmark, August 1808
A division of Spanish soldiers had been stationed in Zealand, Denmark, by Napoleon. When the revolt in Spain began the soldiers were contacted by Rear-Admiral Richard Keats and arrangements were made for them to be evacuated from Denmark and transported to Spain. They first seized control of the port of Nyborg, and two Danish ships in the harbour entrance were captured in a boat attack by British sailors. Other Spanish detached forces were collected, and in the end 10,000 men were taken to Spain. (James 4.303–305; Anderson 326; Clowes 5.250–251)

Nymphe **v.** *Cléopatre*, **18 June 1793**
The frigate *Nymphe* (40; Capt. Edward Pellew) met the French frigate *Cleopatre* (36) in the western Channel. The captains having courteously hailed each other, and the two crews having indulged in rival cheers, they fought. The two ships became entangled more than once, and in the end a party from *Nymphe* boarded *Cléopatre* and hauled down the colours. *Cléopatre* had been effectively disabled by that time, and had lost a quarter of her crew either dead or wounded. (James 1.106–109; *NC* 1.12–14; Clowes 4.476–477)

Nymphe **and** *Circe* **v.** *Espiégle*, **15 November 1793**
The French brig *Espiégle* (16) was captured by the frigates *Nymphe* (36) and *Circe* (28) off Ushant. (Clowes 4.482)

Nyroca v. U-boat, 3 June 1917
The Q-ship *Nyroca* (which also operated as *Mavis*) was torpedoed off the Scilly Isles, but was beached at Cawsand Bay. (Colledge 284)

O

Obligado, Argentina, 13 November 1845
The commanders of the British and French squadrons in the River Plate became involved in fighting the forces of the Argentine dictator Manuel Rosas. Their squadrons, three paddle steamers and eight other ships, sailed up the Paraná River until blocked by a line of hulks chained together, protected by batteries and gunboats. This defence was briefly successful until a boat party bravely attacked and opened the boom of ships, and the landing party captured three of the batteries; the fourth was taken the next day. The remaining Argentine vessel, a schooner, was chased until abandoned. It then became possible for allied ships to sail as far as the Paraguayan capital Asuncion. (Clowes 6.338–343; L.B. MacKinnon, *Steam Warfare on the Paraná*, London 1848; J. Lynch, *Argentine Dictator*, Oxford 1981, 281–283)
See also: **Montevideo**

***Ocean*, Korea, May 1952–May 1953**
The carrier *Ocean* raided communications and positions as required in North Korea. (Wettern 68–69)

***Oceanic II* v. *U-14*, 5 June 1915**
The trawler *Oceanic II* was attacked by *U-14* and replied with gunfire. The submarine was sunk. (Grant 23)

***Ockham* v. Angria's squadron, 1732**
The EIC ship *Ockham*, a large Indiaman, beat off an attack by Angria's ships out of Colaba. (Keay 264)

Odessa, Russia, April–May 1854
The allied fleets in the Black Sea bombarded the Man-of-War harbour at Odessa on 22 April, destroying almost all the ships there. (Lambert 102–103; Clowes 6.400–401)

***Odin* v. *Strale* and *Baleno*, 13 June 1940**
The British submarine *Odin* was sunk by the Italian destroyers *Strale* and *Baleno* off Taranto. (Rohwer 27)

***Oiseau* v. Spanish frigates, 20 May 1797**
The frigate *Oiseau* (36; Capt. Charles Brisbane) met a Spanish frigate north of Rio de la Plata and started to fight, but broke off when threatened by a second frigate. (James 2.94–95)

***Oiseau* v. *Reunion*, 1 September 1798**
Oiseau (36; Capt. Charles Brisbane) captured the French *Reunion* (4) in the East Indies. (Clowes 4.556)

Oiseau and others v. *Dédaigneuse*, 26–28 January 1801

The frigate *Oiseau* (36; Capt. Samuel Linzee) chased the frigate *Dédaigneuse* southwards past Cape Finisterre, where the frigates *Sirius* and *Amethyst* (Capts Richard King and John Cooke) joined the chase. Only on the third day were the ships close enough to exchange shots, but then *Dédaigneuse* surrendered quickly. (James 3.123–124; Clowes 4.331)

Olaf Guthfrithsson and Northumbria, 937 and 939

King Olaf Guthfrithsson of Dublin took an expeditionary force to Britain in 937, in alliance with other enemies of King Athelstan of Wessex. The allies were defeated in battle at Brunanburh. Olaf may have landed in the Clyde, invading England by way of the Humber or the Wash. Two years later, on the death of King Athelstan, Olaf again sailed to Northumbria, presumably landing on the Lancashire coast. He was accepted as king at York, and then invaded Mercia. A stalemate resulted at Leicester, and a peace was patched up by which Olaf secured York and part of Danish Mercia. (*ASC* s.a. 937, 939; Smyth, *Dublin* 36–38)

Olaf the White at Dumbarton, 870–871

Olaf was king in Dublin, a Viking city. In 870 he sailed to Dumbarton, chief place of the Strathclyde kingdom, and was joined by his former colleague Ivar the Boneless in a successful four-month siege of the dun. (Smyth, *Warlords* 158)

Olive Branch v. *U-28*, 2 September 1917

U-28 torpedoed the escort vessel *Olive Branch* off the North Cape of Norway, but was herself then damaged and sunk when her prey's ammunition blew up. The survivors of *Olive Branch* ignored the submarine's survivors. (Grant 67)

Olympia v. French privateer, 2 March 1811

The brig *Olympia* (10; Lt Henry Taylor) was captured by French privateers off Dieppe. (Clowes 5.553)

Olympic v. *U-103*, 12 May 1918

The troop transport *Olympic*, carrying American soldiers, rammed and sank *U-106* in the western Channel. (Newbolt 5.280; Grant 118)

Omoa, Honduras

1779 Two Spanish galleons took refuge at Omoa in September. A landing was made from a British squadron commanded by Capt. Hon. John Luttrell of *Lowestoft* (32), and a menacing approach by the ships allowed the landing force to storm the fort from the land. The galleons were captured along with $3 million in treasure. (Clowes 4.44–45)

1873 A dispute arose at Omoa over British assets seized by a general in command at the town, Honduras being in a state of civil war. The screw sloop *Niobe* (Cmdr Lambton Loraine) bombarded the old castle at Omoa between 18 and 21 August until the general capitulated. (Clowes 7.235–237)

Omrah v. U-boat, 12 May 1918
The troop transport *Omrah*, returning from Marseilles to Alexandria (and so with no troops on board), was sunk by a U-boat. (Newbolt 5.292)

Onore, Malabar, 1783
An assault was made by BM ships and EIC troops on the fort at Onore, held by troops of Sultan Tipu of Mysore. The BM ships bombarded the fort and covered the landing. After the fort's successful capture the ships transported forces to capture Cuddalore further south. Tipu's army then besieged Onore, with the BM ship *Wolfe* helping the defence, until he retook the place. (Low 1.181–183)

Onslow v. *U-102*, 25 February 1918
The destroyer *Onslow* sank *U-102* in the eastern part of the Channel. (Newbolt 5.427; Grant 121)

Onward and others v. German submarines, 11 July 1916
The trawlers *Onward*, *Era*, and *Nellie Nutten* chased a U-boat, but were then attacked by her and three more submarines; all the trawlers were sunk. (Newbolt 4.348)

Onyx v. *Manly*, 1 January 1809
The sloop *Onyx* (Cmdr Charles Gill), in the North Sea, met the Dutch sloop *Manly*. The two ships fought for over two hours until *Manly* surrendered. (James 5.1–2)

Ophelia v. *UB-83*, 10 September 1918
The destroyer *Ophelia* sank *UB-83* in the North Sea at the second attempt. (Newbolt 5.429; Grant 103–104)

Opossum v. Chinese pirates, October 1865–1866
The screw gunboat *Opossum* (Lt Henry St John) captured two pirate boats in Mirs Bay, China, in October 1865, then found and captured three more at Toomiang Island. Next year she campaigned against pirates at Pakshui in February (fifteen ships destroyed), and again in April (nine boats and a battery destroyed). In June, with *Osprey* (Lt William Menzies), she attacked a fleet of twenty pirate ships at Sama and destroyed them and their village. (Clowes 7.211–212, 215–260)

Opossum v. *UC-49*, 8 August 1918
The destroyer *Opossum* sank *UC-49* in the eastern Channel. The submarine had fouled one of its own mines, and was then depth-charged three times. (Newbolt 3.429; Grant 120–121)

Oracle v. *U-44*, 12 August 1917
The submarine *U-44*, already damaged by an encounter with the Q-ship *Chagford* in the southern North Sea, was rammed and sunk by the destroyer *Oracle*. (Newbolt 5.130n, 425; Grant 62–63)

***Orama* v. *U-62*, 19 October 1917**
The AMC *Orama*, escorting convoy HD-17 in the Mediterranean, was torpedoed and sunk by *U-62*. (Newbolt 5.163)

***Orange Tree* and *French Victory* v. Dutch ships, 3 August 1666**
The British ships *Orange Tree* (26; Capt. Christopher Gunman) and *French Victory* (13; Capt. Thomas Scott) met two Dutch warships (36 and 40 guns) out of Flushing, and fought. After several hours the English ships were badly damaged, and the Dutch ships sailed on. (Clowes 2.429)

***Orestes* v. *Loup Garou*, 27 October 1810**
The sloop *Orestes* (16; Cmdr John Lapenotiere) met the privateer brig *Loup Garou* (16) and chased and fought her until she surrendered. (James 5.104–105)

***Orfasay* v. *U-68*, 22 October 1943**
The ASW *Orfasay* was sunk by *U-68* off West Africa. (Rohwer 282)

***Orford* v. privateers, 1703**
Orford (70; Capt. John Norris) fought two privateers, *Philippeaux* (36) and one of 16 guns. (Clowes 2.505)

***Orford* and others v. *Hasard*, November 1703**
A squadron of the Mediterranean fleet, consisting of *Orford* (70; Capt. John Norris), *Warspite* (70; Capt. Edmund Loades), and *Lichfield* (50; Capt. Lord Dursley), captured *Hasard* (53) in the Channel. Despite the odds *Hasard* fought for six hours, and was reduced to wreckage when she surrendered. (Clowes 5.505)

***Orford* and *Revenge* v. *Esperance*, 13 November 1755**
The French ship *Esperance* (74; *en flute*) met a British squadron in mid-Atlantic and was attacked by *Orford* (64; Capt. Charles Steevens) and *Revenge* (64; Capt. Frederick Cornwall). *Esperance* fought until the rest of the squadron arrived; but she was so badly damaged that she was burnt. (Clowes 3.289)

Orkney Islands, Scotland
580–581 In 580 King Aidin mac Gabriain of Dal Riata made an expedition against Orkney; another expedition against the islands is mentioned next year, but by whom is not known. (Thompson 7)

c.682 King Bridei mac Bile of the Picts invaded Orkney and devastated the islands. (Thompson 6)

1534 In a dispute over the rulership of Orkney, the Earl of Caithness was commissioned by King James V to restore William Sinclair to power there. He collected an army and a fleet and landed at Orphir, but the invaders were met and defeated at Summersdale by the Orkneymen. (Thompson 137–138)

1557 An English squadron commanded by Sir John Clere went north to escort home the Iceland fishing fleet. Clere landed a force at Kirkwall on 12 August, which was driven off by the Orkneymen; Clere, three of his captains, and 100 of their men were killed; the English artillery was captured. (Clowes 1.422–423; Rodger 1.192–193; Loades 171; Thompson 141)

1614 A rebellion had developed in Orkney; George, Earl of Caithness, was commissioned by the Scottish government to suppress it. He gathered ships at Caithness and guns from Edinburgh Castle, and landed at Carness, near Kirkwall, on 23 August. Neither side had much support from the Orkneymen. Kirkwall Castle was bombarded until, on 30 September, the rebels inside surrendered. (Thompson 177–178)

1652 General-at-Sea Robert Blake, with the main English fleet, sailed to disrupt the Dutch fishing fleet in the North Sea. Off the Orkneys he captured or sank most of the Dutch guardships, and captured 100 of the fishing boats; the rest scattered. He released the captured fishermen. (Clowes 2.154; Powell 159)

Oronsay v. *Archimede*, 9 October 1942
The transport *Oronsay* was attacked and sunk by the Italian submarine *Archimede* in the Gulf of Guinea. (Rohwer 200)

Orpheus v. *Duguay-Trouin*, 5 May 1794
Orpheus (32 Capt. Henry Newcome), part of a British squadron sailing to India, met *Duguay-Trouin* (34) and the corvette *Vulcan* near Mauritius. *Orpheus* chased *Duguay-Trouin*, caught up with her, and forced her surrender. (James 1.226–227; Clowes 4.464)

Orpheus v. *Zeelast* and *Zeevraght*, 24 October 1799
The frigate *Orpheus* (32; William Hills) came up with two Dutch Indiamen near Ternate in the Moluccas; tackling both at the same time by sailing between them, she forced a quick surrender. (James 2.412)

Orpheus v. *Dolores*, 20 November 1806
The barge of the frigate *Orpheus* (32; Capt. Thomas Briggs) captured the schooner *Dolores* (3) near Campeche. (James 4.185)

Orpheus and *Shelburne* v. *Frolic*, 20 April 1814
The US sloop *Frolic* (22) was chased by the frigate *Orpheus* (36; Capt. Hugh Pigot) and the schooner *Shelburne* (12; Lt David Hope). As soon as the British ships came close, *Orpheus* fired two shots, which did not reach *Frolic*; *Frolic* at once surrendered. (James 8.156–157)

Orpheus v. *Turbine*, 16 June 1940
The submarine *Orpheus* was sunk by the Italian destroyer *Turbine* off Tobruk. (Rohwer 27)

Osprey v. Resource, 26 October 1803

The sloop *Osprey* (Cmdr George Younghusband) was becalmed not far from the French privateer *Resource* (4) near Trinidad. Seventeen men in the ship's cutter attacked and captured the privateer, which had a crew of forty-three. (James 3.195–196; Clowes 5.329)

Osprey v. Egyptienne, 23 May 1804

The sloop *Osprey* (18; Cmdr George Younghusband) met the privateer *Egyptienne* (36) near Barbados. After a fight lasting over an hour *Egyptienne* sailed away. (James 3.257–258; Clowes 5.341)

Osprey and others v. Eole, 16 July 1812

The sloop *Osprey* (16; Cmdr Timothy Clinch) and the brigs *Britomart* (10; Cmdr William Hunt) and *Leveret* (10; Cmdr George Willes) sent boats to capture the privateer lugger *Eole* (14) near Heligoland. After rowing for several hours and boarding against stiff resistance, the lugger was captured. (James 5.327–328; Clowes 5.511)

Otranto Barrage, 1915–1918

Italian ships based in Brindisi and Otranto watched the Strait of Otranto for enemy surface ships, but submarines could evade them. The preferred solution to this was a line of anti-submarine nets laid and maintained by drifters and trawlers sent from Britain. At first sixty were sent in September 1915, then another forty in November, and still more later. The intention was that fifty ships at a time were on patrol, but the actual number was usually less. As a means of catching or even deterring submarines it was a complete failure. One submarine, *U-6* (Austrian), was caught on 10 May 1916, and possibly two others at other times.

The drifters were tempting targets for Austrian ships. The drifter *Beneficent* was attacked and sunk by an Austrian squadron of two destroyers and three torpedo boats on 31 May 1916, and two others on 9 July. On 15 May 1917 three Austrian cruisers attacked the drifters, fourteen of which were sunk and three damaged. The cruisers were attacked on their retirement by an Allied force which included the light cruisers *Bristol* and *Dartmouth*. The Austrian cruiser *Novara* was damaged; *Dartmouth* was hit by a torpedo from *UC-25*. The drifters patrolling the nets had thus to be protected by intermittent destroyer patrols. The existence of the barrage probably had little effect on submarines, but it did help to confine the Austrian surface ships to the Adriatic.

An Austrian attempt to attack the Otranto barrage on 22–23 April 1918 was intercepted by the destroyers *Jackal* and *Hornet* off Valona. The five Austrian destroyers badly damaged *Hornet* and hit *Jackal*; but having been intercepted their purpose was revealed, and Allied destroyers – two British, one Australian, one French – converged on the action. The Austrian force withdrew. On 14 May the destroyer *Phoenix* was torpedoed and sunk by *U-27* while patrolling the barrage. (Newbolt 4.292, 296–297, 5.287–288; Halpern, *Naval History* 159–166, 173; Halpern, *Mediterranean* 24–27, 32–34, 279, 450–459; E.K. Chatterton, *Seas of Adventure*, London 1936)

Otter v. French ships, 28 July 1702
The sloop *Otter* (Cmdr Isaac Andrews) was captured in the Channel by two French frigates; Andrews was killed. (Clowes 2.502)

Otter at Rivière Noire, Mauritius, 14 August 1809
The sloop *Otter* (18; Cmdr Nisbet Willoughby) sent boats into Rivière Noire harbour to attack a brig and two other vessels. Only a single lugger could be taken out. (James 5.57–58; Clowes 5.443)

Otway v. *U-49*, 23 July 1917
The AMC *Otway* was sunk by *U-49* in the Minch. (Colledge 292)

Ouse v. *UC-70*, 28 August 1918
The trawler *Ouse*, together with an aeroplane, sank *UC-70* in the North Sea. (Newbolt 3.429; Grant 128–129)

Ouse and *Star* v. *UB-115*, 29 September 1918
The trawlers *Ouse* and *Star* and other trawlers sank *UB-115*, located by an airship in the North Sea. (Newbolt 5.429; Grant 129)

Oxenham in the Pacific, 1576
John Oxenham crossed the Isthmus of Panamá, built a pinnace by a river flowing into the Pacific, and sailed to the Pearl Islands, where he captured two Spanish ships. The released crews raised the alarm and Oxenham and his men were captured when they attempted to return to the Caribbean. All the men were put to death. (Clowes 1.623–624; Andrews 133; Williamson 132–144)

P

***P-33* v. *Partenope*, 23 August 1941**
The Italian TB *Partenope* sank the British submarine *P-33* off Pantelleria while defending a convoy. (Rohwer 92)

***P-38* v. *Circe* and *Usodimare*, 22 February 1942**
An Italian convoy from Messina to Tripoli was attacked by the British submarine *P-38*, but she was sunk by the TB *Circe* and the destroyer *Usodimare*. (Rohwer 146)

***P-46* v. *Gruppo*, 15 December 1942**
The British submarine *P-46* sank a transport from a convoy near Bizerta, but was itself damaged by an attack by the TB *Gruppo*. (Rohwer 218)

***P-48* v. Italian TBs, 24–25 December 1942**
The British submarine *P-48* was damaged by the TB *Perseo* on 24 December and sunk by the Italian TBs *Ardente* and *Ardito* next day. (Rohwer 219)

***P-51* v. *U-61*, 26 March 1918**
The British patrol boat *P-51* sank *U-61* in the North Channel. (Newbolt 5.427; Grant 111–112)

***P-57* v. *UC-47*, 18 November 1917**
The British patrol boat *P-57* rammed and sank *UC-47* in the North Sea. (Newbolt 5.426; Grant 63)

***P-222* v. *Fortunale*, 12 December 1942**
The British submarine *P-222* was sunk by the Italian TB *Fortunale* off Naples. (Rohwer 218)

***P-615* v. *U-123*, 18 April 1943**
The British submarine *P-615* was sunk by *U-123* off Freetown, Sierra Leone; *U-123* also sank four more ships about this time. (Rohwer 242)

***Pakenham* and *Paladin* v. Italian convoy, 16 April 1943**
An Italian convoy was intercepted by the destroyers *Pakenham* and *Paladin* near Marsala, Sicily. The TBs escorting the convoy turned to attack in order that the convoy could get away, and the TB *Cigno* was sunk. *Pakenham* was badly damaged in the fight and later sank. (Rohwer 241)

***Paladin* v. *U-205*, 17 February 1943**
U-205 attacked a convoy off Derna, North Africa, but was located, depth-charged, and sunk by the destroyer *Paladin*. (Sebag-Montefiore 268–270; Rohwer 226)

Palamos, Spain

1695 A force of soldiers was landed from Admiral Edward Russell's Mediterranean fleet in August to co-operate with Spanish forces in the siege of Palamos. They were quickly re-embarked when news was received that the French fleet had come out. (Corbett 2.181)

1810 A force of 350 seamen and 250 marines was landed at Palamos on 13 December from a squadron commanded by Capt. Thomas Rogers of *Kent* (74). The aim was to destroy several vessels in the harbour. This was done with little opposition, but in retiring the force was attacked and driven back headlong, losing a third of its strength. (James 5.129–130; Clowes 5.476–477; Hall 169–170)

Palermo, Sicily, 3 January 1943
British 'Chariots' – midget submarines – launched by the submarines *Thunderbolt* and *Trooper*, attacked ships in Palermo harbour; they sank the cruiser *Ulpio Traiano* and a transport. (Rohwer 224)

***Pallas* at Conquet Roads, 14 July 1759**
The frigate *Pallas* (36; Capt. Michael Clements) went in to Conquet Roads to cut out four merchant ships. They proved to be Swedish, loaded with contraband cargoes. They were sent to Plymouth for examination. (NRS, *Hawke* nos. 222–223b)

***Pallas* and *Niger* v. *Diadème*, 1760**
The French *Diadème* (74), escorting a convoy from Martinique, was met by *Pallas* (36; Capt. Michael Clements) and *Niger* (32; Capt. John Bentinck) which attacked without success, and were driven off with considerable damage. (Clowes 3.303)

***Pallas* on the Biscay coast, April–May 1806**
The frigate *Pallas* (32; Capt. Lord Cochrane) made a series of destructive raids on signal stations and batteries along the Vendée coast. On 5–6 April a boat party went 20 miles up the estuary of the Gironde and captured the corvette *Tapageuse*, though a second corvette could not be reached. *Pallas* was menaced by three other corvettes (*Garonne*, *Gloire*, and *Malicieuse*), all of which were driven on shore. On 14 May the ship went in close to Ile d'Aix to tempt the frigate *Minerve* (44) to attack. This it did, but the subsequent fight brought both ships to near ruin. (James 4.138–142; Clowes 5.376–379; Thomas 95–96)

***Pancras* v. U-boat, 3 May 1918**
The troop transport *Pancras*, without troops on board, was torpedoed by a U-boat in the Mediterranean, but reached port. (Newbolt 5.292)

***Pandora* v. *Rigault de Genouilly*, 3 July 1940**
The British submarine *Pandora* sank the French sloop *Rigault de Genouilly* off North Africa. This was a follow-up to the bombardment of Mers el-Kebir. (Rohwer 31)

Pandora v. *Cosenz*, 28 September 1940
The British submarine *Pandora* sank one ship from an Italian convoy, and was then driven off by the TB escort *Cosenz*. (Rohwer 41)

Pansy (or *Pensée*) v. *Lion*, 1549
The Scots ship *Lion* attacked the English *Pansy* (or *Pensée*) and captured her; *Lion* was wrecked soon after. (Clowes 1.467)

Pantaleon v. slaver, 26 May 1845
The brig *Pantaleon* (10; Cmdr Edward Wilson) sent three boats to attack a large slaver, which was boarded from both sides and captured after a bitter fight. (Clowes 6.365)

Pantelleria Island
1586 Five ships of the Turkey Company sailed for home from the Levant as a group. They were *Merchant Royal* (Capt. Edward Williamson, elected commodore), *Toby*, *Edward Bonaventure*, *William and John*, and *Susan*. They were intercepted by a Spanish squadron out of Sicily which demanded their surrender. The captains, who had expected this, refused and were attacked. All the English ships survived with little damage, but several of the Spanish ships – eleven galleys and two frigates – were damaged in being driven off. (Clowes 1.481–482)

1943 Pantelleria was shelled on 31 May and 1 June. A landing was made on the island on 10–11 June and the island surrendered at once. The nearby islands of Lampedusa, Linosa, and Lampione were taken in the next few days. (Rohwer 253; Greene and Massignani 286–287)

Panther and *Argo* v. *Santissima Trinidad*, 31 October 1761
Panther (60; Cmdr George Ourry) and *Argo* (28; Capt. Richard King) were sent from Manila in search of the annual Spanish galleon from Acapulco; instead they found and captured the galleon *Santissima Trinidad* which had left Manila three months before but was still in the Philippines. She carried treasure worth $3 million. (Clowes 3.241)

Papillon v. *Concepcion*, 15 April 1805
A boat from the sloop *Papillon* (Cmdr William Woolsey) at Savanna La Mar, Jamaica, captured the Spanish privateer *Concepcion* in a swift assault. (James 4.30)

Pargust v. *UC-29*, 7 June 1917
The Q-ship *Pargust* successfully engaged and sank *UC-29* off southern Ireland, despite having been torpedoed. (Newbolt 3.57, 425; Grant 67)

Parktown and others v. S-boats, 22 June 1942
The German 3rd S-boat Flotilla, operating from Derna, North Africa, attacked British ships leaving Tobruk; the South African Navy minesweeper *Parktown*, two motor launches, and six landing craft and other ships were sunk; *S-58* was damaged. (Rohwer 174)

Parthian v. Greek schooner, 23 September 1827
The sloop *Parthian* (10; Cmdr G.F. Hotham), escorting a convoy from Malta, met a Greek schooner near Cerigo, which refused to stop when challenged and made serious efforts to get away. Hotham fired near her and then into her, and when she stopped found no cargo but plenty of arms. She was detained as a probable pirate. (NRS, *Piracy* 207–210)

Partridge and *Pellew* v. German destroyers, 12 December 1917
An attack on a convoy heading for Scandinavia was mounted by four ships of the German 2nd Destroyer Half-flotilla. Of the convoy escort the destroyer *Partridge* was sunk, and *Pellew* damaged. The whole convoy was sunk. (Newbolt 5.188–193)

Partridge v. *U-565*, 18 December 1942
The destroyer *Partridge* was sunk by *U-565* in the western Mediterranean. (Rohwer 216)

Pasley v. Spanish xebec, 21 July 1801
The brig *Pasley* (16; Lt William Woolridge), off Cabrera, met a Spanish xebec of 22 guns. The two fought. When a calm fell, the xebec got away under sweeps to Ibiza. (James 3.149; Clowes 4.540)

Pasley v. *Virgen del Rosario*, 28 October 1801
The brig *Pasley* (16; Lt William Woolridge) was chased by the Spanish polacre *Virgen del Rosario* off Cape da Gata. The Spanish ship's guns were about to reduce *Pasley* to ruin, when Lt Woolridge ran his ship close under his opponent's bow and boarded and captured her. (James 3.149–150)

Passage of the Var, 30 June 1707
An Austro-Savoyard army invaded Provence from Italy. A party of seamen from the British Mediterranean fleet landed from four ships which also covered the landing with a bombardment. The men assisted the allied army in passing the River Var. (Clowes 2.410)

Patani, Malaya, 17 July 1619
Two EIC ships under the factor John Jourdain were attacked by a Dutch squadron of three ships. Jourdain was killed and the ships were compelled to surrender. (Foster 274)

Pathfinder v. *U-21*, 5 September 1914
The destroyer *Pathfinder* (Capt. Martin Leake) was sunk by a torpedo from *U-21* off St Abbs Head, North Sea. (Corbett 1.163)

Pathfinder and others v. *U-859* and *U-198*, 4–6 July 1944
U-859 and *U-198* were hunted by the destroyer *Pathfinder* and a South African ASW trawler group near Madagascar, without success. (Rohwer 327)

***Patia* v. *UC-49*, 13 June 1918**
The AMC *Patia* was sunk by *UC-49* in the Bristol Channel. (Colledge 299)

***Patriot* v. *Snap*, 29 May 1809**
The Danish ship *Snap* (3) was captured in the North Sea by *Patriot* (10; Lt Edward Mansell). (Clowes 5.565)

***PC-61* v. *UC-33*, 26 September 1917**
The British patrol boat *PC-61* rammed and sank *UC-33* in the Irish Sea. (Newbolt 5.26; Grant 6)

***PC-62* v. *U-84*, 26 January 1918**
The British patrol boat *PC-62* sank *U-84* in the North Channel. (Newbolt 5.427; Grant 109)

***Peacock* v. *Hornet*, 24 February 1813**
The US sloop *Hornet* (20), off Demerara, was attacked by the sloop *Peacock* (18; Cmdr William Peake). *Hornet* fired more efficiently, and *Peacock* surrendered, then sank. Peake was killed. (James 6.46–49; Clowes 6.54–55; NC 5.291–293)

***Pearl* v. Dutch warship, 16 February 1667**
Pearl (22; Capt. Benjamin Carterett) was escorting a convoy of colliers in the North Sea when she was attacked by a Dutch warship of 50 guns. The fighting lasted for several hours, but when *Little Victory* (28), also with the convoy, was able to reach the fighting, the Dutch ship left. (Clowes 2.434)

***Pearl* v. Dutch privateer, February 1673**
Pearl (22; Capt. John Ashby), on the way to Jersey, met a Dutch privateer (22), and fought her to the point of surrender, but could not secure her. (Clowes 2.447)

***Pearl* v. French ship, 1681**
Pearl (22; Capt. Henry Williams) fought a French vessel in the Channel which had refused to salute; the French ship was effectively destroyed. (Clowes 2.457)

***Pearl* and *Lyme* v. *Adventure*, 21 November 1718**
The ship *Adventure* of the pirate Edward Thatch (or Teach, or Blackbeard) was hidden in Ocracoke inlet, Virginia. Lt Robert Maynard of *Pearl* (40) with men also from *Lyme* (20) rowed into the inlet in two hired sloops. Thatch thought he killed many of the sailors by an initial burst of gunfire, but he was wrong. He was killed when the ship was boarded. (Clowes 3.259–260; Earle 194)

***Pearl* v. *Lexington*, October 1776 or 1777**
The frigate *Pearl* (32) captured the rebel American ship *Lexington* in the West Indies, but the captured crew retook the ship later. (Clowes 4.10)

Pearl v. *Santa Monica*, 14 September 1779
The frigate *Pearl* (32; Capt. George Montagu) chased the Spanish frigate *Santa Monica* off Fayal in the Azores, and captured her after a two-hour fight. On the 30th *Pearl* also captured the French frigate *Espérance* (32). (Clowes 4.33; Colledge 300)

Pearl v. *Regenerée* and *Vertu*, 24–25 April 1798
The frigate *Pearl* (32; Capt. Samuel Ballard) encountered the French frigates *Regenerée* (40) and *Vertu* (40), recently arrived from Mauritius, at anchor in the Isles of Los, West Africa. *Pearl* attacked *Regenerée*, but when *Vertu* arrived she was chased away. (James 2.246)

Pearl v. Genoese polacre, 9 February 1800
The frigate *Pearl* (32; Capt. Samuel Ballard), in the Mediterranean, drove a Genoese polacre (14) ashore. (Clowes 4.557)

Pearl at Santa Cruz Island, 12 August 1875
The screw corvette *Pearl* (Commodore James Goodenough) visited Carlisle Bay on Santa Cruz Island in the Solomon Islands. The landing party was attacked as it re-embarked and Goodenough retaliated by burning the village. He and two seamen died of their wounds. (Clowes 7.265–267)

Pegasus v. *Echo* and *Gier*, 12 May 1796
The frigate *Pegasus* (28; Capt. Ross Donnelly), off Friesland, drove the Dutch brigs *Echo* (12) and *Gier* (12) ashore. (Clowes 4.558)

Pegasus v. *Königsberg*, 20 September 1914
The old light cruiser *Pegasus* (Cmdr Ingles) at Zanzibar was attacked by the German light cruiser *Königsberg*, and sank soon afterwards. (Corbett 1.295–296; Halpern, *Naval History* 77)

Pehtang, China, 1 August 1860
A combined Franco-British force was landed at Pehtang in order to attack the Taku forts 50 miles away (which had defeated earlier seaborne attacks). The land attack was assisted by bombardments by British ships in the Peiho estuary and after a day's fighting the forts were taken. The way was thus opened for the expedition to move upriver to capture Peking (Beijing). (Clowes 7.133–135; Graham 396–400)

Pelican v. *Medée*, 23–25 September 1796
The sloop *Pelican* (18; Capt. John Searle) was pursued near Desirade Island, West Indies, by the French frigate *Medée* (36). Although badly undermanned, *Pelican* turned to fight, and after a short engagement, *Medée* left. *Pelican*, recovered and repaired after the fight, saw and captured *Alcyon*, a British army victualler which had been *Medée*'s prize. Next morning, however, *Medée* recaptured the ship. (James 1.396–398; Clowes 4.203)

Pelican v. Trompeur, 17 September 1797
Near St Domingue the sloop *Pelican* (18; Lt Thomas White) chased the privateer *Trompeur* (12). The fight lasted five hours, until *Trompeur* suffered an explosion and sank. *Pelican* rescued sixty of her men. (James 2.100–101)

Pelican v. Laurette, 23 August 1804
The French schooner *Laurette* (5) was captured by the frigate *Pelican* (18; Cmdr John Marshall) off Jamaica. (Clowes 4.556)

Pelican v. Argus, 14 August 1813
The sloop *Pelican* (18; Cmdr John Maples) searched for the US sloop *Argus* (16) which was attacking shipping in the Irish Sea. The two met near St David's Head, and after battering *Argus* into unmanageability, *Pelican* boarded and captured her. (James 6.78–82; Clowes 6.86–88; NC 5.164–165)

Pelican in the Aegean, 1827
Pelican (18; Capt. Charles Irby) campaigned against Greek pirates in the Aegean. *Aphrodite* (4) was captured on 3 January; a Turkish ship was attacked on 2 March (by mistake); the town of Scardamoula was bombarded on 13 June; a pirate vessel was destroyed on 15 June. (Clowes 6.251–252; NRS, *Piracy* 77–79, 114–116)

Pelican and others v. U-342, 26 August 1943
U-342 was damaged by depth-charges in attacks by the sloops *Pelican* and *Egret* and four frigates (the 5th Support Group). (Rohwer 268)

Pellew's squadron at Batavia, 27 November 1806
The squadron of Rear-Admiral Sir Edward Pellew, four line-of-battle ships, two frigates, and a brig, arrived in the roads at Batavia. The Dutch warships there immediately ran themselves ashore, except the corvette *William*, which surrendered. Boats went in to destroy the grounded ships. The frigate *Phoenix* was scuttled: she and the rest were set on fire. (James 4.180–181; Clowes 5.392–393; Parkinson 296–298; NC 3.333–334)

Pellew's squadron at Griessee, Java, 5–6 December 1807
Rear-Admiral Sir Edward Pellew took his squadron (two 74s, two frigates, and four sloops) to Griessee where there were two Dutch warships, *Revolutie* and *Pluto*, each of 68 guns. A party sent in under a flag of truce was detained and the commodore refused Pellew's demands. Pellew then bombarded the place until the council at Surabaya returned the prisoners and agreed to Pellew's demands. The commodore scuttled the ships and the British burned them. (James 4.283–284; Parkinson 306 –307; Clowes 5.239–240)

Pellew's fleet at Cassis, Provence, 18 August 1813
Boats from many of the ships of the Mediterranean fleet, commanded by Vice-Admiral Sir Edmund Pellew, went in to attack the defences of Cassis. Led by the frigate *Undaunted* (36; Capt. Thomas Ussher) and the sloops *Redwing* (Cmdr Sir John Sinclair) and *Kite* (Cmdr Hon. Robert Spencer) the

landing was accomplished with some loss; three gunboats and twenty-five merchant ships were taken or destroyed. (James 6.19; Clowes 5.534)

Pelorus v. slaver, 1835
A slaver in the New Calabar River repeatedly avoided capture by unloading slaves when an attack appeared imminent. Eventually Cmdr Meredith of the sloop *Pelorus* seized the ship anyway; he was fined £1800 for this illegality. (Lloyd 71)

Pembroke v. Dutch ship, spring 1667
Twice in several days *Pembroke* (32; Capt. Arthur Herbert) fought a Dutch ship (34) near Cadiz; neither could claim the victory, but the Dutch ship finally took refuge in neutral waters. (Clowes 2.436)

Pembroke and *Falcon* v. French squadron, 29 December 1709
Pembroke (64; Capt. Edward Rumsey) and *Falcon* (32; Capt. Charles Constable) were chased by a squadron of three French ships, *Sérieux* (70) and others of 60 and 50 guns, in the Mediterranean. Both were battered into a ruinous condition and suffered enormous casualties before surrendering. (Clowes 2.523)

Pembroke v. *Ferme*, 4 August 1746
The French ship *Ferme* (54) was captured by *Pembroke* (60). (Clowes 3.312)

Pendennis and convoy v. French squadron, 20 October 1705
A convoy of English ships from the Baltic, escorted by *Pendennis* (50; Capt. John Foljambe), *Blackwall* (50; Capt. Samuel Martin), and *Sorlings* (32; Capt. William Coney), was attacked by a French squadron of four warships and five armed merchantmen commanded by the Chevalier de St Pol. The English escorts and merchantmen were all captured. Foljambe, Martin, and St Pol were killed. (Clowes 2.509; Owen 127)

Penelope v. *Goeland*, 16 April 1793
The frigate *Penelope* (32; Capt. Bartholomew Rowley) captured the French sloop *Goeland* (16) in the West Indies. (Clowes 4.552)

Penelope and *Iphigenia* v. *Inconstante*, 25 November 1793
The frigates *Penelope* (32; Capt. Bartholomew Rowley) and *Iphigenia* (32; Capt. Patrick Sinclair) met the French frigate *Inconstante* (36) south of St Domingue. *Penelope* caught up with and fought the French ship; *Iphigenia*'s arrival persuaded *Inconstante* to surrender. (James 1.122; Clowes 4.481)

Penelope v. *Vivo* and *Nuestra Senora del Carmen*, 8 July 1799
The hired cutter *Penelope* (Lt David Hamline) sailed from Gibraltar to investigate some firing nearby, only to find herself amid the whole Spanish fleet. Attacked by the corvette *Vivo*, she was eventually captured by the frigate *Nuestra Senora del Carmen*. (James 2.298–299)

Penelope v. *Nuestra Senora del Carmen*, 26 January 1800
The frigate *Penelope* (32; Capt. Hon. Henry Blackwood) captured the Spanish sloop *Nuestra Senora del Carmen* (16) in the Mediterranean. (Clowes 4.561)

Penguin v. *Malicieuse* and *Opale*, 28 March 1760
Penguin (20; Capt. William Harris) was attacked by *Malicieuse* (32) and *Opale* (32) near the Bayona Islands and forced to surrender, and was burned. (Clowes 3.302)

Penguin v. *Oiseau* and *Express*, 21 August 1797
The sloop *Penguin* (16; Cmdr John Pulling) was challenged by two armed brigs and the privateer *Oiseau* (18) and her prize *Express* (14). *Express* was quickly (re-)captured; *Penguin* chased *Oiseau* for a time before she also surrendered. (James 2.99–100)

Penguin v. three French ships, 18 February 1801
The sloop *Penguin* (16; Cmdr Robert Mansel) met a group of three ships, a corvette and two armed merchantmen, near Tenerife. The ships manoeuvred for some time until *Penguin* was able to fire on one of the merchantmen, which surrendered, but then the corvette attacked, and *Penguin* received such damage as permitted her antagonists to reach Tenerife. (James 3.125–127; Clowes 4.537)

Penguin v. *Renommée*, 17–25 March 1804
The sloop *Penguin* (16; Cmdr George Morris) drove the privateer *Renommée* on shore at the estuary of the Senegal River; a week later *Penguin* went in to complete the work. *Renommée* had two other schooners with her. Fire was exchanged for some time, then a boat was sent in to destroy *Renommée*. (James 3.257; Clowes 5.360)

Penguin v. *Hornet*, 23 March 1815
The US sloop *Hornet* (20), off Tristan da Cunha, was challenged by the sloop *Penguin* (18; Cmdr James Dickinson), but in the fight which followed *Penguin* was dismasted and forced to surrender. Dickinson was killed. (James 6.261–266; Clowes 6.173–175)

Penobscot, Maine
1779 Commodore Sir George Collier took a squadron of seven ships, including *Raisonnable* (64), to break the rebel American siege of Penobscot on 13 August. In the river he was confronted by a line of forty-one American vessels; his ships attacked and they scattered; most were captured or destroyed in the pursuit. (Clowes 4.28–29)

1814 A force of soldiers landed from a British squadron in the Penobscot River on 1 September and marched to locate and capture the frigate *Adams* at Hamden. The ship was burnt before it could be captured. (James 6.200–203; Clowes 6.148; *NC* 5.244)

Penshurst v. *UB-19*, 13 November 1916
UB-19 attacked the Q-ship *Penshurst* in the English Channel. The crew of *Penshurst* put on a show of abandoning the ship; when the submarine came close, they sank her. (Grant 38)

Penshurst v. *UB-37*, 14 January 1917
Penshurst was attacked by *UB-37* and apparently abandoned, but when the submarine approached, she was sunk by gunfire and depth-charges. (Grant 64)

Penshurst v. *U-84*, 22 February 1917
Penshurst encountered *U-84* south of Ireland and damaged her by gunfire, but the submarine escaped without having to dive. (Grant 64)

Penshurst v. *U-110*, 24 December 1917
The Q-ship *Penshurst* was sunk by *U-110* in the Bristol Channel. (Colledge 303)

Perak, Malaya, November 1875
The British Resident in Perak was murdered, and a retaliatory attack by a small naval party was defeated. Six ships were brought to the area. Parties from the gunvessels *Thistle* (Cmdr Francis Stirling) and *Fly* (Cmdr John Bruce) were landed and they attacked and burned villages. The ships formed a Naval Brigade from *Thistle*, *Fly*, the screw corvette *Modeste* (14; Capt. Alexander Buller), the screw sloop *Egeria* (Cmdr Ralph Turton), and the screw gunvessels *Ringdove* (Cmdr Uvedale Singleton) and *Philomel* (Cmdr Edward Garforth) for further land operations. (Clowes 7.272–273)

Perdrix v. *Armée d'Italie*, 11 December 1798
The sloop *Perdrix* (22; Capt. William Fahie) found the French privateer *Armée d'Italie* off St Thomas, Leeward Islands; the two ships fought for an hour until *Armée d'Italie*, severely damaged, surrendered. (James 2.272–273)

Perlin v. *Trident* and *Amélie*, 22 November 1811
The frigate *Perlin* (38; Cmdr Joseph Tetley) was chased from Toulon by part of the French fleet which had come out for a brief exercising cruise. *Trident* (74) and the frigate *Amélie* persisted in the chase but were unable to catch *Perlin*, which, by contrast, was able to fire effectually at her pursuers. All three were damaged in the rigging. The French ships in the end turned back to port. (James 5.209–210)

Pernambuco, Brazil, 1594
James Lancaster, in command of a small squadron, seized Pernambuco, which he held for a month, capturing about thirty ships and their cargoes. (Clowes 1.653–654; M. Franks, *The Basingstoke Admiral*, Salisbury 2006, 77–94; Foster 135)

Perseverance v. Lively and Hirondelle, 29 July 1781
The French ships *Lively* (28) and *Hirondelle* (16) met a British fleet in the Channel; *Hirondelle* got away, but *Lively* was captured by *Perseverance* (36; Capt. Skeffington Lutwidge), after a long fight. (Clowes 4.72)

Perseverance v. Alerte, 1781
The frigate *Perseverance* (36; Capt. Skeffington Lutwidge) captured the French sloop *Alerte* (18) in North American waters. (Clowes 4.114)

Persian Gulf
The Portuguese Wars
1620 An EIC fleet under Capt. Andrew Shilling sailed to the Persian Gulf to conduct trade at Jask in December. A Portuguese fleet intervened, and fighting took place; the English ships were victorious, though Shilling was killed

1621–1622 An EIC fleet arrived at the entrance to the Persian Gulf to reinforce the ships already there. The commander, Capt. John Weddell, allied with the Persians to besiege the Portuguese castles on Hormuz Island and Kishm Island. Both were captured

1625 An Anglo-Dutch squadron of eight ships was formed to block a Portuguese attempt to recover Hormuz. The enemies met on 31 January and fought until 4 February. *Royal James* (Capt. John Weddell) particularly fought well, though suffering considerable damage in the process. The Portuguese returned to the fight on 13 February, and Weddell concentrated all his force on the Portuguese flagship, *San Francisco*, which suffered badly until *San Sebastian* came up to interpose and take *Royal James*'s fire. The Portuguese retired, not pursued. On 8 November the EIC ship *Lion*, already badly damaged, reached Gombroon and traded. A Portuguese force of 'frigates' – small heavily manned vessels – attacked. *Lion* was set on fire and the last defenders blew her up. The survivors were beheaded by the Portuguese; one man was spared to give the news to the Company. (Foster 308–311; Clowes 2.40–45, 327)

The Dutch War
1652 A Dutch fleet captured the EIC ships *Roebuck* and *Lannerat* off Jask, and soon after *Blessing* was taken and *Supply* driven on shore and lost

Pirate Wars
1768 Two BM ships and a reluctant Persian fleet attacked the pirate island of Kerak. The pirate fleet was defeated, but attacks on the fort were driven off

1775 A squadron of EIC ships helped resist a Persian attack on Basra. On 10 April as the EIC ships sailed downriver a battle broke out between *Eagle* (16) and *Success* (14) and the Persian fleet of galivats. Two days later the Persians withdrew into the gulf. The EIC ships joined others at Bushire. (Low 1.52–53, 163–171)

1797 The EIC brig *Viper* was attacked unexpectedly by dhows of Joasmi pirates in Bushire Roads in October. She beat off her assailants, but with heavy casualties. (Low 1.313–314)

1805 In reply to several attacks by Joasmi pirates in the gulf, the EIC ship *Mornington* (22) and a squadron of Omani ships blockaded the pirates at Kishm Island. A treaty was made, but lasted only a short time. (Low 1.317)

1808 The EIC schooner *Sylph* (8; Lt W.C. Graham) was captured by boarding by Joasmi pirates. (Low 1.321–322)

1809 A squadron of the frigates *Chiffonne* (36; Capt. John Wainwright) and *Caroline* (36; Capt. Charles Gordon) and six EIC cruisers attacked the pirate towns Ras al-Khaimah, Linga, and Luft on the Arabian coast in November. Almost 100 dhows and other craft were destroyed

1816 The BM ship *Aurora* (14; Capt. Jeakes), escorting a convoy, was attacked by fifteen Joasmi pirate dhows, but resisted effectively, sinking several of them and protecting the convoy. An attempt was made in December to persuade the chief of Ras al-Khaimah to provide restitution of pirate plunder but thus failed; the forts were then bombarded by the EIC ships *Vestal* and *Ariel*, without result. (Low 1.342–346)

1818 The EIC brig *Antelope* (Lt Tanner) fought a fleet of pirate dhows near Kishm, Persian Gulf on 21 December; ships of the Imam of Muscat were rescued and the pirates driven off

1819 An expedition was sent to suppress pirates in the gulf, carried and escorted by *Liverpool* (50; Capt. Francis Collier) with *Eden* (26; Capt. Francis Loch) and *Curlew* (18; Cmdr William Walpole). The defences of Ras al-Khaimah were captured and destroyed, as were ships in the port. Treaties were made with other pirate towns. (Low 1.351–366; Clowes 6.234)

1835 The EIC sloop *Elphinstone* was attacked by seven large dhows off Abu Dhabi, Persian Gulf. Capt. Sawyer sailed between two of the dhows, held his fire to the last moment, then a single broadside destroyed two of the ships; the rest fled. (Low 1.317–318, 325–336, 340–341, 347–348, 2.18–21; James 5.66–67; H. Moyse-Bartlett, *The Pirates of Trucial Oman*, London 1966, 33–34)

The Persian War
1856 An EIC expedition against Persia was sent from Bombay. An opposed landing was made at Hallilah Bay, Bushire, covered by Indian Navy ships which bombarded Persian shore positions. The fort at Bushire was bombarded into surrender

1857 A fleet of transports escorted by a squadron of Indian Navy ships sailed up the Shatt el-Arab to land the army at Mohammerah in March. The fortifications were bombarded and troops landed upstream. The Persian army soon retreated. (Low 2. 340–348, 351–357; B. English, *John Company's Last War*, London 1971, 81–97, 121–134)

More Pirate Wars
1866 The corvette *Highflyer* (Capt. Thomas Pasley), attempting to suppress piracy in the gulf, destroyed two forts and some dhows, and attacked the fort at El Katif; neither a landing nor a bombardment had any effect

1868–1869 The screw gunvessel *Vigilant* (Cmdr Ralph Brown) and BM ships *Sir Hugh Rose*, *Sinde*, and *Clyde* attacked the fort and ships at Bahrain, which had become a base for pirates. The place was bombarded for two days, at the end of which political adjustments were made. The operation had to be repeated next year by the screw sloops *Daphne* (Cmdr George Douglas) and *Nymphe* (Cmdr Edward Meara) and two BM ships. The island was blockaded and Manama fort captured. *Nymphe* and *Daphne* then cruised in the gulf and the Indian Ocean to suppress the slave trade, capturing sixty slavers of various sizes. The paddle sloop *Spiteful* (Cmdr Benjamin Lefroy) also cruised in the gulf for a month, attacking slavers. Six ships were destroyed and 200 slaves set free. (Clowes 7.214, 224–226)

1878 *Vulture* (Cmdr John Pringle) intervened at El Katif fort, which was under attack by a Bedouin force, by attacking a fleet of dhows nearby; twenty were captured; about 100 Arabs were killed or wounded. The siege was lifted. (Clowes 7.289–290)

The Great War
1914 An expedition from India was sent to take control of the waterways near the oil installations at Abadan. The Turkish fort at the mouth of the delta was shelled and a landing was made at Saniyeh. The squadron in the gulf, the sloops *Odin* and *Espiegle* and the Indian Marine ship *Lawrence*, moved up the Shatt el-Arab; *Espiegle* was fired at from an Ottoman position at Bulzanieh, and the Turkish gunboat *Marmaris* was driven off. On 22 November the city of Basra surrendered and was occupied. (Corbett 1.377–379, 387–391; Halpern, *Naval History* 124–125)

Hitler's War
1940 The Italian submarine *Galvani*, having recently sunk the Indian sloop *Pathan*, was attacked and sunk by the sloop *Falmouth* in the gulf on 23 June.

1941 A squadron of RN and RIN ships attacked Iranian bases at Abadan on 25 August. The sloop *Shoreham* sank the gunboat *Palang*. In the Karin estuary *Yarra* (RAN) captured *Chahbaaz* and *Karkass*, and sank *Babr*. At Bandar Abbas a group of German and Italian freighters was seized. (Rohwer 27, 95)

Iraq Wars (Gulf Wars)
1991 A squadron of RN ships was placed in the gulf, originally as the Armilla Patrol to catch contraband heading for Iraq, but then as part of the Allied forces for the invasion of Iraq and the liberation of Kuwait. The main action was by naval helicopters against Iraqi TBs armed with missiles in the Babiyan Channel. On 29 and 30 January many of these TBs were destroyed. The mine-clearing force came under attack on 25 February, but without casualties. (C.J.S. Craig, 'Gulf War: The Maritime Campaign', *RUSI*

Journal 137, 1992, 11–16; Andrew Lambert, 'The Naval War', in J. Pimlott and G. Badsey (eds), *The Gulf War Assessed*, London 1992, 125–126)

2003 An RN contingent in the gulf assisted US forces in the capture of the port of Umm Qais, in clearing mines (the US not having effective mine-hunting capability), and in providing supporting fire for land forces when asked. (Joanna Kidd, 'Campaign Analysis: Maritime Forces', in P. Cornish (ed.), *The Conflict in Iraq 2003*, London 2004)

Perth, Scotland, 1332
King Edward Balliol and his men were besieged in Perth, when their ships in the river were attacked by a Scots squadron under the 'pirate' John Crabbe. One English ship was burned, but the rest were well defended and the Scots were driven off. (Clowes 1.231–232)

***Perugia* v. *U-63*, 3 December 1916**
Perugia, a Q-ship, was sunk by *U-63* in the Gulf of Genoa. (Colledge 304)

***Petard* and others v. *U-559*, 30 October 1942**
U-559 was compelled to surface by the destroyers *Petard*, *Pakenham*, *Hero*, *Dulverton*, and *Hurworth*. Enigma materials were recovered, but the two men in the submarine doing this were killed as she sank. (Rohwer 208; Sebag-Montefiore 256–262; David Kahn, *Seizing the Enigma*, London 1992)

***Petard* v. *Uarsciek*, 15 December 1942**
The Italian submarine *Uarsciek* was forced to the surface by the destroyer *Petard* and the Greek destroyer *Vassilissa Olga* south of Malta. She and her code books were captured; she later sank. (Rohwer 219)

***Peterel* at Finale, 25 April 1796**
The sloop *Peterel* (16; Cmdr John Temple), one of a squadron commanded by Capt. Horatio Nelson, captured a convoy at Finale in Liguria. (James 1.343; Clowes 4.284)

***Peterel* v. three Spanish frigates, 12 November 1798**
The sloop *Peterel* (16; Cmdr Charles Long) was captured by three Spanish frigates on 12 November; next day she was retaken by *Argo* (44; Capt. James Brown). (Clowes 4.550, 560)

***Peterel* and *Mermaid* v. *Ligurienne* and others, 21 March 1800**
The sloop *Peterel* (16; Cmdr Francis Austen) attacked a French convoy off Provence escorted by *Cerf* (14), *Ligurienne* (14), and *Lejoille* (6). The approach of the frigate *Mermaid* (32; Capt. Robert Oliver) persuaded the French ships to leave, but *Peterel* succeeded in forcing the surrender of *Ligurienne*. *Cerf* and the xebec *Lejoille* were driven ashore. (James 3.10–11; Clowes 4.530)

Peterhead, Scotland, 22 December 1715
The Old Pretender, Prince James Stuart ('James III and VIII'), sailed in a

small ship from Dunkirk and landed at Peterhead, carried ashore on the back of a soldier. By the time he arrived the Jacobite rising in Scotland provoked by the union with England had effectively collapsed. (Lavery 40)

Petit Guavas, St Domingue, 23 July 1697
A squadron of English ships under Rear-Admiral George Mees was detached from the main fleet in the West Indies to raid the town of Petit Guavas. It was captured without difficulty by a landing party, but the men got helplessly drunk on local rum; Mees withdrew. (Clowes 2.493–494)

Petropavlovsk, 1854–1855
The Russian port of Petropavlovsk, Kamchatka, was attacked by the allied squadron in the Pacific. The first attack, in August 1854, was a bombardment, but the British commander, Rear-Admiral David Price, committed suicide and the attack was called off. A new attack next year, a combined bombardment and landing, commanded by Rear-Admiral Henry Bruce, was successful. By this time, however, the target of the attacks, Russian warships, had all left. (Clowes 6.429–432, 475; J.D. Grainger, *The First Pacific War*, Woodbridge 2008)

Petunia v. *Barbarigo*, 6 October 1942
The Italian submarine *Barbarigo*, off Freetown, attacked the corvette *Petunia*, unsuccessfully. (Rohwer 200)

Peverel v. *U-63*, 6 November 1917
Peverel, operating as a decoy ship, was sunk by *U-63* off Gibraltar. (Colledge 306)

Phaeton v. *Général Dumouriez*, 14 April 1793
A British squadron bound for the Mediterranean encountered the privateer *Général Dumouriez* (22) and her prize, the Spanish galleon *Santa Rosa*. These were captured after a chase and a fight by *Phaeton* (38; Cmdr Andrew Douglas). *Santa Rosa* had been laden with treasure worth £200,000, which was eventually adjudged prize, a fact which much annoyed the Spanish government. (James 1.100)

Phaeton v. *Prompte*, 28 May 1793
The French sloop *Prompte* was captured by the frigate *Phaeton* (38; Cmdr Andrew Douglas) in the Bay of Biscay. (Clowes 4.552)

Phaeton v. *Echoue*, July 1795
The French frigate *Echoue* (28) was forced ashore on the Ile de Re and then destroyed by the frigate *Phaeton* (38; Capt. Hon. Robert Stopford). (Clowes 4.553)

Phaeton v. *Bonne Citoyenne*, 10 March 1796
Phaeton (36; Capt. Hon. Robert Stopford) and two other frigates chased *Bonne Citoyenne* (20); *Phaeton* performed the capture. (Clowes 4.494)

Phaeton and *Anson* v. *Flore*, 7 September 1798
The frigates *Phaeton* and *Anson* (Capts Hon. Robert Stopford and Philip Durham) chased and captured the privateer *Flore* off the estuary of the Gironde. (James 2.269)

Phaeton and others v. *Hirondelle*, 20 November 1798
The French sloop *Hirondelle* (20) was captured in the English Channel by the frigates *Ambuscade*, *Phaeton*, and *Stag*. (Clowes 4.556)

Phaeton v. *San Josef*, 27 October 1800
The polacre *San Josef* (14), in Fuengirola harbour, Spain, was captured and brought out, after considerable resistance, by a boat party from the frigate *Phaeton* (38; Capt. James Morris). (James 3.33–34; Clowes 4.534)

Phaeton and *Harrier* v. *Semillante*, 2–4 August 1805
The French frigate *Semillante* had taken in a cargo for Mexico at Manila, but was intercepted by the frigate *Phaeton* (Capt. John Wood) and the sloop *Harrier* (18; Cmdr Edward Ratsey). *Semillante* took refuge under the batteries at San Jacinto; the British ships could not approach, and all three ships were damaged by the batteries' fire. *Semillante* went to Mauritius instead. (James 4.52–54; Clowes 5.366)

Philadelphia, Pennsylvania, 26 September 1777
General Sir William Howe took his army from New York to attack the rebel centre at Philadelphia, convoyed by the fleet under his brother, Admiral Lord Howe. The voyage was long and slow, for Howe chose the Chesapeake route rather than the Delaware. Philadelphia was taken on 26 September after a short fight. The city was held until May 1779 when it was evacuated. (Syrett, *American* 78–85; Mackesy, *America* 121–130; Syrett, *Howe* 67–69, 75–76; Clowes 3.390)

Philippine Islands, 1944–1945
Two Australian cruisers and four destroyers were part of covering forces involved in the battle of Leyte Gulf on 17–20 October. Australian ships were among the escorts for the Mindanao landings in January 1945, and in the fleet which escorted the landing force to Lingayen Gulf on 6 January. The cruiser *Australia* (several times) and the destroyer *Arunta* were damaged. The Australian cruiser *Shropshire* was part of the escort for the landing on Luzon on 27 January. (Rohwer 367, 383, 389)

Philomel and *Repulse* v. French frigates, 31 August 1810
Part of the French Toulon fleet came out to cover the arrival of storeships; three frigates (*Pomone, Penelope, Adrienne*) chased the sloop *Philomel* (18; Cmdr Gardiner Guion), which had been watching these moves. They were coming very close when *Repulse* (74; Capt. John Halliday) came up and took station to cover *Philomel*; the frigates turned away and returned to port. (James 5.84–85; Clowes 5.290)

Philpot's squadron v. Mercer's squadron, April 1378

The Scottish adventurer Andrew Mercer of Perth collected a number of Scottish, Flemish, and Castilian ships and raided the coast of northeast England. The London merchant John Philpot in reply collected an English fleet and sought out Mercer's ships; Mercer himself was captured along with several of his ships, mainly Castilian. (Sumption 3.316)

Phipps v. French luggers, 15–16 November 1810

The sloop *Phipps* (Cmdr Christopher Bell) chased a French lugger across the Channel to refuge under the batteries at Calais; another lugger, *Barbier de Seville*, was boarded and captured, then sank. (James 5.108–109; Clowes 5.475)

Phoebe v. *Atalante*, 10 January 1797

The frigate *Phoebe* (36; Capt. Robert Barlow) captured the sloop *Atalante* (16) off the Scilly Isles. (Clowes 4.553)

Phoebe v. *Néréide*, 20 December 1797

The frigate *Phoebe* (36; Capt. Robert Barlow) met the French frigate *Néréide* (36). They manoeuvred and chased for over twelve hours, until *Néréide* surrendered; she was later purchased for the navy. (James 2.103–105; Clowes 4.508)

Phoebe v. *Heureux*, 5 March 1800

The frigate *Phoebe* (36) was attacked by the French privateer *Heureux*, mistaking her for an Indiaman; despite attempts to escape, *Heureux* was forced to surrender. (James 3.8–9)

Phoebe v. *Africaine*, 19 February 1801

The frigate *Phoebe* (36; Capt. Robert Barlow) met the French frigate *Africaine*, heading for Egypt with supplies and reinforcements for the French army, off Ceuta. The ships fired broadsides into each other for half an hour until *Africaine*, extensively damaged and with 200 dead and 143 wounded, surrendered. (James 3.127–129; Clowes 4.537)

Phoebe v. *Essex*, 28 March 1814

The US frigate *Essex*, having cruised in the Pacific for some time, was found in Valparaiso Bay by the frigate *Phoebe* (Capt. James Hillyar) and the sloop *Cherub* (Capt. Thomas Tucker). *Essex* made several attempts to escape without fighting, but was finally brought to battle on the 28th. She was defeated and compelled to surrender. (James 6.149–156; Clowes 6.101–108; NC 5.227)

Phoebe v. *U-161*, 23 October 1942

The cruiser *Phoebe* was torpedoed by *U-161* off the Congo River. (Rohwer 203)

Phoenix v. French ship, October 1650

General-at-Sea Robert Blake, in *Phoenix* (38), and with three frigates, met a

French ship of 17 guns commanded by Chevalier de la Lande in the Strait of Gibraltar. De la Lande surrendered without firing, but then complained that he had been gulled; Blake let him return to his ship to recommence fighting, but his crew refused. De la Lande re-surrendered. (Corbett 1.217)

Phoenix v. Dutch convoy, 21 December 1653
Phoenix (38) took the English ambassador, Bulstrode Whitelocke, to Sweden. On the return voyage she attacked a Dutch Baltic convoy, only to suffer extensive damage, including the loss of all her masts. (Clowes 2.200)

Phoenix v. Zanganian pirate, 19 September 1685
Phoenix (42; Capt. John Tyrrel), in Indian waters, met an evasive ship, apparently a pirate. *Phoenix* attacked. The pirate was damaged and boarded by a party led by Lt George Byng, all of whom were killed or wounded. The captured ship sank. (Clowes 2.458–459)

Phoenix v. French squadron, 12 April 1692
Phoenix (42; Capt. Jacob Banks) was forced on shore in Spain by a French force, and was then burnt to avoid capture. (Clowes 2.468)

Phoenix v. *Opale*, 1762
The French ship *Opale* (20) was captured by the frigate *Phoenix* (44). (Clowes 3.313)

Phoenix and others v. *Sans Pareil*, 26 June 1780
Sans Pareil, a French cutter, was captured by the frigate *Phoenix* (44) and two other frigates. (Clowes 4.52)

Phoenix v. *Resolue*, 1791
The frigate *Phoenix* (36; Capt. Sir Richard Strachan) stopped the French frigate *Resolue* (36) off Tellicherry, India, and demanded to search her for contraband – the EIC was at war with Sultan Tipu. *Resolue*'s captain refused; fighting began. *Phoenix* was supported by the frigate *Perseverance* (36; Capt. Isaac Smith). *Resolue* surrendered, but no contraband was found. (James 1.131–132)

Phoenix v. *Argo*, 12 May 1796
The Dutch frigate *Argo* (38), with three brigs, on its way from Norway to the Texel, was intercepted by a British squadron. The frigate *Phoenix* (36; Capt. Lawrence Halstead) attacked. Surrounded by British ships, *Argo* surrendered; two of the brigs went on shore. (James 1.363–364; Clowes 4.498)

Phoenix v. *Revanche*, 17 June 1800
The French *Revanche* (4) was captured by the frigate *Phoenix* (36; Capt. Lawrence Halstead) in the Mediterranean. (Clowes 4.557)

Phoenix v. *Didon*, 10 August 1805
The frigate *Phoenix* (36; Capt. Thomas Baker) met and was attacked by the

French frigate *Didon* (40) in the Bay of Biscay. The two ships manoeuvred and pounded each other for several hours until *Didon*'s foremast fell and she surrendered. In taking his prize to Gibraltar, Capt. Baker had to evade both the French and Spanish fleets, and put down a rising by his prisoners. (James 4.65–74; Clowes 368–370)

Phoenix v. slavers, 1850
The screw sloop *Phoenix* (Cmdr George Wodehouse), off West Africa, chased a slaver which suddenly turned and collided with her, but which was then captured by a boat's crew; *Phoenix* also captured eight more slavers about this time. (Clowes 6.393)

Phoenix v. Albatros, 16 July 1940
The British submarine *Phoenix* was sunk by the Italian TB *Albatros* off Augusta, Sicily. (Rohwer 32)

Phosphorus v. Eliza, 14 August 1806
The *Phosphorus* fire-brig (4; Lt William Hughes) was attacked by the French privateer *Eliza* (12) off the Isle of Wight; every attempt to board was repelled, though most of the British crew were wounded in the process. (James 4.166–167; Clowes 5.387)

Pickle v. Boladora, 1 January 1828
The schooner *Pickle* (5; Lt John McHardy) attacked the slaver *Boladora*. The fight lasted eighty minutes, during which *Pickle* had eleven casualties (out of thirty-six men) and *Boladora* twenty-four (out of sixty); 335 slaves were freed. (Clowes 6.268–269; Ward 135–137; Lloyd 77–79)

Pictou v. Constitution, 14 February 1814
The schooner *Pictou* (16) was captured by the US frigate *Constitution* near Barbados, and destroyed. (James 6.198)

Pigot's squadron at Jean Rabel, St Domingue, 20–21 April 1797
A squadron under Capt. Hugh Pigot of the frigate *Hermione* was sent to the port of Jean Rabel to bring out ships captured by privateers. The ships' boats succeeded in bringing out nine vessels. (James 2.113–114; Clowes 4.334–335)

Pigot v. French privateers, 17 January and 8 February 1794
The EIC ship *Pigot* (32; Capt. George Ballantyne), refitting at Rat Island near Bencoolen in Sumatra, was attacked by the French privateers *Vengeur* (36) and *Resolue* (26). The harbour entrance was narrow and the French ships could only attack one at a time, so *Pigot* was able to make a stern defence; the privateers withdrew to make repairs. *Pigot* was captured a month later, still at Rat Island, by two other privateers. (James 1.219–220)

Pike v. Spanish *guarda costa*, 30 August 1806
Capt. George Le Geyt, commanding a small squadron, sent *Pike* (4; Lt John Ottley) to stop a Spanish *guarda costa* schooner (10) near the Isle of Pines,

Cuba; the schooner surrendered after an exchange of broadsides. (James 4.171)

Pike v. *Marat*, 20 April 1807
The schooner *Pike* (4; Lt John Ottley) was captured by the French privateer *Marat* (12) near Altavella. *Pike* was soon retaken, by the sloop *Moselle*. (James 4.336)

Pilot at Strongoli, 26 May 1811
The sloop *Pilot* (18; Cmdr John Nicholas) sent boats to a beach at Strongoli, near Taranto; defenders were driven off; three settees on the beach were taken away and a fourth holed. (James 5.257; Clowes 5.585)

Pilot at Castellan, Italy, 6 September 1811
The sloop *Pilot* (18; Cmdr John Nicholas) sent boats to attack a ketch in the harbour at Castellan, which was burnt; the sailors collected some loot before returning to the ship. (James 5.257–258; Clowes 5.492)

Pilot at Policastro, 16 April 1812
A boat party from the sloop *Pilot* (Cmdr John Nicholas) went into Policastro harbour and drove off an enemy force; nine coasting vessels were captured. (James 5.341–344; Clowes 5.503)

Pilot v. *Légère*, 17 June 1815
The sloop *Pilot* (18; Cmdr. John Nicholas) met the French corvette *Légère* near Corsica. *Pilot* fired into *Légère*'s hull, *Légère* at *Pilot*'s masts and rigging. *Légère* was able to get away, though half of her crew were killed or wounded. (James 6.228–229)

Pilot v. Chinese pirates, May–June 1849
The sloop *Pilot* (16; Cmdr Edward Lyons) encountered and fought a series of pirate junks in the estuary of the Canton River. (Clowes 6.353–354)

Pilot Me and *Young Fred* v. *UB-82*, 17 April 1918
The drifters *Pilot Me* and *Young Fred* sank *UB-82* north of Ireland. (Newbolt 5.427; Grant 112)

Pink v. *U-988*, 27 June 1944
The corvette *Pink* was torpedoed by *U-988* in the English Channel; the ship survived, but was not worth repairing. (Rohwer 334)

Pique, *Jason*, and *Mermaid* v. *Seine*, 24 April 1798
The frigate *Seine* (33) made a swift voyage from Mauritius but was prevented from entering Brest by the frigate *Mermaid* (32; Capt. James Newman). She turned to try to reach Lorient, chased by *Mermaid*'s two companions, *Jason* (38; Capt. Charles Stirling) and *Pique* (36; Capt. David Milne), until all three ran aground after a running fight between *Seine* and *Pique*. When the slow-

sailing *Mermaid* came up, *Seine* surrendered. *Pique* could not be refloated, and was burnt. (James 2.247–249; Clowes 4.511)

Pique and Pelican v. Goeland and cutter, October 1803
The French sloop *Goeland* (18) was captured by the frigate *Pique* (36) and the sloop *Pelican* (18), as was a cutter (12), near St Domingue. (Clowes 5.556)

Pique v. Terreur, 18 March 1804
The cutter *Terreur* (10) was captured by the frigate *Pique* (36) near Jamaica. (Clowes 5.556)

Pique v. Orquijo, 8 February 1805
The Spanish sloop *Orquijo* was captured by *Pique* (36; Capt. Charles Ross). (Clowes 5.562)

Pique v. Santa Clara, 17–26 March 1806
The frigate *Pique* (36; Capt. Charles Ross) sent two boats into Ocoe Bay, Santo Domingo on 17 March, to capture the schooner *Santa Clara*. On 26 March she encountered the French corvettes *Voltigeur* and *Phaeton* off St Domingue. After a short fight, a party of twenty-nine men boarded *Phaeton*, but were almost all killed or wounded in the subsequent fight. *Pique* sent another party, which succeeded. *Pique* then compelled *Voltigeur* to surrender without further ado. (James 4.134–135; Clowes 5.375)

Pique v. several ships, 1–2 November 1806
The frigate *Pique* (36; Capt. Charles Ross) sent a boat after a schooner near Cape Roxo, Santo Domingo. She could not be found, but a Spanish brig in Camberet Bay was captured. A battery was destroyed on the way out, and next day a French privateer was forced ashore and a second captured. (James 4.135–136)

Pitt v. Superbe, 23–26 October 1806
The schooner *Pitt* (12; Lt Michael Fitton) chased the French privateer schooner *Superbe* along the St Domingue coast. The chase lasted three days, *Pitt* often having to be propelled by sweeps, until *Superbe* put itself on shore on Cuba. The schooner was refloated by the victors. (James 4.181–184)

Placentia Bay, Newfoundland, August–October 1702
Capt. John Leake, in command of a small squadron, cruised off Placentia in search of French warships; many French fishing boats were captured or destroyed, and a landing party destroyed St Peter's Fort. (Clowes 2.501)

Plantagenet and Rosario v. Atalante, 29 July 1803
The sloop *Rosario* (10; Cmdr William Mounsey) chased the Bordeaux privateer *Atalante* in the Bay of Biscay, but was damaged in attacking her; *Plantagenet* (74; Capt. Graham Hamond) took up the chase and forced *Atalante* to surrender. (Clowes 5.324)

Plantagenet and others v. *General Armstrong*, 26–27 September 1814
The US privateer *General Armstrong* was found at Fayal, Cape Verde Islands, by *Plantagenet* (74; Capt. Robert Lloyd), the frigate *Rota* (38; Capt. Philip Somerville), and the sloop *Carnatian* (18; Cmdr George Bentham). The privateer was deemed to have violated the port's neutrality and was attacked; this attack was soundly defeated with heavy loss. *Carnatian* went in next morning, but the privateer had been burnt by its crew. (James 6.223–224; Clowes 6.155–157)

Plover v. *Aurore* and *Hirondelle*, September–October 1809
The sloop *Plover* (18; Cmdr Philip Browne) captured *Aurore* (16) off Beachy Head on 18 September, and the schooner *Hirondelle* (16) off Plymouth on 22 October. (Clowes 5.559)

Plumper v. *Flor do Mar*, June 1851
The screw sloop *Plumper* captured and sank *Flor do Mar* near Rio de Janeiro; she was carrying slaving equipment to the slaver *Valarozo*. (Bethell 355)

Pluto v. *Lutine*, 25 July 1793
The French *Lutine* (12) was captured at Newfoundland by *Pluto* (14; Cmdr James Morris). (Clowes 4.552)

Pluto v. *Anne D. Richardson*, 14 February 1850
The paddle vessel *Pluto* (Lt William Jolliffe) captured the slaver *Anne D. Richardson* off West Africa. (Clowes 6.393)

Plymouth, Devon
1567 A squadron of Spanish warships attempted to enter Plymouth harbour. They failed to salute the flag of Sir John Hawkins, so he fired and drove them out. Spanish intentions are unclear, but Hawkins's actions met with general approval in England. (Loades 222)

1644 Plymouth, under Royalist siege, was partly relieved by seaborne supplies taken in by a Parliamentary squadron under William Batten. (Rodger 1.421)

1652 A Dutch fleet and convoy under Admiral Michiel de Ruijter met the English fleet under Sir George Ayscue off Plymouth on 12 August. The two fleets fought for a day, without a clear result. The Dutch convoy sailed on. (Clowes 2.156–157; Powell 162–163; Rodger 2.13)

Plymouth v. *Content* and *Trident*, 7 January 1695
An English squadron under Capt. James Killigrew in *Plymouth* (60) patrolling the Sicilian Passage met two French ships, *Content* (60) and *Trident* (50). *Plymouth* fought them until the rest of the squadron came up. Both French ships were then captured. Killigrew was killed, and *Plymouth* suffered fifty casualties. (Clowes 2.484)

Plymouth v. privateers, 27 January–5 February 1697
Plymouth (60; Capt. John Jennings) chased the French privateer *Concorde* (14) on 27 January and captured her. On 5 February *Plymouth* and *Rye* (32; Capt. Richard Haddock) captured the privateers *Nouveau Cherbourg* (36) and *Dauphin* (28) after a hard fight. (Clowes 2.496)

Plymouth and others v. French convoy, 25 February 1697
Plymouth (60; Capt. John Jennings), *Rye* (32), and *Severn* (50) captured six French merchant ships and a small warship out of a convoy. (Clowes 2.496)

Plymouth v. *Adriade*, 20 September 1709
Plymouth (60; Capt. Jonas Hanway), though already damaged from an earlier fight, went in chase of *Adriade* (40) and forced her to surrender. (Clowes 2.522–523)

Polecat v. French ship, 1782
The brig *Polecat* (14; Lt Hon. Patrick Napier) was captured by the French off North America. (Clowes 4.112)

Polyphemus v. *Overijssel*, 22 October 1795
The Dutch line-of-battle ship *Overijssel* (64) was captured by *Polyphemus* (64; Capt. George Lumsdaine) off Queenstown, Ireland. (Clowes 4.558)

Polyphemus v. *Deux Amis*, December 1796
The French privateer schooner *Deux Amis* (14) was captured by *Polyphemus* (64). (Colledge 109)

Polyphemus v. *Tartu*, 5 January 1797
The French frigate *Tartu* (40) was captured by *Polyphemus* (64; Capt. George Lumsdaine). (Clowes 4.506)

Polyphemus and *Lively* v. *Santa Gertrudis*, 7 December 1804
The Spanish frigate *Santa Gertrudis* was captured by *Polyphemus* (64; Capt. Robert Redmill) and *Lively* (38; Capt. Graham Hamond) off Cape St Mary. (Clowes 5.562)

Polyphemus v. *Colibri*, 14 November 1808
Polyphemus (64; Capt. William Cumby), near Santo Domingo, sent boats to capture the French schooner *Colibri* (3), trying to enter the port. (James 4.382; Clowes 5.429)

Polyphemus v. Moorish pirates, 8 November 1848
The brig *Three Sisters* was captured by Moorish pirates. The paddle sloop *Polyphemus* (Cmdr James McLaverty) went to rescue the ship, which was done despite a large force of pirates at the scene, who prevented a landing. (Clowes 6.361)

Pomone v. Curieuse, 26 February 1795
The frigate *Pomone* (44; Capt. Sir John Borlase Warren) captured the French schooner *Curieuse* off the Ile Groix. (Clowes 4.533)

Pomone v. Rude, 2 September 1795
The frigate *Pomone* (44; Capt. Sir John Borlase Warren) captured and burnt the gunvessel *Rude* (12) off the French coast. (Clowes 4.554)

Pomone and squadron v. French convoy, 20 March 1796
The frigate squadron commanded by Capt. Sir John Borlase Warren in *Pomone* (40), with *Anson* (44; Capt. Philip Durham), *Artois* (38; Capt. Sir Edward Nagle), and *Galatea* (32; Capt. Richard Keats), encountered a convoy of sixty ships guarded by four frigates and a corvette. The French lost a storeship and four ships from the convoy, but otherwise reached safety. (James 1.355–357; Clowes 4.495; NRS, *Blockade of Brest* 43)

Pomone v. Petit Diable, 27 August 1797
Pomone (44; Capt. Sir John Borlase Warren) sent a boat to take possession of a cutter, which resisted. *Pomone* fired and the cutter ran ashore. (James 2.96–97)

Pomone v. Cheri, 5 January 1798
The French corvette *Cheri* (26) was captured in the Bay of Biscay by *Pomone* (44; Capt. Robert Reynolds), but then sank. (Clowes 4.555)

Pomone v. Carrère, 3 August 1801
The French frigate *Carrère*, escorting a convoy towards Porto Ferraio, Elba, with supplies for the French besiegers, was attacked by the frigate *Pomone* (44; Capt. Edward Leveson Gower) and forced to surrender. (James 3.78–79; Clowes 5.451)

Pomone v. French convoy, 5 June 1807
The frigate *Pomone* (44; Capt. Robert Barrie), off Brittany, fired at a convoy, some of whose ships ran ashore. Boats went to bring them off; about twenty vessels were captured. (James 4.258–259; Clowes 5.400)

Pomone v. Lucien Charles, 13 June 1809
The frigate *Pomone* (38; Capt. Robert Barrie) captured the Neapolitan privateer *Lucien Charles* (3) off Cape Bon, after a chase. (James 5.32; Clowes 5.439)

Pomone v. French convoy, 23 and 31 October 1809
A French convoy from Toulon for Barcelona was sighted by the Mediterranean fleet. The line-of-battle ships separated off from the convoy and the frigate *Pomone* (38; Capt. Robert Barrie) attacked and destroyed five vessels. The rest of the convoy got into Rosas Bay. A force of brigs and boats from the fleet went in on 31 October; every vessel of the convoy was either burnt or carried off. (James 4.445, 447–449; Clowes 5.432–433)

Pomone v. Etourdie, 14 March 1811
The French sloop *Etourdie* (18), threatened with capture by the frigate *Pomone* (38; Capt. Robert Barrie), was burnt. (Clowes 5.560)

Pomone and others at Sagone, Corsica, 1 May 1811
Three French brigs anchored in the Bay of Sagone, protected by a battery and a gun tower, were attacked by the frigates *Pomone* (38; Capt. Robert Barrie) and *Unite* (36; Capt. Edwin Chamberlayne) and the sloop *Scout* (18; Cmdr Alexander Sharpe). A cannonade set *Girafe* and *Nourrice* on fire and in subsequent explosions the tower was demolished and the battery exploded. (James 5.246–247; Clowes 5.483–484)

Pompée v. Pilade, 14 October 1808
Pompée (74; Capt. George Cockburn) met and captured the French corvette *Pilade* (16) near Barbados. (James 4.332; Clowes 5.427)

Pompée and Recruit v. d'Hautpoult, 14–17 April 1809
D'Hautpoult (74), one of a French squadron driven from refuge at the Saintes, was separated from her fellows in the chase which followed. At first the sloop *Recruit* (18; Cmdr Charles Napier) harassed the bigger ship, and then *Pompée* (74; Capt. Charles Fahie) took over until *d'Hautpoult* was forced to surrender. (James 5.18–22; Clowes 5.435–436)

Pondicherry, India
1748 Rear-Admiral Edward Boscawen landed forces in August to assist in the siege of the French base of Pondicherry. His ships blockaded and bombarded the town, but the siege was unsuccessful. (Clowes 3.131–132)

1758 A British squadron of nine line-of-battle ships under Vice-Admiral George Pocock met a French squadron of eleven line-of-battle ships under Comte d'Ache on 10 September. The fighting was indecisive, leaving several ships on each side badly damaged and both sides with heavy casualties. (Clowes 3.197–199; Tunstall 113)

1760 Pondicherry was besieged by land and blockaded by sea by British forces. In October boats from the British squadron, commanded by Cmdr William Newson of *Southsea Castle* (40), cut out the frigates *Hermione* (36) and *Baleine* (32). (Clowes 3.222)

1778 A small British squadron under Commodore Sir Edward Vernon blockaded Pondicherry from 8 August. Two days later a similar-sized French squadron under Capt. Tronjoly arrived. The two fought. The French had the advantage and went into Pondicherry. Vernon returned on 20 August and Tronjoly sailed away. (Clowes 3.543)

1793 The French fortified town was besieged. The frigate *Minerva* (38) and three EIC ships formed a blockade. The French frigate *Cybèle* and three supply ships were prevented from entering. The town surrendered on 20 August. (James 1.133; Clowes 4.214)

Pongos River, West Africa, 1841
Capt. J. Nourse raided the slave factory at the Pongos River, and destroyed it. (Lloyd 96)

Poole Harbour, Dorset, 896
Six Danish ships raided along the south coast of England. King Alfred sent a squadron of nine ships of a large type against them. They met in a bay which may have been Poole Harbour. Three of the Danish ships were attacked, two being captured; the crews of the others counter-attacked but were defeated. (*ASC* s.a. 896)

Popham's squadron v. *Volontaire*, 4 March 1806
The French frigate *Volontaire* came into Table Bay, recently captured by the British. The Dutch flags had been left flying and the ship surrendered when its situation in the midst of the British squadron under Commodore Sir Home Popham was understood. It was carrying 200 British soldiers as prisoners, who were in great need of attention. (James 4.189; Clowes 5.204)

Porcupine and *Minorca* v. *Montréal*, 30 July 1780
The French ship *Montréal* (32), escorting a convoy along the Algerian coast, was attacked by *Porcupine* (24; Capt. Sir Charles Knowles) and *Minorca*, a xebec (18; Capt. Hugh Lawson). After two hours' fighting the British ships sailed away, defeated. (Clowes 4.54–55)

Porcupine on the coast of Latium, June–August 1808
Porcupine (22; Capt. Hon. Henry Duncan) attacked a French ship coming from Civitavecchia on 23 June. The French ship eventually ran aground, and *Porcupine*'s boats went in to destroy it. In the next month several merchant ships and polacres were captured or destroyed. (James 4.345–347; Clowes 5.420–421)

Porcupine v. *U-602*, 9 December 1942
The destroyer *Porcupine* was torpedoed by *U-602* in the western Mediterranean, and irretrievably damaged. (Rohwer 216)

Porkala, Finland, 7–8 July 1809
Boats from *Implacable* (74; Capt. Thomas Byam Martin) and others attacked Russian vessels in Porkala harbour, sinking six gunboats and a merchantman. (Anderson 340; Clowes 5.441)

Porpoise v. *U-1*, 16 April 1940
The submarine *Porpoise* sank *U-1* off Norway. (Rohwer 21)

Porpoise and *Torbay* v. *Sebastiano Venier*, 9–12 December 1941
The Italian motor vessel *Sebastiano Venier*, carrying 2000 British prisoners of war from North Africa towards Italy, was damaged by the British submarine *Porpoise* on 9 December and sunk by the submarine *Torbay* three days later. (Rohwer 119)

Porpoise v. *Lince* and *Sagittario*, 19 August 1942
The submarine *Porpoise* was badly damaged by the TBs *Lince* and *Sagittario* while attacking a convoy. (Rohwer 188)

Port Castries, St Lucia, 10 March 1942
U-161 went brazenly into Port Castries harbour, and sank two ships at the quayside. (Terraine 421; Rohwer 145)

Port d'Espagne v. *Mercedes*, 6 June 1807
The brig *Port d'Espagne* (14; Lt James Stewart), in the Gulf of Paria, Spanish Main, sent a prize schooner to attack a Spanish privateer, *Mercedes*, which was boarded and taken. (James 4.259; Clowes 5.400)

PORTLAND, Dorset, 18–20 February 1653 (the THREE DAYS' FIGHT)
Admiral Tromp with a returning Dutch convoy was intercepted by the English fleet off Portland. Each side had about eighty warships, but the English were divided while the Dutch had to guard the convoy. Tromp attacked at once, hoping to defeat the English piecemeal. In fact good seamanship by the English admirals – Blake, Deane, Monck, and Penn – brought on a close fight, and late arriving ships threatened the damaged Dutch fleet with a fresh attack. Both sides suffered badly, but the English redistributed their crews and sent the most damaged ships into port for repair.

Next day fighting resumed. Two Dutch warships and a dozen merchantmen were captured, and the convoy began to disperse. Fighting continued on the 20th, by which time the fleets were past Boulogne. Next morning all the Dutch had got away. They lost four ships captured, five sunk, and two or three more abandoned and burned. About fifty of the convoy were captured. The English lost one ship, and three were disabled. (Clowes 2.178–184; Powell 207–223; Rodger 2.16–17)

Portland v. *Coventry* and *Mignon*, 3–6 May 1709
Portland (48; Capt. Stephen Hutchings) chased the French ships *Coventry* (50) and *Mignon* (40) which sailed from Porto Bello. *Mignon* was fought until seriously damaged, then on 6 May *Coventry* was attacked until she surrendered. *Mignon* thereupon got away. (Clowes 2.518–520)

Portland v. *Auguste*, 9 February 1746
Portland (50; Capt. Charles Steevens) met and fought the French *Auguste* (50) in the Channel. *Auguste* surrendered, having 150 casualties to *Portland*'s eighteen. (Clowes 3.282)

Portland v. *Subtile*, 19 November 1746
The French *Subtile* (26) was captured by *Portland* (50). (Clowes 3.312)

Port Louis, Hispaniola, 8 March 1748
Rear-Admiral Charles Knowles's squadron attacked Port Louis. The fort was bombarded, but a fireship attack was deflected. Once Spanish fire was

suppressed the governor was persuaded to surrender. Seven ships were taken and the fort was burnt. (Clowes 3.133–134)

Port Mahon, Minorca, September 1708
The British Mediterranean fleet under Admiral Sir John Leake and a military force under General James Stanhope laid siege to Port Mahon. After Leake left for England, a squadron under Rear-Admiral Sir Edward Whitaker remained to assist, and the ships made landings at various places. The final fort, St Philip's, was taken by assault on 17 September. (Corbett 2.304–330; Clowes 2.412–414; Owen 98–100; Francis 267–268; Rodger 2.173)

***Port Mahon* v. *Galgo*, 30 September 1805**
The Spanish *Galgo* (14) was captured by *Port Mahon* (18; Cmdr Samuel Chambers). (Clowes 5.562)

***Port Mahon* v. *San Josef*, 25–26 June 1806**
Boats from the sloop *Port Mahon* (18; Cmdr Samuel Chambers) went into the harbour at Banes, Cuba, to cut out the Spanish brig *San Josef* (7) which had gone in for refuge. (James 4.155–156; Clowes 5.384)

Porto Bello, Panama
1602 Porto Bello was captured by an English force commanded by William Parker on 7 February. They seized and shared a small fortune. (Clowes 1.531–532)

1739 Vice-Admiral Edward Vernon, commanding six line-of-battle ships, attacked Porto Bello on 21 November. The outlying defence, the Iron Castle, was taken by bombardment and assault, and the squadron entered the bay. Next day the Spanish governor surrendered the town and was allowed to march his garrison out. The ships *Astraea* (20) and *Triunfo* (20) were captured. The British remained in occupation, destroying fortifications, for several weeks, but they were disappointed in the booty they found. (Clowes 3.54–57)

Port-of-Spain, Trinidad, 18 February 1942
U-161 sailed into Trinidad waters and sank two ships at anchor off Port-of-Spain. (Terraine 421; Rohwer 145)

Pôrto Novo, West Africa, 1861
Pôrto Novo was bombarded by the paddle gunboat *Brune* (Lt John Stokes) on 25 February in a campaign against the local slave trade. On 26 April a bombardment by *Brune*, *Fidelity* (Lt Robert Cay), the paddle sloop *Alecto*, the screw frigate *Arrogant*, and the paddle vessel *Bloodhound* set the town on fire. A landing party drove the people away, and then destroyed the slave barracoons. (Clowes 7.187–188; Lloyd 160–161)

Porto Praya, Cape Verde Islands, 16 April 1781
A British squadron of five line-of-battle ships, eleven smaller warships, and

ten Indiamen commanded by Commodore George Johnstone anchored in the bay at Porto Praya. On 16 April a French squadron of five line-of-battle ships arrived. The encounter was unexpected on both sides. Johnstone's ships had many men on shore and the French commander, Vice-Admiral Suffren, at once attacked. Only two of the French ships made a serious effort, and Suffren withdrew; Johnstone made a brief attempt to pursue, then returned to the bay. (Clowes 3.546–549)

Port Royal, Nova Scotia, September 1710
An expeditionary force of British warships and New England soldiers attacked and rapidly captured Port Royal, the French headquarters in Nova Scotia. The place was renamed Annapolis Royal in the queen's honour. (Clowes 2.526–527)

Port Royal v. French ship, 17 May 1797
The schooner *Port Royal* (10; Lt Elias Man) was captured by the French in the West Indies; she was retaken in October. (Clowes 4.549)

Portsmouth, Hampshire, August 1642
The Parliamentary fleet under the Earl of Warwick assisted in the capture of Portsmouth. (Clowes 2.78)

Portsmouth, Virginia
1779   A store of naval equipment at Portsmouth accumulated by the rebel American navy was destroyed in a raid commanded by Commodore Sir George Collier in May; the retreating American forces also destroyed other items, including several partly built ships. (Clowes 4.26; Mackesy, *America* 270; Syrett, *American* 123–124)

1813   A detachment from the British blockading forces went to Portsmouth to remove privateers reported to be there. The town was taken on 11 July and two ships, *Atlas* and *Anaconda*, captured. (James 6.95–96)

Portsmouth v. *Marquis*, 9 August 1689
Portsmouth (46; Capt. George St Loe) was captured by the French *Marquis*; St Loe, despite being seriously wounded, threw important dispatches overboard. (Powley 281; Clowes 2.462)

Portsmouth and *Canterbury* v. French merchant ship, 11 June 1694
A French merchant ship of 36 guns fought very hard against *Portsmouth* (32; Capt. John Clements) and *Canterbury* (60), but was eventually taken. (Clowes 2.480)

Postboy v. *Facteur de Bristol*, 3 July 1695
The advice boat *Postboy* (8) was captured off Plymouth by the French *Facteur de Bristol*. (Colledge 315)

Post Boy v. French ship, 30 May 1702
The brig *Post Boy* (4; Lt Gilbert Frankland) was captured by the French off Beachy Head; Frankland was killed. (Clowes 2.556)

Powerful and Rattlesnake v. Bellone, July 1806
The sloop *Rattlesnake* (16; Cmdr John Bastard) chased the privateer *Bellone* (34) near Ceylon. *Powerful* (74; Capt. Robert Plampin) joined in; after a two-hour running fight, *Bellone* surrendered. (James 4.156–157)

Prescott, Ontario, 13 November 1838
Niagara (20; Capt. William Sansom) was on hand at Brockville and Prescott when those towns were threatened by rebels. Sansom landed forces at Prescott to assist the soldiers against the rebels. (Clowes 6.277)

President and others v. Dutch convoy, 12 May 1652
President (49; Capt. Anthony Young), with the frigates *Nightingale* (20; Capt. Reynolds) and *Recovery* (20; Capt. Chapman), demanded that the three escorts of a Dutch convoy off Start Point strike their flags in salute. One ship did so, but two refused. A short fight ensued; the Dutch gave way. (Clowes 2.143–144; Powell 139–140)

President v. pirates, Malabar, 1683
The EIC ship *President* (Capt. Hyde) was attacked off Malabar by a group of vessels described as Arab pirates from Muscat. One of the attacking grabs was sunk; *President* suffered over forty casualties. (Low 1.71)

President v. Angria's ships, 1716
The EIC ship *President* was attacked off the Malabar coast by six of Kanhoji Angria's fleet. An attempt to board by three grabs failed. Two grabs were sunk and one blew up, setting *President* on fire for a time. (Low 1.97)

President at Anjoxa, East Africa, 1847
President (52; Capt. William Sydney, with Rear-Admiral James Dacres) raided the slave stockade at Anjoxa. (Clowes 6.360)

Preston v. Marseillais, 13 August 1778
Preston (50; Commodore William Hotham) attacked the French *Marseillais* (74), which had been damaged in a storm. The two ships fought for some hours until several other French ships came to *Marseillais*'s rescue. (Clowes 4.17)

Prima v. U-boat, 1 March 1917
The hospital ship *Prima* was sunk by a U-boat off Skokholm Island. (Colledge 116)

Primrose v. Duke of Marlborough, 12 March 1814
The sloop *Primrose* (18; Cmdr Charles Philpott) saw the packet *Duke of Marlborough* (Capt. John Bull) at a distance; neither could read the other's signals and they fell to fighting each other; three men died and over twenty were wounded. (James 6.112–114; Clowes 5.548)

Primrose v. *Veloz Pasajero*, 7 September 1830
Primrose (18; Capt. William Broughton) met the slaver *Veloz Pasajero* (20); when repeated attempts to permit examination (that is, surrender) failed, a long fight took place. *Primrose* suffered sixteen casualties, the slaver crew over sixty; 555 slaves were freed. (Clowes 6.269–278; Ward 129–132)

Primula v. *U-35*, 1 March 1916
The sloop *Primula* was sunk by *U-35* in the Mediterranean. (Colledge 317)

Prince Charles v. *U-36*, 24 July 1915
The trawler *Prince Charles*, a Q-ship, was attacked by *U-36* near Shetland. In the fight which followed the submarine was sunk. (Corbett 3.52; Grant 28)

Prince Frederick v. *St Antoine*, 13 August 1747
Prince Frederick (64; Capt. Harry Norris) captured the sloop *St Antoine*, carrying supplies for Senegal, in the Bay of Biscay. (NRS, *Hawke* no. 27)

Prince of Orange and squadron v. *Diligente*, May 1694
The French warship *Diligente* (36) was chased by *Prince of Orange* (50; Capt. Samuel Vincent) and got away, only to be captured by an English squadron of six ships under Capt. Thomas Warren near the Scilly Isles. Its captain, Duguay-Trouin, was charged with violating the laws of war and imprisoned, but escaped almost at once. (Clowes 2.479)

Prince of Orange and *Dove* v. *Surprise*, 2–3 May 1777
Capt. Gustavus Conyngham, a rebel American sailor, sailed from Dunkirk in the privateer *Surprise*. He captured the packet *Prince of Orange* and the brig *Dove* and took them into port in France. The British government successfully demanded that they be restored. (Syrett, *European* 7; Clowes 4.4)

Prince of Wales at Malwan, India, 1812
Malwan was a pirate base. The EIC ship *Prince of Wales* (14) landed a small force at the port; the piracy was successfully ended. (Low 1.277)

Princess v. Dutch squadron, 18 April 1667
Princess (52; Capt. Henry Dawes) met a Dutch fleet of seventeen ships at Dogger Bank, and was attacked successively by three of the largest ships and by several frigates. She fought clear with only a few casualties. (Clowes 2.435)

Princess v. *Faisant* and *Hardarinne*, 17 May 1667
Princess (52; Capt. Henry Dawes) fought two Danish ships, *Faisant* (38) and *Hardarinne* (38), near Marstrand on the Kattegat coast. Both sides suffered considerable damage. Dawes, his lieutenant, and the master were killed, leaving command to the gunner; after three hours the Danes pulled away. (Clowes 2.435–436; Anderson 102)

Princess Augusta v. **Angria's squadron, 1742**
The EIC ship *Princess Augusta* was captured by a squadron of Tulaji Angria. (Keay 265)

Princess Augusta v. *Union* **and** *Wraak*, **20 September 1803**
The cutter *Princess Augusta* (8; Lt Isaac Scott) was attacked off the Texel by two Dutch schooners, *Union* (12) and *Wraak* (8), first separately then both together. Scott was killed; both ships were driven off. (James 3.194; Clowes 5.327–328)

Princess Caroline v. *Piet Hein*, **20 May 1809**
Boats from *Princess Caroline* (74; Capt. Charles Pater) captured the Dutch schooner *Piet Hein* (7) in the Vlie. (Clowes 5.438)

Princess Caroline **and others at Frederickshamn, Finland, 25 July 1809**
Boats of a squadron commanded by Capt. Charles Pater of *Princess Caroline* (74), with *Minotaur* (74; Capt. John Barrett), the frigate *Cerberus* (Capt. Henry Whitby), and the sloop *Prometheus* (Cmdr Thomas Forrest), went into Frederickshamn. Four Russian gunboats and an armed brig were captured, but at considerable cost. (James 5.41–42; Clowes 5.442)

Princess Charlotte v. *Naiade* **and** *Cyane*, **9 October 1805**
Capt. George Tobin of the frigate *Princess Charlotte* (38), off Tobago, disguised his ship as a merchantman and so attracted the hostile attention of the French corvettes *Naiade* and *Cyane*. *Cyane* came close enough to be fought and captured. (James 4.75–76)

Princess Louise **and** *C-27* v. *U-23*, **20 July 1915**
The armed trawler *Princess Louise* towed the submarine *C-27* underwater as a decoy. She was challenged by *U-23*; *C-27* was released and sank the German vessel. (Corbett 3.48; Grant 25–26)

Princess Royal v. **French privateers, 27 September 1793**
Princess Royal (Capt. James Horncastle), an EIC China ship, was attacked and captured by three French privateers in the Sunda Strait. (James 1.218; Low 1.204–205)

Princess Royal v. *Aventurier*, **21–22 June 1798**
The packet *Princess Royal* (6; Capt. John Skinner) was attacked in the Atlantic by the privateer *Aventurier* (14). After a chase lasting a day, the two ships came to a fight on 22 June, in which the passengers on the packet assisted with the defence. *Aventurier* had to return to Bordeaux for repairs; *Princess Royal* was repaired at once and sailed on. (James 2.253–254)

Privet v. *U-85*, **12 March 1917**
Privet, a Q-ship, was shelled by *U-85* and badly damaged, but replied with gunfire. *U-85* submerged but was unable to resurface. *Privet* grounded to avoid sinking but was repaired. (Grant 64)

Privet v. *U-34*, 8 November 1918
The armed coaster *Privet* sank *U-34* by gunfire and depth-charges near Gibraltar. (Newbolt 5.411; Grant 133)

Prize and *D-6* v. *U-48*, 14 August 1917
The Q-ship *Prize*, sailing in company with the submarine *D-6*, encountered *U-48* northwest of Ireland, which submerged when *Prize* attacked. *D-6* could not get in a shot; *U-48* torpedoed and sank *Prize*. (Newbolt 5.109–110)

Procris v. Dutch convoy, 28 July 1811
The sloop *Procris* (Capt. Robert Maunsell) located a Dutch convoy protected by gunboats at the mouth of the Indramayo River, Java, and sent boats to attack; five gunboats were captured; a sixth blew up. (James 5.300–301)

Prohibition v. French ship, 14 August 1702
The sloop *Prohibition* (6; Lt John Barber) was captured by the French. (Clowes 2.536)

Prometheus v. Moorish pirates, 26 June 1854
Pirates from Cape Treforcas captured the brig *Cuthbert Young*; the paddle sloop *Prometheus* (Cmdr Edward Rice) was sent to recover the ship, which was accomplished despite strong opposition from the shore. (Clowes 6.391)

Prompte v. *Urca Cardagora*, 16 March 1799
The Spanish *Urca Cardagora* (12) was captured and burnt by *Prompte* (20; Capt. Thomas Dundas) in the West Indies. (Clowes 4.560)

Proserpine v. *Sphinx*, 1779
The sloop *Proserpine* (28; Cmdr George Byron) captured the French *Sphinx* (20). (Clowes 4.114)

Proserpine v. *Pauline* and *Penelope*, 28 February 1809
The frigate *Proserpine* (32; Capt. Charles Otter), off Toulon, was ambushed by two French frigates, *Pauline* and *Penelope*, on the night of 27–28 February. *Proserpine* was beaten into surrender. (James 5.11–12; Clowes 5.432; *NC* 4.193–197)

PROVIDIEN, 12 April 1782
The French fleet under Vice-Admiral Pierre Suffren, with twelve ships, laid siege to Trincomalee. Vice-Admiral Sir Edward Hughes, with eleven line-of-battle ships, sailed to reinforce Trincomalee's garrison. The fleets met and the fighting was close, hot, and costly. No ship was taken, but casualties were heavy, about a thousand men in total. Hughes moved out to sea, taunting the aggressive Suffren by keeping just out of fighting range. When he gave the signal to attack, the French fleet was in some disarray so that several French ships were badly damaged in the subsequent fighting, while some scarcely got into the fight at all. (Clowes 3.552–554, 557–561, 4.76–77; Tunstall 185; Mahan 436–442)

Prudente and *Licorne* v. *Capricieuse*, 5 July 1780
The frigates *Prudente* (36; Capt. Hon. William Waldegrave) and *Licorne* (32; Capt. Hon. Thomas Cadogan) chased the frigate *Capricieuse* (32) off Cape Ortegal. *Prudente* reached the French ship first and caused her much damage; *Licorne* then arrived, but *Capricieuse* fought on until she was nearly sinking and had suffered 100 casualties. (Clowes 4.53)

Prudente v. *Jackal*, 1781
The British frigate *Prudente* (36) captured the French privateer *Jackal* (14), which had been a British ship until carried off by her mutinous crew two years before. (Clowes 4.76)

Psyche at Samarang, Java, 31 August 1807
The frigate *Psyche* (36; Capt. Fleetwood Pellew) went into Samarang road, Java, against vessels there. Her boats secured some, but three, the armed merchantmen *Resolutie* and *Ceres* and the corvette *Scipio* (24), attempted to get away. The prizes were burnt, and the three ships were forced aground and bombarded from a distance. In succession they surrendered. (James 4.283; Clowes 5.239)

Puckeridge, Hyacinth, and others v. *U-617*, 6–12 September 1943
U-617 sank the destroyer *Puckeridge* east of Gibraltar on 6 September; she was then attacked from the air, and by the corvette *Hyacinth*, the RAN minesweeper *Wollongong*, and the trawler *Haarlem*, until forced to beach on the Moroccan coast. (Rohwer 266)

Puerto Cabello, Spanish Main, 15–24 April 1743
A squadron under Capt. Charles Knowles attacked the town of Puerto Cabello. An attack on the batteries was repelled, and a bombardment of the main defences failed. The ships were badly damaged by Spanish fire; about 200 men were killed or wounded. (Clowes 3.87–88)

Puketakauere, New Zealand, 27 June 1860
A Naval Brigade from the screw corvette *Pelorus* (Capt. Frederick Seymour) assisted in an attack on a Maori *pa* (a fortified stockade) at Puketakauere. The attack, by about 350 men against a Maori garrison of about 200, was comprehensively defeated; perhaps a third of the British force were killed. (Clowes 7.176; Belich 91–95)

PULO AUR, Malacca Strait, 14–15 February 1804
A fleet of thirty-nine ships from Canton, including sixteen Indiamen, was met off Pulo Aur, at the entrance to the Malacca Strait, by the squadron of Admiral Linois, *Marengo* (74), the frigates *Belle Poule* and *Semillante*, and the corvettes *Berceau* and *Aventurier*. The China fleet had been expecting an attack and responded well to the commands of the commodore, Capt. Nathanial Dance. Linois, surprised to see more ships than expected, and at their discipline, made to attack on the morning of the 15th, aiming to cut off part of the line before him, but was deterred by the aggressive behaviour of

five of the Indiamen, who formed a line ahead and fired broadsides. After less than an hour the French squadron turned away, to find that they were being followed, still aggressively, by the whole fleet. The sheer size and aggressiveness of the Indiamen convinced Linois that he was facing a much stronger force, perhaps Royal Navy ships. Dance was knighted for his achievement, and £50,000 was distributed amongst the crews. (James 3.249–254; *NC* 3.40–45; Parkinson 221–231; Clowes 5.336–338)

Pulo Run, Banda Islands, 1616
Pulo Run was occupied by ships sent by the EIC, commanded by Nathaniel Courthope. A Dutch attack seized these ships, and two relieving ships were captured in 1618; Courthope was killed by a Dutch attack in 1619. (Clowes 2.38)

Punta Delgada, Canary Islands, 16 January–2 February 1942
A troop convoy from Gibraltar was attacked by *U-402* on 16 January; one ship was torpedoed and took refuge at Punta Delgada for repairs; in the meantime *U-581* sank the ASW trawler *Rosemonde* on 22 January. When the repaired ship sailed the destroyer *Westcott* sank *U-581*. (Rohwer 136)

PUNTA STILO, Calabria, 9 July 1940
The British Mediterranean fleet, commanded by Admiral A.B. Cunningham, attacked the Italian fleet; the battleship *Giulio Cesare* and the cruiser *Bolzano* were damaged by fire from the battleship *Warspite*; the cruiser *Gloucester* was damaged. The Italians broke off the fight after about two hours; next day planes from the carrier *Eagle* sank the destroyer *Pancaldo* off Augusta, Sicily. (Greene and Massignani 66–78; Rohwer 32)

***Pursuer* v. German patrol vessels, 20 November 1944**
A raid by aircraft from the carrier *Pursuer* sank *V-6413* off Trondheim, and MTBs attacked and sank *V-5107* north of Lagemen. (Rohwer 371)

***Pylades* and others v. *Crash* and others, 11–14 August 1799**
Three ships from a British squadron went to recapture the Dutch brig *Crash* (12), off the Groningen coast. The cutter *Courier* (Lt Thomas Searle) attacked first, and the sloops *Pylades* and *Espiégle* (Cmdrs Adam McKenzie and James Boorder) came up; *Crash* resisted the fire of all three for an hour before surrendering. Next day boats from several ships, covered by *Crash*, attacked the Dutch schooner *Vengeance*, which lay beneath a battery at Schiermonnikoog, Groningen. Fire from the ships silenced the battery, but the schooner was burnt by her crew; the battery was spiked. Several small craft nearby were captured, the gunboat *Undaunted* next day, *Weerwrack* (6) two days after. (Clowes 4.522–523; James 2.382–384)

***Pylades* v. *Aigle*, 14 December 1809**
The sloop *Pylades* (18; Cmdr George Ferguson) captured the French *Aigle* (14). (Clowes 5.559)

Q

Québec, Canada
1690   Sir William Phipps, governor of Massachusetts, took an expedition of more than thirty ships with 2000 men from New England to attack Québec. They landed on 18 October, but were immediately defeated and swiftly re-embarked. (Clowes 2.464)

1711   An expedition from Britain, nine line-of-battle ships and others, with 5000 troops, aimed to attack Québec. It called first at Boston and Gaspé Bay, but the pilots had no knowledge of the currents or the shoals of the St Lawrence. Several transports were wrecked and more than 800 men were drowned, and Rear-Admiral Sir Hovenden Walker called off the whole enterprise. (Clowes 2.527–529; Rodger 2.179)

1759–1760 (Conquest of QUÉBEC)   The British fleet, commanded by Vice-Admiral Charles Saunders, carried an army up the St Lawrence to attack Québec. Saunders had a fleet of twenty line-of-battle ships and a large number of frigates and smaller vessels, carrying 9000 soldiers commanded by Major General James Wolfe. The expedition reached the environs of Québec on 26 June, but repeated attempts to bring the army directly before the city failed, until Saunders organised the transit of soldiers past the city in September. They climbed to the plain next to the city called the Heights of Abraham, and in a short battle on 13 September the British defeated the French garrison; the city surrendered on the 17th.

Over the winter the British force holding Québec was besieged by a French army. A British naval force relieved the siege on 15 May and next day *Vanguard* (70; Capt. Robert Swanton) fired on the French siege lines and forced their evacuation; *Diana* (36; Capt. Alexander Schomberg) and *Lowestoft* (28; Capt. Joseph Deane) attacked the French flotilla upriver; *Pomone* (30) and *Atalante* (32) were forced ashore and burnt. The army has received much of the acclaim for this achievement, but an objective consideration suggests that the navy was the main element in the success. (Clowes 3.205–209, 227; Mahan 294–296)
See also: **Louisburg, Montreal**

1775–1776   Québec was attacked by a rebel American force commanded by General Montgomery, and was under siege through the winter. On 6 May 1776 Royal Navy ships under Capt. Charles Douglas in *Isis* (50) approached and broke the siege. *Isis* had broken through the sea ice at the mouth of the St Lawrence earlier than anyone expected. (Clowes 3.356–358)

***Québec* and *Rambler* v. *Surveillante* and *Expedition*, 6 October 1779**
Québec (32; Capt. George Farmer), in company with *Rambler* (10; Lt Rupert George), met the French frigate *Surveillante* (32) with *Expedition* (12) off

Ushant. The captains of both frigates were all too eager to fight, and their ships battered each other to ruin; *Québec* eventually caught fire and blew up. Of her 195 men, 125 died; *Surveillante* had about 100 casualties. The smaller ships fought each other until *Expedition* made off. The captains of both frigates died. Their families were rewarded; there is no sign that the surviving crewmen were. (Clowes 4.40–44)

Québec v. Aspic, 10 March 1796
The French cutter *Aspic* was captured by *Québec* (32) in St George's Channel. (Clowes 4.495)

Québec v. Thetis and Pensée, 7 July 1796
The frigate *Québec* (32; Capt. John Cook), escorting a convoy near St Domingue, was challenged by the French frigates *Thetis* (36) and *Pensée* (36). *Québec* began to fight one of the French ships, but the ships of the convoy surrendered to the other frigate, without even being threatened. *Québec* thereupon departed. (James 1.380–381)

Québec v. Africaine, 3 December 1796
The French sloop *Africaine* (18) was captured by the frigate *Québec* (32; Capt. John Cook) near St Domingue. (Clowes 4.555)

Québec v. Prinds Christian Frederik, 1808
Québec (32), carrying part of a subsidy to Sweden, was attacked by the Danish ship *Prinds Christian Frederik* (68). *Québec* barely survived the encounter. (Anderson 322)

Québec v. Jeune Louise, 8 November 1810
Québec (32; Capt. Charles Hawtayne) saw the privateer schooner *Jeune Louise* in the Vlie, attacked and captured her, and brought her out through a very difficult passage. (James 5.105–106; Clowes 5.473–474)

Québec and others v. gunboats, 2 August 1811
The frigate *Québec* (32; Capt. Charles Hawtayne), accompanied by several smaller ships, sent ten boats in to attack a flotilla of gunboats near Norderney. Four gunboats were captured, and one blew up. (James 5.221–222; Clowes 5.489–490)

Queen v. Actionnaire, 22 April 1782
Queen (98; Capt. Hon. Frederick Maitland) chased the French *Actionnaire* (64; *en flute*) carrying naval stores and 550 soldiers to the Ile de France, and captured her in the Bay of Biscay after a single broadside. (Clowes 4.83)

Queen Alexandra v. UB-78, 9 May 1918
The troop transport *Queen Alexandra* rammed and sank *UB-78* in the eastern Channel. (Newbolt 5.428; Grant 116)

Queen Charlotte v. Swan, 29 August 1810
The cutter *Queen Charlotte* (Master, Joseph Thomas), off Alderney, met

and fought the French cutter *Swan*. *Queen Charlotte* was reduced to a ruin before *Swan* sailed away. (James 5.99–100; *NC* 4.338)

Queen Charlotte v. Louis, 1816
The slaver *Louis* was captured by *Queen Charlotte* (104) *en route* from Martinique to Africa. (Lloyd 44)

Quentin and Quiberon v. Dessie, 28 November 1942
The destroyers *Quentin* and *Quiberon*, off Bône, North Africa, sank the Italian submarine *Dessie*. (Rohwer 215)

Quiberon Bay, Brittany
1759 (Battle of QUIBERON BAY)   The French fleet at Brest came out on 20 November and sailed to Quiberon to drive off a British blockading force. It was followed by the British Channel Fleet under Admiral Sir Edward Hawke with twenty-seven line-of-battle ships; the French had twenty-one. The battle was fought in a gale, in gathering darkness, and on a lee shore, and was very confused. Having driven the French towards the land, the British mainly anchored for the night. Six French ships were lost, foundered or wrecked; of the rest half took refuge in the Charente estuary and half in the Vilaine, from which refuges few of them ever emerged. (Clowes 3.216–221; Syrett, *Howe* 26–27; NRS, *Hawke* 327–350; NRS, *Misc* I; Tunstall 115–117)

1795   An expedition aiming to encourage a Royalist rising in Brittany landed 2500 French emigrants, with a large stock of arms, at Quiberon Bay on 27 June from a naval force commanded by Commodore Sir John Borlase Warren in the frigate *Anson* (44). The whole was covered by the British Channel Fleet under Admiral Lord Bridport. Local support was disappointing. On being defeated by a Republican army on 20 July the emigrant forces collapsed. (Clowes 4.266–267; NRS, *Blockade of Brest* 73, 88; *NC* 1.124–133)

1800   A British squadron under Capt. Sir Edward Pellew in *Impetueux* (74) sailed to Quiberon intending to assist the rebellious Chouans. On 4 June the frigate *Thames* (32; Capt. William Lukin) and the sloop *Cynthia* (16; Cmdr Micajah Malbon) bombarded and destroyed the fort at the end of the Quiberon peninsula. A landing on the mainland two days later captured and destroyed several ships. After a brief occupation of Houat Island, the expedition sailed off to Spain. (James 2.427–428; Clowes 4.15; *NC* 2.110)

Quickly v. U-16, 20 July 1915
The armed trawler *Quickly*, acting as a Q-ship, fought *U-16*, assisted by the trawler *Gunner*; it was thought that the submarine was sunk, but she was only damaged. (Corbett 3.51–52)

R

***Racehorse* v. *Andrea Doria*, December 1776**
The bomb *Racehorse* (Lt James Jones) fought the rebel American ship *Andrea Doria* (14), and was captured by her. (Clowes 4.4)

***Racehorse* at Para, Brazil, 1835**
The sloop *Racehorse* (18) assisted Brazilian forces fighting rebels at Para, at one point rescuing over 200 fugitives by a night landing. (Clowes 6.275)

***Racehorse* v. Chinese pirates, 25 June 1855**
The sloop *Racehorse* (18; Cmdr Edward Bernard) chased a group of pirate ships near Foochow, sending a boat to attack them; several junks were burnt or captured; others were attacked in the following days. (Clowes 6.388–389)

***Racehorse* and *Raider* v. *U-537*, 8 July 1944**
U-537 made an unsuccessful attack near Ceylon, and was then hunted for several days by the destroyers *Racehorse* and *Raider*. All three ships survived. (Rohwer 327)

***Racer* v. *Bom Destina*, September 1843**
The slaver *Bom Destina* was captured by the sloop *Racer* off Bahia, Brazil. (Bethell 210)

***Racoon* v. *Intrepide*, 3 December 1799**
Near Dover the sloop *Racoon* (16; Cmdr Robert Lloyd) attacked the French lugger *Intrepide*, which was seen boarding the brig *Melcombe*; after an hour's fight, the lugger surrendered. (James 2.415–416)

***Racoon* off St Domingue, June–October 1803**
The sloop *Racoon* (16; Cmdr Austin Bissell) captured the schooners *Vertu* and *Ami de Colonnot* off St Domingue on 7 June. On 11 July she found the French corvette *Lodi* at anchor in Leogane roads, St Domingue, and anchored close to her. The two ships fired broadsides at each other for half an hour. *Lodi* tried to get away, but when *Racoon* persisted, surrendered. On 17 August *Racoon* approached a brig near Santiago da Cuba, which eventually fired at her. A battle close to shore resulted in the brig, probably *Mutine* (18), being dismasted and wrecked. On 14 October *Racoon* encountered three vessels evacuating French troops from St Domingue and attacked. The brig *Petite Fille*, then the cutter *Amélie*, and finally the schooner *Jeune Adèle*, surrendered. They carried over 300 soldiers between them. The brig's crew overpowered the prize crew and ran the ship ashore, but Bissell recovered his men. (James 3.189–191; Clowes 5.328, 555)

Raglan and *M-23* v. *Goeben* and *Breslau*, 20 January 1918
The German battle-cruiser *Goeben* and the cruiser *Breslau* came through the Dardanelles. *Goeben* hit a mine soon after leaving the strait but the two ships reached Kusu Bay, where they bombarded and destroyed the monitors *Raglan* and *M-23*. The German ships turned to attack Allied shipping in Mudros harbour, but *Breslau* hit several mines and began to sink, though *Goeben* extricated herself from this minefield. Four Turkish destroyers were driven off by the destroyers *Lizard* and *Tigress*. *Goeben* struck another mine on her return to the strait and then ran aground inside the strait. She remained aground and under Allied bombardment until 26 January when she was refloated. The submarine *E-14* went in to attack, but too late, and was sunk on the return voyage. (Newbolt 5.84–92)

Ragusa (Dubrovnik), 15 November 1813–28 January 1814
The population of Ragusa rose against the French, who were besieged in the castle. *Bacchante* (38; Capt. William Hoste) briefly helped with the siege in November 1813 and left some soldiers. When she returned in January, the British troops and some Austrians were leading the siege. By great exertions sailors of *Bacchante* and *Saracen* emplaced a battery on a hill above the city. This persuaded the French to surrender (on 28 January). (James 6.20, 119; T. Pocock, *Remember Nelson*, London 1977, ch. 10; Clowes 5.536)

Rainbow and others v. *Hancock* and others, 6–8 July 1777
The American frigates *Hancock* (32) and *Boston* (30) and their prize *Fox* (28) encountered *Rainbow* (44; Capt. Sir George Collier) and *Victor* (18), who pursued them. The American ships scattered when *Flora* (32; Capt. John Brisbane) joined in. *Hancock* was forced to surrender by *Rainbow*, and *Flora* forced *Fox* to strike. *Boston* got away. (Clowes 4.6–7; Syrett, *American* 71–72; Mackesy, *America* 173)

Rainbow v. *Hebe*, 4 September 1782
Rainbow (44; Capt. Henry Trollope) chased the French frigate *Hebe* near the Ile de Batz. *Hebe* surrendered at the first exchange of fire, under the impression that *Rainbow* was a line-of-battle ship. (Clowes 4.86)

Rainbow and *Avon* v. *Neréide*, 13–14 February 1810
The French frigate *Neréide* (40) arrived at Guadeloupe to find the island in British control. Evading several frigates, she was later chased by the sloop *Rainbow* (28; Capt. James Wooldridge) and the brig *Avon* (18; Cmdr Henry Fraser). The two British ships attacked separately, so *Neréide* was able to beat them off singly without trouble. (James 5.92–95)

Raison v. *Vengeance*, 25 August 1796
Raison (20; Capt. John Beresford) met *Vengeance* (40) and tried to evade, but was challenged. The fight, conducted in a fog, resulted in *Raison* escaping. (James 1.384–385; Clowes 4.492)

Rajputana v. *U-108*, 13 April 1941
The AMC *Rajputana* was sunk by *U-108* in the Denmark Strait. (Rohwer 68)

Raleigh v. *Rio de la Plata*, November 1834
The sloop *Raleigh* captured the Brazilian slaver *Rio de la Plata*, carrying 523 slaves. (Bethell 138)

Rambler v. French privateer, 28 September 1810
A party from *Rambler* (14; Cmdr Robert Hall) landed at the mouth of the River Barbate near Tarifa in southern Spain, and attacked a French privateer anchored several miles upriver. The ship was captured. (James 5.127–128)

Rambler at San Lucar, July 1811
Boats from *Rambler* (14) went into San Lucar to cut out a schooner; met by strong resistance, the exploit had to be abandoned. (Hall 128)

Ramillies and others v. Combined Fleet, 9 August 1780
A large British convoy from the West Indies, escorted by *Ramillies* (74; Capt. John Moutray), was mainly captured by the Franco-Spanish Combined Fleet – fifty-five out of sixty-three ships. The British warships escaped. Moutray was blamed, even though the merchantmen had disobeyed his orders to change course. (Clowes 3.477–478, 4.55; Mackesy, *America* 357)

Ramillies and *Ulysses* v. *Franklin*, 1781
The French privateer *Franklin* (28) was intercepted and captured by *Ramillies* (74) and *Ulysses* (34). (Colledge 278)

Ramsey v. *Meteor*, 8 August 1915
The armed boarding steamer *Ramsey*, near Cromarty, stopped the German minelayer *Meteor*, flying the Russian flag; it suddenly displayed German colours and sank *Ramsey*, using a masked gun. *Meteor* was then hunted across the North Sea by British ships until she was trapped and scuttled. (Corbett 3.122–126; Hore 254)

Rangariri, New Zealand, 20 November 1863
A partly constructed Maori defensive line (*pa*) was attacked by a Naval Brigade from several vessels in combination with a larger army force. A day's assault failed to take the position, at a cost of over 100 casualties. (Clowes 7.180–181; Belich 145–155)

Ranger v. Mahratta fleet, April 1783
The BM brig *Ranger* (12; Lt Pruen) encountered the Mahratta fleet (fifteen ships) on her way to Calicut; after a fight, *Ranger* was boarded and taken. (Low 1.157–161)

Ranger v. French ship, 28 June 1794
The cutter *Ranger* (14; Lt Isaac Cotgrave) was captured by the French off Brest. (Clowes 4.548)

Ranger v. French squadron, 17 July 1805
The French Rochefort squadron, stationed off Finisterre hoping to join Villeneuve's fleet, expected from the West Indies, captured *Ranger* (18; Cmdr Charles Coote). She was so damaged by the crew beforehand that she was burned. (James 4.48; Clowes 5.371)

Rapid v. feluccas, 18 May 1808
The brig *Rapid* (18; Lt Henry Baugh) chased two feluccas near Cape St Vincent but was hit by fire from a shore battery and sunk. (Hall 24)

Rapid v. slaver, 1842
The brig *Rapid* captured a slaver at Bimbia, West Africa, after an exchange of musket fire. (Dike 68)

Raposa v. Spanish ship, 15 February 1808
The brig *Raposa* (10; Lt James Violett) was attacked and captured near Cartagena. (Clowes 5.552)

Rathlin Island, Ireland, 1575
An English squadron under Francis Drake patrolled the North Channel to assist the Earl of Essex's plantation in Ulster. A large number of women and children who took refuge on Rathlin were massacred by some of the English crews. (Rodger 1.243)

Rattler v. Chinese pirates, 28 May 1855
The screw sloop *Rattler* (Cmdr William Fellowes) attacked and destroyed a group of pirate junks at Samchow. (Clowes 6.389)

Rattler and others v. Chinese pirates, 4 August 1855
The screw sloop *Rattler* (Cmdr William Fellowes), the armed steamer *Eaglet*, and the US steam frigate *Powhatan* attacked a pirate base near Canton. Several pirate ships were captured or sunk; casualties were eight killed and sixteen wounded; 500 pirates died and 1000 were captured. (Clowes 6.389–390)

Rattlesnake v. privateers, 14 March 1779
Rattlesnake (10; Lt William Knell) attacked two French privateer cutters. One surrendered after three hours; the second, *Frélon* (12), was captured by boarding; meanwhile the first escaped. (Clowes 4.24)

Rattlesnake v. *Marie Louise*, 22 October 1795
The sloop *Rattlesnake* (16; Cmdr Edward Ramage) captured the Dutch brig *Marie Louise* (14) off the Cape of Good Hope. (Clowes 4.558)

'Rauthabjorg', 1046
Jarl Thorfinn the Mighty of Orkney was challenged by his nephew Rognvald Brusison, who received help from the king of Norway, while Thorfinn had help from Karl Arnisson, ruler of the Hebrides. The two forces fought a sea-

battle at 'Rauthabjorg', which was somewhere in the Pentland Firth. Thorfinn was victorious. (Thompson 51; *Orkneyinga Saga* 26)

Raven v. two French frigates, 1783
The sloop *Raven* (16; Cmdr John Wells) was captured by two French frigates in the West Indies. (Clowes 4.112)

Raven v. French flotilla, 3 July 1812
The sloop *Raven* (Cmdr George Lennock) attacked a flotilla of fourteen brigs coming out of the Scheldt. Three were driven on shore. (James 5.324; Clowes 5.509)

Ravenspur, Yorkshire
1399 A small squadron sailed from Boulogne and landed Henry Duke of Lancaster at 'Ravensrode' in July; Henry was ostensibly claiming his rightful inheritance, but three months later he carried through a *coup* and made himself king as Henry IV. (Clowes 1.302)

1471 Edward IV, driven into exile the year before, returned to reclaim his throne with 1200 men in a fleet of thirty-six ships. An attempted landing at Cromer in Norfolk failed. They sailed north to Ravenspur, by which time Edward was alone, the other ships having been dispersed by a storm. He landed on 11 August; the rest of the ships soon arrived. (Gillingham 189–190; Clowes 1.389–390)

Rawalpindi v. *Scharnhorst*, 23 November 1939
The AMC *Rawalpindi* was sunk by the battle-cruiser *Scharnhorst* in the North Atlantic. (Rohwer 9)

Recruit v. *Diligente*, 6 September 1808
The sloop *Recruit* (Cmdr Charles Napier) met the French corvette *Diligente* heading for Martinique. The two fought for three hours until *Recruit* was disabled; *Diligente*, also damaged, sailed away. (James 4.372–374)

Recruit v. *UB-6*, 1 May 1915
The destroyer *Recruit* (Cmdr C.A.W. Wrightson) was sunk by *UB-6* in the Thames estuary. The destroyer *Brazen* (Lt-Cmdr E.O. Broadley) searched for the submarine unsuccessfully. (Corbett 2.401)

Recruit v. *UB-16*, 9 August 1917
The destroyer *Recruit* was sunk by *UB-16* in the North Sea. (Colledge 353)

Redbreast v. *UC-38*, 15 July 1917
The hired ship *Redbreast*, serving as a decoy ship, was sunk by *UC-38* in the Mediterranean. (Colledge 334)

Redbridge v. French ship, 4 August 1803
The schooner *Redbridge* (12; Midshipman George Lempriere) was captured by the French off Toulon. (Clowes 4.549)

Redmill v. *U-1105*, **27 April 1945**
U-1105 torpedoed the destroyer *Redmill* off the west coast of Scotland; the ship was saved but never repaired. (Rohwer 406)

Redpole v. *Grand Rodeur*, **10 December 1809**
The sloop *Redpole* (16; Cmdr Colin MacDonald) captured the French sloop *Grand Rodeur*. (Clowes 5.561)

Redpole v. *Congress*, **October 1828**
The packet *Redpole* (10) was sunk in a fight with the pirate ship *Congress*, off Cabo Frio. (Clowes 6.505)

Redwing v. **Spanish convoy, 7 May 1808**
The sloop *Redwing* (Cmdr Thomas Ussher) met a Spanish convoy of twelve merchantmen escorted by seven gunboats off Cape Trafalgar. Five of the gunboats were driven ashore by *Redwing*'s fire and seven of the merchantmen and one gunboat were captured; four merchantmen were sunk. (James 4.337–338; Clowes 5.416)

Regent v. *Gabbiano*, **16 April 1943**
The Italian corvette *Gabbiano* sank the submarine *Regent*. (Rohwer 241)

Regina v. *Avorio*, **8 February 1943**
The Italian submarine *Avorio* was sunk by the Canadian corvette *Regina* off Philippeville, Algeria. (Rohwer 225)

Regulus v. *San Pio*, **2 November 1796**
The frigate *Regulus* (44; Capt. William Carthew) captured the sloop *San Pio* (18). (Clowes 4.560)

Regulus at **Puerto Rico, 11 July 1798**
Boats of the frigate *Regulus* (44; Capt. George Eyre) went in to cut out ships at Aguada Bay. Five ships were secured, but only three could be brought out. (James 2.253–254)

Reindeer v. *Voltigeur* and *Phaeton*, **24 March 1806**
The sloop *Reindeer* (18; Cmdr John Fyffe) met the French corvettes *Phaeton* (16) and *Voltigeur* (16) off Puerto Rico. *Reindeer* attacked both ships, firing at each alternately. They eventually got away when *Reindeer*'s rigging was damaged. (James 4.133–134; Clowes 5.375)

Reindeer v. *Wasp*, **28 June 1814**
The sloop *Reindeer* (18; Cmdr William Manners) met and chased the US sloop *Wasp*. *Reindeer* was badly outmatched and was burnt by the victors. Manners was killed. (James 6.161–165; *NC* 5.245)

Relentless v. *Charlotte Schliemann*, **11–12 January 1944**
The German tanker *Charlotte Schliemann*, which replenished U-boats, was

located by air near Mauritius; when approached by the destroyer *Relentless* she was scuttled. (Rohwer 406)

Remembrance v. *U-38*, 14 August 1916
Remembrance, operating as a decoy ship in the Mediterranean, was sunk by *U-38*. (Colledge 355)

Renard v. *Général Ernouf*, 20 March 1805
The sloop *Renard* (18; Cmdr Jeremiah Coghlan) chased the privateer *Général Ernouf* (20) north of St Domingue. After a short fight the privateer blew up; only a third of her people were saved. (James 4.26–27; Clowes 4.359)

Renard v. *Diligent*, 25–27 May 1806
The sloop *Renard* (18; Cmdr Jeremiah Coghlan) chased the French corvette *Diligent* (16) for two days east from Puerto Rico; when *Renard* caught up at last, *Diligent* surrendered without either party having to fire a shot. (James 4.147–148; Clowes 5.382)

Renfrew, Scotland, 1164
Somerled, king of the Isles, invaded Scotland with a fleet of 160 ships gathered from the Hebrides, Argyll, Kintyre, and Dublin. He landed at Renfrew in the Clyde estuary but was defeated and killed in battle nearby, probably at Knock. (MacDonald 61–62)

Renommée, Spain, 1806
The frigate *Renommée* (36; Capt. Sir Thomas Livingstone) attacked the Spanish brig *Vigilante* (18) at anchor under Fort Callartes, near Cartagena, Spain, on 3 April, and quickly captured her and two gunboats. On 3 May boats from *Renommée* and the sloop *Nautilus* (18; Cmdr Edward Palmer) went into the port of Vieja, Spain, to attack the schooner *Giganta* (5). The ship was fully prepared for the attack, but was quickly boarded and taken without serious loss. On 21 October *Renommée*'s boats went into the harbour of Colon, Majorca, and cut out two settees, loaded with grain, and a tartan, which ran aground and was burnt. Next day a party was landed to suppress musket fire from the shore and another settee was captured. (James 4.136–138; Clowes 5.376)

Renommée and *Grasshopper* off Cartagena, November–December 1807
The frigate *Renommée* (36; Capt. Sir Thomas Livingstone) and the sloop *Grasshopper* (18; Cmdr Thomas Searle) sent boats to cut out two vessels at anchor north of Cartagena, Spain, on 6 November. These were captured but the current sent both ships and boats on shore. Heavy fire from the land forced abandonment of the captured vessels. On 11 December 1807 the Spanish brig *San Josef* near Cartagena was attacked and run ashore; under fire, men from *Grasshopper* refloated and brought the ship off. (James 4.270–271, 273; Clowes 5.403–404)

Renown and *Rochester* v. *Guirlande*, 29 June 1758
The French frigate *Guirlande* (22) was captured by *Renown* (32; Capt. George McKenzie), helped by *Rochester* (50; Capt. Robert Duff). (Clowes 3.193)

Renown v. *Languedoc*, 13 August 1778
Renown (50; Capt. George Dawson) attacked *Languedoc* (80), already dismasted in a storm. *Renown* battered at the bigger ship all day and ceased at nightfall, intending to continue in the morning, but *Languedoc* was rescued by six French line-of-battle ships which drove *Renown* away. (Clowes 4.16–17; Syrett, *Howe* 84–85)

Renown v. *Champenoite*, 4 May 1809
The French brig *Champenoite* (12) was captured by *Renown* (74; Capt. Philip Durham) off Toulon. (Clowes 5.559)

Renown v. *Scharnhorst* and *Gneisenau*, 9 April 1940
The battle-cruiser *Renown* briefly exchanged fire with the German battle-cruisers *Scharnhorst* and *Gneisenau* off Norway; *Gneisenau* was damaged. (Rohwer 19)

Reserve and *Foresight* v. French privateer, September 1694
Reserve (48; Capt. James Lance) and *Foresight* (46) captured a French privateer (28) from St Malo in the western Channel. (Clowes 2.480)

Resistance and *Duguay-Trouin* v. *Coquette*, 2 March 1783
Resistance (44; Capt. James King) and *Duguay-Trouin* (18; Capt. John Fish) chased and captured the French frigate *Coquette* (28) in the West Indies. (Clowes 4.94–95)

Resistance v. *Revenge*, October 1794
The French sloop *Revenge* (18) was captured in the Sunda Strait by *Resistance* (44; Capt. Edward Pakenham). (Clowes 4.553)

Resistance v. Dutch ships, October 1797
The frigate *Resistance* (44; Capt. Edward Pakenham) captured a number of small Dutch vessels in the East Indies. (Clowes 4.559)

Resistance at Anchove, Spain, 8 March 1809
The frigate *Resistance* (38; Capt. Charles Adam) raided the harbour at Anchove, northern Spain, capturing a schooner and a *chasse-marée* loaded with French military supplies. (Hall 75)

Resolution v. Dutch privateer, 10 March 1673
Resolution (68; Capt. Sir John Berry) met and captured a Dutch privateer west of Scilly. (Clowes 2.447)

Resolution v. French squadron, 19 March 1707
Resolution (70; Capt. Hon. Henry Mordaunt), with other ships in company near Genoa, was chased by a French squadron which included six line-of-battle ships. The ships with *Resolution* scattered. *Resolution* ran aground at Ventimiglia, but fought off attempts to capture her, and was evacuated and burned. (Clowes 2.515–516)

Resolution and Raikes v. French ships, 6 June 1782
The armed transports *Resolution* (12) and *Raikes* (12) were captured by the French in the East Indies. (Clowes 4.112)

Resource v. Licorne, 20 April 1781
Resource (28; Capt. Bartholomew Rowley) was attacked by the French frigate *Licorne* (28). (Clowes 4.63–64)

Restoration v. Angria's squadron, 1749
Restoration, flagship of the BM, was captured by ships of Tulaji Angria. (Keay 265)

Reunion and others v. Alliantie and others, 22 August 1795
The frigates *Reunion* (36; Capt. James Almes), *Isis* (50; Capt. Robert Watson), *Stag* (32; Capt. Joseph Yorke), and *Vestal* (28; Capt. Charles White) chased the Dutch frigates *Argo* (36) and *Alliantie* (38) and the cutter *Vlugheld* (16) near Norway. *Alliantie* was captured; the other ships took refuge in the Norwegian port of Egeroe. (James 1.324–325; Clowes 4.493)

Revenge and Little Victory v. Algerine raiders, 14–17 December 1670
Revenge (52; Vice-Admiral Sir Edward Spragge) chased two Algerine ships, which pulled away; Spragge sent *Little Victory* (28; Capt. Leonard Harris) to delay them, and *Revenge* then came up and captured one of the Algerines. (Clowes 2.439)

Revenge and Falmouth v. French squadron, 4 August 1704
Revenge (60; Capt. William Kerr) and *Falmouth* (48; Capt. Thomas Kenney) fought a squadron commanded by Duguay-Trouin. *Falmouth* was forced to surrender. (Clowes 2.506; Owen 104)

Revenge v. L'Indienne, 1756
The BM ship *Revenge* (28; Capt. William James) met, fought, and captured the French ship *L'Indienne* (34) which was heading for Mauritius. (Low 1.137)

Revenge and Bombay v. Shumsher Jung, Gheriah, 1775
The BM frigate *Revenge* (Commodore John Moore) and the grab *Bombay* (Capt. Sheriff) attacked the Mahratta fleet. The BM ships concentrated on the largest Mahratta vessel, *Shumsher Jung* (46), which eventually blew up. The rest of the Mahratta fleet retired. (Low 1.156–157)

Revenge at Palamos, 8 November 1813
The boats of *Revenge* (74; Capt. Sir John Gore) went into Palamos and cut out a French privateer. (James 6.35; Clowes 5.539)

Revolutionnaire v. Unité, 12 April 1796
Revolutionnaire (38; Capt. Francis Cole), one of a frigate squadron, went to attack the French frigate *Unité* (36) near Ushant. With four other frigates

approaching, *Unité* made only a slight resistance before surrendering. (James 1.357–358; Clowes 4.495–496)

Revolutionnaire off Ireland, 1799–1800
The frigate *Revolutionnaire* (38; Capt. Thomas Twysden) chased and captured the French privateer *Bordelais* (24) off Ireland in October 1799, and in the next few months captured *Determinée* (24) and the sloop *Trompeuse* (18). (James 2.399–400; Clowes 4.525; Colledge 109, 417)

Rewa v. *U-55*, 4 January 1918
The hospital ship *Rewa* was torpedoed and sunk by *U-55* in the entrance to the Bristol Channel, even though it was fully lit and in supposedly safe waters for hospital ships. (Halpern, *Mediterranean* 324)

Rhode Island, 8 December 1776
A British force from New York occupied Rhode Island and Narragansett Bay to deny the area to privateers and provide a base for the navy. (Clowes 3.386)

Rhododendron v. *U-70*, 5 May 1918
The sloop *Rhododendron* was sunk by *U-70* in the North Sea. (Colledge 359)

Richmond v. *Felicité*, 24 January 1761
Richmond (32; Capt. John Elphinston) followed the French frigate *Felicite* (32) north from Cherbourg. The two ships fought off Scheveningen and continued fighting when they both ran aground. When *Richmond* floated off the French crew escaped ashore and *Felicité* was captured and burnt; her dispatches were saved. (Clowes 3.304)

Richmond v. *Galliard*, 19 April 1807
The brig *Richmond* (18; Lt Samuel Heming) sent in boats to capture the privateer *Galliard* in the harbour of Pedenara, Portugal. (James 4.256; Clowes 5.398)

Rifleman v. *Alban*, 11 May 1811
The Danish cutter *Alban* (12) was chased across the North Sea almost to Shetland by *Rifleman* (8; Cmdr Joseph Pearce), and was there captured. (Anderson 344; Clowes 5.566)

Riflemen v. slavers, 1849–1850
The screw sloop *Rifleman* (Cmdr S.S.L. Crofton) found a Brazilian slaver ashore at Cabo Frio in June 1849, and rescued many of the slaves; the crew had left them to die. On 10 January next year *Rifleman* captured the Brazilian slaver *Providencia* off Santos. (Bethell 310; Lloyd 143–144)

Rinaldo v. *Maraudeur*, 7 December 1810
The sloop *Rinaldo* (10; Cmdr James Anderson) fought two French luggers off Dover on 10 December. *Maraudeur* (14) attempted to board but was repulsed, and was then boarded and captured. The other left. Ten days later

Rinaldo was attacked by four French luggers near the Owers. One, *Vieille Josephine*, was sunk, the others driven off. (James 5.111–113; Clowes 5.475)

Rinaldo and *Redpole* v. French convoy, 3 September 1811
Off Boulogne the sloops *Rinaldo* (10; Cmdr James Anderson) and *Redpole* (10; Cmdr Colin MacDonald) attacked a convoy of brigs and gunboats, which resisted; neither side could claim victory. (James 5.217; Clowes 5.493–494)

Rinaldo, *Bermuda*, and others v. *Apelles*, 3 May 1812
The sloops *Apelles* (14; Cmdr Frederick Hoffman) and *Skylark* (16; Cmdr James Boxer) went ashore near Boulogne and *Apelles* was captured. The sloops *Rinaldo* (Cmdr Sir William Parker) and *Bermuda* (10; Cmdr Alexander Cunningham) bombarded *Apelles* and a party went in to recover her. *Skylark* was burnt by her own crew. (James 5.318–319; Clowes 5.504–505)

Rinaldo at Selangor, Malaya, July 1871
To suppress piracy emanating from Selangor the screw sloop *Rinaldo* (Cmdr George Robinson) and the colonial steamer *Pluto* attacked the town. The sloop, though damaged, bombarded several forts into silence. An Indian Infantry Regiment and a detachment of Royal Artillery then occupied the town without further opposition. (Clowes 7.229–230)

Rio de la Hacha, Spanish Main, 1656
The English fleet based at Jamaica, commanded by William Goodson, sacked Rio de la Hacha. (Capp 96)

Ripon v. *Condé de Chincan*, 1744
Ripon (60) captured the Spanish sloop *Condé de Chincan* (24) in the West Indies. (Clowes 3.315)

Ripon v. *Achille*, 9 March 1761
Ripon (60; Capt. Edward Jekyll) met *Achille* (64) in the Bay of Biscay, and the two fought a running battle for several hours. Both were damaged; *Achille* got away in the dark. (Clowes 3.305)

River Clare, Ireland, 1650
A Parliamentary squadron under William Penn blockaded the ports of western Ireland. He took his ships up the River Clare and attacked settlements along the banks. (Capp 67)

River Nile, Sudan
1884–1885 (Gordon Relief Expedition)   A Naval Brigade was formed from crews of ships of the Mediterranean fleet, under the command of Captain Lord Charles Beresford, to navigate up the Nile. Part of the brigade was in the column which crossed the desert and fought at Abu Klea, but could not reach Khartoum; several small commandeered steamers were equally unable to get through. Part of the brigade was with the army column, which moved so slowly that it was soon withdrawn. (Clowes 7.358–371)

1896–1899 In the conquest of Mahdist Sudan four Egyptian gunboats commanded by naval officers were used in the capture of Dongola and Hafir in 1896, and then in the pursuit as far as Merawe. Next year they reached Berber in September, and bombarded the forts at Metemmah in October. In February 1898 a large Mahdist force crossed the river in the face of fire from the gunboat *Zafir* (Cmdr Colin Keppel). The gunboats were used to dominate the river banks by their fire at the battles of Albara and Omdurman. The flotilla continued in use in the final actions in 1899. (Clowes 7.439–440, 449–451)

River Plate (Rio de la Plata)

1806–1807 The squadron of Capt. Sir Home Popham landed a detachment of troops at Quilmes on 25 June, defeated a Spanish force next day, and on the 27th secured the surrender of the city of Buenos Aires. The city was retaken by local forces a month later. On 29 October Popham landed soldiers at Maldonado at the northern entrance to the River Plate and captured the town, and the fortified island of Goritti nearby.

Popham was superseded by Rear-Admiral Charles Stirling. His squadron of four 64s and three frigates assisted in the successful siege of Montevideo early in February. When further troops arrived, the army landed again on the southern shore, the ships by now under the command of Rear-Admiral George Murray. The attack on Buenos Aires commanded by Lt-General Whitelocke was defeated with considerable loss. An armistice followed so that British prisoners could be brought to the River Plate area for release. The whole force was evacuated in September. (James 4.189–191, 279–282; NRS, *The Royal Navy in the River Plate*, ed. J.D. Grainger, 1996; Clowes 5.204–205, 234–235; *NC* 3.288–310, 4.9–11, 67–74; H. Popham, *A Damned Cunning Fellow*, Tywaedreath 1991, 49–153)

1939 (Battle of the RIVER PLATE) The German pocket battleship *Admiral Graf Spee* was located by three cruisers, *Ajax*, *Exeter*, and RNZS *Achilles*, on 13 December. They attacked from two directions. All ships in the battle were damaged, *Achilles* very badly, and *Exeter* was put out of action. *Graf Spee* took refuge in the Plate estuary at Montevideo, where, given to believe that British reinforcements were arriving, she was scuttled. (Roskill 1.118–121; Rohwer 11)

River Severn, 1049

A fleet of thirty-six Viking ships from Ireland sailed up the River Severn. In alliance with a Welsh king called Gruffudd they ravaged the area. They were opposed by a force led by Bishop Ealdred of Worcester assembled from Worcestershire, Gloucestershire, and Herefordshire, but the Viking-Welsh army learned of its approach. The English army was defeated. (*ASC* s.a. 1050; Maund 124, 164)

Rivoli v. *Melpomène*, 30 April 1815

The French frigate *Melpomène*, carrying the news of Napoleon's return to France to King Joachim Murat, was captured by *Rivoli* (74; Capt. Edward Dickson) near Ischia. (James 6.227)

Roatan Island, Honduras, 1742
An expedition was sent from Jamaica under the convoy of *Lichfield* (50; Capt. James Cusack) and the sloop *Bonetta* (Cmdr William Lea), and landed troops on the island, which was then annexed. (Clowes 3.80)

Robert and *Delight* v. Dutch warships, 1589
Two ships sent out by the Earl of Cumberland, *Robert* and *Delight*, seized a Breton ship and defeated a Flushing warship which attempted to rescue it; later they drove a Rotterdam warship into Calais. (Spence 93)

Robust and *Magnanime* v. *Hoche* and *Embuscade*, 12 October 1798
A French expedition left Brest to land soldiers in Ireland, and was followed by British frigates. Off Tory Island the French commodore *Hoche* (74) was attacked by *Robust* (74; Capt. Edward Thornborough); both ships were reduced to wrecks. The *Magnanime* frigate (44; Capt. Hon. Michael de Courcy) fought the frigate *Embuscade* (36), and came to assist *Robust*; *Hoche* now surrendered. (James 2.139–146)

Rochester v. French merchant ship, August 1696
Rochester (48; Capt. Robert Kirton) captured a merchant ship (20 guns) out of Marseilles in the Mediterranean. (Clowes 2.491)

Rochester v. French ship, September 1697
Rochester (48; Capt. Robert Kirton) captured a French ship of 24 guns in the Channel. (Clowes 2.496–497)

Rochester v. *Gracieuse*, 18 May 1702
The French sloop *Gracieuse* (18) was captured by *Rochester* (48) and renamed *Rochester Prize*. (Colledge 342)

Rochester v. French ships, 1705
Rochester (48; Capt. Edward Owen) captured a French frigate, a privateer of 24 guns, and recaptured a Jamaica ship called *Richard and Sarah*. (Clowes 2.509)

Rochester and others v. *Guirlande*, 18 August 1762
Rochester (50), in company with *Maidstone* and *Renommée*, captured the French frigate *Guirlande* (26) in the Channel. (Clowes 3.308)

Rochester and *Mallow* v. *U-204*, 19 October 1941
Two U-boats stationed off Cape Trafalgar sank two ships, and were hunted by the sloop *Rochester* and the corvette *Mallow*, who sank *U-204*. (Rohwer 109)

Rochester and others v. *U-213*, 31 July 1942
In the Bay of Biscay *U-213* was attacked and sunk by the escort sloops *Rochester*, *Erne*, and *Sandwich*. (Rohwer 185)

Rodney's squadron v. Spanish convoy, 8 January 1780
Admiral Sir George Rodney escorted a convoy taking supplies to blockaded Gibraltar. His squadron of eighteen line-of-battle ships met a Spanish convoy heading for Cadiz. *Bienfaisant* (64) forced the surrender of *Guipozcoana* (64), the largest ship in the Spanish escort; the rest of the convoy, including six smaller warships, was captured. The supplies were taken on to Gibraltar. (Syrett, *European* 85–88; Clowes 3.448)

Rodrigues Island, Indian Ocean, 1809
Rodrigues Island was occupied by a British force as a means to develop supplies for the blockading forces at Mauritius. (Parkinson 366; Low 1.226)

Roebuck and *Medea* v. *Protector*, 1780
The rebel American ship *Protector* (26) was captured by *Roebuck* (44) and *Medea* (28). (Clowes 4.113)

Roebuck and *Orpheus* v. *Confederacy*, 14 April 1781
Roebuck (44; Capt. John Orde) and *Orpheus* (32; Capt. John Colpoys) captured the rebel American frigate *Confederacy* (36), loaded with stores for the rebel army. (Clowes 4.63)

Roebuck v. *Bataaf*, 6 July 1796
The Dutch brig *Bataaf* (12) was captured by the frigate *Roebuck* (44; Capt. Alexander Burrowes) off Barbados. (Clowes 4.558)

Roebuck v. *Brake*, 12 March 1945
The German tanker *Brake*, which replenished U-boats in the Indian Ocean, was approached by the destroyer *Roebuck*, and scuttled. (Rohwer 406; Sebag-Montefiore 319)

Romney v. French vessels, March–August 1696
Romney (48; Capt. Edward Loades) captured the French privateer *Phénix* (30) in the Mediterranean. In July *Romney* and *Canterbury* (60) captured a French merchant ship (18), and in August *Romney* met a Bayonne privateer (54) off the Portuguese coast. The ships fought for two hours, until the privateer took shelter in Portuguese waters. (Clowes 2.491)

Romney off Spain, December 1706–January 1707
Romney (48; Capt. William Coney) bluffed her way into Malaga harbour on 15 December, changed to English colours, captured a French privateer, and escaped, under fire, without suffering any casualties. Next month *Romney*, together with *Milford* (32; Capt. Philip Stanhope) and *Fowey* (32; Capt. Richard Lestock), drove the French ship *Content* (60) ashore near Cape de Gata, where she was burned; in addition *Mercure* (42) was captured. (Clowes 2.510)

Romney v. *Artois* and *Perle*, 1 July 1780
Romney (50; Capt. Roddam Home) captured the French frigate *Artois* (40)

off Finisterre after a short fight, and on the 5th captured *Perle* (18) also near Finisterre; *Perle* surrendered after a single broadside. (Clowes 4.52)

Romney v. *Sybille*, 17 January 1794
Romney (50; Capt. Hon. William Paget), escorting a convoy in the Aegean, met the French frigate *Sibylle* (40) near Mykonos. They manoeuvred to avoid hitting Mykonos town with their fire, then fought. *Sybille* surrendered after an hour, and the three French merchantmen she was guarding were captured. (James 1.231–233; Clowes 4.485)

Romso, Denmark, 19 May 1809
Ardent (64) landed a force of eighty men on the island of Romso in the Great Belt; they were quickly captured by a Danish landing party. (Anderson 338)

Romulus v. French squadron, 25 February 1781
Romulus (44; Capt. George Gayton) encountered a small French squadron of one line-of-battle ship (*Eveille*) and two frigates at the Capes of the Chesapeake, and was captured. (Clowes 3.489, 4.62)

Romulus and *Mahonesa* v. *Nuestra Señora del Rosario*, 24 May 1797
Romulus (56) and *Mahonesa* (34) captured *Nuestra Señora del Rosario* (20) off Cadiz. (Clowes 4.560)

Rook v. two French schooners, 18 August 1808
The schooner *Rook* (4; Lt James Lawrence) was attacked by two French privateer schooners off St Nicolas Mole, St Domingue, and was captured; fifteen out of the twenty men on board were casualties. Lawrence was killed. (James 4.336; Clowes 5.425)

Roos's squadron v. *Cogge de Flandre*, May 1337
Cogge de Flandre, a large merchant ship, was loaded at Calais with supplies for the Scots and carried a contingent of soldiers and dignitaries. It met an English squadron of forty ships from Yarmouth under Sir John Roos which had escorted English ambassadors to Flanders. *Cogge* was captured. (Clowes 1.239; Sumption 1.196)

Rorqual v. *Papa*, 21 August 1940
The submarine *Rorqual* attacked an Italian convoy off Cyrenaica and was then attacked by the TB *Papa*. (Rohwer 38)

Rorqual v. *Capponi*, 21 March 1941
The submarine *Rorqual* sank the Italian submarine *Capponi* and a ship from a convoy west of Sicily. (Rohwer 64)

Rosabelle and *Lady Shirley* v. *U-374*, 11 December 1941
In passing through the Strait of Gibraltar *U-374* sank the ASW trawlers *Rosabelle* and *Lady Shirley*. (Rohwer 121)

Rosamond v. *Papillon*, 17 December 1809
The sloop *Rosamond* (18; Cmdr Benjamin Walker) chased and eventually captured the brig *Papillon* (16) near Santa Cruz. (James 5.47; Clowes 5.448)

Rosario v. *Mamelouck*, 10 December 1810
The sloop *Rosario* (16; Cmdr Booty Harvey) was attacked off Dungeness by two French luggers. One of these, *Mamelouck* (16), was boarded and captured; the second sailed off. (James 5.109–110; Clowes 5.476)

Rosario and *Griffon* v. French flotilla, 27 March 1812
The sloop *Rosario* (16; Cmdr Booty Harvey) met a flotilla of twelve brigs coasting from Boulogne towards Dieppe and was joined by the sloop *Griffon* (16; Capt. George Trollope). The flotilla presented a powerful defence, but *Rosario* managed to break their line. Two brigs were driven on shore, and three captured. (James 5.316–318; Clowes 5.503)

Rosario in the Santa Cruz Islands, 1871
The screw sloop *Rosario* (Lt Albert Markham) cruised in the Santa Cruz Islands making revenge attacks for perceived hostilities committed by the islanders. Villages on Montague Island, Nukapu, Nitendi, and Aurora were destroyed by gunfire. (Clowes 7.230–231)

Rosas, Spain, November–December 1808
The Spanish city of Rosas was under siege by the French. *Excellent* (74; Capt. John West) landed marines and sailors to assist the defence, and the bombs *Meteor* and *Lucifer* were used to harass the besiegers. The ships were eventually driven off by French guns. *Fame* (74; Capt. Richard Bennet) arrived to take *Excellent*'s place, and when *Fame* had to leave, the frigate *Imperieuse* (Capt. Lord Cochrane) took over. The city eventually succumbed on 5 December. (James 4.385–387; Clowes 5.407; Thomas 134–142)

Rose v. Spanish ships, 4 June 1742
Rose (24; Capt. Thomas Frankland) chased four Spanish vessels near Cuba, concentrating on the largest (10). This was battered into a sinking condition; the other three were also damaged. (Clowes 3.268)

Rose v. *Concepcion*, December 1744
Rose (24; Capt. Thomas Frankland) met and fought the treasure ship *Concepcion* (20) on her way from Cartagena to Havana. The Spanish ship was captured along with the treasure. (Clowes 3.279–280)

Rose v. privateers, 28 September 1795
The cutter *Rose* (8; Lt William Walker) met three French privateers off Capraria, and attacked them in succession: the first surrendered, the second sank, the third fled. (James 1.326–328)

Rose v. Dutch ships, 13 October 1800
The hired cutter *Rose* (10; Lt Smith) was captured in the Ems by Dutch ships. (Clowes 4.551)

Rose v. pirates, June–September 1827
The sloop *Rose* (18; Cmdr L. Davies) searched for pirate ships in Greek waters. Several were destroyed near Samothrace on 8 June and more on 12 June. In September *Rose* intercepted more Greek vessels on suspicion of piracy, and in one case retook a recently looted British brig. (NRS, *Piracy* 105–108, 216–217)

Rothesay, Isle of Bute, Scotland
1230 An expedition led by Uspak, appointed as king of the Hebrides by King Hakon IV of Norway, sailed to Orkney with twelve ships; there it was joined by twenty more, and by still more in the Hebrides, to a total of eighty ships. They sailed into the Clyde estuary and besieged Rothesay Castle. The siege was successful but Uspak died. The expedition wintered in Man, ravaged Kintyre next year, then broke up. (MacDonald 90)

1335 A force of Irish ships from Dublin reached the Clyde estuary, aiming to attack Dumbarton Castle, but attacked Rothesay Castle instead. They failed to take it and returned to Dublin later in the year. (Sumption 1.148)

Rover v. *Junon*, 13 September 1780
Rover (18; Cmdr Henry Savage) was attacked and captured by *Junon* (32) in the West Indies. (Clowes 4.57)

Rover v. *Flor de Loanda* and *Cesar*, April 1836
The sloop *Rover* captured the Brazilian slavers *Flor de Loanda* and *Cesar* at the Manica Islands, Brazil. (Bethell 144)

Rover v. *Clio* and *Castone*, 7 January 1941
The British submarine *Rover* attacked an Italian convoy, but was driven off and damaged by the TBs *Clio* and *Castone*. (Rohwer 54)

Roxburgh v. *U-38*, 20 June 1915
The cruiser *Roxburgh* was torpedoed by *U-38* while taking part in a sweep through the North Sea, but survived. (Corbett 3.46)

Roxburgh v. *U-89*, 12 February 1918
The cruiser *Roxburgh* rammed and sank *U-89* in the waters north of Ireland. (Newbolt 5.427; Grant 111)

Royal Edward v. *UB-14*, 15 August 1915
The troop transport *Royal Edward* was torpedoed in the Aegean by *U-14*; about 900 soldiers died when she sank. (Corbett 3.112–113)

Royal Oak and others v. French squadron, 1 May 1707
A convoy of over forty merchant ships, escorted by *Royal Oak* (76; Capt. Baron Wylde), *Hampton Court* (70; Capt. George Clements), and *Grafton* (70; Capt. Edward Aston), sailed from the Downs down-Channel. It was intercepted by a squadron of eight French ships commanded by the Cheva-

lier de Forbin off Brighton. *Grafton* was boarded and captured almost at once; *Hampton Court* was boarded, escaped, but was then attacked by other ships and forced to surrender; *Royal Oak* was very badly damaged. Half the merchant ships were captured. (Clowes 2.511–512)

Royal Oak v. Spanish frigate, 16 January 1719
Royal Oak (70) captured a Spanish frigate. (Clowes 3.364)

Royal Oak v. Nuestra Señora del Rosario, 11 March 1727
Royal Oak (70) captured the new Spanish ship *Nuestra Señora del Rosario*. (Clowes 3.47)

Royal Oak v. U-47, 14 October 1939
On orders from submarine command *U-47* penetrated the incomplete defences of Scapa Flow in the Orkneys and sank the battleship *Royal Oak*, then escaped. This was one of the outstanding feats of the naval war. Much insecurity followed in the Royal Navy. The defences of Scapa Flow were hurried on. (Terraine 223–224; Rohwer 6)

Royalist v. Princesse and others, 1 May 1809
Royalist (18; Cmdr John Maxwell) fought five lugger privateers in the Channel, and captured *Princesse* (16). (Clowes 5.437)

Royalist in the Downs, November–December 1809
While stationed in the Downs, *Royalist* (18; Cmdr John Maxwell) captured the sloop *Grand Napoleon* on 17 November, *Heureuse Etoile* (2) on 6 December, the sloop *Beau Marseille* five days later, and *Françoise* (14) on the 31st. (Clowes 5.559–560)

Ruby and Portsmouth v. Dutch ship, 5 January 1653
Ruby (42; Capt. Anthony Houlding) and *Portsmouth* (36; Capt. Dornford), cruising west along the Channel, met and fought a Dutch ship of 46 guns, without result. (Powell 199)

Ruby v. Entreprenant, April 1694
Ruby (48; Capt. Robert Fairfax), off Ireland, captured the privateer *Entreprenant* (46) after a difficult fight. (Clowes 2.479)

Ruby and Niger v. Minerve, 7 March 1779
The French frigate *Minerve* (32) was attacked by *Ruby* (64) and *Niger* (32); she disabled *Niger* by firing at her rigging, and then got away. (Clowes 4.24)

Ruby and others v. Prudente, 2 June 1779
Ruby (64; Capt. Michael Everitt), in company with the frigate *Aeolus* (32) and the sloop *Jamaica* (18), met the French frigate *Prudente* (36) off St Domingue. *Ruby* chased *Prudente* (36) and eventually forced her to surrender; Everitt was killed. (Clowes 4.27)

Ruby v. *Solitaire*, 6 December 1782
Ruby (64; Capt. John Collins) was one of a squadron near Barbados which encountered a French squadron. She captured *Solitaire* (64) after a stiff battle. (Clowes 4.90–91)

Rupert and others off Brest, 1689
Rupert (66; Capt. Sir Francis Wheler), off Brest, with twelve other ships, captured a French warship carrying dispatches, and a large number of storeships with supplies for the French army in Ireland. (Clowes 2.461)

Rupert and *Adventure* v. French privateers, October 1692
Rupert (66; Capt. Basil Beaumont) and *Adventure* (44; Capt. Thomas Dilkes), off the Irish coast, fought two French privateers, recovered two of their prizes, and captured two enemy merchantmen. They also captured three more privateers in December. (Clowes 2.469)

Rupert and *Conn* v. *U-965*, 30 March 1945
U-965 was sunk by the destroyers *Rupert* and *Conn*. (Rohwer 397)

Russell v. *Betsy*, 3 June 1803
Russell (74) captured and destroyed the French *Betsy* (4). (Clowes 5.555)

RUSSIAN CONVOYS, 1941–1945
Convoys sailed between the UK and/or Iceland and Russian ports, particularly Murmansk. The first had no designation, but when the system was fully organised the codes were:

PQ, JW – westbound
QP, RA – eastbound

Only convoys which came under attack are listed; the dates are those of fighting. The first supply convoy, codenamed 'Dervish', set out from Iceland for Murmansk on 21 August 1941; it made no enemy contact. (Schofield 9)

PQ-7A, 30 December 1941
This convoy moved in two parts. Of the first (7A – two ships), *U-134* sank one of the freighters. (Rohwer 129)

PQ-12/QP-8, 7–8 March 1942
These two convoys set off from Reykjavik and Kola Inlet simultaneously in order that both could be protected by the same escorts. The German battleship *Tirpitz*, with four destroyers, came out from its northern Norwegian base to attack. The convoy escort included an aircraft carrier, three battleships, cruisers, and destroyers. Both forces groped in thick weather to find each other. A flight of aircraft from *Victorious* finally found *Tirpitz*, but all their torpedoes missed. One ship of the convoy was sunk by a German destroyer. (Schofield 31–38; Rohwer 149–150)

QP-9, 21–24 March 1942
The escorting minesweeper *Sharpshooter* located and sank *U-655* in the only action which involved this convoy. (Schofield 42; Rohwer 153)

PQ-13, 27 March–1 April 1942
A violent storm scattered this convoy. On 27 March it was located by a German reconnaissance aircraft, and two ships were sunk by dive-bombers. Three German destroyers came out to attack, but met the cruiser *Trinidad* and the destroyer *Fury*. One destroyer, *Z-26*, was sunk; the others returned to Norway. *Trinidad* was hit by one of her own torpedoes. Of the remaining merchant ships three were sunk by U-boats, but *Fury* sank *U-585*. (Schofield 42–46; Rohwer 151, 153, 157)

PQ-14/QP-10, 10–17 April 1942
Ice damage compelled most of PQ-14 to return to Iceland from Jan Mayen Island for repairs. Eight ships continued; one was sunk by *U-403*. QP-10 was heavily attacked by both aircraft and U-boats and four ships were sunk. (Schofield 46–47; Rohwer 158)

PQ-15/QP-11, 28 April–3 May 1942
These convoys approached and passed each other near Bear Island and were attacked by the same German forces. The cruiser *Edinburgh* was damaged by torpedoes from *U-456* and turned back towards Murmansk, assisted by destroyers and minesweepers. QP-11 was attacked further west by aircraft, U-boats, and three German destroyers in five successive attacks; they were driven off by the escort. The destroyers turned to attack the slow-moving *Edinburgh*. In the fight which followed, the destroyer *Hermann Schoerman* was sunk and two British destroyers were damaged. *Edinburgh* was damaged again, and had to be sunk. The two remaining German destroyers were driven off by the minesweepers. Finally PQ-15 was attacked by aircraft, which sank three ships. (Schofield 48–53; Rohwer 161–162)

PQ-16, 25–30 May 1942
This convoy came under repeated attack by aircraft and U-boats for six days. The continuous daylight permitted attacks for twenty out of twenty-four hours, the only respite being a period of fog. Six ships were sunk by aircraft and one by *U-703*. (Schofield 57–67; Rohwer 167)

PQ-17, 1–24 July 1942
A series of air attacks from Norwegian airfields sank three ships from this convoy by 4 July. In the Admiralty it was believed that a major German surface force, including the battleship *Tirpitz*, the pocket battleship *Admiral Scheer*, and the cruiser *Admiral Hipper*, had sailed to attack the convoy. On 4 July orders were given to the convoy escort to withdraw westwards and for the convoy to scatter, the ships making their way independently to Archangel. The result was the destruction of the convoy: fourteen ships were sunk by aircraft, ten by U-boat; only eleven reached Archangel. The disaster has been a continuous source of controversy ever since. (Schofield 69–98; J. Broome, *Convoy Is to Scatter*, London 1972; D. Irving, *The Destruction of Convoy PQ 17*, London 1968; Rohwer 175–176; Sebag-Montefiore 230–245)

PQ-18, 12–19 September 1942
This convoy, accompanied by a very large escort including the carrier *Avenger*, was attacked by frequent air sorties and by several U-boats. Thirteen out of

forty merchant ships were sunk; the Germans lost thirty-seven aircraft and two submarines: *U-589* was sunk by the destroyer *Onslow*, and *U-457* by *Impulsive*. (Schofield 105–116; Rohwer 195–196)

QP-14, 20–22 September 1942
This small convoy was heavily escorted. It was attacked by aircraft and U-boats in the waters round Spitzbergen and lost four merchant ships; the minesweeper *Leda* was sunk by *U-435* and the destroyer *Somali* by *U-703*. (Schofield 117–123; Rohwer 195)

PQ-19, 29 October 1942
This convoy travelled as single ships, for no escort was available other than single trawlers stationed along the route. Six of the merchant ships were sunk by air and submarine attacks. (Rohwer 207)

QP-15, 23 November 1942
An accumulation of empty ships at the White Sea was brought west. A series of gales prevented interception by surface ships or aircraft, but two vessels were sunk by U-boats. (Schofield 127–128; Rohwer 213)

JW-51B, 22–30 December 1942 (Battle of the BARENTS SEA)
The second half of convoy JW-51 was detected by *U-354*; the cruisers *Admiral Hipper* and *Lutzow* and six destroyers came out from Altenfjord to attack. The destroyers of the escort kept the cruisers from getting near the convoy. The destroyer *Achates* and the minesweeper *Bramble* were sunk; two destroyers were damaged. The cruisers *Sheffield* and *Jamaica* joined in; the German force withdrew with *Hipper* damaged and the destroyer *Eckholdt* sunk. One of the merchant ships was damaged. (Schofield 132–147; Rohwer 219, 221)

JW-52, 23–26 January 1943
Attacked by aircraft and U-boats, this convoy got through without loss. (Schofield 152–153; Rohwer 226)

RA-52, 30 January 1943
One ship of this convoy was sunk by a U-boat. (Schofield 152; Rohwer 226)

JW-53, 27–29 February 1943
Attacked by U-boats and two waves of aircraft, this convoy got through intact to the Russian ports, though with several ships damaged by air attack. (Schofield 152–153; Rohwer 232)

RA-53, 5–6 March 1943
This large convoy of empty ships was attacked by U-boats. Bad weather kept aircraft away except for one foiled attack. Two ships were sunk by submarines and one foundered, out of thirty. (Schofield 153–154; Rohwer 233)

JW-55B, 23–26 December 1943 (Battle of NORTH CAPE)
This convoy of nineteen ships, with a heavy escort and covered by the Home Fleet, was attacked unsuccessfully by aircraft and by U-boats. On 25 December the battlecruiser *Scharnhorst* and a destroyer escort mounted an attack. They were located by radar and *Scharnhorst* was attacked and damaged

by the cruisers *Belfast, Norfolk* and *Suffolk* and destroyers. She turned away and was ambushed by the battleship *Duke of York* and the cruiser *Jamaica*. A torpedo attack by British destroyers then stopped *Scharnhorst* and she was sunk by fire from the British ships. The convoy arrived at Kola Inlet without loss. (Schofield 271–188; Rohwer 292–293)

JW-56A, 12–28 January 1944
This convoy ran into a line of U-boats; three merchant ships were sunk, and the destroyer *Obdurate* damaged. (Schofield 190; Rohwer 300)

JW-56B, 22–30 January 1944
This convoy was located by one U-boat, which reported its position and so attracted others. They were driven away from the merchant ships, and *U-314* was sunk by the destroyers *Whitehall* and *Meteor*; the destroyer *Hardy* was badly damaged and had to be sunk. None of the convoy was hit. (Schofield 190–191; Rohwer 300)

RA-56, 4 February 1944
U-985 sank one ship from this convoy. (Rohwer 300, 304)

JW-57, 23–26 February 1944
This was a very large convoy of forty-three ships with nineteen warships in close escort and three cruisers as distant cover. A double line of fourteen U-boats was formed to assault it, but most of their attacks were thwarted by the escorts. *U-713* was sunk by the destroyer *Keppel*, and *U-601* by a Catalina flying boat. The destroyer *Mahratta* was sunk by *U-990*. The convoy itself arrived safely. (Schofield 191–192; Rohwer 307)

RA-57, 4 March 1944
Initial evasive tactics kept this convoy clear of trouble, and when the U-boats located the ships and sank one of them, *U-472* was sunk by the destroyer *Onslaught* and aircraft from the carrier *Chaser*, and *U-366* and *U-973* by *Chaser*'s planes. (Schofield 192–193; Rohwer 307)

JW-58, 29 March–3 April 1944
This large convoy of forty-seven ships and thirty-one escorts was quickly located by German reconnaissance. Six of their aircraft were brought down by planes from the escort carriers *Activity* and *Tracker*. The sloop *Starling* sank *U-961*; *Tracker*'s aircraft and the destroyer *Beagle* sank *U-355*; *Keppel* sank *U-360*; *Activity*'s and *Tracker*'s planes sank *U-288*. The convoy itself was unscathed. (Schofield 194–195; Rohwer 314)

RA-58, 9–11 April 1944
This convoy evaded early contact with U-boats, and their later attacks were unsuccessful. (Schofield 195; Rohwer 314)

RA-59, 28 April–2 May 1944
This convoy was located early in its passage, and attacked by U-boats near Bear Island. One ship was sunk, but aircraft from the escort carriers *Activity* and *Fencer* sank three U-boats – *U-277, U-674,* and *U-959*. (Schofield 196–197; Rohwer 320)

JW-59 15–25 August 1944
U-344 sank the sloop *Kite*, but was itself then sunk by aircraft from the carrier *Vindex*, and *U-354* by the sloops *Mermaid* and *Peacock*, the frigate *Loch Dunvegan*, and the destroyer *Keppel*. The convoy was not hit. (Schofield 200; Rohwer 350–351)

RA-60, 29 September 1944
This convoy evaded two U-boat packs, but two ships were sunk by *U-310*. (Schofield 202; Rohwer 358)

JW-61, 1 November 1944
The frigate *Mounsey* was damaged, but the merchant vessels got through unscathed, despite an attack by a pack of nineteen U-boats. (Schofield 202; Rohwer 368)

RA-62, 11–14 December 1944
U-387 was sunk by *Bamborough Castle* in a drive to push the ambushing U-boats away before this convoy left Kola. It evaded the waiting line of U-boats, but was attacked later, when *U-365* damaged the destroyer *Cassandra*. Two air attacks failed; *U-365* was sunk by aircraft from the carrier *Campania*. (Schofield 206; Rohwer 375–376)

JW-64, 6–11 February 1945
This convoy survived several air attacks and two lines of U-boats. Several shadowing aircraft were shot down, and one air attack was foiled by a change of course. The corvette *Denbigh Castle* was torpedoed at the entrance to the White Sea and had to be written off. (Schofield 207–209; Rohwer 392)

RA-64, 17–22 February 1945
A decoy force of escort vessels pretended to sweep a channel through a minefield off Kola Inlet, during which *U-425* was sunk by the sloop *Lark* and the corvette *Alnwick Castle*; even so the convoy ran into a group of U-boats lying in wait at Kola. *Lark* was damaged by *U-968*, another ship was sunk, and *U-711* sank the sloop *Bluebell*. Twice the convoy was dispersed by storms and one straggler was sunk by air attack. (Schofield 210–213; Rohwer 394)

JW-65, 20 March 1945
This convoy had a clear passage until close to Kola, where U-boats were concentrated. Three merchant ships and the sloop *Lapwing* (by *U-995*) were sunk. (Schofield 214; Rohwer 399–400)

RA-65, 23–31 March 1945
This convoy, heavily escorted, was menaced by ten U-boats near its destination at Kola. The defensive operation was so well conducted that none of them could get near. (Rohwer 403)

RA-66, 29 April–2 May 1945
This convoy was escorted by over twenty warships, with the 19th Escort Group (five ships) as cover. The Soviet destroyers at Kola drove off fourteen U-boats lying in wait, and *U-286* and *U-307* were sunk by the frigates *Loch Insh*, *Loch Shin*, and *Anguilla* and the destroyer *Cotton*. One ship of the convoy was sunk. (Rohwer 492)

Russian Redoubts, Black Sea, May 1854 and February–March 1855

Redoubt Kaleh was bombarded from the sea on 19 May 1854 by the screw battleship *Agamemnon* (Capt. Thomas Symonds) and the French *Charlemagne*; the Russian garrison soon retreated, whereupon a Turkish force, landed earlier, occupied the redoubt. The Anapa and Soujak Kaleh redoubts were attacked by a British squadron in February 1855, Anapa by the paddle frigate *Leopard* (Capt. George Giffard) while a landing drove off the Russian defenders. On 8 March the fort of Djemetil was attacked by the screw gunvessel *Viper* (Lt Charles Lodder); on 13 March *Leopard*, *Viper*, and the screw frigate *Highflyer* (Capt. John Moore) failed in a new attack at Soujak Kaleh. (Clowes 6.402, 450–451)

Ryukyu Islands, March–May 1945

The British Pacific fleet raided the Sakishima-Gunto Islands in the Ryukyus four times between 26 March and 5 May. The fleet consisted of six carriers, two battleships, one New Zealand and four British cruisers, eleven destroyers, a frigate, and two sloops. On 1 April the carrier *Indefatigable* and the destroyer *Ulster* were damaged by kamikaze attacks, and later the carriers *Formidable* and *Indomitable* also, as were *Victorious* and *Formidable* on 9 May. (Rohwer 402, 404, 408, 409)

S

Saba, Gambia, 21 February 1861
A landing was made upstream on the Gambia River by a force which included a Naval Brigade from the screw frigate *Arrogant* (Commodore William Edmondstone), the screw sloop *Falcon* (Cmdr Algernon Heneage), and the screw gunvessel *Torch* (Cmdr Frederick Smith), to attack the king of Baddiboo, who had incurred British displeasure. The town of Saba was reached after a day's march and was bombarded and destroyed. (Clowes 7.188)

Sabine **at Sabiona, Spain, 26 May 1811**
Boats from the sloop *Sabine* (16; Cmdr George Price) went to capture privateers in the port of Sabiona. Two were dragged ashore to foil the attackers, but three were taken. (James 5.266–267; Clowes 5.486; Hall 128)

SADRAS, India, 17 February 1782
The British and French fleets in the Bay of Bengal met near Madras. Vice-Admiral Sir Edward Hughes had nine line-of-battle ships. The French, with twelve ships, concentrated on attacking half of the British, but their gunnery was poor and all the British survived. The British captured several French transports. (Clowes 3.549–552; Tunstall 185; Mahan 430–432)

Safari **v. *Durazzo*, 14 July 1943**
The British submarine *Safari* sank the Italian minelayer *Durazzo*. (Rohwer 260)

Safeguard **v. Danish gunboats, 29 June 1811**
The brig *Safeguard* (12; Lt Thomas England) was attacked off Jutland by four Danish gunboats, and was compelled to surrender. (Anderson 344)

Sagres, Portugal, April–May 1587
Sir Francis Drake landed sailors from his ships at Cape St Vincent and captured the castle of Sagres, whence he disrupted the Spanish coastal trade, burning fishing vessels, intercepting merchant ships, and destroying, so he claimed, large quantities of barrel staves intended for the use of the Armada. (Clowes 1.488; Andrews 140–142; Williamson 298–301)

Sahib **v. *Gabbiano* and others, 24 April 1943**
The submarine *Sahib* was sunk in attacks by the Italian corvettes *Gabbiano* and *Euterpe*, the TB *Climene*, and aircraft. (Rohwer 241)

St Albans **v. French ship, 18 July 1690**
St Albans (50; Capt. Richard Fitzpatrick) fought a French ship of 36 guns off Rame Head, Ireland, and captured it. (Clowes 2.463)

St Albans and Happy Return v. French convoy, February 1691
St Albans (50; Capt. Richard Fitzpatrick), *Happy Return* (54; Capt. Thomas Monck), and some English privateers encountered a French convoy off Cape Barfleur. The escorting French warships were driven on shore and fourteen of the twenty-two ships in the convoy were captured. (Clowes 2.465)

St Albans v. Loire, 1758
St Albans (60) met and captured the French *Loire* (44) in the Mediterranean. (Clowes 3.298)

St Albans v. Concorde, 15 February, 1783
In the West Indies three French ships were chased by a British squadron; *Concorde* (32) was captured by *St Albans* (64; Capt. Charles Inglis). (Clowes 4.94)

St Augustine, Florida
1586 The Spanish fort was captured and destroyed by the squadron of Sir Francis Drake in April. (Rodger 1.249; Andrews 126)

1741 An attempt was made to capture St Augustine by a land force and a squadron of small ships from South Carolina. The Spanish galleys kept off the British ships and in July both forces were withdrawn. (Clowes 3.270)

St Domingue (San Domingo, Hispaniola, Haiti)
1695 A joint Anglo-Spanish attack was made on the French colony of St Domingue. Four ships under Capt. Robert Wilmot co-operated with Spanish forces to attack Cap François and Port de Paix, which were captured. A dispute over loot then prevented further action. (Clowes 2.486)

1703 Capt. William Whetstone, senior officer in the West Indies, captured several privateers in the seas near St Domingue. (Clowes 2.502–503)

1706 A raid made on Petit Guavas, led by Capt. William Kerr, was a failure. (Clowes 2.509)

1793–1794 French Royalists persuaded Lord Dunmore, governor of Jamaica, and the naval commander Commodore John Ford to send troops to the French colony of St Domingue. Landings at Jérémie and Cape Nicolas Mole produced surrenders, partly under the threat of a slave uprising. On 31 May 1794 an expedition attacked the city of Port-au-Prince. *Belliqueux* (64; Capt. James Brine), *Sceptre* (64; Capt. James Dacres), and *Penelope* (32) bombarded Fort Brissoton, while *Europe* (50; Capt. George Gregory) and *Irresistible* (74; Capt. John Henry) fired at relieving forces. A thunderstorm interrupted the firing, but allowed the fort to be reached and captured. Port-au-Prince was occupied three days later. (James 1.128–131, 251–252; Duffy 97–104; Clowes 4.250–251; *NC* 1.64–66)

1796 A landing was made at Léogane on 21 March covered by the frigates *Ceres* (32; Capt. James Newman) and *Iphigenia* (32; Capt. Roddam Gardner) and three sloops, while *Leviathan* (74; Capt. John Duckworth), *Africa* (64;

Capt. Richard Home), and *Swiftsure* (74; Capt. Robert Parker) bombarded the fort and the town. Resistance was stronger than expected and the troops withdrew at once. (James 1.412–413; Duffy 244–246; Clowes 4.293)

1798 The last British forces on the island, covered by a truce, were evacuated in May. (James 2.280; Duffy 305–310; Clowes 4.378)

SAINTES, West Indies, 9 and 12 April 1782

The British and French fleets in the West Indies were built up to their greatest strength, thirty-six and thirty-five line-of-battle ships respectively, under Admirals Sir George Rodney and Comte de Grasse. The fleets met and fought for a time on 9 April without serious result, then sailed slowly north. On the 12th a series of accidents in the French fleet left *Zélé* (64) isolated. De Grasse turned the fleet to assist her and the two fleets approached each other on opposite courses. In the midst of this approach, Rodney demanded that the British get closer, whereupon a shift in the wind allowed him to lead his flagship and the nearest ships to break the French line, a move copied by other British ships. Five French ships were captured, including the flagship *Ville de Paris*. (Clowes 3.520–536; Mahan 485–492; Tunstall 179–182)

St Firmin v. Spanish ships, May 1781

The sloop *St Firmin* (16; Cmdr Jonathan Faulknor) was captured by the Spaniards near Gibraltar. (Clowes 4.111)

St George at Hyeres, August 1707

Capt. Lord Dursley in *St George* (96) landed a force near the Hyères Islands, Provence, and captured several forts. (Clowes 2.516)

St Helena, South Atlantic, May 1673

Capt. Richard Munden, with *Assistance* and a small squadron, arriving at St Helena, found the Dutch in occupation and succeeded in retaking the island. He then captured the Dutch *Europa* with the new Dutch governor, and two rich Dutch East Indiamen. He was knighted for his work. (Clowes 2.446)

ST JAMES'S DAY FIGHT, 25–26 July 1666

The English fleet, commanded by Prince Rupert and the Duke of Albemarle, was attacked at the mouth of the Thames by the Dutch fleet under Admiral de Ruijter, the two fleets being roughly equal in numbers. The fight broke up into three separate conflicts. The English van under Sir Thomas Allin comprehensively defeated the Dutch van; the Dutch rear under Cornelis Tromp drove the English rear under Sir Jeremy Smyth toward the English coast. The centres fought for several hours until the Dutch began to give way, retreating in good order. The fighting continued during the night and into the next day, when the Dutch rear squadron also retreated, pursued by Smyth's squadron which had seemed to be beaten. Casualties were heaviest amongst the Dutch, who lost perhaps twenty ships; the English lost only one ship and two fireships. (Clowes 2.278–283; Rodger 2.75–76; Tunstall 30–31)

***St John* and *Swansea* v. *U-247*, 1 September 1944**
U-247 was sunk by the Canadian frigates *St John* and *Swansea* in the Bristol Channel. (Rohwer 353)

***St John* v. *U-309*, 25 February 1945**
U-309 was sunk by the Canadian frigate *St John* in the Moray Firth. (Rohwer 390)

St John's, Newfoundland
1762 A small French expedition captured St John's in a surprise attack in August, and was at once blockaded by ships and troops from Halifax and Louisburg. The blockaders were driven off by a gale after a month. The French ships escaped, and the land force surrendered. (Clowes **3.250–251**)

1942 *U-513* entered the roads at St John's, Newfoundland on 5 September, sank two ships, and damaged another. (Rohwer 190)

St Kitts, West Indies
1690 A squadron commanded by Commodore Lawrence Wright in *Mary* (62) landed a force of soldiers at Frigate Bay, St Kitts. The French forces in occupation of the island were soon defeated. (Clowes 2.463–464)

1703 Capt. Hovenden Walker, in command of a British squadron, raided the island. (Clowes 2.503)

1782 (Battle of ST KITTS)   The French West Indian fleet landed French troops and captured most of St Kitts. The British fleet under Rear-Admiral Sir Samuel Hood approached. Admiral de Grasse sailed out to meet the British fleet, but Hood anchored in a powerful position close to the land. De Grasse attacked but was beaten off without difficulty, and a second attack also failed. Hood's manoeuvre, regarded as masterly, certainly drove off the French fleet, but the French land force conquered the island. In a carefully concerted move, the British sailed away on the night of 13 February. (Clowes 3.510–519; Mahan 470–477; Tunstall 177–179)

***St Lawrence* v. *Chasseur*, 26 February 1815**
The schooner *St Lawrence* (Lt James Gordon) was intercepted by the US privateer *Chasseur* and forced to surrender; half of her crew were casualties. (James 6.247; Clowes 5.555)

St Lucia, West Indies
1762 A small British expedition went to take possession of the island of St Lucia. The French governor refused to surrender until an attack was about to begin. (Clowes 3.244)

1778 The British fleet at Barbados, commanded by Rear-Admiral Hon. Samuel Barrington, sailed to St Lucia, landed troops, and captured several positions on the west coast. The French fleet under the Comte d'Estaing came in from Martinique. Barrington brought his ships into the Grand Cul de Sac and formed a defensive line, which the French attacked in vain. French troops were landed but failed to take the key post of La Vigie. In the end d'Estaing sailed away; the governor surrendered on 30 December. (Clowes 3.429–432; Mahan 365–366; NRS, *Rodney* nos. 865–866)

1794–1796   A landing by a British force from Martinique in 1794 captured the island with little resistance. In June next year the British garrison, 2000 men, was evacuated by the armed storeship *Experiment* and a transport, but new landings were made on 27–28 March 1796, covered by a bombardment from *Ganges* (74; Capt. Robert MacDougal), *Hebe* (36; Capt. Matthew Scott), and *Pelican* (18; Cmdr John Searle). The island surrendered on 26 May. (James 1.245, 333, 410–411; Duffy 89–91, 144–145, 225–236; Clowes 4.248, 280; *NC* 1.83)

1803   A squadron commanded by Capt. Samuel Hood, including *Centaur* (74; Commodore Bendall Littlehales) and *Courageux* (74; Capt. Benjamin Hallowell) and several smaller ships, landed a force of soldiers at St Lucia, and captured the town and fort within a day. (James 3.203; Clowes 5.56)

St Martin, West Indies
1800   The half-Dutch, half-French island was attacked by a British force, landed and covered by the frigate *Proselyte* and the brig *Drake*. Both parts surrendered after a short resistance. (Duffy 323–324)

1808   A party of men from the sloop *Wanderer* (Cmdr Edward Crofton) and two schooners landed on the island on 3 July. A battery was captured, but an assault on a fort was repelled with loss, and the landing party was soon captured by the French. (James 4.388; Clowes 5.252)

St Mary's, Georgia, 13–14 December 1814
A landing was made to attack the town of St Mary's, under the command of Capt. Philip Somerville of the frigate *Rota*. A fort, the town, and a new gunboat, *Scorpion*, were captured; the captured Indiaman *Countess of Harcourt* was retaken. (James 6.235–236; Morriss 114–116)

St Nazaire, France, 27–28 March 1942
The only dry dock south of Germany capable of holding the German battleship *Tirpitz* was at St Nazaire (built to hold the liner *Normandie*). A commando raiding force in the destroyer *Campbeltown*, two MTBs, and sixteen motor launches attacked the dock. *Campbeltown* rammed the dock gates; the small ships fought the shore defences and the German 5th S-Boat Flotilla – only four returned. The commandos were all killed or captured. *Campbeltown* blew up next morning, destroying the gates and killing a large number of inspecting Germans. (C.E. Lucas-Philips, *The Greatest Raid of All*, London 1958; Rohwer 155)

St Nicolas Point, Java, 25 January 1794
A squadron of EIC ships came in sight of two French frigates and other ships off Java. After a short action the French ships got away. (Low 1.205)

St Patrick v. *Delft* and *Schakerloo*, 5 February 1667
The Dutch warships *Delft* (34) and *Schakerloo* (28), near the North Foreland, met *St Patrick* (48; Capt. Robert Saunders) and *Malaga Merchant* (Capt. Seeley). *Malaga Merchant* kept clear of the fight, which allowed the Dutch ships to board and capture *St Patrick*. Seeley was court-martialled and shot. (Clowes 2.433–434)

St Pierre, Canada
1693 The island of St Pierre in the Gulf of St Lawrence was ravaged by a naval expedition under Sir Francis Wheler in September. (Clowes 2.471)

1793 The frigate *Alligator*, the schooner *Diligente*, and three transports sailed from Halifax, Nova Scotia, to take possession of the French islands of St Pierre and Miquelon in the Gulf of St Lawrence. A landing was made on St Pierre on 14 May and, after some negotiations, the governor surrendered both islands. (James 1.126; Clowes 4.213)

St Vincent, West Indies, 8 June 1796
A landing on St Vincent was covered by *Arethusa* (38; Capt. Thomas Wolley); the island capitulated on the 11th. (James 1.411–412)

Salamis and *Janus* v. pirates, 12 December 1865
Chinese pirates on the island of Tonqua were attacked by parties from *Salamis* (Cmdr Francis Suttie) and *Janus* (Lt Cecil Johnson). Several pirate vessels were destroyed and a number of pirates killed. (Clowes 7.210)

Saldanha Bay, Cape of Good Hope, 21 July 1781
Five Dutch East Indiamen were found in Saldanha Bay by the British squadron of Capt. George Johnstone which had intended to attack Cape Town. The Dutch ships, trapped, ran on shore and were set on fire by their crews, but the British sailors arrived in boats and put the fires out in four of them. The fifth blew up. (Clowes 4.70–71)

SALERNO, Italy, 9 September 1943
The US 5th Army landed in the Bay of Salerno, covered and supported by British and US ships which bombarded the landing place and provided fire support in the early stages of a very difficult battle. The hospital ship *Newfoundland* was sunk, and the battleship *Warspite*, the monitor *Abercrombie*, the destroyer *Laforey*, and the cruiser *Uganda* were all damaged by return fire from the shore, as were several LSTs. The landing was secure by 15 September, and linked up with forward elements of the 8th Army marching from Reggio next day. (Rohwer 272–273; Greene and Massignani 301–303)

Salisbury and convoy v. French squadron, 10 April 1703
A convoy of merchantmen, guarded by *Salisbury* (52; Capt. Richard Cotten), *Adventure* (40; Capt. John Balchen), and the armed ship *Muscovia Merchant* (Cmdr Daniel Parsons), was attacked by a French squadron commanded by the Chevalier de St Pol (*Adroit* (40), *Ludlow* (32), and *Milford* (13) and

others). *Muscovia Merchant* surrendered at once, and *Adventure* turned away. *Salisbury* fought for two hours, and then had to surrender. Four of the convoy were captured. (Clowes 2.504)

Sallee, Morocco, 1637
A squadron of royal and merchant ships commanded by Capt. Thomas Rainsborough sailed to suppress piracy out of Sallee in Morocco. A tight blockade was maintained for five months, and Rainsborough, skilfully exploiting local divisions, eventually forced a surrender; 340 English captives were freed. (Rodger 1.385; Clowes 2.55)

Salmon v. U-36, 4 December 1939
U-36 was sunk by the British submarine *Salmon* in the North Sea. (Terraine 227; Rohwer 10)

Salmon and Ursula v. German squadron, 13 December 1939
A concentration of German cruisers and destroyers in the North Sea was attacked by the British submarines *Salmon* and *Ursula*. The cruiser *Nürnberg* was damaged and the escort vessel *F-9* sunk. (Rohwer 10–11)

Salonica, Greece, October 1915
After considerable political, diplomatic, and military debate a joint Franco-British force landed at Salonica, with the aim of helping the Serbians and deterring Bulgaria. Many of the troops came from those who had been fighting at Gallipoli. (Corbett 3.155–167)

Salsette v. Apith, 24 June 1808
The Russian brig *Apith* (14) was captured by the frigate *Salsette* (38; Capt. Walter Bathurst) off Nargen. (Clowes 5.566)

Salvia v. U-94, 20 June 1917
The sloop *Salvia* was sunk by *U-94* west of Ireland while operating as a decoy ship. (Colledge 356)

Salvia v. U-568, 2 December 1941
The corvette *Salvia* was sunk by *U-568* off Egypt. (Rohwer 128)

Samarang at Gilolo, Molucca Islands, 3–4 June 1844
Samarang (26; Capt. Sir Edward Belcher) fought Malay pirates near the island of Gilolo, causing them serious damage. (Clowes 6.327)

Sambas, Borneo
1805 The ruler of Sambas captured *Calcutta*, an armed Indiaman. *Les Freres Unis* (Lt Robert Deane) and the armed ship *Belisarius* of the BM searched for the ship. *Calcutta* was in the Sambas River in a strong position with six gunboats and two armed junks. Deane's attack was successful; *Calcutta*, the junks, and two of the gunboats were taken. (Low 1.254–255)

1812–1813 An attack by three RN ships – *Barracouta* (10), *Procris* (10), and *Phoenix* (36) – on the Sambas River in 1812 was defeated by the defending batteries. Next year a squadron of nine warships, led by the frigate *Leda* (Capt. George Sayer) with three battalions of soldiers and some artillery, made a new attack. The troops were carried up to Sambas by boat, and captured the town. (Low 1.256–260)

Samoa, South Pacific

1876 Capt. Charles Stevens of the paddle sloop *Barracouta* intervened in an internal dispute in Samoa, which was none of his business. At one point he attacked the council house in Apia, but was quickly defeated. He then landed guns and formed a battery, but later withdrew. (Clowes 7.280)

1899 A disputed royal succession in Samoa in April brought intervention by British and US forces. The cruisers *Porpoise* and *Royalist* bombarded several villages and sank several boats. Later the cruiser *Tauranga* joined, and sailors were landed to drive back the 'rebels'. An international commission later decided that the intervention was not justified; the islands were divided by treaty between the USA and Germany. (Clowes 7.455–462)

1914 An expeditionary force from New Zealand, escorted by New Zealand and Australian warships, took control of the German part of Samoa on 30 August. (Corbett 1.151)

Samson v. pirates, Mirs Bay, China, 8 June 1857

A boat party from the paddle frigate *Samson* (Capt. George Hand) attacked pirates who had taken refuge in Mirs Bay. A pirate ship was captured, and three captured vessels were recovered. (Clowes 7.109)

San Andres v. *U-86*, 11 May 1918

The trawler *San Andres*, escorting a convoy south of Ireland, was sunk by *U-86*. (Newbolt 5.279)

Sandfly in the Santa Cruz Islands, South Pacific, 1874

The Santa Cruz islanders were hostile as a result of slaving expeditions from Australia. The survey schooner *Sandfly* was attacked at several places and retaliated at Nitendi, and at Tapua and Tasiko in the New Hebrides, in each case destroying whole villages in response to the attacks. (Clowes 7.264–265)

San Domingo, Hispaniola

1586 The fleet of Sir Francis Drake attacked, captured, and looted the town of San Domingo on 1 January. (Rodger 1.249; Andrews 120–122; Williamson 283–285)

1655 A fleet commanded by William Penn landed an army commanded by General Venables near the city of San Domingo on 13 and 14 April. The attack on the city failed and the troops were re-embarked. (Clowes 2.205–206; Rodger 2.23)

1806 (Battle of SAN DOMINGO) A French squadron of five line-of-battle ships and a frigate, commanded by Vice-Admiral Lessiegues, delivered soldiers at San Domingo. As the squadron was about to sail for France, a British squadron of seven line-of-battle ships and two frigates, commanded by Vice-Admiral Sir John Duckworth, arrived. A confused battle followed, which ended with the destruction of the French squadron. *Alexandre* (80) and *Brave* (74) were compelled to surrender, *Jupiter* (74) was captured; *Impérial* (120) and *Diomède* (74) were driven ashore and wrecked and later burnt. (James 4.94–108; Clowes 5.189–193; *NC* 3.261–269; Tunstall 259–262)

Sandwich and *Cormorant* v. French fleet, 24 August 1781
The sloops *Sandwich* (20; Cmdr William Bett) and *Cormorant* (14; Cmdr Robert McEvoy) were captured by the French fleet at Charleston, South Carolina. (Clowes 4.74)

San Fiorenzo, Corsica, 1793
Commodore Robert Linzee with a small squadron detached from the Mediterranean fleet attempted to persuade authorities in Corsica to restore Royalist government. Rejected, he attacked forts at San Fiorenzo, one of which, the Mortella, became the model for the later Martello towers in Britain. This was taken by surprise, but another redoubt resisted bombardment by *Alcide* (74), *Ardent* (64), and *Courageux* (74). The ships were all damaged by return fire and suffered casualties. Linzee retired. (James 1.94–96; Clowes 4.212; *NC* 1.31–36; Gordon 40–42)

San Fiorenzo and *Nymphe* v. *Résistance* and *Constance*, 9 March 1797
The frigates *San Fiorenzo* (36; Capt. Sir Harry Neale) and *Nymphe* (36; Capt. John Cooke) met the French ships *Résistance* (40) and *Constance* (22) returning to France from landing an invasion force at Fishguard in South Wales. The British ships tackled the French ships in turn; both quickly surrendered. (James 2.90–92; Clowes 4.506–507)

San Fiorenzo v. *Passe-Partout*, 14 January 1804
The French *chasse-marée Passe-Partout* (2) was captured by a boat attack from the frigate *San Fiorenzo* (40) in the East Indies. (Clowes 5.556)

San Fiorenzo v. *Psyche* and prizes, 14 February 1805
The frigate *San Fiorenzo* (40; Cmdr Henry Lambert) found the French frigate *Psyche* (36) and two prizes off Vizagapatam, India. One prize, the country ship *Thetis*, was retaken, then *San Fiorenzo* came up to *Psyche* and the two ships fought until *Psyche* surrendered, with half her crew dead or wounded. (James 4.18–20; Clowes 5.355–356)

San Fiorenzo v. *Piémontaise*, 4–6 March 1808
The frigate *San Fiorenzo* (40; Capt. George Hardinge) intercepted the French frigate *Piémontaise* (38), which was aiming to attack three Indiamen, near Ceylon. The two frigates manoeuvred, chased, and fought each other for three days, until *Piémontaise* finally surrendered. Both ships suffered heavy casualties. Hardinge was killed. (James 4.307–311; Clowes 5.407–410)

San Juan, Puerto Rico

1595 and 1598 An English expedition jointly commanded by Sir Francis Drake and Sir John Hawkins attacked San Juan on 12 November 1595, but the Spaniards were warned and the attack failed. Three years later an expedition commanded by the Earl of Cumberland captured the city. Cumberland hoped to make it a permanent English base, but it was unhealthy for his troops and he had to withdraw. (Rodger 1.283, 293; Clowes 1.505–506, 527; Andrews 193–197; Spence 157–175)

1797 An expedition under Rear-Admiral Henry Harvey landed troops to attack San Juan on 17 April, but the city was too strong to be assaulted. The troops re-embarked, having suffered 225 casualties. (James 2.112; Duffy 283–291)

San Juan de Ulloa, Mexico, 17 September 1568

The English trading fleet of Sir John Hawkins occupied the harbour of San Juan de Ulloa intending to make repairs to some of the ships. Next day the Viceroy of New Spain arrived with the annual Spanish fleet. Fighting broke out and ships were sunk on both sides. Two English ships escaped – *Minion* with Hawkins and *Judith* captained by Francis Drake. The English were clearly in the wrong, but both men accused the Spaniards of treachery, and spent much of the rest of their lives seeking revenge. (Rodger 1.201; Andrews 37–39; Williamson 88–92)

San Lorenzo, Argentina, May 1846

On the cliffs at San Lorenzo on the Paraná River batteries obstructed passage along the river. A large convoy of 110 ships coming down the river was clearly vulnerable. Under the command of Lt Lachlan Mackinnon of the paddle sloop *Alecto*, a rocket battery was planted on an island facing the Argentine guns. As the ships arrived the rockets suppressed the gunners' fire. The convoy passed, losing only four ships which ran aground and were burnt. (Clowes 6.344–345; L. MacKinnon, *Steam Warfare on the Parana*, London 1848; D. MacLean, *War, Diplomacy and Informal Empire*, London 1995, 99–100)
See also: **Montevideo, Obligado**

San Sebastian, Spain, July–September 1813

The siege of San Sebastian by British forces was assisted by seamen landed from Capt. Sir George Collier's squadron. A ship's demonstration at the crucial moment helped the assault on the breach. The squadron was up to twelve ships strong. (James 6.16; Clowes 5.529; *NC* 5.192–193; Hall 218–219)

SANTA CRUZ, Tenerife, Canary Islands

1656 The Spanish treasure fleet waited at Santa Cruz; the English blockading fleet under General-at-Sea Robert Blake arrived. The Spanish ships, sixteen in number, were protected by the harbour forts. Blake sent in twelve frigates to fight the ships, and took his larger ships to attack the forts. All the Spanish ships were sunk or burned; all the English ships survived, damaged.

The treasure remained on shore. (Capp 99; NRS, *Misc* II, 125–136; Clowes 2.214–215; Powell 298–305; Rodger 2.26–27)

1797 A boat party from the frigates *Lively* (32; Capt. Benjamin Hallowell) and *Minerve* (38; Capt. George Cockburn) cut out the French brig *Mutine* on 28 May, despite heavy fire from the town. The reported arrival of a rich galleon led to a new attack, commanded by Capt. Horatio Nelson, with three 74s, a 50, and three frigates. Their arrival alerted the garrison, which frustrated all attacks. (James 2.62–68; Colin White, *1797, Nelson's Year of Destiny*, Stroud 1998, 87–131; *NC* 1.193–199; NRS, *Misc* II)

Santa Dorotea and others v. San Leon, 28 November 1798
The Spanish sloop *San Leon* (16) was captured by the British frigate *Santa Dorotea* (34) and other ships off Lisbon. (Clowes 4.560)

Santa Margarita v. Amazone, 29 July 1782
Santa Margarita (38; Capt. Elliot Salter) was chased by the French frigate *Amazone* (36) until out of sight of *Amazone*'s squadron. At the request of the crew, Salter turned to fight. *Amazone* surrendered. (Clowes 4.83–84)

Santa Margarita v. Tamise, 8 June 1796
The frigate *Santa Margarita* (38; Capt. Thomas Byam Martin) fought the French frigate *Tamise* (36). Both separated off from other vessels to fight each other; *Tamise* was badly damaged and surrendered. (James 1.365–366; Clowes 4.498)

Santa Margarita v. Buonaparte and Vengeur, 24–25 October 1796
Santa Margarita (38; Capt. Thomas Byam Martin) captured the privateer *Buonaparte* (16) at the entrance to the Channel, and next morning met *Vengeur* (16) and its prize, *Potomak*. The latter was captured, and when the frigate caught up with *Vengeur*, she quickly surrendered. (James 1.400)

Santa Margarita v. San Francisco, 21 June 1797
The Spanish brig *San Francisco* (14) was captured by the frigate *Santa Margarita* (38; Capt. George Parker) off Ireland. (Clowes 4.560)

Santa Maura, Ionian Islands, 15 March–16 April 1810
A force of soldiers, seamen, and marines was landed at Santa Maura from a squadron commanded by Capt. George Eyre in *Magnificent* (74). The French garrison retired to the main fortress; a brief siege brought their early capitulation. (James 5.79–80)

Santiago, Cape Verde Islands, 17 November 1585
Sir Francis Drake landed a force of soldiers to capture Santiago. The inhabitants fled into the interior. No offer of ransom was made, so Drake burned the town before leaving. (Rodger 1.249; Andrews 119–120; Williamson 282)

Santiago de Cuba, July–November 1741
A landing was made near Santiago in July from the fleet commanded by

Admiral Edward Vernon. Part of the fleet blockaded the harbour, but it proved impossible for a landing force to reach the town by land and it was withdrawn. (Clowes 3.76–77)

Santona, Spain, June–July 1810
Narcissus (32; Capt. Frederick Aylmer) landed a force of Spanish guerrillas at Santona in northern Spain. The batteries were destroyed and a French force driven off. The landing force was then re-embarked. (Hall 193)

Sao Vicente, Brazil, 23 September 1582
Two English ships under Edward Fenton attacked three Spanish ships near Sao Vicente, successfully. (Andrews 100)

Sao Vicente, Cape Verde Islands, 1602
A privateering fleet under William Parker landed a small force at Sao Vicente and plundered and burnt the town. (Clowes 1.531)

Sapphire **v.** *Walcheren,* **January 1654**
Sapphire (36; Capt. Nicholas Heaton) captured the Dutch warship *Walcheren*. (Clowes 2.200)

Sapphire **v. Dutch ships, April 1666**
Sapphire (36; Capt. Jasper Grant) fought a difficult battle against two Dutch warships (of 42 and 36 guns) in the Channel; all three survived. (Clowes 2.428)

Sapphire **v.** *Date Tree* **and** *Golden Horse,* **August–September 1677**
Sapphire (32; Capt. Thomas Harman) captured *Date Tree*, an Algerine warship, in August. On 10 September *Sapphire* met and fought the Algerine warship *Golden Horse*, but Harman was killed and *Sapphire* lost her mainmast; *Golden Horse* got away. (Clowes 2.452)

Sapphire **and** *James* **v.** *Halfmoon,* **October 1681**
Sapphire (32; Capt. Anthony Hastings) and the galley *James* (30; Capt. Cloudisley Shovell), near Tangier, fought and captured the Algerine warship *Halfmoon* (32). The Algerine captain, an Englishman, was hanged. (Clowes 2.457)

Sappho **v.** *Admiral Jawl,* **2 March 1808**
The sloop *Sappho* (18; Cmdr George Langford), near Scarborough, challenged the Danish brig *Admiral Jawl* (28), which threatened some merchant ships; the two fought until the Danish ship surrendered. (James 4.307; Clowes 5.407)

Sappho **v.** *Isabella II,* **1838**
The slaver *Isabella II* was chased and captured by the sloop *Sappho*. (Lloyd 31–32)

***Saracen* v. *U-335*, 3 August 1942**
The submarine *Saracen* sank *U-335* off Norway. (Rohwer 185)

***Saracen* v. *Granito*, 9 November 1942**
The submarine *Saracen* sank the Italian submarine *Granito* off Cape Vito, Sicily. (Rohwer 212)

***Saracen* v. *Minerva*, 14 August 1943**
The submarine *Saracen* was sunk by the Italian corvette *Minerva* off Bastia, Corsica. (Rohwer 260)

Sardinia
1710 An attempt by the French to land on Sardinia in June was defeated by the British Mediterranean fleet under Sir John Norris. (Clowes 2.415)

1940 Aircraft from *Ark Royal* raided Cagliari in August and the airfield at Elmae on 1 September. (Rohwer 34, 36)
See also: **Malta Convoys**

***Satellite* v. slavers, 1833–1835**
The sloop *Satellite* captured the Brazilian slavers *Paquete do Sul* and *Duqueza de Braganza* carrying 300 slaves off Brazil in July 1834. In December 1835 she captured the Brazilian slaver *Orion* near Bahia; the 250 slaves she carried were claimed to be 'free apprentices' in the subsequent court case. (Bethell 137, 141)

***Satyr* v. *U-987*, 11 June 1944**
The submarine *Satyr* sank *U-987* west of the Lofoten Islands. (Rohwer 330)

***Saudadoes* v. French ship, September 1692**
The sloop *Saudadoes* captured a French ship of 36 guns which was taken into the navy as *Saudadoes Prize*; it was retaken by the French in 1696. (Colledge 359)

***Saudadoes Prize* v. French squadron, 23 July 1694**
Saudadoes Prize (32; Capt. William Allin) and the pink *Hind* drove a small French squadron – a ship (26), privateers, and merchantmen – into a bay near La Hougue, where most were forced on shore and burned. (Clowes 2.480)

***Saumarez* and flotilla v. *Haguro* and *Kamikaze*, 16 May 1945**
The Japanese cruiser *Haguro* and the destroyer *Kamikaze* were twice deterred from reaching the Andaman Islands. Near Penang they were attacked by the 26th Destroyer Flotilla, *Saumarez*, *Verulam*, *Vigilant*, *Venus*, and *Virago*. *Haguro* was sunk; *Kamikaze* escaped, damaged. *Saumarez* was badly damaged. (Rohwer 417)

***Savage* v. *Congress*, 6 September 1781**
Savage (16; Cmdr Charles Stirling) was attacked twice by the rebel American

privateer *Congress* off Charleston, which finally forced *Savage*'s surrender. *Savage* was retaken by *Solebay* soon after. (Clowes 4.75)

Savannah, Georgia, September 1779–February 1780
The French fleet under Admiral d'Estaing landed men and guns to attack Savannah; British ships in the port did the same to help the resistance, and the French siege was abandoned after a month. In February 1780 a British expedition sailed from New York with 7500 soldiers, in a squadron commanded by Vice-Admiral Marriott Arbuthnot. At Savannah Fort Royal was captured. (Clowes 3.442, 4.32–33)

Scanderoon (Iskenderun, Alexandretta), Syria, 1628
A squadron of six English ships commanded by Sir Kenelm Digby found four French and four Venetian ships at Iskenderun. The Venetian ships were driven off; three of the French ships were captured and one was sunk. (Clowes 2.71–72)

Scarborough, Yorkshire, April 1557
A group of English exiles landed at Scarborough and seized the castle in the name of Protestantism. They were swiftly defeated and the castle recaptured. The exiles had come from France; their expedition provoked a declaration of war. (Rodger 1.192)

Scarborough v. French privateers, 18 July 1694
Scarborough (32; Capt. Thomas Killingworth) was attacked and captured by two French privateers, of 40 and 26 guns, in the Caribbean. Killingworth was killed. (Clowes 2.480)

Scarborough v. French ship, 1 November 1710
The frigate *Scarborough* (34; Capt. Edward Holland) was captured by the French; the ship was recaptured next year by *Anglesey* (50; Capt. Thomas Legge) and *Fowey* (14; Capt. Robert Chadwick). (Clowes 2.330)

Scarborough v. *Queen Anne's Revenge*, 1717
Kidd the pirate captured a Guineaman and renamed it *Queen Anne's Revenge*. He encountered *Scarborough* (20), which was defeated in the subsequent fight. (Clowes 3.259)

Scarborough v. Spanish ships, Tortugas, 1733
Scarborough (20; Capt. Thomas Durell) was escorting British ships loading salt at the Tortuga Islands. They were attacked by two Spanish *guarda costas*, which captured some of the merchantmen. *Scarborough* intervened; the rest of the merchantmen escaped. (Clowes 3.263)

Scarcies River, West Africa
1858 A naval force intervened in January in a local war along the Scarcies River in West Africa. Bombardments and rockets destroyed a series of towns and villages, with minimal casualties to the ships' crews, but the war

continued until the 1st West India Regiment was put ashore in March and defeated the contumacious people. (Clowes 7.150–151)

1891 The screw sloops *Racer* (Cmdr Henry Royle) and *Swallow* (Lt Ian Fraser), the paddle vessel *Alecto* (Lt Frederick Loane), and the West Indian Regiment attacked the towns of Tambi and Toniatuba to suppress a troublesome chief. (Clowes 4.406–407)

Sceptre v. *Naiade*, 14 April 1783
The French frigate *Naiade* (20) was chased by *Sceptre* (64; Capt. Samuel Graves) in the East Indies. *Naiade* inflicted considerable damage in a two-hour fight before surrendering. (Clowes 4.95)

Sceptre and *X-24* at Bergen, 11 September 1944
The submarine *Sceptre* launched the midget submarine *X-24* in a successful attack on the floating dock at Bergen; two ships were also damaged. (Rohwer 352)

SCHOONEVELD, Netherlands, 28 May–4 June 1673
On 28 May the Dutch fleet (fifty-two line-of-battle ships) under Admiral de Ruijter at Schooneveld attacked a contingent of thirty-five ships of the Anglo-French fleet to lure the rest out. In a confused fight the French lost two ships and one of the Dutch ships succumbed to damage later. Neither side could claim victory. A week later the Dutch fleet emerged again to drive away the Anglo-French fleet. The fighting was as confused as in the first battle. The allies retired to their bases in England and France; the Dutch had thus succeeded in their strategic aim. (Clowes 2.310–316; Rodger 2.83–84; Mahan 151–152; Tunstall 35–36)

Scilly Isles, June 1651
Royalist privateers operated from the Scilly Isles. General-at-Sea Robert Blake with a squadron forced the islands' surrender. (Capp 67; Clowes 2.138–139; Powell 108–119)

Scorpion v. French fleet, January 1794
The EIC ship *Scorpion*, bringing to Britain colours captured at Pondicherry, among other things, was captured by a French fleet as she approached Britain. The crew were released in America. (Low 1.204)

Scorpion and *Beaver* v. *Athalante*, 28 March 1804
The sloops *Scorpion* and *Beaver* (Cmdrs George Hardinge and Charles Pelly) attacked the Dutch corvette *Athalante* in Vlie road. Having boarded, they had a desperate fight to seize the ship, then were struck by a gale. It took three days to get *Athalante* out to the open sea. (James 3.264–267; Clowes 5.342; *NC* 3.32–34)

Scorpion v. *Oreste*, 11–12 January 1810
The sloop *Scorpion* (Cmdr Francis Stanfell) attacked the French corvette

Oreste (16) as she left Basse Terre, Guadeloupe. A running fight followed until *Oreste*, her rigging destroyed, surrendered. (James 5.86–87; Clowes 5.449)

Scotland
866 Olaf the White, king of Dublin, led an expedition to invade Scotland, plundering to the heart of the Pictish kingdom of Fortriu. (Smyth, *Warlords* 158)

934 King Athelstan invaded Scotland by land in 934, paced by his fleet by sea. The army marched as far north as Aberdeenshire, while the fleet sailed as far as Caithness. (*ASC* s.a. 934)

1054 The Earl of Northumbria, Siward, invaded Scotland aiming to displace King Macbeth, accompanied by a fleet. Siward was unsuccessful. (*ASC* s.a. 1054)

1072 King William I the Conqueror invaded Scotland, whose king harboured the claimant to the English kingship, Edgar the Aetheling. The fleet blockaded the coast and the Forth estuary. (*ASC* s.a. 1072)

1091 After an invasion of northern England by King Malcolm III of Scots, William II Rufus marched an army north, with a fleet of fifty ships off the coast. But the fleet was wrecked. (F. Barlow, *William Rufus*, London 1983, 292–293)

1300–1304 King Edward I called up fleets to assist in his campaigns in Scotland. Little naval fighting took place, the fleets being used mainly to carry supplies. An Irish fleet carried an army from Ulster in 1303, and captured Rothesay Castle on the Isle of Bute. (Rodger 1.84; Prestwich 499)

1308–1311 King Edward II of England pursued the Scottish war largely by sea, sending supplies and reinforcements to Aberdeen, Berwick, Perth, and other places. The towns of Hartlepool, Yarmouth, and London and others supplied the ships. In 1310 a fleet was active in the Irish Sea, defending the Isle of Man, and in 1311 in the Hebrides, with some success. (Barrow 279; Clowes 1.215–216)
See also: **Firth of Forth, Firth of Tay, Hebrides, Orkney Islands**

Scott v. *UC-17*, 15 August 1918
The destroyer *Scott* was sunk by *UC-17* in the North Sea. (Colledge 381)

Scourge v. *Sans-Culotte*, 13 March 1793
The sloop *Scourge* (16; Cmdr George Brisac), west of the Scilly Isles, captured the privateer *Sans-Culotte* (12) in a fight lasting three hours. (James 1.98; Clowes 4.475)

Scout v. French frigates, 24 August 1794
The sloop *Scout* (14; Cmdr Charles Robinson) was captured by two French frigates, *Celeste* and another, off Cape Bon, North Africa. (Clowes 4.548)

Scout off Provence, 14 June–14 July 1809
The sloop *Scout* (18; Cmdr William Raitt) sent boats against a convoy near Cape Croisette; seven of the convoy were followed into harbour to capture them. On 14 July a party of seamen and marines from the ship captured a battery at the port of Carri. (James 5.29–30; Clowes 5.439–440)

Scout v. slaver, 11 January 1837
Scout (18; Cmdr Robert Craigie), in the West Indies, captured a Portuguese slaver carrying over 570 slaves. (Clowes 6.277)

Scout v. Chinese pirates, 31 May 1848
The sloop *Scout* (18; Cmdr Frederick Johnstone) chased two Chinese junks identified as pirates near Climmo Island, China. One was captured quickly, the other after a prolonged chase and conflict. (Clowes 6.352)

Scylla, Calabria, 17 February 1808
French forces in Italy reconquered Calabria; Scylla, the last post held by the British, was evacuated by *Montagu* (74; Capt. Robert Otway) and the sloop *Electra* (Cmdr George Trollope) with transports. (James 4.294; Clowes 5.245–246)

Scylla v. Canonnier and convoy, 8 May 1811
The sloop *Scylla* (18; Cmdr Arthur Atchison) chased a convoy escorted by the brig *Canonnier* into rocks off Morlaix; *Canonnier* was boarded and captured; one of the convoy was also taken. (James 5.212–213; Clowes 5.485)

Scylla and Royalist v. Weser, 18–19 October 1813
The Dutch frigate *Weser* (40), damaged by a gale, was chased by the sloop *Scylla* (18; Cmdr Colin MacDonald), and a second sloop, *Royalist* (18; Cmdr James Bremer), joined in. The two sloops attacked, and when *Rippon* (74) approached, *Weser* finally surrendered. (James 6.12–13; Clowes 5.538; NC 5.168)

Seaflower v. Charles, 15 July 1806
The French ketch *Charles* (3) was captured off Rodrigues Island by the sloop *Seaflower* (16). (Clowes 5.557)

Seaford and others v. French ships, summer 1744
Seaford (20; Capt. Thomas Pye), *Grampus* (16; Cmdr Richard Collins), and *Solebay* (20; Capt. Thomas Bury) were captured by the French fleet in the Mediterranean. (Clowes 3.274)

Seagull v. Loug and gunboats, 19 June 1808
The sloop *Seagull* (16; Cmdr Robert Cathcart) attacked the Danish brig *Loug* (20) off Kristiansand, but *Loug* stayed at a distance, which suited her armament, and six gunboats arrived to help. Between them they battered *Seagull* into surrender, and she sank soon after. (James 4.318–319; Anderson 325; Clowes 5.411)

Seahorse v. *Maréchal de Belleisle* and *Chauvelin*, 1 August 1757
Seahorse (24) met the French frigates *Maréchal de Belleisle* (36) and *Chauvelin* (36) off Flushing. *Seahorse* was reduced to a floating wreck in a two-hour fight, but the French failed to complete their capture. (Clowes 3.297)

Seahorse v. *Aigrette*, 10 January 1761
Seahorse (24; Capt. James Smith), on her way to India with astronomers to observe the transit of Venus, was attacked by *Aigrette* (32) and damaged so badly she had to return to port for repairs. (Clowes 3.304)

Seahorse and *Coventry* v. *Sartine*, 25 August 1778
The French frigate *Sartine* (32), attacked by *Seahorse* (24) and *Coventry* (28) in the Indian Ocean, surrendered after being boarded. (Clowes 4.19)

Seahorse v. *Sensible*, 26–27 June 1798
The frigate *Seahorse* (38; Capt. Edward Foote) met the French frigate *Sensible* (36) off Sicily; after a chase they fought near Pantelleria. *Seahorse* carried heavier armament, and *Sensible* quickly surrendered. (James 2.234–236; Clowes 4.510)

Seahorse and *Emerald* v. *Anemone*, 2 September 1798
The French *Anemone* (4) was driven ashore at Marabou in Egypt by *Seahorse* (38) and *Emerald* (36). The French sailors were menaced by local Arabs and an attempt was made to rescue them. Five were brought off; the rest were killed. (Clowes 4.376)

Seahorse at San Pedro, Spain, 4 May 1805
The frigate *Seahorse* (38; Capt. Hon. Courtnay Boyle) discovered a convoy, whose ships went into San Pedro anchorage, guarded by gunboats. *Seahorse* attacked. One gunboat was sunk; a brig, laden with gunpowder and other military stores, was captured. (James 4.31; Clowes 5.361)

Seahorse v. *Badr-i-Zaffer* and *Alis Fezzan*, 1–2 July 1808
The frigate *Seahorse* (38; Capt. John Stewart), in the Aegean, attacked two Turkish frigates, *Badr-i-Zaffer* (52) and *Alis Fezzan* (26). The three manoeuvred and fought each other through the night. *Alis Fezzan* suffered an explosion and withdrew; *Badr-i-Zaffer* was eventually compelled to surrender. (James 4.347–354; Clowes 5.421–423)

Seahorse v. German minesweepers, 7 January 1940
The submarine *Seahorse* was sunk by the German minesweepers *M-122* and *M-123* in the North Sea. (Rohwer 13)

Sea King v. *UC-66*, 12 June 1917
The armed trawler *Sea King* fought and sank *UC-66* in the English Channel. (Newbolt 5.57, 425; Grant 62)

Seal v. UJ-126, 4 May 1940
The minelaying submarine *Seal* was damaged on a mine in the Kattegat. A German flying boat landed and took the captain prisoner, then the patrol vessel *UJ-126* seized the submarine itself. (Rohwer 22; Sebag-Montefiore 93)

Sealark on the Río Grande, Guinea, March 1852
The brig *Sealark* (Cmdr Edward Sotheby) searched the Río Grande for a slaver. When it was found, it was blown up; the slaves were freed. (Ward 47–49)

Sea of Azov, 26 May–6 November 1855
A light squadron of six paddle and eight screw steamships passed into the Sea of Azov on 26 May. For four months every town and store within reach of the coast was attacked to destroy stores accumulated for the Russian army fighting in the Crimea; all ships were burnt. Repeatedly parties landed to do the work of destruction, and more often than not did so without casualties. It was a notable display of the flexibility of sea power. (Clowes 6.453–466)

Seawolf v. Adolf Vinnen, 28 October 1940
The submarine *Seawolf* shelled and sank the German weather ship *Adolf Vinnen* at Sondlandet, Norway. (Rohwer 46)

Seba River, West Africa, December 1849
A group of pirates operated out of the Seba River. Their base was raided and destroyed by the screw tender *Teazer* (Lt Jasper Selwyn) and the French *Rubis*, under the command of Capt. Claude Buckle. (Clowes 6.367)

SEBASTOPOL, Russia, September 1854–September 1855
Sebastopol was put under siege in September 1854; the British and French fleets formed a blockade. A Naval Brigade of marines and seamen assisted in the siege on land. Seaborne bombardments were carried out, principally on 17 October and occasionally thereafter, but the ships could not approach close enough to have a real effect. Once the Russian supply line in the Sea of Azov was cut, Russian forces evacuated Sebastopol. A hundred Russian naval vessels were destroyed. (Clowes 6.432–450, 466–469; Lambert 130–143, 239–248)

Seine v. Vengeance, 20–21 August 1800
The frigate *Seine* (38; Capt. David Milne) chased the French frigate *Vengeance* near St Domingue. The fight left *Seine*'s rigging in tatters, but it was repaired during the night. A second fight reduced *Vengeance* to ruin and surrender. (James 3.23–26; Clowes 4.533)

Seine v. three ships, May–June 1805
The frigate *Seine* (40; Capt. David Atkins) sent two boats to capture the schooner *Concepcion* off Puerto Rico. Two weeks later she captured a felucca also called *Concepcion*, and destroyed a sloop. (James 4.31)

Seine v. *Zephyr*, **October 1809**
The French sloop *Zephyr* (18) was captured in the Channel by the frigate *Seine* (40; Capt. David Atkins). (Clowes 5.559)

Selangor, Malaya, February 1874
A squadron of ships commanded by Vice-Admiral Sir Charles Shadwell in the battleship *Iron Duke* acted against pirates operating from the rivers of Selangor. The sultan was persuaded to help and several stockades were captured and burnt. (Clowes 7.269–270)

Senegal, West Africa, July 1809
In order to deny the use of Senegal to French ships, an expedition consisting of the frigate *Solebay* (32; Capt. Edward Columbine), the sloop *Derwent* (18; Cmdr Frederick Parker), and numerous smaller vessels was sent from Goree. The ships crossed the bar, landed the soldiers, and went upriver to threaten a fort at Babaque, which surrendered before it was attacked. *Solebay* was wrecked, and Parker was drowned, but Senegal surrendered. (James 5.67–69; Clowes 5.282; *NC* 4.278–279)

Senegal and *Thunder* v. **French fleet, 14 August 1778**
The French fleet in North America captured the British ships *Senegal* (18) and *Thunder* (bomb). (Clowes 4.18)

Serapis v. *Bonhomme Richard*, **23 September 1779**
Serapis (44; Capt. Richard Pearson), escorting a Baltic convoy, was attacked by the rebel American frigate *Bonhomme Richard* (Capt. John Paul Jones) off Scarborough. The fight, between equals, lasted several hours, and both suffered great damage. At last, threatened also by *Alliance* (32) and with all her guns useless, *Serapis* surrendered. Jones moved his people across; *Bonhomme Richard* soon sank. (Clowes 4.35–39)

Serbian evacuation, January–April 1916
The defeated Serbian army arrived on the Albanian coast and was evacuated by ships of Britain, France, and Italy from several ports in a continuous naval effort over several months, by which a quarter of a million people were rescued. (Newbolt 4.99–106, 118–125; Halpern, *Naval History* 152–159)

Serpent v. *San Christovel Pano* and a felucca, **28 November 1805**
The sloop *Serpent* (Cmdr John Waller) intercepted the *guarda costa San Christovel Pano* and a felucca near Truxillo, Honduras. A boat party captured the *guarda costa*; the felucca, warned, got away. (James 8.77–78; Clowes 5.372)

Severn and *Woolwich* v. *Terrible*, **1746**
Severn (50; Capt. William Lisle) and *Woolwich* (50; Capt. Joseph Lingen), escorting a convoy from the Leeward Islands, met a French convoy of which *Terrible* (74), commanded by Admiral de Conflans, was the main escort.

Lisle ordered his convoy to disperse and he and *Woolwich* fought *Terrible*. *Severn* was taken; *Woolwich* got away; the convoy escaped. (Clowes 3.122)

Severn and *Pelican* v. *République Triomphante*, December 1797
The French sloop *République Triomphante* (18) was captured by the frigate *Severn* (44) and the sloop *Pelican* (18) in the West Indies. (Clowes 4.555)

Severn and *Mersey* v. *Königsberg*, 6–11 July 1915
To eliminate the threat of the German light cruiser *Königsberg*, holed up in the delta of the Rufiji River in Tanganyika, the monitors *Severn* and *Mersey*, accompanied by tugs, were sent from Malta. On 6 July, with an aircraft spotting their shots, they bombarded *Königsberg*, but were damaged by her return fire. A second bombardment on 11 July resulted in *Königsberg*'s destruction. (Corbett 3.63–67; Halpern, *Naval History* 77–78)

Shah and *Amethyst* v. *Huascar*, July 1877
Huascar was a Peruvian ironclad seized by insurgents. Rear-Admiral Algernon de Horsey intervened with the armoured frigate *Shah* (26) and the screw corvette *Amethyst* (14), which fought *Huascar* for three hours. Each ship received many hits, but little damage; *Huascar* suffered only four casualties. Much interest followed; both *Huascar* and *Shah* were carefully inspected to discover exactly why they had resisted fire so well. (Clowes 7.285–289)

Shah and others v. *U-198*, 10 August 1944
U-198, located by aircraft from the carrier *Shah*, was sunk by the Indian sloop *Godavari* and the frigates *Findhorn* and *Parrett*. (Rohwer 327)

Shakespeare v. *Velella*, 9 September 1943
The submarine *Shakespeare* sank the Italian submarine *Velella*. (Rohwer 260)

Shanghai, China
1842   A British force landed at the city of Shanghai on 19 June. (Graham 217–218)

1854   A threat to the foreign settlement in Shanghai from Chinese forces was countered by the landing of a party of seamen and marines from the screw corvette *Encounter* (Capt. George O'Callaghan), the brig *Grecian* (Cmdr Hon. George Keen), and the US corvette *Plymouth* on 3 April. They captured a fort that day and another next day. Three of the attackers died; 300 Chinese died. (Clowes 6.387–388)

1860   The rebel Taiping army approached Shanghai in August and was driven back from the walls by armed European residents and by bombardment from the gunboats *Kestrel* (Lt Henry Huxham), *Hongkong*, and *Pioneer* (Cmdr Hugh Reilly), even though the Taiping forces did not fire on the city. (Clowes 7.158–159)

1862   A Naval Brigade and a Chinese force landed in February to drive away Taiping forces. A series of massacres of poorly armed forces followed until May. The screw frigates *Imperieuse* (Capt. George Willes) and *Vulcan* (Cmdr Augustus Strode) and the screw corvette *Pearl* (Capt. John Borlase) contributed forces to the brigade. (Clowes 7.165–167)

1941 The gunboat *Peterel* was sunk in a fight with the Japanese cruiser *Izumo* on 8 December. (Rohwer 123)

Shannon v. *Chesapeake*, 1 June 1813
The frigate *Shannon* (38; Capt. Philip Broke) hovered outside Boston taunting US ships in the harbour. *Chesapeake*, a frigate of approximately equal size and armament, came out. After some early broadsides, the two ships became hooked together and *Chesapeake* was captured by boarding. Casualties were heavy: in *Shannon* over 80, in *Chesapeake* 150. (James 6.50–69; Clowes 6.75–86; *NC* 5.154)

Shark v. French ship, 29 March 1703
The sloop *Shark* (6; Cmdr George Fisher) was captured by the French. (Clowes 2.556)

Sharpshooter v. *Polka*, June 1850–July 1851
The screw gunship *Sharpshooter* cruised against slavers off Brazil. In June 1850 the slaver *Polka*, even under the protection of the fort, was captured in the harbour of Macahe, and the slavers *Malteza* and *Conceicao* were taken near Rio de Janeiro; *Malteza* was burned. In July 1851 the Sardinian slaver *Valarozo* was captured near Rio de Janeiro (and eventually returned to the Sardinian government), and the Brazilian coaster *Piratinim*, carrying slaves recently landed at Bahia, was taken. (Bethell 327, 329, 355; Lloyd 143; Clowes 6.392)

Shawinigan v. *U-1228*, 24 November 1944
U-1228 sank the RCN corvette *Shawinigan* in the Cabot Strait. (Rohwer 373)

Shebar River, West Africa, 1840
Capt. H.W. Hill with men from the sloop *Saracen* and the brig *Ferret* raided slave bases in the Shebar River, liberating slaves and destroying the barracoons. (Lloyd 96; Ward 175)

Sheerness v. French privateers, January 1694
The frigate *Sheerness* (32; Capt. James Lance) off the Kenmare River in Ireland fought two French privateers (32 and 24 guns), who had captured two prizes. *Sheerness* was unable to defeat the privateers, even after five hours' fighting. (Clowes 2.478)

Sheerness v. *Espérance* and *Prince Charles*, November 1745–March 1746
A French squadron carrying troops and stores to Scotland was scattered by a storm; *Espérance* was captured by *Sheerness* (24), and burned. Next March *Sheerness* (24; Capt. Lucius O'Brien) attacked *Prince Charles* (14), which was carrying funds for Prince Charles Edward, and sank her in the Pentland Firth. (Lavery 52, 59)

Sheerness v. two *chasse-marées*, 9 September 1803
The cutter *Sheerness* (Lt Henry Rowed) sent boats after two French *chasse-marées* attempting to get into Brest. Both were taken, and were then defended against French attempts to retake them. (James 3.191–194; Clowes 5.326–327)

Sheikh Syed, Yemen, 8–9 November 1914
A force of Turks and Arabs gathered on the border of the Aden Protectorate. The cruiser *Duke of Edinburgh* arrived with troops in three transports, shelled and destroyed a fort, and landed troops who dispersed the Turkish forces. The Indian troops then re-embarked. (Corbett 1.378–379)

Shelanagig v. French ship, September 1781
The sloop *Shelanagig* (16; Cmdr James Shephard) was captured by the French in the West Indies. (Clowes 4.111)

Sheldrake and convoy v. Danish gunboats, 4–5 July 1811
A British convoy, escorted by *Sheldrake* (14), at anchor in the Great Belt, was attacked by seventeen Danish gunboats and ten fireships. Five gunboats were captured, but several of the merchant ships were set on fire. (Anderson 344)

Sherbro Island, West Africa, 25 December 1853
Cmdr Phillips of the paddle sloop *Polyphemus* raided slave barracoons at Sherbro; they were destroyed and the slaves, who were driven 50 miles inland, were followed and released. (Lloyd 151)

Shetland and Faeroe, 1390
In a confused account of the adventures of two Venetians, Nicolo and Antonio Zeo, the ruler of Orkney, who must have been Earl Henry I Sinclair, is said to have sent expeditions to Shetland and Faeroe (and a voyage of exploration to Greenland). (Thompson 99–100)

SHIMONOSEKI, Japan, 5–8 September 1864
A combined squadron consisting of ten British, four Dutch, one American, and three French ships, under the command of Vice-Admiral Sir Augustus Kuper, bombarded batteries belonging to the *daimyo* of Choshu in Shimonoseki Strait. Landing parties systematically destroyed the batteries once they were silenced. Over seventy casualties were incurred, but Choshu submitted in the end. (Clowes 7.203–208; Hore, *Seapower* 153–161)
See also: **Kagoshima**

Shoreham v. pirate ship, 1700
Shoreham (32) fought a pirate ship off the coast of Virginia for several hours; the pirate was deprived of the two ships he had captured. (Clowes 2.498)

Sibyl v. *Hummer* and convoy, 24 September 1943
The submarine *Sibyl* sank the German escort ship *Hummer* and a ship from her convoy near Sardinia. (Rohwer 274)

SICILY, 10 July–17 August 1943
Landings by Allied forces took place at several places in southern and eastern Sicily on 10 July: by the British 8th Army south of Syracuse on the east coast, and by the US 7th Army near Gela and Licata on the south coast. British warships in support included six battleships, ten cruisers, three AA ships, three monitors, two carriers, and over 100 smaller ships, and included Indian and Australian vessels. Direct support for the campaign on land was provided by bombardments by some of the larger ships – the battleships *Howe* and *King George V* at Favignana, the cruisers *Dido* and *Sirius* at Marsala, the monitor *Erebus* and the battleship *Warspite* and others at Catania.

The monitor *Erebus* and the carrier *Indomitable* were damaged in Italian and German air attacks. Five German torpedo boats were sunk; two British MTBs were sunk by the Italian cruiser *Scipione Africano*. The cruiser *Cleopatra* was torpedoed by the Italian submarine *Dandolo*, and *MTB-641* was sunk by *Nichelio*. Three British MTBs sank the submarine *Flutto*. *MTB-81* sank *U-561*, the submarine *Unruly* sank *Acciaio*, *United* sank *Remo*, *Trooper* sank *Micca*; the destroyer *Inconstant* sank *U-409*, *Echo* and *Ilex* sank *Nereide*, and the submarine *Bronzo* was captured. *U-407* torpedoed the cruiser *Newfoundland*. By 17 August the island had been conquered. (Greene and Massignani 288–292; Rohwer 262; C. D'Este, *Bitter Victory: The Battle for Sicily 1943*, London 1988)

Sickle v. U-303 and UJ-2213, 15–21 May 1943
The submarine *Sickle* sank the German ASW trawler *UJ-2213* off Provence, and on 21 May she sank *U-303* off Toulon. (Rohwer 244, 249, 252)

Sickle v. German escort vessels, 29 August 1943
The submarine *Sickle* sank the German escort vessels *SG-7* and *SG-10* on 29 August 1943. (Rohwer 269)

Sierra Leone, West Africa
1853 The screw tender *Teazer*, towing boats of the brig *Linnet* (Cmdr Henry Need), in March attacked the village of Medina in the Sierra Leone River, where a British subject was detained; the village was shelled. (Clowes 6.394)

1898 A rebellion in the interior of the colony against a new tax was contained by several ships sailing up various rivers. The cruiser *Fox*, the paddle vessel *Alecto*, and the cruiser *Blonde* were particularly busy, and other ships assisted. The rebellion was eventually crushed by a large army expedition. (Clowes 7.452–454)

Sikh and others v. Italian cruisers, 13 December 1941
The Italian cruisers *Alberigo da Barbariano* and *Alberto da Giussano* were located by Ultra decrypts and sunk off Cape Bon by the destroyers *Sikh*, *Legion*, *Maori*, and a Dutch destroyer. (Rohwer 120)

***Sikh* and others v. *U-372*, 4 August 1942**
U-372 was sunk by the destroyers *Sikh*, *Zulu*, *Croome*, and *Telcott*. (Rohwer 183)

***Simoom* v. *Garibaldi* and *Gioberti*, 9 August 1943**
The submarine *Simoom* attacked the cruiser *Garibaldi* and the destroyer *Gioberti* off La Spezia on 9 August; *Gioberti* was sunk. (Rohwer 260)

Singapore
1943 The Australian drifter *Krait* sailed through Indonesian waters and launched an expedition in six canoes against Japanese-occupied Singapore harbour on 18 September. Limpet mines sank two ships on the 21st; the canoes and their occupants were recovered. (Rohwer 270)

1945 Two British midget submarines penetrated the harbour on 30–31 July, sinking the cruiser *Takao*; the Singapore–Saigon cable was cut by another craft. (Rohwer 425)

***Siren* v. pirates, Stanchio Island, 1846**
Siren (16; Cmdr Henry Edgell) sent boats to capture four pirate craft near to the Turkish island of Stanchio. (Clowes 6.361)

***Sir Francis Drake* v. Dutch gunboats, 23 May 1811**
The frigate *Sir Francis Drake* (32; Capt. George Harris) met a flotilla of Dutch gunboats near Rembang, Java. On being attacked, five surrendered; the others headed for the shore where the frigate's boats captured them. (James 5.296–297; Clowes 5.298)

***Sir Thomas Pasley* v. Spanish gunboats, 2 December 1800**
The brig *Sir Thomas Pasley* (16; Lt Charles Niven) was captured by two Spanish gunboats in the Mediterranean. (Clowes 4.551)

***Sirius* v. *Waakzaamheid* and *Furie*, 24 October 1798**
The frigate *Sirius* (36; Capt. Richard King) encountered two Dutch ships off the Texel. *Sirius* tackled them singly, compelling the corvette *Waakzaamheid* (26) to surrender, then chasing and fighting the frigate *Furie* (36), which also surrendered, though not so quickly; 6000 stand of arms and 122 French soldiers were captured. (James 2.270–271; Clowes 4.516–517)

***Sirius* v. *Bergère* and flotilla, 17 August 1806**
The frigate *Sirius* (36; Capt. William Prowse) met a French flotilla off the mouth of the Tiber – the corvettes *Bergère*, *Abeille*, *Légère*, and *Janus* and five smaller vessels. *Sirius* attacked and eventually forced *Bergère* (18) to yield, but the rest of them got away; *Sirius* was badly damaged. (James 4.142–143; Clowes 5.379–380)

***Sirius* v. *Edward*, 9 July 1810**
The privateer *Edward* attempted to get away from Bourbon Island when the

British took it. *Sirius* (36; Capt. Samuel Pym) sent a barge in chase, which captured *Edward*, after a twelve-hour row. (James 5.144; Clowes 5.458)

Skerries, Ireland, September 1689
Capt. George Rooke led a squadron south along the Irish coast. He raided the Skerries, landing 200 men, who destroyed a number of small vessels before they re-embarked. (Powley 296)

Skipjack v. Maria, November 1827
The schooner *Skipjack* chased the Spanish slaver *Maria* until she went ashore on Cuba; she was blown up by her crew as they left. (Ward 134–135)

Skylark v. Ville de Caen, 21 July 1812
The schooner *Skylark* (10; Lt Thomas Warrand) found the lugger *Ville de Caen* attacking two West Indiamen off Start Point. *Skylark* chased and collided with the lugger, resulting in a fierce fight until the lugger was captured by boarding. (James 5.324–325)

Smerwick, Ireland, March 1580
A Spanish squadron under Juan Martínez de Recalde landed troops at Smerwick. Sir William Winter had earlier patrolled the area and now returned and bombarded the soldiers. They surrendered, and were immediately killed. (Rodger 1.245; Clowes 1.482; Silke 21)

Smyrna, Turkey, 5–15 March 1915
A rumour that the governor was disaffected induced a British squadron to go into the Gulf of Smyrna. Forts were bombarded, with no reply and little result. Minesweepers went in but were driven out. Negotiations with the governor were futile. The seaplane carrier *Annie Rickmers* was torpedoed by the Turkish torpedo boat *Demir Hissar*. On 15 March the force was ordered away. (Corbett 2.195–202, 209–210; Halpern, *Mediterranean* 67)

Snaefell v. U-105, 3 June 1918
The armed boarding steamer *Snaefell* was sunk by *U-105* in the Mediterranean. (Colledge 374)

Snake v. American privateers, 13 June 1781
Snake (14; Cmdr William Jackson) was attacked and captured by two rebel American privateers, *Pilgrim* and *Rambler*. (Clowes 4.70)

Snake v. Christiania, October 1809
The Danish brig *Christiania* (8) was captured by *Snake* (18; Cmdr Thomas Young) off Bergen. (Clowes 5.586)

Snake v. Maria da Gloria, November 1833
The sloop *Snake* (16) captured the Brazilian slaver *Maria da Gloria* off Rio de Janeiro, carrying over 300 slaves. This became a notable case because the owner claimed Portuguese nationality, though living in Brazil. (Bethell 135)

Snake v. *Arrogante* and *Matilda*, 1837
Snake (16; Cmdr Alexander Milne), in the West Indies, captured the slavers *Arrogante* on 23 November and *Matilda* on 5 December, freeing over 900 slaves. (Clowes 6.277)

Snapdragon, Cradosin, and *Queensland* v. *UB-68*, October 1918
The sloop *Snapdragon*, the trawler *Cradosin*, and the armed steamer *Queensland*, escorting a convoy south of Malta, sank *UB-68* (whose captain was Oberleutnant Karl von Donitz). (Newbolt 5.411; Grant 133)

Snapper v. *Rapace*, 15 July 1811
Snapper (4; Lt Henry Thackstone) was captured by the French *Rapace* off Brest. (Clowes 5.553)

Snapper v. German minesweepers, 11 April 1940
The submarine *Snapper* sank a merchant ship and the minesweepers *M-1701* and *M-1702* off Norway. (Rohwer 18)

SOLEBAY, 27 May 1672
The Anglo-French fleet, commanded by the Duke of York and anchored in Sole (or Southwold) Bay with many watering parties ashore, was surprised by the approach of the Dutch fleet commanded by Admiral De Ruijter (which had captured *French Victory* (38) earlier). The allied fleet got to sea before fighting began, but in separate sections. Part of the Dutch fleet held off the French ships, and the rest fought the English, where the fight was hottest. The battle was effectively a draw, though a strategic success for the Dutch. The Dutch lost one ship captured and one sunk; the English lost four destroyed and one captured. (Clowes 2.302–308; Rodger 2.81–82; Mahan 146–148; Tunstall 32–34)

Solebay and *Dolphin* v. *Maréchal de Belleisle*, 26 May 1758
The French frigate *Maréchal de Belleisle* (44) was challenged by *Solebay* (28; Capt. Robert Craig) and *Dolphin* (24; Capt. Benjamin Marlow) who were badly damaged in the masts and rigging; the French ship got away. (Clowes 3.298)

Solebay v. French squadron, 24 November 1799
The frigate *Solebay* (32; Capt. Stephen Poyntz) followed a French squadron, consisting of the storeship *Egyptienne*, two corvettes, *Levrier* and *Eole*, and the schooner *Vengeur*, off St Domingue until they were becalmed and separated into two pairs. *Solebay* then captured them in succession. (James 2.414–415; Clowes 5.528)

Sollum, Egypt, 23 November 1915
As a result of increased hostility from the Senussi nomads, the Egyptian army garrison at Sollum was evacuated by the sloop *Clematis* and six trawlers. (Corbett 3.224–225; Halpern, *Naval History* 109)

Solomon Islands, South Pacific

1868 The screw sloop *Blanche* (Capt. John Montgomerie) bombarded villages in Roduna Bay in revenge for local hostility. (Clowes 7.223–224)

1943 The RAN cruiser *Australia* and destroyers *Arunta* and *Warramunga* took part in the landing on New Georgia, supported by the carrier *Victorious* and others. RNZS *Leander* was damaged in the battle of Kaloobangara on 12–13 July. The RAN cruiser *Hobart* was torpedoed by *I-11* on 20 July; the RNZS corvette *Tui* and US aircraft sank *I-17* on 19 August. Two Australian cruisers and four destroyers supported the US landing at Cape Gloucester on New Ireland on 26 December. (Rohwer 258–259, 263, 294)

Somali v. *Munchen*, 7 May 1941

The German weather ship *Munchen* was surprised and captured by the destroyer *Somali* near Jan Mayen Island. *Somali* was covered by a large task force, and Enigma codes were recovered. (Rohwer 72; Sebag-Montefiore 144–148)

Somaliland

1890 An expedition including a Naval Brigade from the screw gunvessel *Ranger* (Cmdr Samuel Johnson) attacked the Esa tribe in Somaliland. The expedition defeated two counter-attacks, destroyed many wells, and rustled cattle. (Clowes 7.400)

1940–1941 British Somaliland was invaded by Italian forces in 1940. The destroyer *Kimberley* and the sloop *Auckland* bombarded invading Italian troops on the coast road near Berbera on 13 August; troops and civilians were evacuated from Berbera and other ports to Aden on 17–19 August. In reply Zante in Italian Somaliland was bombarded by the cruiser *Devonshire* on 18 November, and Mogadishu was shelled by the cruiser *Leander* on 29 November and attacked by aircraft from the carrier *Formidable* on 2 February 1941. At Kismayu on 10–14 February the German and Italian ships in the harbour, under threat of British attack, sailed to escape; the cruiser *Shropshire* gave supporting fire to the attackers; most of the escaping ships were captured or sunk. Two Indian battalions and a Somali detachment successfully landed at Berbera in British Somaliland on 16 March; naval gunfire helped to break Italian resistance. (Rohwer 36, 49, 50, 57, 59, 64)

Soroy, Norway, February 1945

A conflict on the island of Soroy, north Norway, between German troops and Norwegian resisters, ended when four British destroyers from Murmansk rescued 500 Norwegians and took them to Britain. (Schofield 209–210; Rohwer 393–394)

South Africa

1878 In the Transkei War, the screw corvette *Active* (Capt. Francis Sulivan) bombarded a large enemy force at Bowker's Bay; a Naval Brigade participated in the battle of Quintana. (Clowes 7.302)

1899–1900 The South African (Boer) War began in October 1899 and involved the navy in its first year. Capt. Percy Scott of the cruiser *Terrible* converted naval guns to army use and assisted in the defence of Ladysmith. A Naval Brigade, made up of men from *Terrible*, *Forte*, *Tartar*, and *Philomel*, assisted in the relief of Ladysmith, then moved up to the Transvaal border. A second Naval Brigade, from the cruisers *Doris*, *Monarch*, and *Powerful*, also using converted ships' guns, was part of the advance to relieve Kimberley. It suffered severe casualties in the battle of Graspan, assisted in the victory at Paardeburg, and assisted in the capture of Bloemfontein and Pretoria. The men returned to their ships late in 1900 and had no part in the guerrilla war which followed. (Clowes 7.463–519; Hore, *Seapower* 181–207)
See also: **Cape of Good Hope**

Southampton, Hampshire, April 1470
The Earl of Warwick fled from the enmity of Edward IV, heading for Calais. On the way he raided Southampton in order to increase his fleet, but was beaten off by Earl Rivers, losing one or two of his ships. (Gillingham 176)

Southampton v. *Maréchal de Belleisle* and *Chauvelin*, 25 July 1756
Two French frigates, *Maréchal de Belleisle* (36) and *Chauvelin* (36), met and attacked the frigate *Southampton* (32; Capt. James Gilchrist), but were driven off. (Clowes 3.296)

Southampton v. *Emeraude*, 23 September 1757
Southampton (32; Capt. James Gilchrist) encountered *Emeraude* (28) near Brest; the two ships fought and suffered heavy casualties; *Emeraude* surrendered. (Clowes 3.297)

Southampton and *Melampe* v. *Danae* and another, 28 March 1759
In the North Sea *Southampton* (32; Capt. James Gilchrist) and *Melampe* (24; Capt. William Hotham) met and fought two French frigates. *Melampe* fought both for a time; when *Southampton* came up, one sailed off; *Danae* surrendered. (Clowes 3.301)

Southampton v. *Fée*, 27–28 June 1781
The French frigate *Fée* (32), already damaged after a fight with an unknown British ship, met and fought *Southampton* (32; Capt. William Afleck), indecisively. (Clowes 4.69–70)

Southampton v. *Vestale*, 29 September 1795
The frigate *Southampton* (32; Capt. James Macnamara) challenged a group of French ships which came out of Genoa. The largest of the French, the frigate *Vestale* (36), brought down *Southampton*'s mainmast, and then sailed off, without attempting capture. (James 1.325–326; Clowes 4.494)

Southampton v. *Utile*, 9 June 1796
The frigate *Southampton* (32; Capt. James Macnamara), pretending to be a neutral, managed to get close to the corvette *Utile* (24) off the island of

Porquerolles. After a challenge and three broadsides, *Utile* was boarded and captured. (James 1.370–372; Clowes 4.499)

Southampton v. Corso, 2 December 1796
The frigate *Southampton* (32; Capt. James Macnamara) captured the Spanish *Corso* (18) off Morocco. (Clowes 4.560)

Southampton v. Amethyste, 3 February 1812
The frigate *Amethyste* was a Haitian privateer licensed by a rebel regime; the frigate *Southampton* (32; Capt. Sir James Yeo) challenged her, was defied, and in half an hour reduced *Amethyste* to a dismasted wreck. The ship was eventually returned to Henri Christophe, the Haitian ruler, from whom she had originally rebelled. (James 5.351–354)

Southampton v. Vixen, 22 November 1812
The frigate *Southampton* (32) captured the US sloop *Vixen* (14), but she sank later near the Bahamas. (Clowes 5.567)

Southern Italy, 3–9 September 1943
A landing in Calabria by the 8th Army took place on 3 September, covered by the Mediterranean fleet with preliminary bombardments at Reggio and Pessaro from 31 August. Allied troops were landed at Taranto on 9 September, covered by the 12th Cruiser Squadron and the battleships *Howe* and *King George V*. The minelayer *Abdiel* was sunk on a mine in Taranto harbour during the operation. Elements of the Italian fleet surrendered to the Allies on 9 September as part of the Italian armistice terms, and were sailed to Malta and other ports. German attacks sank some ships, including the battleship *Roma*. (Rohwer 270–272)

Southern Maid and *Protea* v. *Ondina*, 11 July 1942
The Italian submarine *Ondina* was sunk by the South African ASW trawlers *Southern Maid* and *Protea* and an aircraft off the coast of Syria. (Rohwer 179)

Southland v. U-14, 2 September 1915
The transport *Southland* was torpedoed south of Mudros by *U-14*; most of the men on board were rescued, and the ship itself survived. (Corbett 3.113)

South of France, 15 August 1944
Allied forces, mainly US and French, landed on the French coast between Cannes and Toulon. Naval support was mainly by US ships, but the British battleship *Ramillies*, eleven cruisers, nine destroyers, and seven carriers were included. (Rohwer 349–350)

South Wales
Viking forces repeatedly raided various parts of South Wales. St David's cathedral harboured wealth and was a frequent target for raiders based in Ireland.

988–991 A Viking force raided Llanbadarn, St David's, Llanilltid, Llandeudoch, and Llancarfan, and Morgannwg was ravaged by a Viking force from Ireland in the pay of Maredudd ap Owain. Next year a Viking fleet led by Godfrey Haraldsson ravaged Dyfed, including St David's. St David's was raided again in 991. (Maund 13, 158–160)

1001 St David's was raided by a Viking fleet. (Maund 160)

1022 A Viking force out of England led by Eilaf (or Eglaf) raided Morgannwg and plundered St David's. (Maund 161)

1033 The ruler of South Wales, Rhydderch ab Iestyn, was killed during a raid by 'Irish', that is, Irish Vikings. (Maund 162; F.M. Stenton, *Anglo-Saxon England*, Oxford 1947, 403–404, 416)

1039 The king of Morgannwg, Meurig ap Hywel, was captured by Vikings during a raid. (Maund 11)

1042–1044 A Viking fleet, probably from Ireland, ravaged Dyfed until defeated by Hywel ap Edwin of Deheubarth at the battle of Pwlldyfach; two years later a Viking fleet from Ireland allied with Hywel but was defeated in a battle at the mouth of the Tywi River by Gruffudd ap Llywelyn; Hywel died in the fight. (Maund 22–23)

1049 A Viking Irish fleet allied with Gruffudd ap Rhyderch and raided in South Wales. (Maund 64, 163; Hudson 131)

1080–1081 St David's was raided in 1080 and next year Gruffudd ap Llywelyn in alliance with a Viking fleet from Ireland fought and defeated Caradog ap Gruffudd at the battle of Mynydd Carn. (Maund 33)

1088–1091 Rhys ap Tewdwr, driven from his kingdom of Deheubarth by the sons of Bleddyn ap Cynfyn, went to Ireland and hired a Viking fleet with whose aid he returned, defeated his enemies at the battle of Llch-y-Crau, and recovered his throne. St David's was raided next year and in 1091. (Maund 159–160, 168)

See also: **Bristol Channel, Milford Haven, North Wales, River Severn**

THE SPANISH ARMADA, 1588

King Philip II of Spain dispatched a fleet of 130 ships, commanded by the Duke of Medina Sidonia, from Lisbon in May with the aim of collecting an army in Flanders to invade England. Delayed by a storm, the Armada arrived off the Scilly Isles on 19 July. The English had two fleets waiting, one based at Plymouth to counter the Armada itself, the second at the Strait of Dover to watch for any move by the Spanish army in Flanders.

The Armada pursued its course along the Channel for the next nine days, fighting four battles on the way. On 20 July, off Devon, the Armada's formation resembled a crescent, with the best fighting ships in the trailing wings shielding the transports. The English attacked both wings, the Admiral Lord Howard of Effingham attacking one, and a squadron under the Vice-Admiral Sir Francis Drake, the other. Neither attack had any effect, though two Spanish ships were disabled by accidents. (Drake captured one of these during the night.) On 22 July, off Portland Bill, one Spanish ship, *Gran Grifon*, fell behind and was attacked by several Englishmen, but was rescued by other Spanish ships.

On 25 July the English feared that the Spaniards might seize the Isle of Wight as a base, and attacked to forestall this. Medina Sidonia had intended to anchor in Spithead, but not to land, and the English attack prevented this.

On 27–28 July, Medina Sidonia anchored the Armada off the French coast at Gravelines, hoping to contact the Prince of Parma, Philip II's commander in Flanders. The two English fleets now united. The commanders feared a possible invasion by the fleet which they had been unable to damage in the past week. Eight fireships were sent in, none of which damaged any of the Spanish ships, but which did compel the Armada's formation to break up. The English ships now closed with the Spaniards, who had largely expended their ammunition. A gale moved the fighting into the North Sea, where some Spanish ships, perhaps three, were sunk.

Medina Sidonia ordered the surviving ships to sail home round Scotland and Ireland. Perhaps twenty ships were wrecked on these coasts; over ninety ships returned home, but a third of the men had died. The whole of Spain went into mourning; the English celebrated, cautiously, when their victory became clear. (Rodger 1.252–271; Clowes 1.539–604; Loades 244–255; E. Martín and G. Parker, *The Spanish Armada*, London 1988; G. Mattingly, *The Defeat of the Spanish Armada*, London 1940)

Spanish Main, December 1595
An English expedition under Sir Francis Drake raided and burnt Rio de la Hacha and Santa Marta. (Rodger 1.283; Clowes 1.506; Andrews 198; Williamson 82–85)

***Spartan* v. French polacre, 14 May 1807**
The frigate *Spartan* (38; Capt. Jahleel Brenton) chased a French polacre near Nice. Being becalmed, two boats were sent to attack the French vessel, but the boarders were driven off with twenty-eight men killed. (James 4.257–258; Clowes 5.400)

***Spartan*, *Success*, and *Espoir* v. convoy, 25 April 1810**
The frigates *Spartan* (38; Capt. Jahleel Brenton) and *Success* (32; Capt. John Ayscough) and the sloop *Espoir* (18; Cmdr Robert Mitford) attacked a convoy near Terracina, Italy. Four prizes were seized and brought out. (James 5.114; Clowes 5.453)

***Spartan* v. *Cerere* and others, 2 May 1810**
The frigate *Spartan* (38; Capt. Jahleel Brenton) tempted the Neapolitan frigate *Cerere* to come out of Naples. *Cerere* was accompanied by the corvette *Fama* (30), the brig *Sparviero* (8), the cutter *Achille* (8), and seven gunboats. An initial triple-shotted broadside put *Cerere* temporarily out of action; *Fama* and *Sparviero* were then attacked in succession. The gunboats joined in a combined attack, but a breeze carried *Spartan* clear. *Cerere* and *Fama* got under the protection of batteries at Baia, but *Sparviero* was compelled to

surrender. The gunboats *Cerere* and *Fama* returned to Naples; *Spartan*, towing her prize, flaunted her success directly in front of Naples harbour. (James 5.114–119; Clowes 5.453–454)

Spearfish v. *Lutzow*, 11 April 1940
The submarine *Spearfish* damaged the pocket battleship *Lutzow* in a torpedo attack. (Rohwer 18)

Spearfish v. *U-34*, 1 August 1940
U-34, on its way home, sank the British submarine *Spearfish* off Cape Noss Head, Scotland. (Rohwer 30)

Speedwell and *Shoreham* v. French convoy, June 1706
Speedwell (28; Capt. George Camocke) and *Shoreham* (20; Capt. George Sanders) met a French convoy of ten ships headed for the West Indies; five were captured. (Clowes 2.510)

Speedwell v. privateers, May 1709
Speedwell (28; Capt. George Camocke) fought two privateers off Bantry Bay, Ireland. One was captured, and their prize, the West Indiaman *Ruth*, was retaken. (Clowes 2.522)

Speedwell v. *Achille*, 4 April 1761
The cutter *Speedwell* was captured by the French *Achille* at Vigo. (Clowes 3.311)

Speedwell v. slavers, 1832
The schooner *Speedwell* (5; Lt William Warren) captured the slavers *Planeta* (on 6 April), *Aquila* (on 3 June), and *Indagadera* (on 25 June). *Aquila* fought for over an hour before surrendering. Over 1000 slaves were freed from the ships. Warren was promoted. (Clowes 6.272)

Speedy v. French frigate, 28 June 1794
The sloop *Speedy* (14; Cmdr George Eyre) was captured off Nice by a French frigate. (Clowes 4.548)

Speedy on the Coast of Spain, August–November 1799
The sloop *Speedy* (14; Cmdr Jahleel Brenton) and the privateer *Defender* chased three Spanish vessels into a bay near Cape de Gata on 9 August; a lengthy cannonade persuaded the Spanish crews to leave; two of their ships drove ashore, but all three were taken by the British ships. On 3 October *Speedy* chased a group of coasters from Algeciras and drove three ashore, where they were wrecked. On 6 November, guarding a small convoy, *Speedy* was attacked by twelve Spanish gunboats from Algeciras; after three hours the ships in the convoy were safe in Gibraltar Bay, and the gunboats retired. (James 2.395–397; Clowes 4.528)

Speedy v. *Gamo* and *Desaix*, May–June 1801
The sloop *Speedy* (14; Cmdr Lord Cochrane) at first evaded a fight with the

Spanish xebec *Gamo* (32), but when they met again on 6 May they fought; *Gamo* was boarded and taken – *Speedy*'s crew of fifty-four defeated *Gamo*'s 319. A month later *Speedy* was attacked near Alicante by three French line-of-battle ships. *Desaix* (74) captured her after Cochrane had manoeuvred for two hours to escape. (James 3.132–134; Clowes 4.538–539; Thomas 64–68, 171–173)

Spencer v. Volcan, 4 May 1796
The sloop *Spencer* (16; Cmdr Andrew Evans) chased and fought the gun brig *Volcan* (12), which eventually surrendered. (James 1.363; Clowes 4.497–498)

Sphinx v. Amphitrite, September 1779
Sphinx (20; Cmdr Robert Sutton) was captured by the French frigate *Amphitrite* (32), but was recaptured on 29 December by *Proserpine* (32). (Clowes 4.31)

Sphinx v. Trompeuse, 12 January 1794
The French sloop *Trompeuse* (18) was captured off Cape Clear, Ireland, by the sloop *Sphinx* (20; Capt. Richard Lucas). (Clowes 4.552)

Spitfire v. Allegre, 12 January 1797
The French storeship *Allegre* was captured by the fireship *Spitfire* (16; Cmdr Michael Seymour) off Ushant. (Clowes 4.555)

Spitfire v. Wilding, 28 December 1798
The French armed transport *Wilding* (14) was captured by the fireship *Spitfire* (16; Cmdr Michael Seymour) in the Bay of Biscay. (Clowes 4.557)

Spitzbergen, Arctic Ocean, 2 July 1943
The submarine *Seadog* evacuated a Norwegian commando unit from Spitzbergen, where a German weather station on the island had been destroyed. (Rohwer 258)

Splendid v. Velite, 21 November 1942
The submarine *Splendid* damaged the Italian destroyer *Velite* in an attack in the Bay of Naples. (Rohwer 214)

Splendid v. Aviere, 17 December 1942
The submarine *Splendid* sank the destroyer *Aviere*. (Rohwer 218)

Splendid v. Hermes, 21 April 1943
The German destroyer *Hermes* sank the British submarine *Splendid*. (Rohwer 241)

Spy v. Esperenza, May 1843
The brig *Spy* captured the Brazilian slaver *Esperanza* off Little Popo, West Africa. (Bethell 196)

Squirrel v. French privateers, 21 September 1703
Squirrel (20; Cmdr Gilbert Talbot) was captured by two French privateers off Hythe, Kent. (Clowes 2.56)

Squirrel v. French ship, 7 July 1706
Squirrel (24; Cmdr Daniel Butler) was captured by the French. (Clowes 2.557)

Squirrel v. Spanish sloop, 28 April 1740
Squirrel (24; Capt. Peter Warren) captured a Spanish sloop off St Augustine, Florida, on 28 April 1740, and next year captured a large Spanish privateer out of Santiago de Cuba; it had information of the imminent arrival of a French squadron. (Clowes 3.269, 272)

Standard and Active v. Friedland, 26 March 1808
The Italian sloop *Friedland* (16) was captured by *Standard* (64) and *Active* (38) off Cape Blanco. (Clowes 5.558)

Stanley v. César, August 1778
The brig *Stanley* (10) was captured by the French *César* (74). (Clowes 4.18)

Starfish v. M-7, 9 January 1940
The submarine *Starfish* was forced to the surface in the Heligoland Bight by the German minesweeper *M-7*; the crew were taken prisoner, having scuttled the submarine. (Rohwer 13)

Starling v. U-202 and U-119, June 1943
The sloop *Starling* sank *U-202* on 1 June, helped by an air search, after a fifteen-hour search. On 20 June *Starling* rammed and sank *U-119*, a U-tanker, in the Bay of Biscay. (Rohwer 253, 257)

Starling and others v. U-592, U-653, and U-473, January–May 1944
U-592, already damaged by air attack, was sunk by the sloops *Starling*, *Wild Goose*, and *Magpie*, part of the 2nd Escort Group, on 31 January; on 14 March *Wild Goose* and *Starling* and aircraft from the carrier *Vindex* sank *U-653*; on 5 May *U-473* was forced to the surface by *Starling*, *Wild Goose*, and *Wren* and sunk by gunfire. (Rohwer 304, 309, 313)

Stately and Nassau v. Prinds Christian Frederik, 22 March 1808
Stately (64; Capt. George Parker) and *Nassau* (64; Capt. Robert Campbell) chased the Danish *Prinds Christian Frederik* (74) near Jutland. The Dane fought her two antagonists for two hours, and when she finally surrendered, she ran aground and could not be refloated. The crew was removed; the ship was set on fire and soon exploded. (James 4.319–320; Anderson 323–324; Clowes 5.414)

Staunch v. pirates, 4 August 1858
The screw gunboat *Staunch* (Lt Leveson Wildman) chased three pirate junks

off Taonpung; the Chinese resisted successfully at first, but finally two of the junks were captured. (Clowes 7.121)

Staunch and *M-15* v. *UC-38*, 11 November 1917
The submarine *UC-38* located the Allied ships at Deir el-Belah, Palestine, got past the guarding net and drifters, and torpedoed the destroyer *Staunch* and the monitor *M-15*. This had the effect of driving the Allied warships back to Port Said. (Newbolt 5.80–81; Halpern, *Naval History* 396)

Sterlet v. German submarine chasers, 12 April 1940
The submarine *Sterlet* was depth-charged and sunk by four German submarine chasers. (Rohwer 19)

Steven Furness v. *UB-64*, 13 December 1917
The armed boarding steamer *Steven Furness* was sunk by *UB-64* in the Irish Sea. (Colledge 384)

Stirling Castle v. *Gyldenlove*, 11 August 1694
The Danish *Gyldenlove* (56) failed to salute *Stirling Castle* (70; Sir Cloudisley Shovell) in the Downs and was attacked. The arrival of a second English ship persuaded Capt. Barfod to surrender, after suffering twenty casualties. The ship was taken to Sheerness and detained for two months. (Anderson 132)

Stirling Castle v. *Volage*, 4 April 1745
The French *Volage* (30) became separated from her squadron and was found off Cape San Martin by *Stirling Castle* (70; Cmdr John Fawler), and fought and captured, but the arrival of *Volage*'s squadron led to her recapture the next day. (Clowes 3.281)

Stockforce v. *UB-80*, 30 July 1918
The Q-ship *Stockforce* was attacked by *UB-80* in the Channel; both were damaged; *Stockforce* later sank under tow. (Grant 91; Colledge 384)

Stonecrop v. *U-151*, 17 September 1917
The Q-ship *Stonecrop* fought *U-151*, but without result. (Grant 66)

Stork v. *Palmier*, August 1758
The French *Palmier* (74) captured *Stork* (10; Lt William Tucker) in the West Indies. (Clowes 3.300)

Stork v. *Coquette*, 24 February 1804
The sloop *Stork* (18; Cmdr George Le Geyt) captured the schooner *Coquette* near Jamaica. (Clowes 5.556)

Stork v. *Antelope*, 23 March 1805
The sloop *Stork* (18; Cmdr George Le Geyt) sent in two boats to cut out the Dutch privateer *Antelope* in the harbour of Cape Roxo, Puerto Rico. The

capture was accomplished quickly; the privateer's crew mostly jumped into the harbour when attacked. (James 4.27–28)

Stour estuary, Essex, 885
King Alfred sent a naval force to intercept a raiding group of Vikings. They were found in the estuary of the River Stour in East Anglia and were defeated and the crews killed. On its return, however, the English force met a larger Danish fleet and was defeated. (*ASC* s.a. 885)

Sir Richard Strachan's Action, 4 November 1805
Four French ships under Rear-Admiral Dumanoir le Pelley escaped destruction at Trafalgar and sailed north into the Bay of Biscay. They were found by the frigate *Phoenix* (36; Capt. Thomas Baker) which enticed them towards the British force blockading Ferrol, five line-of-battle ships under Capt. Sir Richard Strachan. After a long chase, the two squadrons met and fought. All four of the French ships were beaten into surrender. (James 4.2–11; Clowes 5.170–174; *NC* 3.241–243; Tunstall 259)

Strait of Dover
The Strait of Dover is the narrowest stretch of sea between England and the continent, linking the North Sea and the English Channel; here it is taken to be the Kent coast from the North Foreland to Dungeness and the French coast from Boulogne to Gravelines
See also: **English Channel, North Sea**

1217 (Battle of DOVER) A French expedition of about eighty ships carrying an army sailed from Calais under the command of Eustace the Monk. An English squadron commanded by Hubert de Burgh sailed from Dover to intercept. De Burgh manoeuvred to gain the weather gauge and attacked the French ships singly. The fighting consisted of grappling and boarding, and the English galleys were used to ram. Most of the French ships were sunk or captured; fifteen escaped. Eustace the Monk, who had changed sides repeatedly in the past, was executed. (Clowes 1.186, 198; Rose 29–31; Rodger 1.55)

The Early Hundred Years' War
1340 Intelligence received in England showed that French galleys at Boulogne were poorly guarded. In January, a fleet from the Cinque Ports raided the harbour, burned all eighteen galleys, and more merchant ships. The French galley fleet was effectively destroyed. (Sumption 1.320–321; Rodger 1.97)

1346–1347 (Siege of CALAIS) Edward III's army, having defeated the French main army at Crecy, besieged the town of Calais for eleven months, supplied from England by ship. The first convoy was intercepted and destroyed by French galleys (17 September); later convoys were more heavily protected. Two French supply convoys reached the town in March and April 1347, but a little later the town was finally fully surrounded, and the English fleet established control over the passage between Calais and England. A French attempt to run supplies in on 25 June was intercepted and defeated, and an attempt by eight barges from Dieppe failed in July. The town surrendered on 3 August, after the French army failed to relieve it. (Sumption 1.ch. 15; Clowes 1.266; Rose 60–61)

The Continuing War
1377   An English squadron under Sir Thomas Percy intercepted a Spanish-Flemish convoy and captured two ships. A raid by an English force from Calais in October burnt part of Boulogne, destroying twenty-eight vessels in the harbour. (Sumption 3.181–183)

1385   As a French fleet dispersed in September, some ships were attacked by English ships from Calais; a considerable number were captured, and others sunk. (Clowes 1.297)

1387   A Franco-Burgundian fleet was intercepted in the strait by an English squadron commanded by the Earl of Arundel and was chased as far as the Flemish coast; most of the ships were captured. (Clowes 1.300; Rodger 1.113–114)

1405   The Captain of Calais captured seventeen ships laden with wine. (Clowes 1.362)

1436 (Siege of Calais)   Burgundian forces besieged Calais, and an English fleet under the Duke of Gloucester sailed in relief. A Burgundian attempt to block the harbour entrance by sinking ships laden with stones was foiled by men from the town who burnt the ships; Gloucester landed his army; the Burgundians retired and Gloucester conducted a raid into France. (Clowes 1.383–384; Barker 252–253)

The Wars of the Roses
1458   The Earl of Warwick, Captain of Calais, short of money due to the parsimony of the royal government, captured six Spanish merchant ships, then attacked the Hanseatic Bay fleet carrying salt from Biscay to Germany. Warwick was summoned to court to explain his conduct but failed to attend in fear of his life. (Gillingham 101–102)

1460   The English royal government attempted to replace the Earl of Warwick as Captain of Calais, but the ships sent against him deserted to him. A royal squadron gathered at Sandwich, but Warwick's own ships captured them. In June he sailed to Kent, defeating another royal squadron on the way. He landed at Sandwich, which he burnt on being opposed. (Clowes 1.386–387; Rose 91)

1470   The Earl of Warwick, commanding a rebel fleet, attacked a large convoy of Flemish ships in August, capturing sixty or more of them. He was then attacked by a royal fleet under Lord Howard and was defeated. (Gillingham 177)

1495   Perkin Warbeck, the pretended son of Edward IV, landed at Sandwich on 7 July with a small force, claiming the throne. He was swiftly defeated and expelled. (Clowes 1.446)

Tudor Wars

1523 The Duke of Albany, Regent of Scotland, was attacked while sailing from France to Scotland by the English fleet under Sir William Fitzwilliam. Two French ships were captured and the rest took refuge in Boulogne and Dieppe. The English fleet then burnt Treport. Albany sailed on when the English retired. (Clowes 1.458–459)

1524 A squadron of six French ships met the *Katherine Galey* off Sandwich on 19 January. A ship came out of Sandwich to assist the galley, but both were taken by the French. An attack was made by land out of Calais on Boulogne, supported at sea by a squadron of English royal ships commanded by Christopher Coo. The harbour was blockaded. The fishing fleet of Rye was attacked near the town by a French squadron in February. Before much damage could be done, however, an English squadron arrived. Two French ships were captured. (Loades 107–109; Clowes 1.458)

1544 The town of Boulogne was besieged by an English army, and ships from Calais blockaded the port; the town was surrendered to Henry VIII in September. (Loades 128–129)

1558 (Loss of Calais)   Calais was unexpectedly attacked by the French in winter, and fell in a short time. An attempt was made to relieve the town by sea, but it failed. (Loades 170–174; Rodger 1.192–194; Clowes 1.472–473)

1588 The Armada at Gravelines – see: **Spanish Armada**

1602 A squadron of nine Spanish galleys sailed from Cezimbra to reinforce others based at Dunkirk. The English and Dutch, forewarned, intercepted them in the strait. Only two got through. (Rodger 1.292–293)

First Dutch War

1652 (Battle of DOVER)   A Dutch fleet driven by weather anchored off Dover on 19 May, saluting part of the English fleet under Admiral Nehemiah Bourne in the Downs. Bourne feared an attack and sent for the rest of the fleet under Admiral Blake, which was off Rye. As Blake approached, the Dutch, commanded by Admiral Maarten Tromp, turned to challenge his fleet. Bourne came down from the Downs to join in. Tromp had a fleet of forty-two ships; Blake had twelve and Bourne nine. The battle lasted all day, during which two Dutch ships were taken, one of which was abandoned as sinking. (Clowes 2.144–149; Powell 140–144)

In July, Sir George Ayscue's squadron of fourteen or fifteen ships in the Downs was attacked by Admiral Tromp's Dutch fleet, perhaps four times that number. Ayscue sheltered under the guns of Deal Castle; the Dutch ships could not close and a gale drove them off. (Clowes 2.153–154; Powell 157–158)

On 4 September General-at-Sea Robert Blake, off Calais, intercepted and destroyed a French convoy heading to relieve the Spanish siege of Dunkirk. Seven of the eight warships of the escort were captured and the transports scattered. (Capp 71; Clowes 2.159; Powell 165–166)

See also: **Dungeness, Kentish Knock, Gabbard**

The French Wars
1694–1696 The Anglo-Dutch Channel fleet bombarded Calais in September 1694, August 1695, and April 1696. In each case damage was caused to some houses, and batteries were silenced, but little other effect resulted. (Clowes 2.478, 482, 487)

1762 A Dutch convoy of four ships escorted by a frigate in the Downs refused to allow an inspection, and fired on the boats sent to do so. The British inspecting squadron thereupon attacked and captured all the ships and detained the merchantmen carrying contraband; the frigate was released. (Clowes 3.252–253)

The French Revolutionary War
1801 The Invasion Threat The French flotilla of boats for the invasion of England was concentrated at Boulogne. Vice-Admiral Lord Nelson was put in charge of the defence of the coast. He organised two raids intended to destroy as many of the flotilla as possible. On 4 August bomb vessels shelled Boulogne harbour, and on 15 August three divisions of boats made a full-scale raid; none got nearer the harbour than the wall of the mole and the guard boats, at a cost of forty-four men killed and 122 wounded.

At Etaples on 20 August a wrecked ship was set on fire by boats from the sloop *Hound* and the gunvessel *Mallard*. Six French gunboats came out and were driven on shore; these were later attacked by boats from *Jamaica* (24; Capt. Jonas Rose). Three were taken off, and the others scuttled or damaged. (James 3.64–68; Clowes 4.444–446)

The Napoleonic War
1803 The Channel fleet occasionally bombarded Calais, as on 27 September 1803 by the sloop *Autumn* (Cmdr Samuel Jackson) with a group of bombs and other vessels. On 27 October boats of the sloop *Merlin* (Cmdr Edward Brenton) chased the privateer *Sept Frères* ashore near Gravelines; in the evening it was destroyed by the schooner *Milbrook* (Lt Mauritius de Starck). (Clowes 5.51, 72, 329; James 3.173–174, 196, 235–236; NC 3.65–67)

A group of French gunboats sailed from Calais to Boulogne, chased ineffectually by the frigate *Leda* (Capt. Robert Honeyman). Another group of boats, twenty-five strong, was also chased by *Leda*; only two were prevented from reaching Boulogne. On 31 October 1803 a French gun brig, with six schooners and sloops, came out of Etaples and headed for Boulogne. The hired cutter *Admiral Mitchell* (12; Lt Alexander Shippard) chased them. The gun brig and one of the sloops were forced on shore, even though *Admiral Mitchell* had to brave the fire of a shore battery; she had only four casualties, all wounded. On 8 November 1803 *Conflict* (14; Lt David Chambers) captured the French *Gunboat no. 86* off Calais. (James 3.172–173; Clowes 5.50–51, 556)

1804 The sloops *Rattler* and *Cruizer* (Cmdrs Francis Mason and John Hancock) attacked a flotilla of invasion gunboats moving along the Flemish coast. *Cruizer* captured one vessel; both sloops were attacked by the prame *Ville d'Anvers*, several schooners, schuyts, and shore batteries. On 20 February the cutter *Active* (14; Lt John Williams) chased a group of fifteen gunboats off Gravelines, capturing one; the rest reached the shelter of batteries. The frigates *Aimable* (Capt. William Bolton) and *Penelope* (Capt. William Broughton) with *Antelope* (50; Capt. Sir Sidney Smith) came to assist. The fighting ended when the tide fell, forcing the British ships to retreat into deeper water; the surviving Dutch vessels went into Ostend. Several of the Dutch ships, including *Ville d'Anvers*, were driven ashore; they were later refloated. French gunboats were gathered mainly at Boulogne by August, and the army of 80,000 men was encamped there and at Montreuil. Several squadrons of British frigates and smaller craft were placed to intercept any invasion.

Attempts to disrupt the French preparations had not been effective. French success had been due largely to the presence of shore batteries along the routes the gunboats had travelled to the gathering place. An attempt on 26 August by several ships to disrupt a large group of gunboats was fairly successful, but at some cost – the hired cutter *Constitution* (Lt James Dennis) was hit by a shell and sunk – but (Napoleon was a witness) only the shore batteries preserved the gunboats from destruction. On 1 October an attack by explosive ships, called 'catamarans', failed to have much effect. On 8 December, an explosive vessel, *Susannah*, and two 'catamarans' were sent against a seaward fort at Calais, without effect. *Mallard* was captured at Calais on 25 December. (James 3.173–174, 218, 235–236, 390; Clowes 5.51, 69–72; *NC* 2.245–249, 3.23, 56–67, 181–182, 240)

1805   The fighting continued after the winter, during which the weather was unsuitable for an invasion. On the night of 23 April a division of gunboats and schuyts sailed from Dunkirk roads for Ambleteuse; in the morning they were seen in some disorder by a squadron commanded by Capt. Robert Honeyman in *Leda*. The brigs *Gallant* (Lt Thomas Shirly) and *Watchful* (Lt James Marshall) attacked a separated group of eight schuyts. *Gallant* was quickly holed and turned away, *Watchful* captured one schuyt. The other six were attacked by the sloop *Railleur* (Capt. Valentine Collard) and the brigs *Locust* and *Starling* (Lts John Lake and Charles Napier) and surrendered after a stiff fight. Next day two more schuyts were taken by the brig *Archer* (Lt William Price).

A division of gunboats sailed from Dunkirk on 16 July, while a second came out from Boulogne to distract British attention. The gunboats advanced steadily, bombarded by every British ship in the area, and suffered some losses, usually by going ashore; the British suffered damage to many of their ships from the French shore batteries. By 23 July the French had gathered, in seven ports from Etaples to Ostend, about 2300 vessels, intended to carry 160,000 men and 9000 horses. But there they stuck. War with Austria began in August; the invasion of Britain was postponed, as it proved, indefinitely. The invasion flotillas were dispersed later in 1805. (James 3.172, 174, 222–234, 315–326; Clowes 5.65–66, 176–177)

The Great War
1914   The gunboat *Niger* (Lt-Cmdr A.T. Muir), part of the Dover Patrol, was sunk by the submarine *U-12* in the Downs on 11 November. (Corbett 1.254, 2.8)

1916–1918 (The DOVER BARRAGE) A line of nets and mines was laid in 1916 to deter U-boats from passing the strait, and this became a target for German surface ships. On 26 October 1916 a raid by German destroyers of the 3rd and 9th Flotillas, based in Flanders, broke through the line of drifters, sinking three and setting one on fire. The transport *Queen* was sunk, as were the destroyers *Flirt* and *Nubian*; several others were damaged. Another raid on 23–24 November accomplished little, but in a raid on 25 February 1917, one destroyer passed through the picket line of drifters, and was then engaged by the destroyer *Laverack*; the rest turned for home. A second group of destroyers bombarded Margate and Westgate briefly but then also headed for home. Three groups of German destroyers raided on 17 March; the destroyer *Paragon* was sunk and the destroyer *Llewellyn* damaged. Ramsgate and Broadstairs were shelled, and SS *Greypoint* was sunk. On 20–21 April German destroyers shelled Calais and Dover, but one group met the British destroyers *Swift* and *Broke* which sank *G-85* and *G-42*, the latter rammed by *Broke*. On 24 November the destroyer *Gipsy*, together with drifters tending the Dover Strait barrage, attacked and sank *U-48*, which had been stranded on the Goodwin Sands. (Newbolt 5.426; Grant 48)

The drifter *Clover Bank*, part of the net patrol, was attacked on 23 January 1918 by German destroyers out of Zeebrugge. The drifter retreated towards the supporting ships; the German destroyers then retired. On 14–15 February German destroyers attacked the drifters' line again. On the British side all was muddle and confusion; seven drifters and a trawler were sunk and seven other vessels damaged. The German raiders faced no opposition to speak of. German destroyers and TBs made an attempt on 20–21 March to bombard coastal installations between Dunkirk and Nieuport, but were driven off by British and French destroyers, losing two TBs; one British destroyer was badly damaged. (Newbolt 4.52–66, 353–355, 361–388, 5.208–218, 224–227; Halpern, *Naval History* 346–350, 408–410)

Hitler's War
The strait was dominated by shore batteries on both sides, and by air attacks. Most fighting was thus done in the North Sea and the Channel, mainly against convoys.

1940 The destroyer *Grafton* was damaged by *U-62* off Dunkirk, and later sunk. In an attack off Dover on 27 July, the destroyer *Codrington* was sunk and the destroyer *Walpole* and the sloop *Sandhurst* were damaged. Convoy CW-9 was attacked off Newhaven on 8 August by S-boats, which sank three of the ships. (Rohwer 25, 33)

1941 On 23 July MTBs sank the German patrol vessel *V-1508* near Boulogne. The German 4th S-boat Flotilla attacked a convoy off Dungeness on 11 August, sinking one ship. MTBs attacked a German convoy off Boulogne on 9 September, sinking one ship. An MTB sank the German patrol vessel *Nordland* off Dunkirk on 25 November. (Rohwer 88, 92, 118)

1942 On 16 August five MGBs attacked the German 10th Minesweeping Flotilla off Calais; the minesweeper *R-184* was sunk by *MGB-330* by ramming. (Rohwer 189)

See also: **English Channel ('Channel Dash')**

1943 On 7–8 March the German 8th Destroyer Flotilla passed through the strait, attacked unsuccessfully by shore batteries and MTBs. On 11–12 March three MTBs attacked a German convoy off Boulogne. The German destroyers *Z-27* and *ZH-1* fought off attacks by MTBs in the Strait of Dover on 3 and 4 November. (Rohwer 236, 237, 284)

1944 MTBs attacked the German 36th Minesweeping Flotilla near Gravelines on 14–15 March, and sank two German ships; one MTB was also sunk. The German convoy 'Hecht' was attacked in the strait by four MTBs on 20 March 1944; a tanker was sunk by shore artillery. The 8th S-boat Flotilla attempted to raid convoys off Dover on 17–18 August and Beachy Head on 23–24 August; one ship was sunk; the raiders were driven off by the destroyer escorts.

1945 German two-man submarines attacked in the Strait of Dover on 1 January 1945 and sank one ship; one submarine was sunk by the destroyer *Cowdray* and one by the frigate *Ekins*. Later attempts during January were unsuccessful. (Rohwer 311, 312, 352–353, 382)

Strait of Gibraltar

1590 A squadron of ten English Levant Company ships was attacked by twelve Spanish galleys on 24 April. The attack was beaten off, the galleys suffering considerable damage. (Clowes 1.494)

1664 An English squadron under Admiral Sir Thomas Allin intercepted a Dutch Smyrna convoy in December; two merchantmen were captured and two sunk; three Dutch escorting warships escaped. (Corbett, *Mediterranean* 49–50; Clowes 2.423–424)

1693 Smyrna Convoy A convoy of 400 British, Dutch, and German ships heading for Smyrna and other ports in the eastern Mediterranean, escorted by a joint Anglo-Dutch fleet, was ambushed by the French fleet under Admiral Comte de Tourville at Lagos Bay, southwest Spain. Two Dutch warships were taken while attempting to distract the French, and a quarter of the merchantmen were lost or sunk. (Corbett, *Mediterranean* 147–148; Clowes 2.357–360; Rodger 2.153; Aubrey 156–160; Tunstall 58–59)

1757 A squadron of five ships commanded by Rear-Admiral Charles Saunders left Gibraltar to intercept four French ships sailing from Toulon for North America. On 5 April the two squadrons met and fired at each other; but during the night the French got away and later reached their destination. (Clowes 3.169–170)

1940 The ASW trawler *Arctic Ranger* attacked the Italian submarine *Cappellini* off Gibraltar on 14 June; the destroyer *Vidette* then chased the submarine into Ceuta. (Rohwer 26)

1944 *U-731*, located by aircraft on 15 May in the strait, was sunk by the submarine chasers *Kilmarnock* and *Blackfly*. (Rohwer 325)
See also: **Gibraltar**

Strait of Malacca

1592 Three ships under Capt. George Raymond were to attempt to open English trade with the countries of the Indian Ocean. Only one ship, the *Edward Bonaventure* (Capt. James Lancaster), reached the Indies, the first English ship to do so. In the Strait of Malacca Lancaster seized cargoes from ships which he identified as Portuguese. (Foster 140–141; Clowes 1.652; M. Franks, *The Basingstoke Admiral*, Salisbury 2006, 71–73)

1597 An expedition of three ships under Benjamin Wood sailed to the Indian Ocean. Two reached India and went on to the Malacca Strait, where they met and fought a Portuguese squadron for a week; one ship was abandoned and burned; the last was wrecked. Only one man, a Frenchman, survived. (Foster 140–141)

1943 The British submarine *Taurus* sank the Japanese submarine *I-34* off Penang on 13 November. (Rohwer 274)

1944–1945 A British submarine campaign was waged in the strait from 1944. *Tally Ho!* sank the Japanese cruiser *Kuma*, two transports, and the submarine *UIT-23*, and damaged the TB *Kari* between 11 and 14 January. *Stonehenge* sank the minesweeper *Wa-4*, but was later itself sunk. *Templar* torpedoed the cruiser *Kitakami* on 25 February; *Storm* sank the minesweeper *W-7* on 15 April; *Telemachus* sank *I-166* on 17 July; *Trenchant* sank *U-859* off Penang on 23 September; *Tally Ho!* sank the Japanese submarine chaser *Cha-135* on 6 October. (Rohwer 299, 313, 334, 355)

On 2 November near Singapore *Tantalus* damaged the submarine chaser *Ch-1*; *Terrapin* sank the minesweeper *W-5* on the 4th; *Shalimar* bombarded Car Nicobar; *Tally Ho!* sank the minelayer *Wa-4* on the 20th; *Stratagem* was sunk, probably by a Japanese destroyer, about 30 November; *Shalimar* sank a minesweeper on 5 December; *Stoic* sank the gun carrier *Shoei Maru* near Sunda Strait on 16 December. The submarine *Supreme* damaged a minelayer and the submarine chaser *Ch-63* in a surface gunfight on 8 February 1945; *Trenchant* and *Terrapin* sank the submarine chaser *Tokumu Tei* on 4 March. On 19 May *Terrapin* was badly damaged by a depth-charge attack by Japanese ASW ships. (Rohwer 372–373, 377, 382, 392, 418)

Strangford Lough, Ireland

877 Halfdan, one of the kings in the Danish Great Army, attempted to capture Dublin, but was defeated and killed in battle with the Dublin fleet in Strangford Lough. (Smyth, *Warlords* 194)

1204 Ragnvald, king of Man, assisted John de Courcy in his attempt to recover lost lands in Ulster. A fleet of 100 Manx ships helped at the siege of Moira. (MacDonald 87)

Streatham and others v. *Caroline*, 31 May 1809

The Indiamen *Streatham* (30), *Europe* (30), and *Lord Keith* (10) were intercepted in the Bay of Bengal by the French frigate *Caroline* (40). The three ships formed a line for defence, but *Caroline* was able to tackle them one at a time, first *Europe*, reduced to helplessness, surrendered, then *Streatham*; Lord Keith got away. (James 5.54–57; Clowes 5.439)

Strongbow and convoy v. *Brummer* and *Bremse*, 17 October 1917
The German minelaying cruisers *Brummer* and *Bremse* raided the regular convoy sailing between Bergen in Norway and Lerwick in Shetland. The protecting destroyers *Strongbow* and *Mary Rose* were sunk, as were nine of the ships in the convoy (all neutrals); three ships and two armed trawlers escaped. (Newbolt 5.152–156; Halpern, *Naval History* 378)

Stronghold v. *Maya* and others, 2 March 1942
The destroyer *Stronghold* was sunk in the Java Sea by the Japanese cruiser *Maya* and two destroyers. (Rohwer 148)

Stuart v. *Gondar*, 3 October 1940
The Italian submarine *Gondar* was sunk by the RAN destroyer *Stuart* and a Sunderland aircraft. (Rohwer 43)

Stubborn v. German convoy, 13 February 1944
The submarine *Stubborn* was damaged by depth-charges from the escort of a convoy it was attacking off Foldafjord, Norway. (Rohwer 301)

Stubborn v. *Nadakaze*, 25 July 1945
The submarine *Stubborn* sank the Japanese patrol boat *Nadakaze* in the Java Sea. (Rohwer 422)

Sturgeon v. *V-209*, 20 November 1939
The British submarine *Sturgeon*, operating near Heligoland, sank the German patrol vessel *V-209*. (Rohwer 9)

Stygian v. *Wa-104* and others, March 1945
The submarine *Stygian* sank the minesweeper *Wa-104* on 4 March 1945 off Nhe-Trang, Indo-China, damaged the minelayer *Wakataka* on 27 March, and sank the submarine chasers *Cha-130* and *Cha-104*. (Rohwer 396, 405)

Suakin, Sudan
1883–1885 The Egyptian garrisons of forts at Suakin were attacked by Mahdists commanded by Osman Digna. The screw gunvessel *Ranger* supported the garrisons with her fire, and the screw corvette *Euryalus* (Capt. Alexander Hastings) and the screw gunboat *Coquette* (Lt Fritz Crowe) arrived. A party of seamen and marines was landed to assist the defence, and a Naval Brigade formed from the crews of six ships took part in the subsequent advance to el-Teb where the Mahdists were defeated. In March a new advance resulted in a battle at Tamai, where the Naval Brigade came into considerable danger as a result of botched commands. Next year a Naval Brigade was part of an expedition from Suakin to Tamai again, on 20 March, fighting two battles on the way; the brigade was then recalled to Suakin and re-embarked. (Clowes 7.350–353, 371–374)

1888 The screw sloop *Dolphin* (Cmdr George Neville) shelled a fort occupied by Mahdists on 4 March, to assist an assault by the Suakin garrison; one of its shells fell among the attackers; the attack thereby failed. (Clowes 7.379)

1890 An expedition including men from the screw sloop *Dolphin* and the gunboat *Sandfly* attacked Mahdists inland from Suakin in January, inflicting a serious defeat. (Clowes 7.400–401)

Success and *Vernon* v. *Santa Catalina*, 16 March 1782
Success (32; Capt. Charles Pole), with the storeship *Vernon* (22), met the Spanish frigate *Santa Catalina* (34) near Cape Spartel. Pole avoided a blunt broadside attack; *Santa Catalina*, badly damaged, surrendered and was burnt. (Clowes 4.77–79)

Success v. *Bella Aurora*, 9 June 1799
The frigate *Success* (32; Capt. Shuldham Peard) drove the polacre *Bella Aurora* into the harbour of La Selva near Cape Creux; boats sent in captured her. (James 2.383)

Success v. *Diane* and *Justice*, 24 August 1800
The French frigates *Diane* and *Justice* broke out of Valetta, Malta; *Diane* was chased, fought, and captured by the frigate *Success* (32; Capt. Shuldham Peard); *Justice* escaped to Toulon. Valetta surrendered on 5 September. (James 2.436–444; NC 2.80–83; Clowes 4.422)

Success and *Sprightly* v. Ganteaume's squadron, 10–13 February 1801
The frigate *Success* (32; Capt. Shuldham Peard) followed the squadron of Rear-Admiral Ganteaume eastwards from Gibraltar. The cutter *Sprightly* (Lt Robert Jump) was captured and sunk on 10 February, and *Success* was attacked and forced to surrender on the 13th. The prisoners misled their captors into believing that there was a great force of British ships at Alexandria, Ganteaume's destination; Ganteaume turned aside to Toulon. (James 3.71–72; Clowes 4.448)

Success v. *Vengeur*, 20 November 1806
The frigate *Success* (32; Capt. John Ayscough) sent boats into Hidden Port, Cuba, to cut out the felucca *Vengeur*. The crew were ashore and proved impossible to defeat or dislodge; the felucca was taken. (James 4.184; Clowes 5.393)

Suez Canal, Egypt
1915 Turkish forces crossed the Sinai Peninsula as far as the Suez Canal, reaching it on 27 January. The battleships *Ocean* and *Swiftsure*, the sloop *Clio*, the AMC *Himalaya*, the light cruiser *Minerva*, and the Indian Marine ship *Hardinge* served as mobile artillery in the canal, along with several smaller French craft. (Corbett 2.110–118; Halpern, *Naval History* 107–108)

1956 An Anglo-French fleet launched air strikes, and landed paratroops and helicopter-borne troops at sites along the Suez Canal in November. A ceasefire was soon agreed, and these forces were evacuated. (Wettern 130–132)

Suffisante v. Revanche, 27 May 1796
The sloop *Suffisante* (14; Cmdr Nicholas Tomlinson) chased the privateer *Revanche* (12) across the Channel to Ushant; after half an hour's fight, she was forced to surrender amid the rocks. (James 1.365; Clowes 4.498)

Suffolk and Fame Prize v. Galliard and other, 3 May 1710
Suffolk (70; Capt. William Clevland) and *Fame Prize* (Capt. Streynsham), part of the British fleet in the Mediterranean, chased two French ships near Messina, Sicily. *Suffolk* captured *Galliard* (56) and *Fame Prize* a smaller ship. (Clowes 2.525)

Suffolk at Vladivostok, August 1918
The cruiser *Suffolk* was part of an Allied force at Vladivostok. A battalion of the Middlesex Regiment was landed; two of *Suffolk*'s guns mounted on trains accompanied some of the regiment along the Trans-Siberian Railway for 4000 miles as far as Omsk. (Newbolt 5.326)

Suffolk at Stavanger, Norway, 17 April 1940
The cruiser *Suffolk* shelled the German seaplane base at Stavanger, destroying four flying boats; *Suffolk* herself was damaged by a bomb. (Rohwer 21)

Sultan v. settee and brig, 4 December 1811
Boats from *Sultan* (74; Capt. John West) captured a settee (8) and a brig (6) off Bastia, Corsica. (Clowes 5.561)

Sultanpur, Gujarat, 1734
Sultanpur was the base of ships regarded by the EIC as pirates, but which were actually competitors. The Bombay government sent the sloop *London* (Capt. Richard Nunn), a bomb, and five galivats against the port; five ships and fourteen other vessels were captured, and fifty more ships burned. (Low 1.116)

Sumatra, February 1844
The sloops *Wanderer* (16; Cmdr George Seymour) and *Harlequin* (16; Cmdr Hon. George Hastings) raided settlements in Sumatra which were identified as pirate bases. (Clowes 6.326)

Sunda Strait, Indonesia
1794 A squadron of EIC ships – *William Pitt, Britannia, Houghton, Nautilus* – lay near the Sunda Strait on 24 January; *Nonsuch*, with two prizes, was 6 miles away. A French squadron – the frigates *Prudente* (36) and *Cybèle* (40), *Duguay-Trouin* (formerly the EIC ship *Princess Royal*), and the corvette *Vulcain* – chased *Nonsuch*, which led them towards the main EIC force, where they were driven off. (James 1.220–221)

1942 A Japanese landing in northeast Java, close to the Sunda Strait, on the night of 28 February, was attacked by the RAN cruiser *Perth* and the US cruiser *Houston*. The Japanese force was quickly reinforced by supporting ships; both Allied ships were sunk. (Rohwer 148)

Sungei Ujong, Malaya, November 1874
The ruler of Sungei Ujong asked for help against a rebel. A small British force of soldiers, sailors, and marines from *Charybdis* (Capt. Thomas Smith) and *Hart* (Cmdr Thomas Royse) marched to the rebel stockade, which was captured and burnt. (Clowes 7.270–272)

Sunn Prize v. French ships, 17 June 1693
Sunn Prize (24; Capt. Francis Manley) was captured by the French while on fishing protection duties in the North Sea. (Clowes 2.472)

Superieure and others at Cuba, 3 September 1806
Superieure (14; Cmdr Edward Rushworth) with *Flying Fish* (12) and *Stork* (18) went into the Gulf of Matamano, Cuba, where they captured the fort at Batabano and captured and destroyed eleven enemy ships. (Clowes 5.389)

Surat, India
1610   Sir Henry Middleton with ships of the EIC's sixth voyage fought a group of Portuguese vessels off Surat, with indecisive results. (Clowes 2.33)

1612   Two EIC ships, awaiting permission to trade, were attacked by four Portuguese warships accompanied by twenty-five smaller vessels. The Portuguese, with very large crews, hoped to board, so the English bombarded them from a safe distance. The English ships, commanded by Capt. Thomas Best, sailed to Kathiawar for provisions; the Portuguese followed, but were again defeated by the same tactics. (Foster 236–237; Clowes 2.33–34)

1615   An EIC squadron of four ships under Nicolas Downton was menaced by a large Portuguese squadron out of Goa. Downton anchored his ships behind a sandbank, and was able to repel Portuguese attacks by small vessels and fireships. (Foster 242–243; Clowes 2.35–36; Low 1.20–21)

1630   A Portuguese fleet attempted to prevent an EIC squadron reaching Surat, resulting in several indecisive skirmishes on land and sea. (Low 1.48–50)

Surinam, South America
1799   A small expedition under Vice-Admiral Hon. Hugh Seymour sailed from Martinique to Surinam. The governor was summoned on 16 August; after a pause, he agreed to surrender. Two corvettes were captured. (James 2.420–241; *NC* 2.68; Duffy 314–315; Clowes 4.412–413)

1804   A squadron of ships under Capt. Murray Maxwell of *Centaur* (74) landed a force of 2000 troops at Surinam on 25 April. They conquered the colony in the next ten days. The frigate *Proserpine*, the corvette *Pylades*, and several gunboats were captured. (James 3.296–298; Clowes 5.82–84)

Surprise v. *Arlequin*, 16 June 1780
The French sloop *Arlequin* was captured by *Surprise* (28). (Colledge 314)

Surprise v. *Hermione*, 24 October 1799
The frigate *Surprise* (28; Capt. Edward Hamilton) located the former British

mutinous frigate *Hermione* at Puerto Cabello, Spanish Main. Boats went in that night; the ship was boarded and carried in a desperate fight, and sailed out of the harbour. (James 2.405–412; *NC* 2.67–68; Clowes 4.427–428)

Surprise v. Chinese pirates, 21 August 1858
The screw gunvessel *Surprise* (Cmdr Samuel Cresswell), with the boats of *Cambrian* (36), attacked a group of pirate junks at Lintin Island, near Hong Kong. Nineteen ships were destroyed, and seven captured. (Clowes 7.122)

Surveillante v. *Milan*, 30 October 1809
The frigate *Surveillante* (38; Capt. Sir George Collier) captured the French corvette *Milan* (18), carrying dispatches, in the Bay of Biscay. (Clowes 5.445)

Surveillante v. *Comtesse Laure*, 3 December 1809
The frigate *Surveillante* (38; Capt. Sir George Collier) captured the French brig *Comtesse Laure*. (Clowes 5.559)

Surveillante and *Constant* on the Breton coast, 5–6 September 1810
Boats from the frigate *Surveillante* (38; Capt. Sir George Collier) and the brig *Constant* (14; Lt John Stokes) went in to St Gildas, Brittany, to capture a French brig; a new battery at the estuary of the River Canche was destroyed next day. (James 5.100–101; Clowes 5.470)

Surveillante off northern Spain, 1811
The frigate *Surveillante* (38; Capt. Sir George Collier) captured a series of small ships in a cruise along the Basque coast. Landings were made, but with little success. (Hall 196–197)

Suvarnadrug, India, 2–4 April 1755
Tulaji Angria was attacked by Mahratta and Bombay EIC forces. The BM frigate *Protector* (40; Capt. William James), with *Bombay* (28), *Swallow* (16), *Triumph*, and *Viper* (bombs), entered Suvarnadrug harbour, burnt the vessels there, and bombarded the castle and three nearby forts. The main castle was set alight and the magazine exploded. All the forts surrendered. (Low 1.128–131; Keay 266–267)

Sveaborg, Finland, 9–10 August 1855
The fortress at Sveaborg, by Helsinki, was systematically bombarded by the British and French fleets, and was effectively destroyed. The Russians took note of the ease with which this operation had succeeded, and negotiated peace during the next winter. (Clowes 6.491–498, Hore, *Seapower* 96–129)

Svensksund, Sweden, 25 July 1809
A convoy of seven Russian storeships and twenty-five gunboats was attacked by boats from *Princess Caroline* (74), *Minotaur* (74), *Cerberus* (32), and *Prometheus* (18) near Svensksund. Three gunboats and one storeship were captured. (Anderson 340; Clowes 5.442)

Swallow v. **French privateer, 31 March 1703**
The sloop *Swallow* (Cmdr Peter Chamberlain) was captured by a French privateer in the North Sea. (Clowes 2.536)

Swallow v. **French frigate, March 1704**
Swallow (54) captured a French frigate, which was taken into the navy as *Swallow Prize* (32). (Colledge 391)

Swallow **and convoy v. French squadron, 11 July 1707**
Swallow (54; Capt. Richard Haddock), escorting a convoy from Russia, was attacked off the Lofoten Islands by a French squadron commanded by the Chevalier de Forbin. Fifteen of the ships of the convoy were captured; *Swallow* escaped. (Clowes 2.512)

Swallow v. **pirates, 21 February 1722**
Swallow (54; Capt. Chaloner Ogle) encountered three pirate ships off Cape Lopez, West Africa. One, captained by Skyrm, was decoyed away and captured; *Royal Fortune* (40), captained by Bartholomew Roberts, was then attacked and captured after a vigorous fight. (Clowes 3.260–261; Earle 197–198)

Swallow v. **US privateers, 26 August 1781**
The sloop *Swallow* was attacked by four rebel American privateers, and driven ashore and wrecked on Long Island. (Clowes 111)

Swallow v. *Renard* **and** *Goeland*, **16 June 1812**
The French corvette *Renard* (14) and the schooner *Goeland* (12) defended their convoy when challenged by the sloop *Swallow* (18; Cmdr Edward Sibly). The three ships fought without result; the convoy reached safety at Fréjus. (James 5.344–346; Clowes 5.507–508)

Swallow v. *Guerrier*, **16 September 1813**
Swallow (18; Cmdr Edward Sibly) sent a boat to capture a brig and xebec seen close inshore near Anzio, Italy. The brig, *Guerrier* (4), was captured by boarding. (James 6.33–34; Clowes 5.534–535)

Swan v. **Danish cutter, 24 May 1808**
Swan (10; Lt Mark Lewis) was challenged by a Danish cutter off the island of Bornholm, and came under fire also from the island's battery; the cutters fought for a time, until the Dane blew up. (James 4.321–322; Anderson 325; Clowes 5.419)

Swan v. **Danish gunboats, 23 April 1811**
The cutter *Swan* (10) was attacked by three Danish gunboats near Udevala, Sweden, and was sunk. (Anderson 344; Clowes 5.553)

Swansea **and** *Pelican* v. *U-448*, **14 April 1944**
U-448 attacked the carrier *Biter*, but was then sunk by the RCN frigate *Swansea* and the British sloop *Pelican*. (Rohwer 313)

Swatow, China, January 1869
The screw gunboat *Cockchafer* was attacked by the people of Swatow, and eleven men were wounded. In reply an expedition of six ships was sent to 'punish' the villagers; three villages were burned down and eighty-eight Chinese killed or wounded. (Clowes 7.225–226)

Sweepstake v. privateers, 16 April 1709
Sweepstake (32; Capt. Samuel Meads) was attacked and captured by two French privateers; as a result Meads was temporarily dismissed the service. (Clowes 2.523)

Swift v. *Duc de Bourgogne*, 18 August 1702
The sloop *Swift* (10; Cmdr John Brokus) was captured by the French privateer *Duc de Bourgogne* off the Scilly Isles. Brokus was killed. (Clowes 2.536; Colledge 392)

Swift v. *Resolue*, 11 August 1782
The sloop *Swift* (16), formerly an American vessel, was captured by the French frigate *Resolue*. (Clowes 4.85)

Swift v. pirates, August 1802
The EIC ship *Swift* (20; Cmdr John Hayes) campaigned against pirates from Mindanao, Philippine Islands, who threatened the company post on Sulawesi. An attack by forty or fifty of their ships was defeated, and seventeen of them were sunk. (Low 1.212–213)

Swift v. *Esperance*, 3 April 1804
The cutter *Swift* (8; Lt. William Leake) was captured by the privateer *Espérance*, a French xebec. (James 3.267)

Swift v. *Mariamne*, 1805
The Spanish schooner *Mariamne* was captured by *Swift* (18; Cmdr John Wright) in the Bay of Honduras. (Clowes 370–371)

Swiftsure v. Spanish galleon, 21 October 1602
Swiftsure (40; Capt. Sir William Monson) chased a galleon close to shore near Cape St Vincent; both ships suffered damage before Monson retired. (Clowes 1.558)

Swiftsure and *Warspite* v. French squadron, February 1707
A convoy of fourteen ships from Lisbon, escorted by *Swiftsure* (70; Capt. Richard Griffith) and *Warspite* (70; Capt. Thomas Butler), was attacked by a French squadron; several of the merchant ships were captured. (Clowes 2.514)

Swiftsure v. *Atalante*, 5–7 May 1794
Swiftsure (74; Capt. Charles Boyle), escorting a convoy southwest of Ireland, was threatened by two French frigates. *Swiftsure* chased *Atalante* (36)

through the night and the next day. Both ships suffered damage aloft from long-range firing. *Atalante* surrendered early on the 7th. (James 1.227–228; Clowes 4.484–485)

Swiftsure v. Fortune, August–October 1798
Swiftsure (74; Capt. Benjamin Hallowell) captured the French sloop *Fortune* (18) off the coast of Egypt. In October boats from *Swiftsure* bombarded the castle at Aboukir and the nearby French camp, with little effect on the former but causing damage to the latter. French officers complained that the bombardment of their camp was by 'unfair' weapons, which were shown to be French weapons taken from the ship *Spartiate* after the battle of the Nile. (James 2.218; Clowes 4.377, 556)

Swiftsure v. Jean Bart and Constitution, 25 June 1801
Swiftsure (74; Capt. Benjamin Hallowell) was overtaken by Admiral Ganteaume's squadron of four line-of-battle ships and a frigate. After fighting *Jean Bart* and *Constitution* for an hour and a half, *Swiftsure* surrendered. (James 3.76–77; Clowes 4.453)

Swiftsure v. Charlemagne, 26 November 1813
Swiftsure (74; Capt. Edward Dickson) sent boats to attack the French privateer *Charlemagne* (8) off Corsica; she resisted but was captured in the end. (James 6.36; Clowes 5.539)

Sybille and Fox in the Philippines, January 1798
The frigates *Sybille* and *Fox* (Capts Edward Cooke and Pulteney Malcolm) sailed from Macao to Manila, where by disguises and ruses they captured several gunboats and numerous sailors; then they sailed to Samboanga, where they attempted to land, but were beaten off by the well-served fort. (James 2.237–243; Clowes 4.509; NC 1.236–238)

Sybille v. Forte, 28 February 1799
The frigate *Sybille* (48; Capt. Edward Cooke) met *Forte* (52) in the Bay of Bengal, the latter having just captured a rich Indiaman. A stealthy approach in darkness enabled *Sybille* to get close to *Forte* before firing, and after two hours *Forte* surrendered. The two prizes, *Mornington* and *Endeavour*, escaped, still in French hands. (James 2.365–375; Parkinson 125–129; Clowes 4.520–522)

Sybille v. Chiffonne, 19 April 1801
The frigate *Sybille* (38; Capt. Charles Adam) attacked the French frigate *Chiffonne* (36) in Mahe roads, Seychelles; having negotiated a very tricky passage, *Sybille* bombarded both the ship and a nearby battery until both gave in. (James 3.131–132; Clowes 4.541)

Sybille v. Hirondelle, 1802
The frigate *Sybille* (38; Capt. Charles Adam) searched for the privateer

Hirondelle in the Mergui Islands; she was chased and forced to surrender. (Low 1.234–235)

Sybille v. Espiégle, 16 August 1808
The frigate *Sybille* (38; Capt. Clotworthy Upton) met two French corvettes; one escaped; the second, *Espiégle* (16), was captured. (James 4.372; Clowes 5.424)

Sybille v. Greek pirates, 18 June 1826
Sybille (Capt. Sir John Pechell) attacked a group of Greek pirate misticos in a small harbour in Crete, destroying several of them. (Clowes 6.251)

Sybille v. Henriquetta, 1828
The slaver *Henriquetta* was captured by the frigate *Sybille*, condemned at the court in Sierra Leone, and then taken into the navy and renamed *Black Joke*. (Lloyd 71)

Sydney v. Emden, 9 November 1914
The German light cruiser *Emden*, having raided shipping in the Indian Ocean, was attacked at Cocos Island by the RAN light cruiser *Sydney*, larger and better armed. *Emden*, which was soon in flames, beached on Keeling Island, north of Cocos. (Corbett 1.380–385)

Sydney v. Kormoran, 19 November 1941
The German raider *Kormoran* attacked British shipping off Western Australia. Approached by the RAN light cruiser *Sydney*, she torpedoed her, but was then shelled. *Sydney*, on fire, disappeared and sank. *Kormoran* escaped but was so badly damaged her raiding career was ended; she was scuttled and the crew reached Australia. The remains of *Sydney* have been located, about 15 miles from the scene of the action. (S.K. Roskill, *The Navy at War*, London 1961, 141; Hore, *passim*)

Sylph v. Mercurius, 12 May 1796
The sloop *Sylph* (18; Cmdr John White) captured the Dutch brig *Mercurius* (12) off the Texel. (Clowes 4.558)

Sylph v. Fouine, 17 November 1798
The French lugger *Fouine* (8) was captured by the sloop *Sylph* (16; Cmdr John White) off Brest. (Clowes 4.556)

Sylph v. Artémise, 21 July and 28 September 1801
The brig *Sylph* (18; Cmdr Charles Dashwood) twice met and fought a frigate, probably *Artémise*, off Santander. In the first encounter both ships were damaged and had to go to port for repair; in the second the frigate escaped, further damaged. (James 3.145–148; Clowes 4.540)

Sylvia in the Sunda Strait, 6–26 April 1810
The cutter *Sylvia* (10; Lt Augustus Drury) was menaced by praus in the

Strait of Sunda on 6 and 7 April. Two were captured and an attack four days later was foiled. On 26 April she attacked the Dutch brig *Echo*, one of three escorting a two-ship convoy near Middelburg, Java. *Echo* was captured after a short fight. The other brigs escaped, but the two ships in the convoy, laden with military stores, were captured. (James 5.130–131)

Syria, June–July 1941
A British and Free French campaign to seize control of Syria from the Vichy government was assisted by a seaborne landing from the assault ship *Glengyle*. Two French destroyers opposed the British naval forces, damaging the destroyers *Janus* and *Jackal*. The submarine *Parthian* sank the French submarine *Souffleur* in the Bay of Jounieh. British ships frequently shelled the French positions along the coast, and several French supply ships were sunk. (Rohwer 48)

T

Taku forts, China, 1858–1859
A squadron of British and French gunboats ran past the forts at the mouth of the Peiho River on 28 May 1858, and other ships bombarded the forts. Landings were made on the flanks of the Chinese positions; both north and south forts were quickly captured and more forts upstream were taken. Next year, however, the estuary had been blocked by three successive booms overlooked by the forts. On 25 June the British squadron, under Admiral Sir William Seymour, attempted to get through but was bombarded by the guns of the forts and was completely unable to break the booms. Four ships were sunk or grounded, including the screw gunboats *Plover*, *Lee*, and *Kestrel*, and a landing failed to capture the south fort. Casualties were heavy. (Clowes 7.117–118, 123–131; Graham 348–349, 371–378)
See also: **Pehtang**

***Taku* v. Italian minesweepers, 13–15 July 1941**
The British submarine *Taku* sank the Italian minesweeper *Caldea* off Benghazi on 13 July, and two auxiliary minesweepers two days later. (Rohwer 86)

***Talbot* v. French privateers, 12 July 1691**
The ketch *Talbot* (Capt. Charles Staggins) was captured by privateers in the North Sea. (Clowes 2.465)

***Talisman* off Greece, 5–14 December 1941**
The submarine *Talisman*, operating south of Greece, fired at and missed several warships, and was slightly damaged by the Italian TB *Orione*. She also met *U-581* and damaged her by gunfire. (Rohwer 121)

***Tamar* v. *Républicaine*, 25–26 August 1799**
The frigate *Tamar* (38; Capt. Thomas Western) chased the French frigate *Républicaine* (28) into shallows off Surinam. *Tamar* caught up next day and forced the French ship to surrender. (James 2.387–388; Clowes 4.523)

Tanga, Tanganyika, 4–6 November 1914
A landing was made at Tanga, German Tanganyika, on 4 November but the troops were defeated and were quickly evacuated. Two days later a collier was sunk in the Rufiji River to block in the German light cruiser *Königsberg*. (Corbett 1.374)

Tangier, Morocco
1662 Tangier was part of the dowry of Catherine of Braganza, but the Moroccan sultan was hostile to the transfer from Portuguese to English control. The Earl of Sandwich landed a force of seamen under Sir Richard

Stayner in January to hold the town, and later in the year an English military garrison arrived and took control. (Corbett 2.30)

1665 A convoy of English Levant Company ships was attacked by a Dutch squadron. Four out of twenty merchantmen were lost, but the English control of Tangier gave the survivors refuge. (Corbett 2.51)

1684 Lord Dartmouth's fleet evacuated English forces from Tangier on 5 March, having destroyed the newly built mole and blocked the harbour. (Corbett 2.140; Clowes 2.457–458; A.J. Smithers, *The Tangier Campaign*, Stroud 2003; E.M.G. Routh, *Tangier, England's Lost Atlantic Outpost*, London 1912)
See also: **Gibraltar, Strait of Gibraltar**

Tapir v. *U-486*, **12 April 1945**
The submarine *Tapir* sank *U-486* off Norway. (Rohwer 401)

Tara v. *U-35*, **5 November 1915**
The armed boarding steamer *Tara* (Lt Tanner) was sunk by *U-35* off Sollum; the survivors were towed by the submarine to Bardia in boats for imprisonment. (Corbett 3.224)

Taranaki and *C-24* v. *U-40*, **24 June 1915**
The armed trawler *Taranaki* towed the submarine *C-24* underwater as a decoy. When challenged by *U-40*, *C-24* was released and sank the German vessel. (Corbett 3.46–47; Grant 25)

TARANTO, 11–12 November 1940
Aircraft from the carrier *Illustrious* raided Taranto harbour, sinking the battleship *Conte di Cavour* and damaging the battleships *Littorio* and *Caio Duillio*; the cruiser *Trento* and the destroyer *Libeccio* were damaged; only two of the aircraft were shot down. The Italian main battle fleet retired to Naples as a result. This was the first clear indication of the vulnerability of large surface ships to air attack. Meanwhile a British cruiser squadron – *Orion*, *Sydney*, and *Ajax*, and two destroyers – located an Italian convoy in the Strait of Otranto: four ships were sunk. (Rohwer 47–48; T.P. Lowry and J.W.G. Willhem, *The Attack on Toronto*, Mechanicsburg, PA 1995; Greene and Massignani 101–107)

Tarpon v. *Schiff 40*, **11 April 1940**
The submarine *Tarpon* was sunk by the German Q-ship *Schiff 40*. (Rohwer 19)

Tarragona, Spain, May–June 1812
A French army laid siege to Tarragona. Ships of the Mediterranean fleet under Capt. Edward Codrington attempted to retard their advance, hampering the siege by bombarding the siege lines and running in Spanish troops. The city fell on 28 June. (Hall 172–176; *NC* 5.79–83)

Tartar v. privateers, 1756–1758
Tartar (28; Capt. John Lockhart) was a most successful cruiser in the Channel, capturing a succession of privateers, including *Victoire*, taken into the navy as *Tartar Prize* (28), and *Melampe* (36). (Clowes 3.293)

Tartar v. Santa Margarita, 11 November 1779
The Spanish frigate *Santa Margarita* (28) encountered a British squadron commanded by Commodore George Johnstone off Cape Finisterre. *Tartar* (28; Capt. Alexander Graeme) went in chase, and the Spanish ship surrendered after a brief contest. (Clowes 4.45–46)

Tartar v. Hirondelle, 31 July 1804
The frigate *Tartar* (32; Capt. Keith Maxwell) chased the privateer *Hirondelle* (10) near St Domingue. *Hirondelle* anchored, and *Tartar* sent in boats which, despite heavy fire, boarded and captured her. (James 3.277–278; Clowes 5.347)

Tartar v. Observateur, 9 June 1806
The French *Observateur* (18) was captured by the frigate *Tartar* (32; Capt. Edward Hawker) in the West Indies. (Clowes 5.557)

Tartar at Bergen, 15 May 1808
The frigate *Tartar* (32; Capt. George Bettesworth) raided Bergen in search of a Dutch convoy. A guard boat roused the town, and Danish gunboats came out to resist. *Tartar* sank one, but was severely damaged and had to return to Leith for extensive repairs. Bettesworth was killed. (James 4.322–324; Anderson 324–325; Clowes 5.416–418)

Tartar at Felixburg, Courland, 15 May 1809
The frigate *Tartar* (32; Capt. Joseph Baker) sent boats to destroy a grounded Danish privateer. The crew left a candle burning close to the powder, but a sailor detected this in time; the ship was safely taken off. (James 5.38–39; Clowes 5.438)

Tartar v. Anna Maria, March 1821
The Cuban slaver *Anna Maria* was captured by *Tartar* (36) off West Africa; 450 slaves, mostly starving, were freed. (Lloyd 70)

Tartar and others v. convoy, 5 January 1945
The destroyers *Tartar*, *Eskimo*, and *Nubian* sank the Japanese submarine chaser *Ch-57* and a freighter in a convoy. (Rohwer 431)

TB-5 v. U-boat, 3 September 1916
A German submarine attacked the merchantman *John Swan* in the eastern Channel but was driven away by *TB-5*. (Newbolt 4.334)

TB-10 and TB-12 v. U-boat, 10 June 1915
TB-10 was torpedoed off the Nore by a U-boat, and was being towed toward

safety by *TB-12*, when the latter was also torpedoed, presumably by the same boat. Both boats were sunk. (Corbett 3.55n)

Teignmouth v. privateer, 1803
The EIC ship *Teignmouth* (16; Lt Hewitson) fought and defeated a French privateer, but *Teignmouth* suffered an explosion; the privateer then got away. (Low 1.225–226)

Telegraph v. *Hirondelle*, 18 March 1799
The brig *Telegraph* (16; Lt James Worth) met the privateer *Hirondelle* off Ile de Batz; the two ships, approximately equal in power, fought each other for three hours, each attempting to board more than once, until *Hirondelle* surrendered. (James 2.375–376)

Telegraph v. *Flibustier*, 13 October 1813
The corvette *Flibustier* (16) came out of St Jean de Luz, but was challenged by the sloop *Telegraph* (12; Cmdr Timothy Scriven). *Flibustier*'s crew quickly abandoned her and set her on fire; she later exploded. (James 6.10–12; Clowes 5.537; Hall 222–223)

Tempest v. *Circe*, 13 February 1942
The submarine *Tempest* was sunk by the Italian TB *Circe* in the Gulf of Taranto. (Rohwer 248)

Temple and *Griffin* v. *Vierge*, September 1760
The French ship *Vierge* (12) was captured by *Temple* (70) and *Griffin* (28). (Clowes 3.313)

Termagent v. *Capricieuse*, 1 September 1800
The French *Capricieuse* (6) was captured by *Termagent* (18; Cmdr William Skipsey) off Corsica. (Clowes 4.557)

Ternate, Moluccas, 1801
The Dutch island of Ternate in the Moluccas was besieged by EIC forces. The fort held out for over seven weeks before surrendering on 21 June. (James 3.151; Low 1.210–212)

Ternate v. pirates, 5 April 1816
The EIC ship *Ternate* (Capt. Davidson) met two large war praus off the Tenette River, Sulawesi, and drove them ashore. (Low 1.268)

Terpsichore v. *Mahonesa*, 13 October 1796
Terpsichore (32; Capt. Richard Bowen) met and fought the Spanish frigate *Mahonesa* (34) near Cartagena. Both were badly damaged but *Terpsichore* recovered first; *Mahonesa* surrendered. (James 1.398–400; Clowes 4.504)

Terpsichore v. *Vestale*, 12–14 December 1796
Terpsichore (32; Capt. Richard Bowen) chased the French frigate *Vestale* (36)

near Cadiz. After a day and a night's chase, they fought at close quarters for two hours, then *Vestale* surrendered; next day the crew took back the ship from the prize crew. (James 1.402–406; Clowes 4.504–505)

Terpsichore v. San Antonio, 23 June 1799
The frigate *Terpsichore* (32; Capt. William Gage) captured *San Antonio* (14) in the Mediterranean. (Clowes 4.560)

Terpsichore v. Semillante, 15–20 March 1808
The French frigate *Semillante* (36) met the frigate *Terpsichore* (32) near Ceylon. The two ships fought each other on the 15th, then for four days *Semillante* headed for Mauritius with *Terpsichore* vainly attempting to catch up. Both ships were severely damaged in the fighting. (James 4.359–363)

Terrapin v. Schwabenland, 24 March 1944
The submarine *Terrapin* damaged a transport and the catapult ship *Schwabenland* off Egerness, Norway; the German ships ran aground and were later destroyed. (Rohwer 310)

Terrible v. Rising States, 15 April 1777
Terrible (74) chased and captured the US privateer *Rising States* off Belle Isle. (Syrett, *European* 9)

Tervani v. Acciaio, 7 February 1943
The Italian submarine *Acciaio* sank the ASW trawler *Tervani*. (Rohwer 230)

Tetrarch v. Italian minesweeper, 20 July 1941
The submarine *Tetrarch* sank a minesweeper in the Aegean. (Rohwer 87)

Texel, Netherlands
1627 An English squadron commanded by Sir Sackville Trevor cruised off the Dutch coast to intercept ships being built there for France. In the Texel he seized and brought out *St Esprit* without any interference from the Dutch. (Clowes 2.70)

1653 (Battle of TEXEL) Two Dutch fleets, one from the Maas under Admiral Tromp and one from the Texel under Admiral de With, joined and met the English fleet under General-at-Sea George Monck on 31 July. The Dutch fleet was about 120 ships, the English rather fewer, but the battle ended with the Dutch forced to return to the Texel, with Admiral Tromp killed. The English lost two ships, the Dutch perhaps twenty. Neither fleet could put to sea for some time, so the English blockade was broken, and Dutch convoys were able to sail once more. Both sides came to the conclusion that it was time to make peace. (Clowes 2.195–200; Powell 244–245; Rodger 2.18; Tunstall 36–37)

1673 (Battle of TEXEL) The Anglo-French fleet (ninety-two ships and frigates), under Prince Rupert, threatened landings at several places on the Dutch coast. The Dutch fleet (seventy-five ships), under Admiral de Ruijter, sailed northwards along the Dutch coast. On 11 August it had the weather gauge, and turned to attack. The Dutch van drove off the French who were in the allied van, and the two rears also fought each other. The Dutch centre, under de Ruijter himself, concentrated a larger force against the English centre, and was soon assisted by the return of the Dutch van. The overall result was an allied repulse, which was the Dutch aim. Neither side lost any ships. (Clowes 2.316–322; Rodger 2.84–85)

Thalia v. *Requin*, 20 February 1795
The frigate *Thalia* (36; Capt. Richard Grindall) captured *Requin* (12) off Dunkirk. (Clowes 4.490)

Thalia v. *Espoir*, 1 September 1797
The sloop *Espoir* (14) was captured by *Thalia* (36; Capt. Lord Henry Powlett) in the Mediterranean. (Clowes 4.555)

Thames and *Coventry* v. *Palmier* and another, October 1759
The French *Palmier* (74) and a frigate were returning from the West Indies when they met the frigates *Thames* (32) and *Coventry* (28). The French ships were harried all the way to safety in Brest. (Clowes 3.302)

Thames v. *Uranie*, 24 October 1793
The frigate *Thames* (32; Capt. James Cotes) encountered the French frigate *Uranie* (40) in the Bay of Biscay. They fought for several hours, both being severely damaged. They lay two miles apart for the night, making repairs. A French squadron came up in the morning; *Thames*, helpless, surrendered. (James 1.118–122; Clowes 4.480–481)

Thames v *Aurore*, 18 January 1801
The frigate *Thames* (32; Capt. James Lukin) captured *Aurore* (16) in the Channel. (Clowes 4.567)

Thames and *Cephalus* at Porto dei Infreschi, Italy, 21 July 1811
A landing party went into Porto dei Infreschi from the frigate *Thames* (32; Capt. Charles Napier) and the sloop *Cephalus* (18; Cmdr Augustus Clifford) and attacked a battery and a tower which protected a large convoy. The defences taken, most of the convoy was captured. (James 5.255–256; Clowes 4.487)

Thames and *Pilot* at Sapri, Italy, 14 May 1812
The frigate *Thames* (32; Capt. Charles Napier) and the sloop *Pilot* (16; Cmdr John Nicholas) raided the port of Sapri in the Gulf of Policastro. A two-hour cannonade brought the surrender of a battery defending the town; twenty-eight vessels were seized and brought out. (James 5.342; Clowes 5.506)

Thames and *Furieuse* at Ponza, Italy, 26 February 1813
The frigates *Thames* (32; Capt. Charles Napier) and *Furieuse* (36; Capt. William Mounsey) carried the second battalion of the 10th Foot to land on

Ponza Island in the Bay of Naples. Under considerable fire the troops were landed and quickly forced the surrender of the French garrison. (James 6.19–20; Clowes 5.522–523)

Thane v. *U-1172*, 15 January 1945
U-1172 damaged the escort carrier *Thane* and another ship in the Clyde estuary. (Rohwer 384)

Thanet and *Vampire* v. Japanese squadron, 26–27 January 1942
The destroyers *Thanet* and *Vampire* (RAN) attacked Japanese transports near Endau, Malaya; *Thanet* was sunk by the destroyer *Yugiri*, the cruiser *Sendai*, the destroyers *Fubuki* and *Asagiri*, and the minesweeper *W-1*. (Rohwer 137)

Themis v. *Luchs*, 26 July 1940
The submarine *Themis* sank the German TB *Luchs* off Norway. (Rohwer 30)

Theseus v. *Sagesse*, 8 September 1803
The French frigate *Sagesse* (28) was captured by *Theseus* (74) at Port Dauphin, St Domingue. (Clowes 5.556)

Theseus off Korea, September 1950–May 1951
The carrier *Theseus* raided communications and positions as required in North Korea. (Wettern 41)

Thetis and *Hussar* v. French squadron, 17 May 1795
The frigates *Thetis* (36; Capt. Hon. Alexander Cochrane) and *Hussar* (38; Capt. John Beresford) met five French ships, *en flute*, off Chesapeake Bay. The French ships formed a line of battle; *Hussar* attacked the two foremost, and *Thetis* the centre ship, the frigate *Prevoyante*. *Hussar*'s enemies broke off and sailed away; *Prevoyante* surrendered; the two rearmost ships surrendered then escaped, but *Raison* (14) was recaptured. (James 1.319–320; Clowes 4.492)

Thetis and others v. *Nisus*, 12 December 1809
A squadron of small vessels headed by the frigate *Thetis* (38; Capt. George Miller) sent a party to cut out the corvette *Nisus* from the harbour of Deshaies, Guadeloupe. One party climbed to capture a fort, while the brig *Attentive* (12; Lt Robert Carr) and the sloop *Pultusk* (16; Cmdr William Elliott) went into the harbour. *Nisus*, loaded with a cargo of coffee, was seized, and the fort destroyed. Casualties were minimal. (James 5.45–46)

Thetis at Vancouver Island, 1853
A dispute having arisen with some Indians on Vancouver Island, *Thetis* (36; Capt. Augustus Kuper) sent a party against them; two murderers were apprehended without much violence. (Clowes 6.394; B.M. Gough, *The Royal Navy on the Northwest Coast of North America, 1815–1914*, Vancouver 1971, 90)

Thetis v. slavers, East Africa, 1876–1877
The screw corvette *Thetis* (Capt. Thomas Ward) was active in suppressing

the slave trade in East Africa, and captured a number of slave dhows during its time there. (Clowes 7.279)

The THIRD CRUSADE, 1190
A fleet of ships gathered at Dartmouth and sailed to meet King Richard I at Marseilles. On the way the Crusaders made a nuisance of themselves at Lisbon, and some assisted in defeating a Muslim attack there. King and fleet finally met up at Messina, where there was more fighting. Richard also felt compelled to conquer Cyprus, where two of his squadrons swept around the Cypriot coast, destroying and capturing all the ships they could find. Off the Palestinian coast a large Turkish ship was sunk. The fleet then had little to do in the fighting in Palestine. (S. Runciman, *History of the Crusades*, vol. 3, London 1954, 34–75; Clowes 1.66–174)

Thistle v. *Havik*, 10 February 1810
The schooner *Thistle* (10; Lt. Peter Proctor) challenged the Dutch corvette *Havik* (10) in the western Atlantic; after a seven-hour chase, and a fight lasting five hours, *Havik* finally surrendered. (James 5.90–91; Clowes 5.450–451)

Thistle v. *Anna Maria*, March 1821
The gun brig *Thistle* (Lt Hogan) captured the Spanish schooner *Anna Maria*, a slaver, in the Bonny River, West Africa. (Ward 103–105)

Thistle v. *U-4*, 10 April 1940
U-4 sank the submarine *Thistle* off Stavanger, Norway. (Rohwer 18)

Thomas Collard v. U-boat, 1 March 1918
The trawler *Thomas Collard* was sunk by a U-boat north of Rathlin Island. (Colledge 403)

Thorn v. American frigate, 1779
Thorn (14; Cmdr William Wardlaw) was captured by a rebel American ship, but was soon retaken. (Clowes 4.110)

Thorn v. *Courier National*, 25 May 1795
The sloop *Thorn* (14; Cmdr Robert Otway) met, fought, and captured the corvette *Courier National* (18) in the Windward Islands. (James 1.320–321; Clowes 4.492)

Thorn v. *Medusa*, 30 January 1942
The submarine *Thorn* sank the Italian submarine *Medusa* in the Adriatic. (Rohwer 139)

Thorn v. *Vivaldi* and *Pegaso*, 7 May 1942
The submarine *Thorn* attacked an Italian convoy heading for Benghazi, but was driven off by the TBs *Vivaldi* and *Pegaso*. (Rohwer 163)

***Thorn* v. *Pegaso*, 7 August 1942**
The submarine *Thorn* was sunk by the Italian TB *Pegaso* southwest of Crete. (Rohwer 182)

***Thrasher* v. *UC-39*, 8 February 1917**
The submarine *UC-39*, operating off the Yorkshire coast, was intercepted by the destroyer *Thrasher*, and sunk near Flamborough Head. (Newbolt 4.357n; Grant 66)

***Thrasher* and *Turbulent* v. *Diana* and convoy, 23–29 June 1942**
The submarines *Thrasher* and *Turbulent* attacked an Italian convoy on 23–24 June 1942; each submarine sank a ship; on 29 June *Thrasher* sank the Italian sloop *Diana*. (Rohwer 176)

***Thunder* v. French privateer, 3 March 1696**
The bomb *Thunder* (Cmdr Nathaniel Symonds) was captured by a French privateer off the Dutch coast. (Clowes 2.556; Colledge 405)

***Thunder* v. *Neptune*, 9 October 1813**
The bomb *Thunder* (Cmdr Watkin Pell), in the Channel, lured the French privateer *Neptune* (16) into attacking, then boarded and captured her. (James 6.14–15; Clowes 5.535–536)

***Thunderbolt* v. *UJ-2210* or *Cicogna*, 14 March 1943**
The submarine *Thunderbolt* was sunk either by the Italian corvette *Cicogna* or the German submarine chaser *UJ-2210*. (Rohwer 231; Greene and Massignani 282)

***Thunderer* and others v. *Achille* and *Bouffonne*, 17 July 1761**
Thunderer (74; Capt. Charles Proby), leading a squadron consisting of *Modeste* (64; Capt. Robert Walsingham), *Thetis* (32; Capt. John Moutray), and the sloop *Favourite* (Cmdr Philemon Pownoll), intercepted *Achille* (64) and *Bouffonne* (32) out of Cadiz. *Achille* was captured by boarding from *Thunderer*, *Bouffonne* surrendered to *Thetis*. (Clowes 3.306)

***Thunderer* and *Pomone* v. *Eveille*, 15 October 1795**
Thunderer (74; Capt. Albemarle Bertie) and *Pomone* (40; Commodore Sir John Borlase Warren) fired on *Eveille* (16). The latter jettisoned her guns, then surrendered. (James 1.329–331)

***Thunderer* and *Valiant* v. *Hermione*, 15–16 April 1797**
Hermione (36) ran into the port of Maregot, St Domingue, where *Thunderer* (74; Cmdr William Ogilvy) and *Valiant* (74; Capt. Edmund Crawley) attacked her. After a day *Hermione* was abandoned and burnt by her crew. (James 2.112–113)

***Tickler* v. French frigate, 1783**
The brig *Tickler* (12) was captured by a French frigate in the West Indies. (Clowes 4.112)

Tickler v. Danish gunboats, 4 June 1808
The brig *Tickler* (14; Lt John Skinner) was attacked by four Danish gunboats in the Great Belt and forced to surrender. Skinner was killed. (James 4.368; Anderson 325; Clowes 5.420)

Tienpak, China, 7 September 1849
The paddle sloop *Medea* (Lt William Lockyer) searched for pirates who had captured ships near Hong Kong. Five ships were located at Tienpak and captured after a stiff fight. Soon afterwards the armed vessel *Canton*, carrying Lt William Mould and some seamen and marines from *Amazon* (28), attacked pirates there, burning three junks. (Clowes 6.354–355)

Tiger v. Dutch ships, June 1652
Tiger (32; Capt. James Peacock) with *Laurel* (50) in company fought two Dutch warships off the coast of Holland. One was captured by boarding but then sank; the other was run ashore. (Clowes 2.152; Powell 150)

Tiger v. *Morgenstar*, 18 October 1652
Tiger (38; Capt. James Peacock) captured the Dutch warship *Morgenstar* after a hard fight, though no one on *Tiger* was killed. *Morgenstar* was retained and renamed *Plover*. (Clowes 2.170)

Tiger v. Zealand privateer, 2 May 1666
Tiger (32; Capt. Phineas Pett) fought a Zealand privateer (40). Pett died, and his lieutenant fought on for several hours. *Tiger* was badly damaged, and the privateer got away. (Clowes 2.428)

Tiger v. Dutch privateers, March 1672
Tiger (32; Capt. Thomas Harman), escorting a fleet of colliers from Newcastle to the Thames, was attacked by eight Dutch privateers. *Tiger* drove them all off, and no collier was lost. (Clowes 2.444)

Tiger v. *Schakerloo*, Cadiz, April 1674
Capt. Thomas Harman of *Tiger* (32) taunted Capt. Passchier de Witte of the Dutch *Schakerloo* (28) in Cadiz to such effect that the two ships left the harbour and fought each other nearby. *Schakerloo* was compelled to strike. Both captains were wounded; seventy-four seamen died. (Corbett 2.80–81; Clowes 2.447)

Tiger v. Spanish sloop, 1742
Tiger (50; Capt. Edward Herbert) was wrecked on a key near Tortuga. The Spanish *Fuerte* (60), attempting to attack the survivors, was also wrecked; the British sailors captured a Spanish sloop and returned to Jamaica. (Clowes 3.272)

Tigress v. Danish gunboats, 2 August 1808
The brig *Tigress* (12; Lt Edward Greensword) was attacked by sixteen Danish

gunboats in the Great Belt, and forced to surrender. (James 4.368–369; Anderson 326)

Tigris v. *Bianchi*, 5 July 1941
The submarine *Tigris* sank the Italian submarine *Bianchi* in the Bay of Biscay. (Rohwer 82)

Tigris v. *Perfido*, 6 December 1942
The submarine *Tigris* sank the Italian submarine *Perfido* off Sardinia. (Rohwer 214)

Tigris v. *UJ-2210*, 27 February 1943
The submarine *Tigris* was sunk by the German submarine chaser *UJ-2210*. (Rohwer 231)

Tilbury, Essex, 23 July 1667
English frigates and fireships at Hope Reach near Gravesend were attacked by a Dutch squadron. They retreated to Tilbury Fort, then turned to counter-attack. Six or seven ships were destroyed on the English side; the Dutch lost twice that number of fireships. (Clowes 2.296–297)

Timor, 9–10 January 1943
The RAN destroyer *Arunta* evacuated over 300 people from Timor to Australia. (Rohwer 225)

Tiptoft's fleet v. French fleet, 14 April 1293
A quarrel between Norman and English seamen escalated by reprisal raids to a pre-arranged full-scale battle in mid-Channel. On 14 April the two forces met. The English, mainly from the Cinque Ports, were reinforced by Fleming, Gascon, and Irish ships, all commanded by Sir John Tiptoft; the French, probably more numerous, were commanded by Charles, Count of Valois. These commanders make the encounter semi-official, rather than piracy, which was the reason for the confrontation. In the battle, fought in very bad weather, the English were victorious, capturing, it is said, 240 ships. The fight was a cause of a new Anglo-French war. (Clowes 1.204–205; Prestwich 376–378)

Tithonus v. U-boat, 28 March 1918
The armed boarding steamer *Tithonus* was sunk by a U-boat in the North Sea. (Colledge 408)

Tobago, West Indies
1672 *St David* (54; Capt. William Poole) convoyed ships carrying an infantry regiment to Tobago. A first landing on the island in December failed, but a second succeeded, despite fire from the forts. (Clowes 2.446)

1793 An expedition commanded by Vice-Admiral Sir John Laforey was mounted from Barbados to Tobago. *Trusty* (50; Capt. John Drew) and other ships carried the soldiers. A brief assault on 14 April captured the main enemy fort at Scarborough. (James 1.126–127; Duffy 34–35)

Tobago v. *Général Ernouf*, 18 October 1806
The schooner *Tobago* (10) was captured by the French privateer *Général Ernouf* in the West Indies. (Clowes 5.551)

Tondern, Schleswig, Germany
1916 A seaplane raid on the Zeppelin base at Tondern on 4 May was combined with a mining expedition, in the hope that part of the German High Seas Fleet would come out. Only one of eleven seaplanes was able to bomb, and none of the hoped-for events took place. Damage to Tondern was only minor. (Corbett 3.309–311)

1918 The carrier *Furious* sent planes to bomb the Zeppelin airship base at Tondern on 19 July. (Newbolt 5.347; Halpern, *Naval History* 442–443)

Tonga, South Pacific, June 1840
A civil war in Tonga attracted the intervention of the sloop *Favourite* (Cmdr Walter Croker). Croker attacked a fort without proper support and he and several others were killed. (Clowes 6.323)

Topaze v. *Elizabeth*, 28 August 1796
Topaze (38; Capt. Stephen Church) chased three French ships off Cape Henry, Virginia. *Elizabeth* (36) was the rearmost and swiftly surrendered. (James 1.385–386; Clowes 4.502)

Topaze v. *Joubert* and others, December 1809
The frigate *Topaze* (38; Capt. Henry Hope) captured three French brigs, *Joubert*, *Mentor*, and *Esperance*, in the Mediterranean. (Clowes 5.560)

TORBAY, Devon, 5 November 1688
William, Prince of Orange, in command of a large Dutch fleet, sailed along the Channel from the Netherlands carrying six British regiments, and arrived in Torbay. The regiments landed as quickly as possible, and the prince landed as soon as it was clear that there was no local opposition. The English fleet under Lord Dartmouth followed the Dutch fleet, but evaded contact. (E.B. Powley, *The English Navy in the Revolution of 1688*, Cambridge 1928; Clowes 2.325–326)

Torbay v. *Arc en Ciel*, Louisbourg, 12 July 1756
Torbay (90) intercepted and captured *Arc en Ciel* (50) as the latter was taking stores to Louisbourg. (Clowes 3.293)

Torbay v. *Rostan*, October 1758
Torbay (90; Capt. Hon. Augustus Keppel) captured the privateer *Rostan* (26). (Clowes 3.299)

Torbay v. Jantina, 5 July 1941
The submarine *Torbay* sank the Italian submarine *Jantina* in the Aegean. (Rohwer 84)

Torbay v. Partenope, 12 August 1941
The submarine *Torbay* attacked a convoy off Benghazi, but was then depth-charged by the Italian TB *Partenope*; all ships involved survived. (Rohwer 92)

Torbay v. Aviere, 23 December 1941
The submarine *Torbay*, having sunk eight small sailing ships in the Aegean, torpedoed the Italian destroyer *Aviere* in Navarino Bay. (Rohwer 124)

Tostig's raids, 1066
Tostig, King Harold II's exiled brother, brought a fleet from Flanders aiming to recover his earldom of Northumbria. He first went to Sandwich, but left when the king approached, then raided several places along the east coast of England, being forced back to sea each time. (*ASC* s.a. 1066)

TOULON, France
1707 An Austro-Savoyard army besieged the French naval base at Toulon in July, assisted by the British Mediterranean fleet under Sir Cloudisley Shovell. The siege was unsuccessful but many French ships were destroyed, partly by bombardment by bomb vessels, and partly because the French sank twenty or more warships to block access to the port. The port was unusable for some time afterwards. (Clowes 2.410; Francis 253–256; Rodger 2.171)

1744 (Battle of TOULON) The joint Franco-Spanish fleet came out of Toulon on 11 February and attacked the British Mediterranean fleet under Vice-Admiral Thomas Mathews. The battle was ragged and inconclusive. The only ship captured was the Spanish *Poder*, battered into surrender by *Berwick* (Capt. Edward Hawke). Many captains on both sides were reluctant to fight at close quarters. *Poder* was recaptured during the night, but was then blown up to prevent re-recapture.

The battle was succeeded by courts martial in Britain on Mathews, his second-in-command, Vice-Admiral Richard Lestock, and ten captains: Mathews and most of the captains were convicted, Lestock was acquitted. In the midst of one trial the president of the court was himself arrested on a charge of illegal imprisonment of a lieutenant some time earlier in the West Indies. The other members protested so strongly at this that they were themselves about to be arrested when they apologised. It was hardly the best atmosphere for fighting a war. (Clowes 3.92–106; Mahan 265–267; Tunstall 83–91)

1793 (Occupation of TOULON) Toulon, royalist in sentiment in 1793, was threatened by republicans from inland. Delegates asked for help from the British Mediterranean fleet, commanded by Vice-Admiral Lord Hood. Hood landed troops on 27 August and took possession of Fort Lamalgue guarding the harbour entrance. The French ships were moved into the inner harbour, and British ships occupied the outer.

Toulon was soon besieged by a republican army, in which the artillery was commanded by Capt. Napoleon Buonaparte. British forces were reinforced by Spanish, Sardinian, and Neapolitan troops and ships, though the mixture of units and languages and authorities confused the defence. Eventually it became impossible to maintain control of the city; British concern reverted to removing or destroying the French ships. Capt. Sir Sidney Smith organised the destruction of the arsenal and the burning of unwanted ships. Capt. George Elphinstone managed the land retreat; 17,000 refugees were taken off. Of the ships originally captured, nine line-of-battle ships, three frigates, and two sloops were destroyed; one 120, three 74s, two frigates, and four smaller ships were removed. One 120, three 80s, and eleven 74s were left with the French. The French Mediterranean fleet was temporarily eliminated. (James 1.69–94; *NC* 1.19–31; Clowes 4.202–211)

1804 A squadron of French ships came out of Toulon on 24 May and menaced the blockading squadron. Some shots were exchanged. The squadron, under Rear-Admiral George Campbell, tried to draw the French onto Admiral Nelson's fleet but the French turned back. (*NC* 3.49–50)

1810 Part of the French fleet in Toulon came out on 20 July to cover the move of two ships into the harbour. The British watching ships, the sloop *Shearwater* (Cmdr Edward Sibly) and the frigate *Euryalus* (Capt. Hon. George Dundas), were fired at, without receiving damage. *Warspite* (74; Capt. Hon. Henry Blackwood), *Conqueror* (74; Capt. Richard Fellowes), and *Ajax* (74; Capt. Robert Otway) clashed briefly with the French ships before the latter returned to port. (James 5.80–84; *NC* 5.340; Clowes 5.296)

TRAFALGAR, 21 October 1805

The combined Franco-Spanish fleet of thirty-three line-of-battle ships commanded by Admiral Villeneuve came out of Cadiz. They faced a British fleet of twenty-seven line-of-battle ships commanded by Vice-Admiral Lord Nelson. Light winds allowed both fleets to organise themselves as they wished. The Combined Fleet was in line ahead, the British in two columns. The aim of the British was to break the enemy line in two places and so tackle parts of the fleet separately. The breaks were accomplished, and several of the Combined Fleet in the van were left out of the action.

This has been perhaps the most intensively investigated naval battle in European history, and the fates and actions of every ship have been minutely scrutinised. The net result was the destruction of the Combined Fleet: sixteen ships were destroyed or wrecked and the rest badly damaged. Almost 1700 men on the British side were killed or wounded, notably Nelson himself; on the allied side the Spanish Admiral Gravina was also killed, and Admiral Villeneuve taken prisoner; French and Spanish casualties were probably twice or three times the British; almost 5000 men became prisoners. (James 3.380–474; Clowes 5.127–162; *NC* 3.194–238; Tunstall 247–259)
See also: **Sir Richard Strachan's Action**

Transylvania v. *U-63*, 3 May 1917

The troopship *Transylvania* was torpedoed by *U-63* near Genoa; the Japanese destroyer *Matsu*, one of the escorts, rescued most of the 3000 soldiers on board. (Halpern, *Mediterranean* 344; Newbolt 4.276)

Transylvania v. *U-56*, 10 August 1940
The AMC *Transylvania* was sunk by *U-56* in the North Atlantic. (Rohwer 34)

Tremendous and *Adamant* v. *Preneuse*, 11 December 1799
Tremendous (74) and *Adamant* (50) chased the French frigate *Preneuse* (36) as far as Mauritius; boat parties went in to burn her. (Clowes 4.529)

Tremendous v. *Canonnière*, 21 April 1806
Tremendous (74; Capt. John Osborn), escorting a fleet of eleven Indiamen off Natal, saw the frigate *Canonnière* (40) nearby. A chase ensued for several hours, but when *Tremendous* finally caught up, *Canonnière* carefully fired at *Tremendous*'s rigging, and got away. (James 4.143–146; Clowes 5.380–381)

Trenchant v. *Wa-105* and *Ashigara*, May–June 1945
The submarine *Trenchant* sank the Japanese minesweeper *Wa-105* on 25 May, then on 8 June sank the Japanese cruiser *Ashigara* in the Banka Strait, Indonesia. (Rohwer 419, 443)

Trent and *Sparrow* at Puerto Rico, 30 March 1799
The frigate *Trent* (Capt. Robert Otway) and the cutter *Sparrow* (Lt John Wiley) sent boats into a bay near Cape Roxo; one party stormed a battery, and another cut out a ship and a schooner; two other schooners were scuttled. (James 2.376)

Trent v. French gunboats, 3 April 1801
The frigate *Trent* (Capt. Sir Edward Hamilton), off Brehat, Brittany, sent boats to recapture a British merchantman. The boats drove off the French escorts and succeeded. (James 3.130–131)

Triad v. *Enrico Toti*, 15 October 1940
The Italian submarine *Enrico Toti*, unable to submerge, fought a gun duel with the British submarine *Triad* off Calabria; *Triad* was sunk. (Rohwer 43)

Tribune and *Hydra* v. gunboats, 30 January 1804
The frigates *Tribune* (38) and *Hydra* (36) captured three gun brigs and a lugger in the Channel. (Clowes 5.556)

Tribune v. Danish brigs, 12 May 1810
The frigate *Tribune* (38; Capt. George Reynolds) chased two Danish brigs, *Samso* (20) and *Seagull* (16); they escaped into a rocky channel near Lindesnaes, Norway, and were joined by *Alsen* (20) and *Allart* (18). The four brigs formed a line of battle and attacked *Tribune*; the fighting was inconclusive. (Anderson 342–343; James 5.98–99; Clowes 5.455)

Trident v. *U-31*, 8 October 1940
U-31 fought a gun duel with the submarine *Trident* in the Bay of Biscay; neither was damaged. (Rohwer 43)

Trident v. *Prinz Eugen*, 23 February 1942
The submarine *Trident* torpedoed the cruiser *Prinz Eugen* at Grimstadfjord, Norway. (Rohwer 146)

Trincomalee, Ceylon, 1782
The Dutch fort and harbour at Trincomalee were attacked by a force of sepoys, sailors, and marines from the fleet of Vice-Admiral Sir Edward Hughes in January. The storming of Fort Oosterberg by marines and sailors on the 11th led to the fall of the town. (Clowes 3.552–554, 557–561, 4.76–77)

Trincomalee and others v. *Iphigénie*, 7–12 October 1799
The privateer *Iphigénie* captured the packet *Pearl* at the entrance to the Persian Gulf, but was then intercepted and attacked by the sloop *Trincomalee*, while the schooner *Comet* attempted to retake *Pearl*. *Trincomalee* and *Iphigénie* fought a close battle, until *Trincomalee* suddenly exploded, damaging *Iphigénie* so badly that she also sank almost at once. *Pearl* had beaten off *Comet*, and collected the survivors. (James 2.400; Parkinson 162–163; Clowes 4.525)

Trinculo at Bonny, West Africa, January 1836
The sloop *Trinculo* (Lt Tryon) went into Bonny port and seized four Spanish slavers. (Dike 70)

Trinidad, West Indies
1595 An expedition commanded by Sir Robert Dudley landed at Trinidad in March, intending to raid, but his crew refused to stay and he withdrew. (Clowes 1.651)

1797 An expeditionary force consisting of *Prince of Wales* (98), three 74s, one 64, and several frigates and sloops arrived on 15 February and found four Spanish line-of-battle ships and a frigate in the Gulf of Paria. Carefully watching these, the transports with the troops on board moved up the gulf and the frigates blockaded Port of Spain. That night four of the Spanish ships were abandoned and burnt; one, *San Damaso* (74), was captured. The island capitulated as soon as the British troops entered the town. (James 2.109–111; Duffy 276–283; Clowes 4.333–334; *NC* 1.203–205)

Tripoli, North Africa, 1675–1676
Tripoli was blockaded, and several ships captured. In January 1676 Lt Cloudisley Shovell led a raid on the harbour; four ships were destroyed and another raid destroyed naval stores. In February Admiral Sir John Narbrough with *Hampshire* and a frigate attacked four Tripolitan warships and drove them into the harbour in defeat. The Dey, at last, made a treaty, and was then overthrown; his successor was constrained to ratify. (Corbett, *Mediterranean* 98–99; Clowes 2.450)

Tripolitania, North Africa, February 1943
The British Inshore Squadron landed supplies for the 8th Army as it advanced along the coast. *U-617* sank four of the ships, including the minelayer *Welshman*, on 1 February; *U-205* was sunk by air attack and the destroyer *Paladin* on 17 February. *U-562* was damaged by air attack and then sunk by the destroyers *Isis* and *Hursley* on 19 February. In addition Force K bombarded the Italian and German escape roads near Zara. (Rohwer 225–226)

Triton v. *St Jacques*, 13 September 1799
The French brig *St Jacques* was captured by the frigate *Triton* (36; Capt. John Gore) off Lorient. (Clowes 4.556)

Triton v. *Vedette*, 10 February 1800
The frigate *Triton* (Capt John Gore) captured the French brig *Vedette* off the French coast. (Clowes 4.557)

Triton v. *V-1507*, 11 April 1940
The submarine *Triton* sank two ships and the German patrol vessel *V-1507* off Norway. (Rohwer 18)

Triton v. *Clio*, 6 December 1940
The British submarine *Triton* sank one ship, but was then itself sunk by a depth-charge attack from the TB *Clio* off Corfu. (Rohwer 51)

Triumph v. *U-21*, 25 May 1915
The submarine *U-21* was the first German submarine to reach the Aegean. She sailed through the Allied fleet at the Dardanelles causing consternation, and finally fired at the battleship *Triumph* (Capt. Fitzmaurice) at Anzac beach, which sank in ten minutes; most of her men were saved. (Corbett 3.28–30; Halpern, *Naval History* 118)

Triumph off Cyrenaica, May–August 1941
The submarine *Triumph* torpedoed the Italian AMC *RAMB III* off Benghazi on 30 May, sank the Italian gunboat *Valoroso* and two smaller ships by gunfire off Cyrenaica, the Italian submarine *Salpe* and an Italian freighter off Sollum on 28 June, an Italian freighter, and, after a gun battle, the gunboat *De Lutti* on 7 July, though *Triumph* was damaged. On 25 August she torpedoed the Italian cruiser *Bolzano* near Sardinia, but did not sink her. (Rohwer 76, 81, 85, 94)

Triumph in the Aegean, October–December 1941
The submarine *Triumph* attacked an Italian convoy in the Gulf of Athens, sinking one ship, but was then driven off by the destroyer *Sella* and TBs *Libera* and *Sirio*. On 31 December *Triumph* was probably sunk by the TB *Orsa*, also in the Gulf of Athens. (Rohwer 109, 131)

Triumph and others, Korea, 1950
The carrier *Triumph*, the cruiser *Jamaica*, and several destroyers bombarded enemy targets in Korea. *Jamaica* and the destroyer *Comus* were damaged by air attacks. (Wettern 35)

Tromso, Norway, 1940–1941
Aircraft from the carrier *Furious* bombed Tromso on 16 October 1940, and from *Victorious* on 3–7 September 1941. (Rohwer 45, 93)

Troubridge and others v. *U-407*, 19 September 1944
U-407 was sunk by the destroyers *Troubridge*, *Terpsichore*, and the Polish destroyer *Garland*. (Rohwer 343)

Truant v. *Karlsruhe*, 11 April 1940
The submarine *Truant* damaged the cruiser *Karlsruhe* by a torpedo hit, off Norway; the ship was later sunk by a German TB. (Rohwer 18)

Truant v. *Vanna*, 17 April 1941
The submarine *Truant* attacked Italian ships off Apollonia, Cyrenaica, sinking the patrol boat *Vanna*. (Rohwer 69)

Truant v. *Alcione*, 11 December 1941
The submarine *Truant* torpedoed the Italian TB *Alcione* in Suda Bay, Crete. The TB was beached. (Rohwer 121)

Truculent v. *U-308*, 4 June 1943
U-308 was sunk by the submarine *Truculent* off Trondheim, Norway. (Rohwer 254)

True Briton v. French ship, 1780
The cutter *True Briton* (10; Lt Hon. Patrick Napier) was captured by the French, but soon retaken. (Clowes 4.110)

Truk and Balikpapan, Caroline Islands, June–July 1945
A British naval force centred on the carrier *Implacable* raided Truk on 12–15 June 1945, and Balikpapan on 1 July, preceded by six days' bombardment. (Rohwer 420)

Tryton v. privateers, 1705
Tryton (42) on 3 March captured the French privateer *Royal*, which became *Tryton Prize* (28), and a ship which was taken into the navy as *Fox* (24). (Colledge 150)

Tsekee, Ningpo River, China, 15 March 1842
A Chinese army was gathered near Tsekee. An expeditionary force landed at the village and drove the Chinese force away. (Clowes 6.297)

Tulip v. U-62, 30 April 1917
The sloop *Tulip*, operating as a decoy ship, was torpedoed by *U-62* in the Atlantic, and sank while under tow. (Colledge 418)

Tumult and others v. U-223, 29–30 March 1944
U-223 sank the destroyer *Laforey* north of Sicily and was then sunk by the destroyers *Tumult, Hambledon,* and *Blencathra*. (Rohwer 311)

Tuna v. Ostmark, 24 September 1940
The submarine *Tuna* sank the German catapult ship *Ostmark* in the Bay of Biscay. (Rohwer 38)

Tunis, North Africa
1655 General-at-Sea Robert Blake took a squadron to Tunis in February and demanded the release of a captured English ship and any English captives. Nine Tunisian warships were blockaded by four frigates at Porto Farina. After two attempts at negotiation Blake lost patience, and in April took his whole squadron in to destroy the ships. Goleta castle had to be heavily bombarded to achieve this, but the Tunisian ships were burned. The action was a revelation of the power of concentrated broadside fire on well-built castles. (Corbett 1.300–312; Clowes 2.210–212; Powell 258–264; Capp 94; Rodger 2.21–22)

1796 *Barfleur* (98) and four 74s commanded by Vice-Admiral Hon. William Waldegrave went to take from Tunis harbour the British frigate *Nemesis* (28) and its captor the French corvette *Sardine*. On 9 April boats of the squadron accomplished this with little opposition. (James 1.305, 342–343)

Turbulent and Thunder v. Danish gunboats, 9 June 1808
A convoy of seventy merchant ships, escorted from Malmo, Sweden, by several small British warships, was becalmed near the island of Saltholm and attacked by twenty-five Danish gunvessels. The brig *Turbulent* (Lt George Wood) was boarded and captured; the bomb *Thunder* was attacked and damaged, but survived. A dozen of the merchant ships were taken. (James 4.368; Anderson 325; Clowes 5.420)

Turbulent v. Pessagno and convoy, 29 May 1942
An Italian convoy for Benghazi was attacked by the submarine *Turbulent*, which sank the destroyer *Pessagno* and a ship from the convoy. (Rohwer 166)

Turbulent v. Bengasi, 10 November 1942
The submarine *Turbulent* sank the German submarine depot ship *Bengasi* off Cagliari. (Rohwer 212)

Turbulent v. UJ-2208, March 1943
The submarine *Turbulent* was sunk off Tunisia by the German submarine chaser *UJ-2208*. (Rohwer 231)

Turks Island, West Indies, 2 March 1783
A French force seized Turks Island; *Drake* (14; Cmdr Charles Dixon) and *Albemarle* (28; Capt. Horatio Nelson) landed a force to recover the island, but it was defeated. (Clowes 4.95)

Turquoise v. slavers, 30 May 1887
The pinnace of the screw corvette *Turquoise* (Capt. Robert Woodward) challenged a slave dhow. A fierce fight ensued during which the dhow went ashore. Fifty-three slaves were rescued; one of *Turquoise*'s sailors died. (Clowes 7.387–388)

Tuzla River raid, 24 July 1916
A group of irregulars, mainly Ottoman refugees, supported by the destroyer *Renard*, the monitor *M-33*, and smaller craft, raided the estuary of the Tuzla River, Anatolia; over 3000 animals were rustled. (Halpern, *Mediterranean* 292)

Tweed v. *U-305*, 7 January 1944
U-305 sank the frigate *Tweed* off the coast of Spain. (Rohwer 295)

Tyler and others v. *U-1172*, 27 January 1945
U-1172 was sunk by the destroyers *Tyler*, *Keats*, and *Bligh* in the Irish Sea. (Rohwer 384)

Tyne and *Thracian* v. *Zaragozana*, 31 March 1823
The frigate *Tyne* (26; Capt. John Walcott) and the sloop *Thracian* (18; Cmdr John Roberts) approached the pirate ship *Zaragozana* in disguise, but were detected. *Zaragozana* went into Mata, Cuba. Boats from both ships attacked and, under heavy fire, the pirate ship was stormed and taken. (Clowes 6.235; James 6.270–274)

Tyrwhitt's squadron v. Zeppelin *L-53*, 10 August 1918
The British cruiser and destroyer squadron out of Harwich, under Admiral Tyrwhitt, was being observed by Zeppelin *L-53* until a Camel aircraft was launched and shot the Zeppelin down. (Newbolt 5.346–347)

U

***Ulleswater* v. *U-60*, 15 September 1918**
The destroyer *Ulleswater* was sunk by *U-60* in the North Sea. (Colledge 420)

Ulster, Ireland
668   The 'voyage of the sons of Gartnait to Ireland with the people of Skye', an incident in the continuing feud between royal families in Ulster and Skye, indicates an invasion of Ulster, or at least a raid. (Smyth, *Warlords* 79)

682–709   Mercenaries from Britain were active in Ulster and eastern Ireland, possibly refugees from the British kingdom of Rheged (Galloway-Cumbria). Their arrival marks an invasion of Ireland. (Smyth, *Warlords* 25–26)

1022   The Dublin fleet raided the Ulster kingdom of Ulaid, but was met at sea by an Ulaid fleet commanded by Niall mac Eochaid, and defeated; the whole Dublin fleet was captured. (Hudson 108)

1103   King Magnus of Norway brought his fleet to anchor off County Down on 24 August. His men landed to collect supplies and were attacked by local men; the king was killed. (Hudson 197)
See also: **King Magnus's Expedition**

1313   Robert Bruce of Scots sent a galley force to attack Ulster; it was repelled by the local people. (Duncan 102)

1315   A Scottish expedition under the command of Edward Bruce landed near Larne on 26 May. The army campaigned very destructively on the island for the next three years. (Clowes 1.218; *NHI* II, 282–283; Duncan 105)
See also: **Belfast Lough, Carrickfergus, Derry, Rathlin Island, Strangford Lough**

***Ultimatum* v. *Millo*, 14 March 1942**
The submarine *Ultimatum* sank the Italian submarine *Millo* off Cape Spartivento. (Rohwer 151)

***Ultimatum* v. submarine chaser, 27 July 1944**
The submarine *Ultimatum* sank a submarine chaser and two ferry barges off Provence. (Rohwer 337)

***Ultor* v. *Lince*, July 1943**
The submarine *Ultor* sank the Italian TB *Lince* in the central Mediterranean. (Rohwer 260)

***Ultor* v. *FC-01* and *Alice Robert*, 22 May–2 June 1944**
The submarine *Ultor* sank the patrol vessel *FC-01* on 22 May and the escort *Alice Robert* on 2 June off Provence. (Rohwer 324)

Ultor v. *UJ-2211*, 21 July 1944
The submarine *Ultor* sank the submarine chaser *UJ-2211* west of Genoa. (Rohwer 337)

Ulysses v. *Semillante*, 5 June 1781
Ulysses (44; Capt. John Thomas) fought the French frigate *Semillante* (40) in the West Indies. Both ships were badly damaged, and the fight was without result. (Clowes 4.69)

Unbeaten v. *U-374*, 12 January 1942
The submarine *Unbeaten* sank *U-374* in the central Mediterranean. (Rohwer 131)

Unbeaten v. *Guglielmotti*, 17 March 1942
The submarine *Unbeaten* sank the Italian submarine *Guglielmotti* off Cape dell'Armi on 17 March. (Rohwer 151)

Unbending and others v. *Da Verrazano* and convoy, 19 October 1942
An Italian convoy from Naples to Tripoli was attacked by the submarine *Unbending*, which sank a ship and the destroyer *Da Verrazano*. Other submarines sank two other ships. (Rohwer 204)

Unbroken v. *Westmark*, 26 December 1942
The submarine *Unbroken* torpedoed the German minelayer *Westmark* off Naples. (Rohwer 219)

Undaunted at Carri, 18 March 1813
In order to attack a tartan sheltering at Carri, Provence, the marines of the frigate *Undaunted* (Capt. Thomas Ussher) captured a battery; the tartan was then taken out. (James 6.17; Clowes 5.523–524)

Undaunted and *Guadeloupe* at Port Nouvelle, 9 November 1813
Boats of the frigate *Undaunted* (Capt. Thomas Ussher) and the brig *Guadeloupe* went into Port Nouvelle, Provence; they captured two vessels and destroyed five more. (James 6.35–36; Clowes 5.539)

Undaunted and destroyers v. German destroyers, 17 October 1914
Four German ships of the 7th Destroyer Half-flotilla were met off Texel by the light cruiser *Undaunted* (Capt. Cecil Fox) leading the destroyers *Lance, Lennox, Legion,* and *Loyal*. The British ships had the speed of the Germans and all four of the latter, *S-115, S-117, S-118,* and *S-119*, were sunk. (Corbett 1.217–218)

Undaunted v. *Pleiadi*, 12 May 1941
The submarine *Undaunted* was sunk by the Italian TB *Pleiadi* off Tripoli. (Rohwer 71)

Undine v. German minesweepers, 6 January 1940
The British submarine *Undine* attacked three German minesweepers –

M-1201, M-1204, and *M-1207* – in the North Sea without success; in its turn *Undine* was forced to surrender after a depth-charge attack. British code books were captured. (Rohwer 13)

Unicorn v. Invincible, 1757
The French privateer *Invincible* (24), out of St Malo, was defeated and captured by *Unicorn* (28; Capt. John Rawling). (Clowes 3.296)

Unicorn v. Vestale, 8 January 1761
Unicorn (28; Capt. Joseph Hunt) met and captured *Vestale* (32) near the Penmarcks; both captains were killed. (Clowes 3.304)

Unicorn v. French squadron, 4 September 1780
Unicorn (20; Capt. Thomas Frederick) was captured by the French frigate *Andromaque* and two line-of-battle ships off Tortuga. (Clowes 4.57)

Unicorn v. Komeet, 28 August 1795
The Dutch sloop *Komeet* (18) was captured off Ireland by the frigate *Unicorn* (36; Capt. Thomas Williams). (Clowes 4.558)

Unicorn v. Tribune, 8 June 1796
The frigate *Unicorn* (36; Capt. Thomas Williams) chased the French frigate *Tribune* (32) for ten hours, the two ships repeatedly firing at each other. *Unicorn* finally caught up, and the two fought a close action for an hour, until *Tribune* surrendered. (James 1.365–369; Clowes 4.498–499)

Unicorn v. Tape-a-Bord, 6 May 1805
The frigate *Unicorn* (36; Capt. Lucius Hardyman), off St Domingue, sent boats to attack the French lugger *Tape-a-Bord*; after a row of several miles, the lugger was boarded and taken. (James 4.30–31; Clowes 5.361)

Unicorn v. Espérance, 12 April 1810
The frigate *Unicorn* (36; Capt. Alexander Kerr) captured *Espérance* (22) off the Ile de Re. (Clowes 5.451)

Union v. Circe, 20 July 1941
The British submarine *Union* was sunk by the Italian TB *Circe* while attacking a convoy off Pantelleria. (Rohwer 87)

Unique v. French privateer, 23 February 1806
The schooner *Unique* (10; Lt George Broad) was captured by a French privateer in the West Indies. (Clowes 5.550)

Unique v. German ASW ships, 13 October 1942
The submarine *Unique* was sunk by German ASW ships near La Rochelle. (Rohwer 206)

Unite v. *Découverte*, 9 October 1797
The French sloop *Découverte* (18) was captured in the Channel by the frigate *Unite* (36; Capt. Charles Rowley). (Clowes 4.555)

Unite and *Cephalus* v. *St François de Paule* and others, 4 July 1811
The frigate *Unite* (36; Capt. Edwin Chamberlayne) sent boats to capture the armed brig *St François de Paule* (8) at Porto Ercole, Latium. Despite vigorous resistance this was achieved with no loss. The sloop *Cephalus* (18; Cmdr Augustus Clifford) now arrived, and the two ships bombarded a battery into silence; merchant ships were captured. (James 5.254–255; Clowes 5.487)

Unite v. *Persanne*, 29 November 1811
Unite (36; Capt. Edwin Chamberlayne) was detached to chase *Persanne* (26). After five hours a single exchange of broadsides persuaded *Persanne* to surrender. She was carrying 150 cannon. (James 5.262–265; Clowes 5.496–497)

United v. *Bombardière*, 17 January 1943
The Italian destroyer *Bombardière* was sunk by the submarine *United* off Marettimo. (Rohwer 225)

Universal off Provence, May–July 1944
The submarine *Universal* sank the former French gunboat *Ysère* and the escort vessel *SG-15*, the German patrol boat *FM-06* and two blockships on 20–21 June, a submarine chaser on 3 July, and the auxiliary minesweeper *Petrel* off La Ciotat. (Rohwer 324, 337, 341)

Unrivalled v. German submarine chasers, 29 March 1943
The submarine *Unrivalled* sank the German submarine chasers *UJ-2201* and *UJ-2202* in the Bay of Picarenzi. (Rohwer 241)

Unruly v. *TA-15*, 7 January 1944
The submarine *Unruly* failed to sink a tanker and was then driven off by the German TB *TA-15*. (Rohwer 297)

Unseen v. *Brandenburg* and *Kreta*, 21 September 1943
The submarine *Unseen* sank the minelayer *Brandenburg* and the night fighter direction ship *Kreta* during the German evacuation of Sardinia. (Rohwer 274)

Unshaken v. *Climene*, 28 April 1943
The submarine *Unshaken* sank the Italian TB *Climene*. (Rohwer 241)

Unsparing v. *UJ-2106*, 21 June 1944
The submarine *Unsparing* sank the German minesweeper *UJ-2106* and two barges off Monemvasia, Greece. (Rohwer 328, 329)

Untiring off Provence, April–June 1944
The submarine *Untiring* sank the minesweeper *M-6022* and two ships off Cannes on 11–12 April, and the minesweeper *UJ-6075* on 27 April. On 10 June she sank the submarine chaser *UJ-6078* off La Ciotat. (Rohwer 312, 321, 325)

Upholder's campaign, January 1941–April 1942
Upholder (Lt-Cmdr Wanklyn) was the most successful British submarine operating from Malta.

The Italian TB *Aldebaran* damaged the submarine in an attack on a convoy north of Zavia on 30 January 1941. On 25 May *Upholder* sank the Italian troopship *Conte Rosso* in a convoy off the Tunisian coast; over 800 soldiers died. On 28 July she torpedoed the Italian cruiser *Giuseppe Garibaldi*, part of a convoy escort. Between 20 and 24 August she sank two ships near Cape San Vito, Sicily, but had to manoeuvre to escape attacks by TBs *Circe* and *Pegaso*. An attack on the cruiser *Luigi de Savoia* failed. On 20 September a large Italian troop convoy was attacked by a British submarine pack off Tripoli: *Upholder* sank two transports but other submarines were unsuccessful or were driven off.

On 4 January 1942 *Upholder* sank the Italian submarine *Saint Bon* (transporting petrol); on 5 February she attacked an Italian convoy off Cape San Vito, Sicily, without success, but was then harassed by the Italian TBs *Orsa* and *Aretusa*. She sank the Italian submarine *Tricheto* off Bari on 18 March, but on 13 April in attacking an Italian convoy was sunk by the Italian torpedo boat *Pegaso*. (Rohwer 56, 76, 87, 92, 100, 131, 141, 151, 159)

Upright v. *Diaz*, 25 February 1941
The submarine *Upright* sank the Italian cruiser *Diaz*, part of a convoy escort from Naples to Tripoli. (Rohwer 61)

Upright v. *Albatros*, 25 September 1941
The submarine *Upright* sank the Italian TB *Albatros* near Sicily. (Rohwer 101)

Upstart v. *Niedersachsen*, 15 February 1944
The submarine *Upstart* sank the minelayer *Niedersachsen* off Cape Cepet. (Rohwer 304)

Urge v. *Vittorio Veneto*, 13–14 December 1941
A major Italian attempt to run supplies to North Africa was frustrated by British submarines. *Urge* torpedoed the battleship *Vittorio Veneto* on 14 December, while *Upright* had sunk two of the ships the day before. (Rohwer 124–125)

Urge v. *Banda Nere*, 1 April 1942
Off Stromboli the submarine *Urge* sank the Italian cruiser *Banda Nere*. (Rohwer 156)

Urge v. *San Giusto*, 29 April 1942

The submarine *Urge* attacked the motor vessel *San Giusto*, but was damaged by gunfire and then sunk either by air attack or by the Italian TB *Pegaso*. (Rohwer 161)

USHANT, 27 July 1778
The British Channel Fleet under Admiral Sir Augustus Keppel met the French Brest fleet under Admiral Comte d'Orvilliers, twenty-seven and thirty line-of-battle ships respectively, west of Ushant. They manoeuvred for several days before coming close enough for battle, passing each other on opposite courses. By firing at the masts and rigging the French disabled several of the British ships, but did not follow up this advantage. Neither fleet lost any ship; the action was thus indecisive. (Syrett, *European* 40–46; Clowes 3.413–426; Mahan 351–353; Tunstall 137–142)

Usurper v. *UJ-2208*, **3 October 1943**
The submarine *Usurper* was sunk by the ASW vessel *UJ-2208* in the Gulf of Genoa. (Rohwer 379)

Utmost v. *Trieste*, **22 November 1941**
A major Italian effort to move supplies to North Africa was attacked by air and by the submarine *Utmost*, which damaged the cruiser *Trieste* with a torpedo. (Rohwer 117)

Utmost v. *Ardente* and *Gruppo*, **25 November 1942**
The submarine *Utmost* was damaged by the TB *Ardente* and then sunk by the TB *Gruppo* off Sicily. (Rohwer 214)

V

Vaagso, Norway, 27–28 December 1941
A squadron from Scapa Flow raided Vaagso and Maaloy. Fish processing factories and communications apparatus were destroyed; five freighters were run on to the beach, and the patrol boat *Donner* was sunk. The cruiser *Kenya* was damaged. (Rohwer 128; Sebag-Montefiore 220–226)

Vado, Italy, 27 March 1944
A German convoy was destroyed off Vado by an Allied force of MTBs and US PT boats. (Rohwer 312)

Vala v. UB-54, 21 August 1917
The collier *Vala*, operating as a decoy ship in the Atlantic, was sunk by *UB-54*. (Colledge 425)

Valeur v. French ship, 6 September 1710
Valeur (18; Cmdr John Hare) was captured by the French. (Clowes 2.537)

Valiant v. Confiance, 3 February 1810
Valiant (74; Capt. John Bligh) captured *Confiance* (14) off Belle Isle; she carried a cargo worth £150,000. (Clowes 5.450)

Valorous and Vancouver v. Vyepr, 28 July 1919
The Soviet submarine *Vyepr* attacked the destroyers *Valorous* and *Vancouver* in the Gulf of Finland, but the destroyers charged and drove her away. (Bennett 132–133)

Vanguard v. Perdrix, June 1795
Vanguard (74; Capt. Simon Miller) captured *Perdrix* (24) off Antigua. (Clowes 4.553)

Vanguard v. Superbe, 10 October 1795
Vanguard (74; Capt. Simon Miller) captured *Superbe* (22) in the West Indies. (Clowes 4.554)

Vanguard and others in the Caribbean, June–September 1803
Near St Domingue the frigate *Creole* (40) was seen by *Cumberland* (74) and *Vanguard* (74; Capt. James Walker) on 30 June and captured by the latter after a short fight. On 24 July *Duquesne* (74) came out of Cap François, St Domingue, and was chased first by *Bellerophon* and others, and then by *Vanguard*, the frigate *Tartar* (Capt. John Perkins), and other ships. They caught up with her on the 25th and, after a brief exchange of fire, *Duquesne* surrendered. On 4 September *Vanguard* captured the French *Papillon* (6)

and the schooner *Coureur de Nantes* (2) off St Marc in St Domingue. (James 3.182, 185–186; Clowes 5.318, 321–322, 556)

Vanoc and *Affleck* v. *U-392*, 16 March 1944
U-392, located by aircraft, was sunk by the destroyers *Vanoc* and *Affleck* in the Strait of Gibraltar. (Rohwer 311)

Vanquisher and *Tintagel Castle* v. *U-878*, 10 April 1945
U-878 was sunk by the destroyer *Vanquisher* and the corvette *Tintagel Castle* off southwest Ireland. (Rohwer 406)

Vascama v. *U-452*, 25 August 1941
U-452 was attacked by a Catalina aircraft of 209 Squadron and finally sunk by the trawler *Vascama*. (Rohwer 90)

'Vatzfiord', Scotland, 1039
Jarl Thorfinn Skull-splitter of Orkney and his nephew Rognvald raided in western Scotland. They won a victory at 'Vatzfiord', which may be Loch Watten in Skye. (Thompson 50; *Orkneyinga Saga* 22)

Velez Malaga, Spain, October 1650
The Royalist squadron of Prince Rupert attacked and burned several English merchant ships in Velez Malaga harbour, despite Spanish protests. (Corbett 1.218; Powell 103)

Vencejo v. gunboats, 8 May 1804
The sloop *Vencejo* (Capt. John Wesley Wright), becalmed at the mouth of the River Morbihan, was attacked by seventeen armed vessels and captured after a two-hour fight. Capt. Wright later died, notoriously, in the Temple prison in Paris. He had been an important British intelligence agent, and it was presumably this which brought such a large force against the ship. (James 3.218–221; Clowes 5.63–64; E. Sparrow, *Secret Service*, Woodbridge 1999, 293)

Venerable and others v. *Alcmene* and *Iphigénie*, 16–20 January 1814
The French frigates *Alcmene* and *Iphigénie* near the Canary Islands were chased by *Venerable* (74; Capt. James Worth) which caught up with and captured *Alcmene*. *Iphigénie* was chased by the brig *Jason* (12; Lt Thomas Moffat), and *Cyane* (22; Capt. Thomas Forrest), but it was only when *Venerable* arrived that she surrendered. (James 6.122–124; Clowes 5.543–544)

Vengeance v. *Entreprenant*, 13 March 1761
Vengeance (26; Capt. Gamaliel Nightingale) captured *Entreprenant*, a privateer of similar strength. (Clowes 3.305)

Vengeance and convoy v. French squadron, 2 May 1781
A large British convoy, escorted by *Vengeance* (Commodore William Hotham) and carrying much of the plunder of St Eustatius, was intercepted

in the Channel approaches by a French squadron commanded by Admiral La Motte Picquet. Hotham ordered the convoy to scatter, but twenty-two out of thirty merchantmen were taken into Brest. (Clowes 3.503–504; Mackesy, *America* 392–393)

Venturer v. *U-771*, 11 November 1944
The submarine *Venturer* sank *U-771* north of the Lofoten Islands. (Rohwer 370)

Venturer off Norway, 9–12 February 1945
The submarine *Venturer* sank *U-864* on 9 February and the German minesweeper *M-381* on the 12th, off Stavanger, Norway. (Rohwer 388)

Venus and others v. *Aréthuse*, 18 May 1759
Aréthuse (36) was captured by *Venus* (36; Capt. Thomas Harrison) near the Breton coast; *Chatham* (50) and *Thames* (32) were also involved. (Clowes 3.302)

Venus and *Juno* v. *Brune*, 30 January 1761
Brune (32) was encountered in the Soundings of the Channel by *Venus* (36; Capt. Thomas Harrison) and *Juno* (32), and was captured by them. (Clowes 3.305)

Venus v. *Boulogne*, January–October 1762
Venus (36; Capt. Thomas Harrison) fought and captured *Boulogne* (20), which had a valuable cargo from the east. From March to June *Venus* cruised off northern Spain and captured several French and Spanish privateers. On 18 October she captured the schooner *Crozon* (6). (Clowes 3.308, 313)

Venus v. *Semillante*, 27 May 1793
The frigate *Venus* (32; Capt. Jonathan Faulknor) met the French frigate *Semillante* (36) off Cape Finisterre. They fought a close action, in which *Semillante* was badly damaged. She made attempts to escape, while *Venus* tried to close once more. The approach of the French frigate *Cleopatre* ended the contest with both ships partly disabled. (James 1.103–105; Clowes 4.476)

Veronica v. *UB-42*, April 1917
The sloop *Veronica* was torpedoed by *UB-42* near Alexandria; she survived. (Newbolt 4.312)

Versatile and others v. *Azard* and *Gavriil*, 9 June 1919
The Soviet destroyers *Azard* and *Gavriil* attacked the destroyers *Versatile*, *Vivacious*, and *Walrus*. Fire was returned; neither side scored any hits. (Bennett 121)

Vestal v. *Bellone*, 21 February 1759
The frigate *Vestal* (32; Capt. Samuel Hood), sailing in advance of a squadron from North America, chased *Bellone* (32). After a stubborn fight *Bellone*

surrendered, completely dismasted. *Vestal* was almost as badly damaged. (Clowes 3.300–301)

Vestal and Fairy v. Mercury, 10 September 1780
Mercury, an American packet, was captured by *Vestal* (28; Capt. George Keppel) and *Fairy* (6). Important dispatches, including a copy of the treaty of alliance between the United States and the Netherlands, were captured. (Clowes 4.57)

Vestal v. Jalouse, 13 May 1797
The sloop *Jalouse* (18) was captured by *Vestal* (28; Capt. Charles White) in the North Sea. (Clowes 4.555)

Vestal v. Intrepide, 19 November 1809
The French ship *Intrepide* (20) was captured by *Vestal* (28; Capt. Edwards Graham) off Newfoundland. (Clowes 5.559)

Vestal v. Venus, 1852
Vestal (26; Capt. Cospatrick Hulton), refitting at Havana, saw the slaver *Venus* leave at night, and chased and captured her next day in the Bahamas. She was then used to capture two other slavers sheltering in shallow waters nearby. (Clowes 6.392–393; Lloyd 166–167)

Vestale v. French storeships, June 1801
The frigate *Vestale* (28, *en flute*; Cmdr Valentine Collard) captured two French storeships near Benghazi; these had been intended for the French forces in Egypt, but Alexandria was inaccessible to them. (James 3.76)

Vesuvius at St Jean de Luz, 10 November 1814
The bomb vessel *Vesuvius* and three smaller vessels bombarded French batteries at St Jean de Luz to assist the army's advance. (Hall 223)

Victor v. Fleche, 2–7 September 1801
The sloop *Victor* (18; Cmdr George Collier) chased the brig *Fleche* (18) near the Seychelles for three days. On the 6th, *Victor* went into Mahe roads, delicately threading the passage, and fought in the harbour with broadsides. *Fleche* was eventually captured, but sank. (James 3.143–145; Clowes 4.541)

Victor v. Bellone, 2 November 1809
The sloop *Victor* (18; Cmdr Edward Stopford) met the French frigate *Bellone* in the Bay of Bengal. After a fight in which she was partly dismasted, *Victor* was captured. (James 5.65–66; Clowes 5.445)

Victorious v. U-517, 21 November 1942
U-517 was sunk by aircraft from the carrier *Victorious*. (Rohwer 214)

Victory and fleet v. French convoy, 12 December 1781
A British fleet commanded by Rear-Admiral Richard Kempenfelt in *Victory*

(100) encountered a French convoy in the Bay of Biscay. The strong French escort commanded by Admiral de Guichen was out of position and the British attack scattered the convoy's ships. Fifteen ships, laden with naval and military stores for the West Indies, were captured. Most of the rest returned to Brest. (Clowes 3.509–510)

Victory v. *Embuscade*, 28 May 1803
Victory (100; Capt. Samuel Sutton) captured *Embuscade* in the Bay of Biscay. *Embuscade* was partly disarmed at the time. (James 3.176; Clowes 5.53)

Victory v. gunvessels, 20 September 1811
Victory (100) captured two Danish gunvessels in Wigo Sound. (Clowes 5.566)

Vigilant v. Sanganian pirates, 13 January 1797
The BM ship *Vigilant* (6; Lt John Hayes) was attacked by four Sanganian pirate ships in the Rann of Cutch, all of which attempted to board simultaneously. Hayes led a determined resistance which ended with success as the attackers sailed away. (Low 1.202–203)

Vigo, Spain
1585 Sir Francis Drake took his fleet into Vigo harbour to redistribute victuals before sailing to the West Indies. While there he raided the land and seized several ships. (Rodger 1.249. Andrews 118–119; Williamson 281–282)

1589 The English fleet, returning from its unsuccessful attack on Lisbon, raided and burnt Vigo as it passed. (Clowes 1.492; Andrews 166)

1656 *Cullen*, carrying siege equipment, was captured on 18 May by an Ostend ship and taken into Vigo. On 12 June *Fairfax* (56; Capt. Edward Blagge) and seven frigates sailed into the harbour to recover her. Two Ostend privateers, *Santa Teresa* and *St Peter*, were destroyed, but *Cullen* was too well protected to be retaken. (Powell 283–284)

1702 (Battle of VIGO) The Spanish *flota*, escorted by a French fleet, evaded Anglo-Dutch interceptors and reached Vigo. The Anglo-Dutch fleet made a landing which captured the batteries overlooking the anchorage. Vice-Admiral Sir Thomas Hopsonn in *Torbay* (80) broke the boom, and the allied fleet entered the anchorage. Seven French warships, including the flagship, were burned, four were captured, and the rest driven ashore. Most of the treasure had been sent inland, but considerable wealth was seized. (Corbett, *Mediterranean* 221–225; Owen 82–88; Clowes 2.380–386; Francis 53–54; Rodger 2.166; Mahan 207–208)

1719 A squadron under Vice-Admiral James Mighells entered and took the harbour, the forts, and the citadel at Vigo. Seven ships were captured, and guns, small arms, and gunpowder were seized. (Clowes 3.261–262)

1800 Boats from ships of Rear-Admiral Sir John Borlase Warren's squadron went into Vigo and cut out *Guèpe*, a large French privateer. (James 3.26–27; Gordon 97)

Ville de Paris v. *Messager*, 10 November 1803
Boats from *Ville de Paris* (110) captured the French lugger *Messager* off Ushant. (Clowes 5.556)

Viper v. *Virgin Maria*, 13 March 1797
The cutter *Viper* (14; Lt John Pengelly) fought and captured the Spanish privateer *Virgin Maria* near Alboran Island. (James 2.92)

Viper v. *Furet*, 26 December 1799
The cutter *Viper* (14; Lt John Pengelly) found the privateer *Furet* acting suspiciously off the Dodman. They fought for an hour, until *Furet* got away. *Viper* chased, and they fought for another hour until *Furet* surrendered. (James 2.419–420)

Viper v. *Cerbère*, 26 July 1800
Boats from the cutter *Viper* and other ships of the squadron blockading Port Louis, France, commanded by Lt Jeremiah Coghlan, went in to cut out the brig *Cerbère* at the harbour entrance. They were detected as they approached and were twice repulsed in attempts to board, but at the third attempt captured *Cerbère*. (James 3.20–22; Clowes 4.532)

Viper v. *Nova Granada*, 1844
The schooner *Viper* captured the Brazilian slaver *Nova Granada* off Brazil. (Bethell 213)

Virgin v. French ship, 17 May 1760
The brig *Virgin* (12; Cmdr Edward St Loe) was captured by the French, but was retaken in September. St Loe was killed. (Clowes 3.311)

Virginie v. Dutch ships, 26 April 1799
Virginie (44; Capt. George Astle) captured three small Dutch vessels in the East Indies. (Clowes 4.559)

Virginie v. *Guelderland*, 19 May 1808
The frigate *Virginie* (44; Capt. Edward Brace) chased and fought the Dutch frigate *Guelderland* (36). *Guelderland* lost three masts and her bowsprit and, having many casualties, surrendered. (James 4.324–326)

Vittoria v. *Pantera*, 31 August 1919
The Soviet submarine *Pantera* sank the destroyer *Vittoria* in the Gulf of Finland. (Bennett 162)

Vitu, East Africa, 1890–1894
An expedition involving eleven warships and a substantial ground force attacked the town of Vitu to avenge the murder of some German traders. A careful advance was needed and the sultan's army had to be defeated three times before the town was taken. Three years later another expedition by a Naval Brigade made up from the cruiser *Blanche* (Capt. George Lindley),

the screw sloop *Swallow* (Cmdr Lewis Sampson), and the screw gunboat *Sparrow* (Lt Francis Cole) attacked the sultan again, destroying two towns. This was repeated a year later, by the Lamu Forest Expedition; one of the towns was destroyed again. (Clowes 7.394–397, 408)

Vizalma v. U-551, 23 March 1941
The trawler *Vizalma* sank *U-551* in an encounter between Iceland and the Faeroe Islands. (Rohwer 64)

Volage v. Succès, 6 November 1807
The sloop *Volage* (22; Capt. Philip Rosenhagen) captured the cutter *Succès* in the Mediterranean. (Clowes 5.558)

Volage v. Requin, 28 July 1808
The sloop *Volage* (22; Capt. Philip Rosenhagen) captured the sloop *Requin* (16) in the Mediterranean. (Clowes 4.558)

Volage and Hyacinth in the Canton River, October 1839
Chinese resistance to imports of Indian opium led to conflict between armed junks and *Volage* (28; Capt. Henry Smith) and *Hyacinth* (18; Cmdr William Warren). Several junks were sunk before a cease-fire was arranged. (Clowes 6.281–282)

Volontaire and others v. French convoy, 29 April 1812
Boats from the frigate *Volontaire* (38; Capt. Charles Bullen) and the sloops *Undaunted* (Capt. Richard Thomas) and *Blossom* (Cmdr William Stewart) attacked a large convoy near the mouth of the Rhône. Seven ships were captured, two driven on shore, and twelve burnt. (James 5.342)

Voltaire v. Thor, April 1940
The AMC *Voltaire* fought the German AMC *Thor* in mid-Atlantic; *Voltaire* was sunk. (Rohwer 67; Hore 255)

W

Waireka, New Zealand, 28 March 1860
A party of seamen and marines from the screw sloop *Niger* (Capt. Peter Cracroft) landed in Taranaki to assist the army in a campaign. Cracroft attacked a supposed Maori *pa* (fortified stockade), which was quickly overrun. This was greeted as a triumph, with many Maori casualties; in fact, the *pa* was not fortified, and only one man was killed. (Clowes 7.174–176; Belich 84–88)

WALCHEREN Expedition, July–September 1809
Partly to support a new war launched by Austria against Napoleon, and partly to attack French naval installations in the Scheldt estuary, a major expedition was launched into the Netherlands. The precise objectives were the islands and peninsulas at the mouth of the Rhine and the city and naval base at Antwerp; 40,000 soldiers carried in 400 transports and escorted and supported by 245 warships were employed. Flushing on Walcheren was besieged and eventually captured, partly as a result of a heavy bombardment by seven line-of-battle ships. By then enemy defensive forces outnumbered the invaders, and the soldiers were suffering from a contagious fever. The difficulty of moving upriver to Antwerp and its squadron of French line-of-battle ships became steadily clearer. On 26 August the decision was made to abandon the expedition. Walcheren was held for a few months, but was evacuated in December. The naval result was the capture of a frigate, *Fidellee*, and timbers prepared for a line-of-battle ship, later assembled as *Chatham*, and the destruction of the new naval base at Flushing. (James 4.431–443; Clowes 5.271–278; NC 4.260–277, 282–298, 305–309; G.C. Bond, *The Grand Expedition*, Athens, GA 1979; Morriss 65–69)

***Wallflower* v. *U-32*, 8 May 1918**
The sloop *Wallflower*, escorting a convoy, fought and sank *U-32* by gunfire south of Sicily. (Newbolt 5.411; Halpern, *Naval History* 454; Grant 131)

Walney Island, Lancashire, 29 January 1915
U-21 reconnoitred the Vickers armament works on Walney Island for a time, then opened fire; the defending battery replied and *U-21* retired. Little was accomplished on either side. (Corbett 2.135)

***Wanderer* and *Glenavon* v. *U-305*, 17 January 1944**
U-305 was sunk by the destroyer *Wanderer* and the frigate *Glenavon* in the Atlantic. (Rohwer 298)

Wareham, Connecticut, 14 June 1814
Boats from *Superb* (74; Capt. Hon. Charles Paget) and the sloop *Nimrod* (Cmdr George Hilton) destroyed ships and boats and a large cotton factory in Wareham. (James 6.196–197)

Warner v. U-61, 13 March 1917
Warner, a cargo ship operating as a decoy ship, was sunk by *U-61* west of Ireland. (Colledge 439)

Warren's squadron v. *Volontaire*, 23 August 1794
A frigate squadron commanded by Capt. Sir John Borlase Warren in *Flora* (38) found the French frigate *Volontaire* off the Penmarcks rocks. *Diamond* (38; Capt. Sir Sidney Smith), *Artois* (38; Capt. Sir Edmund Nagle), *Santa Margarita* (38; Capt. Eliab Harvey), and *Diana* (38; Capt. Jonathan Faulknor) forced *Volontaire* onto the rocks, leaving her disabled. The frigates *Flora* and *Arethusa* chased the corvettes *Alerte* (18) and *Espion* (18) onto rocks in the Bay of Audierne. Boats were sent in to destroy them, but they were already wrecked. (James 1.233–234; Clowes 4.486–487)

Warren's squadron v. French convoys, 11 June–1 July 1800
A squadron commanded by Rear-Admiral Sir John Borlase Warren sent in eight boats from *Fishguard* (44), *Renown* (74), and *Defence* (74) against a convoy in the harbour of St Croix in the Penmarcks on 11 June. Against considerable fire, this was done. Three armed vessels and eight merchant ships were captured, the rest driven onto the rocks.

On 23 June a similar raid on Glenans resulted only in the destruction of a battery, the ships having retired upriver. On 1 July a raid on Noirmoutier Island resulted in the destruction of fifteen merchant ships, a corvette, and three armed vessels. On their return the raiding party was trapped by the tide in the sands and half the men were killed or captured. (James 3.15–17; Clowes 4.529)

Warren Hastings v. *Piemontaise*, 21 June 1806
The EIC China ship *Warren Hastings* (56; Capt. Thomas Larkins) was intercepted south of Mauritius by the frigate *Piemontaise* (46), which passed back and forth firing broadsides at the ship until its rudder was destroyed and its foremast down, at which point it surrendered. (James 4.149–154; Clowes 5.382–384)

Warspite and others v. Dutch squadron, 25 December 1666
A convoy from Gothenburg, escorted by six English warships under the command of Capt. Robert Robinson in *Warspite*, was attacked by five Dutch warships. Three of the Dutch ships, *Cleen Harderwyk* (38), *Leijden* (36), and *Els* (36), were captured. (Clowes 2.431)

Warspite and *Breda* v. *Maure*, 13 December 1710
Maure (60) was attacked by *Breda* (70; Capt. Thomas Long), and surrendered when *Warspite* (70; Capt. Josiah Crow) joined in. She became a Royal Navy ship, as *Moor*. Long was killed. (Clowes 2.525)

Warspite v. U-64, 13 April 1940
U-64 was sunk by an aircraft from the battleship *Warspite* in the Norwegian Sea. (Rohwer 18)

Warwick v. *Glorioso*, 14 September 1747
The Spanish treasure ship *Glorioso* (74) met *Warwick* (60; Capt. Robert Erskine) and *Lark* (40; Capt. John Crookshanks) in the Azores. *Warwick* attacked but was beaten off; *Lark* gave no support, for which Capt. Crookshanks was cashiered. (Clowes 3.285)

Warwick v. *Prudent* and others, 11 March 1756
Warwick (60; Capt. Molyneux Shuldham), near Martinique, was attacked by the French *Prudent* (74) and the frigates *Atalante* and *Zephyr*. *Warwick*, an old and crank ship with a sickly crew, was forced to surrender after being reduced to unmanageability. (Clowes 3.290–291)

Warwick v. *Rotterdam*, 5 January 1781
The Dutch *Rotterdam* (50), which had escaped two earlier encounters with British ships, was taken by *Warwick* (50; Capt. Hon. George Elphinston) in the Channel. (Clowes 4.60)

Warwick and others v. *Aigle* and *Gloire*, 12–14 September 1782
The French frigates *Aigle* (32) and *Gloire* (32) captured *Raccoon* (14; Cmdr Edmund Nagle) and were then chased into Delaware Bay by a squadron led by *Warwick* (50; Capt. Hon. George Elphinston), with *Lion* (64), *Vestal* (28), *Bonetta* (14), and a prize, *Sophie*. *Gloire* escaped upriver, but *Aigle* went aground and was captured and refloated. (Clowes 4.89)

Wasp v. *Felicidade*, February–March 1845
The sloop *Wasp* (Cmdr Sydney Ussher) captured the slaver *Felicidade*, which was sent with a prize crew to Sierra Leone. On the way *Felicidade* captured another slaver, *Echo*, and half the prize crew transferred to it. The crew of *Echo* went to *Felicidade* as prisoners, where they seized the ship. It was then recaptured by the brig *Star* (6; Cmdr Robert Dunlop). (Clowes 6.364–365; Bethell 274; Lloyd 85–88)

Wasp v. slaver, East Africa, 12 May 1865
The boat of the screw sloop *Wasp* (Capt. William Bowden) attacked a large dhow carrying 280 slaves. It had a crew of seventy-six, but the twenty-six men on the boat captured it after a fierce fight. (Clowes 7.209–210)

Watchet, Devon, 988
Godfrey Haraldsson, king of the Isles and Man, raided Watchet. He was defeated, but two Devon nobles died. (*ASC* s.a. 988; Hudson 62)

Waterford, Ireland, 917
Ragnall, king of Northumbria, and the Viking leader Sitric, sailed to Waterford, which was captured. Sitric defeated an Irish counter-attack, then made his way to Dublin, where he made himself king. (Hudson 23)

Waterwitch v. *Ermelinda*, October 1841
The sloop *Waterwitch* captured the slaver *Ermelinda* off Angola. (Bethell 194)

Waterwitch and Rapid v. Romeo Primero, 22 July 1847
The sloop *Waterwitch* (10; Cmdr Thomas Birch) and the brig *Rapid* (Cmdr Edward Dixon) captured the slaver *Romeo Primero*, which was sent in to Sierra Leone; the slaver's crew attempted to retake the ship on the way, but failed. (Clowes 6.366)

Weazel v. Boudeuse, 13 January 1779
Near St Eustatius *Weazel* (16; Cmdr Lewis Robertson), carrying dispatches, was intercepted and captured by *Boudeuse* (32). (Clowes 4.22)

Weazel off Corfu, 23–24 August 1804
The sloop *Weazel* (18; Lt John Clavell) discovered that Corfu was receiving a French garrison, and on 24 August encountered six vessels carrying French troops. Three were driven ashore, and three captured, as was another vessel. *Weazel* then, with 280 prisoners, sailed to Malta with the news. (James 4.265–266; Clowes 5.401–402)

Wellholme v. U-boat, 30 January 1918
The auxiliary ketch *Wellholme*, operating as a decoy, was sunk by a U-boat in the Channel. (Colledge 442)

West Africa
1562 and 1564 Sir John Hawkins sailed to West Africa in 1562 with four ships, and in 1564 with seven. He bought slaves from Portuguese slavers between Cape Verde and Sierra Leone, and raided the mainland to kidnap others. (Clowes 1.617–618; Williamson 53–54, 62–63)

1664 A dispute having arisen between the English and Dutch over the European forts in West Africa, Commodore Robert Holmes with a small squadron enforced English claims. He captured Goree, Cape Coast Castle, and other places, but failed to capture Elmina, the main Dutch base. (Clowes 2.423)

1758 *Harwich* (50; Commodore Henry Marsh), *Nassau* (64; Capt. James Sayer), and four smaller ships attacked the French posts in West Africa. In May Fort Louis in the Senegal River was captured, with booty valued at £200,000. Marsh then attacked Goree, but was driven off. A second, stronger, expedition was sent to complete the work, with five line-of-battle ships and seven smaller vessels, commanded by Commodore Hon. Augustus Keppel. Goree was bombarded into surrender on 29 December. (Clowes 3.187–189)

West Indies
1593 Five ships sent out by the Earl of Cumberland raided in the islands. A frigate was captured near San Domingo, Margarita was raided for pearls, two barks were captured near Jamaica, and seven ships taken after bombarding Puerto de Caballos, Honduras. (Spence 118)

1705 The English squadron in the West Indies, commanded by Rear-Admiral Sir William Whetstone, captured a French warship of 46 guns and a series of privateers. (Clowes 2.508)

See also: the several islands, **St Domingue, Spanish Main**

Westphalia v. U-boat, 11 February 1918
The hired ship *Westphalia*, operating as a decoy, was sunk by a U-boat in the Irish Sea. (Colledge 443)

Weymouth, Dorset, April 1471
Queen Margaret and her son Prince Edward landed at Weymouth intending to recover the throne for her husband Henry VI. (Gillingham 201)

Weymouth and *Dunkirk* v. *Invincible* and others, June–September 1694
Weymouth (48; Capt. William Jumper) and *Dunkirk* (60; Capt. Thomas Aitken) met the French *Invincible* (54) in the Channel on 10 June. The fighting was almost entirely between *Weymouth* and *Invincible*, and lasted almost a full day until *Invincible* was captured. *Weymouth* then cruised in the Channel, capturing French privateers in June and August; on 23 September in a fight with another privateer, *Comte de Toulouse*, she was dismasted and the enemy escaped. (Clowes 2.479–480)

Weymouth v. *Comte de Revelle* and others, May–November 1695
Weymouth (Capt. William Jumper) captured two French privateers in the Channel in May, the privateer *Comte de Revelle* (36) in July, and in November a French naval ship used as a privateer (26). (Clowes 2.484–485)

Weymouth and *Dover* v. *Fougeux*, December 1696
Weymouth (48; Capt. William Jumper) and *Dover* (48; Capt. William Cross) fought *Fougeux* (48); the French ship struck a rock and foundered soon after surrendering. (Clowes 2.489)

Weymouth v. French ship, December 1696
Weymouth (48; Capt. William Jumper) fought a French ship of 50 guns off Cape Clear, southern Ireland, but was dismasted in the encounter; the French ship got away. (Clowes 2.489)

Weymouth v. *Aurore* and a privateer, April–July 1697
Weymouth (48; Capt. William Jumper) captured a privateer (18) out of Granville, and in July captured the French warship *Aurore* (24) off Olonne, in a widely admired skilful fight. (Clowes 2.496)

Weymouth v. *Helgoland*, 6 February 1916
The cruiser *Weymouth* and the French destroyer *Bouclier* met the Austrian cruiser *Helgoland* with six TBs, which aimed to interfere with the evacuation of the Serbian army and refugees from Durazzo. The Austrians fought briefly, then headed for home; two of the TBs collided; this was the only damage. (Halpern, *Naval History* 158; Newbolt 4.122–123)

Wheatland and others v. *Asteria* and *U-443*, February 1943
The Italian submarine *Asteria* was sunk by the destroyers *Wheatland, Easton,*

Lamerton, and *Bicester* off Algeria on 17 February; six days later they sank *U-443*. (Rohwer 230)

Whetstone's squadron v. *Oland*, 6 August 1704
The Swedish ship *Oland* (50) failed to salute an English fleet under Commodore Sir William Whetstone off Orfordness. Eight English ships then attacked; *Oland* eventually surrendered, having suffered over fifty casualties. (Anderson 141; Rodger 2.175; Owen 106–107)

Whirlwind v. *U-34*, 5 July 1940
The destroyer *Whirlwind* was sunk by *U-34* south of Ireland. (Rohwer 29)

Whitaker v. *U-483*, 1 November 1944
U-483 sank the destroyer *Whitaker* in the North Channel. (Rohwer 360)

Whitehaven, Cumberland, 22–23 April 1778
Capt. John Paul Jones in the rebel American brig *Ranger* (18) landed a force at Whitehaven, spiked the guns in an old fort, and tried to burn a ship in the harbour. The alarm being raised, he retreated. (Clowes 4.11–12)

White Sea, August 1854
A small British squadron was sent to blockade the Russian White Sea ports. The Solovetskoi monastery and Kola were bombarded and landings made at Kola and on Shapley Island. (Clowes 6.428–429)

Whiting v. *Diligente*, 22 August 1812
The schooner *Whiting* (4; Lt Lewis Maxey) was captured by the French privateer *Diligente*. (Clowes 5.554)

Whitsand Bay, Cornwall, 27 September 1497
Perkin Warbeck, pretended son of Edward IV, landed with a few followers. He failed in his attempt to seize the throne. (Clowes 1.447)

Whitsand Bay at Kunsan, Korea, September 1950
The frigate *Whitsand Bay* carried out a landing at Kunsan by British and US marines as a diversion connected with the main invasion at Inchon. (Wettern 36)

Wild Boar v. French schooner, 12 April 1808
The sloop *Wild Boar* (10) captured a French schooner off Cape Machichura, Spain. (Hall 75)

Wild Goose and others v. *U-449* and *U-504*, June–July 1943
U-449 was sunk by the corvettes *Wild Goose*, *Woodpecker*, *Kite*, and *Wren* in the Bay of Biscay on 15 June; on 30 July they sank *U-504*. (Rohwer 257)

Wild Swan at Chuluwan, Mozambique, February 1881
The screw sloop *Wild Swan* (Cmdr Seymour Dacres) assisted a Portuguese

force attempting to suppress the slave trade and fired at hostile forces ashore, but the expedition overall was not successful. (Clowes 7.314)

Wilhelmina v. *Psyche*, 9–12 April 1804
The frigate *Wilhelmina* (*en flute*; Cmdr Henry Lambert), escorting a ship from Trincomalee towards Madras, was attacked by the French privateer *Psyche* (30). The two ships tracked each other for two days, and began fighting only on the 12th; both were seriously damaged. *Psyche*, badly holed, sailed away. (James 3.267–272)

Willamette Valley v. *U-66*, 26 June 1940
The hired ship *Willamette Valley*, operating as a decoy ship, was sunk by *U-66* in the Atlantic. (Colledge 446)

Willemstadt, Netherlands, 15–16 March 1793
The fort of Willemstadt, on an island in the Hollands Diep, was under siege by the French who had established five forts around it. Three gunboats from the *Syren* (32; Capt. John Manley) bombarded the forts, so persuading the French to leave, assisted by fog which magnified apparent British strength. Dutch forces thereupon reinforced the garrison. (James 1.98–99)

William Pitt v. Spanish ship, 6 June 1798
The lugger *William Pitt* (10; Lt Charles Haswell) was captured by Spanish gunboats in the Mediterranean. (Clowes 4.550)

Willow Branch v. *U-153* and *U-154*, 24 April 1918
The collier *Willow Branch*, operating as a decoy near the Cape Verde Islands, was sunk by *U-153* and *U-154*, operating together. (Colledge 449)

Winchelsea v. French force, 6 June 1706
Winchelsea (32; Capt. John Castle) was captured by four French privateers near Hastings. Castle was killed. (Clowes 2.510)

Winchelsea v. *Bizarre*, 11 October 1758
Winchelsea (24; Capt. John Hale), escorting a convoy from Carolina, was intercepted by *Bizarre* (60). *Winchelsea* fought to defend the convoy but was overcome, and forced to surrender. (Clowes 3.299–300)

Winchester and others v. Chinese pirates, November 1854
Winchester (50; Capt. Thomas Wilson) and other ships of the China squadron attacked pirate ships and bases in the Macao River, at Tyloo and Coulan Bay. (Clowes 6.388)

Windau, Latvia, February 1919
Bolshevik troops captured the port of Windau and threatened Libau. Rear-Admiral Walter Cowan sent the light cruiser *Caledon* to bombard the Bolsheviks, who rapidly left. (Bennett 74)

***Windham* and others v. *Manche* and others, 18–22 November 1809**
Three Indiamen, *Windham*, *United Kingdom*, and *Charlton*, each with 20 to 30 guns, were intercepted by the French frigates *Manche* (40) and *Vénus* (44), and the corvette *Créole* (14). *Windham* (Capt. John Stewart) attacked *Manche*, but the other Indiamen stayed clear. After a fight *Windham* broke away and, while *Manche* and *Créole* captured *United Kingdom* and *Charlton*, *Vénus* chased and eventually captured *Windham*. *Windham* was later retaken by the frigate *Magicienne* (32; Capt. Lucius Curtis) near Mauritius. (James 5.63–65)

***Windsor* v. *Duc de Chartres*, 27 March 1759**
Near Lisbon *Windsor* (60; Capt. Samuel Faulkner) intercepted a convoy of four French East Indiamen. *Duc de Chartres* (24) was captured; the rest escaped. (Clowes 3.301)

***Windsor Castle* v. *Jeune Richard*, 1 October 1807**
The packet *Windsor Castle* (Cmdr William Rogers), making for Barbados, was attacked unsuccessfully by the French privateer *Jeune Richard* (7). In the end Rogers and five of his men boarded and captured the privateer; of the privateer's crew of ninety-two, twenty-one were killed and thirty-three wounded. The survivors were locked in their own chains for the rest of the journey. (James 4.266–268; Clowes 5.402)

Wirral, Cheshire, 902
A group of Norse led by Ingimund, expelled from Dublin by the Irish, attempted to settle in Wales, but were driven off, then settled in the Wirral of Cheshire by agreement with Aethelflaed, Lady of the Mercians. They were joined by others until in 907 they were numerous enough to threaten Chester, only to be foiled by Aethelflaed, who occupied the old Roman city and refortified it. (F.T. Wainwright, 'Ingimund's invasion', *Scandinavian England*, Chichester 1975)

***Wishart* v. *Glauco*, 27 June 1941**
The destroyer *Wishart* sank the Italian submarine *Glauco* west of Gibraltar. (Rohwer 80)

***Wishart* and *Wrestler* v. *U-74*, 2 May 1942**
U-74 was sunk by the destroyers *Wishart* and *Wrestler* and a Catalina from 202 Squadron in the western Mediterranean. (Rohwer 161)

***Wizard* v. *Requin*, 10–13 May 1808**
The sloop *Wizard* (16; Cmdr Abel Ferris) chased the French sloop *Requin* (16) towards Tunisia. After two fights and a chase of over 350 miles *Requin* went into Goleta. (James 4.338–342; Clowes 5.418–419)

***Wizard* v. slavers, 1838–1840**
The sloop *Wizard* captured the slaver *Brilhante*, carrying 250 slaves, off Rio de Janeiro in May 1838, the slaver *Feliz*, carrying 236 slaves, in January 1839,

and in January 1840 the Brazilian slaver *Congresso* out of Rio de Janeiro. *Congresso* was heading for Africa, and was the first to be taken near Brazil solely on the grounds of having slaver equipment. Later that year *Wizard* captured the Brazilian slaver *Tentador*. (Bethell 144, 149, 167, 202, 203)

Wolf v. French ship, 1745

The sloop *Wolf* (14) was captured by the French, and was retaken two years later. (Clowes 3.284)

Wolf and *Malabar* v. *Regulateur* and *Napoleon*, 2 January 1806

The sloop *Wolf* (18; Cmdr George Mackenzie) went through the reef at Azeraderos, Cuba, with the boats of *Malabar* (54; Capt. Robert Hall). Two privateers, *Regulateur* and *Napoleon*, were bombarded by *Wolf* and then captured by the boats; *Regulateur* sank. (James 4.126–127; Clowes 5.372)

Wolverine v. *Furet* and *Ruse*, 4 January 1797

The sloop *Wolverine* (12; Cmdr Lewis Mortlock) attacked the French privateers *Furet* (4) and *Ruse* (8) off Boulogne. In a desperate struggle the French several times attempted to board, but then drew off, having briefly set *Wolverine* on fire. (James 2.352–353; NC 2.4–5; Clowes 4.519)

Wolverine and *Arrow* v. *Gier* and *Draak*, 12 September 1799

The sloops *Wolverine* (12; Cmdr William Bolton) and *Arrow* (12; Cmdr Nathaniel Portlock) were sent by Vice-Admiral Mitchell in search of the Dutch brigs *Gier* and *Draak*, located behind Vlie Island. Once the British ships reached them, *Gier* surrendered, but *Draak* fought briefly and then gave up. Two days later they also captured *Dolphijn* (24). (Clowes 4.524; James 2.388–389)

Wolverine v. *Blonde*, 24 March 1804

The brig *Wolverine* (12; Cmdr Henry Gordon), escorting a convoy, was challenged by two privateers and attacked by *Blonde* (30). After an hour's fight *Wolverine*, badly holed, surrendered, and sank a few minutes later. All but two of the convoy got away. (James 3.259–261)

Wolverine v. *Tremeuse*, 12 March 1806

Wolverine (18; Cmdr Francis Collier) captured the French schooner *Tremeuse* in the West Indies. (Clowes 5.557)

Wolverine v. French lugger, 7 October 1813

The sloop *Wolverine* (18; Cmdr Charles Kerr) captured the French lugger *No. 961*. (Clowes 5.559)

Wolverine v. slavers, 1839–1840

The sloop *Wolverine* (16; Cmdr William Tucker) captured the slaver *Emprehendador* in June, and on 25 July the slaver *Firmeza* off Whydah, as they prepared to take on cargoes of slaves. In November she captured the slaver *Veloz* off the mouth of the Congo, and in May 1840 a party from the sloop captured and destroyed the slaving base on the island of Corisco, Gabon. (Clowes 6.306; Bethell 175, 177, 182)

Wolverine and *Scorpion* v. German minelayer, 1 November 1914

The destroyers *Wolverine* and *Scorpion* investigated a supposed German minelayer in the Gulf of Smyrna. She was burnt before they arrived and may actually have been a Turkish gunboat. (Corbett 1.363; Halpern, *Naval History* 64)

Woodcot and *Raymond* v. *Preneuse*, 21 April 1798

The French frigate *Preneuse* followed an EIC ship into Tellicherry harbour, where the Indiamen *Woodcot* and *Raymond* were captured after a single exchange of fire. (James 2.243–244; Parkinson 121)

Woolf v. French ship, 24 June 1704

The sloop *Woolf* was captured by the French. (Clowes 2.535)

Woosung, China, 16–17 June 1842

The British squadron in the Yangzi attacked Chinese forces at Woosung, the steamers towing the wooden ships into position. Chinese resistance was tough, but the British naval guns outranged those on land and destroyed the many Chinese batteries before unopposed landings completed the fighting. (Graham 214–217)

Worcester v. *Jason*, 13 January 1705

Worcester (48; Capt. Richard Canning) attacked the French *Jason* (54) and was assisted by other ships; the fight stopped at nightfall; *Jason* got away, badly damaged. (Clowes 2.508)

Worcester v. *Valeur*, 1707

Worcester (48; Capt. Richard Canning) captured the French warship *Valeur* (24) in the Channel. (Clowes 2.515; Owen 123)

Worcester v. Spanish dispatch boat, August 1741

Worcester (60), in the West Indies, captured a Spanish frigate (24) carrying dispatches to the Viceroy of Mexico. (Clowes 3.272)

Wynnington's captures, 2 April 1449

Robert Wynnington was commissioned to campaign against pirates and robbers in the Channel; he deviated from this to capture a great fleet of Hanseatic, Fleming, and Dutch ships carrying salt from the Bay of Bourgneuf to northern Europe. Diplomatically this led to the final alienation of the Dukes of Brittany and Burgundy from the English side in the war with France. (Barker 378)

X

X-craft v. *Tirpitz*, 22 September 1943
The German battleship *Tirpitz*, located in fjords in northern Norway during 1942 and 1943, was a standing threat to the Russian and Atlantic convoys. Several bombing attacks had not damaged the ship, and it lay too far up Altenfjord for surface or submarine attack. Six X-craft, midget submarines, were towed to a point near the entrance to the fjord and released. Three reached the ship and left their explosives beneath it. Some of the crews were captured. The ship's captain appreciated what had been done but was unable to move the ship very far, so when the explosives blew, the ship was badly disabled. It took no further part in the war, though it was bombed and sunk later. (Schofield 158–163; Rohwer 277)

Y

Yangzi estuary, China, August 1862
With the implied permission of Rear-Admiral Sir James Hope, Capt. Roderick Dew of the screw corvette *Encounter*, with the screw gunboat *Hardy* and the French gunboat *Confucius*, raided and massacred along the southern shore of the Yangzi River estuary on the pretence of keeping the Taiping rebels away from Ningpo. (Clowes 7.51–72)

Yap, Caroline Islands, 12 August 1914
The cruisers *Minotaur* and *Newcastle* sailed from Hong Kong to Yap in the Caroline Islands, a German colony; they shelled the radio station on the island to ruin. (Corbett 1.142–143; Halpern, *Naval History* 73)

***Yarmouth* and others v. *Eendracht* and *Jonge Leeuw*, North Sea, February 1665**
Three English ships, *Yarmouth* (44), *Diamond* (40), and *Mermaid* (22), met the Dutch ships *Eendracht* (32) and *Jonge Leeuw* (22) in the North Sea. Both forces were scouting for their respective fleets; in the fighting the Dutch ships were defeated and captured. (Clowes 2.425)

***Yarmouth* v. *Randolph*, 7 March 1778**
Yarmouth (64; Capt. Nicholas Vincent) chased a group of rebel American ships near Barbados and fought *Randolph* (32), which blew up. (Clowes 4.10)

***Yarra* and convoy v. Japanese squadron, 4 March 1942**
The RAN sloop *Yarra*, escorting a convoy south of Java, was attacked by a squadron of three Japanese cruisers and two destroyers. *Yarra* and all the convoy were sunk. (Rohwer 148)

Yell Sound, Shetland, 1135
The earldom of Orkney was claimed by Rognvald, son of St Magnus, who came from Norway with a fleet; he was defeated in Yell Sound by the incumbent Earl Paul. (Thompson 62)

***York* and *Dover* v. *St Antoine* and *Mariana*, 12 January 1693**
The French privateers *St Antoine* (26) and *Mariana* (16), having captured the ketch *Scarborough* (Capt. Thomas Taylor) off Ireland, were themselves captured by *York* (60; Capt. George Mees) and *Dover* (48; Capt. Edward Whitaker), and *Scarborough* was recovered. (Clowes 2.472)

***York* v. *Prince of Wales*, April 1693**
Prince of Wales (14), a privateer with a letter of marque from James II, was captured by *York* (60; Capt. George Mees). (Clowes 2.472)

York v. French ship, 1778
The tender *York* (14; Lt Thomas Walbeoff) was captured off the American coast. (Clowes 4.109)

York v. *Sandoval*, July 1799
The Spanish ship *Sandoval* (14) was captured by *York* (64) and other ships in the West Indies. (Clowes 4.560)

York v. Italian motor boats, 26 March 1941
Six Italian explosive motor boats were sent in to Suda Bay, Crete, where they sank a tanker and damaged the cruiser *York*. (Rohwer 65)

Yorkshire, 1066
A Norwegian fleet, with ships from Orkney and Ireland, and commanded by King Harald Hardrada, sailed to the Humber and captured York, aiming to reinstate Tostig as earl of Northumbria and install Harald as king of England. The invasion was defeated by King Harold II at the battle of Stamford Bridge. (Hudson 153–155; Thompson 54)

Yorkshire coast, 16 December 1914
German battle-cruisers crossed the North Sea to bombard seaside resorts on the Yorkshire coast, covered by the High Seas Fleet. Several British squadrons were at sea, and when the High Seas Fleet collided with a destroyer screen it turned away. The battle-cruisers also turned away, and though they were sighted twice on their retirement, no British ship would open fire without direct orders. Only minor damage was done on shore, and a few ships on each side were also damaged; the main result was confusion. (Corbett 2.23–44; Halpern, *Naval History* 41–42; Massie 319–360)

Yorktown, Virginia, September 1781
Several British ships were at Yorktown during the siege of the British army of Lord Cornwallis; *Charon* (44; Capt. Thomas Symonds), *Guadeloupe* (28; Capt. Hugh Robinson), *Fowey* (24; Capt. Peter Aplin), and the fireship *Vulcan* (Cmdr George Palmer) were destroyed by a red-hot shot from the shore during the siege; *Bonetta* (14; Cmdr Ralph Dundas) was captured when the army surrendered. (Clowes 4.75–76)

Young Crow v. *UB-103*, 16 September 1918
The drifter *Young Crow* combined with an airship to sink *UB-103* near Dover. (Newbolt 5.429; Grant 93)

Z

Zanzibar, 25–26 August 1896
When the sultan of Zanzibar died, a relative seized power, contrary to British wishes. A squadron of British ships led by the cruiser *St George* (Capt. George Egerton, with Rear-Admiral Henry Rawson) took station to threaten the palace. When an ultimatum expired, the ships fired on the palace and on some armed ships in the harbour. A new sultan was then installed. (Clowes 7.436–439)

***Zealous* v. *Courier*, March 1799**
The sloop *Courier* (16) was captured by *Zealous* (74; Capt. Samuel Hood) in the Mediterranean. (Clowes 4.556)

***Zebra* v. *Carmagnole*, 30 November 1794**
The French schooner *Carmagnole* (10) was captured by the sloop *Zebra* (16; Capt. Robert Faulknor) in the West Indies. (Clowes 4.554)

***Zebra* v. pirates, February–March 1827**
The sloop *Zebra* (Cmdr Richard Williams) searched bays and villages in the Peloponnese in February for rumoured pirate ships; those he found were burned or impounded. In March the sloop chased two pirate ships near Zea; one was caught and burned. (NRS, *Piracy* 52–59, 93)

***Zebra* v. *Maraquita*, 1862**
The screw sloop *Zebra* (Cmdr Antony Hoskins) captured the slaver *Maraquita* off the West African coast. (Clowes 7.189)

***Zephyr* v. French frigate, 23 August 1778**
The sloop *Zephyr* (14; Cmdr Thomas West) was captured by a French frigate in the Mediterranean. (Clowes 4.19)

***Zephyr* v. *Sénégal*, 2 November 1780**
The sloop *Zephyr* (14; Cmdr John Inglis) attacked and captured *Sénégal* (18) in the Gambia River, West Africa. (Clowes 4.58)

***Zephyr* v. *Victoire*, December 1811**
The sloop *Zephyr* (16; Capt. Francis Dickins) captured the sloop *Victoire* off Dieppe. (Clowes 5.561)

***Zephyr* v. *U-1020*, 31 December 1944**
The destroyer *Zephyr* was torpedoed by *U-1020*, which was lost on a mine soon after. (Rohwer 373)

***Zubian* v. *UC-50*, 4 February 1918**
The destroyer *Zubian* sank *UC-50* in the Channel. (Newbolt 5.427; Grant 81)

Zululand, 1878–1879
Naval Brigades, formed from the screw corvette *Active* (Commodore Francis Sulivan), the screw sloop *Tenedos* (Capt. Edward Adeane), the armoured frigate *Shah* (Capt. Richard Bradshaw), and the screw corvette *Boadicea* (Cmdr Frederick Richards), took part in operations to relieve Ekoma, constructed bridges, and took part in the battle of Ginginhlovo. (Clowes 7.305–308)

***Zylpha* v. *U-82* or *U-96*, 11 June 1917**
The collier *Zylpha*, operating as a decoy ship, was torpedoed by *U-82* or *U-96* southwest of Ireland; she sank four days later. (Colledge 460)

1 British waters

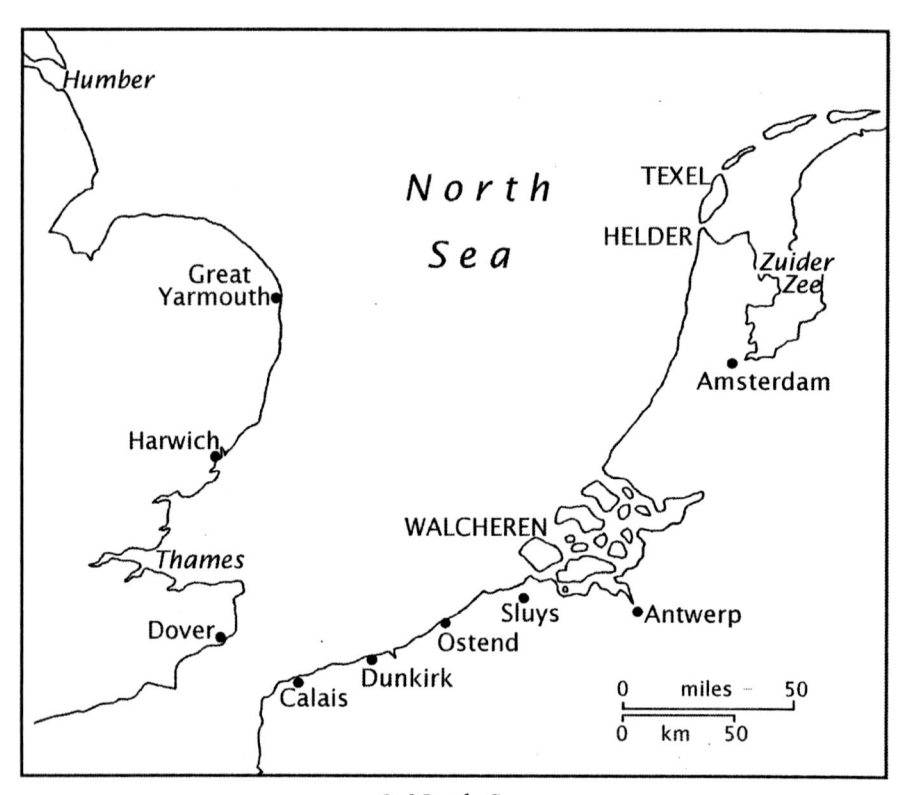

2 North Sea

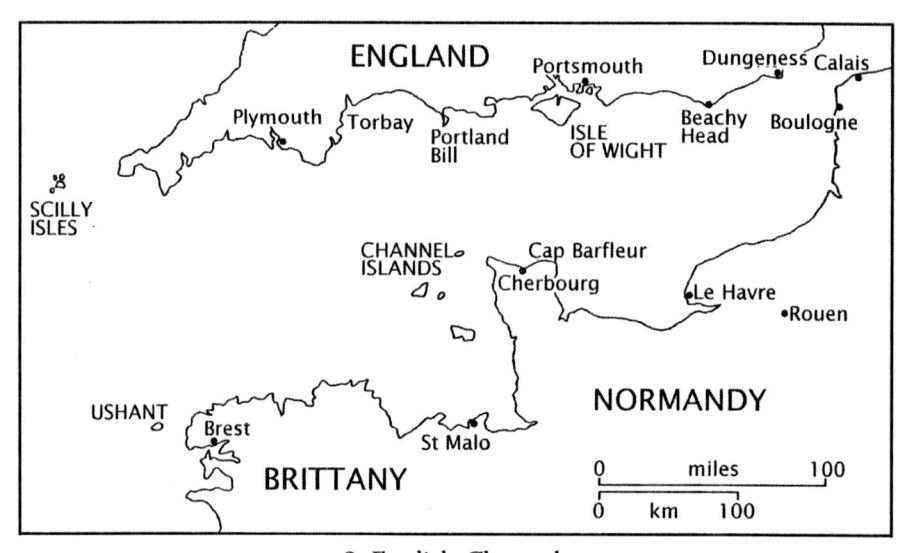

3 English Channel

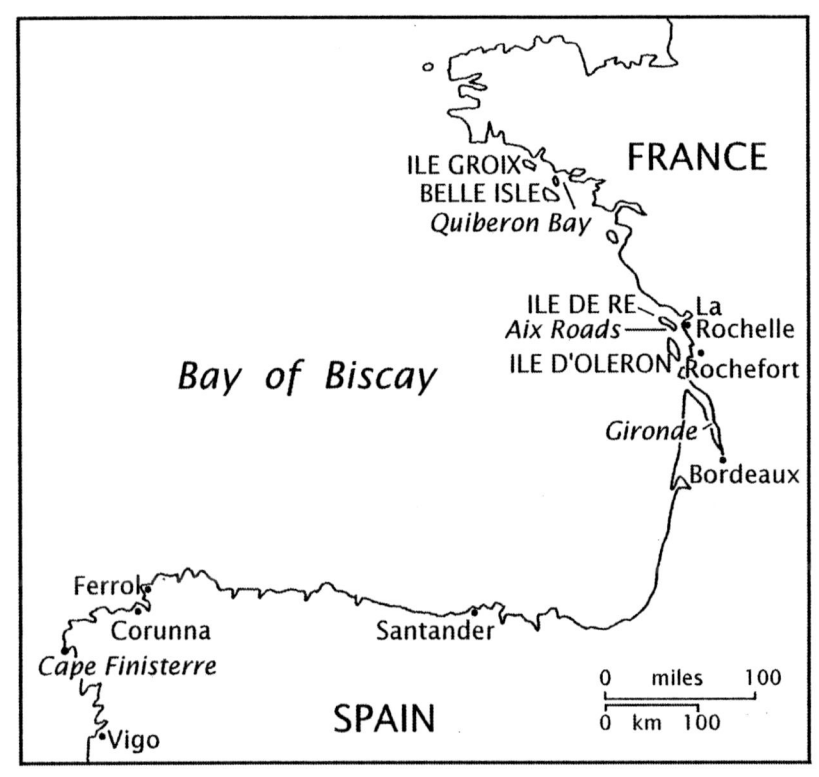

4 Bay of Biscay

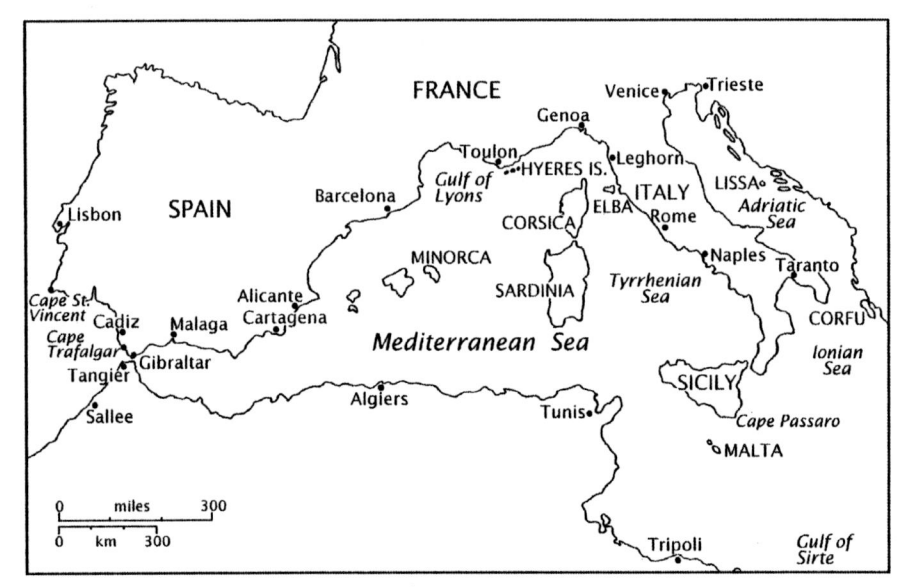

5 Mediterranean Sea

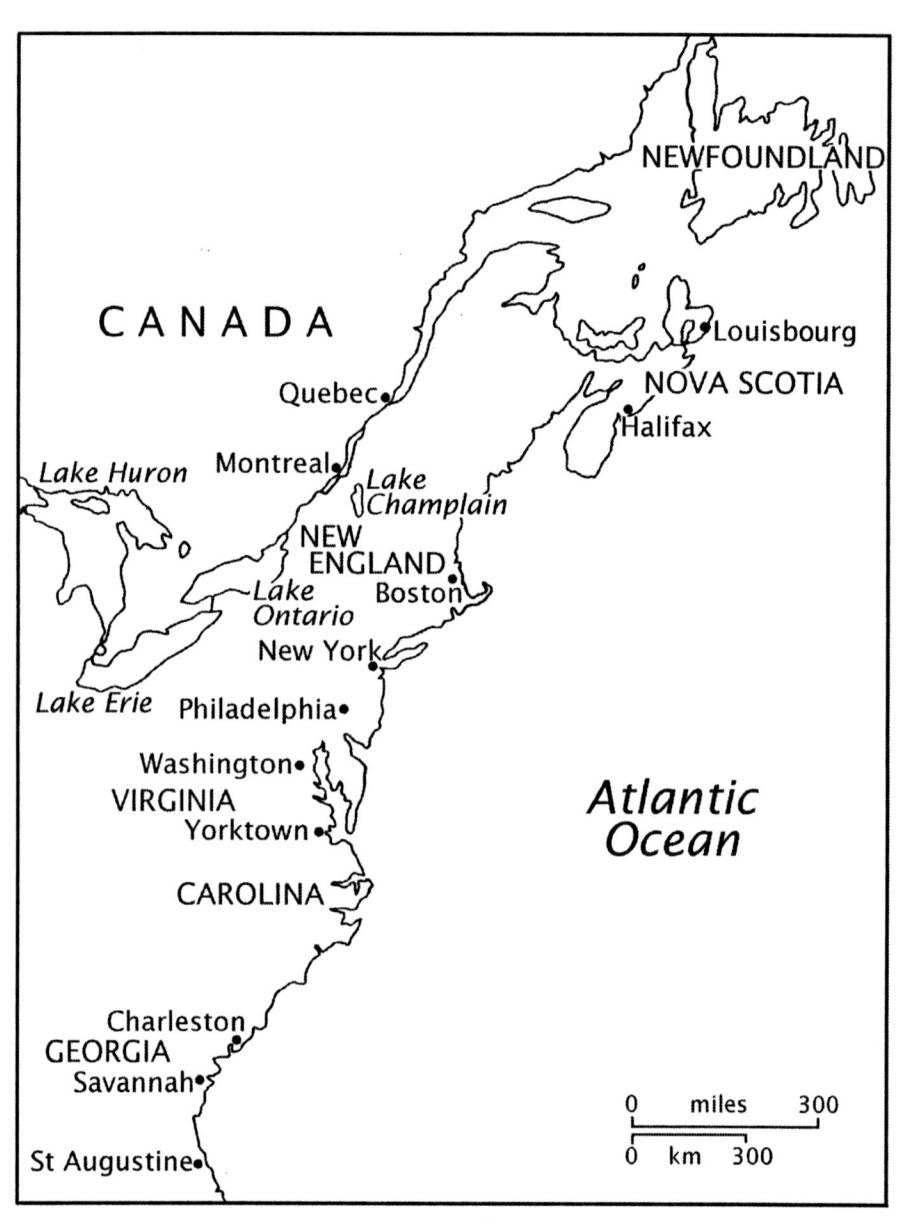

6 Eastern North America

7 Caribbean Sea

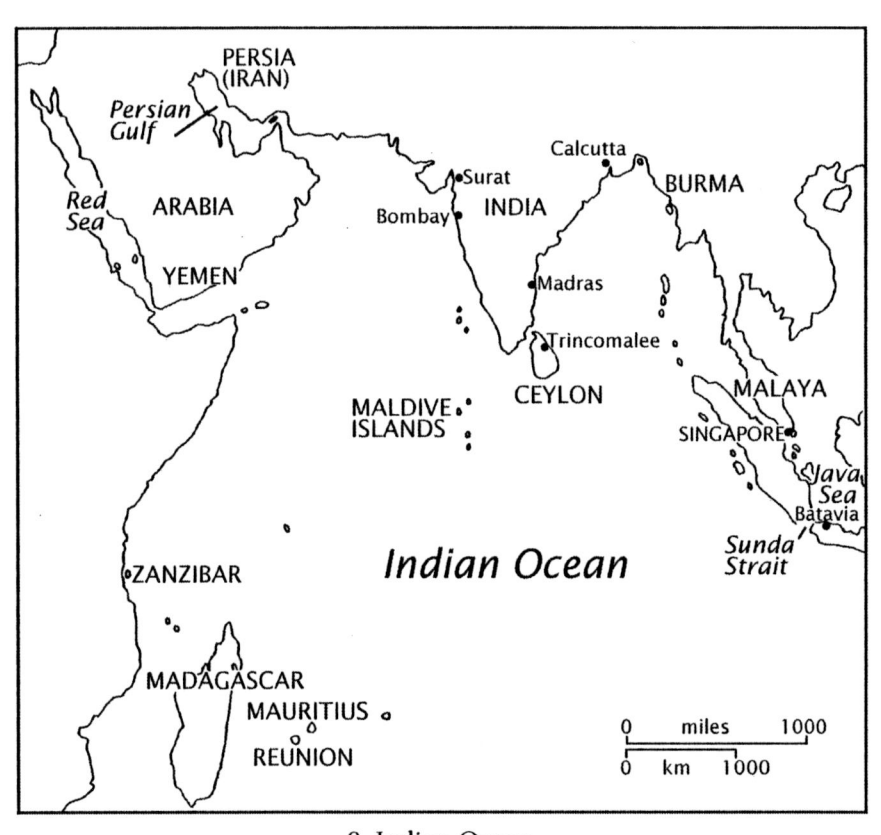

8 Indian Ocean

Index

Ranks of people are not included in this index, since they changed so much. Ships' names were used and re-used, and here no attempt is made to distinguish each ship, apart from nationality; ships are British except where indicated by letters in parentheses, as follows:

(A) – Australian
(Cn) – Canadian
(D) – Dutch
(Dan) – Danish
(F) – French
(G) – German
(I) – Italian

(In) – Indian
(J) – Japanese
(NZ) – New Zealand
(S) – Spanish
(SA) – South African
(US) – United States

Other nationalities are indicated in full.

A-2 (G) 125
A-6 (G) 125
A-7 (G) 86
A-19 (G) 86
Aachen (G) 162
Aalborg (Dan) 166
Abadan, Iran 352
Abbeville, France 178
Abdiel 141, 159, 431
Abeille (F) 11, 157, 426
Abercrombie 407
Abercromby, Sir Ralph 1
Aberdeen, Aberdeenshire, Scotland 417
Aberffraw, Anglesey 329
Abergavenny 331
Abigail (Dan) 220
Aboukir 1
Aboukir Bay, Egypt 1, 210, 316, 453
Abriza, West Africa 96
Abu Dhabi, Persian Gulf 351
Abyssinia (Ethiopia) 1
Acadia (Nova Scotia), Canada 1
Acapulco, Mexico 113, 342
Acasta 2, 209, 263
Accra, Ghana 210
Acciaio (I) 425, 460
Acertif (D) 144
Achates 21, 319, 398
d'Ache, Comte 136, 311, 364
Acheron 2, 29
Achille (F) 90, 210, 388, 434, 464; (Neapolitan) 433

Achilles 2, 154; (NZ) 215, 389
Aconit (F) 51
Acorn 2, 5
Acre, Palestine 2–3
Actaeon 13
Actéon (F) 167, 319
Actif (F) 28, 318
Actionnaire (F) 376
Active 3, 5–6, 12, 16, 55, 127, 176, 269, 429, 436, 503
Activity 399
Acton 4
Adam, Charles 124, 177, 385, 453
Adamant 470
Adams, John 2
Adams (US) 348
Addaya Creek, Minorca 299
Adeane, Edward 503
Aden, South Arabia 4, 424, 429
Admiral Graf Spee (G) 389
Admiral Hipper (G) 36, 210, 397, 398
Admiral Jawl (Dan) 413
Admiral Mitchell 441
Admiral Pasley 4
Admiral Rainier 4
Admiral Scheer (G) 35, 397
Admiralty Islands, Melanesia 4
Adolf Vinnen (G) 420
Adour River, France 4
Adour (F) 170
Adriade (F) 362
Adriatic Sea 4–8, 158, 302, 463

Adrienne (F) 11, 87, 355
Adroit (F) 273, 407
Adua (I) 281
Adventure 6, 9, 90, 396, 407; (pirate) 344
Advice 9, 265
Advice Prize 9
AE-2 (A) 9
Aegean Sea 26, 61, 114, 210, 346, 391, 394, 419, 460, 468, 472
Aelfgar, earl of Mercia 240
Aeolus 109, 240, 395
Aethelflaed, Lady of the Mercians 496
Aethelred II, King of England 283
Aetna 9
Affaire (F) 89
Affleck 9, 104, 483
Affronteur (F) 154
Afleck, William 430
Africa 317, 497
Africa 9, 10, 403; (S) 184
Africaine 290–291; (F) 356, 376
Agamemnon 10, 401
Agay, France 12, 266
Agberi, Nigeria 315
Agde, France 260
Agile (F) 13
Aguada Bay, Puerto Rico 383
Aidin mac Gabriain, King 336
Aigle 10; (F) 7, 158, 225, 374, 491
Aigrette (F) 27, 419
Aikiko Maru (J) 76
Aimable 10–11, 209, 442
Aimable Nelly (F) 118
Aircraft: Catalina 46, 79, 400, 483, 496; Condor (G) 36, 37, 39, 40, 42, 43, 169; Halifax 198; Hurricane 28, 39, 279, 280; Spitfire 282; Sunderland 32, 41
Airone (I) 279
Aitape, New Guinea 383
Aitken, Thomas 493
Aix Roads, France 11
Ajaccio, Corsica 238
Ajax 11, 144, 279, 389, 457, 469
Akado, Nigeria 315
Akitoye, king of Lagos 257
Akyab peninsula, Burma 94
Alaart 11
Alacrity 11
Alagi (I) 282
Alan of Galloway 284
Alarm 11, 75, 222, 314
Alassio, Corsica 132, 257
Albacore 12
Alban 12; (Dan) 387
Albania 130, 421
Albany, Duke of 440
Albany 12

Albara, India 389
Albatros (I) 60, 358, 480
Albatross 320
Albemarle, Earl of 222
Albemarle 475
Alberigo da Barbariano (I) 425
Alberni (Cn) 182
Alberto da Giussano (I) 425
Albion 12; (F) 81
Alboran I. 294, 487
Albrighton 179, 180
Alcantara 12
Alceste 6, 12, 13, 101; (F) 78, 112
Alcide 13, 410; (F) 167, 233
Alcinous (F) 7
Alcion (F) 11, 231, 309
Alcione (I) 473
Alcmène 13, 308; (F) 483
Alcudia (S) 308
Alcyon 345
Aldborough 175
Aldebaran (I) 480
Aldenham 44, 183
Aldergrove, Ireland 52
Alderney, Channel Is., 149, 182, 225, 376
Alderson, W.J.S. 157
Aldred, John 313
Alecto 203, 315, 367, 411, 416, 425
Alert 13, 26, 328
Alerte 14; (F) 110, 112, 130, 350, 490
Alexander III, King of Scots 284
Alexander, James 110
Alexander, John 28
Alexander 14
Alexandre (F) 242, 291, 410
Alexandria, Egypt 1, 14, 26, 60, 107, 141, 149, 167, 203, 213, 252, 254, 279, 283, 291, 292, 335, 484, 485
Alexandria, Virginia 120
Alexandria 14
Alexandrian 15
Alfieri (I) 290
Alfred, King of Wessex 365, 438
Alfred 15; (US) 28
Algeciras, Spain 15, 220, 434
Algeria 155, 230, 233, 319, 320, 365, 494
Algerine (ships) 253, 386
Algerine 16, 89, 120, 198, 249, 318
Alghero, Sardinia 280
Algier 16
Algiers 16, 308, 318–319, 320; Dey of 16, 86, 308
Algoa Bay, South Africa 100, 247
Alicante, Spain 17, 435
Alice Robert (G) 476
Alimnia I., Dodecanese Is., 152
Alis Fezzan (Turkish) 419

Allart (Dan) 470
Allegre (F) 435
Allemand, Rear-Admiral (F) 98
Alliance 2; (US) 31, 421
Alliantie (D) 386
Alligator 17, 210, 407
Allin, Sir Thomas 16, 17, 404, 444
Allin, William 231, 414
Allington, Argenton 16
Almes, James 222, 386
Almirante (slaver) 80
Almunecar, Spain 232
Alnwick Castle 400
Alphaea 17
Alsen (Dan) 470
Altavela, Spain 150, 359
Altenfjord, Norway 398, 499
Altham, E. 60
Altmark (G) 133
Alvise da Mosto (I) 61
Alysse (F) 43
Amaranthe 17, 288; (F) 149
Amazon 18, 155, 236, 272, 324, 465
Amazone (F) 28, 78, 137, 150
Ambleteuse, France 442
Amboyna, Molucca Is, 66, 131
Ambra (I) 213
Ambrose 70
Ambuscade 18, 355
Ameer 161
Amelia 18, 19, 78
Amélie (F) 11, 349, 378
America 19, 104, 132, 257, 297
Amethyst 19, 59, 334, 422
Améthyste (F) 298; (Haitian) 431
Amfitrite (S) 135, 291; (I) 213
Amherst, Lord 13
Ami de Colonnot (F) 378
Amitié (F) 81
Amlaibh – see Olaf the White
Amoy, China 19–20, 212
Amphion 5, 20, 98, 236, 260, 266, 269
Amphitrite (F) 27, 435
Amrum I., Denmark 91
Anaconda (US) 368
Anagassan, Ireland 217
Anapa redoubt, Russia 401
Anatolia 20
Anchove, Spain 385
Anchusa 20
Ancona, Italy 5, 6, 7, 92, 269, 294
Andalsnes, Norway 214, 331
Andaman Islands, Bay of Bengal 20, 84, 414
Andania 20
Anderson, James 387, 388
Anderson, Kenneth 9

Anderson, W. 207
Andes 12
Andrea Doria (US) 378
Andrew, John 6
Andrews, Isaac 339
Andromache 20, 21, 101
Andromaque (F) 202, 329, 478
Anemone 26; (F) 287, 419
Anglesey, Wales 239, 253, 329, 330
Anglesey 21, 415
Angola 491
Angria family 117, 124, 148, 206, 216, 221
Angria, Kanhoji 206, 252, 305, 369
Angria, Manaji 124
Angria, Samboji 124, 303
Angria, Tulaji 371, 450
Anguilla, West Indies 260
Anguilla 400
Angus Og – see MacDonald
Anholt Island, Denmark 21, 214
Anjou, France 261
Anjoxa, Wast Africa 369
Anna Maria (slaver) 458, 463
Annan 22
Annapolis Royal, Nova Scotia 368
Anne 22
Anne D. Richardson (slaver) 361
Annie Rickmers 427
Anoh, Nigeria 315
Anse la Barque, Guadeloupe 215
Anson, George 22, 103, 113
Anson 22, 27, 138, 355, 363, 377
Antelope 23, 32, 35, 189, 250, 351, 442; (D) 437
Anthony 24, 275
Antibes, France 24
Antigua, West Indies 67, 228, 313, 482
Antigua 24
Antilope (S) 293
Anton Schmitt (G) 310
Antrim 189
Antwerp, Belgium 489
Anzac beach, Gallipoli, Turkey 145, 472
Anzio, Italy 24–25, 186, 451
Apelles 388
Aphis 141, 202
Aphrodite (pirate) 346
Apia, Samoa 409
Apith (R) 408
Aplin, Peter 501
Apollo 6–7, 25, 247
Apollon (F) 21
Apollonia, Cyrenaica 473
Appleton, Henry 264
Apropos (F) 169
Apulia, Italy 6, 7, 8
Aquila (slaver) 434

Aquilon (F) 23, 124
Arab 25, 264
Arabe (F) 277
Arabi Pasha 14
Arabic 25
Arabis 25, 26, 39
Aradam (I) 223
Aragon 26
Arakan, Burma 93
Arandora Star 33
Arbuthnot, Hon. James 61
Arbuthnot, Marriot 103, 415
Arbutus 26, 37, 43
Arc (F) 186
Arcachon, France 26
Arcadian 26
Arc en Ciel (F) 467
Archangel, Russia 60, 397
Archer, Anthony 211
Archer 26, 84, 177, 217, 442
Archimède (I) 337
Arctic Ranger 444
Ardea, Italy 72
Ardent 26, 176, 209, 392; (F) 70
Ardente (I) 340, 481
Ardito (I) 340
Arensburg I., Gulf of Riga 217
Arethusa 19, 26, 27, 116, 138, 226, 283, 407, 490
Arethuse (F) 19, 186, 484
Aretusa (I) 480
Argall, Governor of Virginia 313
Argeles, George 316
Argent 61, 410
Argentina 189, 303, 333, 411
Argilla, North Africa 200
Argo 27, 28, 238, 342, 353; (I) 35 (D) 386
Argonaut 28
Argonauta (S) 233
Argonaute (F) 319
Argus (US) 245, 346
Argyll, Scotland 193, 260, 384; Earl of 83, 253
Ariadne 28, 313; (G) 226
Ariane (F) 329
Arica, Chile 112, 156
Ariel 28, 60, 314; (In) 351; (I) 279
Ariguani 41
Ark Royal 29, 107, 264, 279–281, 296, 414
Arlequin (F) 449
Armée d'Italie (F) 349
Armide 69, 121; (F) 98, 302
Armies: Eighth (British) 202, 425, 431; Fifth (US) 407; Seventh (US) 24
Armilla Patrol 352
Arnemuiden, Flanders 321
Arnold, Benedict 358

Arran, Scotland 28, 94, 13, 238, 254; Earl of 109, 224
Arrogant 28, 216–217, 367, 402
Arrogante (F) 244 (S) 149 (slaver) 428
Arrow 29, 30, 497
Artémise (F) 151, 454
Artésien (F) 221
Arthur, Richard 118
Arthur 30
Artigliere (I) 279
Artois 30, 363, 490; (F) 391–392
Arundel, Sussex 170; Earl of 72, 88, 172–173, 439
Arundel (Norwegian)
Arunta (A) 4, 313, 320, 355, 429, 466
Asama 30
Asagiri (J) 462
Ascania 182
Ascension 30
Ascension I. 145, 149
Ascianghi (I) 318
Ascot 30
Ashanti, Ghana 30
Ashanti 181
Ashby, John 130, 344
Ashigara (J) 470
Asia (S) 135
Asigamo (J) 245
Asp (US) 127
Asphodel 58
Aspic (F) 376
Assab, Eritrea 151
Assaye (In) 274
Assemblé Nationale (F) 177
Assiniboine (Cn) 30, 45
Assistance 30, 157, 404
Assurance 30, 31, 251
Astell 115
Aster 20
Asteria (I) 493
Astle, George 487
Aston, Edward 394
Astraea 134, 145, 221, 275; (S) 367
Astree (F) 117, 290
Asturias 31
Asuncion, Paraguay 333
Atalanta 31
Atalante 31; (F) 23, 113, 239, 277, 356, 360, 452–453, 491
Atchison, Arthur 418
Atendolo (I) 282
Athabascan (Cn) 181
Athalante (D) 416
Atheling 161
Athelstan, King of England 170, 218, 334, 417
Athenia 31

Athénienne (F) 12
Atholl, Earl of 83
Atkins, David 420
Atkinson, William 2
Atlantic Ocean 31–59, 73, 83, 85, 86, 122, 153, 164, 165, 167, 170, 176, 205, 216, 230, 256, 275, 289, 312, 336, 371, 463, 474, 482, 488, 489, 495
Atlantis (G) 149
Atlas (US) 368
Attack 26, 59, 60, 125
Attendant 308
Attentive 60, 462
Aubrietia 38
Auckland 60, 429
Aud (Norwegian) 83
Audacieux (F) 69, 143
Audacious 192, 316
Audacity 40, 42
Audierne Bay, France 23, 154, 270, 291, 489
Augusta, Sicily 60, 212, 358, 374
Augusta 147
Auguste (F) 7, 95, 168, 301, 366
August Wriedt (G) 79
Ault, France 171
Aurangzeb, Mogul emperor 65, 168
Aurania 41
Auricula 275
Aurora I., Melanesia 393
Aurora 60, 61, 79, 152, 153, 178, 205, 281, 319, 351; (slaver) 141
Aurore (F) 122 361, 461, 493
Austen, Francis 393
Austerlitz (F) 122
Australia 61, 69, 140–141, 313, 409, 454, 466
Australia *II*; (A) *143, 313, 355, 429*
Austria 3, 24, 442, 489
Autumn 441
Ava, Burma 93
Avenger 48, 397
Aventure (F) 103
Aventurier (F) 210, 29, 371, 373
Avieri (I) 435, 468
Aviles, Spain 125
Aviso no. 25 (F) 290
Avon 61, 62, 127, 315, 379
Avon Vale (A) 141
Avorio (I) 383
Avranches, France 250
Avtroil (Russian) 108
Axum (I) 282
Aylmer, Frederick 413
Aylmer 78, 285
Ayscough, John 433, 447
Ayscue, Sir George 67, 270, 361, 440

Azard (Russian) 123, 484
Azeraderos, Cuba 497
Azores Is 13, 36, 38, 57, 61, 62–63, 277, 491

B-11 64
Babaque, Senegal 421
Babet 64; (F) 116
Babiyan Channel, Persian Gulf 352
Babr (Persian) 352
Bacchante 6, 7, 64, 111, 379; (F) 170
Bacchus 64
Baddiboo, Gambia, king of 402
Badger 64, 65
Badiley, Richard 264, 303
Badr-i-Zaffer (Turkish) 419
Baetan mac Cairill, King of Dal Fiatach 283
Bagnolini (I) 140
Bagur, Spain 232
Bahama Is 90, 431, 485
Bahamas Strait 222
Bahia, Brazil 213, 378, 414, 423
Bahrain, Persian Gulf 352
Baia, Italy 433
Baja California, Mexico 112
Baker, Francis 82
Baker, John 65, 302
Baker, Joseph 21, 99, 135, 458
Baker, Thomas 311, 357–358, 438
Balasore, India 65
Balchen, John 137, 210, 407
Baldur (Dan) 75
Balearic Islands 69, 234
Baleine (F) 20, 186, 364
Baleno (I) 333
Balfour 182
Balikpapan, Caroline Is 473
Ball, Alexander 8, 28
Ball, Henry 142
Ballahou 65
Ballantyne, George 358
Ballard, Samuel 345
Ballard, Volant 215
Balsam 55
Baltic Sea, 10, 65, 108, 123, 129, 133, 144, 153, 164, 235, 277, 310, 347, 357, 421; Baltic squadron 108, 123
Baltimore, Maryland 120
Baltimore 270
Bamborough Castle 400
Bamburgh, Northumberland 65–66
Banda Is, Indonesia 66
Banda Neira, Banda Is 66
Banda Nere (I) 480
Bandar Abbas, Persia 352
Banes, Cuba 367

Bangor, Wales 330
Bangor Bay, Ireland 74
Banka Strait, Indonesia 66, 470
Banks, Jacob 357
Bann 66
Bannow, Ireland 239
Banterer 309
Bantry Bay, Ireland 66–67, 239, 434
Baquio, Spain 60
Baracca (I) 135
Baralong 67
Barbadoes 67
Barbados, West Indies 12, 15, 67, 85, 138, 148, 215, 227, 245, 288, 290, 338, 358, 364, 391, 396, 405, 466, 496, 500
Barbara 67
Barbarigo (I) 354
Barbarossa Khair-ed-din (Turkish) 163
Barbate River, Spain 380
Barber, John 372
Barbier de Seville (F) 356
Barbuda, West Indies 67, 293
Barcelona, Spain 68, 111, 234, 289 299, 363
Barcelona, Spanish Main 203
Barcoo (A) 320
Bardia, Cyrenaica 140–141, 210, 457
Bardsey Island, Bristol Channel 90
Barents Sea 398
Barfleur, France 78, 298
Barfleur 474
Barfod, Capt. (Dan) 437
Barham 68–69, 143
Bari, Italy 480
Barid son of Oitir 283
Barker, John 137
Barkley, Andrew 82
Barlow, Robert 120, 356
Barnaby 113
Barnet, Curtis 66, 107
Barossa 247
Barra, Scotland 83
Barracoe, Ghana 260
Barracouta 66, 301, 409
de Barras, Admiral (F) 119, 239
Barrete, George 154
Barrett, John 9, 371
Barrie, Robert 363, 364
Barrington, Hon. Samuel 2, 71, 154, 405
Bartella, Italy 5
Bartolemeo Colleoni (I) 106
Barton, Andrew 211
Barton, Robert 126, 260
Basilisk 69, 232, 325
Baskerville, Sir Thomas 242
Basque (F) 157
Basque Roads, France 69–70

Basra, Iraq 201, 350, 352
Bassein River, Burma 93
Basse Terre, Guadeloupe 215, 417
Bass Rock, Scotland 194
Bastard, John 369
Bastia, Corsica 132, 206, 414, 448
Bataaf (D) 391
Batabano, Cuba 70, 449
Batavia (Jakarta), Indonesia 121, 161, 245, 346
Batavia (D) 214
Batavian Republic 225
Bateman, Richard 255
Bath 40
Bathurst Walter 408
Batrun, Lebanon 74
Batten, Sir William 89, 361
Battle Cruiser Squadron, 1st 226
Baugh, Henry 212, 381
Bayano 70
Bayard 56
Bayeux, France 171
Bayntun 57, 70
Bay of Bengal 66, 118, 301, 305, 311, 402, 445, 453, 485
Bay of Biscay 4, 11, 19, 21, 25, 30, 43, 60, 61, 70–71, 75, 96, 125, 143, 165, 184, 214, 240, 241–242, 268, 272, 287, 302, 306, 308, 309, 341, 358, 360, 363, 370, 388, 390, 435, 436, 438, 439, 450, 461, 466, 471, 474, 486, 494
Bay of Bourgneuf, France 71–72, 498
Bay of Fundy, Canada 314
Bay of Guayaquil 112
Bay of Honduras 452
Bay of Hyéres, France 309
Bay of Jounieh, Lebanon 455
Bay of La Hougue, France 68
Bay of Lebedos, Aegean Sea 72
Bay of Naples 72, 435, 462
Bay of Picarenzi, Italy 479
Bay of Rocks, Spain 298
Bay of Sagone, Corsica 364
Bay of St Eufemia, Italy
Bayona Islands 348
Bayonnaise (F) 18, 26
Bayonne, France 71, 391
Bazely, Henry 221
Bazely, John 13, 20
Bazely 57, 72
Beach 128
Beachy Head, Sussex 28, 72–73, 180, 182, 361, 368, 444
Beagle 399
Bear Island 298, 397, 399
Béarnais (F) 293
Beatty, David 153, 248

Beauclerk, Lord Amelius 157
Beauclerk, Lord Aubrey 229
Beaulieu 73
Beau Marseille (F) 395
Beaumont, Basil 396
Beau Narcisse (F) 305
Beaver, Philip 2, 205
Beaver 73, 416
Bedford, Duke of 173
Bedford 73, 151, 198, 250
Bedouin 282
Begonia 73
Beijerland (D) 179
Beirut, Lebanon 73–74, 232
Belchen (G) 79
Belcher, Sir Edward 408
Belfast 398
Belfast Lough, Ireland 74, 156, 239
Belgica (D) 214
Belgium 324
Belisarius 408; (US) 291
Belize, Central America 74
Bell, Christopher 356
Bella Aurora (I) 447
Bella Dura (slaver) 306
Bella Miquelina (slaver) 212
Bellamy, John 257
Belle Isle, France 18, 70, 131, 241, 242, 460, 482
Belleisle 74
Belle Poule 6, 74, 208; (F) 26–27, 82, 91, 271–272, 318, 373
Bellerophon 65, 74, 316, 482
Belliqueux 75, 403; (F) 23
Bellona 74, 75, 112, 166, 251, 286; (I) 269; (slaver) 267
Bellone (F) 115, 118, 134, 166, 185, 270, 272, 290, 297, 369, 484, 485
Belmont 43
Belvidera 75
Benbow, John 75–76, 175
Bencoolen, Indonesia 76, 358
Beneficent 338
Bengal, India 76
Bengal (In) 76
Bengasi (G) 474
Benghazi, Cyrenaica 61, 140, 222, 280, 456, 463, 468, 472, 474, 485
Benin City and River, Nigeria 76, 184
Benjamin Stevenson 76
Ben Lawer 76
Ben-My-Chree 76, 163
Bennet, Richard 305, 393
Bennett, George 203
Bennett, James 286
Bentham, George 89, 361
Bentinck, John 315, 341

Bentinck 72, 98, 285
Beorht 329
Berber, Sudan 389
Berbera, Somaliland 429
Berbice, West Indies 161
Berceau (F) 373
Berc-i-Satvet (Turkish) 163
Beresford, Lord Charles 388
Beresford, John 99, 379, 462
Bergamot 77
Bergen, Norway 77, 78, 109, 149, 305, 331, 416, 427, 446, 458
Bergère (F) 209, 426
Berillo (I) 222
Berkeley, Lord (1) 297; (2) 70
Berkeley, Hon. George 11
Berkeley, George 239
Berkeley, Velters 240
Berkeley 179
Berkeley Castle 77
Bermuda I. 27, 77, 99, 267
Bermuda 388
Bernard, Edward 378
Bernd von Arnim (G) 210
Berry Head, Devon 156
Berry, Sir Edward 268
Berry, Sir John 16, 312, 385
Bertie, Albemarle 464
Bertie, Peregrine 137
Bertin (F) 227
Berwick, Northumberland 77–78, 417
Berwick 36, 78, 103, 107, 468
Beryl III 78
Best, Henry 289
Best, Thomas 204, 449
Betsy (F) 18
Bett, William 411
Bettesworth, George 138, 458
Betty 78
Beverley 50, 53
Beveziers (F) 275
Beyt, Kathiawar, India 249–250
Biak I., New Guinea 312
Bianchi (I) 37, 466
Bias Bay, China 78
Bicester 72, 494
Bickerton 78, 181, 237
Biddeford 90
Bien Aimé (F) 155
Bienfaisant 78, 391; (F) 273
Bien Trouvé (F) 208
Bienvenue (F) 288
Biggs, Robert 269
Bight of Benin 140
Big Sandy Creek, New York 259
Bilbao, Spain 321
Billingsley, Rupert 266

Bimbia, West Africa 381
Bingham, Arthur 269
Bingham, Joseph 130
Birch, Thomas 492
Birdlip 79
Birmingham 77
Bismarck (G) 79
Bissell, Austin 82
Biter (US) 53, 451
Bittern 79, 80
Bizarre (F) 495
Bizerta, Tunisia 340
Bjorneborg, Finland 216
Black, James 7
Blackfly 444
Black Joke 80, 454
Blackmore 8
Blackness, Scotland 193, 194
Black Prince 108
Black Sea 185, 333, 400–401
Black Swan 52
Blackwall 347
Black Watch (G) 310
Blackwood, Hon. Henry 89, 144, 268, 348, 469
Blackwood, Hon. Price 101
Blackwood 57, 181
Blagge, Edward 486
Blake, Robert 80, 109, 116, 160, 251, 269, 37, 356, 366, 411, 416, 440, 474
Blake 81
Blanchard (F) 174
Blanche 81, 255, 298, 429, 487; (F) 247, 276
Blanc Sablon Bay, France 88, 302
Bland, Loftus 184, 227
Blandford 81, 82
Blankett, John 104
Blankney 42, 186
Blast 82
Blaxland, John 214
Blaye, France 208
Blaze 331
Blazer 82
Blean 82
Bleddyn ap Cynfyn 432
Blencathra 186, 327, 474
Blenheim 20, 82
Blennerhasset, Goddard 115
Blessing 350
Bletchley Park 39
Bligh, John 138, 482
Bligh, Richard 14
Bligh, Thomas 176
Bligh 78, 475
Bloemfontein, South Africa 430

Blonde 19, 82, 215, 304, 425; (F) 109, 240, 262, 271, 497
Bloodhound 367
Bloody Bay, Toberbory, Mull 83
Bloom 83
Blossom 83, 488
Blow, John 89
Blücher (G) 153
Bluebell 83, 400
Bluefields, Nicaragua 314
Blyth, Samuel 87
Boadicea 83, 84, 195, 291, 503
Bocca Tigris, China 101
Bodø, Norway 159
Bodrum, Turkey 64
Boger, Coryndon 207
Bogue (US) 55
Bogue forts, China 102
Bokenham, Robert 95, 118, 168
Bolador (S) 277
Boladora (slaver) 358
Bolsheviks 60, 495
Bolton, Charles 317
Bolton, Sir William 138, 157, 442, 497
Bolton 84
Bolzano (I) 282, 374, 472
Bomarsund, Finland 84
Bombarde (F) 83
Bombardière (F) 479
Bombay (Mumbai), India 1, 13, 23, 84, 101, 124, 168, 201, 206, 216, 252, 351
Bombay 84, 216, 386, 450
Bombay Castle 75
Bombay Marine 23, 101, 206, 278, 335, 350–352, 386, 408, 450
Bom Destina (slaver) 378
Bomstead, John 246
Bonaparte, Prince Jerome (F) 116
Bonaparte (F) 228
Bonaventure 84, 213, 231, 283
Bonbee, Nigeria 84
Bond, Francis 312
Bone, Algeria 84, 319, 377
Bonetta 20, 84, 85, 390, 491, 501
Bonhomme Richard (US) 421
Bonne Citoyenne 85; (F) 354
Bonny City and River, West Africa 238, 306–307, 463, 471
Boorder, James 374
Booth, Richard 204
Booth, William 8, 90
Bordeaux, France 13, 18, 72, 179, 208, 360, 371
Bordelais (F) 387
Bordelaise 85
Bordentown, New Jersey 85
Borea (I) 140

Boreas 85, 220
Borée (F) 289
Borkum I., Germany 164
Borlase, John 423
Borneo 151, 245, 320
Bornholm I., Denmark 136, 451
Bosanquet, Charles 265
Boscawen, Edward 85, 236, 212, 257, 273, 364
Boston, Massachusetts 86, 118, 187, 231, 375, 423
Boston 86; (US) 200, 379
Bostonian 86
Bosworth, Northants 297
Botha 86
Bouclier (F) 493
Boudeuse (F) 492
Bouffonne (F) 464
Bougainville 314
Bougainville (F) 275
Bougie, Algeria 86, 101, 286, 319
Boulogne, France 174, 178, 181, 183, 308, 366, 382, 388, 393, 438, 439, 440, 441, 442, 443, 444, 497
Boulogne (F) 484
Bouncer 86, 87
Bounty, John 128
Bourbon I. 87, 426
Bourchier, Henry 223
Bourchier, John 225
Bourchier, Thomas 19–20, 78
Bourg, France 208
Bourgogne (F) 304
Bourne, Nehemiah 251, 440
Bourne, Sampson 312
Bouverie, Duncombe 295
Bouverie, Hon. Pleydell 26
Bouvet (F) 144
Bowden, William 491
Bowen, James 27, 28
Bowen, John 286, 288
Bowen, Richard 459
Bowker's Bay, South Africa 429
Bowles, Valentine 331
Boxer, James 388
Boxer 87, 315
Boxers (Chinese rebels) 120
Boyle, Hon. A.D. 64, 419
Boyle, Charles 225, 452
Boyle, Hon. Courtney 309
Boyle, Robert 85
Boyne 87, 288
Boys, Charles 18–19
Boys, Henry 305
Braave 275
Brace, Edward 22, 78, 296, 487
Brace, F. 204

Bradford City 87
Bradshaw, Richard 113, 127
Bradshaw, Robert 503
Braeneil 87
Braimer, David 61
Braithwaite 70
Brake (G) 391
Bramble 398
Brandenburg (G) 479
Brandon, Finland 216
Brave (F) 410
Bravoure (F) 126, 298–299
Brazen 32, 191, 382
Brazil 12, 75, 107 108, 112, 118, 131, 138, 153, 230, 245, 269, 378, 414, 423, 427, 487, 497
Breconshire 280, 281
Breda 75, 490
Bredon 50
Bréhat I., France 88, 173, 470
Bremer, Sir James 121, 418
Bremse (G) 61, 446
Brenton, Edward 17, 288, 295, 441
Brenton, Jahleel 5, 238, 299, 433, 434
Breslau (G) 210, 379
Brest, France 13, 18, 25, 30, 68, 69, 71, 72, 79, 80, 82, 87–88, 109, 120, 126, 128, 130, 156, 172, 174, 175, 176, 178, 181, 182, 185, 192, 195, 200, 203, 221, 242, 244, 269, 270, 271, 300, 308, 359, 377, 380, 396, 424, 428, 430, 454, 461, 484
Bretagne (F) 296
Brett, John 120
Brett, Piercy 268
Brevdrageren 82, 89
Brian Boru, king of Munster, High King 264, 263
Brice, Nathaniel 243
Bridei mac Bile, King of the Picts 336
Bridges, John 113
Bridgewater 89
Bridlington, Yorkshire 89
Briel (D) 196
Brigandine 174
Briggs, Thomas 337
Brighton, Sussex 174, 182, 395
Brighton 83
Brilhante (slaver) 496
Brilliant 75, 89, 109, 319; (F) 205
Brin (I) 39
Brindisi, Italy 7, 8
Brine, Augustus 292
Brine, James 403
Brisac, George 417
Brisbane, Charles 27, 73, 138, 211, 333
Brisbane, James 6, 74
Brisbane, John 309, 379

Briseis 89
Brisk 89
Bristol 90, 171, 193, 330
Bristol 90, 107, 117, 338
Bristol Channel 90, 178, 344, 349, 387, 405
Britannia 90, 91, 448
Britiff, Charles 148
British Queen 325
British Transport 91
Britomart 328
Briton 91, 255
Brittany, France 25, 88, 108, 151, 172, 173, 175, 180, 182, 183, 363, 377, 484; Duke of 498
Broad, George 478
Broadley, E.O. 382
Broadstairs, Kent 443
Broadwater 41
Broadway 38, 54
Brockville, Ontario 389
Broke, Philip 423
Broke 319, 443
Brokus, John 452
Bromley, Robert 116
Bronzo (I) 86, 425
Brooke, Arthur 315
Brooke, James 151
Broom 186
Broughton, John 293
Broughton, William 370, 442
Broughty Crag, Scotland 195
Brown, Guillermo (Argentine) 303
Brown, James 353
Brown, John 244
Brown, Ralph 352
Browne, Joseph 188
Browne, Philip 361
Browning, Micaiah 148
Brownrigg, Charles 272
Bruce, Edward 239, 476
Bruce, John 349
Bruce, Henry 257, 354
Bruges 178
Bruges Canal, Belgium 323, 325
Bruiser 89
Brummer (G) 446
Brunanburh 334
Brune 91, 367; (F) 484
Brunei, Sultan of 320
Brunsbuttel, Germany 82
Brunswick 91–92
Brutus (F) 295
Bucephalus 92
Buchan Ness, Scotland 195
Buchanan, John 27
Buck, James 117

Buckingham, Duke of 241
Buckingham 92
Buckle, Claude 214
Buckle, Matthew 253
Bueleng Roads, Gulf of Thailand 217
Buena Dicha (F) 276
Buenos Aires 188, 389
Bulair, Turkey 163
Bulgaria 408
Bulgaria (G) 152
Bull, John 369
Bull, Stephen 193
Bulldog 38, 92, 182, 294; (F) 115
Bullen, Charles 488
Bullen 92
Buller, Alexander 349
Bulteel, Rowley 75
Bulzanieh, Persian Gulf 352
Bunker Hill, Massachusetts 86, 92
Buonaparte (F) 114, 166, 412
Burburata, Spanish Main 92
Burdon, George 156
Burgess, John 127
Burgh, Sir John 62
Burgoyne, General 231
Burgundy, Duke of 498
Burlington, Vermont 258
Burlton, George 270
Burma (Myanmar) 93–94
Burnaby, Sir William 297
Burntisland, Scotland 194
Burr, John 297, 315
Burrard, Sir Harry 10
Burrowes, Alexander 127, 391
Burton, James 308
Burwell 40
Bury, Thomas 418
Bushire, Persia 350, 351
Bustard 5, 94
Bustow, William 204
Busum, Holstein 94
Butchart, John 27
Butcher, Samuel 23
Bute I., Scotland 94, 193, 414
Butler, Daniel 436
Butler, Thomas 452
Buttercup 95
Butterfield, E.W. 190
Butterfield, Edward 89
Butterfield, William 223
Buzzard 95
Buzzard's Bay, Massachusetts 95
Bylandt, Graaf van (D) 191
Byng, Sir George 17, 65, 68, 95, 104, 194, 257
Byng, Hon. Henry 119, 128
Byron, Hon. John 213, 299

Byron, George 372
Byron, Richard 75
Byron 195, 196

C-7 96
C-15 96
C-24 457
C-27 371
C-34 96
Cabinda, West Africa 96
Cabo Frio, Brazil 131, 212, 383, 387
Cabot Strait, Canada 423
Cabot (US) 197
Cabrera 343
Cachalot 96
Cadiz, Spain 3, 15, 96–97, 103, 105, 111, 176, 191, 207, 233, 236, 246, 265, 291, 347, 392, 460, 464, 465, 469
Cagni (I) 31
Cadogan, Hon. George 6, 139
Cadogan, Hon. Thomas 373
Cadzand, Flanders 321
Caen, France 182
Caesar 97, 320
Cagliari, Sardinia 97, 274, 309, 414, 474
Caicos 328
Caio Duillio (I) 457
Ca-Ira (F) 205
Cairndale 97
Cairn-na-Burgh Castle, Treshnish Is., Scotland 224
Cairo, Egypt 167
Cairo 282
Caithness, Scotland 98, 337, 417; Earl of (1) 336; (2) 337
Calabar, Nigeria 80, 300
Calabash (Algerine) 8
Calabria, Italy 98, 418, 431, 470
Calais, France 59, 80, 172, 173, 175, 178, 221, 227, 250, 304, 322, 356, 390, 392, 429, 438–439, 440, 441, 442, 443
Calcutta (Kolkata), India 76
Calcutta 98, 120, 135, 40; (F) 69, 209
Caldagues Bay, Catalonia 234
Caldea (I) 456
Calder, Sir Robert 98
Calder 98, 285
Caledon 495
Caledonia 64, 87
Calgarian 98
Calgary (Cn) 57
Calicut, India 98, 380
California 156
Callao, Peru 99, 156
Calliope 99, 314; (F) 22
Callis, Smith 137, 159
Calvi, Corsica 132

Calvi (I) 45
Calvia 99
Calypso 99, 134–135, 140, 150, 310; (F) 97, 270
Calyx 99
Camaret Bay, France 73, 99
Camarinas Bay, Spain 271
Cambay, India 23
Camberet Bay, St Domingue 360
Cambrian 99, 450
Cambridge 90
Camel 100
Cameleon 100, 308
Camellia 27
Cameron, Hugh 122, 224
Cameronia 100
Cameronian 10
Cameroon River, West Africa 158
Camilla 211, 296; (slaver) 294
Camito 100
Camocke, George 302, 434
Campania 400
Campanula 100
Campbell, Capt. 159
Campbell, Cmdr 160
Campbell, Charles 76, 315
Campbell, Colin 146
Campbell, George 264, 469
Campbell, Patrick 5, 132, 257, 266, 324
Campbell, Robert 140, 436
Campbell 50
Campbeltown 406
Campeche, Mexico 200, 337
Camperdown, Netherlands 100
Camperdown 135
Campion 126
Camrose (Cn) 57
Canada 33, 41, 176, 198, 231, 241, 258
Canada 14, 101
Canary Islands 37, 126, 227, 236, 483
Canberra (A) 215
Cancale Bay, France 101
Canche River, France 450
Candytuft 101
Cannaday, Moses 80
Cannanore, India 101
Cannes, France 431, 480
Canning, George 117
Canning, John 90
Canning, Richard 498
Canonnier (F) 418
Canonnière (F) 262, 317, 470
Canopus 289
Cantabro (S) 25
Canterbury 110, 368, 391
Canton, city and river, China 101–102, 359, 373, 381, 488

Canton 78, 465
Cap Blanc Nez, France 234
Cap d'Antifer 327
Cap de la Hague, France 179, 180
Cap de la Heve, France 174
Cape Antonio, Jamaica 208
Cape Barfleur, France 68, 133, 181, 403
Cape Blanco 436
Cape Bon, North Africa 100, 102, 139, 282, 363, 417, 425
Cape Breton I., Canada 117
Cape Carteret. France 292
Cape Cepet 480
Cape Clear, Ireland 223, 435, 493
Cape Coast Castle, Ghana 492
Cape Corso 25
Cape Creux, France 447
Cape Croisette, France 418
Cape de Gata, Spain 8, 101, 343, 391, 434
Cape dell'Armi, Italy 477
Cape Finisterre, Spain 15, 26, 32, 36, 55, 98, 103, 149, 176, 308, 334, 458, 484
Cape Fréhel, France 127, 221
Cape Gloucester, New Ireland 429
Cape Hatteras, North Carolina 269
Cape Helles, Gallipoli, Turkey 145, 277
Cape Henry, Virginia 103–104, 467
Capel, Hon. Thomas 127
Capel 104
Cape Lopez, West Africa 451
Cape Machichura, Spain 494
Cape Matapan, Greece 242, 290
Cape Noli, Italy 205
Cape Noss Head, Scotland 434
Cape of Good Hope, South Africa 104, 109, 114, 220, 381
Cape Oropesa, Spain 112
Cape Ortegal, Spain 103, 114, 373
Cape Otranto, Italy 6
Cape Palos, Spain 80
Cape Passaro, Sicily 104
Cape Race 43
Cape Roman, 266
Cape Roxo, Puerto Rico 437, 470
Cape Roxo, St Domingue 104, 360
Cape St Mary 362
Cape St Nicolas, St Domingue 105
Cape St Vincent, Portugal 40, 50, 105–106, 198, 381, 402, 452
Cape San Antonio, Cuba 64
Cape San Francisco, Peru 156
Cape San Martin 437
Cape San Vito, Sicily 414, 480
Cape Sicie, France 83, 112
Cape Spartel, Spain 106–107, 134, 136, 196, 207, 235, 447

Cape Spartivento, Sardinia 107, 279, 280, 476
Cape Tiburon, St Domingue 99, 232
Cape Town, South Africa 104, 259, 407
Capetown 107, 140
Cape Trafalgar, Spain 91, 383, 390
Cape Treforcas, Morocco 190, 372
Cape Verde 492
Cape Verde Islands 107, 124, 243, 271, 315, 495
Cap François, St Domingue 107, 118, 168, 220, 403, 482
Cap Gris Nez, France 78, 177
Cap Haitien, Haiti 92
Cap Nicolas-Mole, St Domingue 227, 403
Caporetto, Italy 302
Cappellini (I) 444
Capponi (I) 392
Capraria, Italy 293
Capri I., Italy 202
Capricieuse (F) 373, 459
Captain 106, 107, 108, 112
Cap Trafalgar (G) 108
Carabiniere (I) 281
Caracas, Spanish Main 122
Caracciolo (I) 190
Caradoc 108, 310
Caradog ap Gruffudd 432
Carbisdale, Scotland 304
Carden, John 275
Cardigan Bay 220
Carducci (I) 290
Caribbean Sea 67, 131, 201, 243, 339, 415, 482–483
Caridad Perfecta (slaver) 286
Carinthia 108
Carleton, Sir Guy, governor of Canada 258
Carleton, John 175, 313
Carleton 258
Carlile, Charles 200
Carlingford Lough, Ireland 108
Carlisle *135, 152*
Carlisle Bay, Santa Cruz I. 345
Carmagnole (F) 502
Carmania 108
Carmen (S) 261, 265, 276
Carnarvon 85–86
Carnarvon Castle 108
Carnatian 108, 361
Carness, Orkney 337
Car Nicobar, Nicobar Is 445
Carolina, 495
Carolina (US) 198; (slaver) 168
Caroline 66, 108, 109, 351; (F) 87, 445
Carpenter, Hon. Charles 75, 238
Carpenter, James 265

Carr, H. C. 70
Carr, Sir Robert 314, 462
Carr, William 116, 312
Carrère (F) 363
Carri, France 477
Carrickfergus, Ireland 74, 109
Carrier Fleet, 1st (J) 115
Carrigan Head 109
Cartagena, Spain 102, 109, 268, 298, 381, 384, 459
Cartagena, Spanish Main 109–110, 145, 169, 331, 393
Carter, Richard 135
Carteret, Peter 157
Carteret, Philip 308
Carterett, Benjamin 344
Carthew, William 105, 383
Carysfort 10, 110
Casablanca, Morocco 318
Cascais, Portugal 268
Casement, Sir Roger 83
Casilha Bay, China 110–111
Casquets, Is, France 317
Cassandra 400
Cassis, France 346
Casteel Belgica, Banda Neira 66
Castellan, Italy 359
Castello Nuova, Cattaro 111
Castelorizo I., Anatolia 76–77, 111
Castile, Castilian 88, 172, 173, 184, 262, 355
Castilian 91
Castle, John 495
Castlehaven, Ireland 111
Castle of Comfort 62
Castone (I) 394
Castor, Spain 321
Castor 111, 321; (F) 110; (D) 196
Castro 83
Castro Urdiales, Spain 111
Catalonia 234, 291
Catania, Sicily 425
Cathcart, Robert 14, 418
Catherine of Braganza, queen 456
Cato 111, 182
Cattaro (Kotor), Dalmatia 7, 111–112, 219
Catterick 152
Caulfield, Toby 107
Cautela (S) 309
Cauveri (In) 94
Cavalière road, Toulon, France 78
Cavendish, Philip 23
Cavendish, Thomas 112
Cay, Robert 367
Cayenne, Guiana 112
Cawnpore (Kanpur), India 237
Cawsand Bay, Cornwall 332

Cecina, Italy 305
Cedeira, Spain 60
Celandine 39
Celebes (Sulawesi) 150, 214
Celeste (F) 417
Censeur 112; (F) 198, 205
Centaur 61, 112, 145, 235, 302, 406, 449
Centurion 113, 114
Cephalonia, Ionian Is 238
Cephalus 461, 479
Ceram, Indonesia 113
Cerbère (F) 487
Cerberus 5–7, 114, 177, 269, 286, 371, 450
Ceredigion, Wales 330
Cerere (Neapolitan) 139, 433–434
Ceres 28, 99, 114, 221, 403; (F) 298, 315; (D) 373
Cerf (F) 353
Cerf Volant (F) 276
Cerigo, Ionian Is 197, 238, 343
César (F) 83, 208, 240, 436; (slaver) 394
Cesenatico, Italy 5
Cestrian 114
Cette, France 289
Ceuta, Morocco 4, 356, 444
Cevita Bay, Cuba 21
Ceylon (Shri Lanka) 82, 92, 114–115, 369, 378, 410, 460
Ceylon 84, 115, 291
Cezimbra Roads, Portugal 115, 269, 440
Ch-1 (J) 445
Ch-34 (J) 20
Ch-57 (J) 458
Ch-63 (J) 445
Cha-104 (J) 446
Cha-105 (J) 217
Cha-130 (J) 446
Cha-135 (J) 445
Chads, Henry 101
Chadwick, Robert 21, 415
de Chaffault, Admiral 85
Chagford 115, 335
Chagres, Panamá 115
Chahbaaz (Persian) 352
Challenger 115, 158, 192
Chamberlain, Peter 451
Chamberlayne, Edwin 11, 364, 479
Chamberlayne, Thomas 156
Chambers, David 441
Chambers, Samuel 367
Chambly (Cn) 40
Chameau (F) 114
Champain, William 244
Champenoite (F) 385
Champion 115, 116
Chandernagore, India 76
Channel Fleet 26, 71, 95, 103, 176

Channel Islands 115, 176, 178
Chanticleer 57, 285
Chapman, Capt. 369
Chapman, William 28
Chapoo, China 116
Charente, river, France 69, 377
Charente (F) 10
Chariot Royal (F) 266
Charity 116
Charlemagne (F) 401, 453
Charles I, king of England 194
Charles III, claimant king of Spain 68, 206
Charles Edward, Prince 208, 269, 270, 423
Charles, Count of Valois 466
Charles 117; (F) 418
Charleston, South Carolina 117, 130, 410, 415
Charleston 151
Charlestown, Boston 92
Charlestown 115
Charlotte 115, 118
Charlotte Schliemann (G) 383
Charlottetown (Cn) 46
Charlton 496
Charmante (F) 3
Charon 78, 501
Charwell 258
Charybdis 110, 118, 180, 449
Chaser 118, 399
Chasseur (F) 291 (US) 405
Chatham 95, 118, 168, 302, 331, 484, 489
Chaudière (Cn) 58, 182
Chauvelin (F) 419, 430
Chawton 320
Cheap, Thomas 90
Cheboque (Cn) 59
Cheduba Island, Burma 93, 94
Chelmer 278
Cherbourg, France 17, 68, 104, 150, 171, 174, 176, 181, 182, 185, 299, 387
Cheri (F) 363
Cheribon, Indonesia 245
Cherokee 118
Cherub 356
Chesapeake Bay 3, 28, 103, 120, 239, 355, 391, 462
Chesapeake (US) 265, 423
Cheshire 45, 120
Chester, Cheshire 166, 496; Earl of 253, 330
Chester 90, 120, 137, 248
Chetham, Edward 143, 220
Chevette (F) 73
Cheyne, George 4
Chichester 238

Chiffonne 177, 351; (F) 154, 453
Child, Sir John 168
Childers 120, 293
Chile 251
Chilliwack (Cn) 58
Chimmo, William 310
China 13, 120
China Squadron 190, 495
Chingkiang, China 121
Chinhai, China 121
Chinsura, India 121
Chios Channel, Aegean Sea 146
Choshu, *daimyo* of 424
Christ 121
Christenestad, Finland 217
Christian VII 121
Christian, Hugh 147
Christianborg (Dan) 136
Christiania (Dan) 427
Christie, Alexander 220, 221
Christopher 321
Chuchi, China 94
Chuenpen fort, China 102
Chuluwan, Mozambique 494–495
Church, Stephen 467
Churchill, John, Duke of Marlborough 130
Churchill, Orford 314
Churchill, Winston 24
Chusan, China 102
Cicogna (I) 464
Cigne (F) 288
Cigno (I) 340
Cilicia, Turkey 154
Cinco Chagas (Portuguese) 62
Cinque Ports 171, 173, 438, 466
Circe 122, 286, 288, 332; (I) 340, 459, 478, 480
Cirie (I) 212
Citoyenne Française (F) 239–240
Citron Tree (Algerine) 90
City of Oxford 205
Civitavecchia, Italy 137, 294, 365
Clara (S) 236; (slaver) 35
Clare River, Ireland 388
Claridge, Charles 230
Clark, William 29
Clarke, Henry 229
Clarke, Robert 9
Clavell, John 492
Clayoquot (Cn) 122
Cleen Harderwyk (D) 490
Cleland, John 259, 295
Clematis 428
Clements, John 368
Clements, George 394
Clements, Michael 109, 341
Cleopatra 21, 122, 123, 230, 320, 425

Cléopatre (F) 332, 484
Clephane, Robert 5
Clere, Sir John 337
van Cleve-Ravenstein, Philip 322
Clevland, William 292 448
Clifford, Augustus 461, 479
Climene (I) 402, 479
Climmo Island, China 418
Clinch, Timothy 67, 338
Clinker 177
Clinton, Lord 194
Clinton, Sir Henry 231
Clio 123, 188, 296, 447; (I) 212, 394, 472
Clive, Robert 76, 121, 206
Clontarf, Ireland 123
Clorinde (F) 185, 275
Clover Bank 443
Clyde 123, 352
Cnut, King of England 124, 330
Coastal Command, RAF 177
Cochrane, Lord 26, 69, 234, 249, 393, 434–435
Cochrane, Hon. Sir Alexander 288, 462
Cochrane, Sir Thomas 245, 320
Cochrane 124
Cock, William 273
Cockburn, George 119–120, 298, 364, 412
Cockchafer 452
Cocos I. 454
Codrington, Christopher 287
Codrington, Sir Edward 311, 457
Codrington 443
Coetquen (F) 222
Cog Edward 321
Cogge de Flandre (Flemish) 392
Coghlan, Jeremiah 384, 487
Colaba, India 124, 333
Colby, Stephen 12
Colchester 124
Col de Balaguer, Catalonia, Spain 124
Cole, Christopher 66
Cole, Francis 386, 488
Coleman, William 209
Coleraine, Ireland 148
Colibri (F) 293, 362
Collard, Valentine 157, 442, 485
Collier Francis 146, 288, 351, 497
Collier, Sir George 101, 111, 263, 298, 348, 368, 379, 411, 450, 485
Collingwood, Cuthbert 106
Collins, John 396
Collins, Richard 396
Colombe (F) 156, 324
Colombo, Ceylon 115
Colon, Majorca 384
Colonia, Rio de la Plata 124
Colossus 125

Colpoys, John 391
Colpoys 125
Colsay 328
Columbia 125
Columbine, Edward 421
Columbine 78, 125
Colville, Sir John 241
Combined Fleet (French and Spanish) 98
Comet 125, 205, 296, 471
Comète (F) 73
Commandos, British 24, 271
Commendah, Ghana 126, 210
Commode (F) 234
Comoro Is 117
Company of Scotland 145
Compas (F) 85
Comte d'Artois (F) 78
Comte de Giraldin (F) 302
Comte de Gramont (F) 259
Comte de Revelle (F) 493
Comte de St Florentine (F) 2
Comte de Toulouse (F) 155, 493
Comtesse d'Hambourg (F) 99
Comtesse Laure (F) 450
Compton, William 267
Comus 126, 473
Conan IV, Count of Brittany 171
Conceicao (slaver) 423
Concepcion (S) 342, 393, 420
Concord 126
Concorde 116, 126; (F) 75, 89, 251, 298, 362, 403
Condé de Chincan (S) 388
Condon, David 222
Coney, William 347, 391
Confederacy (US) 391
Confiance 112, 126; (F) 251, 271, 482
Confiante (F) 232
Confidencia (slaver) 267
de Conflans, Admiral 105, 421
Conflict 266, 324, 441
Confucius (F) 500
Congalton, Andrew 83
Congo River 26, 85, 125, 126–127, 356, 497
Congress (pirate) 383
Congresso (slaver) 497
Conil Bay, Spain 240
Conn 127, 396
Connaught, Ireland 238
Connecticut River 127
Connetable (F) 118
Conqueror 137, 189, 469
Conquest 273
Conquet Roads, France 341
Consort 19, 127
Constable, Charles 347

Constance 127; (F) 122, 410
Constant 450
Constantinople 1, 144, 210
Constant Reformation 286
Constant Warwick 117, 127, 128
Constitution 127, 442; (US) 139, 216, 245, 263, 358; (F) 453
Conte di Cavour (I) 457
Content 112, 127; (F) 329, 361, 391
Conte Rosso (I) 480
Contest 127
Contre Amiral Magon (F) 136
Conventive 286
Conwy Castle, Wales 330
Conyngham, Gustavus 370
Coo, Christopher 322, 440
Cooban, R. 30
Coode, John 208
Cook, John 376
Cooke, Edward 453
Cooke, Isaac 206
Cooke, John 19, 334, 411
Cooke 182
Coolie pirates 23
Coombe, William 228
Cooper, Thomas 206
Coote, Charles 381
Coote (In) 4
Copenhagen, Denmark 9, 129
Coq (F) 15
Coquette 446; (F) 385, 437
Coquille (F) 101
Coralo (I) 170
Corbet, Robert 79, 290–291, 312
Corcubion, Spain 170
Corceyre (F) 6
Corcyre (F) 197
Córdoba, Admiral 106
Coregou, France 293
Coreopsis 130
Corfu, Ionian Is 5, 6, 7, 11, 130, 472, 492
Corisco Is, Gabon 80, 498
Cork, Ireland 30, 130, 207
Cormorant 112, 130, 131, 410
Cormorant IV 131
Cornélie (F) 18
Cornish, Sir Samuel 277, 285
Cornwall 90
Cornwall, Frederick 336
Cornwall, Woolfran 148
Cornwall 115, 131
Cornwallis, Earl 77, 82, 118–119, 501
Cornwallis, Sir William 99, 107, 131
Cornwallis 131
Coro, Spanish Main 131
Coromandel, India 110
Corona (F) 269

Coronation 312
Coronel, Chile 132, 189
Corsica 11, 78, 132, 168, 186, 205, 206, 238–239, 359, 410, 453, 459
Corso 132, 295; (S) 431
Cortellazzo, Italy 5
Cortez (S) 197
Corunna, Spain 62, 91, 98, 132–133, 137, 195, 272
Corvesse (F) 132
Cosenz (I) 342
Cossack 41, 133, 217, 220, 280
Costante (slaver) 212
Cotentin Peninsula, France 68, 176, 182
Cotes, James 461
Cotgrave, Isaac 380
Cotswold 328
Cotten, Richard 407
Cotton, Sir Thomas 254
Cotton 400
Coulan, China 133, 495
Countess, George 185,
Countess of Harcourt 406
Countess of Scarborough 133
Courageous 133
Courageuse (F) 112
Courageux 133, 406, 410; (F) 13, 75
de Courcy, John 445
de Courcy, Hon. Michael 110, 306, 390
de Courcy, Nevinson 306
Coureer (Dan) 89
Coureur 133; (F) 26–27
Coureur de Nantes (F) 483
Courier 133, 374; (F) 267, 502
Courier National (F) 463
Courrieur Bay, Madagascar 275
Courteen's Association 101
Courtenay, George 86, 186
Courthope, Nathaniel 374
Coutances, France 101
Coventry 134, 140, 141, 189, 419, 461; (F) 366
Cowan, Walter 123, 495
Cowdray 444
Cowslip 134
Cox, Edward 264
Crabbe, John 353
Crache-feu (F) 292
Cracraft, William 143
Cracroft, Peter 489
Cradosin 428
Crafty 134
Craig, Major General 104
Craig, Robert 428
Craigie, Robert 418
Crane 57, 58
Crash 134; (D) 374

INDEX 527

Crawley, Edmund 464
Crawley, George 238
Creagh, J.V. 60
Crècy, France 172, 438
Creole 134, 221; (F) 122, 235, 482, 496
Crescent 111, 116, 134, 135, 196, 275
Cresswell, Samuel 450
Cressy 1
Crete 135, 142, 204, 211, 280, 190, 454, 464
Cribb, Richard 67
Crimea 185, 420
Crispi (I) 213
Crocodile 135
Crocus 135
Crofton, Edward 406
Crofton, S.S.L. 387
Croker, Walter 467
Cromarty, Scotland 380
Cromarty 86
Cromer, Norfolk 326, 327, 382
Cromie, F.N. 164
Crookhaven, Ireland 302
Crookshanks, John 491
Croome 135, 426
Cross, William 168, 493
Crotone, Italy 98
Crow, Josiah 490
Crowe, Fritz 446
Crown 135
Crown Point, New York 303
Crozon (F) 484
Cruden Bay, Scotland 210
Cruelle (F) 296
Cruiser Squadron: 12th 431
Cruiser 4, 136, 185, 234, 324, 441
Crul, Willem (Dan) 302
Crusade, Second 268; Third 463
Cuba 23, 136, 261, 305, 393, 427
Cuba 183; (S) 25
Cubugua, West Indies 136
Cuckmere 320
Cuckoo *216*
Cuddalore, India 136, 291, 335
Cuervo (S) 11
Cullen 486
Culloden, Scotland 270
Culloden 137
Culmore, Ireland 148
Cumberland, Earl of 62, 137, 260, 390, 411, 492
Cumberland 76, 137, 158, 482
Cumbria 137–138, 283, 476
Cumby, William 362
Cumming, Arthur 266
Cunningham, A.B. 290, 374
Cunningham, Alexander 388

Cunningham, Charles 73, 123
Curacao, West Indies 81, 138, 166
Curieuse (F) 82, 270, 363
Curieux 138; (F) 85, 112, 235
Curlew 138, 139, 351
Curnas Bay, Spain 60
Curtis, Capt. 23
Curtis, Lucius 290, 496
Curtis, Roger 192
Curzola I., Dalmatia 5, 6, 8, 11
Curzon 182, 328
Curzon-Howe, Hon. Assheton 84
Cusack, James 390
Custennin ap Iago 330
Cutch, India 23
Cuthbert Young 372
Cutter No. 79 (Dan) 230
Cuxhaven, Germany 82, 139
Cyane 139, 263, 483; (F) 371
Cybèle (F) 29, 97, 364, 448
Cyclamen 139
Cyclops 139, 245
Cygne (F) 17
Cygnet 58, 139, 149, 314
Cynthia 377
Cyprus 463
Cyrenaica, North Africa 140–141, 222, 392, 472
Cyrène 141

D-2 142
D-4 142
D-6 142, 372
D-7 142
Daba, Egypt 141, 183
Dacres, Barrington 92, 137
Dacres, James 28, 64, 216, 369, 403
Dacres, Richard 114, 120
Dacres, Seymour 494
Daedalus 142, 277
Dagabur (I) 282
Dagerort, Latvia 162
Dainty 99, 142
Dakar, West Africa 142–143
Dale, Sir Thomas 243
Dalmatia 5–7
Dal Riada, Ireland 65; Scotland 163, 224
Daly, Cuthbert 125
Damaon, India 143
Dame Ambert (F) 267
Dame de Grace 199
Dame Ernouf (F) 138
Damme, Flanders 321
Dampo (I) 320
Danabyu, Burma 93
Danae 143, 221; (F) 5, 101, 430
Dance, Nathanial 373–374

Dandolo (I) 425
Danube River 192
Danzig, Prussia 143
Daphne 143, 144, 255, 352; (F) 22
Darby, George 176
Darcy, Francis 204
D'Arcy, Edward 67
D'Arcy, J. 146, 254
Dardanelles 64, 144–145, 162, 163, 211, 379, 472
Da Reccio (I) 161
Dar-es-Salaam, Tanzania 145
Darien, Panama 145
Daring 145
Darkdale 145
Darling 300
Darrel, Nathaniel 260
Dart 145, 146, 324; (S) 25
Dartmouth, Devon 172, 463
Dartmouth, Lord 457, 467
Dartmouth 146, 148, 253, 338
Darwin, Australia 146
Dashwood, Charles 64, 200, 454
D'Asass (F) 216
Date Tree (Algerine) 413
Dauntless 143
Dauphin (F) 27, 154, 362
Da Verrazano (I) 477
Davers, Charles 10
Davidson, Capt. 459
Davidson, James 30, 84
Davidson, James 30, 84
Davie, John 190
Davies, Henry 12
Davies, L. 394
Davis, John 113
Davis Strait 79
Dawes, Henry 370
Dawson, George 239, 385
Day, S.M. 2
Deal Castle 440
Deale Castle 146
Deane, Joseph 73, 375
Deane, Richard 366
Deane, Robert 408
Deane (US) 243
Decade (F) 276
Decatur (US) 154
Décius (F) 260
Découverte 146; (F) 479
Decoy 142, 146
Dédaigneuse (F) 3, 334
Dedeagatch, Greece 146
Dee, River 166
Deerness, Orkney 146–147
Defence (In) 65, 97, 126, 316, 490
Defender 142, 434

Defiance 113, 147
Deheubarth, Wales 432
Deir el-Belah, Palestine 437
Delaware Bay and river 85, 147, 205, 247, 262, 295, 312, 491
Delaware 147
Delft (D) 407
Delgarno, Arthur 228
Delight 147, 178, 390
Deloraine (A) 146
De Lutti (I) 472
Demerara, Guiana 161, 344
Demerara 147
Demir Hissar (Turkish) 146, 427
Denbigh, Earl of 262
Denbigh Castle 400
Denbydale 207
Denia, Spain 147, 219, 259
Denis, Peter 154
Denman, Hon. Joseph 138, 203
Denmark 65, 79, 117, 124, 126, 129, 264, 312; King of 77
Denmark Strait 380
Dennis, James 442
Dentelle (F) 268
D'Entrecasteaux (F) 275
Département des Landes (F) 286
Deptford 42, 66, 74, 147
Derby, Earl and Countess of 285
Derby 148
Dermot mac Morrough 239
Derna, North Africa 340, 342
Derry (Londonderry), Ireland 148, 235
Derwent 421
Désaix (F) 435
Deshaies, Guadeloupe 462
Désirade I., West Indies 81, 148, 285, 345
Desire 112
Desirée 148; (F) 64, 324
Despatch 148–149
Desperate 217
Dessie (I) 282
Destimado (slaver) 157
Destroyer Flotillas, British: 2nd 310; 5th 178; 10th 181, 182, 294; 14th 246; German: 3rd 443; 6th 324; 7th 477; 8th 71, 179, 181, 224, 445; 9th 443; Italian: 11th 279
Destroyer Half-flotillas, German 2nd 343; 7th 477
Determinée 149; (F) 387
Deux Amis (F) 362
Devil's I., Ionian Is 7
Devon 90, 300, 432
Devon, Thomas 82, 89
Devonshire 137, 149, 429
Dew, Roderick 500

Dexterous 149
D'Hautpoult (F) 364
Diableto (S) 168
Diadem 149
Diadème (F) 213, 341
Diamante (I) 140
Diamond 30, 136, 149, 150, 176, 177, 195, 213, 293, 490, 500
Diamond Rock, Martinique 122, 150
Diana 150, 208, 375, 490; (I) 464
Diane (F) 85, 101, 447
Dianthus 45
Diarmait ua Conchobair 224
Diaz (I) 420
Dickins, Francis 502
Dickinson, James 317, 348
Dickson, Edward 211, 389, 453
Dictator 150, 213
Dido 72, 141, 151, 425
Didon (40) 358
Diego Suarez, Madagascar 275
Dieppe, France 118, 170, 171, 174, 175, 177, 179, 183, 304, 334, 393, 439, 440, 502
Digby, Hon. Francis 246
Digby, George 133
Digby, Henry 13, 60, 61, 308
Digby, Sir Kenelm 415
Digby, Hon. Robert 151
Diligencia (S) 150
Diligent 151; (F) 262, 370, 384
Diligente 407; (F) 99, 185216, 382, 494; (slaver) 168
Dilkes, Thomas 250, 396
Dillon, William 120
Diogenes (slaver) 265
Diomède 151; (F) 410
Dispatch 152, 185
Divisions, British: 1st 24; 52nd 254; German: 22nd Infantry 152; US 3rd 24
Dixon, Charles 475
Dixon, Edward 492
Dixon, Manley 268
Djemetil fort 401
Dobbie, Hugh 4
Dobree, Daniel 243
Docwra, Sir Henry 148
Dod, Edmund 270
Dodd, Edward 81
Dodecanese Is, Aegean Sea 152, 280
Dodman 487
Dogger Bank, North Sea 1, 152–153, 370
Dolores (S) 377
Dolphijn (D) 497
Dolphin 126, 143, 153, 231, 428, 447
Dolphin's Prize 153
Domchad, king of Munster 158
Domett 182

Domiat (Egyptian) 313
Dominica, West Indies 64, 120, 140, 154, 246
Dominica 154
Domville, Compton 16
Donald Dubh 225, 239
Donegal, Ireland 22, 293
Donegal 97, 150, 291
Dongola, Sudan 389
Donitz, Karl von 256, 428
Donmall mac Taidc 224
Donnelly, Ross 309, 345
Donner (G) 482
Dorade (F) 26, 146
Doris 25, 73, 154, 155
Dornford, Capt. 395
Dorothy Gray 154
Dorsetshire 79, 115, 154, 155
Douglas, Andrew 118, 354
Douglas, Billy 104
Douglas, Charles 375
Douglas, George 139, 352
Douglas, John 74
Douglas, Stair 303
Douglas 38, 370
Douillan River, France 125
Dous Amigos (slaver) 139
Dove 155, 370
Dove Bay, New Guinea 314
Dover, Kent 165, 172, 211, 378, 387, 438, 440, 443, 444, 501
Dover 18, 155, 493, 500
Dover Castle 155
Dover Patrol 324
Dowers, William 215, 288
Down, County, Ireland 476
Down, Edward 5
Downes, Henry 80
Downpatrick, Ireland 155
Downs, Kent 199, 394, 395, 437, 440, 441, 442
Downton, Nicolas 449
Doyle, Bentinck 266
Draak (D) 267, 497
Dragon 107, 156, 198, 242; (F) 99
Dragonfly 161
Drake, Sir Francis 62, 96, 109, 132, 156, 262, 268, 317, 381, 402
Drake 82, 156, 216, 406, 475
Dreadful 175
Dreadnaught 157, 265
Dreadnaught Prize 157
Dresden (G) 189, 251
Drew, Andrew 198
Drew, John 114
Driver 216–217, 230
Drogheda, Ireland 239

Droits de l'Homme (F) 236
Dromédaire (F) 11
Druid 116, 154, 157
Druides (S) 127
Drumheller (Cn) 54
Drury, Augustus 454
Drury, Thomas 15, 100
Drury 57, 72
Dryad 157, 158, 185
Duala, Cameroon 158
Duart, Scotland 83
Dublin, Ireland 90, 108, 123, 130, 158, 166, 201, 217, 224, 226, 240, 254, 283, 284, 285, 306, 329, 330, 334, 384, 394, 445, 476, 491, 496
Dublin 158
Dublin Bay, Ireland 158
Dubordieu, Capt. 269
Duc d'Aquitaine (F) 165
Duc de Bourgogne (F) 452
Duc de Chartres 158; (F) 137, 496
Duc de Choiseul (F) 220
Duc d'Estissac (F) 114
Duc d'Hanovre (F) 270
Duckworth, Sir John 1, 144, 264, 265, 299, 403, 411
Duckworth 158, 182, 183
Dudley, Andrew 322
Dudley, John, Lord Dudley, 159, 195
Dudley, Sir Robert 471
Duff, George 209
Duff, Robert 384
Duffus, Lord 9
Duguay-Trouin, Capt. (F) 21, 30, 95, 134, 137, 196, 210, 211, 301, 318, 396
Duguay-Trouin 385; (F) 83, 137, 168, 337, 448
Duin, Istria 5
Duke 159
Duke of Albany 159
Duke of Edinburgh 424
Duke of Marlborough 369
Duke of York 159, 398
Dulverton 152, 353
Dumanoir le Pelley 438
Dumbarton 225, 334, 394
Dumbarton Castle 159
Dun, Thomas 330
Dunamonde, Latvia 159
Dunaverty castle, Scotland 159
Duncan, Adam, Lord Duncan 100, 159, 225
Duncan, Adam 245
Duncan, Hon. Henry 5, 24, 234, 365
Duncan 41, 56, 160
Dundas, Hon. George 24, 168, 185, 469
Dundas, Ralph 501

Dundas, Thomas 372
Dundee, Scotland 195
Dundee 2, 34
Dunedin 79, 160
Dungeness, Sussex 17, 160, 180, 214, 393, 438, 443
Dunivaig Castle, Scotland 160
Dunkirk, France 9, 80, 109, 113, 146, 191, 194, 221, 304, 316, 323, 325, 327, 328, 354, 370, 440, 442, 443, 461
Dunkirk 160, 175, 259, 493
Dunkirk Prize 160
Dunlop, Robert 491
Dunmore, Lord 403
Dunn, Richard 69, 415
Dunottar Castle, Scotland 193
Dunquerque (F) 296
Dunraven 160
Dunvegan Castle 160
Duquesne (F) 482
Duqueza de Braganza (slaver) 414
Duras (F) 75
Durazzo (Durres), Albania 8, 146, 150, 493
Durazzo (I) 402
Durban, South Africa 31
Durbo (I) 192
Durell, Thomas 264, 415
Durham, Sir Philip 22, 215, 363, 385
Dursley, Lord 336, 404
Dursley Galley 161
Dvina River, Russia 60
Dwarf 158, 161
Dyfed, Wales 330, 432

E-1 162
E-2 163
E-3 162
E-7 162
E-8 162
E-9 162
E-11 162, 163
E-12 163
E-13 163
E-14 163, 379
E-15 164–165
E-16 164
E-19 164
E-20 164
E-22 164
E-23 164
E-34 164
E-35 164
E-38 164
E-40 165
E-42 165
E-45 165

E-52 165
E-54 165
Eagle 6, 7–8, 60, 79, 140, 152, 165, 166, 202, 282, 350, 374; (slaver) 95; (US) 258
Eaglet 165, 381
Ealdred, Bishop of Worcester 389
Earl of Peterborough 302
Earn Islands, Ireland 30
Earnest 166
East Africa 84, 91, 125, 214, 265, 301, 463, 491
East Anglia 327, 329
East Asiatic Squadron (G) 132
Eastern Fleet 115, 161
East India Company 13, 76, 101, 117, 124, 143, 167, 168, 206, 245, 249, 252, 257, 300, 301, 306, 320, 335, 343, 350–352, 370, 371, 374, 448, 449, 450, 452, 459
East Indies (Indonesia) 29, 137, 142, 155, 161, 214, 291, 331, 333, 385, 386, 410, 416, 487
East Indies squadron 278, 442
Easton 493
Ecgfrith, King of Northumbria 319
Echmarcach, king of Galloway and Man 158, 240, 283
Echo 104, 152, 166, 425; (D) 345, 455; (slaver) 491
Echoué (F) 254
Eckholdt (G) 398
Eckness, Finland 29
Eclair 166, 257; (F) 204, 264, 292
Eclipse 152, 275
Ecureuil (F) 190, 315
Eddercop (Dan) 277
Eddystone I., English Channel 179
Eden 351
Edgar, King of England 166
Edgar the Aetheling 417
Edgar 213
Edge, Joseph 314
Edgecumbe, Hon. George 259
Edgell, Henry 426
Edinburgh, Scotlan 194, 357
Edinburgh 24, 166, 397
Edmondston (Cn) 59
Edmondstone, William 402
Edsall (US) 146
Edward the Confessor, King of England 166
Edward I, King of England 77, 193, 339, 417
Edward II, King of England 285, 417
Edward III, King of England 77, 94, 172, 193, 321, 439
Edward IV, King of England 201, 382, 430, 439, 494

Edward VI, King of England 201
Edward, Prince, son of Henry VI 493
Edward Balliol, king of Scots 253, 353
Edward (F) 426–427
Edward Bonaventure 342, 445
Edwards, Frederick 252
Edwards, Richard 137
Edwards, Sampson 31
Edwin, King of Northumbria 283, 329
Eendracht (D) 500
Egalité (F) 60
Egeo (I) 246
Egeria 166, 349
Egerness, Norway 460
Egeroe, Norway 386
Egersund, Norway 167, 318
Egerton, George 76, 502
Eglinton 327
Egmond, Netherlands 225
Egmont 157, 349
Egret 346
Egypt 1,2, 3, 13, 14, 100, 167, 213, 279–280, 294, 311, 316, 356, 408, 452
Egypt (F) 227
Egyptienne 267; (F) 228, 338, 428
Eiachnae mac Baetan, King 283
Eilaf (or Eglaf) 432
Eilean Donan Castle, Scotland 225
Einar Wry-mouth, Jarl of Orkney 261
Ekins, Charles 126
Ekins 182, 328, 329, 444
Ekoma, South Africa 503
Elba I. 168, 215
Elbe River, Germany 94, 148
Eleanore Woermann (G) 61
Electra 168, 245, 458
Elephant 168; (F) 120
Elise (F) 276
Eliza 168; (F) 150, 201, 358
Elizabeth I, Queen of England 174–175
Elizabeth 7, 168; (S) 64; (F) 268, 467
Ellengreg Castle, Scotland 253
Elliott, Hon. George 301, 309
Elliott, John 109, 231, 240
Elliott, Stephen 117
Elliott, William 462
Ellis, John 14
Elmina, Ghana 210, 492
Elmae, Sardinia 414
Elobey Is, West Africa 80
Elphinston, John 387
Elphinstone, Sir George, Lord Keith 1, 104, 241, 469, 491
Elphinstone, Charles 213
Elphinstone (In) 351
Els (D) 490
Eltham 169

Elton, Jacob 21
Emblana, Nigeria 315
Embuscade (F) 86, 147, 390, 486
Emden, Germany 169
Emden (G) 454
Emerald 112, 169, 240, 265, 317, 419
Emeraude (F) 430
Emilieu (F) 137
Emo (I) 318
Empire MacAlpine 56
Empire Wave 41
Emprehendador (slaver) 497
Empress 139
Empress of Britain 169
Ems River, Germany 3, 122, 148, 191, 219, 285, 393
Enchantress 170
Encounter 127, 245, 422, 500
Endau, Malaya 462
Endeavour 453
Endelau, Denmark 188
Endymion 156, 170
Enfant Prodigue (F) 169
Engadine 139
Engageante (F) 116
England, Thomas 150, 402
English Channel 8, 9, 13, 18, 19, 32, 76, 77, 86, 91, 95, 96, 99, 113, 114, 123, 133, 134, 137, 146, 147, 148, 165–183, 188, 191, 196, 198, 199, 204, 206, 209, 217, 219, 220, 229, 241, 246, 256, 263, 266, 267, 285, 291, 297, 301, 332, 334, 335, 336, 339, 344, 349, 350, 355, 356, 359, 366, 376, 385, 390, 394–395, 412, 413, 419, 421, 437, 438, 443, 448, 458, 461, 464, 466, 467, 470, 479, 484, 491, 492, 493, 498, 503
Enigma decryption 38, 79, 87, 209, 271, 290, 353
Enquiry 183
Enrico Toti(I) (I) 470
Enson, Robert 128
Enterprise (Cn) 71, 183, 225; (US) 87
Entreprenant (F) 246, 395, 463
Entreprenante 183
Eole (F) 338, 428
Epervier 183; (F) 114, 167, 188
Epicharis (F) 15
Epreuve (F) 315
Era 335
Erebus 178, 183, 324, 325, 425
Eridge 183–184, 227, 228
Ermelinda (slaver) 491
Erne 184, 390
Erqui, France 177
Erskine, Robert 491
Escapade 56

Escape Creek, China 184
Escarboucle (F) 240
Escort 32, 184, 310
Escort Groups: 2nd 56, 58, 436; 5th 346; 23rd 271; 26th 313
Esk 184
Eskdale (Norwegian) 180
Eskimo 94 (Cn) 181, 182, 458
Esmeralda (S) 299
Especulador (slaver) 168
Esperance (F) 28, 85, 345, 423, 452, 467, 478
Esperanza 6; (S) 261, 271; (slaver) 435
Espero (I) 279
Espiègle 296, 352, 374; (F) 214, 238, 332, 454
Espion 184; (F) 270, 490
Espoir 139, 184, 314, 433; (F) 461
Esquimault (Cn) 184
Essex 185; Earl of 63, 381
Essex 185; (US) 13, 356
Essex Prize 185
Essington, William 60
Essington 182
Essiquibo, Guiana 161
Estafette (F) 290
d'Estaing, Comte (F) 213, 405, 406, 415
Estonia 108, 310
Etaples, France 441, 442
Ethalion 185, 308
Etna (F) 293
Etoile (F) 34, 149, 185, 225
Etonnant (F) 298
Etourdie (F) 365
Eudo of Porhoet 171
Eugenie (F) 305
Eupatoria, Crimea 185
Euphrates River 296
Euro (I) 140
Europa (D) 404
Europe 87, 403, 445–446
Eurotas 185
Euryalus 78, 186, 446, 469
Eurydice 116, 186
Eustace the Monk 438
Euterpe (I) 402
Evans, Andrew 435
Evans, John 113
Eveille (F) 31, 213, 392, 464
Eveleigh, John 134
Everitt, Charles 27
Everitt, Michael 395
Ewen, King of the Isles 284
Excellent 5, 106, 186, 393
Exertion 186
Exe 57
Exeter, Devon 186

Exeter 75, 245, 389
Exmoor 42, 186, 326
Exmouth, Lord (see Pellew, Edward)
Exmouth 186, 324
Expedition 110, 186; (F) 375–376
Experiment 101, 117, 186, 187, 265
Express 288, 348
Eyre, George 383, 412, 434
Eystein, King in Dublin 158

F-9 (G) 408
Faaborg (Dan) 91
Faa di Bruno (I) 223
Facteur de Bristol (F) 368
Faeroe Islands 81, 109, 217, 424, 488
Fahie, Charles 364
Fahie, William 349
Fairborne, Sir Stafford 97, 302, 323
Fairfax, William 13, 26
Fairfax, Robert 395
Fairfax 486
Fair Isle 79
Fair Rosamond 188
Fairy 188, 221, 485
Faisant (Dan) 370
Falcon, Gordon 139
Falcon 177, 188, 318, 324, 347, 402
Falkland, Viscount 227
Falkland 189, 313
Falkland Islands 61, 188–89, 251
Falmouth, Maine 189
Falmouth 189, 352, 386
Fama (Neapolitan) 139, 433, 434 (S) 236
Fame 47, 50, 147, 181, 190, 393
Fame Prize 448
Fanfaron (F) 169
Fanshaw, Henry 212
Fanshawe, Edward 217, 220
Fantome 190
Farasina, Istria 7
Far Eastern Squadron (G) 132; 189,
Farmer, George 375
Farnborough 190
Farndale 190, 328
Faro, Portugal 183, 212
Farquhar, Arthur 29, 320
Fastnet Rock 256
Fatshan Creek, China 190
Fauconberg, Bastard of 250
Faulkes de Breaute 284
Faulkner, Samuel 18, 476
Faulknor, Jonathan 404, 484, 490
Faulknor, Robert 75, 81, 288, 502
Faulknor, William 128
Faulknor 29, *152*, *190*
Faune (F) 211
Favignana, Italy 425

Favorette (F) 292
Favori (F) 232
Favourite 3, 188, 190, 464, 467; (F) 15, 245, 269
Fawler, John 437
Fayal, Azores Is 63, 345, 361
FC-01 (G) 476
Fearless 32, 191, 226, 280
Fécamp, France 123, 171, 173, 177, 182
Fée (F) 430
Feilding, Charles 191
Felicidade (slaver) 491
Felicité (F) 262, 491
Felix (F) 18; (S) 64
Felixburg, Latvia 458
Feliz (S) 11; (slaver) 496
Fellowes, Edward 11
Fellowes, Richard 469
Fellowes, William 381
Fencer 399
Fenix (S) 222
Fennel 58
Fenner, George 62
Fenton, Edward 413
Ferguson, George 374
Ferme (F) 347
Fernie 178
Ferraris (I) 41
Ferret 191, 261, 423
Ferreter 191
Ferris, Abel 496
Ferris, Solomon 15
Ferris, William 75, 82, 208, 230, 251
Ferrol, Spain 11, 18, 98, 191
Fiachnae mac Baetan, king 65
Fidèle (F) 124, 294
Fidelity 49, 367
Fidellee (F) 489
Fife, Scotland 60, 195
Fifi 259
Figg, William 12
Fiji 192
Fiji *135*
Finale, Liguria 353
Findhorn 422
Fine (F) 304
Fingal, king of Man and the Isles 283
Finisterre, Spain 2, 83, 98, 114, 126, 247, 276, 298, 381, 392
Finnis, Frank 203
Fiorentina (S) 265
Firebrand 192
Fire Bredre (D) 166
Firedrake 29, 49, 192
Firefly 216–217
Firme (S) 98; (slaver) 153
Firme Union (S) 168

Firmeza (slaver) 497
Firth of Clyde, Scotland 159, 209, 334, 384, 394, 462
Firth of Forth, Scotland 193–195, 329, 417
Firth of Tay, Scotland 159, 209
Fisalia (I) 232
Fish, John 385
Fish Bay, West Africa 232
Fisher, George 423
Fishguard, Wales 410
Fis(h)guard 99, 138, 195, 236, 490
Fishtown, Nigeria 315
Fiskerton 195
Fitton, Michael 191, 20, 331, 360
FitzGerald, Maurice 239
FitzGerald, Thomas 274
Fitzmaurice, Capt. 472
Fitzpatrick, Richard 402, 403
Fitzroy, Lord Augustus 264–265
Fitzroy 195, 196
FitzStephen, Robert 239
FitzWilliam, Sir William 174, 440
Fiume, Istria 7
Fiume (I) 290
Fladstrand, Denmark 143, 196
Flamborough 196, 225
Flamborough Head, Yorkshire 28, 464
Flamborough Prize 196
Flamer 150
Flamingo 94
Flanders, Flemings 166, 184, 209, 321, 322, 324, 325, 356, 392, 432, 433, 443, 468
Flèche (F) 485
Fleetwood 4, 196
Fletcher, John 231
Fleur de Lys 41; (F) 220
Flibustier (F) 65, 459
Flirt 443
Flodden Field 109
Flora 116, 169, 196, 197, 309, 379, 490
Flor de Loanda (slaver) 394
Flor do Mar (S) 361
Flore (F) 5, 269, 355
Flores, Azores Is 62
Floria 246
Florida 216, 302
Florissant (F) 92
Florvag, Norway 331
flota (Spanish treasure convoy) 62, 63, 96, 97
Flower de Luce 174
Flower-pot (Algerine) 9
Flushing, Netherlands 8, 336, 390, 419, 489
Flutto (I) 425
Fly 197, 349

Flying Fish 70, 197, 449
FM-06 (G) 479
Fodeh Cabbah 203
Fodeh Sillah 204
Fogg, Christopher 75
Foggia, Italy 8
Foldafjord, Norway 446
Foley 57
Folgore (I) 61
Foljambe, John 347
Folkstone, Kent 172
Folkstone 197
Foochow, China 378
Foote, Charles 66
Foote, Edward 315, 419
Forbes, Edwyn 85
Forbes, Robert 316
Forbin, Chevalier de (F) 137, 194, 394–395
Force B 281; Force H 79, 97, 107, 184, 190, 279–281, 296; Force K 61, 281, 472; Force Q 61
Ford, John 403
Foresight 143, 197, 198, 282, 385
Forester 58, 182
Forfar 35
Formidable 198, 236, 244, 289, 290, 401; (F) 242; (slaver) 95
Formosa (Taiwan) 198
Forrest, Arthur 112
Forrest, Thomas 371, 483
Forsyth, William 315
Fort Beausejour, Nova Scotia 198
Fort Brissoton, St Domingue 403
Fort Callartes, Cartagena, Spain 384
Fort Capuzzo, Cyrenaica 140
Fort Churchill, Hudson's Bay 231
Fort Désaix, Martinique 289
Fort Diamond 169
Forte 430; (F) 29, 453
Fort Erie, New York 258
Fortescue, William 227
Fortescue 199
Fort Gustafvard, Hango Head, Finland 198
Fotheringham, Patrick 200
Fortified Island, India 278
Fortitude 132, 198
Fort Izzedin, Crete 135
Fort Louis, Guadeloupe 215
Fort Louis, West Africa 492
Fort Marrack, Java 245
Fort Matilda, Guadeloupe
Fort Mifflin, Delaware Bay 147
Fort Moultrie, Charleston 17
Fort Nelson, Hudson's Bay 231
Fort Nurasier, Kathiawar, India 250
Fortone River, Italy 7

Fortriu, Scotland 417
Fort Royal, Martinique 198, 287, 288
Fort Schlosser, New York 198
Fortunale (I) 340
Fortune 199, 280; (F) 148, 197, 453
Fortunée (F) 276
Forward 144, 199
Fort William, Calcutta 76
Foudroyant 14, 71, 268, 272; (F) 22, 103, 107
Fougeux (F) 493
Fouine (F) 454
Foul Point, Madagascar 275
Fowey 21, 32, 177, 199, 200, 391, 501
Fox, Cecil 477
Fox, Thomas 70
Fox 93, 142, 188, 200, 276, 379, 425, 453, 473
Foxhound 29
Foyle Bank 178
France, French 56, 65, 71, 88, 120, 122, 143, 171, 188, 205, 212, 225, 236, 254, 293, 298, 311, 370, 416, 421, 439, 440, 498
Franconia 200
Français (F) 318
Franchise 81, 200; (F) 75, 299
Francis 200, 204
François (F) 21
Françoise (F) 395
Franctireur 327
Frankland, Gilbert 368
Frankland, Thomas 393
Franklin (F) 380
Fraser, Henry 416
Fraser, Ian 416
Frederick, Thomas 151, 205, 478
Frederickscoarn (Dan) 126
Fredericksvaern, Norway 316
Frederikshamn, Finland 217, 371
Freetown, Sierra Leone 19, 340, 354
Freija 201; (Dan) 311
Fréjus, France 12, 294, 451
Frélon (F) 381
Fremantle, Charles 235
Fremantle, Thomas 6–8, 235, 264
Fremantle, Australia 161
French, George 232
French Ruby 17
Frenchtown, Virginia 119
French Victory 336, 428
Friedland (F) 436
Friesland, Netherlands 345
Frigate Bay, St Kitts 405
Fripon (F) 158
Friponne (F) 111
Frodsham, John 17, 210

Frolic 201; (US) 337
Frost, Capt. 305
Fubuki (J) 462
Fuengirola, Spain 355
Fuerte (S) 465
Fuerte de Gibraltar (S) 295
Fulminante (F) 184
Fulmine (I) 61
Furet (F) 233, 487, 497
Furie (D) 426
Furieuse 201, 461; (F) 85, 299
Furious 236, 255, 282, 467, 473
Furness, Lancashire 201
Fury 78, 125, 152, 192, 201, 397
Fyffe, John 383

G-2 202
G-13 202
G-41 (G) 254
G-42 (G) 443
G-85 (G) 443
G-88 (G) 324
G-132 (G) 163
G-194 (G) 230
GA-45 (G) 152
Gabbard, North Sea 202
Gabbiano (I) 383, 402
Gabes, Tunisia 202
Gabon 202
Gabriel (slaver) 2
Gaeta, Italy 139, 202
Gage, William 73, 460
Gaieté (F) 127
Galatea 2, 202, 203, 275, 363
Galatée (F) 185, 230
Galen, Johann van (D) 264, 303
Galgo (S) 11, 135, 220, 367
Galianna (slaver) 140
Galilei (I) 304
Gallant 203, 442
Galliard (F) 387, 448
Gallinas River, West Africa 203, 306
Gallipoli Peninsula, Turkey 115, 144–145, 163, 211, 408
Gallito (slaver) 317
Galloway, Scotland 203, 224, 238, 284, 476
Galvani (I) 352
Galway, Ireland 267
Galway, Edward 158
Gambia 203, 402, 502
Gambia 71
Gambier, James, Lord 69, 129
Gamla Carleby, Finland 204
Gamo (S) 435
Ganges River, India 76, 237
Ganges 204, 442; (slaver) 212

Ganilly 182
Gannet 204
Ganteaume, Rear-Admiral (F) 99, 447, 453
Gardiner, Arthur 103
Gardiner, John 167
Gardner, Sir Alan 11, 216–217, 277
Gardner, Alan Hyde 114
Gardner, Roddam 403
Garforth, Edward 289, 349
Garibaldi, Giuseppe (I) 303
Garibaldi (I) 426
Garigliano River, Italy 208
Garland 19, 204
Garlies, Lord 215
Garonne (F) 341
Garrety, James 177
Garry 154, 204
Garth, Thomas 7
Garth 326, 327
Gartnait 476
Gascony, France 208
Gaspé Bay, Canada 375
Gaspe 204
Gate *Pa*, New Zealand 205
Gatineau (Cn) 58, 182
Gauloise (F) 234
Gavriil (R) 123, 256, 484
Gayton, George 392
Gawen, William 232
Gaza, Palestine 205
Geary, Francis 71, 120
Gedania (G) 79
Gela, Italy 425
Gell, John 304
Gemaizeh, Sudan 205
General Armstrong (US) 361
General Belgrano (Argentine) 189
Général Brune (F) 19
Général Dumouriez (F) 354
Général Ernouf (F) 67, 384, 467
Général Lally (F) 196
Général Leveau (F) 296
General Monck 118, 205
General Washington (US) 118
Généreux (F) 14, 203, 263
Genie (F) 219
Genista 43, 205; (F) 275
Gentille (F) 199, 221
Genoa, Genoese 24, 73, 88, 91, 173, 174, 184, 204, 205–206, 322, 345, 385, 430, 469, 477
Genua (G) 167
George, Rupert 375
George 206
George and Molly 206
Georgiana 177

Geraldine 127
Germaine 206
Geranium 56
German Bight (also Heligoland Bight) 16, 294
Germany 225, 272, 274, 406, 409, 439
Gheriah, India 206, 386
Giada (I) 282
Gibraltar, Spain 22, 29, 31, 41, 42, 59, 96, 97, 103, 106, 107, 113, 134, 135, 149, 151, 155, 184, 190 196, 203, 206–207, 222, 225, 226, 256, 257, 278, 279–282, 285, 296, 299, 300, 347, 354, 358, 372, 373, 374, 391, 404, 444, 447, 496
Gibraltar 207; (S) 22
Gibraltar Bay, Spain 15, 206, 207, 434
Gibraltar Prize 207
Gidoin, John 271
Gier (D) 345, 497
Giffard, George 401
Giganta (S) 384
Gigha Island, Scotland 254
Gilchrist, James 430
Gill, Charles 335
Gilli, Jarl of the Hebrides 123, 283
Gilolo, Indonesia 408
Gilt Lime Tree (Algerine) 16
Ginginhlovo, South Africa 503
Gioberti (I) 426
Giovanni Berta (I) 140
Giovanni delle Banda Nere (I) 106
Gipsy 207, 208
Girafe (F) 364
Gironde River, France 10, 11, 179, 208, 341, 355
Gironde (F) 83
Giulia Nova, Italy 7
Giulio Cesare (I) 374
Giuppana, Dalmatia 7
Giuseppe Garibaldi (I) 480
Gladiolus 33, 39, 41, 178
Glaisdale 180
Glasgow 71, 92, 132, 208, 251
Glass, Frederic 204
Glatton 209
Glauco (I) 36, 496
Gleaner 209
Glen, Nisbet 177
Glen 209
Glenans, France 490
Glenavon 489
Glengyle 455
Glenmore 209
Globe 117
Gloire (F) 12, 90, 111, 221, 225, 267, 297, 302, 341, 491
Glorieux (F) 120, 216

Glorioso (S) 253, 491
Glorious 209
Glory 209, 246, 314
Gloucester 135, 140, 209, 210, 279, 301, 374; Duke of 439
Gloucestershire 389
Glover, Bonovrier 107
Glowworm 210
Gluckstadt, Germany 148
Gnat 210
Gneisenau (G) 36, 37, 123, 178, 189, 209, 385
Goa, India 449
Goate, William 139
Goathland 180
Godavari (In) 422
Godfred, King of Man 284
Godfrey Haraldsson, king of the Isles and Man 143, 224, 283, 329–330, 432, 491
Godred Crovan, king of the Isles and Man 158, 283–284
Godred, Olaf's son 284
Godwin, son of Harold II 90
Godwine, Earl 166
Goeben (G) 210, 379
Goeland (F) 347, 360, 451
Gold Coast 201, 210
Golden Grove 92
Golden Horse (Algerine) 8–9, 413
Golden Hind (also *Pelican*) 156
Goldfinch 210
Goleta Castle, Tunis 474, 496
Golfe de Juan 91
Goliath 145, 210, 211, 316
Gombroon, Persian Gulf 350
Gondar (I) 446
Gonzenheim (G) 79
Gooch, Samuel 100
Goodall 92
Goodenough, James 345
Goodenough I., New Guinea 313
Goodhart, F.H.H. 162
Good Hope 132, 211
Gooding, James 70
Goodson, William 323, 388
Goodson 182
Goodwin 211
Goodwin Sands, Kent 211, 244, 443
Gordon, Charles 291, 351
Gordon, James 5, 405
Gordon, Henry 497
Gordon, Thomas 195
Gordon, Thornhaugh 198
Gore, Henry 90
Gore, Sir John 236, 291, 308, 386, 472
Gore 9
Goree, West Africa 211, 273, 41, 492

Goritti I., Uruguay 389
Gorleston, Norfolk 219
Goro, Italy 6, 7
Goshawk 67, 78
Gosier, Guadeloupe 215
Gosport 211
Gossen, Norway 251
Gothenburg, Sweden 109, 136, 490
Gotland, Sweden 162
Gould 9
Goulet, France 99
Gourly, John 97
Gower, Erasmus 291
Gower, Edward Leveson 7, 295, 298–299, 363
Gozo, Malta 278
Grabusa I., Crete 211
Grace, Percy 141
Gracieuse 211–212; ((F) 81, 390
Graciosa, Azores 62, 63
Grado, Italy 5
Graeme, Alexander 458
Grafton 205, 325, 394–395, 443
Graham, W.C. 351
Graham, Edwards 13, 485
Gramont 212
Grampus 157, 212, 418
Grana (S) 114
Granada, Spain 232
Granado 175
Grand Banks of Newfoundland, 167, 212
Grand Canal, china 121
Grand Canaria, Canary Is 126
Grand Cul de Sac, St Lucia 405
Grand Décide (F) 147, 166
Grande Ile, France 176
Grand Fleet 157, 248, 331
Grand Napoleon (F) 395
Grand Port, Mauritius 290, 291
Grand Rodeur (F) 383
Grange, John 231
Granger, William 247
Gran Grifon (S) 433
Granito (I) 414
Grant, Charles 93, 150
Grant, Jasper 413
Grant, John 273
Grant, N. 108
Granville, France 175, 176, 177, 250, 493
Graph 40
Graspan, South Africa 430
Grasse, Comte de (F) 3, 118–119, 216, 288, 404, 405
Grasshopper 161, 212, 384
Gravelines, France 173, 433, 438, 440, 441, 442, 444
Graves, Samuel 416

Graves, Sir Thomas 3, 82, 118–119, 276
Gravesend, Kent 466
Gravina, Admiral (S) 469
Great Belt, Denmark 165, 186, 293, 300, 392, 424, 465
Great Heart 324
Great Yarmouth (also Yarmouth), Norfolk 100, 212, 325, 326, 327
Grecian 212, 422
Greece 100, 213, 245, 290, 304, 311, 394, 456
Greenland 38, 39, 40, 424
Greensword, Edward 465
Greenwich 213
Gregory, Charles 108
Gregory, George 403
Greif (G) 12
Grenaa, Denmark 213
Grenada, West Indies 213
Grenada 136
Grenade 25
Grenville, Sir Richard 62
Grenville 72
Grey, Francis 301
Greyhound 135, 148, 213, 214, 270, 283
Greypoint 443
Grey Shark 180
Griessee, Java 346
Griffin 29–30, 203, 214, 459
Griffith, Richard 452
Griffiths, Anselm 5, 31
Griffon 214, 393; (S) 64, 103
Grimstadfjord, Norway 471
Grindall, Richard 461
Grindall 214
Grinder 214
Grive 214
Grosser Kurfürst (G) 243
Grove 44, 214
Growler 127, 214, 329; (US) 258
Gruffyddd ap Llywelyn, King of Gwynnedd 330, 432
Gruffudd ap Rhyderch 432
Gruppo (I) 340, 481
Guadalcanal, Solomon Is 215
Guadalupe (S) 112
Guadeloupe, West Indies 10, 15, 24, 67, 75, 122, 156, 166, 169, 204, 207, 215, 224, 247, 262, 276, 296, 293, 295, 379
Guadeloupe 216, 501
Guajara, Cuba 168
Gualulco, Mexico 112, 156
Guardia, Portugal 126
Guardian 216
Guelderland (D) 487
Guèpe (F) 216, 486
Guernsey, Channel is 116, 181

Guernsey 16, 216
Guerrier (F) 133, 451
Guerrière 216; (F) 81, 83, 137, 168
Guetaria, Spain 320
Guglielmotti (I) 477
Guiana 161
Guichen, Comte de (F) 250, 288, 486
Guillaume Tell (F) 268
Guillemot 328
Guinea, West Africa 189
Guinea 117
Guion, Gardiner 345
Guipozcoana (S) 391
Guirlande (22) (F) 176, 384, 390
Gujerat, India 270
Gul Djemal (Turkish) 163
Gulf of Athens, 472
Gulf of Bothnia 204, 216
Gulf of Finland 123, 216, 482, 487
Gulf of Florida 11
Gulf of Gaeta, Italy 72
Gulf of Genoa 296, 353, 481
Gulf of Guinea 337
Gulf of Lions 294
Gulf of Matamano, Cuba 449
Gulf of Mexico 25
Gulf of Paria, Spanish Main 366, 471
Gulf of Policastro, Italy 461
Gulf of Riga 159, 162, 217, 266
Gulf of St Lawrence 44, 45, 46, 47, 122, 217, 407
Gulf of Salonica 286
Gulf of Smyrna 217, 498
Gulf of Taranto 459
Gulf of Thailand 217
Gulf of Trieste 302
Gulf of Venice 295
Gunboat no. 4 (S) 149, 298
Gunboat no. 86 (F) 441
Gunboat no. 360 (F) 154
Gunboat no. 436 (F) 69
Gunman, Christopher 336
Gunner 377
Gun Vessel no. 1 (F) 126
Gun Vessel no. 8 (F) 6
Gurkha 217, 281
Guthfrith, King of Dublin 217–218
Guyana 245
Guysborough (Cn) 218
Gwilliam, Thomas 148
Gwrmid, Viking commander 329
Gwynn, Richard 18
Gwynnedd, Wales 330
Gyldenlove (Dan) 437

H-4 219
H-5 219

H-31 219
H-47 325
H-49 219, 325
Haakon IV, King of Norway 260, 284, 394
Haarlem 219, 373
Haasje (D) 108
Haddock, Nicholas 130, 273
Haddock, Richard 362, 451
Haddock 219
Hafir, Sudan 398
Haguro (J) 414
Haida (Cn) 181
Haifa, Palestine 232, 292
Haiti 92, 431
Halcyon 219
Hale, John 495
Hale, Henry 216
Halfaya Pass, Cyrenaica 141
Halfdan, Jarl of Orkney 321
Halfdan, Viking king 158, 445
Halfmoon (Algerine) 413
Halidon Hill, Scotland 78
Halifax, Nova Scotia 31, 59, 75, 85, 86, 184, 198, 272, 314, 405, 407
Halifax 221
Halkett, Peter 25
Hall, Edmund 264
Hall, Robert 380, 497
Hall, William 29, 102
Halliday, John 355
Hallilah Bay, Persian Gulf 351
Hallowell, Benjamin 406, 412, 453
Hallowell-Carew, Lt-Cmdr 25
Halstaar (D) 138
Halstead, Lawrence 298, 357
Hamadryad 220
Hambledon 474
Hamburg, Germany 23, 196, 211
Hamden, Maine 348
Hamline, David 347
Hamilton, Lord Archibald 266
Hamilton, Sir Charles 14, 293
Hamilton, Sir Edward 449, 470
Hamilton, J. 3
Hamilton, James 253
Hamilton, Thomas 117, 128, 253
Hamilton, William 244
Hammick, Robert 314
Hamond, Andrew 147
Hamond, Graham 236, 360, 362
Hampshire 8, 230, 210, 220, 231, 265, 471
Hampton, Virginia 119
Hampton Court 220, 394–395
Hancock, John 234, 324, 441
Hancock (US) 200, 379
Hand, George 315, 409
Handfield, Philip 147, 167

Han River, Korea 220
Hango, Finland 74
Hango Head, Finland 220
Hannah 220
Hannibal 15, 220, 221
Hanseatic League 439
Hanway, James 7
Hanway, Jonas 250, 362
Happy Entrance 23
Happy Return 221, 403
Harald, King of Man 203, 284
Harald Hardrada, King of Norway 501
Harald Maddadsson, Jarl of Orkney 331
Haraldssons, Kings of Man 264
Hardarinne (Dan) 370
Hardi (F) 223
Hardinge, George 411, 416
Hardinge (In) 447
Hardy, Sir Charles 176, 217, 246
Hardy, Temple 104
Hardy, Sir Thomas 103, 250
Hardy 30, 399, 500
Hardyman, Lucius 121, 478
Hare, John 313, 482
Hare (F) 137
Harfleur, France 172, 173, 174, 183, 287
Hargood, William 74, 482
Harland, Robert 331
Harlequin 448
Harlow, Thomas 221
Harman, James 216
Harman, Sir John 287
Harman, Thomas 413, 465
Harman, William 265
Harmonie (F) 82
Harold II, King of England 90, 66, 170, 330, 468, 501
Harper, John 7
Harpy 221
Harrier 213–214, 216, 221, 355
Harriette (F) 10
Harrington, William 14
Harrington 221
Harris, Scotland 83
Harris, George 208, 426
Harris, Leonard 386
Harris, William 348
Harrison, Thomas 227, 484
Harstad, Norway 32, 331
Harston, Frank 15
Hart 222, 449
Hartland 319
Hartlepool, Durham 417
Hartwell, Brodrick 270
Hartwell, Francis 91
Harvester 51, 169, 222
Harvey, Lt-Cmdr 8

Harvey, Booty 393
Harvey, Eliab 490
Harvey, Henry 411
Harvey, Thomas 5
Harward, Richard 67
Harwich, Suffolk 125, 259, 260, 273, 316, 324, 327, 475
Harwich 492
Hasard (F) 166, 36
Hastings, Sussex 172, 180, 181, 495
Hastings, Alexander 446
Hastings, Anthony 413
Hastings, Hon. George 441, 448
Hastings 78
Hasty 222, 282
Haswell, Charles 495
Haugesund, Norway 306
Haughty 7
Havana, Cuba 22–23, 25, 27, 64, 136, 222, 393, 485
Havannah 6, 7
Havant 325
Havelock 181, 223
Havfru (Dan) 169
Havik (D) 463
Havock 6, 222, 223
Havre de Grace, Virginia 119
Haward, Charles 295
Hawk 78, 223
Hawke, Sir Edward 15, 71, 103, 241, 377, 468
Hawke 223
Hawker, Edward 293, 458
Hawker, James 239, 295
Hawkesbury (A) 320
Hawkins, Edward 149
Hawkins, Sir John 92, 262, 361, 411, 492
Hawkins, Richard 99, 298
Hawkins, William 107
Hawtayne, Charles 376
Hay, Lord John 321
Hayes, John 13, 197, 201, 277, 306, 452, 486
Hazard 122, 223, 224, 314
Hearty Knoll, North Sea 327
Heath, Capt. 65
Heath, Leopold 1
Heathcote, Edward 217
Heathcote, Henry 203
Heaton, Nicholas 413
Hebe 292, 406; (F) 271, 379
Hebrides, Scotland (See also Western Isles) 29, 98, 123, 155, 195, 224–225, 260, 384, 394
Hebrus 225
Hecla 29, 84, 225
Hector 115, 225

Hedwig von Wissmann (G) 259
Hela (G) 162
Helder, Netherlands 225–226, 327
Helena 226
Helene (F) 18
Helga 226
Helgoland 226; (Austria) 493
Heligoland I. Germany 90, 148, 262, 227, 338, 446
Heligoland Bight (also German Bight) 226, 436
Helmsdale 59
Helsinki, Finland 450
Helvoetsluis, Netherlands 23
Heming, Samuel 387
Heneage, Algernon 92, 402
Hennebont Castle, France 70
Henri Christophe, Haitian emperor 431
Henrietta Maria, Queen 89
Henriquetta (slaver) 454
Henry I, King of England 171
Henry II, King of England 171, 239
Henry III, King of England 171, 261
Henry IV, Duke of Lancaster, King of England 65, 192, 382, 493
Henry V, King of England 172, 174
Henry VI, King of England 65, 493
Henry VII, Earl of Richmond, King of England 201, 297, 322
Henry VIII, King of England 121, 193, 440
Henry I Sinclair, Earl of Orkney 424
Henry, John 85, 403
Herald 5, 102
Herbert, Lt 164
Herbert, Arthur, Earl of Torrington 66, 72–73, 90, 156, 289, 347
Herbert, Hon. Charles 18
Herbert, Edward 465
Herbert 227
Hercule 227; (F) 287
Hercules 227
Herefordshire 389
Hereward 135, 140
Herière de l'Etenduere, Commodore (F) 103
Hermann Schoerman (G) 397
Hermes 93, 115, 227, 300; (G) 435
Hermione 227, 280, 282, 358; (S) 3 (F) 75, 117, 139, 239
L'Hermitte, Commodore (F) 191
Hero 212, 227, 353
Heroine 114
Heron (F) 223
Héros (F) 221
Hervey, Hon. Augustus 242
Hesperus 42, 49, 53, 54, 222
Hesse, Prince of 206

INDEX

Heugh, John 315
Heureuse Etoile (F) 395
Heureux 227, 228; (F) 111, 356
Hewett, Sir William 127, 314
Hewitson, Lt 459
Heysham, Lancashire 218
Heythrop 228
Heywood, Edmund 126, 221
Hicks, Edmund 9
Hidden Port, Cuba 447
Highflyer 228, 352, 401
Highlander 169, 222
High Seas Fleet (G) 164, 165, 248, 331, 467, 501
Hilary 228
Hill, H.W. 423
Hills, John 227
Hills, William 337
Hillyar, James 275, 299, 315, 356
Hilton, George 489
Himalaya 447
Hinchinbrooke 228
Hind 228, 414; (F) 292
Hindman, Michael 229
Hipper, Admiral (G) 248
Hippomenes 228–229
Hirondelle 209; (F) 79, 350, 355, 361, 453–454, 458, 459
Hispaniola (also St Domingue, San Domingo, Haiti) 105, 229
Hoare, Edward 245
Hobart 114 (A) 161, 320, 429
Hoche (F) 390
Hoedie I. France 70
Hoffman, Frederick 388
Hogan, Lt 463
Hogue 1, 127
Hokoko Maru (J) 76
Holbrook, D.N. 64
Holcombe 320
Holland 134, 225, 465
Holland, Edward 415
Hollandia, New Guinea 313
Hollands Diep, Netherlands 495
Hollingsworth, John 214, 300
Hollyhock 115
Holm I., Prussia 143
Holmes, Charles 169, 222
Holmes, Sir Robert 229, 314, 492
Holmes 229
Holstock, William 229, 323
Holyhead, Wales 83, 330
Holy River, Sweden 124
Home, Richard 404
Home, Roddam 391
Home Fleet 52, 79, 159
Honduras 74, 334

Honeyman, Robert 441, 442
Hong Kong, China 78, 127, 229, 237, 450, 465, 500
Hongkong 422
Hony, George 5
Hood, Alexander (1) 287, 468; (2) Lord Bridport 242, 377; (3) Lord Hood 23, 132, 298,
Hood, Horace 324
Hood, Sir Samuel (1) 15, 150, 208, 235, 246, 276, 302, 406, 502; Viscount Hood 119, 288, 301, 405, 406, 484
Hood 79, 296
Hook of Holland, Netherlands 110, 327, 328
Hoop (D) 155, 266
Hope, David 337
Hope, Henry 170, 467
Hope, Sir James 500
Hope 21, 229, 230
Hopkins, Esek (US) 84
Hopsonn, Sir Thomas 486
Horatio 230
Hormuz Island, Persian Gulf 350
Horncastle, James 371
Hornet 102, 230, 338; (US) 344, 348
Horsey, Algernon de 422
Horta, Azores 62
Hortense (F) 29, 139
Horton, Joshua 188, 221
Horton, Max 162
Hoseason, John 237
Hoskins, Antony 502
Hoste, William 5, 6, 20, 98, 111, 379
Hotham, G.F. 343
Hotham, Hon. Henry 234, 329
Hotham, William 199, 205, 233, 369, 430, 483
Hotspur 203, 222
Houat I., France 70, 377
Houghton 448
Houlding, Anthony 395
Hound 230, 441
Houston (US) 448
Howard, Lord 439
Howard, Lord Edward 88, 211
Howard, Lord John 193
Howard, Lord Thomas (1) 62; (2) 211
Howard, Lord William 174
Howard of Effingham, Lord 432
Howe, Richard, Earl 95, 175, 176, 192, 207, 259, 314, 355
Howe, Tyringham 208
Howe 425, 41
Hoxa, Orkney Islands 154
Hoyer, Germany 230
Huascar (Peruvian) 422

Hubert de Burgh 438
Hudson, Charles 239
Hudson River, New York 231, 258
Hudson's Bay 231
Hudson's Bay Company 231
Hughes, Sir Edward 136, 285, 311 372, 402, 471
Hughes, Thomas 313
Hughes, William 358
Hugh Gallant 112
Hugh Rose (In) 289
Huilbo, Denmark 293
Hull, Yorkshire 231
Hulton, Cospatrick 485
Humber River 189, 253, 326, 327, 328, 329, 334, 501
Hummer (G) 424
Humphreys, Salusbury 265
Hundisson, Karl 147
Hunt, Joseph 478
Hunt, William 338
Hunter, Charles 253, 262
Hunter 213, 231, 310
Huntingdon, Earl of 173, 174
Huntly, Earl of 84
Huron (Cn) 181, 182
Hurricane 57
Hursley 152, 472
Hurst Castle 59
Hurworth 152, 227, 353
Huskisson, Thomas 67, 224
Husky 197
Hussar 19, 85, 231, 462
Hussard (F) 19, 318
Hutchings, Stephen 366
Hutchinson, William 228
Hutt, John 24, 192
Huxham, Henry 422
Hyacinth 232, 373, 488
Hyacinthe (F) 148
Hyaena 232
Hyde, Capt. 369
Hyderabad, Sind, Pakistan 232
Hyderabad (In) 55
Hyder Ali, Raja of Mysore 98, 278, 285
Hyder Ali (US) 205
Hydra 177, 182, 232, 233, 470
Hydrangea 39
Hyène (F) 232, 236
Hyères Is, France 10, 233, 404
Hyperion 140, 233, 280
Hypolite (F) 160; (slaver) 141
Hythe, Kent 436
Hythe 233
Hywel ap Edwin 432
Hywel ap Ieuaf 330
I-10 (J) 237

I-11 (J) 429
I-16 (J) 275
I-17 (J) 429
I-20 (J) 275
I-22 (J) 255
I-24 (J) 255
I-27 (J) 237, 255
I-34 (J) 445
I-60 (J) 161
I-124 (J) 146
I-166 (J) 166
I-177 (J) 61
I-365 (J) 313
Iago ap Idwal Foel 330
Ibah, Nigeria 315
Ibiza, Balearic Is 234, 343
Icarus 12, 58, 253
Iceland 22, 30, 37, 38, 49, 79, 84, 396, 397, 488
Ijmuiden, Netherlands 326, 328
Ilderim (Swedish) 65
Iltis (G) 179
Ile d'Aix, France 71, 121, 241, 341
Ile de Bas, France 181
Ile de Batz, France 271, 379, 459
Ile de Cezèbre, France 183
Ile de France (see also Mauritius) 311, 376
Ile de la Passe, Mauritius 290
Ile de Ré, France 14, 70, 236, 241, 354, 478
Ile d'Oléron, France 69
Ile d'Yeu, France 75, 158, 240, 241
Ile Groix, France 10, 70, 242, 363
Ile Réunion 290
Ile St Jean, Canada (see also Prince Edward I.) 217
Ilex 32, 142, 152, 425
Ilfracombe, Devon 23
Illustrious 152, 161, 205, 275, 280, 291, 457
Imart mac Arailt 240
Immortalité 177, 234; (F) 195
Imogen 32, 310
Imogene 101
Impatiente (F) 239, 308
Imperial 135; (F) 410
Impériale (F) 140
Imperialist 155
Impérieuse 24, 69, 234, 393, 423; (F) 108
Impetueux 235, 377; (F) 74
Implacable 65, 235, 365, 473
Imprenable (F) 261
Impulsive 398
Inabordable (F) 234
Ina Williams 235
Incendiary 235, 277
Inch Island, Lough Swilly, Ireland 235

INDEX

Inchkeith, Scotland 193, 194
Inchon, Korea 494
Incomparable (F) 103, 169
Incomprehensivel (slaver) 153
Inconstant 181, 211, 235, 264, 425
Inconstante (F) 347
Incorruptable (F) 29
Indagadera (slaver) 434
Indefatigable 235–236, 244, 248, 251, 401; (F) 185, 302
India 133, 167, 227, 237, 291, 337, 352, 419, 445
India 237
Indian Ocean 71, 76, 144, 221, 237, 294, 352, 357, 391, 419, 445
L'Indienne (F) 386
Indivisible (F) 235
Indo-China 278
Indomitable 282, 401, 425
Indonesia, Indonesians 161, 195, 289, 426
Indramayo River, Java 372
Industry 237; (slaver) 294
Infanta Amalia (S) 294
Infanta Don Carlos (S) 150
Infernal (F) 9
Inflexible 144, 189, 237, 258
Ingham, Capt. 12
Ingham (US) 49
Ingimund 496
Inglefield, Samuel 64
Inglefield 24, 32, 143, 310
Ingles, Cdr 345
Inglis, Charles 403
Inglis, John 502
Inis Cathaig, Ireland 237–238
Inishowen, Ireland 238
Inshore Squadron 472
Insolente (F) 235
Intrepid 32, 152, 238
Intrépide (F) 378, 485
Invade (US) 59
Invention (F) 234
Inverlyon 238
Invincible 124, 189, 238, 248; (F) 306, 438, 493
L'Invincible General Bonaparte (F) 83
Iona, Scotland 143
Ionian Is 238
Ionian Sea 210
Iphigenia 238, 290, 347, 403
Iphigénie (F) 114, 199, 270, 290, 471, 483
Ipswich 238–239, 265
Iraq 252
Irby, Charles 346
Irby, Hon. Frederick 18,19, 78
Ireland 9, 13, 20, 31, 2, 33, 34, 35, 36, 37, 38, 52, 66, 67, 74, 80, 90, 94, 96, 98, 101, 109, 110, 115, 131, 138, 142, 148, 154, 160, 169, 170, 190, 195, 196, 210, 223, 224, 226, 236, 238, 239, 261, 263, 273, 293, 286, 291, 296, 297, 302, 329, 332, 342, 349, 359, 372, 387, 388, 389, 394, 395, 396, 408, 409, 412, 431, 432, 433, 452, 476, 478, 483, 490, 494, 500, 501, 503
Ireland's Eye 239
Iride (I) 140, 223
Iris 239; (F) 11
Irish Sea 74, 158, 166, 240, 254, 270, 285, 329, 344, 346, 417, 437, 475, 493,
Irois, St Domingue 105
Iron Duke 421
Irrawaddy River, Burma 93
Irresistible 144, 240, 403
Isabella II (slaver) 413
Ischia, Italy 139, 240, 389
Isigny River, France 177, 295
Isis 211, 240, 241, 375, 386, 472
Islay, Scotland 109, 224
Islay 242
Isle of Pines, Cuba 242, 358
Isle of Wight 166, 172, 178, 180, 181, 199, 261, 358, 433
Isles of Los, West Africa 345
Islet de Ramiers, Martinique 288
Issehoved, Denmark 274
Isthmus of Panamá 145, 339
Istria 5–7
Italian Riviera 272
Italienne (F) 97
Italy 225, 343, 365, 418, 421
Itchen (Cn) 56, 242
Ithaca, Ionian Is 238
Ivanhoe 32
Ivar of Limerick 238
Ivar the Boneless 334
Ivernia 242
Izabel (slaver) 261
Izat, George 315
Izumo (J) 423

J-1 243
J-2 242
Jacinth 243
Jack 117
Jackal 84, 141, 243, 338, 455; (F) 373
Jackdaw 243
Jackson, Samuel 441
Jackson, William 243, 427
Jacobin (F) 204
Jacobites 74, 148, 194, 265
Jacolet anchorage, Mauritius 290
Jaffa, Palestine 3
Jaffna, Ceylon 114

Jaguar 243
Jakarta, Java 243
Jalouse 234; (F) 485
Jamaica, West Indies 2, 17, 75, 76, 81, 85, 107, 109, 110, 135, 148, 183, 191, 200, 238, 243–244, 261, 346, 360, 390, 403, 437, 465, 492
Jamaica 244, 395, 398, 473
James IV, King of Scots 159, 193, 224
James V, King of Scots 336
James VII and II, King 66, 68, 72, 253, 254, 274, 500
James, Prince, son of Robert III 196
James, William 216, 386, 450
James 9, 117, 413
James Fletcher 244
James Madison (US) 67
James River, Virginia 84, 429
James Stuart, Prince, The Old Pretender 194, 304, 353
Janet 244
Jan Mayen I. 79, 397, 429
Jantina (I) 468
Janus 24, 107, 244, 252, 407, 455; (F) 426
Japan 304
Jaseur (F) 84
Jask, Persian Gulf 350
Jason 122, 244, 245, 359, 483; (F) 137, 168–169, 196, 211, 226, 301, 498
Jasper 179, 245
Java 109, 150, 161, 245, 406, 446, 448, 500
Java 245
Java Sea 245
Javelin 178, 197, 246
Jeakes, Capt. 351
Jean Bart (F) 114, 310, 453
Jean de Vienne 172, 173
Jean Rabel, St Domingue 358
Jebail, Lebanon 74
Jed 53, 54, 55
Jeddah, Arabia 245
Jekyll, Edward 388
Jellicoe, John 248
Jena (F) 115, 136, 301
Jenkins, Robert 221
Jenkins, Henry 18
Jenkins, William 120
Jennings, John 362
Jérémie, St Domingue 403
Jermy, Seth 316
Jersey, Channel Is 101, 165, 180, 287, 344
Jersey 137, 246; (F) 302
Jervis, Sir John 71, 105–106
Jervis 14, 24, 246, 252
Jervis Bay 35
Jessamine 246

Jessop, J. de B. 164
Jeune Adèle (F) 378
Jeune Louise (F) 376
Jeune Richard (F) 496
Jezzar Pasha, Governor of Acre 2
Joaquina (slaver) 317
Joasmi pirates 350–351
John, King of England 171, 261, 284
John of Argyll 25
John II, Lord of the Isles 83
John Broome 246
John Gillman 246
John of Gaunt, Duke of Lancaster 88, 132, 172, 173
John Swan 458
Johnson, Cecil 94, 407
Johnson, Edward 277
Johnson, Robert 251
Johnson, Samuel 429
Johnstone, Frederick 418
Johnstone, George 11, 407
Johnstone, Henry 127
Johnstone, James 261
Joie (F) 10
Jolie (F) 244
Jolliffe, William 361
Jon, Jarl of Orkney 224
Jones, Hon. Charles 25
Jones, Daniel 197
Jones, James 73
Jones, John Paul (US) 133, 156, 423, 494
Jones, Thomas 17
Jones, William 309
Jonge Leeuw (D) 500
de la Jonquière, Admiral (F) 103
Joseph (S) 28
Josepha (slaver) 302
Josephine (slaver) 190
Jossingfjord, Norway 133
Jouba, Lebanon 74
Joubert (F) 467
Jourdain, John 343
Joven Carolina (slaver) 95
Juan Fernandez I. 22
Judith 411
Julie (F) 234
Julnar 255
Juminda (G) 305
Jumna (In) 94
Jump, Robert 447
Jumper, William 493
Junge Trautman (Dan) 82
Juniper 209
Juno 132, 135, 246, 484
Junon 247; (F) 13, 112, 200, 230, 394
Jupiter 161, 245, 247; (F) 410
Justice (F) 447

Jutland, Denmark 248, 402, 436

Kaa Fjord, Norway 237
Kagoshima Bay, Japan 249
Kaiser Wilhelm der Grösse (G) 228
Kaiyo (J) 244
Kaleh, redoubt 401
Kalemi, Lake Tanganyika 259
Kallebostrand, Amager, Denmark 91
Kaloobangara, Solomon Is 429
Kamahashi (J) 217
Kamikaze (J) 161, 414
Kandahar 249, 281
Kangaroo 22, 249, 296
Kangaw, Burma 94
Kansiala Bay, Gulf of Finland 216
Karachi, Pakistan 249
Karada, Turkey 249
Karakisi Bay, Turkey 249
Karapara *155*
Kari (J) 445
Karin River, Persia 352
Karkass (Persian) 352
Karl Arnisson, ruler of the Hebrides 381
Karlebago, Istria 7
Karlskrona, Sweden 10, 129
Karlsruhe (G) 90, 473
Kashmir *135, 253*
Katcha, Crimea 185
Katherine Galey 440
Kathiawar, India 249, 449
el-Katif, Persian Gulf 352
Katoomba (A) 146
Kattegat 21, 59, 370, 420
Katwijk, Netherlands 250
Kearny (US) 41
Keats, Richard 15, 83, 202, 332, 363
Keats 214, 475
Keeling I. 454
Keen, Hon. George 422
Keith, Lord (see Elphinstone)
Keith 325
Kelibia, North Africa 223
Kelly 135, 250
Kelvin *197, 246, 255*
Kempenfelt, Richard 250, 485
Kempthorne, James 271
Kempthorne, John 16
Kempthorne, Morgan 253
Kempthorne, William 150
Kenah, Richard 66
Kenilworth Castle 58, 183
Kenmare River, Ireland 423
Kennedy, Archibald 190
Kennet 64, 146, 250
Kenney, Thomas 386
Kent 250, 439; Earl of 173, 241

Kent 70, 76, 140, 250, 251, 264, 341
Kentish Knock 251–252
Kenya 79, 282, 482
Keppel, Sir Augustus 297, 467, 481, 492
Keppel, Colin 389
Keppel, George 208, 485
Keppel, Hon. Henry 151
Keppel, Leicester 127
Keppel 56, 400
Ker, George 177
Kerak, Persian Gulf 350
Kercher, Thomas 153
Kerkennah I., North Africa 246, 252
Kerr, Alexander 263, 478
Kerr, Charles 497
Kerr, Lord Mark 130
Kerr, William 147, 386, 403
Kertch Strait 252
Kestrel 252, 422, 456
Ketil Flatnose, Jarl of the Hebrides 306
Key, Astley Cooper 266
Khanderi, India 13, 252
Khartoum, Sudan 388
Khartoum 249
Kidd (pirate) 415
Kiel (Dan) 89, 150
Killigrew, James 130, 361
Killingworth, Thomas 415
Kilmarnock 444
Kimberley, South Africa 430
Kimberley 152, 252, 263, 429
Kinburn, Russia 252
Kincardine, Scotland 195
Kinfauns Castle 276
King, Richard 334, 342, 426
King, James 385
King, Norfolk 65
King, William 156
Kingani (G) 259
Kingfish 253
Kingfisher 7, 67, 113, 253
King George 253
King George V 79, 425, 431
Kinghorn, Fife 193, 253
Kings Island, Limerick, Ireland 267
King Stephen 254
Kingston, Ontario 259
Kingston 249
Kingstonian 254
Kinsale, Ireland 21, 25, 89, 109, 254, 274
Kintyre, Scotland 224, 238, 254, 384, 394
Kipling 141, 254, 255
Kirkenes, Norway 255
Kirkwall, Orkney 337
Kirton, Robert 302, 390
Kishm Island, Persian Gulf 350, 351
Kismayu, Somaliland 255, 429

Kitakami (J) 445
Kitchener, Lord 220
Kite 58, 300, 346, 400, 494
Kittywake 326, 328
Kiunga, East Africa 255
Kiwi (NZ) 215
Knapp, John 9
Kneeshaw, Joshua 177
Knell, William 381
Knight, John 151
Knock, Scotland 384
Knowles, Charles 136, 222, 257, 365, 366, 373
Knyvett, Thomas 16
Kola Inlet, Russia 224, 396, 400, 494
Kolangsu Island, Amoy, china 20
Kolberg (G) 153
Kolli Bardarsson, Viking King 267
Koln (G) 226
Komeet (D) 478
Komet (G) 179
Königin Luise (G) 259
Königsberg (G) 145, 226, 422, 456
Kootenay (Cn) 182
Korea 116, 304, 473
Kormoran (G) 454
Kos I., Dodecanese Is 152
Kosoko, king of Lagos 257
Kosseir, Egypt 142
Kota Tinggi River, Malaya 313
Kotka, Gulf of Finland 217
Kra Isthmus, Burma 94, 161
Krait (S) 426
Krebs (G) 271
Kreta (G) 479
Kristiansand, Norway 251 418
Kriti (Greek) 152
Kronprinz (G) 243
Kronprinz Wilhelm (G) 210
Kronstadt, Russia 123, 129, 165, 216
Kuma (I) 445
Kumasi, Ghana 30
Kunsan, Korea 494
Kuper, Sir Augustus 424, 462
Kuphorisi, Crete 255
Kusu Bay 379
Kut el-Amara, Mesopotamia 255, 296
Kuttabal (A) 255
Kuwait 352
Kwakowiak (Polish) 179
Kyholm, Denmark 188

L-10 256
L-12 256
L-55 256
Laaland (Dan) 150

La Bourdonnais, governor of Ile de France (F) 311
La Ciotat, France 479, 480
Lacedemonian 256
Lachlan (A) 320
La Combattante 328; (F) 180, 181
Laconia 256
Ladybird 140
Lady Nelson 256
Lady Olive 256
Lady Patricia 256
Lady Shirley 392
Ladysmith, South Africa 430
Lady Somers 257
Laertes 257, 273
Lafole (I) 203
Laforey, Francis 110, 177, 232
Laforey, Sir John 466
Laforey 72, 407, 474
Lagan 54, 56
Lagemen, Norway 374
Lagman, King of the Isles 224
Lagos, Nigeria 118, 257
Lagos Bay, Spain 8, 253, 257, 444
Lagosta I., Dalmatia 6
La Guaira/Guayra, Spanish Main 2, 257
La Hougue, France 114, 150, 414
La Hulloise (Cn) 59
Laigueglia, Italy 257
Lake Borgne, Louisiana 257
Lake Champlain, New York 258
Lake Huron, North America 258
Lake Erie, North America 258
Lake Nyasa, Central Africa 258–259
Lake Ontario, North America 259
Lake Tanganyika, Central Africa 259
Lake, John 442
Lalpan, Burma 94
Lambert, Henry 245, 290, 411, 495
Lambert, Rowley 192
Lambert Simnel 201
Lamerton 41, 494
Lamu, East Africa 488
Lampedusa I., Italy 342
Lampione I. Italy 342
Lancashire 218, 334
Lancaster, James 167, 349, 445
Lancaster, Robert 260
Lancaster 259
Lance, James 385, 423
Lance 61, 259–260, 477
Lanciere (I) 107, 281
Landguard Fort, Suffolk 260
Landrail 259–260
Land's End, Cornwall 176, 190
Langa, Sulawesi 26o
Langadille Bay, Puerto Rico 166

Langeland (Dan) 89
Langford, George 413
Languedoc, France 234, 260
Languedoc (F) 385
Langueglia, Corsica 132
Lannerat 350
Lanzarote, Canary Is 260
Lapenotiere, John 336
la Perouse, Comte de (F) 231
Lapwing 260, 400
La Rancheria, Cubugua, West Indies 136
Larcom, Thomas 228
Largs, Scotland 260–261
Lark 261, 283, 400, 491
Larkins, Thomas 490
Larne, Ireland 261, 476
Larne 93, 261
la Roche-Courbon-Blenac, Comte de (F) 148
La Rochelle, France 72, 121, 149, 208, 241, 261–261, 478
Larut River, Malaya 62
La Selva, 447
Las Palmas, Canary Is 37, 262
La Spezia, Italy 108, 262, 264, 426
Latona 138, 141, 230, 262, 292
Lauenberg (G) 79
Laugharne, Morgan 215
Laugharne, Thomas 13
Laura 262
Laurel 262, 465
Laurentic 263
Laurette (F) 29, 346
Lavender 263
Laverack 443
Lavie, Sir Thomas 81
La Vigie, St Lucia 406
Lawrence, Henry 134
Lawrence, James 392
Lawrence, Peter 105
Lawrence, Thomas 89
Lawrence (In) 296, 352
Lawrie, Robert 21, 122
Lawson, Hugh 365
Lawson, Sir John 16
Layton, John 303
Lea, William 390
Leader, John 302
Leake, Capt. 2
Leake, Sir John 17, 68, 97, 106, 148, 207, 360, 367
Leake, Martin 343
Leake, Richard 9
Leake, William 452
Leal (slaver) 212
Leamington 40, 44
Leander 122, 210, 263, 316; (NZ) 429

Leasowe Castle 263
Leaver, Charles 243
Le Blanc, George 300
Lechmere, Edward 274
Le Conquet, France 88, 174, 241
Leda 264, 398, 409, 441, 442; (F) 5
Ledbury 8
Lee 309, 456
Leeke, Capt. 306
Leeward Islands 10, 157, 200, 421
Lefroy, Benjamin 352
Léger (F) 5
Légère (F) 13, 25, 312, 318, 359, 426
Le Geyt, George 70, 288, 358, 437
Legge, Arthur 292
Legge, Thomas 21, 250, 415
Leghorn (Livorno), Italy 264, 303
Legion 281, 425, 477
Legouille (F) 353
Le Havre, France 9, 117, 150, 174, 175, 176, 177, 178, 179, 181, 182, 232
Le Hocquart (F) 160
Leicester 34
Leighton, Thomas 283
Leijden (D) 490
Leinster, Ireland 90
Leipzig (G) 189
Leith, Scotland 120, 193, 194, 458
Lemma Is, China 237
Lempriere, George 382
Lennock, George 382
Lennox, Earl of 193
Lennox 477
Lenox 105, 222, 264, 265
Leocadia (S) 226
Leogane, St Domingue 265–266, 403
Leonardo da Vinci (I) 55
Leopard 195, 219, 265, 401; (G) 2; (F) 45
Leopold 58
Leopoldville 265
Leotung, China 80
Lequitio, Spain 27, 321
Leros I., Dodecanese Is 152
Lerwick, Shetland 446
Les Frères Unis 408
Lestock, Richard 65, 70, 199, 391, 468
le Testu, Guillaume 317
Le Tiger 44
Letsoe, Norway 251
Leure, France 172
Levant 113, 342
Levant 139, 263, 265
Leveret 265, 338
Leveson, Sir Richard 63, 111, 115, 254
Leviathan 27, 132, 257, 265, 266
Levis (Cn) 40
Levrier (F) 428

Lewes, Sussex 172
Lewis, Mark 451
Lexington (US) 13, 344
Leyte Gulf, Philippines 355
Libau, Latvia 162, 266, 495
Libau (G) 83
Libeccio (I) 61, 457
Libera (I) 472
Liberia 79
Liberté (F) 11, 17
Liberty 266
Libre (F) 167
Libya 279
Licata, Sicily 425
Lichfield 266, 336, 390
Licorne 373; (F) 297, 386
Liddesdale 152
Liebe (Dan) 82
Liffey River, Ireland 158
Liffey 93
Lightning 266
Liguria, Italy 296, 306
Liguria (Genoese) 184
Ligurienne (F) 353
Lijnx (D) 122
Lilburne, James 67, 78
Lilizzi (I) 142
Lily 92, 267
Limbourne 180
Limerick, Ireland 267
Lince (I) 366, 476
Lindesnaes, Norway 470
Lindley, George 255, 487
Lindorm (Dan) 183
Lindsey, Lord 262
Linga, Persian Gulf 351
Lingayen Gulf, Philippines 355
Lingen, Joseph 421
Linnet 267, 425
Linosa I., italy 342
Lintin Island, China 101, 450
Linzee, Robert 411
Linzee, Samuel 311, 334
Lion 107, 143, 153, 190, 248, 268, 342, 350, 491; (F) 277, 289, 322
Lion Eveille (F) 155
Lisbon, Portjal 10, 60, 105, 127, 190, 197, 268–269, 312, 412, 432, 452, 463, 486, 496
Lisle, Nicholas 127
Lisle, William 421–422
Lissa I. 6, 269
Listerfjord, Norway 251
Lithgow, C. 60
Lithgow (A) 146
Little Belt 269
Littlehales, Bendall 406

Littlehales, Edward 153
Littlejohn, Adam 78
Little Popo, West Africa 435
Littleton, James 110
Little Victory 86, 127, 344, 386
Littorio (I) 457
Lively 61, 169, 219, 220, 236, 249, 269–270, 362, 412; (F) 350
Lively Prize 197, 270
Liverpool 32, 387
Liverpool 140, 152, 279, 351
Livingstone, Sir Thomas 384
Livorno – see Leghorn
Lizard, Cornwall 12, 17, 87, 128, 137, 158, 180, 183, 226, 251, 270, 318
Lizard 270, 379
Llanbadarn, Wales 432
Llancarfan, wales 432
Llandeudoch, Wales 432
Llanilltid, Wales 432
Llch-y-Crau, Wales 432
Llewellyn 443
Lloyd, Robert 361
Lloyd, Rodney 91
Lloyd, William 137
Llyn, Wales 329
Loades, Edmund 336
Loades, Edward 391
Loane, Frederick 416
Loango (Portuguese) 127
Lobb, William 134–135
Loch, Francis 225, 351
Loch, Granville 314
Loch Alsh, Scotland 225
Loch Broom, Scotland 208
Loch Dunvegan 400
Loch Eck 70
Loch Fada 183
Loch Glendhu 270
Loch Insh 92, 320, 400
Loch Killin 59, 182
Loch Nan Uamh, Scotland 270
Loch Osaig 155
Loch Scavaig 271
Loch Shin 271, 400
Loch Watten, Scotland 483
Lockhart, John 458
Lockyer, Nicolas 257
Lockyer, William 465
Locust 442
Lodder, Charles 401
Lodi (F) 378
Lodwick, John 214
Lofoten Islands, Norway 271, 414, 451, 484
Logie, Gustavus 243
Logie, James 75, 109

Loire 17, 167, 170, 221, 271; (F) 22, 215, 247, 296, 403
London 72, 166, 236, 250, 286, 291, 356, 417
London 271, 272, 448
Londonderry (also Derry), Ireland 148
Long, Charles 353
Long, Henry 110
Long, Thomas 490
Long Island, New York 103, 314, 451
Long Island, Gulf of Smyrna 217
Lookout 72, 272, 276
Loosestrife 53
Loraine, Lambton 334
Lord Clive 124, 324
Lord Eldon 272
Lord Keith 445–446
Lord Nelson 272
Lord Nuffield 319
Lorient, France 10, 19, 69, 70, 97, 186, 317, 329, 359, 472
Loring, John 150, 317
Loring, Joshua 78
Lorna 272
Losack, Woodley 275
Los Magellanes (S) 155
Los Negros, Manus I., Melanesia 4
Lothian, Scotland 193
Lothringen (G) 79
Lottery (US) 119
Lotus 319
Loug (Dan) 418
Lougen (Dan) 120
Lough Corrib, Ireland 267
Lough Derg, Ireland 267
Lough Erne, Ireland 267
Lough Foyle, Ireland 148
Lough Neagh, Ireland 267
Lough Ree, Ireland 267
Louis, Sir Thomas 137, 149, 299
Louis 272; (F) 377
Louisbourg, Cape Breton I., 85, 107, 266, 272–273, 405, 467
Louisbourg (Cn) 319
Loup (F) 18
Loup Garou (F) 336
Louvain 273
Loviso, Gulf of Finland 217
Lowestoffe 151
Lowestoft, Suffolk 133, 238, 254, 273, 325, 326, 327, 328, 329
Lowestoft 334, 375
Lowfield, William 69
Loxley, A.N. 198
Loyal 477
Loyalist 215
Loyalty 182

Lucas, Richard 29, 435
Luce, J. 251
Luchs (G) 462
Lucien Charles (F) 363
Lucifer 393
Lucknow (Laknau), India 237
de Lucy, Geoffrey 171
Ludlow 273; (F) 407
Ludlow Castle 273
Luft, Persian Gulf 351
Lugen (Dan) 89
Lugger no. 28 (Dan) 150
lugger no. 432 (F) 26
lugger no. 961 (F) 497
Luigi de Savoia (I) 480
Luke, William 108
Lukin, James 461
Lukin, William 377
Lumley, Henry 301
Lumley, John 301, 309
Lulworth 45
Lumsdaine, George 362
Lundy, Lt-Col. 148
Lupo (I) 135, 246
Lurat River, Malaya 273
Lurcher 316
Lusitania 274
Lusk, Ireland 239
Lutine (F) 10, 244, 361
Luttrell, Hon. John 291, 334
Lutwidge, Skeffington 350
Lutzow (G) 248, 398, 434
Luzon, Philippines 355
Lyall, William 267
Lychnis 274
Lydiard, Charles 22, 27, 138
Lydonia (US) 69
Lye, William 84
Lyme, town and bay, Dorset 179, 272, 274
Lyme 124, 274, 303, 344
Lyngoe Creek, Norway 150
Lynslager (Consul) 300
Lynx 274; (F) 203
Lyons, Edward 304, 359
Lyra 274
Lys (F) 137
Lysekil, Norway 289

M-7 (G) 436
M-8 (G) 327
M-15 437
M-23 379
M-25 60
M-26 (G) 179
M-30 217
M-31 205
M-32 205

M-33 475
M-39 (G) 181
M-122 (G) 419
M-123 (G) 419
M-133 (G) 182
M-153 (G) 180
M-156 (G) 180
M-263 (G) 318
M-273 (G) 318
M-381 (G) 484
M-416 (G) 251
M-427 (G) 251
M-469 (G) 328
M-486 (G) 75
M-534 (G) 180
M-1201 (G) 478
M-1204 (G) 478
M-1207 (G) 478
M-1701 (G) 428
M-1702 (G) 428
M-3411 (G) 327
M-4611 (G) 182
M-4618 (G) 180
M-4620 (G) 182
M-4623 (G) 181
M-6022 (G) 480
Maaloy, Norway 482
Maas River, Netherlands 250, 460
Maasnah, Gulf of Oman 289
Mabbott, William 189
Macahe, Brazil 423
Macao, China 101, 111, 453
Macao River, China 495
Macbeth, King of Scots 417
MacBride, John 78
MacCulloch, Thomas 158
MacDonald, Lt 270
MacDonald, Angus Og 29, 83
MacDonald, Colin 383, 398, 418
MacDonald, Randall 283
MacDonalds of Islay 159, 160
MacDougal, Robert 406
Macedonia (G) 210, 275
Macedonian 275
McEvoy, Robert 130, 411
McHardy, John 258
Machault (F) 295
Machias, Maine 151
Macht Haraldsson, 329
McInstry, Frederick 203
Mackay 179
McKenzie, Adam 276, 374
Mackenzie, Thomas 28
McKenzie, George 134, 185, 384, 497
McKenzie, James 22
McKenzie, Kenneth 228
McKerlie, John 99

Mackinnon, Lachlan 411
McLaverty, James 362
Maclean of Duart 83
MacLeod of Lewis 83
Macnamara, Capt. 124
Macnamara, James 78, 114, 430, 431
McNamara, Jeremiah 95
MacNeill of barra 83
Madagascar 44, 275–276, 343
Madagascar 96
Madeira 48, 139, 209, 276, 301
Madison (US) 186
Madras (Chennai), India 66, 76, 16, 402, 495
Madre de Deus (Portuguese) 62
Madura, Java 245
Maelbrigte Tusk 98
Mafia I., Tanganyika 276
Magic 111, 182
Magicienne 104–105, 133, 216–217, 231, 276, 290, 496; (F) 118
Magnanime 276, 390; (F) 98, 265, 331
Magnificent 276, 412
Magnus, King of Norway 158
Magnus Haraldsson, King of the Isles 237–238
Magog (Cn) 59
Magpie 58, 277, 436
Maguire, Rochfort 92
Mahaut, Guadeloupe 201, 228
Mahé, India 277
Mahé roads, Seychelles 453, 485
Mahé (In) 4
Mahonesa 392; (S) 459
Mahratta 399
Maida, Italy 98
Maidstone 277, 309, 390
Mainwaring, Lt 197
Mainwaring, Jemmett 10, 64
Mainwaring, Karl 86
Mainz (G) 226
Maitland, Sir Frederick 167, 169, 220, 249, 271, 376
Maitland, John 83
Maitland, Thomas 121, 249
Majestic 164, 227, 277, 316
Major, Christopher 133
Majorca, Balearic Is 27, 220, 234, 277–278
Makaronia, Turkey 278
Makrel (D) 166
Malabar, India 278, 285, 369
Malabar 161, 497
Malacca, Malaya 278
Malaga, Spain 130, 278, 391
Malaga Merchant 407
Malaspina (I) 41

Malaya 161, 27, 278
Malaya 37, 183, 306
Malays 13, 289, 408
Malbon, Micajah 377
Malcolm III, King of Scots 417
Malcolm, Charles 309
Malcolm, Pulteney 150, 453
Malcolm 39, 325
Maldive Is 237, 263
Maldonado, Uruguay 389
Malen, John 322
Malero, Ionian Is 7
Maletta Creek, Congo 127
Malicieuse (F) 75, 190, 341, 348
Malindi, East Africa 306
Mallard 441, 442
Mallow 390
Malmo, Sweden 9, 474
Malta 14, 29, 100, 104, 131, 197, 200, 245, 246, 278–283, 303, 316, 319, 343, 353, 422, 428, 431, 480, 492
Malteza (slaver) 423
Maltby, William 92, 188
Malwan, India 370
Mamelouck (F) 319, 393
Mamora, Morocco 283
Man, Isle of 203, 238, 253, 260, 283–285, 329, 330, 394, 417, 445
Man, Elias 368
Man, Robert 73, 114
Manama, Bahrain 352
Manby, Thomas 85
Manche (F) 290, 496
Manchester 280, 282
Mandalay, Burma 93
Mandarin 66
Manette (F) 154
Mangalore, India 278, 285
Manhattan, New York 314
Manica Is, Brazil 294
Manila, Philippines 113, 265, 342, 355, 453
Manin (I) 165
Manistee 285
Manley, Francis 449
Manley, John 25, 495
Manly 285; (D) 335
Mann, Robert 297
Manners, William 383
Manners 285
Mansel, Robert 16, 348
Mansell, Edward 344
Mansfield, Charles 20, 300
Manus I., Melanesia 4
Manxman 285
Maori 280, 281, 425
Mapia Is, New Guinea 313

Maples, John 346
Maplin 39
Marabou, Egypt 419
Maraquita (slaver) 502
Marat (F) 359
Maraudeur (F) 387
Marbella, Spain 184, 207
Marcello (I) 36
Marconi (I) 41, 97, 184
Mardoe, Norway 150
Mardyke, Flanders 323
Maréchal de Belleisle (F) 109, 419, 428, 430
Maredudd, king of Gwynnedd 330
Maredudd ap Owain 330, 432
Maregot, St Domingue 464
Marengo (F) 82, 91, 113, 271, 373
Marettimo, Italy 479
Margaret, Queen of Henry VI 65, 493
Margaretta (D) 131
Margarita, Spanish Main 492
Margate, Kent 443
Maria 69, 258, 286; (S) 88; (slaver) 427
Maria Antonia (S) 157
Maria Carlota (slaver) 212
Maria da Gloria (slaver) 427
Mariamne 286; (S) 452
Mariana (F) 500
Maria Reijgersbergen (D) 109
Maria Teresa (slaver) 153
Marie (F) 244
Marie de Cordelière (F) 88
Mariegalante I., west Indies 215, 286
Marie Guiton (F) 303
Mariel, Cuba 64, 147
Marie Louise (F) 381
Marie-Thérèse (F) 304
Marigold 286
Marin, Martinique 82, 150
Marinerito (slaver) 80
Marischal, Earl 225
Markham, Albert 393
Markham, John 221
Markland, John 5, 7, 94
Marlborough 286
Marlow, Benjamin 231, 428
Marmaduke 286
Marmaris (Turkish) 352
Marmora 286
Marne 286
Maron 286
Marquette 286
Marquis (F) 362
Marryat, Frederick 231, 428
Mars 131, 287, 302; (D) 301; (F) 19, 270, 329, 331
Marsala, Sicily 340, 425

Marsdale 79
Marseillais (F) 369
Marseilles, France 335, 390, 463
Marsh, Henry 492
Marshall, James 274, 442
Marshall, John 346
Marshall, Samuel 24, 26
Marshall Soult 324
Marsouin (F) 73
Marstrand, Denmak 370
Martaban 94
Marte (S) 147
Martello towers – see Mortella
Marten, Francis 26
Martha's Vineyard 95
Martin, George 240, 289
Martin, Samuel 347
Martin, Sir Thomas Byam 65, 195, 235, 365, 412
Martin, William 239
Martin 243, 247, 287, 318
Martinique, West Indies 11, 15, 64, 65, 82, 108, 138, 150, 198, 213, 265, 287–288, 331, 341, 377, 382, 405, 406, 449, 491
Marwick Head, Orkney 220
Mary I, Queen 174
Mary II, Queen 72
Mary 109, 117, 189, 289, 405; (slaver) 146
Mary Adeline 126
Mary Antrim 268
Mary Rose 16, 127, 174, 231, 446
Maryton 289, 320
Mary Willoughby 285
MAS-213 (I) 107
MAS 228 (I) 184
MAS-537 (I) 152
Mas a Tierra I. 251
Masefield, Joseph 31
Mason, Francis 143, 441
Massachusetts 1, 375
Massawa, Eritrea 1, 263, 289
Master Standfast 289
Masulipatam, India 289
Mata, Cuba 475
Matai (NZ) 215
Matane (Cn) 289
Matapan – see Cape Matapan
Mathews, Capt. 124
Mathews, Thomas 90, 120, 155 468
Matilda, Empress 171
Matilda 290; (S) 99, 287, 291; (slaver) 428
Matson, H.J. 96
Matsu (J) 470
Maude, William 122
Maunsell, Robert 372
Mauny, Sir Walter 70, 172, 321
Maure (F) 490

Maurice, Prince 286
Mauritius 87, 115, 262, 290–291, 339, 345, 359, 384, 386, 391, 460, 470, 490, 496
Mauritius 149, 291
Mavis 332
Maxey, Lewis 494
Maxwell, Henry 317
Maxwell, John 395
Maxwell, Keith 458
Maxwell, Murray 6, 12–13, 101, 449
May, Henry 205
Maya (J) 446
Maynard, Robert 344
Mayne, Coville 264
Mayo 24
Mayo I., Cape Verde Is 134
Mazagaon, India 84
Mazagran, Morocco 9
MB-20 86
Meads, Samuel 452
Meads, Thomas 301
Meara, Edward 352
Meath, Ireland 329
Mechanician 291
Medea 247, 291,391, 465; (S) 236
Medée (F) 75, 157, 345
Mediator 291
Medina, Sierra Leone 425
Mediterranean Sea 1, 2, 17, 30, 79, 82, 91, 125, 130, 132, 151, 187, 188, 235, 240, 263, 264, 265, 258, 273, 277, 285, 298, 312, 316, 336, 341, 343, 345, 347, 348, 354, 357, 365, 370, 382, 384, 390, 391, 403, 418, 426, 427, 444, 448, 460, 461, 467, 476, 477, 488, 495, 496, 502
Medley, Henry 24
Medlycott, Mervyn 127
Medusa 26, 230, 236, 291; (I) 463
Meduse 92
Medway 292
Medway River, Kent 269, 292
Medway's Prize 292, 313
Mees, George 354, 500
Megas Is, Spain 292
Mehell, John 113
Melada I. 5
Melampe 430; (F) 458
Melampus 74, 116, 292, 293
Melbourne (A) 312
Melbreak 180
Melcombe, John 130
Melcombe 378
Meleager 293
Melos, Greece 26
Melpomene 65, 177, 293, 324; (F) 132, 389
Menai Strait, Wales 330

Menai 293–294
Mendip 326
Mends, Robert 19, 27
Menelaus 294
Mentor 294; (F) 467
Menzies, William 335
Mercer, Andrew 356
Merawe, Sudan 389
Mercedes (S) 236
Mercedita (slaver) 135
Merchant Royal 342
Mercia 334
Mercian 294
Mercure (F) 309, 391
Mercurius (D) 454
Mercury 5, 294, 295; (US) 485
Meredith, Cmdr 347
Mergui Is 454
Merinos (F) 25
Merion 295
Merlin 74, 147, 216, 259, 295, 441
Mermaid 213, 295, 296, 353, 359–360, 400, 500
Merriman, Lt-Cmdr 3
Mers, France 172
Mersa Matruh, Egypt 141, 254, 296
Mers el-Kebir, Algeria 296, 341
Mersey 422
Messager (F) 487
Messina, Sicily 104, 281, 340, 448, 463
Messudiyeh (Turkish) 64
Metemmah, Sudan 389
Meteor 296, 393, 399; (G) 380
Meurig ap Hywel 432
Mexico 27, 113, 308, 355
Mezzo, Dalmatia 7
MGB-35 179
MGB-330 443
Miaoulis (Greek) 152
Micca (I) 425
Michael 109, 297
Michel (G) 178
Michilimackinac 258
Midas (slaver) 302
Middelburg, Java 455
Middleton, Sir Henry 300, 449
Middleton, Robert 151, 197
Middleton 180
Midge 273
Mighells, James 220, 486
Mignon (F) 366
Mignone River, Italy 294
Mignonette 55, 196
Mignonne (F) 211, 240
Milan (F) 450
Milbrook 286, 297, 441
Milford 7–8, 202, 297, 304, 391; (F) 407

Milford Haven, Wales 90, 297
Miller, George 215, 299, 462
Miller, Simon 482
Millo (I) 476
Milne, Alexander 122, 135, 428
Milne, David 11, 359, 420
Milne 297, 298
Milne Bay, New Guinea 313
Mimi 259
Mimose (F) 44
Minch, Minches, Scotland 127, 339
Mindanao, Philippine Is 355, 452
Minden 245
Minerva 133, 243, 298, 364, 447; (I) 414
Minerve 298, 299, 412; (F) 78, 94, 115, 132, 133, 151, 290, 341, 395
Mingary, Ardnamurchan, Scotland 224
Minion 411
Minorca, Balearic Is 151, 299
Minorca 299, 365
Minotaur 137, 299, 316, 371, 450, 500
Minotaure (G) 182
Minstrel 300
Minturno, Italy 72
Minx 300
Miquelon, Canada 407
Mirs Bay, China 16, 375, 409
Mississippi River 120
Missouri (US) 244
Mitchell, Andrew 134, 225
Mitchell, Charles 93
Mitchell, Cornelius 105
Mitchell 300
Mitford, Henry 290
Mitford, Robert 139, 433
Mizen Head, Ireland 235
ML-263 204, 300
Moa (NZ) 215
Mobile, Alabama 300
Mocenigo (I) 28, 35
Mocha, Yemen 300–301
Moderate 301
Modeste 301, 349, 464; (F) 73, 200
Moffat, Thomas 483
Mogadishu, Somaliland 429
Mohammerah, Iraq 351
Mohawk 119, 127, 252
Moira, Ireland 445
Moldavia 301
Molly 301
Moltke (G) 162, 165
Moluccas, Indonesia 66, 459
Mombasa, East Africa 301
Monado, Sulawesi 150
Mona Passage, Caribbean Sea 276, 301
Monarch 103, 301–302, 329, 430

Monck, George, Duke of Albemarle 199, 250, 366, 404, 460
Monck, Thomas 403
Monck 302
Monckton, Lt-Col 192
Mondego Bay, Portugal 302
Mondovi (F) 197
Monemvasia, Greece 479
Money, B.M. 60
Mongat, Catalonia 234
Monge (F) 275
Monkey 274, 302, 317
Monmouth, Duke of 274
Monmouth 103. 132, 302, 303
Monson, Sir William 269, 452
Montagne (F) 192
Montagu, Sir George 200, 303, 345
Montagu, James 247
Montagu, John 103
Montagu, William 131
Montagu 103, 204, 303, 418
Montague 303
Montague I., Melanesia 393
Montbretia (Norwegian) 48
Monte Christi, St Domingue 81, 303
Montevideo, Uruguay 149, 303, 389
Montfort, Countess of 70
Montgomerie, John 429
Montgomery, Augustus 198
Montgomery 36
Montréal, Canada 303
Montréal 303–304; (F) 365
Montreuil, France 442
Montrose, Scotland 223, 304; Earl of 304
Montrose 326
Moodie/Moody, James 128, 259
Moonstone 304
Moor, John 401
Moor 490
Moore, Graham 236, 293
Moore, Sir John 132
Moore, John 215, 287, 386
Moose Jaw (Cn) 40
Morant, George 212
Moray Firth, Scotland 186, 405
Morbihan, France 316, 483
Mordaunt, Hon. Henry 385
Mordaunt 197
Morden (Cn) 46
Morea Castle, Greece 304
Morecambe Bay 220, 304
Moresby, Fairfax 293
Moresby, John 69
Morgannwg, Wales 432
Morgenstar (D) 465
Morgiou, France 304
Morib, Malaya 304

Morlacca Channel 306
Morlaix, france 174, 418
Morne Fortunée 288
Morning Star 305
Mornington (In) 305, 351, 453
Moro Castle, Havana 27, 222
Morocco 4, 24, 204, 373, 431
Morotai I., New Guinea 313
Morrice, Salmon 9
Morris, George 348
Morris, James 355, 31
Morris, John 117
Morrison, Isaac 21
Mortella, Corsica 132, 410
Mortlock, Lewis 497
Morto Bay, Gallipoli Peninsula 211
Mosambique (F) 169
Moselle 305, 359; (F) 10
Mosquito 139, 305, 325; (S) 261
Moss, John 74
Mouat, Patrick 212
Moubray, Richard 277, 304
Mouche (F) 18, 80, 133, 210
Mould, William 465
Moulton, Capt. 127
Mounsey, William 85, 201, 360, 461
Mounsey 400
Mountagu, Edward 323
Mountjoy, Lord 254
Mountjoy 148
Mounts Bay 127, 220
Mourne 181
Mourree, Ghana 310
Moutray, John 380, 464
Mowatt, Henry 189
Mozambique 122, 265
Mozambique Channel or Passage 115, 117
MTB-22 178
MTB-31 178
MTB-32 178
MTB-79 326
MTB-81 425
MTB 90 181
MTB-241 327
MTB-256 179
MTB-260 197
MTB-266 305
MTB-330 179
MTB-315 305
MTB-345 305
MTB-347 328
MTB-360 328
MTB-458 328
MTB-494 29
MTB-508 289
MTB-622 326
MTB 633 305

MTB 637 305
MTB-639 305
MTB-641 425
MTB-666 327
MTB-681 327
MTB-670 306
MTB-697 306
MTB-5001 329
Muavinet-i-Miliet (Turkish) 211
Muckee, Sumatra 306
Muckle Flugga, Shetland Is 202
Mudge, Zachary 81, 127
Mudros, Greece 295, 379, 431
Mudyugski I., Russia 60
Muir, A. T. 442
Muirchertach mac Lochlainn, king of Cenel nEoghan 238
Muirchertach mac Niell, king of Ailech 224
Muletive, Ceylon 114
Mull, Scotland 83
Mull 306
Mull of Kintyre, Scotland 244
Mullanda Bay, Brunei 320
München (G) 165, 429
Munden, Richard 404
Mundy, George 232, 233
Munster, Ireland 239, 306
Murchad, King of Dublin 283
Murmansk, Russia 60, 255, 396, 397, 429
Muros, Spain 167, 271
Murray, George 389
Muscat 369
Muscovia Merchant 407–408
Musette (F) 223
Musketeer 296
Mutine 306; (F) 85, 176, 247, 378, 412
Mwele, East Africa 306
Mykonos, Greece 392
Myngs, Christopher 131
Mynydd Carn, Wales 432
Myrmidon 127, 306–307

Nabob 237, 306–307
Nadakaze (J) 446
Nagle, Sir Edmund 30, 363, 490, 491
Naiad 84, 135, 244, 276, 308
Naiade (I) 140 (F) 371, 416
Nailaka I., Banda Is 308
Nairana 60
Namsos, Norway 60, 331
Namtao, China 309
Namur 309
Nancy (Cn) 258
Nani (I) 36
Nankin 102, 309
Nanking, China 19, 309

Nanna's Town, Nigeria 315
Nanning, Raja of 276
Nantes, France 71, 166
Nantucket, Massachusetts 170, 228
Napier, Charles 78, 234, 364, 382, 442, 461
Napier, Hon. Patrick 362, 473
Napier, Sir Robert 1
Napier 93–94, 141
Naples, Italy 61, 107, 139, 202, 247, 280, 340, 433–434, 457, 477, 480
Napoleon Bonaparte, emperor 2,7, 99, 29, 308, 316, 442, 469, 489
Napoleon (F) 497
Narbada (In) 20, 94
Narbrough, Sir John 16, 471
Narcisse (F) 60
Narcissus 309, 413
Nargen 408
Narragansett, Rhode I. 103, 309–310, 387
Narrawassa 258
Narva, Estonia 310
Narvalo (I) 197
Narvik, Norway 310, 331
Narwhal 310
Naskon River, Denmark 185
Nassau 301, 10, 436, 492
Nasturtium 39
Natal, South Africa 142, 470
Natal (SA) 310
Nautilus 310, 384, 448
Naval Brigades 1, 30, 76, 120, 203, 204, 205, 237, 349, 373, 380, 388, 402, 420, 422, 429, 430, 446, 487
Navarino Bay, Greece 310–311, 468
Navarre 172–173
Nayaden (Dan) 150
Neale, Sir Harry 18, 69, 411
Néarque (F) 317
Necessité (F) 20
Necker (F) 220
Need, Henry 267, 425
Neghelli (I) 140, 214
Negombo, Ceylon 115
Negapatam, India 311
Negrais, Burma 93
Nellie Nutten 335
Nelson, Sir Horatio, Vt Nelson 10, 14, 97, 106, 129, 137, 168, 298, 316, 353, 412, 441, 469, 475
Nelson 281
Nembo (I) 140
Nemesis 75, 1–2, 121, 311, 317, 320, 474; (F) 167
Nene 58
Nepal 237
Nepal (A) 93

Neptune 79, 281; (F) 223, 464
Neptuno (S) 195, 219
Nereide 87, 138, 290, 312; (F) 275, 292, 379; (I) 425
Nerja, Spain 232
Ness 55
Nestor 248, 282; (A) 42, 312
Netherlands 23, 89, 253, 467, 485, 489
Netley 67, 258, 312
Nettuno (F) 5
Netuno (slaver) 184
Neville, George 447
Neville, John 109–110
Nevin, Charles 4
Nevis, West Indies 312
New Amsterdam (New York) 314
Newark, Nottinghamshire 201
New Bedford, Massachusetts 95
New Britain 312
New Calabar, Nigeria 127, 347
Newcastle, Northumberland 193, 465
Newcastle 126, 263, 280, 312, 313, 500
Newcombe, Francis 272
Newcome, Henry 337
New England 1, 9, 189, 198, 272, 313, 318, 368, 375
Newfoundland 36, 41, 46, 111, 133, 268, 303, 313, 318, 361, 485
Newfoundland 313, 407, 425
New Georgia, Solomon Is, 429
New Glasgow (Cn) 313
New Guinea 313–314
Newhaven, Kent 443
New Hebrides 40
New Ireland 314, 429
Newman, James 212, 221, 296, 359, 403
New Orleans, Louisiana 257
Newport, Rhode Island 119
Newport 314
Newson, William 364
New York 3, 86, 95, 117, 118, 170, 274, 314, 355, 387, 415
New Zealand 314, 409
Nhe-Trang, Indo-China 446
Niagara Falls 198
Niagara River 258
Niall mac Eochaid 476
Nias, Joseph 102
Nias Island, Sumatra 161
Niblett, G.T. 201
Nicaragua, Central America
Nice, France 433, 434
Nichelio (I) 425
Nicholas, John 359, 461
Nicholas, Robert 261
Nicholls, Edward 153
Nicholson, Sir Frederick 190

Nicholson, James 80
Nicobar Islands, Bay of Bengal 314
Nicosian 67
Niedersachsen (G) 480
Niemen (F) 19
Nieuport, Belgium 243, 323, 324, 443
Nieuwe Diep, Netherlands 212
Niger 292, 299, 315, 341, 395, 442, 489
Niger River 300, 314–315
Nigeria 61, 282
Nightingale, Gamaliel 483
Nightingale 135, 316, 369; (F) 273
Nile 316
Nile River 263, 316, 388–389
Nimbi, Nigeria 315
Nimble 289, 317
Nimrod 489
Ninfa (S) 240
Ningpo, China 121, 317, 500
Niobe 78, 150, 317, 334; (G) 8
Nisus (F) 462
Nitendi I. Melanesia 393, 409
Niven, Charles 426
Noel, Thomas 270
Nogu I., Solomon Islands 317
Noirmoutier I., France 71, 72, 490
Noli, Italy 251
Nomad 248
Nombre de Dios, Panamá 317
Nonpareil 317
Nonsuch 8, 90, 168, 204, 254, 313, 318
Norbury, Coningsby 220
Norderney I. 376
Nordhav II (Norwegian) 310
Nordland (G) 443
Nore, Kent 458
Norfolk 325, 326
Norfolk, Virginia 119, 247
Norfolk 79, 318, 398
Normandie (F) 406
Normandy, France 67, 115, 171, 172, 181
Norris, Harry 370
Norris, Sir John (1) 65, 233, 260, 336, 414
Norris, Sir John (2) 175
Norris, Richard 159
North Africa 31, 48, 190, 318–320, 341, 365, 480, 481
North America 32, 85, 137, 154, 362, 421, 444, 484
North Atlantic 20, 31, 285, 382, 470
North Berwick, Scotland 195
North Borneo 320
North Cape, Norway 334, 398–399
North Channel 26, 33, 36, 40, 70, 130, 240, 246, 271, 340, 344, 381, 494
Northern Chief 40
Northern Patrol 12, 70, 228

Northern Rover 320
Northesk, Earl of 66
North Foreland, Kent 202, 328, 407, 438
North Korea 209, 244, 333, 462
North Ronaldsay, Orkney 321
North Sea 1, 9, 16, 76, 77, 86, 89, 91, 96, 99, 100, 108, 125, 135, 136, 147, 159, 164, 165, 179, 188, 191, 192, 202, 214, 219, 223, 250, 297, 321–329, 335, 339, 340, 344, 380, 382, 387, 394, 408, 417, 419, 430, 433, 438, 443, 449, 451, 456, 466, 476, 478, 485, 500, 501
North Sea Fleet 194
North Star 314
Northumberland 329
Northumbria 330, 334, 468
Northwest Approaches 33
North-West Company 258
Norway 32, 61, 77, 89, 120, 124, 126, 132, 133, 145, 186, 191, 209, 237, 253, 284, 310, 321, 331, 334, 357, 365, 381, 385, 386, 396, 397, 414, 428, 446, 457, 462, 472, 473, 499, 500
Norwegian Sea 210, 242, 490
Norwich 331
Nottingham 166, 331
Nourrice (F) 365
Nourse, Joseph 67
Nouveau Cherbourg (F) 362
Nova Granada (S) 487
Novara (Austrian) 338
Nova Scotia 44, 198, 216, 297
Nubian 197, 252, 331, 443, 458
Nuestra Señora de Covadonga (S) 113
Nuestra Señora de la Buen Confeso (S) 231
Nuestra Señora de la Concepcion, alias *Cacafuega* (S) 156
Nuestra Señora de la Dolores 331–332
Nuestra Señora del Carmen (S) 85, 347, 348
Nuestra Señora del Rosario (S) 392, 395
Nukapu I., Melanesia 393
Nulla (I) 263
Nunn, Richard 448
Nupe, Nigeria 315
Nürnberg (G) 189, 408
Nusa (G) 312
Nyasaland 271, 332
Nyborg, Denmark 332
Nymphe 116, 332, 352, 410; (F) 27, 93, 196, 220
Nyroca 332
Nystadt, Finland 216

Oakville (Cn) 46
Obdurate 399
Obligado, Argentina 333
O'Brien, Lucius 124, 423
O'Bryen, James 169, 293
Observateur 247; (F) 458
O'Callaghan, George 422
Ocean 144, 333, 447
Oceanic II 333
Ockham 333
Ocoe Bay, Santo Domingo 360
Ocracoke inlet, Virginia 344
Octavia 1; (I) 38
Odessa, Russia 333
Odin 84, 204, 296, 333, 352
Ofotfjord, Norway 310
Ogilvy, William 464
Ogle, Chaloner 451
Ohio (US) 258, 282
Oil Pioneer 209
Oiseau 333, 334; (F) 25, 91, 348
O'Keefe, Yelverton 86–87
Olaf, King of Man 284
Olaf, King of Norway 124
Olaf, ruler in Lewis, 284
Olaf Guthfrithsson, King of Dublin and York 267, 334
Olaf mac Taidc 284
Olaf of Anglesey 238
Olaf the White, King of Dublin 306, 329, 334, 417
Olaf Sitricsson, King of Dublin 130
Oland (Swedish) 494
Oldfield, R.B. 274
Olive Branch 334
Oliver, Robert 69, 177, 287, 353
Oliver Cromwell (US) 73
Olonne, France 70, 493
Olympia 334
Olympic 334
Omago, Istria 7
Oman 351
Omdurman, Sudan 389
Omoa, Honduras 334
Omrah 335
Omsk, Russia 448
Ondina (D) 76; (I) 431
Onitsha, Nigeria 315
Onore, India 278, 335
Onslaught 399
Onslow, John 188
Onslow, Richard 188, 286
Onslow 335, 396
Onward 335
Onyx 335
Opal 315
Opale (F) 190, 348, 357
Ophelia 335
Oporto, Portugal 297

Opossum 335
Oracle 335
Orama 209, 251, 336
Oran, Algeria 184, 296, 318–319
Orange Tree 336; (Algerine) 8
Orbetello, Italy 294
Orchis 182
Orde, John 391
Oreste (F) 417
Orestes 336
Orfasay 336
Orford 264–265, 336
Orfordness, Suffolk 326, 328, 494
Oribi 53
Orient (F) 316
Oriflamme (F) 103, 240
Orion 72, 106, 152, 296, 316, 457; (slaver) 414
Orione (I) 456
Orissa, India 134
Orkney Islands, Scotland 98, 123, 138, 157, 224, 240, 253, 260, 261, 304, 321, 326–327, 394, 395, 500, 501
Orkan (Polish) 56
Orne River, France 232
Oronsay 337
Oropesa, Spain 249
Orphée (F) 103
Orpheus 29, 337, 391
Orphir, Orkney Is 376
Orquijo (S) 360
Orrok, James 9
Orsa (I) 472, 480
Ortenzia (Venetian) 300
Ortona, Italy 6
d'Orvilliers, Comte (F) 481
Orwell River, Suffolk 322
Osborn, Edward 29
Osborn, Henry 102
Osborn, John 410
Osborn, Samuel 114
Osbourne, Robert 175
Osgood, Henry 200
Osiris 8
Osman 320
Osman Digna 446
Osprey 67, 314, 335, 338
Ostend, Belgium 25, 323, 324, 325, 328, 442, 486
Ostmark (G) 475
Ostro (I) 140
Oswald 279
Oswego, Lake Ontario 259
Otranto, Italy 5, 7, 338
Otranto 132
Ottawa (Cn) 46, 182
Otter, Charles 372

Otter, Henry 216
Otter 339
Ottley, John 70, 358, 359
Otto (G) 75
Ottoman Empire (see also Turkey) 2, 100, 144, 310–311
Otway, Robert 11, 213, 295, 418, 463, 469, 470
Otway 339
Ourry, George 342
Ouse 339
Overijssel (D) 362
Owain Glyn Dwr 90, 173, 297, 330
Owen, Edward 123, 177, 234, 390
Owen Glendower 21
Owen Sound 58
Oxenham, John 339
Oxford 159, 287

P-33 340
P-36 281
P-38 340
P-39 281
P-46 340
P-48 340
P-51 340
P-57 340
P-222 340
P-615 340
Paardeburg, South Africa 430
Pacific Fleet 161
Pacific Ocean 22, 99, 112, 113, 339, 354, 356
Padagia I., Dodecanese Is 152
Padang, Sumatra 161
Page, Benjamin 109, 114
Paget, Alfred 205
Paget, Hon. Charles 150, 167, 170, 489
Paget, Hon. William 392
Pajaro (S) 11
Pakenham, Edward 385
Pakenham, Hon. Thomas 196
Pakenham 197, 340, 353
Pakshui, China 335
Paladin 237, 331, 340, 472
Palamos, Spain 341, 386
Palang (Persian) 352
Palembang, Sumatra 161
Palermo, Sicily 102, 341
Palestine 1, 268, 463
Palestro (I) 8
Palinure (F) 108, 122
Palinuro, Calabria 234
Pallas 101, 109, 341; (US) 133; (D) 214, 221
Palliser, Hugh 135, 165
Palmer, Edward 225, 384

Palmer, George 501
Palmer, Nisbet 11
Palmier (F) 157, 437, 461
Palomares 24
Palsgrave 143
Panamá 317
Pancaldo (I) 60, 374
Pancras 341
Panda (pirate) 138
Pandora 127, 341, 342
Pandore (F) 108
Pansy (or *Pensée*) 342
Pantaleon 342
Pantelleria I. 340, 32, 419, 478
Pantera (Russian) 165, 487
Panther 65, 152, 302, 342
Papa (I) 96, 392
Papillon 342; (F) 393, 482
Papua 271
Papwell, John 78
Paquete do Sul (slaver) 414
Para, Brazil 378
Paragon 443
Paraná River 333, 411
Parenza, Italy 6
Pargust 342
Paris 483
Paris (G) 306
Parker, Christopher 81
Parker, Frederick 421
Parker, George 412, 436
Parker, Hyde 129, 153, 192
Parker, Peter 241, 293, 294
Parker, Robert 404
Parker, William (1) 136, 367, 413
Parker, William (2) 192
Parker, William (3) 18, 272
Parker, Sir William (4) 388
Parktown (SA) 342
Parr, Alfred 118
Parr, Thomas 161
Parramatta (A) 141
Parrett 422
Parsons, Daniel 407
Partenope (I) 280, 340, 468
Parthian 140, 343, 455
Partridge 343
Pasley, Thomas 352
Pasley 343
Passage de Raz, France 287
Passages, spain 27
Passe-Partout (F) 410
Patani, Nigeria 315
Pater, Charles 371
Patey, Sir George 61
Pathan (In) 352
Pathfinder 53, 152, 343

Patia 344
Patriot 344
Patriote (F) 111
Patroclus 263
Patrol Boat Flotillas, German: 12th 327; 13th 180; 14th 180; 15th 183
Patrol boat 109 (J) 217
Patterson, John 62
Paul, Earl of Orkney 500
Paulet, Lord Henry 221
Paulina (slaver) 131
Pauline (F) 12, 289, 372
Paxo I. 5
Payne, John 263
Payta, Chile 22
Paxton, Wentworth 314
Paxton 256
Paz (S) 299
PC-56 95
PC-61 344
PC-62 344
Peacock, James 465
Peacock 344, 400; (US) 183, 310
Peake, William 344
Pearce, Joseph 387
Pearce, Marle 147
Peard, Shuldham 14, 447
Pearl 16, 237, 344, 345, 423, 471
Pearl Is, Panama 339
Pearl Rock, Martinique 169
Pearse, Henry 219
Pearson, Richard 154, 421
Pechell, Sir John 122, 454
Pechenga Bay, Russia 124
Pedaso, Italy 8
Pedenara, Portugal 387
Peel, Isle of Man 284
Peel, William 237
Pégase (F) 71
Pegaso (I) 463, 464, 480, 481
Pegasus 345
Pegu, Burma 93
Pegun I., New Guinea 313
Pehtang, China 345
Peiho River, China 345, 456
Peking (Beijing), China 120, 345
Pelican 44, 53, 55, 156, 244, 345, 346, 360, 406, 422, 451; (F) 231
Pell, Watkin 464
Pellew, Sir Edward, Lord Exmouth 16, 106, 137, 235–236, 272, 332, 346, 377
Pellew, Fleetwoodv373
Pellew, Israel 21
Pellew 343
Pelly, Charles 92, 416
Peloponnese, Greece 502
Pelorus 224, 347, 373

Pembroke, Earl of 261
Pembroke 347
Penang, Malaya 66, 414, 445
Pendennis 347
Penelope 24, 61, 71, 152, 268, 273, 281, 347, 348, 403, 442; (F) 355, 372
Pengelly, Lt John 487
Penguin 348
Peniche, Portugal 268
Penmarcks, France 22, 131, 236, 312, 315, 478, 490
Penn, William 243, 251, 268, 366, 388, 409
Penn 152
Pennerf River, France 31
Penny, Taylor 286
Penobscot, Maine 348
Penriche (F) 221
Penrose, Charles 208
Pensée (F) 10, 143, 376
Penshurst 349
Penthièvre (F) 179
Pentland Firth, Scotland 382, 423
Pentstemon 42
Penylan 179
Penzance 33
Peppercorn 300
Perak, Malaya 62, 349
Pératy (F) 216
Percante (F) 238
Percy, Henry (Hotspur), 90
Percy, Sir Thomas 439
Percy, Hon. William 300
Perdrix 349; (F) 482
Perfido (I) 466
Perim Island 249
Periwinkle 38
Perkin Warbeck, 193, 439, 494
Perkins, John 264, 482
Perla (I) 232
Perle (F) 391–392
Perlin 349
Pernambuco, Brazil 349
Perros, France 277
Perry, John 139–140
Perry (US) 65
Persanne (F) 479
Perseo (I) 331, 340
Perseus (D) 122
Perseverance 350, 357
Persian Gulf 168, 197, 350–353, 471
Persia, Persians (see also Iran) 350, 351
Perth, Scotland 353, 354, 417
Perth (A) 448
Peru 3, 422
Perugia 353
Pescara, Istria 6

Pessagno (I) 474
Pessaro, Italy 431
Petard 237, 331, 353
Peterborough, Earl of 68
Peterel 27, 353, 423
Peterhead, Scotland 210, 223, 353–354
Petit Bourg, Guadeloupe 215
Petite Armée (slaver) 305
Petite Fille (F) 378
Petit Guavas, St Domingue 354, 403
Petrel (G) 479
Petropavlovsk, Russia 354
Petropavlovsk (Russian) 123
Petsamo, Russia 255
Pett, Phineas 465
Pettipague Point, Connecticut 127
Petunia 354
Pevensey, Sussex 170
Pevensey Castle 183
Peverel 354
Peyton, Edward 311
Peyton, John 300
Phaeton 262, 308, 354, 355; (F) 360, 383
Phénix (F) 391
Philadelphia, Pennsylvania 147, 355
Philip I, King of France 321
Philip II, King of Spain 432–433
Philip V, King of Spain 68
Philippeaux (F) 336
Philippeville, Algeria 383
Philippine Is. 22, 113, 285, 342, 355
Phillimore, John 185
Phillips, master of privateer 14
Phillips, James 113
Phillips, Tom 178
Phillips, Cmdr 424
Phillipson, John 66
Philomel 238, 289, 315, 349, 355, 430
Philpot, Robert 166
Philpot, John 356
Philpott, Charles 369
Philpotts, Arthur 255
Phipps, Hon. Charles 18
Phipps, Constantine 133
Phipps, Sir William 1, 375
Phipps 356
Phlegethon 93, 120, 201, 317, 320
Phoebe 94, 275, 315, 356
Phoenix 60, 264, 298, 303, 338, 356, 357, 358, 438; (D) 346
Phosphorus 358
Piave River, Italy 5
Picardy, France 172, 173
Pickard, Peter 221, 302
Pickle 12, 358
Picotee (Cn) 39
Pictou 358

Piémontaise 66; (F) 410, 490
Piercy, Richard 230
Piercy, Thomas 133
Pierrepont, William 308
Piet Hein (D) 371
Pigeon 286
Piggott, Cmdr 4
Pigot, Hugh 122, 227, 230, 262, 286, 317, 358
Pigot 358
Pike 70, 358, 359
Pilade (F) 364
Pilgrim (US) 289, 427
Pillau, East Prussia 89
Pilot 359, 461
Pilote (F) 247
Pilot Me 359
Pincher 359
Pine 180
Pinguin (G) 131
Pink 182, 359
Pinkie Cleugh, Scotland 194
Pinn, Edward 8
Pioneer 315, 422
Pipon, John 93
Pipon, Philip 195, 315
Pique 150, 321, 359–360; (F) 81
Piraeus, Greece 213, 214, 280
Piratinim (slaver) 423
Piscopi I., Dodecanese Is 152
Pitt 360
Piumas Is, Brazil 123
Placentia Bay, Newfoundland 360
Plampin, Robert 364
Planeta (slaver) 434
Plantagenet 360, 361
Plassey, India 76
Plate, River – see Rio de la Plata
Platino (I) 319
Plattsburg, New York 258
Pléiade (F) 103
Pleiadi (I) 477
Plover 127, 320, 361, 456
Plumper 177, 361
Plumridge, James 276
Pluto 185, 320, 361, 388; (D) 346
Pluvier (F) 208
Plymouth, Devon 88, 96, 132, 137, 172, 176, 178, 179, 318, 340, 361, 368, 432
Plymouth 361, 362; (US) 422
Pocock, Sir George 136, 222, 311, 364
Podargus 150
Poder (S) 468
Point-a-Pitre, Guadeloupe 215
Pointe de Ché, France 69
de Pointis, Admiral (F) 106, 109, 207, 221
Poitou, france 171, 261

Pola, Istria 6
Pola (I) 290
Poland, James 127
Polares (G) 214
Pole, Charles 447
Polecat 362
Polka (slaver) 423
Polluce (I) 212
Polyanthus 56
Polyphemus 239, 362, 424
Pommern (G) 248
Pomona (S) 27
Pomone 170, 298, 363, 364, 375, 464; (F) 12, 116, 355
Pompée 364
Poncelet (F) 202
Pontchartrain (F) 292
Porlock, Somerset 166
Policastro, Italy 359
Pondicherry, India 136, 364, 416
Pongos River, West Africa 267, 365
Pontevedra, Spain 308
Ponza I., Italy 461–462
Poole, Dorset 172, 241, 365
Poole, William 466
Poole 86
Popham, Alexander 117
Popham, Sir Home 104, 149, 320–321, 323, 365, 389
Porcola Point, Finland 65
Porcupine 5, 208, 365; (US) 258
Porkala, Finland 365
Porpoise 365, 366, 409
Porquerolles, France 431
Porta Coeli (S) 250
Port Arthur (Cn) 319
Port-au-Prince, St Domingue 403
Port Blair, Andaman Is 20, 161
Port Castries, St. Lucia 366
Portchester Castle 59
Port Dauphin, St Domingue 462
Port de Paix, St Domingue 220, 403
Port d'Espagne 366
Port Elmas, Sardinia 279
Portent 24
Porter, Jervis 227
Portland, Maine 87
Portland 313, 331, 366
Portland Bill, Dorset 178, 198, 365, 433
Port Lemo, Italy 6
Portlock, Nathaniel 497
Port Louis, France 487
Port Louis, St Domingue 366
Port Mahon, Minorca 220, 299, 367
Port Mahon 367
Port Niagara, Lake Ontario 259
Port Nouvelle, France 477

Porto Bello, Panama 366, 367
Porto dei Infreschi, Italy 461
Porto Ercole, Italy 294, 479
Porto Farina, Tunis 474
Porto Ferraio, Elba 11, 168, 264, 298, 363
Port-of-Spain, Trinidad 367
Porto Maria, Cuba 136
Pôrto Novo, West Africa 367
Porto Praya, Cape Verde Is 263, 367–368
Porto-Re, Istria 7
Porto San Stefano, Italy 294
Port Royal, Martinique 112
Port Royal, Nova Scotia 1, 368
Port Royal 368
Port Said, Egypt 292, 437
Portsmouth, Hampshire 66, 134, 171, 172, 174, 208, 368
Portsmouth, Virginia 369
Portsmouth 177, 148, 368, 395
Port Sudan, Red Sea 107, 165
Portugal 28, 62, 65, 126, 155, 157, 199, 236, 268–269, 276, 277, 298, 350, 391, 427, 445, 449
Poshtra, India 250
Positano, Italy 234
Postboy 268
Postillon (S) 261
Potomak 412
Poursuivante (F) 227
Pourvoyeuse (F) 167
Powell, Francis 315
Powell, Richard 192, 244
Powerful 369, 430
Powhatan (US) 381
Powlett, Lord Henry 461
Pownoll, Philemon 3, 25, 247, 464
Poynings, Sir Edward 322
Poyntz, Stephen 73, 74, 428
Pozzuoli, Italy 139
Praed, Buckley 134
Prendergast of Great Yarmouth 196
Preneuse (F) 100, 247–248, 470, 498
Prescott, Ontario 369
Prescott (Cn) 51
President 369; (US) 14, 75, 170, 228, 269
Presidente (F) 148–149; (slaver) 80
Preston, D'Arcy 298
Preston 66, 369
Pretoria, South Africa 430
Prevail 24
Prévoyante (F) 462
Price, Charles 64, 65
Price, David 354
Price, George 402
Price, John 113, 188
Price, William 177
Prima 369; (Genoese) 205

Primrose 369, 370
Primula 370
Prince Charles 370; (F) 423
Prince de Neufchatel (F) 170
Prince Edward (F) 220
Prince Edward Island, Canada 217
Prince Frederick 370
Prince Leopold 182
Prince of Orange 370
Prince Rupert 324
Prince of Wales 79, 278, 370, 471, 500
Princesa (S) 264–265
Princess 370
Princess Augusta 371
Princess Caroline 371, 450
Princess Charlotte 113, 371
Princesse (F) 395
Princess Louise 371
Princess Margaret 294
Princess Royal 371, 448
Principe I., West Africa 138
Principe de Guinea (slaver) 277
Pringle, John 352
Pringle, Thomas 28
Prins Christian Frederik (Dan) 376, 436
Prinses Carolina (D) 286
Prinz Adalbert (G) 162
Prinz Eugen (G) 79, 178, 471
Privet 371, 372
Prize 372
Proby, Charles 464
Proby, Lord 221
Procida, Italy 139, 240
Procris 372, 409
Proctor, Peter 463
Progresso (slaver) 122
Prohibition 372
Prometheus 65, 371, 372, 450
Prompte 372; (F) 354
Prosecco, Italy 302
Proselyte 406; (F) 132
Proserpine 93, 372, 435; (F) 151; (S) 27; (D) 449
Prospère (F) 21
Protea (SA) 431
Protée (F) 151
Protector 450; (US) 391
Provence, France 24, 343, 353, 418, 425, 476
Provence (F) 296
Providence (US) 151; (F) 308
Providencia (slaver) 80, 387
Providien 372
Prower, William 21
Prowse, William 426
Prudent (F) 491
Prudente 373; (F) 29, 142, 273, 395, 448

Prueba (slaver) 89
Pruen, Lt 380
Prussia 241
Psara, Greece 11
Psyche 373; (F) 410, 495
Puckeridge 373
Pudner, Humphrey 313
Puerto Cabello, Spanish Main 203, 373, 450
Puerto de Caballos, Honduras 492
Puerto de Haz, Canary Is 126
Puerto Rico, West Indies 11, 81, 169, 227, 363, 384, 420
Pugliése (F) 5
Puketakauere, New Zealand 373
Pullen, William 245
Pulling, George 249
Pulling, John 157, 348
Pulo Arroa, Indonesia 221
Pulo Aur, Indonesia 373–374
Pulo Leat, Indonesia 12
Pulo Run, Indonesia 374
Pulo Sujee, Indonesia 221
Pulteney 221
Pultusk 122, 463
Puna, Peru 112
Puncheston 289
Punta Delgada, Canary Is 374
Punta Stilo, Calabria 374
Pursuer 374
Purvis, George 160, 313
Purvis, John 315
Purvis, John Child 158
Pwlldyfach, Wales 432
Pye, Thomas 418
Pylades 182, 374; (D) 449
Pym, Samuel 290, 427
Python (G) 155

Québec, Canada 23, 85, 116, 303, 375
Québec 151, 227, 323, 375, 376
Queen 28, 192, 376, 443
Queen Alexandra 376
Queen Anne's Revenge (pirate) 415
Queen Charlotte 192, 256, 376–377
Queen Elizabeth 14, 94
Queen Mary 248
Queensland 438
Quelimane, Mozambique 266
Quentin 61, 377
Quiberon Bay, France 31, 70, 186, 235, 242, 317, 377
Quiberon 377
Quickly 377
Quidproquo (F) 207
Quilmes, Argentina 389
Quimper, France 71

Quintana, South Africa 429
Quintero, Chile 112

R-41 (G) 180
R-89 (G) 251
R-111 (G) 328
R-184 (G) 179, 443
R-192 (G) 305
RA-251 (G) 91
RA-255 (G) 91
RA-259 (G) 91
Racehorse 275, 378
Racer 205, 378, 416
Racoon 378, 491
Radcliff, Sir Robert 192
RAF Squadrons: 58th 196; 202nd 496; 209th 483; 269th 40
Raglan 205, 379
Ragnall, king of York 283, 491
Ragnvald, king of Man 284, 330, 445
Ragosniza, Istria 6, 7
Ragusa (Dubrovnik), Dalmatia 5, 6, 7, 379
Raider 378
Raikes 386
Railleur 221, 442; (F) 139
Railleuse (F) 318
Rainbow 379
Rainier, Peter 66, 109, 114, 315
Rainsborough, Thomas 408
Raison 379; (F) 462
Raisonnable 87, 348;(F) 154
Raleigh (US) 28, 157, 187
Raitt, William 418
Rajputana 380
Raleigh 380
Ramage, Edward 381
RAMB I (I) 263, 289
RAMB III (I) 472
Rambler 375, 380; (US) 427
Rame Head, Ireland 402
Ramillies 36, 107, 275, 380, 431
Ramree Island, Burma 94
Ramsay, William 80
Ramsgate, Kent 443
Ramsey, Isle of Man 284
Ramsey 380
Randolph (US) 500
Ranee 320
Rangariri, New Zealand 380
Ranger 93, 380, 381, 429, 446; (F) 236; (US) 156, 494
Rangoon (Yangon), Burma 93–94
Rangwa, Burma 94
Rann of Cutch, India 486
Rapace (F) 428
Raper, Henry 209
Rapid 20, 212, 381, 492

Raposa 381;(S) 200
Raposo (S) 308
Ras al-Khaimah, Persian Gulf 351
Rat Island, Sumatra 358
Rathlin Island, Ireland 156, 240, 381, 463
Ratsey, Edward 355
Rattler 324, 381, 441
Rattlesnake 100, 369, 381; (US) 31, 263
Rattray, James 128
Raumo, Finland 216
'Rauthabjorg', Scotland 381–382
Raven 382
Ravenspur, also 'Ravensrode' 382
Rawalpindi 382
Rawling, John 478
Rawson, Henry 502
Raymond, George 445
Raymond 498
Raynor, John 240
Real Carlos (S) 15, 289
Rebecca 80; (F) 80
de Recalde, Juan Martínez (S) 427
Recanati, Italy 8
Receviso (S) 60
Recovery 133, 369
Recruit 382; (US) 59
Recuperador (slaver) 212
Redbreast 382
Redbridge 382
Rede, R. 86
Redgauntlet 327
Redingfield, Norman 314
Redmill, Robert 362
Redmill 135, 383
Redoubt 323
Redoubtable 324
Redpole 383, 388
Red River, China 201
Red Sea 1, 142, 151, 263, 304
Redstart 229
Redwing 5, 304, 346, 383
Reeve, Samuel 108, 147
Regenerée (F) 29, 89, 345
Regent 88, 383
Reggio, Italy 147, 431
Regiments: 10th Foot 461; 62nd Foot; 65th Foot 250; 74th Foot 104; 79th Foot 285; Middlesex 448; Tanganyika Rifles 145; 1st West India 416
Regina (Cn) 182, 383
Regulateur (F) 497
Regulus 105, 383; (F) 208
Reilly, Hugh 422
Reina Luisa (S) 228
Reindeer 383
Reitrada (S) 126
Rejouie (F) 19

Relentless 383
Rembang, Java 426
Rembang (D) 155
Remembrance 394
Remo (I) 425
Renard 394, 385; (F) 17, 91, 114, 293, 451
Rena (Norwegian) 2
Reneger, Robert 105
Renfrew, Scotland 384
Renommée 384, 390; (F) 5, 18, 155, 223, 247, 272, 275, 348
Renown 107, 176, 205, 384, 385, 490
Réolaise (F) 22, 316
Républicaine (F) 295
République Triomphante (F) 422
Repulse 226, 278, 304, 355
Requain, Grenada 129
Requin (F) 461, 488, 496
Reserve 385
Resistance 385; (F) 410
Resolucion (S) 25
Resolue (F) 90, 116, 293, 357, 358, 452
Resolutie (D) 373
Resolution 23, 143, 151, 302, 385, 386
Resource 296, 386; (F) 338
Restoration 386
Retalick 328
Reuben James (US) 41
Reunion 386; (F) 134, 203, 333
Reval, Estonia 129
Revanche (F) 138, 357, 448
Revenge 62, 103, 150, 178, 239, 336, 386; (F) 385
Revolutie (D) 346
Revolutionnaire 386, 387; (F) 30, 81, 192
Rewa 387
Reykjavik, Iceland 59, 346
Reynolds, Francis 147, 247, 302
Reynolds, George 470
Reynolds, Robert 18, 236, 363, 470
Rheged 476
Rhin (F) 287
Rhine, River 489
Rhinoceros (F) 240
Rhode Island 387
Rhodes I., Dodecanese Is 152, 282
Rhododendron 387
Rhodri ab Owain 330
Rhône, River 488
Rhydderch ab Iestyn 432
Rhys ap Tewdwr 432
Ribotteur (F) 133
Rice, Edward 372
Richard I, King of England 463
Richard III, King of England 297
Richards, Frederick 503
Richard and Sarah 390

INDEX

Richard Strongbow, earl of Pembroke 239
Richelieu (F) 142
Richery, Rear-Admiral (F) 112, 198
Richmond 101, 239, 387
Richthofen (G) 291
Ricketts, William 104, 132, 276, 295
Riddell, Walter 189
Riflemen 301, 388
Rigault de Genouilly (F) 341
Rinaldo 387, 388
Ringdove 215, 349
Rio de Janeiro, Brazil 12, 131, 138, 139, 212, 361, 423, 427, 496–497
Rio de la Hacha, Spanish Main 388, 433
Rio de la Plata (River Plate) 124, 333, 389
Rio de la Plata (slaver) 380
Rio de Oro, West Africa 228
Río Grande, West Africa 420
Rion 329
Rio Paranagua, Brazil 131
Riou, Edward 73
Ripon 329
de Rippe, James 275
Rippon 287, 388
Rising States (US) 460
Rival (slaver) 131
Rivers, Earl 430
Riviera 139
Rivière Noire, Martinique 339
Rivoli 389; (F) 6
Ro-33 (J) 313
Roatan I., Honduras 390
Robari, Sierra Leone 32
Robert I Bruce, King of Scots 159, 284–285, 476
Robert III, King of Scots 196
Robert the Steward 94
Robert of Artois 71
Robert of Normandy 170–171
Robert 390
Roberts, Bartholomew 451
Roberts, Francis 226
Roberts, John 475
Robertson, Lewis 199, 492
Robilliard, William 150
Robina (I) 142
Robinson, Charles 417
Robinson, George 388
Robinson, Hugh 501
Robinson, Henry 21
Robinson, Robert 490
Robust 390
Robuste (F) 13, 289
Rochambeau, General (F) 118–119, 288
Rochefort, France 11, 6, 71, 98, 123, 124, 154, 167, 211, 292, 381
Rochester 43, 55, 184, 313, 384, *390*

Rochester Prize 390
Rockall I. 35, 43, 223
Rockwood 152
Roddam, Robert 213
Rodgers, Commodore (US) 14
Rodent *20*
Rodi 5
Rodney, Sir George 3, 103, 105, 165, 176, 225, 287, 288, 391, 404
Rodney 37, 79, 182
Rodrigues I. 87, 391, 418
Roduna Bay, Solomon Is 429
Roebuck 20, 21, 80, 94, 302, 350, 391
Rogers, Josias 205, 219
Rogers, Thomas 251, 294, 341
Rogers, William 496
Rogerswick, Russia 235
Rognvald 483
Rognvald, son of St Magnus 500
Rognvald Brusison 381
Rolla 203
Rolles, Robert 11
Roma (I) 431
Rome 24, 137
Romeo Primero (slaver) 492
Romney 391, 392
Romsdal, Norway 29
Romso, Denmark 392
Romulus 392; (F) 87
Rona, Italy 235
Ronaldsway, Isle of Man 284
Ronco (F) 5
Rook 392
Rooke, Sir George 68, 74, 129, 130, 254, 278, 427
Roomcoyle, Thomas 318
Roos, Sir John 392
Rorqual 392
Rosa (S) 66
Rosabelle 392
Rosamond 393
Rosario 360, 393
Rosas, Manuel 333
Rosas, Spain 20, 363, 393
Roscanvel, France 175
Rose 393, 394; (F) 166, 303
Rose, Jonas 441
Rosemonde 374
Rosenhagen, Philip 488
Ross, Charles 360
Ross, Hon. Henry 321
Ross, John 89
Rostan (F) 467
Rota, Spain 97
Rota 361, 406
Rotchensalm, Gulf of Finland 217
Rotherham *20*

Rothesay, Isle of Bute 394, 417
Rotterdam 179, 390
Rotterdam (D) 241, 491
Rottingdean, Sussex 171
Rouen, France 174, 175
Rous, John 198
Rover 394
Rovigno, Istria 5, 7
Rowed, Henry 424
Rowley, Charles 6, 122, 202, 479
Rowley, Bartholomew 347, 386
Rowley, Josias 83, 132, 205, 257, 262, 291
Rowley, Joshua 103, 276
Rowley 181, 183
Roxburgh 394
Royal (F) 473
Royal Charles 109, 292
Royal Edward 394
Royal Fortune (pirate) 451
Royalist 320, 395, 409, 418
Royal James 127, 350
Royal Marines 124, 255
Royal Niger Company 215
Royal Oak 137, 34, 395
Royal Sovereign 131
Royle, Henry 416
Royse, Thomas 449
Ruari, son of Ranald 148
Rubis (F) 17, 19, 103, 145, 420
Ruby 75, 137, 276–277, 395, 396
Ruddach, Alexander 223
Rude (F) 363
Rufiji River, Tanzania 145, 276, 421, 456
de Ruijter, Michiel (D) 199, 361, 404, 416, 428, 460–461
Rumsey, Edward 347
Rupert, Prince 23, 80, 199, 254, 269, 286, 404, 460, 483
Rupert 289, 396
Ruse (F) 214, 497
Rushen Castle, Isle of Man 285
Rushworth, Edward 67, 70, 449
Russell, Edward 68, 341
Russell, F.A.H. 64
Russell, Thomas 231
Russell, William 143
Russell 253, 324, 396
Russia 62, 65, 129, 220, 225, 269, 311, 396–400, 450, 451
Ruth 190, 434
Rutlandshire 60
Ryder, Alfred 314
Rye, Sussex 171, 172, 173, 440
Rye 361
Ryukyu Is 401

S-20 (G) 325

S-28 (G) 326, 327
S-30 (G) 325, 326
S-31 (G) 250
S-33 (G) 256
S-38 (G) 325
S-55 (G) 266
S-58 (G) 230, 325, 342
S-63 (G) 327
S-65 (G) 180
S-70 (G) 326
S-71 (G) 327
S-74 (G) 327
S-75 (G) 326
S-76 (G) 329
S-77 (G) 327
S-81 (G) 179
S-88 (G) 327
S-90 (G) 180
S-94 (G) 327
S-96 (G) 327
S-104 (G) 326
S-111 (G) 326
S-112 (G) 180
S-115 (G) 179, 477
S-116 (G) 162
S-117 (G) 477
S-118 (G) 477
S-119 (G) 477
S-128 (G) 327
S-132 (G) 327
S-141 (G) 181
S-143 (G) 180
S-145 (G) 182
S-147 (G) 181
S-148 (G) 162
S-177 (G) 329
S-183 (G) 329
S-190 (G) 182
S-193 (G) 328
S-200 (G) 328
S-202 (G) 329
S-203 (G) 329
S-223 (G) 329
S-228 (G) 328
S-701 (G) 328
S-702 (G) 328
Saba, Gambia 402
Saba I., West Indies 264
Sabang, Sumatra 161
Sabina (F) 298
Sabine 402
Sabiona, Spain 402
Sables d'Olonne, France 22, 97, 291
Sabogrega, Nigeria 315
Sabyn, William 193
Sackett's Harbor, New York 259
Sador, New Guinea 313

INDEX 567

Sadras, India 402
Safari 402
Safeguard 402
Safo (Venetian) 5
Sagami Bay. Japan 244
Sagittario (I) 305, 366
Sagesse (F) 462
Sagres, Portugal 402
Sagu Island, Burma 94
Saguenay (Cn) 35
Sahib 402
Sailau, China 309
St Abbs Head, Northumerland 343
St Albans 39, 402, 403
St Ann, Curacao 137
St Anne's Bay, Martinique 287
St Antoine (F) 370, 500
St Augustine, Florida 403, 436
St Bartholomew, West Indies 264
Saint Bon (I) 480
St Brieux, France 120, 181
St Catherines (Cn) 58
St Clair, Hon. Archibald 80
St Clair, James 70
St Croix, France 71, 490
St Croix (Cn) 45, 51, 56
St David 466
St David's, Wales 330, 431, 432
St David's Head 346
St Denis, France 172
St Domingue (also Haiti, San Domingo, Hispaniola) 3, 15, 71, 81, 83, 146, 160, 200, 201, 227, 238, 271, 276, 346, 347, 360, 376, 379, 384, 395, 403–403, 420, 428, 458, 478
Ste Anne (F) 112
Sainte Famille (F) 235
Saintes, West Indies 203, 301, 364, 404
St Esprit (F) 103, 246, 294; (D) 460
St Eustatius, West Indies 92, 483, 492
St Firmin 404
St François de Paule (F) 479
St George 76, 315, 404, 502
St George's, Grenada 295
St George's Channel 26, 376
St Gildas, France 450
St Helena I. 131, 404
St Helen's, Hampshire 159
St Jacques (F) 472
St Jean de Luz, France 71, 459, 485
S*t John* (Cn) 405
St John, Henry 335
St John, West Indies 264
St John's, Newfoundland 212, 405
St Joseph (F) 294; (slaver) 305
St Kitts, West Indies 260, 270, 405
St Lawrence 405

St Lawrence River, Canada 45, 303, 375
St Laurent (Cn) 58
St Loe, Edward 487
St Loe, George 368
St Louis (F) 21
St Lucia, West Indies 114, 169, 198, 405–406
St Malo, France 101, 118, 171, 172, 173, 175, 176, 178, 182, 188, 385
St Marc, St Domingue 483
St Marcouf Is, France 64, 65, 177, 223
St Martin Castle, Ile de Re 241
St Martin, West Indies 264, 406
St Martin's Island, Burma 93
St Mary's, Georgia 406
St Mary's River, Florida 99
St Mathieu, France 173
St Monans, Scotland 194
St Nazaire, France 71, 406
St Nicolas Mole, St Domingue 392
St Nicolas Point, Java 406
St Patrick 407
St Paul, Bourbon I. 87
St Peter (Ostend) 486
St Peter's Fort, Newfoundland 360
St Pierre, Canada 407
St Pierre, Martinique 82, 154, 287, 288
St Pol, Chevalier de (F) 347, 407
St Thomas (Cn) 59
St Thomas, West Indies 200, 262, 349
St Tropez, France 159
St Vaast-la-Hougue, France 172, 178
St Valéry, France 177, 178
St Vincent, West Indies 213, 407
Sakishima-Gunto Islands 401
Salamander 93
Salamandre (F) 127, 302
Salamine (F) 112, 199
Salamis 407
Salas, Colonel 314
Saldanha Bay, Cape of Good Hope 104, 407
Salerno, Italy 407
Salisbury, Earl of 172, 321
Salisbury 407–408; (F) 194
Sallee, Morocco 8, 89, 204, 228, 229, 253, 283, 408
Sally 143
Salmon 408
Salonica, Greece 408
Salopian 38
Salpe (I) 472
Salsette 408
Salter, Elliot 231, 412
Saltholm I., Denmark 163
Salvador (S) 22
Salvador del Mondo (S) 106

INDEX

Salvia 408
Sama, China 335
Samara Bay, St Domingue 271
Samarang, Java 373
Samarang 408
Sambas, Borneo 408–409
Samboanga, Philippines 453
Samchow, China 381
Saméa (F) 186
Samoa 409
Samos, Greece 20, 152, 249
Samothrace, Greece 394
Samphire 42 (Cn) 319
Sampson, Lewis 488
Samso (Dan) 470
Samson 102, 409
Sana, Imam of 301
San Andres 409
San Antonio (Portuguese) 66; (S) 170, 460
San Carlos, Falkland Is 189
San Cataldo, Italy 6, 7
San Christovel Pano (S) 421
Sanda 324
San Damaso (S) 471
San Demetrio 35
Sanders, George 177, 434
Sanders, James 247
Sandfly 65, 317, 409, 447
Sandheads, Bengal 251
Sandhurst 443
San Domingo, Hispaniola 28, 409–410, 492
Sandoval (S) 501
Sandwich, Kent 172, 250, 439, 440, 468; Earl of 16, 77, 456
Sandwich 184, 288, 390, 410
San Felipe (Portuguese) 66
San Fiorenzo, Corsica 132, 410
San Fiorenzo 18, 132, 410
San Francisco (Portuguese) 350; (S) 412
San Giorgio (I) 140
San Giorgio I., Cattaro 111
San Giusto (I) 480–481
Sangro (I) 100
San Hermenegildo (S) 15
San Isidro (S) 238
Saniyeh, Persian Gulf 351
San Jacinto, Philippines 355
San Jose (S) 106
San Josef (S) 110, 355, 367, 384
San Juan, Puerto Rico 411
San Juan de Baptista (S) 277
San Juan de Ulloa, Mexico 411
San Leon (S) 412
San Lorenzo, Argentina 411
San Lucar, Spain 105, 380
San Miguel (S) 312

San Nicolas (S) 106
San Pedro, Spain 419
San Pio (S) 383
San Rafael (S) 98
San Remo, Italy 206, 296
San Salvador (S) 105
Sans-Culotte (F) 10, 81, 417
San Sebastian (Portuguese) 350
San Sebastian, Spain 321, 411
Sansom, William 369
Sans Pareil (F) 357
Sans-Pareille (F) 294
Sans Quartier (F) 143
Sans Souci (F) 89
San Stefano, Italy 305
Santa Ana (S) 112
Santa Brigida (S) 308
Santa Catalina (S) 200, 447
Santa Clara (S) 360
Santa Cruz (slaver) 131
Santa Cruz, Rio de Janeiro 212
Santa Cruz, Tenerife, Canary Is. 89, 411–412
Santa Cruz, West Indies 264, 393
Santa Cruz Is 345, 393, 409
Santa Dorotea 294, 412; (S) 268
Santa Elena (S) 240
Santa Getrudis (S) 362
Santa Leocadia (S) 101
Santa Margarita 114, 412, 490; (S) 458
Santa Maria (S) 331–332
Santa Marinella, Italy 201
Santa Marta, Spanish Main 64, 75, 433
Santa Maura, Ionian Is 5, 412
Santa Monica (S) 345
Santander, Spain 18, 80, 321, 454
Santarosa (I) 197
Santa Rosa (S) 354
Santa Teresa 112, 204, 254; (S) 27, 250; (Ostend) 486
San Thomé (S) 62
Santiago, Cape Verde Is 412
Santiago de Cuba 191, 293, 378, 412–413, 436
Santissima Trinidad (S) 105–106, 343
San Ysidro (S) 106
Sardoine (F) 287
Santo Domingo 212, 362
Santona, Spain 413
Santos, Brazil 123, 387
Sao Miguel, Azores 62
Sao Valentinho (Portuguese) 115
Sao Vicente, Brazil 413
Sao Vicente, Cape Verde Is 413
Sapphire 413
Sappho 413
Sapri, Italy 461

Saracen 7, 111–112, 203, 379, 414
Sarah 92; (Brazil) 131
Saratoga, New York 231
Sarawak, Malaysia 12
Sardine (F) 167, 474
Sardinia 10, 107, 197, 254, 274, 282, 294, 309, 414, 423, 424, 466, 479
Sark, Channel Is 116
Sartaine, Stephen 165
Sartine 98; (F) 419
Satellite 1, 314, 414
Satsuma, *daimyo* of (J) 249
Satyr 414
Saudadoes 414
Saudadoes Prize 414
Saumarez, Sir James 15, 106, 116, 134, 177
Saumarez, Philip 331
Saumarez 20, 130, 320, 414
Saunders, Charles 210, 375, 444
Saunders, Richard 206
Saunders, Robert 407
Sauro (I) 165
Savage, Henry 394
Savage 414–415
Savannah, Georgia 415
Savanna La Mar, Jamaica 342
Savill, Capt. 220
Savona, Italy 206
Sawyer, Capt. 351
Sawyer, Herbert 3
Saxton, Charles 238
Sayer, George 203, 409
Sayer, James 492
S-boat Flotillas, German 1st 325, 326; 2nd 178, 180, 326, 327, 328, 329; 3rd 178, 179, 230, 325, 342; 4th 180, 326, 327, 328, 329, 443; 5th 179, 180, 181, 328, 406; 6th 326, 327, 328, 329; 8th 327, 328, 444; 9th 180, 181, 328, 329; 10th 328
Scandinavia 343
Scanderoon (Iskenderun, Alexandretta) 232, 415
Scapa Flow, Orkney 209, 331, 395, 482
Scarborough, Tobago 467
Scarborough, Yorkshire 413, 415, 421
Scarborough 38, 415, 500; (F) 21
Scarcies River, West Africa 415–416
Scardamoula, Greece 346
Scarpanto I. Dodecanese Is 152, 279
Scattery I., Ireland 238
Sceptre 403, 500
Schakerloo (D) 407, 465
Scharnhorst (G) 36, 37, 178, 189, 209, 382, 385
Scheer, Admiral (G) 248

Scheldt, River, Belgium 23, 326, 328, 329, 382, 489
Scheveningen, Netherlands 327, 387
Schiermonnikoog, Groningen 374
Schiff 37 (G) 29–30
Schiff 36 (G) 29–30
Schiff 40 (G) 457
Schomberg, Alexander 271, 409
Schomberg, Charles 275
Schomberg, Herbert 130–131
Schooneveld, Netherlands 416
Schouwen Bank, North Sea 165
Schwabenland (G) 460
Scilly Islands, Cornwall 117, 134, 154, 155, 176, 186, 188, 199, 221, 230, 270, 318, 332, 356, 380, 385, 416, 417, 432, 452
Scimitar 39
Scipio (D) 373
Scipion (F) 15, 271
Scipione Africano (I) 425
Scire (I) 14, 207, 242
Scirocco (I) 281
schooner no. 114 (Dan) 230
Scorpion 161, 416, 498; (US) 127, 258, 406
Scotia 325
Scotland 28, 92, 109, 113, 138, 145, 159, 193–195, 212, 252, 253, 260, 268, 284, 304, 320, 322, 356, 383, 384, 417, 423, 433, 440, 483
Scots Navy 109, 159, 244
Scotstoun 33
Scott, Alexander 117
Scott, Francis 232
Scott, George 230
Scott, Isaac 371
Scott, Matthew 406
Scott, Percy 430
Scott, Thomas 336
Scott 417
Scourge 417
Scout 364, 417, 418
Scriven, Timothy 459
Scylla, Italy 418
Scylla 418
Seadog 435
Seaflower 418
Seaford 231, 331, 418
Seagull 272, 418; (Dan) 470
Seaham 86
Seahorse 169, 309, 419
Sea King 419
Seal 420
Sealark 420
Sealy, Capt. 260
Sea of Azov 252, 420
Sea of Marmara 9, 144, 162, 163, 164
Searle, John 345, 406

Searle, Thomas 133, 212, 374, 384
Sea Scout 217
Seawolf 420
Seba River, West Africa 420
Sebastiano Venier (I) 365
Sebastopol, Russia 420
Seccombe, Thomas 209
Seeadler (G) 179
Seeley, Capt. 207
Segundo Rosario (slaver) 122
Seine, River France 171, 172, 173, 174, 175, 177
Seine 420, 421; (F) 29, 215, 230, 247, 359–360
Selangor, Malaya 126, 388, 421
Selby, William 21, 177, 206
Sella (I) 213, 472
Selsey Bill, Sussex 181
Selwyn, Jasper 420
Semarap, Java 245
Semillante (F) 18, 113, 301, 355, 373, 460, 477, 484
Semiramis 208
Sendai (J) 462
Senegal, West Africa 370, 421
Senegal 421; (F) 293, 502
Senegal River, West Africa 293, 348, 492
Senhouse, Humphrey 247
Senhouse, William 15
Sensible (F) 226, 429
Senussi, Libya 296, 428
Sept Frères (F) 441
Sept Iles, France 180
Serapis 421
Serbia 408, 421, 493
Sercey, Rear-Admiral (F) 29
Sérieux (F) 347
Serpent 93, 421; (F) 2
Serpente (I) 233, 280; (F) 318
Sesostris 317
Severn, River 90, 389
Severn 54, 362, 421–422
Seychelles Islands 131, 485
Seydlitz (G) 153, 273
Seymour, Sir Beauchamp 14
Seymour, Edward 127
Seymour, Frederick 373
Seymour, George 448
Seymour, Hon. Hugh 449
Seymour, Sir Michael 19, 190, 221, 435
Seymour, Sir William 456
Seymour 328
Seyne (F) 189
Sewolod (Russian) 235
SG-7 (G) 425
SG-10 (G) 425
SG-15 (G) 479

SGB-7 179
Shadwell, Sir Charles 421
Shah 422, 503
Shakespeare 422
Shalimar 445
Shanghai, China 422–423
Shannon, River, Ireland 237–238, 267
Shannon 237, 295, 423
Shapley I., White Sea 494
'Shap'n'gtzui' 201
Shark 248, 423
Sharpe, Alexander 364
Sharpshooter 127, 396, 423
Shatt el-Arab 351, 352
Shawinigan (Cn) 423
Shearwater 328, 469
Shebar River, West Africa 423
Shediac (Cn) 51
Sheerness, Kent 292
Sheerness 194, 331, 423–424
Sheffield 189, 206, 398
Sheikh Syed, Yemen 424
Shelanagig 424
Shelburne 337
Sheldrake 21, 326, 424
Shenpu, china 80
Shephard, James 424
Shepheard, William 69
Sherbro I., West Africa 424
Sherer, Joseph 302, 317
Sheriff, Capt. 386
Sherriff, John 26, 138
Shetland Islands 30, 60, 70, 72, 142, 228, 253, 370, 387, 424, 446
Shiels, David 144
Shilling, Andrew 350
Shimonoseki Strait, Japan 424
Shipley, Conway 126, 228
Shippard, Alexander 441
Shirley, Thomas 210
Shirley, Hon. Washington 18
Shirly, Thomas 442
Shirreff, James 247
Shoei Maru (J) 445
Shoreham, Sussex 174
Shoreham 93, 136, 249, 352, 424, 434
Shortland, John 247
Shovell, Sir Cloudisley 9, 68, 158, 323, 413, 437, 468, 471
Shrewsbury, Earl of 254, 330
Shrewsbury 135
Shropshire (A) 313, 355, 429
Shuldham, Molyneux 491
Shumsher Jung (Mahratta) 386
Sibly, Edward 451, 469
Sibyl 302, 424
Sicilian Channel 233, 361

Sicily 17, 61, 98, 104, 107, 234, 262, 274, 305, 342, 39, 419, 425, 474, 480, 481, 489
Sickle 425
Sidi Barrani, Egypt 140
Sidon, Lebanon 74
Sierra Leone 2, 36, 138, 425, 453, 491, 492
Sigli, Sumatra 161
Signi, Lesbos 209
Sigurd, King of Norway 224
Sigurd the Mighty, Jarl of Orkney 98
Sigurd the Stout, Jarl of Orkney 123, 263
Sikh 141, 425, 426
Silba Island, Italy 8
Silivri, Turkey 163
Simonds, Richard 59, 285
Simonstown, South Africa 104
Simonton, Robert 98
Simoom 324, 426
Simpathia (slaver) 274
Sinai Peninsula 447
Sinclair, Sir John 34, 346
Sinclair, Patrick 238, 347
Sinclair, William 336
Sincocke, Robert 318
Sind, Pakistan 23
Sinde (In) 352
Singapore 161, 278, 319, 426, 445
Singleton, Uvedale 349
Sinn Fein 83
Sion, Bombay I, India 84
Siren 426; (US) 292
Sirène (F) 209, 220, 238
Sir Francis Drake 426
Sir Galahad 189
Sir Hugh Rose (In) 352
Sirio (I) 472
Sirius 61, 152, 290, 334, 425, 426–427
Sir John Moore 324
Sir Thomas Pasley 426
Sir Thomas Picton 302
Si Tallah 320
Sitric, King of Dublin 123, 283, 330, 491
Sitric, king of York 217
Sitric Camm 239
Siward, Earl of Northumbria 417
Skagen, Denmark 12, 91
Skagerrak 256
Skerki Bank 61
Skerries, Ireland 427
Skene, Alexander 216
Skinner, FitzOwen 210
Skinner, George 209
Skinner, John 371, 465
Skipjack 325, 427
Skipsey, William 459

Skipwith, Grey 233
Skokholm Island 369
Skye, Scotland 476
Skylark 388, 427
Skynner, Lancelot 73
Skyrm (pirate) 451
Skyros, Greece 146
Slaney 93
Sluys, Flanders 321–322, 324
Smerwick, Ireland 427
Smith, Lt 393
Smith, Charles 13
Smith, Edward 169
Smith, Eustace 278
Smith, Frederick 402
Smith, Henry 488
Smith, Isaac 357
Smith, James 386, 419
Smith, John B. 211
Smith, Matthew 297
Smith, Sir Sidney 1, 2–3, 98, 176–177, 202, 269, 292, 442, 469, 490
Smith, Thomas 449
Smith, William 197
Smith's Knoll, North sea 336
Smyrna, Turkey 229, 303, 311, 437, 444
Smyth, James 297
Smyth, Sir Jeremy 404
Snaefell 427
Snake 427, 428
Snap (Dan) 344
Snapdragon 428
Snapper 428
Sneyd, Clement 160
Sneyd, Edward 84
Snowberry (Cn) 57
Snowflake 53
Society 186
Soldadoes 274
Sole (or Southwold) Bay 428
Solebay 415, 418, 421, 428; (F) 14
Soleil Royal (F) 68
Solent, Hampshire 173, 174
Solent 217
Solitaire (F) 396
Sollum, Egypt 140, 227, 228, 308, 428, 457, 472
Solomon 308
Solomon Is 314, 345, 429
Solovetskoi monastery, Russia 494
Somali 271, 398, 429
Somaliland 429
Somerled, Lord of the Isles 224, 284, 384
Somers (US) 258
Somerset 90
Somerville, Sir James 107
Somerville, Philip 361, 406

Somme, river, France 172, 180
Sondlandet, Norway 420
Sophie 491
Sorlings 347
Soroka, Russia 60
Soroy, Norway 429
Sotheby, Edmund 237
Sotheby, Edward 420
Sotheby, Thomas 157
Souffleur (F) 455
Soujak Kaleh, redoubt 401
Soult, Marshal (F) 132
Sound, Denmark 10
Sound of Arisaig, Scotland 270
Souris (F) 64
South Africa 31, 51, 429–430
South America 99, 112, 156, 189
Southampton, Hampshire 105, 172, 173–74, 241, 430
Southampton 280, 430, 431
South Atlantic 155, 160
South Carolina 403
South Carolina (US) 151
Southdown 326, 327
Southern Maid (SA) 431
South Korea 244
Southland 431
Southsea Castle 364
South Wales 90, 431
Souverain (F) 227
Spain 3, 4, 54, 55, 62, 97, 113, 188, 195, 196, 216, 223, 229, 232, 233, 236, 265, 272, 315, 320–321, 332, 357, 433, 450, 475, 484
Spanish Main 2, 75, 161, 261
Sparrow 470, 488
Spartak (Russian) 108
Spartan 5, 24, 238, 433
Spartiate (F) 453
Sparviero (Neapolitan) 433
Spear, Joseph 146
Spear, Richard 285
Spearfish 434
Specucie Island, Virginia 119
von Spee, Graf (G) 132
Speedwell 39, 434
Speedy 73, 224, 249, 434–435; (F) 235
Speerbrecher 7 (G) 149
Speerbrecher 157 (G) 70, 291
Spencer, Hon. Frederick 304
Spencer, Richard 134
Spencer, Hon. Sir Robert 84, 308, 346
Spencer 435; (US) 50, 53
Spey 44, 58
Sphinx 435; (F) 372
Spice Is (also Moluccas) 66
Spikenard (Cn) 43

Spiteful 127, 352
Spitfire 14, 435
Spithead, Hampshire 433
Spitzbergen 398, 435
Splendid 435
Spottiswood, Robert 272
Spragge, Sir Edward 86, 386
Spranger, John 238, 275
Sprightly 447
Springbank 41
Spry, Richard 272
Spy 435
Squire, Matthew 28
Squirrel 436; (F) 273
Stag 355
Staggins, Charles 456
Staines, Sir Thomas 139, 211
Stamford Bridge, Yorkshire 501
Stamphalia I., Dodecanese Is 152
Stanchio, Turkey 426
Standard 5, 436
Stanfell, Francis 416
Stanhope, James 367
Stanhope, Philip 391
Stanhope, Thomas 103
Stanislas (F) 25
Stanley 42, 436
Stapleton, Sir William 200
Star 339, 491
Starck, Mauritius de 441
Starfish 436
Starling 55, 56, 57, 58, 182, 205, 399, 436
Starling Inlet, China 87
Start Point, Devon 179, 310, 369, 427
Starwort 319
Stately 104, 436
Staten I., New York 314
Statesman 217
Statira 18
Staunch 205, 436, 437
Stavanger, Norway 164, 331, 448, 463, 484
Stayner, Sir Richard 97, 456–457
Stayner 182, 358
Steevens, Charles 331, 336, 366
Stephen, King of England 171
Sterlet 437
Steven Furness 437
Stevens, Charles 409
Stewards, M. 289
Stewart, Henry 169
Stewart, James 21, 150, 186, 366
Stewart, John 419, 496
Stewart, William 83, 488
Stickland, Sir Roger 289
Stier (G) 179
Stirling, Scotland 193, 194

INDEX

Stirling, Charles 359, 389, 414
Stirling, Francis 349
Stirling Castle 220, 276, 437
Stockforce 437
Stoic 445
Stokes, John 367
Stoll, John 85
Stonecrop 52, 55, 437
Stonehenge 445
Stopford, Edward 485
Stopford, Hon. Robert 3, 73, 97, 245, 354, 355
Stork 42, 44, 55, 70, 258, 318, 437, 449
Storm 445
Stornoway, Scotland 225
Storr, John 1o3
Story, Admiral (D) 225
Story, Henry 216
Stott, John 298
Stour, river, Essex 438
Strachan, John 186
Strachan, Sir Richard 140, 177, 291, 292, 357, 438
Strachey, Christopher 143, 234
Strait of Dover 179, 266, 328, 432, 438–444
Strait of Gaspar, Indonesia 13
Strait of Gibraltar 83, 169, 304, 357, 392, 444, 463
Strait of Magellan 99, 112, 156
Strait of Malacca 168, 221, 373, 445
Strait of Messina 86, 87
Strait of Otranto 280, 338, 457
Strale (I) 333
Stralsund (G) 191
Strange, James 84
Strangford, Lord 269
Strangford Lough, Ireland 445
Strasbourg (F) 196
Stratagem 445
Strathadam (Cn) 59
Strathclyde, Scotland 334
Streatham 87, 445–446
Strenuous 127
Streynsham, Capt. 448
Strode, Augustus 423
Stromboli 480
Strombolo 97, 169
Strongbow 446
Stronghold 161, 446
Strongoli, Italy 359
Stuart, Lord George 10, 230, 263
Stuart, Henry 142
Stuart, Sir John 98
Stuart, Lord William 115
Stuart 446
Stubborn 446

Studtland, Norway 75
Sturdee, Sir Doveton 189
Sturgeon 446
Stygian 161, 446
Suakin, Sudan 446–447
Subtile (F) 18, 366
Succès (F) 298–299, 488
Success 14, 206, 350, 433, 447
Suckling, Maurice 157
Suda Bay, Crete 213, 279, 473, 501
Sudan 388–389
Suez, Egypt 313
Suez Canal 167, 447
Suffisante 448; (F) 159
Suffolk 79, 90, 276, 398, 448
Suffren, Pierre (F) 136, 311, 372
Suffren (F) 277
Sulawesi (Celebes) 452
Sulivan, Francis 429, 503
Sulivan, George 301
Sulpa (I) 142
Sultan 448
Sultane (F) 134, 221
Sultan Hissar (Turkish) 9
Sultan of Sokoto 315
Sultanpur, Gujarat 23, 448
Sulu, Borneo 320
Sulu Sea 310
Sumatra, Indonesia 29, 161, 448
Summersdale, Orkney 336
Sunda Strait, Indonesia 90, 161, 301, 310, 371, 385, 445, 448, 455
Sunderland 120
Sunflower 56
Sungei Ujong, Malaya 449; Sultan of 449
Sunn Prize 449; (F) 266
Superb 15, 489
Superbe (F) 251, 360, 482
Supérieure 70, 230, 449
Supply 350
Support Groups, British: 52, 53, 54; 1st 9; 3rd 56; 6th 71
Supreme 445
Surabaya, Java 92, 161, 346
Suraj-ud-Dawla, Nawab of Bengal 76
Surat, India 143, 449
Surinam 449, 456
Surinam 138; (D) 138
Surprise 449, 450; (US) 370
Surrey, Earl of 174
Surridge, Thomas 17
Surveillante 111, 239, 450; (F) 197, 239, 375–376
Surveyor (US) 309
Susan 342
Susannah 442
Sussex 166

Suttie, Francis 407
Sutton, Evelyn 241
Sutton, Robert 435
Sutton, Samuel 236, 486
Suvarnadrug, India 124, 148, 450
Suvla, Gallipoli 145
Sveaborg, Finland 450
Svensksund, Sweden 450
Swale 54, 58
Swallow 148, 203, 225, 416, 450, 451, 488
Swallow Prize 451
Swain, Thomas 125
Swan 113, 451; (F) (F) 377
Swansea (Cn) 58, 289, 405, 451
Swanton, Vermont 258
Swanton, Robert 375
Swatow, China 94, 452
Sweaborg (Russian) 23
Sweden 65, 129, 264, 341, 357, 376
Sweepstake 452
Swegn, son of Harald 283
Swift 82, 320, 443, 452
Swiftsure 103, 404, 447, 452, 453
Switzerland 225
Sybille 102, 453, 454; (F) 231–232, 271, 276, 392
Sydney, William 369
Sydney, Australia 255
Sydney, Nova Scotia 32
Sydney (A) 106, 279, 454, 457
Sylph 22, 202, 235; (In) 351, 454; (F) 243
Sylphe (F) 125
Sylvia 454
Symonds, George 331
Symonds, Nathaniel 464
Symonds, Thomas 401, 501
Syphax 275
Syracuse, Sicily 425
Syren 292, 495; (US) 260
Syria 2, 73, 154, 199, 431, 455

T-22 (G) 180
T-23 (G) 180
T-24 (G) 181, 327
T-25 (G) 71, 327
T-26 (G) 71, 180
T-27 (G) 71
T-29 (G) 181
TA-10 (G) 152
TA-12 (G) 152
TA-15 (G) 479
TA-24 (G) 296
TA-29 (G) 296
TA-45 (G) 306
Table Bay, South Africa 365
Taciturn 217
Tactique (F) 216

Taggal, Java 245
Tagus, River, Portugal 126, 128, 268, 269, 329
Tagus 315
Taiping 309, 422
Taiwan 198
Takao (J) 426
Taku 456
Taku forts, China 120, 345, 456
Talbot, Capt. 277
Talbot, C.P. 164
Talbot, Gilbert 436
Talbot, John 6, 122
Talbot 127, 304, 456
Talisman 456
Tally Ho! 445
Tamai, Sudan 446
Tamar 456
Tamar mac Ailche, 267
Tamarisk 43
Tamatave, Madagascar 275
Tambi, West Africa 416
Tamega (slaver) 118
Tamise (F) 412
Tanga, Tanganyika 456
Tanganyika 422, 456
Tangier, Morocco 8, 90, 117, 295, 413, 456–457
Tanner, Lt 23, 351, 457
Tantalus 445
Taonpung, China 437
Tapageuse (F) 341
Tape-a-Bord (F) 478
Tapir 457
Tapua I., New Hebrides 409
Tara 457
Tarakan, Burma 320
Taranaki, New Zealand 489
Taranaki 457
Taranto, Italy 8, 279, 281, 333, 359, 431, 457
Tarifa, Spain 22, 380
Tarigo (I) 252
Tarpon 457
Tarragona, Spain 81, 457
Tarrant, Lt-Cmdr 3
Tarrebas, Malaya 252
Tartar 9, 21, 181, 430, 458, 482
Tartar Prize 458
Tartarus 143
Tartu (F) 362
Tasiko I., New Hebrides 409
Tauranga 409
Taurus 445
Tavy 182
Tawe, river, Devon 90
Tay, river, Scotland 243

Tay 54, 237
Taylor, Bridges 6, 25
Taylor, Henry 334
Taylor, Thomas 198, 318, 500
TB-5 458
TB-10 458–459
TB-12 458–459
Teazer 177, 208, 420, 425
el-Teb, Sudan 446
Teddeman, Sir Thomas 77
Teignmouth 249, 260, 459
Telcott 426
Telegraph 459
Telemachus 445
Telemaque (F) 186
Tellicherry, India 216, 357, 498
Tembien (I) 227, 280
Teme 59
Téméraire (F) 130, 151
Tempest 459
Tempête (F) 244
Templar 445
Temple, John 126, 353
Temple 459
Tenacious 8
Tenasserim, Burma 93
Tenedos 115, 170, 503
Tenerife, Canary Is 348
Tenette river, Sulawesi 459
Tentador (slaver) 497
Terceira, Azores 63
Termagent 232, 459
Ternate, Molucca Is 337, 459
Ternate (In) 13, 249, 459
Ternay, Commodore de 77
Terpsichore 459, 460, 473; (F) 109, 277
Terracina, Italy 433
Terrapin 161, 445, 460
Terre Neuve (F) 296
Terreur (F) 360
Terrible 430, 460; (F) 421–422
Terror 97, 206, 270, 324
Terschelling, Netherlands 219, 229, 325, 326, 327
Tervani 460
Test 54
Tetley, Joseph 216, 349
Tetrarch 102, 460
Teulie (F) 5
Tewodros, Emperor of Ethiopia 1
Texel, Netherlands 153, 159, 211, 250, 256, 261, 325, 326, 357, 371, 426, 454, 460–461, 477
Thackstone, Henry 428
Thalia 273, 461
Thames, river, England 88, 202, 260, 292, 326, 328, 329, 382, 404, 465

Thames 234, 377, 461, 464
Thane 462
Thanet 462
Thatch, Edward (or Teach, or Blackbeard) 344
Themis 462
Theseus 2–3, 76, 138, 316, 462
Thetford Mines (Cn) 59
Thetis 215, 303–304, 410, 462, 464; (F) 19, 95, 376; (D) 161; (S) 222, 308
Thicknesse, John 118
Thistle 349, 463
Thomas of Galloway 148, 224
Thomas, son of Henry IV 322
Thomas, Joseph 376
Thomas, Richard 266, 292, 488
Thomas, Samuel 12
Thomas, Sidney 249
Thomas Collard 463
Thompson, Charles 85
Thompson, Thomas 263
Thor (G) 12, 108, 488; (Dan) 75
Thorfinn Skull-splitter, Jarl of Orkney 137, 146, 483
Thorfinn the Mighty, Jarl of Orkney 381–382
Thorn 463, 464
Thornborough, Edward 262, 390
Thornborough 328
Thorough 217
Thorstein the Red, Jarl of the Hebrides 98
Thracian 229, 475
Thrasher 464
Three Sisters 362
Thunder 10, 97, 421, 464, 474
Thunderbolt 341, 464
Thunderer 464
Thuno, Denmark 188
Tichborne, William 197, 270
Tickler 464, 465
Tienpak, China 465
Tientsin, China 120
Tiger 76, 117, 295, 465
Tigre 2; (F) 242, 262, 266; (pirate) 295
Tigress 379, 465; (US) 258
Tigris 466
Tilbury Fort, Essex 466
Tillard, James 11
Timor 466
Tinchebrai, France 171
Tinghai, China 121
Tintagel Castle 483
Tinwald, Isle of Man 284
Tippet, Lt-Cmdr 28
Tiptoe 217
Tiptoft, Sir John 466
Tipu, Sultan of Mysore 335

Tir Connaill, Ireland 238
Tiree, Scotland 224
Tirpitz battery, Belgium 324
Tirpitz (G) 237, 396, 397, 406, 499
Tisiphone (F) 6
Tithonus 466
Tobago, West Indies 371, 466
Tobago 467
Tobermory, Scotland 83
Tobin, George 21, 371
Tobruk, Libya 140–14, 243, 279, 337, 342
Toby 342
Toirrdelbach ua Conchobair, king of Connaught 238
Toker, Thomas 136
Tokumu Tei (J) 445
Tokyo, Japan 244
Tollat, Anthony 30
Tomlinson, Nicholas 448
Tondern, Schleswig, Germany 467
Tonga 467
Toniatuba, West Africa 416
Tonnante (F) 7
Tonqua I., China 407
Tonyn, George 91
Toomiang I., China 335
Topaze 5, 301, 467; (F) 5, 81, 122
Torbay, Devon 176, 467
Torbay 271, 365, 467, 468, 486
Torch 402
Torelli (I) 36, 41
Torf-Einar, Jarl of Orkney 321
Torpedo Boat Flotillas, Italian: 1st 279; German: 2nd 294; 10th 296
Torpley, John 8
Torquand, William 221
Torricelli (I) 249
Torride (F) 210
Torrington 328
Tortola, West Indies 166
Tortosa, Lebanon 74
Tortue (F) 239, 292
Tortuga Is, West Indies 415, 465, 478
Tory Island, Ireland 77, 101, 185, 390
Tostig, Earl of Northumbria 330, 468, 501
Tottenham, John 232
Totty, Thomas 15
Touches, Commodore des 103
Toulon, France 11, 14, 15, 68, 78, 87, 106, 132, 135, 137, 198, 205, 233, 246, 257, 296, 305, 349, 355, 363, 372, 382, 385, 425, 431, 444, 447, 468–469
Totland 50
Toulouse (F) 220
Touques, France 174
Tourterelle (F) 270
Tourville, Comte de 68, 72–73, 278, 444

Tou-tou 259
Townsend, Isaac 198, 265
Towry, George 151
Tracey, John 267
Tracker 399
Trades Increase 300
Trafalgar, Spain 69, 240, 438, 469
Tralee, Ireland 83
Transkei, South Africa 429
Trans-Siberian Railway 448
Transsund, Gulf of Finland 217
Transvaal, South Africa 430
Transylvania 469, 470
Trave (D) 21
Tregonatec, France 172
Tremendous 470
Tremeuse (F) 497
Tremiti, Italy 295
Trenchant 161, 445, 470
Trent 470
Trento (I) 282, 457
Trentonian 183
Trepassy 31
Treport, France 171, 174, 439
Treshnish Islands, Scotland 224
Trevanion, Nicholas 155
Trevanion, Richard 274
Trevor, Sir Sackville 460
Triad 470
Trial 232
Tribune 470; (F) 478
Tricheto (I) 480
Trident 471; (F) 220, 349, 361
Trieste, Istria 8
Trieste (I) 61, 481
Trincomalee, Ceylon 114, 115, 161, 372, 471, 495
Trincomalee 471
Trinculo 471
Trinidad, West Indies 49, 338, 471
Trinidad 397
Trinidad Island, South Atlantic 108
Trinité, Martinique 156
Tripoli, Libya 61, 102, 197, 247–248, 339, 477, 480; Dey of 471
Tripoli (Algerine) 308
Tripolitania, North Africa 472
Tristan da Cunha, South Atlantic 348
Triton 308, 472; (F) 247
Tritone (I) 319
Tritton, Ewell 7
Triumph 8, 131, 163, 450, 472, 473
Triunfo (S) 367
Trois Couleurs (F) 18
Trois Rivières, Guadeloupe 204
Trollope, George 393
Trollope, Henry 209, 379

Trollope 182
Tromp, Cornelis 404
Tromp, Maarten 160, 202, 250, 366, 440, 460
Trompeur (F) 346
Trompeuse (F) 387, 435; (pirate) 200
Tromso, Norway 230, 473
Trondheim, Norway 123, 331, 374, 473
Tronjoly, Capt. 364
Trooper 341, 425
Trotten, Richard 28
Trotter, Henry 138
Troubridge, Edward 214
Troubridge, Sir Thomas 82, 111, 137
Troubridge 8, 473
Truant 93, 473
Truculent 473
True Briton 473
Truk, Caroline Is 473
Trumbull (US) 239
Trump 217
Trumpeter 251
Trusty 466
Truxillo, Honduras 206, 421
Tryall 208
Tryon, Lt 471
Tryton 473
Tryton Prize 473
Tsingtao, China 250
Tsekee, Ningpo River, China 473
Tucker, John 125
Tucker, Robert 138
Tucker, Thomas 356
Tucker, William 435, 497
Tui (NZ) 429
Tuijncelaar (D) 301
Tuke, Stratford 301
Tulip 474
Tulo (I) 61
Tumult 8, 72, 474
Tuna 474
Tunis 167, 226, 280, 305, 474
Tunisia 331, 474, 480, 496
Turbine (I) 337
Turbulent 464, 474
Turkey Company 342
Turks Island, West Indies 475
Turner, R.R. 164
Turquoise 475; (F) 164
Turton, Ralph 349
Tuscany, Grand Duke of 264
Tuzla River, Anatolia 475
Tweed 475
Twysden, Thomas 387
Tyger 318
Tyler, Charles 10, 66
Tyler 475

Tyloo, China 495
Tyne 475
Tynedale 320
Tynemouth, Northumberland 65
Tynwald 318
Tyrannicide (F) 152
Tyre, Lebanon 75
Tyrell, Richard 92
Tyrian 72
Tyrrel, John 197, 357
Tyrwhitt, Reginald 273. 475
Tywi River, Wales 432
Tywyn, Wales 329

(All *U*-, *UB*-, *UC*-, and *UJ*- ships are German, except where mentioned.)
U-A 20, 37, 155
U-1 365
U-4 (Austrian); 158 (G) 463
U-6 (Austrian); 338 (G) 164
U-8 213
U-9 1, 223
U-12 28, 60, 442
U-13 325
U-14 333, 394, 431
U-15 79
U-16 377
U-18 154
U-19 83, 98
U-20 70, 274
U-21 277, 343, 472, 489
U-22 26, 186, 237
U-23 145, 371
U-24 25, 198
U-25 33
U-26 33, 178
U-27 67, 162, 199, 227, 338
U-28 33, 34, 334
U-29 133, 155
U-30 31, 68
U-31 32, 35, 160, 471
U-32 34, 131, 169, 222, 489
U-33 100, 209
U-34 33, 372, 434, 494
U-35 235, 253, 286, 291, 370, 457
U-36 370, 408
U-37 32, 33, 36
U-38 32, 69, 294, 384, 394
U-39 29, 101
U-40 457
U-41 32, 67
U-42 32
U-43 42
U-44 115
U-45 32, 142
U-46 38, 108, 160, 256
U-47 32, 33, 34, 35, 36, 395

U-48 32, 33, 34, 37, 372, 443
U-49 32, 91, 191, 339
U-50 256
U-51 96, 219
U-52 35, 96, 331
U-53 32, 33, 86, 217
U-54 20
U-55 32, 177, 387
U-56 33, 470
U-57 205
U-58 32, 33, 34
U-59 320
U-60 476
U-61 340, 490
U-62 325, 336, 443, 474
U-63 32, 189, 353, 354, 469
U-64 274, 310, 490
U-65 32, 34, 38, 310
U-66 189, 495
U-67 123
U-68 123, 145, 155, 190, 336
U-69 36, 46, 83
U-70 37, 387
U-71 45
U-73 282
U-74 38, 40, 252, 496
U-75 254
U-76 38, 202
U-77 214, 252, 318, 319
U-78 202
U-79 156, 210, 222
U-81 40, 165, 281, 286
U-82 41, 43, 503
U-83 41, 190
U-84 41, 43, 77, 344, 349
U-85 371
U-86 42, 57, 409
U-87 42, 51, 95
U-88 228
U-89 54, 394
U-90 45
U-91 9, 46
U-92 48
U-93 34, 36, 42, 87
U-94 35, 38, 40, 43, 46, 408
U-96 35, 36, 41, 503
U-97 37, 100
U-98 38, 319
U-99 33, 35, 37, 242, 263
U-100 33, 35, 37
U-101 35
U-102 335
U-103 35, 41
U-104 246
U-105 36, 37, 38, 43, 427
U-106 37, 334
U-107 38, 40, 43, 51, 285

U-108 380
U-109 78
U-110 38, 297, 349
U-111 123
U-116 44
U-119 436
U-123 35, 41, 349
U-124 33, 37, 44, 52, 160
U-125 53
U-126 149
U-127 42, 312
U-128 44
U-130 42, 45
U-131 42
U-132 44, 45, 48
U-133 281
U-134 396
U-135 42, 46, 55
U-136 34, 43, 45
U-137 120
U-138 34, 79, 190
U-141 39
U-147 38
U-151 437
U-153 495
U-154 43, 164, 495
U-155 43 48
U-156 47, 256
U-159 44
U-160 51
U-161 356, 367
U-163 51
U-175 53
U-177 55
U-178 55
U-179 3
U-184 48
U-186 54
U-187 50
U-188 53
U-189 53
U-190 184
U-191 53
U-192 53
U-194 55
U-196 55, 237
U-198 54, 237, 343, 422
U-201 38, 41, 50, 257
U-202 45, 55, 436
U-203 43, 53
U-204 40, 390
U-205 340, 472
U-206 41
U-207 40
U-208 222
U-210 45
U-211 49, 57

U-212 182
U-213 184, 390
U-214 46, 182
U-215 44
U-216 46
U-218 48
U-221 47, 51
U-223 54, 320, 474
U-224 319
U-226 57
U-229 56
U-231 57
U-238 56, 57, 58
U-245 329
U-246 59
U-247 405
U-252 44
U-254 48
U-255 58
U-256 46, 58
U-257 58
U-258 54
U-260 47, 56
U-261 46
U-262 48, 53
U-264 58
U-265 49
U-266 54
U-268 49
U-269 181
U-270 56
U-273 54
U-274 56
U-277 399
U-282 56
U-285 214
U-286 400
U-288 399
U-289 298
U-300 59
U-302 58
U-303 425
U-304 55
U-305 56, 475, 489
U-306 56
U-307 400
U-308 473
U-309 405
U-310 400
U-311 58, 289
U-314 399
U-322 *30*
U-331 68–69
U-333 42, 43, 57, 182
U-334 55
U-335 414
U-336 51

U-338 52, 56
U-339 158
U-342 346
U-340 3
U-343 306
U-344 400
U-353 47, 135
U-354 237, 398, 400
U-355 399
U-356 49
U-357 49
U-358 9
U-360 399
U-365 400
U-366 399
U-371 39, 233, 320
U-372 292, 426
U-373 48
U-374 41, 392, 477
U-375 285, 319
U-378 56
U-379 45
U-381 54
U-384 52
U-386 58
U-387 400
U-390 182
U-392 483
U-400 332
U-401 39
U-402 50, 54, 374
U-403 54, 397
U-404 47
U-405 51
U-406 44, 58
U-407 425, 473
U-409 425
U-410 51, 319
U-413 49, 180, 182
U-414 319
U-415 57, 58
U-419 56
U-424 58
U-425 400
U-431 318
U-432 51
U-433 286
U-434 42
U-435 49, 319, 398
U-436 55
U-438 53
U-439 54
U-440 46
U-441 56
U-442 50
U-443 47, 82
U-444 51

U-445 272
U-447 54
U-448 56
U-449 494
U-450 186
U-452 483
U-454 45
U-456 49, 54, 55, 397
U-457 398
U-470 56
U-472 399
U-473 436
U-480 182, 183
U-482 59
U-483 494
U-484 59
U-486 104, 457
U-501 40
U-504 54, 494
U-510 237
U-511 46
U-513 405
U-514 49
U-515 54, 56, 57, 225
U-517 46, 47, 485
U-520 48
U-521 50
U-522 50
U-523 55
U-528 196
U-529 50
U-531 53
U-535 55
U-536 57
U-537 378
U-538 57
U-540 56
U-542 57
U-547 79
U-548 58
U-565 319
U-551 488
U-552 37, 41, 44, 45
U-553 41, 42
U-556 38, 39
U-557 40, 203
U-558 40
U-559 353
U-561 42, 425
U-562 41, 472
U-563 41
U-564 40
U-565 308, 319, 343
U-566 46
U-567 42
U-568 39, 227, 408
U-569 55

U-570 40
U-574 42
U-575 58
U-581 374, 456
U-582 43
U-584 53, 182
U-585 397
U-587 44
U-588 43, 45
U-589 398
U-590 44
U-591 43
U-592 436
U-593 45, 319, 20
U-595 45
U-596 319
U-597 47
U-599 141
U-600 57
U-601 399
U-602 365
U-604 50
U-605 46
U-606 50
U-608 182
U-609 46, 49
U-610 47, 56
U-611 48
U-614 50
U-616 320
U-617 47, 373, 472
U-618 182
U-619 47
U-620 50
U-621 181, 182
U-623 50
U-626 48
U-630 53
U-631 56
U-632 49
U-634 55
U-636 72
U-640 54
U-641 57
U-643 56
U-645 56
U-646 54
U-648 57
U-651 39
U-652 228, 243
U-653 436
U-654 43
U-655 396
U-657 54
U-658 48
U-659 54
U-660 319

INDEX

U-661 47
U-664 50
U-667 182
U-671 182
U-672 182
U-674 399
U-678 182
U-679 50
U-703 397, 398
U-707 57
U-710 53
U-711 310, 400
U-713 399
U-714 310
U-719 182
U-722 195
U-731 444
U-732 155
U-734 58
U-736 182
U-741 182
U-744 58
U-751 43
U-752 55
U-753 54
U-756 46
U-757 57
U-761 24
U-762 58
U-763 181
U-764 181
U-765 78
U-767 181
U-771 484
U-772 59
U-774 98
U-775 92
U-806 122
U-841 56
U-842 57
U-844 56
U-845 58
U-859 58, 343, 445
U-864 484
U-868 218
U-877 59
U-878 483
U-905 127
U-952 54, 56
U-954 54
U-959 399
U-961 399
U-962 58
U-964 56
U-965 396
U-968 400
U-971 181

U-973 399
U-978 183
U-984 182
U-985 399
U-987 414
U-988 182, 359
U-990 399
U-995 400
U-1001 196
U-1003 313
U-1004 183
U-1006 22
U-1014 271
U-1018 183
U-1020 502
U-1024 270
U-1051 285
U-1063 59
U-1105 383
U-1169 158
U-1172 462
U-1195 183
U-1200 183
U-1223 59
U-1227 59
U-1228 423
U-1274 329
U-1276 59
U-1278 70
U-1279 70
U-1302 59
U-2329 329
U-2336 329
Uarsciek (I) 353
UB-4 239
UB-6 382
UB-8 295
UB-10 96
UB-13 273
UB-14 162, 164
UB-16 164, 382
UB-18 76, 164
UB-19 349
UB-23 91
UB-27 159, 219
UB-29 260
UB-30 246
UB-35 291
UB-37 349
UB-39 209
UB-40 238
UB-42 484
UB-47 200, 242
UB-50 91
UB-52 219
UB-54 482
UB-57 301

582 INDEX

UB-63 131
UB-64 286, 437
UB-65 26
UB-66 100, 419
UB-67 30
UB-68 428
UB-69 139
UB-70 69
UB-71 300
UB-72 142
UB-73 142
UB-74 272
UB-78 376
UB-80 437
UB-82 359
UB-83 335
UB-85 130
UB-90 256
UB-103 501
UB-105 134
UB-107 99
UB-110 204
UB-115 339
UB-124 286
Ubean I., Sulu Sea 161
UC-5 273
UC-6 244
UC-10 165
UC-17 417
UC-18 256
UC-19 28
UC-22 273
UC-25 338
UC-26 297
UC-29 342
UC-33 344
UC-34 26, 60
UC-38 382, 437
UC-39 464
UC-41 243
UC-43 202
UC-46 266
UC-47 340
UC-49 335, 344
UC-50 503
UC-51 192
UC-62 165
UC-63 165
UC-65 28, 96
UC-66 419
UC-67 155
UC-70 339
UC-71 160
UC-72 4
UC-74 26
UC-75 188, 263
Udevala, Sweden 451

Uebi Scelebi (I_ 142
Uganda 407
UIT-23 (G) 445
UJ-126 219, 420
UJ-1402 180
UJ-2104 152
UJ-2106 479
UJ-2109 152
UJ-2201 479
UJ-2202 479
UJ-2207 306
UJ-2208 474, 481
UJ-2210 464, 466
UJ-2211 477
UJ-2213 425
UJ-6075 480
UJ-6078 480
Ulaid, Ireland 476
Ulleswater 476
Ullswater 179
Ulpio Traiano (I) 341
Ulster, Ireland 65, 148, 158, 254, 381, 417, 445, 476
Ulster 401
Ultimatum 476
Ultor 476, 477
Ulysse (F) 6
Ulysses 380, 477
Umbra (I) 282
Umfravill, Sir Robert 193, 322
Umm Qais, Itaq 353
Unaio (slaver) 233
Unbeaten 477
Unbending 477
Unbroken 282, 477
Undaunted 231, 266, 292, 304, 346, 477, 488; (D) 374
Underdown, John 189, 313
Undine 477, 478; (G) 164
Unicorn 101, 117, 154, 187, 478
Union 478; (D) 371
Unique 102, 478
Unite 5, 11, 108, 364, 479; (F) 13, 235, 386–387
United 425, 479
United Kingdom 496
United States 139, 154, 256, 274, 409, 485
United States (US) 275
Unity 292
Unruly 152, 425, 479
Universal 479
Unrivalled 479
Unseen 479
Unshaken 479
Unsparing 479
Untiring 480
Upholder 61, 102, 480

INDEX 583

Upper Marlborough, Maryland 120
Upright 480
Upstart 480
Upton, Clotworthy 454
Urania 89
Uranie 73; (F) 461
Urbino 67
Urca Cardagora (S) 372
Urge 480–481
Ursula 102, 408
Ushant, France 22, 27, 30, 73, 80, 127, 154, 156, 157, 160, 180, 196, 236, 250, 262, 270, 277, 303, 318, 332, 376, 386, 435, 448, 481, 487
Usodimare (I) 340
Uspak, king of the Hebrides 394
Ussher, Thomas 125, 232, 304, 346, 383, 477
Ussher, Sydney 491
Usurper 481
Utile (F) 83, 430–431
Utmost 481
Uvedale, Samuel 220

V-27 (G) 248
V-29 (G) 248
V-69 (G) 324
V-187 (G) 226
V-188 (G) 164
V-202 (G) 179
V-208 (G) 182
V-209 (G) 9
V-210 (G) 182
V-211 (G) 181
V-414 (G) 75
V-1241 (G) 327
V-1253 (G) 327
V-1303 (G) 328
V-1304 (G) 327
V-1308 (G) 327
V-1311 (G) 327
V-1314 (G) 327
V-1409 (G) 180
V-1411 (G) 328
V-1412 (G) 327
V-1501 (G) 180
V-1507 (G) 472
V-1508 (G) 443
V-1525 (G) 180
V-1605 (G) 186
V-1606 (G) 289
V-2009 (G) 328
V-2016 (G) 328
V-2020 (G) 327
V-2021 (G) 327
V-5107 (G) 374
V-5560 (G) 186

V-5716 (G) 186
V-6413 (G) 374
V-6801 (G) 186
Vaagso, Norway 482
Vado, Italy 482
Vaga (slaver) 274
Vaillante (F) 236, 260
Vainqueur (F) 18
Vala 482
Valarozo (slaver) 131, 361, 423
Valetta, Malta 14, 268, 278, 447
Valeur 313, 482; (F) 168, 220, 498
Valiant 8, 14, 69, 133, 464, 482
Valiente (S) 130
Valleyfield (Cn) 58
Valmy (F) 32
Valona, Albania 8, 74
Valorosa (I) 472
Valorous 482
Valparaiso, Chile 112, 156, 356
Vampire 115; (A) 462
Vancouver 482
Vancouver I., Canada 462
Vanessa 49, 99
Vanguard 316, 375, 482
Vanna (I) 473
Vanneau (F) 125
Vannes, France 70
Vanoc 37, 483
Vanquisher 56, 483
Vansittart, Henry 85
Vansittart, Nicholas 133, 216
Vansittart, Westby 80
Vansittart 33
Var (F) 74
Var, river, France 343
Varna, Romania 185
Vascama 483
Vassall, Spencer 221
Vassilissa Olgas (Greek) 353
Vasto, Istria 7
'Vatzfiord' 483
Vaughan, Roger 146, 397
Vautour (F) 83
Vedette (F) 472
Vega (I) 280
Velella (I) 422
Velez Malaga, Spain 483
Velite (I) 435
Véloce (F) 7
Velos Aragonesa (S) 61
Veloz (S) 12, 312; (slaver) 497
Veloz Pasajero (slaver) 370
Venables, General 409
Vence, Rear-Admiral (F) 131
Vencedora (slaver) 201, 230
Vencejo 483; (S) 22, 130

Vendée, France 341
Venerable 15, 324, 483; (D) 100
Vengador (slaver) 80
Venganza (S) 147
Vengeance 276, 483; (F) 18, 295–296, 379, 420; (D) 374
Vengeur (F) 17, 81, 90, 177, 358, 412, 428, 447
Venice 5, 6, 7, 300, 302
Venteux (F) 271
Ventimiglia, Italy 385
Ventura (S) 200
Venturer 484
Venturier (F) 203
Venus 227, 414, 484; (F) 84, 236, 290291, 329, 496; (slaver) 485
Verniero (I) 37
Verity 325
Vernon, Edward 110, 115, 124, 314, 364, 367, 413
Vernon 447
Veronica 484
Versatile 484
Vertu (F) 29, 89, 345, 378
Verulam 414
Vervain 59
Vesey, Francis 17
Vesper 178
Vestal 161, 386, 484, 485, 491; (In) 351
Vestale 485; (F) 78, 123, 430, 459, 478
Vésuve (F) 232, 292
Vesuvius 192, 208, 232, 485
Vetch 44, 319
Veteran 40, 319; (F) 116
Vian, Philip 261
Viceroy 329
Vickers, Lewis 230
Victor 379, 485; (F) 290–291
Victoire (F) 304, 458, 502
Victorieuse (F) 159
Victorious 6, 29, 79, 84, 244, 255, 396, 401, 419, 473, 485
Victory 62, 485, 486
Vidette 53, 56, 182, 444
Vieja, Spain 384
Vieille Josephine (F) 388
25 de Mayo (Argentine) 189
Vièrge (F) 459
Vigilant 147, 352, 414, 486; (US) 265
Vigilante (F) 7, 120, 251, 272, 384
Vigo, Spain 75, 127, 308, 434, 486–487
Vilaine, river, France 317, 377
Villaret-Joyeuse, Admiral (F) 131, 12, 242
Ville d'Anvers (F) 441, 442
Ville de Caen (F) 427
Ville de Lorient (F) 154
Ville de Lyon (F) 308

Ville de Milan (F) 122
Ville de Paris 487; (F) 404
Ville de Québec (Cn) 319
Villeneuve, Admiral (F) 98, 469
Villers-sur-Mer, France 182
Villiers, Arthur 309
Vimy 41 (Cn) 50
Vincent, Nicholas 500
Vincent, Richard 29
Vincent, Samuel 370
Vindex 78, 230, 400, 436
Vingorla, India 197
Viola 246
Violet 39, 57
Violett, James 381
Viper 350, 401, 450, 487; (US) 309
Vipère (F) 196
Virago 414
Virgen del Carmen (S) 315
Virgen del Rosario (S) 343
Virgin 487
Virginia 9, 74, 118–119, 424
Virginie 487; (F) 236
Virgin Is, West Indies 230
Virgin Maria (F) 487
Viscount 47, 50
Vistula River, Prussia 143
Vittoria 487; (D) 214
Vittorio Veneto (I) 282, 290, 480
Vitu, East Africa 487–488
Vivacious 484
Vivaldi (I) 279, 463
Vivero, Spain 169
Vivien 327
Vivo (S) 195, 347
Vixen 314; (US) 431
Vizagapatam, India 113, 200, 410
Vizalma 488
Vladivostok, Russia 448
Vlie river, Netherlands 371, 376, 416
Vlieg (D) 150
Vlieland, Netherlands 327, 497
Vlugheld (D) 386
Volage 4, 20, 130, 488; (F) 437
Volcan (F) 435
Volontaire 302, 488; (F) 365, 490
Volpe (Neapolitan) 5
Voltaire 488
Voltigeur (F) 360, 383
Volturno River, Italy 72
Volunteer 304, 180
Vortigern 326
Voyager 142
Vrijheid (D) 291
Vryheit (D) 100
Vulcan 423, 501; (F) 337
Vulcain (F) 448

Vulture 195, 204, 352
Vyepr (Russian) 482

W-1 (J) 462
W-5 (J) 445
W-7 (J) 445
Wa-4 (J) 445
Wa-104 (J) 446
Wa-105 (J) 470
Waakzaamheid (D) 426
Wager, Sir Charles 110, 207
Wainwright, John 351
Waireka, New Zealand 489
Wakataka (J) 446
Wake, Charles 92
Wakeful 310, 325
Walbeoff, Thomas 151, 501
Walcheren, Netherlands 489
Walcheren (D) 413
Walcott, John 475
Waldegrave, Hon. George 304
Waldegrave, Hon. William 373, 474
Wales 173, 329, 340
Wales, Richard 183
Walker, Benjamin 393
Walker, Charles 161
Walker, George 253
Walker, Sir Hovenden 215, 375, 405
Walker, James 482
Walker, William 393
Walker 37
Wallace, Sir James 101, 187, 318
Wallasea 180
Waller, John 421
Waller, Thomas 265
Wallflower 55, 489
Wallis, James 308
Walney I., Lancashire 489
Walney 318
Walpole, William 351
Walpole 178, 328, 443
Walrus 484
Walsingham, Robert 464
Walton, George 75, 331
Wanderer 38, 55, 178, 182, 203, 406, 448, 489
Wanklyn, Lt-Cmdr 480
Warburton-Lee, Capt. 310
Ward, Thomas 462
Wardlaw, William 463
Wardle, Capt. 12
Wareham, Connecticut 489
Warner 490
Warramunga (A) 4, 313, 320, 429
Warrand, Thomas 427
Warre, Henry 295
Warree, Nigeria 84

Warren, C. H. 164
Warren, Sir John Borlase 71, 101, 116, 191, 241, 271, 363, 377, 464, 486, 490
Warren, Peter 149, 272, 436
Warren, Samuel 74
Warren, Thomas 287, 370
Warren, William 434, 488
Warren Hastings 490
Warrior 238
Warspite 8, 182, 310, 336, 374, 407, 425, 452, 469, 490
Warwick, Earl of (1) 322, 430, 439; (2) 186, 274, 368
Warwick 180, 241, 303, 491; (F) 298
Wash 334
Washington (US) 200
Washington, DC 120
Washington, George (US) 86, 118–119
Waskesiu)Cn) 58
Wasp 314, 491; (US) 61, 201, 383
Wassenaes, Jacob van, lord of Opdam (D) 273
Watchet, Devon 491
Watchful 442
Watchman 165, 183
Waterford, Ireland 159, 239, 283, 491
Waterwitch 96, 491, 492
Watkins, Frederick 138, 312
Watkins, John 137
Watkins, Richard 82
Watson, Charles 76, 206
Watson, Robert 386
Watson, Thomas 329
Wear 146
Weatherall, Frederick 247
Weazel 6, 7, 492
Webley, William 235
Weddell, John 101, 350
Weeks, John 329
Weerwrack (D) 374
Weir, Henry 150
Wellard, John 157
Wellesley 20, 121, 249
Wellholme 492
Wellington, Duke of 4
Wells, John 382
Wells, Thomas 136
Welshman 282, 472
Wensleydale 180, 182
Werolax Bay, Gulf of Finland 217
Weser, river, Germany 148
Weser (D) 418
West, John 5, 393, 448
West, Thomas 502
West Africa 2, 17, 28, 32, 37, 38, 45, 54, 80, 85, 138, 145, 191, 214, 257, 274, 277, 336, 358, 361, 458, 492, 502

West African Slave Patrol 203
Westcott 319, 374
Westcott, George 277
Wester Eems, Germany 142
Western, Thomas 456
Western Approaches 133, 177
Western Australia 454
Western Desert, Egypt 69, 184
Western Isles, Scotland (also Hebrides) 29, 83, 94, 148, 224–225, 239, 240, 253, 283–284,
Westfalen (G) 164
Westgate, Kent 443
Westmark (G) 477
West Indies 9, 10, 12, 21, 24, 27, 28, 64, 73, 81, 85, 91, 103, 112, 118, 122, 128, 130, 135, 139, 147, 149, 197, 199, 201, 206, 210, 222, 235, 238, 239, 242, 243, 250, 251, 253, 256, 272, 301, 302, 305, 312, 317, 331, 344, 347, 354, 368, 372, 380, 381, 382, 385, 388, 394, 403, 404, 418, 422, 424, 428, 434, 437, 458, 461, 464, 467, 468, 477, 478, 482, 486, 492, 497, 498, 501, 502
West Indies Squadron 110, 148, 204, 286
Westminster 327
Weston 325
Westphalia 493
Wetaskiwin (Cn) 45
Wewak, New Guinea 314
Wexford, Ireland 239
Weymouth, Dorset 493
Weymouth 146, 160, 493
Whampoa, China 101, 102
Wheatland 493
Wheeler, Edward 240
Wheler, Sir Francis 8, 253, 287, 396
Whetstone, Sir William 403, 492, 494
Whinyates, Thomas 201
Whirlwind 494
Whitaker, Sir Edward 155, 367, 500
Whitaker 494
Whitby, Yorkshire 246
Whitby, Henry 6, 371
Whitby, John 131
Whitby Abbey 20, 72, 278
White, Charles 386, 485
White, John 22, 202, 454
White, John Chambers 272
White, Martin 285
White, Richard 23, 217
White, Thomas 305, 346
Whitehall 56, 399
Whitehaven, Cumbria 494
White Horse (Algerine) 216
Whitekirk, Scotland 193
Whitelocke, Lt-General 389

Whitelocke, Bulstrode 357
White Sea 60, 398, 400, 494
Whiting 494
Whitsand Bay, Cornwall 494
Whitsand Bay 494
Whitshed 32, 177, 327
Whittaker, Samuel 331
Whydah, West Africa 153, 497
Wickham, Henry 149
Widgeon 203, 255, 327
Wiesbaden (G) 248
Wigo Sound, Gulf of Finland 485
Wilcox, James 198
Wild Boar 494
Wild Cat (US) 167
Wild Goose 37, 58, 436, 494
Wilding (F) 435
Wildman, Leveson 436
Wild Swan 494
Wiley, John 470
Wilhelmina 495
Wilhelm Heidcamp (G) 310
Wilhelmshafen, Germany 178
Willamette Valley 495
Willaumez, Admiral (F) 22, 69
Willemstadt, Netherlands 495
Willes, George 338, 423
William I the Conqueror, King of England 170, 417
William II Rufus, King of England 171, 417
William III, Prince of Orange, King of England 74, 467
William (D) 214, 346
William and John 342
William Pitt 90, 448, 495
William Sugden 327
Williams, Henry 394
Williams, James 201
Williams, John 441
Williams, Richard 502
Williams, Peter 183
Williams, Thomas 478
Williams, William 3, 196
Williamson, Edward 342
Willoughby, Nesbit 390, 339
Willoughby de Broke, Lord 193
Willow Branch 495
Willshaw, Thomas 126, 195
Wilmington, North Carolina 82
Wilmot, Robert 403
Wilmot-Smith, A. 67
Wilson, Capt. 121
Wilson, Edward 342
Wilson, George 75
Wilson, Thomas 261, 495
Wilson, W. J. 76
Wimbledon, Viscount 97

Winchelsea, Sussex 172, 184
Winchelsea 215, 495
Winchester, Hampshire 171
Winchester 495
Windham 115, 496
Windsor, Hon. Thomas 200
Windsor 326, 327, 496
Windsor Castle 98, 496
Windward Is 92, 463
Windward Passage, Caribbean Sea 45, 46
Windau, Latvia 495
Wingo Sound, Baltic Sea 166
Winter, Sir William 116, 194
Winthrop, Robert 12, 26, 122
Wirral, Cheshire 496
Wishart, James 117
Wishart 24, 496
Wissant, France 171
With, Witte de (D) 250, 251–252, 460
Witherington 3
Witte, Passchier de (D) 465
Wivern 110
Wizard 251, 496
Wodehouse, George 358
Wolf 177, 437
Wolfe, George 10
Wolfe, James 375
Wolfe 335
Wolley, Thomas 27, 407
Wollongong (A) 373
Wolseley, William 134
Wolverine 37, 38, 146, 282, 497, 498
Wood, Sir Andrew 193
Wood, Benjamin 445
Wood, George 474
Wood, John 353
Woodcock 56
Woodcot 498
Wooden, John 331
Woodlark 4, 93
Woodpecker 58, 494
Woodriff, Daniel 98
Woods, Lt-Cmdr 8
Woodward, Robert 475
Woolcombe, John 262
Wooldridge, James 379
Woolf 498
Woollcombe, Henry 273
Woolridge, William 343
Woolsey, William 342
Woolwich 421–422
Woosung, China 498
Worcester 178, 225, 326, 498
Worcestershire 389
Worcestershire 38
Worsley, Miller 258
Worth, James 226, 459, 483

Wraak (D) 371
Wrangler 59–60
Wren 192, 319, 496
Wrench, Matthew 256
Wrenn, Ralph 148, 253
Wrestler 213
Wright, John 452
Wright, John Wesley 483
Wright, Lawrence 405
Wrightson, C.A.W. 382
Wryneck 213
Wyborn, John 90
Wyld, Charles 90
Wylde, Baron 137, 394
Wynnington, Robert 498
Wyvill, Christopher 122
Wyvill, Francis 113

X-24 416
Xabia, Spain 147
X-craft 499

Yangzi River, China 19, 121, 498, 500
Yap, Caroline Islands 500
Yar Hissar (Turkish) 163
Yarmouth (also Great Yarmouth), Norfolk 9, 273, 392, 417
Yarmouth, Isle of Wight 261
Yarmouth 500
Yarra (A) 352, 500
Yell Sound, Shetland 500
Yelverton, Hastings 29, 216
Yeo, Sir James 112, 126, 259, 431
Yeocomico River 127
Yokohama, Japan 244, 249
Yoni, Sierra Leone 2
York 217, 334, 501
York, Hudson's Bay 231
York, Duke of (James VII and II) 273, 428
York 251, 500, 501
York River, Virginia 309
Yorke, Sir Joseph 121, 386
Yorkshire 25, 170, 204, 464, 501
Yorktown, Virginia 20, 84, 118–119, 501
Young, Capt. 12
Young, Anthony 23, 369
Young, Benjamin 16
Young, James 308
Young, Thomas 427
Young Crow 501
Young Fred 131, 359
Younghusband, George 338
Ysère (G) 479
Yugiri (J) 462

Z-26 (G) 397
Z-27 (G) 71, 444

Z-32 (G) 181
Z-81 (G) 181
Zafir 389
Zanganian pirates 358
Zante, Ionian Is 238, 429
Zanzibar 144, 145, 272, 274, 294, 306, 345, 502; Sultan of 274, 301, 502
Zara, Dalmatia 5
Zara, Tripolitania 472
Zara (I) 290
Zaragozana (pirate) 475
Zavia, Italy 480
Zea, Greece 480, 502
Zealand, Denmark 332, 465
Zealous 316, 502
Zebra 288, 502
Zeebrugge, Belgium 244, 324–325, 443
Zeerop (D) 109
Zeffiro (I) 40
Zélé (F) 404
Zeo, Nicolo and Antonio 424
Zephir (slaver) 305
Zephyr 502; (D) 150; (F) 268, 421, 491
Zeppelin airships 164, 230, 467
Zeppelin *L-53* (G) 475
ZH-1 (G) 444
Zibara I., Italy 7
Zinnia 40
Zubian 503
Zuider Zee, Netherlands 225
Zula, Eritrea 1
Zulu 141, 426
Zululand, South Africa 503
Zupiano, Dalmatia 5
Zwyn, river, Flanders 321
Zylpha 503